THE ORIGINS OF
HUMAN SOCIETY

THE BLACKWELL HISTORY OF THE WORLD (HOTW)

General Editor: **R. I. Moore**

Published

A History of Latin America
Peter Bakewell

The Origins of Human Society
Peter Bogucki

A History of Russia, Central Asia and Mongolia: Volume I
David Christian

A History of India
Burton Stein

In Preparation

A History of the Mediterranean World
David Abulafia

The Birth of the Modern World
C. A. Bayly

A History of Western Europe
c. 400–1914
Robin Briggs

A History of Russia, Central Asia and Mongolia: Volume II
David Christian

A History of Australia, New Zealand and the Pacific
Donald Denoon

A History of Africa
Paul Lovejoy

Elements of World History
R. I. Moore

A History of the Middle East
David Morgan

A History of the Ancient Mediterranean
Ian Morris

A History of South-East Asia
Anthony Reid

A History of China
Morris Rossabi

A History of the Ancient Americas
Fred Spier

The Early Modern World
Sanjay Subrahmanyam

A History of Japan
Conrad Totman

The Beginnings of Civilization
Robert Wenke

THE ORIGINS OF HUMAN SOCIETY

PETER BOGUCKI

First published 1999

2 4 6 8 10 9 7 5 3 1

Blackwell Publishers Inc.
350 Main Street
Malden, Massachusetts 02148
USA

Blackwell Publishers Ltd
108 Cowley Road
Oxford OX4 1JF
UK

Library of Congress Cataloging-in-Publication Data

Bogucki, Peter I.
    The origins of human society / Peter Bogucki.
      p. cm. — (The Blackwell history of the world)
    Includes bibliographical references and index.
    ISBN 1–55786–349–0 (hb: alk. paper). — ISBN 1–57718–112–3 (pb)
    1. Culture—Origin. 2. Primitive societies. 3. Social evolution.
  I. Title. II. Series
  GN358.B64 1999
  306—dc21
                                          98–56285
                                               CIP

British Library Cataloguing in Publication Data
A CIP catalogue record for this book is available from the British Library.

Typeset in 10 on 12 pt Plantin by Newgen Imaging Systems (P) Ltd, Chennai, India
Printed in Great Britain by TJ International, Padstow, Cornwall
This book is printed on acid-free paper

CONTENTS

LIST OF FIGURES AND TABLES

FIGURES

NOTE ON MAP SOURCES

Base maps for the outline maps in this volume were prepared using the inter-active GIS map server at the Institute for the Study of the Continents (INSTOC), Department of Geological Sciences, Cornell University (http://atlas.geo.cornell.edu), except for figures 3.3 and 7.15 which are based on maps generated by the Online Map Creation facility provided by Körsgen, Kantz + Weinelt Digitale Kartografie (http://www.aquarius.geomar.de/omc/) in Kiel, Germany.

TABLE

SERIES EDITOR'S PREFACE

THERE is nothing new in the attempt to understand history as a whole. To know how humanity began and how it has come to its present condition is one of the oldest and most universal of human needs, expressed in the religious and philosophical systems of every civilization. But only in the last few decades has it begun to appear both necessary and possible to meet that need by means of a rational and systematic appraisal of current knowledge. History claimed its independence as a field of scholarship with its own subject matter and its own rules and methods, not simply a branch of literature, rhetoric, law, philosophy or religion, in the second half of the nineteenth century. World History has begun to do so only in the second half of the twentieth. Its emergence has been delayed on the one hand by simple ignorance – for the history of enormous stretches of space and time has been known not at all, or so patchily and superficially as not to be worth revisiting – and on the other by the lack of a widely acceptable basis upon which to organize and discuss what is nevertheless the enormous and enormously diverse knowledge that we have.

Both obstacles are now being rapidly overcome. There is almost no part of the world or period of its history that is not the subject of vigorous and sophisticated investigation by archaeologists and historians. It is truer than it has ever been that knowledge is growing and perspectives changing and multiplying more quickly than it is possible to assimilate and record them in synthetic form. Nevertheless the attempt to grasp the human past as a whole can and must be made. Facing a common future of headlong and potentially catastrophic transformation, the world needs its common history. Since we no longer believe that a complete or definitive account is ultimately attainable by the mere accumulation of knowledge we are free to offer the best we can manage at the moment. Since we no longer suppose that it is our business as historians to detect or proclaim "The End of History" in the fruition of any grand design, human or divine, there is no single path to trace, or golden key to turn. There is also a growing wealth of ways in which world history can be written. The oldest and simplest view, that world history is best understood as the history of contacts between peoples previously isolated from one another, from which (some think) all change arises, is now seen to be capable of application since the earliest times. An influential alternative focuses upon the tendency of economic exchanges to create self-sufficient but ever expanding "worlds" which sustain successive systems of power and culture. Others seek to understand the differences between societies and cultures, and therefore the particular character of each, by comparing the ways in which they have developed their values, social relationships and structures of power. The rapidly developing field of ecological history returns to a very ancient tradition of seeing interaction with the physical environment, and with other animals, at the center of the human predicament, while insisting that its understanding demands an approach which is culturally, chronologically and geographically comprehensive.

The Blackwell History of the World does not seek to embody any of these approaches, but to support them all, as it will use them all, by providing a modern, comprehensive and accessible account of the entire human past. Its plan is that of a barrel, in which the indispensable narratives of very long-term regional development are bound together by global surveys of the interaction between regions at particular times, and of the great transformations which they have experienced in common, or visited upon one another. Each volume, of course, reflects the idiosyncrasies of its sources and its subjects, as well as the judgment and experience of its author, but in combination they offer a framework in which the history of every part of the world can be viewed, and a basis upon which most aspects of human activity can be compared. A frame imparts perspective. Comparison implies respect for difference. That is the beginning of what the past has to offer the future.

R. I. Moore

SERIES EDITOR'S ACKNOWLEDGMENTS

The Editor is grateful to all of the contributors to the Blackwell History of the World for advice and assistance on the design and contents of the series as a whole as well as on individual volumes. Both Editor and Contributors wish to place on record their immense debt, individually and collectively, to John Davey, formerly of Blackwell Publishers. The series would not have been initiated without his vision and enthusiasm, and could not have been realized without his energy, skill and diplomacy.

PREFACE

ANY attempt to write a book on world prehistory seems an exercise in hubris. The explosion in archaeological data over the last five decades has meant that the record of 2.5 million years of human accomplishments and failures has expanded to the point where no single person can hope to be an expert. An author charged with the task of covering this expanse of time on a global scale should become paralyzed by the immensity of the task. Nonetheless, in a moment of extreme self-confidence, I agreed to take on this assignment.

The result, for better or worse, is the book that you now hold. My goal in writing it was to provide a summary of the current state of knowledge and ignorance about human affairs from the first glimmers of social behavior to the emergence of societies which have a scale of organizational complexity comparable to our own. Writing it has induced a profound sense of humility about my own breadth of knowledge while at the same time providing a remarkable opportunity for me to explore the archaeological record of parts of the world and of periods of the past about which I previously had only superficial knowledge. This book is aimed at a broad readership. Some of these readers may be archaeologists like myself, while many others will be intelligent and informed individuals with a curiosity about the past beyond the reach of written records who claim no particular expertise in archaeology and prehistory as scholarly disciplines.

In writing this book, I have attempted to convey some sense of the life of the discipline of prehistoric archaeology, especially the fact that there are few certainties. Archaeological data are frequently cited as having "proven" something about life in the distant past, but these claims should be examined critically. Archaeological data are in themselves objective and concrete. Yet all interpretations of them, no matter how grounded they are in scientific method and social science theory, are always subject to revision. Throughout this book, issues about which there is considerable disagreement are discussed. I have attempted to convey the flavor of this disagreement, and sometimes I have taken sides.

This book is a summary of the information that I have been able to soak up during the 25 years that I have had an academic interest in archaeology. Any attempt to acknowledge all the people who have contributed to it in some way would simply be a catalog of everyone whom I have met in the field, so it would serve little purpose to enumerate a list of them. Particular thanks, however, are due to my instructors at the University of Pennsylvania and at Harvard who encouraged me to become broadly informed outside my narrow topics of specialization and to look at prehistoric archaeology as a global comparative discipline.

A few particular thanks are in order. John Davey and Bob Moore persuaded me that I would be a good candidate to write such a volume. I believe that Graeme Barker steered them to me, so I must implicate him as well. Tessa Harvey and Anthony Grahame have been patient with me as I have completed the manuscript at a glacial pace. My superiors at Princeton – John Gager of Forbes College; Nancy Malkiel of the Office of the Dean of the College; and since 1994, James Wei, Brad Dickinson, Rob Stengel, and Sundar Sundaresan of the School of Engineering and Applied Science – have generously not given me such onerous duties that might have prevented me from diverting time to this project from my administrative responsibilities and have supported my attendance at archaeological conferences. D. Whitney Coe and the other bibliographers at Firestone Library have made sure that the holdings in prehistoric archaeology are comprehensive. Cheryl Cantore and Caroline Bogucki read large parts of the manuscript and did not hesitate to point out where it made no sense.

The greatest thanks, of course, are owed to my wife Virginia and daughters Caroline and Marianna for not only tolerating but even sometimes encouraging my continued involvement in the study of archaeology.

A NOTE ON DATING

ARCHAEOLOGISTS who study different periods use various dating conventions. Those who work on more recent millennia, generally from 10,000 years ago onward, normally use the BC/AD convention. For remains prior to about 10,000 years ago, terms like "before the present" (BP) and "years ago" are used interchangeably. For the most part, "years ago" is used in chapters 2, 3, and 4, while BC/AD is used in chapters 6, 7 and 8. Chapter 5 is a swing chapter, in which both types of expressions occur, but where it is always clear which one is in use. When dating is based on radiocarbon age determinations after 10,000 years ago, a recalibrated scale is used to reflect calendar years.

In memory of
John L. Cotter
1911–1999
Pioneer Archaeologist

[1] THE GATEWAY TO HUMAN PREHISTORY

INTRODUCTION

Even with a very conservative definition of what it means to be a human being, over 99 percent of the existence of the genus Homo to date occurred prior to the development of written records. Many millennia have yet to pass before this proportion falls even one percent. Were this not already a staggering statement, it is also important to remember that there are parts of the world which did not produce their own written records even a generation ago and that even in the world of ancient literate civilizations what is recorded in documents reflects a very narrow segment of society.

Another way of looking at this is to consider that, for all intents and purposes, the record of human life on this planet is prehistoric. Patterns of human behavior which govern our existence today were established deep in this misty past. No one wrote about the first leader, the first battle, the first treaty, the first crime. No critic commented on the earliest monumental architecture or the first artistic achievements. Institutions such as the family and social differentiation began in this unrecorded past.

The scope of human prehistory is very difficult for us who are used to thinking in years, decades, and centuries to comprehend. Barely fifty centuries have passed since the development of written records, 250 generations at best. The thousands of centuries of human existence which preceded literacy were scarcely less eventful, although the events might have been more banal. Still, the successful killing of a mastodon 500 generations ago in eastern North America would have been an event which was talked about for months, if not years. In our global society we tend to minimize the importance of events which do not have international or national significance. Yet for the hunter-gatherer band that killed the mastodon, it would have been as defining an experience in its existence as anything deemed worthy for a history book.

The only problem is that we do not know the people. They are faceless and nameless, both individually and collectively. Only recently have historians begun to examine the faceless and nameless people of historical epochs, but the archaeologists who study prehistory have always had to deal with this greater gap between them and their subjects. When one becomes a prehistorian, one accepts the fact that he or she will remain ignorant of personalities and, except when their literate neighbors gave them names, the collective identities of the people they study. Archaeologists give them names – "Lucy," the Jaguar King, Venus of Willendorf, Burial 3 – but of course these are made-up tags to help give some humanity to the dry remains or to write on a catalog card.

But there is not any question that they are *human*, and we can identify them clearly as our ancestors. Even the earliest hominids who might have headed down unsuccessful evolutionary paths share with us a common earlier past. Once anatomically modern humans emerge in the last 100,000 years, we can no longer deny that our genetic code directly comes from theirs.

The goal of this book is to explore this human past as a prelude to history, not as something apart from it. Although the techniques that are used by archaeologists to investigate this past might be different from those of the historian, they are no less intellectually rigorous and systematic. The primary data of archaeologists are manufactured objects and the physical remains of their makers instead of texts and documents, but the scholarly goals are the same. A key theme in this volume will be the scholarship behind the knowledge of the archaeological past, to give the reader a sense of *why* and *how* we say what we do about the distant past.

THE IDEA OF PREHISTORY

The concept of a span of human existence before recorded history may seem intuitively obvious to the readers of this volume, but such was not always the case. What the eminent British historian of archaeology Glyn Daniel (1914–86) called "the idea of prehistory" crystallized only in the early part of the nineteenth century (Daniel 1964). Between 1820 and 1860, the study of the past moved from an antiquarian interest in old curiosities to a scholarly discipline which recognized that there was a considerable amount of human experience before historical records and which attempted to understand and explain this period in precise and rational terms. There are many excellent histories of archaeology (two good recent volumes are Bahn 1996 and Trigger 1989), and this section will not attempt to duplicate them. Instead, a few points will be made which will preface the discussion that follows.

In its European roots, the study of human prehistory evolved along two major lines. The first could generally be called "antiquarian," and it involved the exploration of sites and the connoisseurship of artifacts, usually those of later prehistory. Beginning in the late Renaissance, antiquarianism developed through the seventeenth and eighteenth centuries, until it came of age in the nineteenth-century Romantic era. The Past lent itself readily to the sentiments of this period and the collection and curation of artifacts came to be systematic. Museums, and eventually university departments, were organized and archaeology took its place alongside other "human sciences" as a legitimate field of scholarly inquiry.

The second major current in the development of archaeology in the Old World happened along with the development of the natural sciences, particularly the life and earth sciences. The study of geological strata revealed human remains, artifacts, and animal bones, all of which were studied, quite appropriately, as related finds. This line of archaeological development touched more the earlier prehistoric periods, especially the Palaeolithic or Old Stone Age. As such, it was linked to the developing interest in human origins which emerged in the early nineteenth century, as well as to the refinement of biological taxonomy and nomenclature seen in the life sciences.

In the New World, archaeology developed along somewhat different lines. In the New World, European colonists had encountered truly prehistoric peoples, and so the initial question became "who are (soon, were) they?" After an initial antiquarian stage of curiosity about the vanishing indigenous peoples and the monuments of the civilizations of Mesoamerica and the Andes, prehistoric archaeology became firmly linked to the nascent discipline of anthropology and has continued that connection ever since.

A major intellectual barrier had to be broken down for the true study of prehistory to occur. The study of the past needed to be disconnected from the biblical chronology pegged to the Flood which had been promoted by clerics since the first antiquarian discussions began in the seventeenth century. Primary credit for this is given to a French pharmacist named Paul Tournal (1805–72) who studied cave deposits near Narbonne (Chippindale 1988). Tournal broke from the "pre-flood" and "post-flood" mentality and wrote about a "période anté-historique." This firmly situated early humans in a period before modern times, beyond the reach of written records.

It seems only an accident of etymology that we use the term "prehistory" to describe this period instead of Tournal's "antehistory." "Préhistorique" came to be used in France during the 1840s and "antehistory" disappeared into oblivion. The first use of the term "prehistoric" in English appears to have been in Daniel Wilson's (1816–92) *The Archaeology and Prehistoric Annals of Scotland*, 1851, although no one seems to have been terribly troubled by the oxymoron "prehistoric annals." This was followed by "prehistory" in Edward Tylor's (1832–1917) *Primitive Culture* and "prehistorian" for someone who studies prehistory in the *American Catholic Quarterly Review* in 1892 (Chippindale 1988). As Chippindale notes, there is to this day no single good word to describe a *person* who lived in prehistoric times!

Nonetheless, naming the subject and disconnecting it from the Bible were only two parts of giving structure to this amorphous subject. It required a body of method and theory. Method was supplied by the progressively more meticulous excavation and documentation of prehistoric sites, such as Ramsauer's excavations at Hallstatt in Austria and Stephens' and Catherwood's expeditions to Yucatan. Theory was somewhat more elusive. It was supplied largely by a unilinear view of human cultural evolution, a translation of Darwinian thought to the archaeological record (Trigger 1989: 114). One of the key figures in articulating this model was John Lubbock (1834–1913) whose book *Pre-historic Times* in 1865 drew parallels between modern band and tribal societies and the supposed way of life of the ancients.

In North America, the field of anthropology embraced ethnology, biological evolution, linguistics, and archaeology, all of which overlapped in a Venn diagram of sorts in the study of indigenous peoples. It was not unusual for an early American anthropologist to publish papers which dealt variously with the ethnology of modern pueblos, the prehistoric pottery found in the bottom layers of the rubbish heaps, the osteometric characteristics of the human bones also found, and the linguistic relationships of the language spoken by the living tribes. Such a "four-field" approach was a classic feature of North American anthropology, unlike the Prehistory of the Old World, before each field went its separate way.

ARCHAEOLOGY AND ITS NEIGHBORS

The intellectual location of prehistoric archaeology on the map of the world of scholarship is difficult to pin down exactly. The glib explanation given by many prehistorians is that it is "the most humanistic of the sciences and the most scientific of the humanities," which makes a good sound bite but does not really answer the question. The composite nature of archaeological data and interpretation clouds the issue considerably. Like the natural science and some of the social sciences, archaeology collects empirical data which can be quantified and observed. Like the natural sciences and some of the social sciences, it has a problem-oriented approach in which research is designed to address a particular unsolved problem rather than having a vague "because it's there" rationale. Like the humanities, however, archaeology relies on imaginative reconstruction and many intuitive leaps-of-faith in the interpretation of its data. Despite efforts to reduce the width of the chasms over which these leaps occur, archaeology is far from being able to have its results replicated in laboratory experiments as in chemistry or physics.

Throughout its history, archaeology has wrestled with the question of its intellectual location, particularly as these locations across the landscape of scholarship became increasingly defined in the late nineteenth century. Nonetheless, by the first half of the twentieth century, New World archaeology and Old World archaeology looked very similar. The prevailing interest was in chronology and taxonomic units. Perhaps the crucial distinction was that in much of Europe, the accepted unit of analysis was the archaeological "culture," which had a much different meaning from the use of the word "culture" in anthropological archaeology. In central Europe especially, the archaeological cultures of later prehistory took on a quasi-ethnic significance, an idea which was rooted in modern nationalism and the concomitant definition of ethnic differences. In both hemispheres, the goal of archaeology became the refinement of a matrix in which one axis was time and the other was space. Through this matrix, the inception, spread, and demise of particular traits, such as a style of pottery decoration, could be traced. The mechanisms of change in the archaeological record were migration and "diffusion," the latter an ill-defined process of the transmission of cultural traits which was difficult for an archaeologist to explain, but he knew it when he saw it. The androcentric usage "he" is entirely appropriate here, for it was not until the 1950s that archaeology opened its doors to more than the occasional women scholar.

Despite the occasional critic, prehistoric archaeology continued in this interpretive vein until after World War II. Not until the 1960s did the discipline begin to assume the form it takes today. During this decade, a widespread concern with the specific character of archaeological evidence and its interpretation moved archaeology away from its earlier role as an extension of history into the pre-literate past. So, before characterizing prehistoric archaeology as it exists at the close of the twentieth century, it would be useful first to consider the key differences between it and history and to examine the nature of archaeological evidence a bit more closely before returning to the development of its interpretive framework.

ARCHAEOLOGY AND HISTORY

History, as a discipline, examines conditions during particular spans of recorded time or change over short periods. A historian might study the Romans or medieval times, but the actual temporal scope of any historical inquiry is very narrow. No historian today would try to trace the development of European society from Classical Greece to the late twentieth century: the subject, as defined by the organization of the field and the amount of evidence at hand, would be overwhelming and such a study would by definition be superficial. Yet shift the temporal frame of reference even two millennia backward and you have a fairly common, even esoteric, period for the study of human prehistory.

Perhaps it could be argued that the changes in human society between 2000 BC and 1 BC were significantly less than between AD 1 and AD 2000. But were they? During the first period agriculture came to North America, the Pacific Islands were colonized, bronze and iron metallurgy transformed Europe, and Greek, Roman, and Egyptian civilization flourished. This highlights another important aspect of human prehistory: it must be understood in its global context rather than on the scale of any smaller part of the globe. True, most people who study human prehistory focus on one particular area. I, for example, study prehistoric Europe. On the other hand, whereas medieval England can be understood with reference to little beyond the adjacent areas of Europe, the early farming cultures must be understood in terms of their Near Eastern precursors and their parallels in Mesoamerica, sub-Saharan Africa, and Southeast Asia.

Prehistory is the study of processes, not of events. We do not know exactly when farming was invented or who had the idea to plant seeds. Indeed, the fact that plants grow from seeds was probably known since earliest human times, as soon as the observational faculties of the human brain were able to process such information. The transitions to agriculture which have taken place in the last ten millennia (very recently, that is) were not the result of a sudden invention but the products of string of changes in the behavior of humans, plants, animals, and the environment which suddenly made agriculture an attractive way to make a living. Similarly, humans did not suddenly have the bright idea to draw on cave walls 30,000 years ago. They had probably already been doing it for a long time, but using impermanent materials and to such a low degree that such art did not survive. The question that confronts archaeologists and prehistorians is why all of a sudden it became an important aspect of human existence in a number of parts of the world. The search is no longer for the first and the most spectacular; instead, it is for an understanding of the causal factors that led to long-term change in human society.

ARCHAEOLOGY AND ANTHROPOLOGY

Archaeology and anthropology have a much more tangled relationship. In the Americas, archaeology emerged as an extension of ethnology and a complement to biological anthropology. When he studied the rapidly-disappearing New World indigenous peoples in the nineteenth and early twentieth centuries, the anthropologist was expected to concern himself with their prehistory, their modern condition, and their anatomical characteristics. In Europe, anthropology and archaeology remained distinct for the most part when it came to understanding the local past, but when Europeans went to other lands in the Old World where they encountered the remnants of indigenous peoples (such as in colonial possessions), the mingling of extant and prehistoric data occurred frequently.

In North America, the academic study of prehistoric archaeology came to be anchored in departments of anthropology and in comprehensive research institutions such as the Smithsonian Institution and the university museums at Harvard and Pennsylvania. At the individual level, however, there was rapid specialization over the first half of the twentieth century into archaeologists and cultural and biological anthropologists. Very few individuals were able to maintain scholarly standing as generalists and could move freely throughout the discipline. In cultural anthropology, the notion of cultural evolution fell into disfavor, yet for archaeologists this model began to appear all the more compelling for the interpretation of their data. Then, suddenly, the agendas of the two subfields shifted back towards each other, with cultural anthropologists, especially at the University of Michigan, embracing an evolutionary model of cultural development. This rapprochement had profound effects on the relationship between archaeology and anthropology.

One of the fundamental tenets of the "New Archaeology" of the 1960s and 1970s was that archaeology should be more like anthropology, or more to the point, the sort of anthropology that many archaeologists had studied in the required ethnography and kinship courses they had taken in the subject as anthropology majors. A fascination with kinship systems and social organization emerged, and attempts to determine whether a society was matrilineal or patrilineal or whether it used a "Big Man" form of socio-political organization were held up as examples of the accomplishments of the "New Archaeology" (e.g., Deetz 1965; Hill 1970; Longacre 1970, etc.). Unfortunately, these relied either on extending a historically known pattern back into shallow prehistory or on spurious assumptions such as "women made the pots" which could not easily be documented.

Viewed in retrospect, such attempts to do ethnography through archaeology luckily turned out to be more or less dead ends as fields for the pursuit of research, although they did have powerful political impact within the field to help reorient it away from the focus on chronology and systematics. Kinship systems and general categories of socio-political organization were the ethnographic equivalent of time–space systematics in archaeology, and to shift archaeology over to the study of such arid topics would have been truly dull.

Yoffee (1985: 45) makes the point that "archaeological data are perhaps more important in the assessment of long-term social changes than are the evanescent materials and emic systems with which ethnographers work. Archaeologists can and should use ethnographic research, but they must use it within their own rigorous standards and in their own distinctive research agendas." I strongly concur with this position. As will be echoed throughout this book, archaeology has a unique capacity for tracing long-term change and is generally unsuited for illustrating the continuity or discontinuity of an ethnographic record.

At this point, I would like to introduce the somewhat heretical position (for the United States) that archaeology is also not properly a subfield of anthropology – a super-discipline which has become too broad and theoretically inflated to support diverse subfields like archaeology and physical anthropology. Of course, in most other parts of the world, this disconnection seems obvious, but in the United States there has been a sustained effort to hold American anthropology together, like an incompatible husband and wife staying together for the sake of the children. Archaeology can learn quite a bit from social anthropology, just as it can from virtually every other discipline, but it has relatively little to *contribute* to these fields *as disciplines*. In order to understand this position further, however, it will be necessary to work back around to it through a consideration of the unique nature of archaeological evidence and archaeological reasoning.

THE NATURE OF ARCHAEOLOGICAL EVIDENCE

For historians, primary sources consist of written documents – treaties, letters, bills, hieroglyphs, dispatches – and in a supporting role, objects and buildings that illuminate life in a particular period. An important element of historical research is the critical analysis of primary sources and the assessment of how well they inform the historian about the issue under study. Archaeologists have their primary sources as well, although they are not usually subjected to the intense critical scrutiny historical sources are. Perhaps because an archaeological theory or model rarely turns on a single potsherd or a single radiocarbon date, scholarly discourse in the field usually involves debate about the *interpretation* of sources instead of the reliability of the sources themselves.

The primary sources of prehistoric archaeologists include *sites*, *features*, and *artifacts*. Sites are locations where archaeological remains are found. They may have structure, such as settlements and cemeteries, or they may be amorphous, such as scatters of flints or bones, or even isolated stray finds. Features are unmovable human constructions, such as burials, hearths, and house foundations. Their arrangement on a site provides its structure and the context for the finds therein. These finds consist largely of artifacts, the portable products of human hands which have taken raw materials and altered and shaped them in some way. Over the broad sweep of prehistory, these materials included stone, wood, plant fiber, bone, metals, and clay. It is important to realize that it was not until very recently that the range of raw materials used by humans was expanded to the range that we know today.

Another important source of information for archaeologists comes from the organic residues of human activity: such as seeds, bones, and charcoal. Well-meaning archaeologists of the 1960s attempted to coin the term "ecofacts" to cover this category of finds, but many are thankful that this word has not taken root. I have not included them among the main archaeological primary sources because their information value comes primarily after their interpretation by an intermediate specialist, who may be either the archaeologist or someone else. This analysis would more properly be considered the primary source used for the actual archaeological interpretation. Many of my colleagues might quarrel with this position, but I write as an archaeologist who specializes in the study of animal bones. In any event, the distinction is academic, since in the end the archaeologist weaves many different sources of data together to produce a coherent synthesis.

BIASES IN THE EVIDENCE

Although archaeological evidence is relatively immune from deliberate attempts by its prehistoric creators to bias and skew it, it is not immune from two other key sources of error. First, it is confined to what survives of the material remains of prehistoric society. Second, it is limited by the archaeologists' ability to recover these traces from the ground in a way which preserves the materials themselves and permits the observation of their context, as well as the degree to which an archaeologist selects the evidence relevant to a particular inquiry. The result is a progressive diminution in the amount of data available from the time it is discarded or otherwise enters the archaeological record to the time that the archaeologist draws his or her conclusions about prehistoric society.

The interaction of microbes, ground water, soil chemistry, physical agents of destruction, and the composition of material remains themselves results in a precipitous decline in the amount of archaeological data between the time artifacts leave the hands of their prehistoric makers and when they present themselves in the soil for recovery. The processes of decay in organic materials are well-known to anyone familiar with rotting wood. Organic materials rapidly lose their form and structure and are broken down and consumed by agents of decomposition. Less familiar to many are the roles played by the chemistry of various soil types and other agents of consumption. For instance, bone is not usually preserved in the decalcified loess soil of central Europe. At the Neolithic site of Bylany in Bohemia, a tiny sample of no more than a few thousand animal bones was found on an enormous site where on any given afternoon about 5200 BC there were probably several million. In the Netherlands at this time, Neolithic cemeteries are known only from pits with offerings of pots and stone axes. The skeletons in them have left only faint dark stains in the golden-colored soil. Dogs wreak havoc on collections of animal bones. The late American archaeozoologist John Guilday (1971) estimated that if dogs can be shown to have been present on a site, 96 percent of the animal bones once there have disappeared, chewed and digested by man's best friend. Iron artifacts in contact with ground water oxidize, leaving a shell of rust around a void which was once the original artifact. The archaeological record is continually under siege by development, highway construction, warfare, and carelessness. It is a wonder that anything survives at all.

Perhaps the greatest damage to the archaeological record, however, is done by archaeologists themselves. Some of this is of necessity, for the excavation of an archaeological site is by its nature destructive of the physical associations of finds. Yet an archaeologist can also unwittingly destroy archaeological evidence through the choice of excavation techniques, the care with which finds are removed from the soil, the handling of finds once removed from the soil, and the eventual method of their storage. Much of this is unavoidable. No archaeologist can be fully prepared for every contingency in the field. Choices and decisions are made about field strategy which may not appear to require changing until some damage to materials comes to light.

By definition, someone who deliberately destroys archaeological data is not an archaeologist, but there are times when archaeologists inadvertently fail to record associations or other observations which might strike them at the time to be irrelevant but which in hindsight may prove crucial. The advent of non-destructive techniques of prospection and the use of video cameras for recording archaeological excavations have been great advances in reducing the accidental loss of data in recent years. Yet in separating data from the soil it is very possible for artifacts to get lost. Few archaeologists have not had the experience of finding an artifact on the backdirt pile, devoid of any associations. Careless handling during washing and packing can cause fragile artifacts to crumble. Boxes piled high in a museum short of space can crush even robust pottery specimens and turn large animal bones to powder.

Thus archaeological evidence has passed through a number of increasingly fine sieves in its route from prehistoric culture to modern archaeologist. The result has been likened to attempting to reconstruct the contents of a room by looking through the keyhole. Another metaphor is to compare archaeological research to working a giant jigsaw puzzle in which there is no picture on the box and from which someone has thrown out most of the pieces.

This incomplete nature of archaeological data has two different effects on those who become engaged by it. Some archaeologists despair of being able to say anything with any degree of certainty and become increasingly frustrated by the gaps in the data. Others are excited by the possibility of finding one or two more pieces to the jigsaw puzzle and putting them into some rough location in the picture. The most exciting moment is when a piece actually fits with the others already there.

ARCHAEOLOGICAL METHODS

In understanding human prehistory, it is important to understand something of the methods of archaeology. For most people, archaeologists are seen as contented, if somewhat obsessive, folks who dig in fields, deserts, and caves to find relics of ancient times. Indeed, most archaeologists do carry out excavations: some once or twice in their careers, others regularly each year for decades. There was a time, a century or more ago, when virtually all of archaeology consisted of fieldwork, largely for its own sake. Ancient tombs were opened and the artifacts within were removed for display or collection. Cave sediments were dug into for cataloging. There was relatively little concern with context, that primary element which gives archaeological data their meaning.

In retrospect, perhaps the greatest measure of progress in archaeological data collection over the last century and the foundation for the rational interpretation of those data has been the elevation of *context* to a position of importance equal to, or even greater than, that of the artifacts themselves. Without the proper documentation and analysis of the relationship of artifacts to other artifacts, to layers and other deposits, and to the ecological and environmental data that those deposits contain, the information content of artifacts is limited to basic characteristics which describe their final shape and decoration and the raw material from which they were made. In the absence of information about context, it is impossible to draw further inferences about technology, economy, and social organization which only come from the patterns that are observable in the associations and distributions of different types of remains.

Without the recording of context, the revolution in archaeological dating caused by carbon-14 would have been impossible, for this method analyzes organic material found with inorganic artifacts like pottery and stone tools, not the artifacts themselves. The reconstruction of ancient diet through the study of animal bones and seeds also would be impossible, for again such materials only take on analytical value through their association with datable artifacts and features like houses and soils. Archaeology would be a fairly dull descriptive exercise and, one can guess, would be now confined to the study of discrete collections of finds such as the contents of royal tombs, had not archaeologists discerned the insights that were possible once context and associations came to be considered primary data. An understanding of the importance of context is the foundation of an appreciation of the accomplishments of prehistoric archaeology over the last 150 years.

RECOVERY OF EVIDENCE

Archaeologists recover primary data on prehistoric life through *survey* to find sites and *excavation* to retrieve the remains in a controlled and orderly fashion. Prehistoric sites are seldom found in the open air, save for unusual circumstances in deserts and other arid environments, and even in these circumstances the artifacts were once buried and the wind has done the work for the archaeologist. Archaeological research inevitably involves someone or something moving some soil. For anyone to claim the title of "archaeologist," he or she must have used a shovel or a trowel at some point, even if all they do now is to sit at the computer and write books.

Virtually all archaeological sites are discovered accidentally. By this I mean that the uniform processes of sedimentation and soil formation that occur throughout the globe will cover archaeological remains forever unless they are disturbed through some sort of natural or human activity. Such disturbances occur locally and, for the most part, randomly. A farmer ploughs a field, a road is built, a drought leads to cropmarks, or lake levels recede. Archaeologists can speed up this process of discovery by conducting archaeological surveys, but for the most part these too rely on human intervention to produce evidence of sites. Survey of ploughed fields will result in the discovery of archaeological sites, but in forested terrain the archaeologist must often put spade in ground at intervals in the hopes that one in a hundred shovel pits will turn up evidence of prehistoric life. One archaeologist who worked in forested conditions in Europe told me that his best allies in finding sites were the wild boars who inhabited the woods and who periodically churned up traces of prehistoric settlements in their rootings and wallowings.

Modern archaeologists are aided in their discovery of sites by prospection devices such as the magnetometer and ground-penetrating radar. Recently, remote-sensing techniques involving satellite imagery have also permitted the discovery of sites, especially if they produce a sufficiently large signature such as Prehispanic wetland argiculture in Mesoamerica and buried urban centers in the Arabian Peninsula. For most archaeologists, however, the walking of ploughed fields or arid wastelands, peering into pipeline trenches and road cuts, and interrogating local farmers and antiquarians about their finds are still fundamental methods of site discovery and will continue to be for years to come.

Once a site is found, the archaeologist must assess its significance and decide whether to conduct excavations. In some cases, the decision is made for the archaeologist, due to an imminent threat to a large concentration of prehistoric materials by some planned development activity, such as a super-highway or a reservoir. In the world today, most archaeological excavation can probably be said to occur under such circumstances. An extraordinary amount of soil is moved in all parts of the world, not just in Europe and North America, and there are very few places where archaeological sites are not threatened with destruction. The archaeological community, therefore, gives priority to sites which may be destroyed (preferring to do it scientifically and to record context, which the bulldozer is not capable of doing) and leaves sites which are safe for future generations.

The threat may come not only from large-scale construction, but may also result from the cumulative effects of small-scale activity such as ploughing. For example, in 1990 my Polish colleagues and I excavated a remarkable 6000-year-old burial in which a woman had been buried with a copper diadem around her head (Grygiel and Bogucki 1997). In this field, erosion had caused a small amount of soil to slide downslope each year, allowing the plough to dig a tiny bit deeper. The plough had just rubbed across the top of this woman's skull but had not yet shattered it and scattered the pieces of the diadem. Had another year passed, we would not have found this burial in such remarkable condition, and in particular, we would not have been able to connect the skull fragments with the diadem so clearly as to have such full documentation of context.

There are long manuals that cover the techniques of archaeological excavation, so a few paragraphs will not adequately describe the process. In general, it can be said that the dimensions of the site determine in large measure the techniques of excavation used. A deep site in which the stratification of the layers provides important information on context will emphasize the vertical dimension. Deep trenches or cuts will generally be made. Unfortunately, such excavations do not provide information on the horizontal patterning of human activity unless they are expanded at critical levels to examine larger areas. A large, shallow, open site (such as are typically found in temperate Europe or midcontinental North America) usually requires a broad-exposure approach to excavation. Such sites may not have much in the way of stratification except in very localized situations where rubbish deposits of features might overlap.

The degree of meticulousness of such excavation depends on the nature of the deposits. A popular image of archaeologists' tools is that of the dental pick and the artist's brush. It may come as a surprise to some how frequently the shovel and even the backhoe are used as primary excavating devices. In many cases, the site is burdened with layers of ploughed-through soil which may contain artifacts that lack context. When time and money are important limitations, as they almost always are, the archaeologist may choose to remove the plough-zone with a backhoe in order to get to the undisturbed layers beneath. In these layers, it may be more appropriate to use a dental-pick or even a vacuum cleaner to remove the soil from some delicate remains. A "dirt archaeologist" is practical and uses the right tool for the job.

Every modern archaeologist sieves some or all of the soil that he or she excavates. The effect of sieving on the recovery of artifacts, particularly of small fragmentary remains and animal bones, is dramatic. Artifacts and bones tend to take on the color of the soil in which they are found, and it is only on the screen that they can be recognized and separated from the soil in which they have been lying for centuries of millennia. In addition, a portion of the soil is often processed through water, either to make small, soft items (such as charred seeds) float or to permit the retrieval of heavier tiny items (like fish bones) when the surrounding matrix is washed away.

ORGANIZING THE DATA

The recognition of context made possible the definition of other fundamental units of archaeological data beyond that of the individual artifact. Features are archaeological finds which cannot be removed from the ground, such as houses, pits, graves, and postholes. The associations among features and artifacts are as important as those among artifacts themselves. Archaeological sites are the locations where artifacts and features are found, normally in some numbers and with further information on context. Sites themselves have a form of context: they are located in relation to characteristics of the natural environment and to other sites of the same or different periods. The larger context of sites makes possible the study of patterns in their distribution and setting, a form of archaeological analysis which came of age in the mid-twentieth century.

The idea of context made possible the fundamental organizational principle of archaeological research: the identification of similar groupings, or "assemblages," of artifacts and their geographical extent. While the size of an assemblage may vary from the artifacts found in a single pit to the collection of pottery from a single site, it always is defined in terms of both its content and its context as a collective term for a group of archaeological specimens. Thus archaeologists were able to progress from concentrating on individual artifacts to looking at patterns of finds distributed over regions and continents. The notion of assemblages found in context means that archaeologists did not have to rely on accidental finds of identical artifacts to make distant comparisons but rather could argue that a collection of finds from Site A was similar to the collection from Site B and draw conclusions based on that fact.

They were also able to note which types of assemblages were stratified over other types of assemblages, thus permitting a measure of chronological order in the growing thicket of archaeological finds.

The term "assemblage" is neutral, and simply describes a collection of artifacts from a given context. Groups of assemblages in a geographical context, however, have traditionally assumed considerable significance for archaeologists and have been given a variety of names which are laden with meaning and conceptual baggage. For example, similar assemblages of chipped-stone tools are frequently referred to (especially in the Old World) as "industries." The choice of term is far from neutral, and implies organized production, a coherent technology, and skilled workers in a collective enterprise. Whether or not these conditions prevailed in the prehistoric situation being so characterized, archaeological terminology has introduced certain fundamental assumptions which color the discussion.

An even more complicated term is the archaeological "culture," a conceptual and analytical unit which continues to be employed widely. The notion of the archaeological culture emerged from the late nineteenth century, was given substance as an analytical tool in the writings of the German prehistorian Carl Schuchhardt (1859–1943), and was made a fundamental concept in the English-speaking archaeological community by the Australian-born British prehistorian V. Gordon Childe (1892–1957). The classic definition of an archaeological culture is that given by Childe in the preface to his 1929 volume *The Danube in Prehistory*:

> We find certain types of remains – pots, implements, ornaments, burial rites, house forms – constantly recurring together. Such a complex of regularly associated traits we shall term a "cultural group" or just a "culture" (Childe 1929: v–vi).

Use of the term "culture" to describe recurring assemblages of artifacts (and in some cases types of features, such as house and burial styles) implies a set of shared customs, values, and beliefs on the part of the makers of the artifacts. Clearly, this is a leap-of-faith. Indeed, in taking a step back and considering this assumption, one is struck by its enormity. Modern material culture provides it with relatively little empirical support, although among tribal peoples perhaps a stronger case can be made for a frequent correlation between distinctive techniques of artifact manufacture and decoration and their cultural identity. Although this is far from universal, the use of the term "culture" introduced another layer of implications and assumptions: among "simpler" peoples as might have existed in prehistory, artifact types reflect non-material aspects of society and discontinuities in artifact styles reflect differences in social and ideological practices.

Over the last century, archaeologists have embraced these assumptions to differing degrees. Until the 1960s, they were largely unspoken and taken as fact. An archaeological culture was equated with a group of people having a distinct ethnic identity as manifested in their material remains. Sequences of archeological cultures were then developed to create a "culture history" of a particular region, and then these would be placed alongside sequences from neighboring regions to trace directions of influence. The form that this influence took was modeled either by using the appropriately diffuse term "diffusion" (a vague form of acculturation and transmission of cultural traits) or by calling it "migration" or even "invasion."

Thus, for many archaeologists in the first half of the twentieth century, the ultimate goal of archaeology was the refinement of a grid in which time ran along the vertical axis and space along the horizontal. Cultures were further subdivided into "groups" or into lettered or numbered phases. This approach was carried to extremes, particularly in the archaeology of east-central Europe of the 1920s and 1930s, in which rival German and Polish archaeologists used similar methods and data to claim the antiquity of either Germanic or Slavic peoples in the area between the Oder and Vistula. Indeed, the spurious equation of the archaeological culture with a distinct group of people is one of the residual caricatures of European prehistorians in the modern global archaeological community.

TELLING TIME

Archaeologists have always been obsessed with time, since this dimension defines one axis (the other being space) of the framework within which all archaeological interpretation occurs. Yet until 1948, almost all archaeological chronology was based largely on guesswork and a set of suppositions about what happened when one group of people and their artifacts met another. The exceptions to this were those cases where an archaeologist studied a late prehistoric period where there was a nearby historical chronology or where preserved wood could be dated by its annual rings. For most of the world and its prehistoric past, however, there were no clear temporal yardsticks by which time could be measured in meaningful units. Nonetheless, this did not stop archaeologists before the advent of scientific dating methods from developing useful conventions for organizing the past in a way which could provide some temporal structure to the archaeological record.

From the early decades of the nineteenth century, when geologists and archaeologists recognized the Law of Superposition (primacy in articulating this principle is given to the seventeenth-century naturalist Nicolaus Steno), some types of archaeological remains could be seen to be older than others. In some cases, such as in caves, they might be stratified in neat, layer-cake deposits, but more commonly it was much more complicated to unravel. A pit on a site might cut through a house foundation which disturbed a grave dug into a lower layer and so forth. After a while, numerous local instances of such stratification were built up so that consistencies could be recognized. Thus over the second half of the nineteenth century, meticulous scholars such as Oskar Montelius (1843–1921), Sophus Müller (1846–1934), and Jaroslav Palliardi (1861–1922) built up the maze of interconnections and superpositions among different types of artifacts over many parts of Europe. They were followed by early twentieth-century culture historians such as

Carl Schuchhardt (1859–1943), V. Gordon Childe (1892–1958), and Paul Reinecke (1872–1958). Each of these scholars possessed an encylopedic grasp of artifact types and their relative positions to each other.

In the New World, where the archaeological record was somewhat more shallow, relatively few such stratigraphic scholars were found. Not until Nels Nelson (1875–1964), who had excavated in Europe, and Alfred V. Kidder (1885–1963), who had studied with Egyptologists at Harvard, undertook excavations in stratified deposits in the southwest United States did such regional chronologies begin to be constructed. In the eastern part of North America and in much of South America, relatively few stratified sites were excavated at this point and few intersecting features had been recognized. Individual sites were largely floating in time.

The common currencies of such analyses were units such as "cultures," "industries" (in the case of Stone Age assemblages), and "groups" (along with other subdivisions) in the Old World and "periods," "phases," "foci," and "components" (again with finer subdivisions) in the New World. In both hemispheres, specific artifact styles (usually pottery) were the defining elements of these divisions. V. Gordon Childe (1929: v–vi) offered the classic definition of an archaeological culture: "certain types of remains – pots, implements, ornaments, burial rites, house forms – constantly recurring together," although in practice these came to be defined on the basis of a single diagnostic type of artifact. The archaeological use of the word "culture" was particularly unfortunate, for it came to be conflated with ethnographic cultures and the anthropological concept of culture. In the New World, the use of terms which had more chronological and classificatory connotation was introduced by the Midwestern Taxonomic System (McKern 1939), although these resulted in a bewildering terminological morass as archaeologists named phases and their subdivisions after administrative units, natural landmarks, and celebrated local diggers.

The major problem with such relative dating, of course, is that the cultural timescale is quite elastic. The Neolithic (or "New Stone Age," characterized by agriculture and pottery) in Europe was said to begin at 5000 BC by some and 3000 BC by others. Who could say which chronology was right? Of course, this made for heated debates among archaeologists, but in the final analysis, the accepted result was determined by strength of personality, force of persuasion, and prolixity of publication.

The revolution in archaeological dating (and it can be considered to be truly a revolution, in that it ultimately caused a radical revision in the aims and goals of archaeology rather than being simply a technical advance) was the discovery of the radiocarbon dating technique by Willard Libby (1908–80) in the late 1940s *and* his recognition that it could be applied to archaeological finds. Many good descriptions of this dating technique are available (e.g., Renfrew 1973: 48–54) so an exhaustive discussion will not be presented here. Fundamentally, it is predicated on the decay of the radioactive isotope ^{14}C at a relatively constant rate over a half-life of 5730 years and extrapolating from the amount present in the dated material in order to ascertain an approximate age.

There are several fundamental principles that must be kept in mind about radiocarbon dating. First of all, a radiocarbon "date" is actually a statistical statement of probability rather than a metrical reading of a gauge. Many factors go into determining the amount of ^{14}C left in a sample: sample size, background cosmic radiation, counting errors, and simply the length of time that the frequency with which decay particles are given off is counted. Second, radiocarbon dating only works on materials that once absorbed carbon, which limits it to materials of a biological origin. For example, a flint tool cannot be radiocarbon-dated, but the piece of charcoal found with it can. Therefore context becomes of supreme importance. Third, a key assumption of radiocarbon dating, that the production of atmospheric ^{14}C has been constant over the millennia, has been proven false. At certain times there was more ^{14}C, while at others, less. Much effort has been expended over recent decades to determine the pattern of these fluctuations, with the result being that many early radiocarbon dates are now shown to be much older, in some cases by as much as a millennium. Finally, conventional radiocarbon dating only works at dates of 50,000 years or younger, while the superior technique of radiocarbon dating using an accelerator mass-spectrometer (AMS) can date materials as old as 100,000 years. Prior to 100,000 years, there is a substantial gap which is filled by other, less proven dating methods, back to about 500,000 years ago when the reliable range of potassium-argon dating, another radiometric technique, is reached.

Archaeologists are probably responsible for most of the errors in the application of radiocarbon dating. Pure, uncontaminated samples are a *sine qua non* of this method. Samples that are contaminated from carbon-bearing natural deposits (such as coal seams) or even by someone smoking in the excavation will produce either spuriously old or recent dates, for example. Archaeologists also have a tendency to forget that radiocarbon dates are statistical expressions of probability, not direct readings of a clock. I have heard one archaeologist telling another that since his material had a single date of 2800 ± 130 BC it was certainly older than his colleague's which had a single date of 2700 ± 120 BC. Statistically, of course, such a statement is ridiculous, and in any event single dates are so dependent on sampling and counting factors that they could be wildly inaccurate. It is far better to have a series of dates which can show some central tendency before pronouncements about absolute chronology can be made.

A modern archaeologist will use a combination of relative and absolute dating methods and conventions. The definition of periods, cultures, groups, and phases now provides a useful qualitative shorthand to describe the characteristics of assemblages and sites in an economical way and their relative temporal relationship to other sites and collections. At the same time, absolute dating – primarily radiocarbon – is used to establish tighter control over chronology and to date specific important remains in a more precise way. Yet rarely is a site occupied for such a long duration that the radiocarbon dating of individual features will enable an archaeologist to unravel its internal development. There is still no substitute for old-fashioned stratigraphic observation during careful excavation and the meticulous documentation of the context of each object, at least to the level of the feature in which it was found.

ARCHAEOLOGICAL INTERPRETATION

Once archaeologists have artifacts, features, and sites in their appropriate context and assigned to the proper cultures, phases, and periods, the question then becomes one of explaining how things got to be the way they were and why they changed from that state into the one that follows. It is here that archaeologists enter into the realm of interpretation, the final frontier for archaeological inquiry.

THE POSTULATES OF ARCHAEOLOGY

Archaeological interpretation is founded on several key postulates. These assertions are of such a basic nature that no attempt is made to deduce them from others. From time to time, these postulates are called into question, but they have stood the test of time and continue to be accepted on faith by most archaeologists. Among these postulates are the Postulate of Uniformitarianism, the Postulate of Interconnectivity, and the Postulate of Inevitable Change.

THE POSTULATE OF UNIFORMITARIANISM

The Postulate of Uniformitarianism states that in the past, the processes which operated on human societies were similar to the ones that continue to operate today. Populations grew, kinship bonds were formed, resources were procured and distributed, and people required food, shelter, and warmth. In other words, we cannot assume that prehistoric people had different needs than we do today, although our modern ways of meeting these needs are significantly different. Moreover, there were not some hidden dimensions of human existence that were so totally alien as to make them completely unknowable to a modern archaeologist.

On the other hand, this postulate cannot be extended uncritically to justify the assumption that modern social, economic, and symbolic forms can be equated with prehistoric cases which share certain formal characteristics. This practice, known as "ethnographic analogy," has been practiced at one time or another by almost every archaeologist, but there are certain rules which control its use (Binford 1967). It is a very useful tool for the generation of hypotheses, but in order for these hypotheses to be considered supportable, some additional logical foundation must be added. It is not sufficient for an archaeologist to say, for example, that because small-scale agriculturalists in the tropics today use shifting agriculture, then Neolithic farmers in Europe did likewise. It may be (as is indeed the case) that other conditions would make this position untenable (Bogucki 1988).

THE POSTULATE OF INTERCONNECTIVITY

The Postulate of Interconnectivity is that variability in one aspect of society will be coupled with or reflected in variability in other elements (Dent 1995: 131). This means that archaeologists assume that the study of raw material procurement or settlement patterns will have something to say about social organization. Such a reliance on proxy evidence is what permits archaeologists to draw conclusions about the far greater proportion of human existence which does not leave any physical trace in the archaeological record.

Faith in this postulate was a distinguishing characteristic of the thinking that came to characterize American and British archaeology in the 1960s and 1970s, and it is still viewed skeptically in many other parts of the world, particularly continental Europe. Yet without the assumption of interconnectivity, archaeology would be little more than an arid exercise in the recovery, classification, and dating of prehistoric remains. This postulate provides archaeology with intellectual excitement and gives the archaeologist freedom to practice social science.

THE POSTULATE OF INEVITABLE CHANGE

Archaeologists assume that change will occur. It may be slow or fast, widespread or limited geographically, but archaeological remains found at a particular time and in a particular area are assumed to be distinctive within a certain geographical and temporal extent. Without change, there would be nothing to study, so archaeology *demands* change as a precondition for its existence.

This postulate may appear so obvious as to seem risible, but there are very many fields in which conditions are viewed as static. Historical fields such as geology and art history also presuppose change, but only archaeology makes the *processes* of change its focus of synthesis and reason for existence (even so-called "post-processual" archaeologists deal with process, but simply have a different interpretive framework for defining it.).

LEAPS OF INFERENCE

Archaeology is unusual, perhaps even exceptional, among all the fields of scholarly inquiry in the degree to which it uses proxy evidence to infer the properties and behavior of its subjects. Pots, stone tools, and animal bones are not people nor are they historical documents; they are the residue of human activities which are not directly observed or reported. This aspect of archaeological evidence has its good points and its bad points. Unlike historical documents, archaeological data is rarely, if ever, manipulated by those who produced it. The sense of history among literate humans is so strong that they are aware when they are writing a document of substance that it may survive their times. Thus the historian must carefully analyze primary sources to isolate bias and deception. The archaeologist almost never has to confront such willful behavior on the part of his or her subjects. The discard of animal bones, broken pottery, worn-out stone tools, and other refuse is done without regard for the patterns that they might produce.

The problem with archaeological data is that in order to get from the data to the human subjects behind it requires an inferential leap into the unknown. Other fields of scholarly inquiry about human behavior are based on direct observations, however flawed. In contrast, the recovery of archaeological materials takes place centuries or millennia distant from the behavior that produced them. This leap-of-inference is the Achilles heel of archaeology, yet it is the hub around which debate and discussion in the field most commonly occur and which generates the key advances in archaeological thinking. The archaeologist who avoids making inferences about human behavior is condemned to a life of sorting pottery over and over, examining the same stone tool dozens of times, or figuring out better ways of moving dirt. Some archaeologists are very cautious and preface each statement with a "perhaps" or a "maybe." Others boldly leap off the edge and risk being shown to have not landed in the right spot only in the hindsight of future generations.

Archaeology is very much constrained by what the modern imagination allows in the range of human behavior. Moreover, there are biases introduced by modern practices and customs. For example, on the sites that I study in Poland, we typically find the remains of shellfish – freshwater clams – in rubbish deposits. These shells are opened and fragmented, and the mussels inside had clearly been extracted. Some of my Polish colleagues until recently insisted that these must be ritual offerings. The idea that the shellfish were consumption remains apparently had never been a possibility for them, for shellfish are not to be found on the twentieth-century Polish menu. Meanwhile, although I do not like clams, I have certainly seen enough remains of clambakes on the New England coast to know that they are edible and that a small number of them can produce a large quantity of shell debris. Is my interpretation correct? I believe so.

CHANGING INTERPRETIVE FRAMEWORKS

As is the case with any discipline, the interpretive frameworks used by archaeologists have changed over time. In general, until recently the history of archaeology has been characterized by two major paradigms to explain prehistoric change: diffusionism and functionalism. Diffusionism is rooted in the traditional archaeological goals of organizing prehistoric remains in a matrix of time and space. Its exclusive agenda is to explain the similarities and differences observed between adjacent cells in this matrix. Functionalism is connected to the view of culture as "adaptation," in which humans respond to conditions in their natural and social environment. In this view, change in the archaeological record is a reaction to a problem presented by changes in conditions beyond a society's control.

Before the 1960s, the predominant paradigm was almost exclusively diffusionist. Prehistoric change was seen as the result of the spread of ideas and techniques either through contact between donor and recipient cultures or the actual movement of peoples. Within this paradigm, there were extremes which ranged from hyperdiffusionism, like that of Grafton Eliot Smith (who saw Egyptian civilization as the progenitor of all subsequent civilizations), to a modified diffusionism which allowed some in situ development (although what caused it was never fully explained). The diffusionist paradigm never really addressed the issue of what really caused prehistoric change. It was sufficient that a different cultural trait or an alien people appeared nearby which led to similar change in artifacts, houses, and economy. The meeting of two different styles of artifact led to hybrid forms which implicitly followed a biological model of mating. Within this paradigm, it was also relatively easy to avoid asking hard questions of the data and to retreat into descriptions and cataloging of materials. The goals of the archaeologist were seen as (1) the recovery of data; (2) its assignment to the proper phase or culture, and (3) the identification of its connections to neighboring groups to trace the direction and source of "influences" on the assemblage.

Since diffusionist models rely only on "contact" to explain changes, they quickly became simple descriptions of how the archaeological record appeared at various points in time and space. There was a nagging suspicion that the underlying reasons for this change were going unexplored. This dissatisfaction was brought into the open somewhat contentiously by Walter Taylor in 1948, although it was almost two decades before a true shift in the agenda of archaeological interpretation can be said to have occurred. In the meantime, however, the impoverishment of the diffusionist paradigm became clearer as archaeologists began to explore key transitions in human prehistory, such as the shift from foraging to farming.

The 1960s saw tremendous upheaval in many scholarly fields, and archaeology was no exception. In the middle of the decade, the diffusionist paradigm came to be replaced by the functionalist approach. This replacement is only apparent in hindsight, for at the time the push was for greater scientific rigor, the explicit testing of hypotheses, and the search for causality and process. Archaeological interpretation discarded diffusionism (along with its mechanisms such as colonization and migration) and embraced adaptation as the underlying mechanism of cultural change. As a philosophical rationalization of this approach, logical positivism was adopted, with its rigorous insistence on deductive reasoning.

The causes of this replacement are varied. Shifts in funding sources after World War II had led American anthropology to be situated unambiguously among the social sciences and thus open to scrutiny about how well it functioned as a social science. It was no longer sufficient to pay lip-service to archaeology as being a subfield of anthropology, and archaeologists came to realize that they actually needed to *practice* anthropology, with cultural anthropology setting the agenda. This was easier said than done, for many investigations in cultural anthropology would be impossible without living informants. Archaeologists gravitated towards particular segments of anthropology, such as cultural evolution and human ecology, which enjoyed legitimacy in the field yet could also be addressed archaeologically. Some ambitious attempts were made to study kinship patterns (e.g., Deetz 1965;

Hill 1970) but these were essentially demonstrations of methodology which did not expand knowledge far beyond that already known ethnohistorically.

This shift was paralleled in other parts of the world, particularly in the British Isles. Although archaeology had never formally been a part of anthropology, there were efforts at integrating the field with the natural sciences and with the more "empirical" social sciences such as geography. Despite the slight difference in emphasis between the British and American trends on archaeology during the late 1960s, the net effect was similar and archaeologists on both sides of the North Atlantic continued to find common interests.

Meanwhile in most other parts of the world, indigenous archaeologists continued their interests in description, chronology, and culture history. Although greater efforts were made to involve the physical sciences in archaeological analysis, the goals of archaeology itself remained unchanged. Indeed, a certain degree of skepticism emerged about expanding the goals of archaeology. Models which were not firmly grounded in empirical data were viewed with suspicion and disapproval (a condition which continues today in some European countries.) It is also possible that US involvement in the Vietnam war led to a distaste for any new ideas which seemed to emanate from America.

The emphasis on functionalist interpretations was abetted by the increasingly interdisciplinary nature of archaeological practice and its collaboration with the natural sciences. The availability of funding from sources such as National Science Foundation and the British Academy encouraged the formation of multidisciplinary teams which included geologists, botanists, zoologists, and other sciences which had previously been ancillary to the main thrust of archaeological investigation. The functionalist embedding of archaeology within human ecology and cultural evolution meshed very well with such organization of research, even if the results were rarely integrated in a systematic way. Very importantly, the rewards structure of academic promotion, particularly in the United States, came to favor the natural science model of competitive research, grant acquisition, and graduate student production.

Inevitably a reaction to the functionalist paradigm set in, which went beyond disagreement with the overstatements of the more strident "New Archaeologists" and which represented a serious challenge to the positivism and scientism which spawned the earlier upheaval. By the mid-1980s, a movement calling itself "post-processual archaeology" emerged, primarily in the United Kingdom, stimulated by marxian social and literary philosophers such as Feyerabend, Derrida, Foucault, and Barthes. The search for causality and explanation in explicitly scientific terms was replaced by attempts to discover the "meaning" that was embodied in various aspects of the archaeological record. For some, this meaning is construed as the abstract symbolic significance that can be uncovered in archaeological remains. Others, following the Continental philosophers more closely, saw meaning as the hidden ways in which power and authority are constructed.

The post-processual (or "*anti*-processual," which might be a better characterization of the approach) has taken root in some quarters, including a number of archaeology departments in the British Isles, where it has appropriated the rubric of "archaeological theory." Elsewhere, particularly in the United States, it is viewed as a virus against which all good processual archaeologists must be inoculated. Interestingly, to embrace this approach would bring American archaeologists back to having more in common with the social anthropologists with whom they continue to cohabit in anthropology departments. The fact that they choose not to is persuasive evidence of how much the two disciplines have diverged in the last three decades.

MODERN ARCHAEOLOGY

Despite the interest in making American archaeology a part of anthropology during the 1960s, in the 1970s and 1980s social anthropology moved away from archaeology. While archaeologists embraced the traditional interests of earlier generations of anthropologists in human ecology, economics, and social organization, the newer generation of social anthropologists shifted its attention towards symbolism and beyond that, the hermeneutic analysis of ethnography as text. Biological anthropology also enlarged its scope to become essentially human population biology, leaving the emerging field of palaeoantropology to cover the traditional intersection of this field with archaeology. Thus disciplinary lines became markedly redrawn, and while archaeologists and social anthropologists continued to belong to one department on many American campuses, there was often very little intellectual common interest between the occupants of neighboring offices in these departments.

In the Old World during the 1960s and 1970s, archaeology never really had the pretension to be considered a part of anthropology. On the other hand, it did, in parallel with American archaeology, embrace the core values of traditional anthropology in ecology, trade, and social structure, even if its approach was not couched in American-style social science jargon. The increased availability of radiocarbon dating meant that the long-standing concentration on chronology and typology could be abandoned in favor of social questions. In general, this was very beneficial in that it rescued archaeology from being an arid exercise in systematics and refocused attention on the people behind the pots.

The collapse of communism in the Soviet Union and its satellites in the late 1980s and early 1990s brought a whole new group of archaeologists into the global archaeological community. Actually, archaeologists in these countries had never been completely isolated, but the technical advancements in archaeology in western Europe and the Americas of the 1960s and 1970s had never been fully available to them and, moreover, the shifts in interpretive frameworks had often penetrated the Iron Curtain in a very garbled way. Thus, calls for more scientific rigor in the West were sometimes interpreted in the East as a need to bear down more on systematics. The words were coming through but not the intellectual context. Now, the archaeologists of these countries are in a position to contribute their own perspective to world archaeology and to learn directly from the experience of others.

Archaeology at the close of the twentieth century now is effectively a free-standing field of scholarship, but not in the finite and bounded sense in

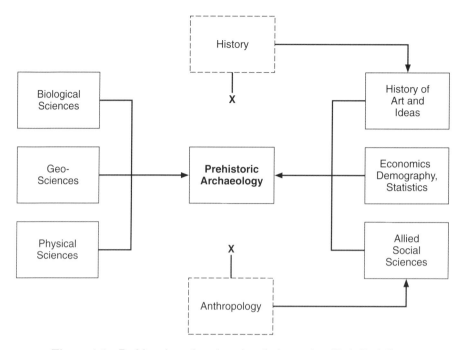

Figure 1.1 Prehistoric archaeology in relation to its allied disciplines.

which disciplines were defined a century ago. In an earlier era, archaeology was viewed as a bridge between history and anthropology. Today, it is a modern multidisciplinary field with extensions to a large number of allied fields, while its two ancestral disciplines have generally remained much more limited in scope, despite their pretensions of breadth. Figure 1.1 potrays this relationship in which archaeology has a core body of method and theory, while using analytical tools derived from a variety of other disciplines which may not be related to each other independently.

Modern archaeology is really a "meta-discipline": a discipline of disciplines. In this sense, it has much in common with another meta-discipline, namely engineering. This observation is perhaps conditioned by my current employment situation within a School of Engineering, but on a daily basis I am struck by the similarities between the two fields, in that they both apply analytical tools derived from a number of other disciplines (in engineering: math, physics, chemistry, geology, economics; in archaeology: anthropology, botany, zoology, chemistry, geology, economics) within a distinctive body of method and theory. This perception of archaeology as a meta-discipline, akin to engineering, is in sharp contrast to the traditional definition of fields in the humanities, social sciences, and natural sciences. Although there are notable exceptions among individual scholars, these fields are largely defined by a fairly narrow and to some extent ingrown body of method and theory. While endorsement is given to "multidiscipinary approaches" in the humanities and social sciences, these usually consist of discourse with scholars in other fields rather than the integration of these in the same way that is done in archaeology and engineering.

If one is seeking a kindred spirit for the core of archaeology among the physical sciences, I would suggest astrophysics rather than the more familiar chemical or biological sciences. Astrophysics also deals with immense spans of time – of hundreds of millions of years, which dwarf the two million years that form the domain of archaeology. More importantly, it tries to reconstruct the behavior of celestial bodies through the properties of a product, their light. By the time their reflected light reaches the telescopes of the astrophysicists, the body being studied may no longer exist or may have changed form significantly. Given the enormity of the universe, the part of it that a single astrophysicist is actually able to study in a lifetime is infinitesimal, so these scientists also make generalizations on the basis of a very small sample. Alongside their technical terminology, they devise metaphors to make processes more intelligible. Although their time scales differ considerably, the frames of reference used by archaeology and astrophysics are remarkably similar.

At the close of the twentieth century, it is clear that modern prehistoric archaeology is not what it was even a few decades ago, much less than at the beginning of the century. Can the same said for many other fields? Not only has archaeology's basic corpus of data been exponentially expanded, but the techniques of obtaining those data have also been revolutionized. Alongside these technical developments, however, the changes in the paradigm of archaeological interpretation have shifted so markedly that articles and books published even a decade or two ago are cited either for the empirical data they contain or as "indicator fossils" of obsolete interpretive approaches. Most significantly, archaeology has become a pluralistic discipline in which a wide variety of interpretations can be accommodated. Some now try to speak of different "archaeologies," but I would strongly resist this tendency. Instead, I believe that the fact that these frameworks can all be accommodated civilly within one discipline is a sign of the maturity and vigor of the field.

ORGANIZATION AND THEMES OF THIS VOLUME

STARTING POINT – ENDING POINTS

Even though human prehistory is only a segment of a continuum that began with our pre-human ancestors and continued into historical periods, a book like this must have a definite temporal beginning and end. As it is, the scope of time is enormous. Moreover, these are largely calendarless tracts of time, into which some order has been introduced through chronometric dating techniques, so there is not the luxury of having the scope defined simply as a particular recent century or era.

I propose to confine this book to the members of our own genus, *Homo*, despite the fact that there is archaeology to be found among our possible immediate precursors, the australopithecines. While not wanting to offend my colleagues who study the archaeology of "Lucy" and her cousins, I am arbitrarily choosing to start this volume with the appearance of *people*, not just hominids. This puts the beginning point of this volume somewhere just before 2 million years ago in Africa, which still leaves plenty of time to cover!

Since this is a book about prehistory, it will have multiple ending points in different parts of the world when literate complex societies appear on the scene. Thus, in the Near East, it will close about 2500 BC; in Europe, when the Romans show up; and in the Americas and Africa, when Europeans are on the horizon. The book will not come to a crashing conclusion in any of these areas, but it will simply fade off as prehistory inexorably shifts into history.

MAJOR THEMES OF THIS BOOK

This volume is organized around a number of recurring themes which will continue throughout. They can be summarized as follows:

1 The interplay of technology and society; the procurement, allocation, and consumption of raw materials.
2 Humans as self-interested decision-makers responding to risk and uncertainty; identification of key units of decision-making in various periods and regions.
3 The behavior through time of these fundamental decision-making units of society, specifically the *household*, as they respond to internal and external demands.
4 Humans as functioning within a *landscape* which has physical, biotic, and social dimensions.
5 The intellectual history of prehistoric archaeology as an evolving meta-discipline rather than a static antiquarian curiosity.

THEORETICAL APPROACH

Although this book aims to be an overview of world prehistory for a generalist audience, it does have a specific theoretical slant of which the reader should be aware. Essentially, the position taken in this book is that the overall sweep of prehistoric society was the cumulative result of decisions made by generations of self-interested individuals. This perspective diverges from the "problem-solving" perspective of the functionalist archaeologists of the 1960s and 1970s as well as from the search for hidden meaning of the post-processualists. Technological development, agriculture, and social inequality were unexpected consequences of the conscious choices made by many individuals who were interested in improving their situations in life, however such improvement was measured in their cultural setting: hunting success, access to mates, offspring, allies, status, wealth, prestige, or authority. Basically, most people act in what they perceive to be their own best interest.

Some might regard this as a Republican Party view of human prehistory. To spare the reader the curiosity, this is indeed my nominal political affiliation.

But I would maintain that this has nothing to do with my writing of prehistory (as my erratic voting record would demonstrate!) although I am sure that some reviewers will deconstruct this volume in such a light. My argument is more grounded in a common-sense and minimalist view of prehistory in which people rather than systems are the primary agents of change.

This is not to say that humans do not respond to external forces, such as environmental change. Such phenomena surely did occur, and people had to respond to them. Even here, however, their responses parlayed the new conditions and circumstances into advantages rather than being passive reactions leading to whatever end dealt tactically with the situation. Moreover, people are constrained by their past practice and social norms as well as by available technology. Clearly there are limits to their initiative and resourcefulness in any given context. The point is that they are always looking out for something better for themselves and taking advantage of every opportunity to do so. Altruism as a social value rather than a strategy for eventual personal success probably does not have very deep roots, despite claims to the contrary. The developmental trajectory of human society was made possible by people as social actors taking care of themselves first.

This view of human prehistory becomes especially helpful, I feel, in explaining the events of the last 10,000 years, which include the establishment of agricultural communities in virtually every part of the world and the rise of societies characterized by institutionalized social inequality and political privilege. It also has relevance to the preceding 99 percent of human existence, in that observable change during this period was largely technological. Nonetheless, a myriad of unobservable social decisions also were made during this period which established human society as we know it and which differentiate fundamental human social relationships from the other higher primates. Again, these were not merely responses to external stimuli but the cumulative result of many conscious decisions.

TWO APHORISMS

A number of years ago, I recorded the following aphorism: "Good intentions randomize behavior." The context of this was in academic advising and enforcement of academic regulations, and the aphorism was an exhortation to maintain consistency and even judgement. On the other hand, the aphorism is equally apt in a discussion of prehistoric society. Prehistoric people did *not* behave randomly. They engaged in consistent and regular behavior which accounts for the patterning seen in the archaeological record. Social, ecological, and economic rules governed these patterns, but underlying these rules, I would argue, was a fundamental motivation by self-interest. All human beings who are active members of society essentially seek to advance their own economic and social standing and that of the family group to which they belong. Ego is at the center of anyone's social sphere.

Despite attempts to portray "primitive" society as being one in which altruism, reciprocity, and generosity prevail, it is clear from ethnographic studies that even such practices as sharing are driven by a desire for social standing and tempered by the need to ensure a reliable food source for the procurer's family. These principles of self-interest were a powerful underlying force in human social development from the depths of the Pleistocene to modern times. Once they are recognized, the vast scope of the human experience becomes much more understandable. Related to, but different from, self-interest is ambition, and this is the variable which is sometimes mistaken for self-interest. All human beings are self-interested, but how they choose to direct their ambitions varies considerably from one individual to another within each one's social context.

The other aphorism, which I heard only recently, is "Nothing worth doing is worth doing perfectly." It is the motto of the optimizer who is trying to juggle a number of competing matters. Human beings, no matter how busy or how idle, are constantly making choices about how to allocate their time and energy. They can never do anything perfectly. Once they accomplish a task adequately, they rarely devote additional time and attempt to achieve a flawless outcome. Choices are another critical dimension of human life which have affected every person who has ever lived.

Our modern week is divided into 168 hours. Everyone, from a derelict to the president of the United States, must accomplish everything he or she needs to do within those 168 hours. The same constraint applied to a Palaeolithic hunter or a Neolithic farmer, even if their accounting of time used different units. Time allocation is even more fundamental to human organization than work or space, since it is universal and inevitable. Trade-offs based on time must be made constantly throughout the lifetime of an individual. Nothing can ever really be done to perfection, unless one has the luxury of excluding so many options that life suffers from overall impoverishment.

On that happy note, let us begin to examine the long trajectory of human decisions and their consequences.

FURTHER READING

While it would be cruel to immerse the reader in the debates over the last several decades about the proper aims and methods of prehistoric archaeology, several volumes provide a good historical perspective on the development of archaeology and prehistory. Prominent among these are the *Cambridge Illustrated History of Archaeology* edited by Paul Bahn (1996) and *The History of Archaeological Thought* by Bruce Trigger (1989). A comprehensive overview of the techniques of prehistoric archaeology and its interpretive frameworks is *Archaeology: Theories, Methods and Practice* (second edition) by Colin Renfrew and Paul Bahn (1996). The *Routledge Companion Encyclopedia of Archaeology* edited by Graeme Barker (1999) contains chapters by leading archaeologists on important archaeological research topics and finds. Most countries have popular archaeology journals which describe recent finds, such as *Archaeology* in the United States and *Current Archaeology* in Great Britain. *National Geographic* frequently has authoritative articles on archaeology, especially on early humans in the Old World and New World civilizations. Some scholarly journals might also be available in libraries, such as *American Antiquity* in North America and *Antiquity* in Great Britain. Another good way to learn about recent discoveries is to attend public lectures offered by departments of anthropology and archaeology at universities and by archaeological societies. Finally, many archaeological projects welcome volunteers, and the only way to experience the long stretches of tedium interrupted by brilliant flashes of discovery that make archaeological research so rewarding is to take trowel in hand and join in.

[2] THE EARLIEST HUMAN SOCIETIES

CHAPTER SYNOPSIS

INTRODUCTION

The human story began over four million years ago on the plains of East Africa. At this remote date, which has been pushed back by about a million years in each of the three most recent decades, it is very difficult to speak about *human* society. Certainly some forms of social behavior existed, for people and the other higher primates are cousins, and all such creatures engage in such activity. The fundamental question, debated among palaeo-anthropologists, is about the date when we see the earliest sparks of *humanity* among the primates to whom we can trace our ancestry.

Since the discovery of *Zinjanthropus* in Olduvai Gorge by Mary Leakey in 1959, there has been an explosion of knowledge about our hominid ances-tors, both direct and indirect. To provide a comprehensive account of these discoveries would take far more than the single chapter allotted here, so all that is possible in this limited space is to highlight some key issues. It is important to realize, however, that our understanding of human phylogeny can be radically altered by a single discovery, and the shelf life of the data in this chapter may be measured in months, or at best a few years.

Although the beginnings are hazy, human society comes into much sharper focus after about 500,000 years ago. By about 100,000 years ago, with the first appearance of anatomically-modern humans, we can begin to see the existence of behavior which we can relate to that of extant foragers. An important development during these hundreds of millennia, concurrent with human biological and technological evolution, was what I call "Pleistocene band society," a form of social organization about which we can make only indirect inferences from the behavior of modern foragers and higher primates. Yet under this social regime, humans made the fundamental technological, behavioral, and social changes which advanced them from being one of many great apes to being the dominant species on Earth, for better or worse, and which positioned them to assume even greater ability to transform the physical and biological world in the last fifty millennia.

EARLY HUMAN EVOLUTION AND SOCIETY

PLEISTOCENE ENVIRONMENTS

The human story takes place during the three most recent geological epochs of the Cenozoic Era: the Pliocene, the Pleistocene, and the Holocene. These cover the last five million years of the earth's history, roughly 0.1 percent of the total existence of the planet. Dating the divisions between these epochs is not easy and is the subject of debate, but a consensus view is presented in figure 2.1. Additional terminology crops up in the literature: the Pleistocene and the Holocene together are often referred to as the Quaternary, while the Pliocene and several of its predecessors form the Tertiary.

Although the immediate precursors of humans were primarily creatures of the Pliocene, humans themselves came on the stage during the earliest millennia of the Pleistocene, at least as far as current dating evidence shows. For this reason, the Pleistocene holds particular significance for the emergence of human society. By the end of the Pliocene, the continents had more or less reached their current locations. The Pleistocene world, however, looked much different from that of the last 10,000 years. It was a world of spreading and contracting ice caps, climatic fluctuations, marked changes in sea level, and changes in oceanic circulation. Traditionally, it has been divided into three segments, based on landmarks in climate and changes in the earth's magnetic field (figure 2.1). The separation between the Lower and the Middle Pleistocene is placed about 730,000 years ago, while the dividing line between the Middle and Upper Pleistocene is about 130,000 years ago.

The fact that the Pleistocene in the Northern Hemisphere was characterized by widespread ice cover was first recognized by Louis Agassiz in the early nineteenth century. Terrestrial indicators of ice movement, such as

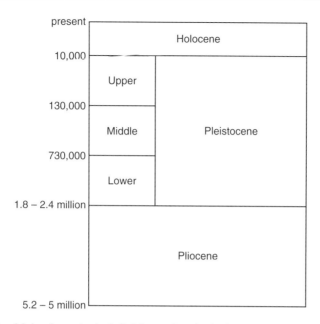

Figure 2.1   Main chronological divisions of geological time in last 5,000,000 years.

moraines and sediments, produced a fairly simple picture of glacial advances and retreats. Until the early 1970s, most geologists believed that there were four, perhaps five, major glaciations, which were separated by interglacial periods. The names of these were memorized in introductory anthropology: Günz–Mindel–Riss–Würm (the names come from small tributaries of the Danube on the north side of the Alps). These glaciations were thought to be nicely spaced out over the last million or so years. Over the last 30 years, however, research in the ocean basins and on the polar ice caps has produced a much finer-grained picture of Pleistocene climate. The picture that has emerged is one of many oscillations of varying intensity and duration between warmer and colder conditions, such that it is now possible to identify about 30 glacial advances in the Northern Hemisphere (van Andel 1994: 66).

What caused the Ice Age? There are many hypotheses, none fully proven. A very plausible scenario has been described by Tjeerd van Andel (1994: 226–7), primarily involving major changes in oceanic circulation. By themselves the individual changes would not have caused the buildup and expansion of polar ice sheets, but taken together and acting over time their cumulative effect may have had dramatic effects. Two major oceanographic changes associated with continental drift played a crucial role. The first was the opening of a passage completely around Antarctica when Australia moved northward around 25 million years ago. This permitted the establishment of a cold Circum-Antarctic Current, which was augmented by cold water from the North Atlantic traveling south in the ocean depths, leading to the continual coverage of Antarctica by ice from around 15 million years ago onward. The second was the closing of the Isthmus of Panama between five and three million years ago, which cut off the warm Circum-Equatorial Current. Rather than escaping west from Atlantic to Pacific, much of this warm water fed into the Gulf Stream, which in turn increased rainfall and snowfall in northwestern Europe and northeastern North America. Two additional factors played a supporting role. Around six million years ago, a drop in world sea levels led to the severing of the Mediterranean from the Atlantic. The water in the Mediterranean promptly evaporated, causing world salinity levels to drop about 6 percent which resulted in greater formation of sea ice in the northern oceans. It is also possible that the emergence of the Rocky Mountains and the Himalayas led to changes in low-level wind circulation that had profound effects on continental vegetation and climate in the Northern Hemisphere, perhaps the final push needed to establish widespread glacial conditions.

The concatenation of these and other developments may have led to the global Ice Age and especially to the emergence of the great ice sheets of the Northern Hemisphere, but future research may introduce additional factors. Why, however, did the ice sheets wax and wane over the last two million years? One theory, which was advanced by the Yugoslav astronomer M. Milankovitch in the 1920s, is that minute cyclical change in the earth's orbit and precession on its axis causes variation in the amount of solar energy it receives, and this variation causes warm and cold episodes. Milankovitch's theory was long disregarded because it did not appear to match the four-glaciation model, but it was revived in the 1970s once the glacial record became better known (Hays, Imbrie, and Shackleton 1976). Van Andel (1994: 96–7) proposes that it is also necessary to take the influence of oceanic and atmospheric circulation into account to explain the sudden onset and cessation of glacial conditions.

The world beyond the ice sheets was also affected by these changes. As the ice sheets advanced and retreated, they pushed before them a zone of tundra and permafrost, then a zone of steppe vegetation populated by herds of large herbivores. Closer to the equator, climatic variations are expressed largely in the form of variations in rainfall and aridity. These variations do not match the glacial advances exactly, so they cannot be explained by some global theory. Many local factors must have contributed to the palaeoenvironmental history of each region of the globe.

RECENT DEBATES ON PHYLOGENY

Most discussions of human evolution have a starting point approximately four or five million years ago, although clearly primate evolution and speciation had been occurring for millions of years prior to this. It is believed that somewhere between six and eight million years ago hominids (humans and their congeners) and the African apes (most notably chimpanzees) shared a common ancestor, but the fossil record between eight million and four million years ago for members of the hominid line is still poorly known. Then approximately four million years ago in eastern Africa, members of the genus

Australopithecus made their appearance in the fossil record. From then on, the story of human evolution is that of two genera: *Australopithecus*, of which many species have now come to light and which existed between four and one million years ago, and *Homo*, of which fewer species are known from about 2.5 million years ago onward.

When I first started studying anthropology nearly thirty years ago, the model of human evolution was fairly simple (and probably simplified even further for presentation to new undergraduates!). There had been two species of *Australopithecus* which had been identified in South Africa in the 1920s, of which one had survived and evolved into *Homo erectus*, then onward to *Homo sapiens neanderthalensis*, and then finally to us, *Homo sapiens sapiens*. The two species of *Australopithecus* were *A. africanus*, a gracile form, and *A. robustus*, a much larger and more massive form. The 1959 discovery of *Zinjanthropus boisei* (so named by Louis Leakey but clearly a robust australopithecine) established the presence of *Australopithecus* in eastern Africa, while the subsequent discovery of a transitional specimen between *Australopithecus* and *Homo*, classified as *Homo habilis* because of its association with stone tools, completed the sequence at the dawn of the 1970s.

An explosion of field research and the recovery of fossil hominid specimens that began in the late 1960s and continues today has changed this simple picture substantially. Of considerable importance was the fact that it became possible to assign dates to these specimens using the potassium-argon method, and the duration of the evolutionary sequence described above was extended from about a million years to the current four million and possibly more. The number of species of *Australopithecus* has grown substantially beyond the original two, and *Homo erectus* has acquired some cousins as well. The previously simple evolutionary path between *Homo erectus* and *Homo sapiens* has become the topic of heated debate, leaving the Neanderthals' role in our lineage in question. Most recently, the discovery of primitive hominid fossils in the Middle Awash region of Ethiopia which have now been assigned to the species *Ardipithecus ramidus* and dated to about 4.4 million years ago (White, Suwa, and Asfaw 1994, 1995) may begin to fill in the gap between the divergence of the hominid and ape lines and the appearance of *Australopithecus*.

Although its name means "southern ape," *Australopithecus* was not an ape nor was its distribution within Africa exclusively in the south. It was also not a human, but rather comprised the evolutionary stock from which humans subsequently arose. All species of *Australopithecus* walked upright on two legs, although probably not with the same smooth gait that modern humans have developed. None of the apes walk consistently upright. Bipedal locomotion is confirmed not only by the anatomical evidence of fossils but also through the discovery of footprints made by two hominids who walked across a patch of wet volcanic ash at Laetoli in northern Tanzania about 3.6 million years ago (Feibel et al. 1995; Agnew and Demas 1998). Thus australopithecines or their immediate ancestors had made a sharp break from their primate precursors and had committed themselves to life on the ground, not in the trees. Another key difference between *Australopithecus* and

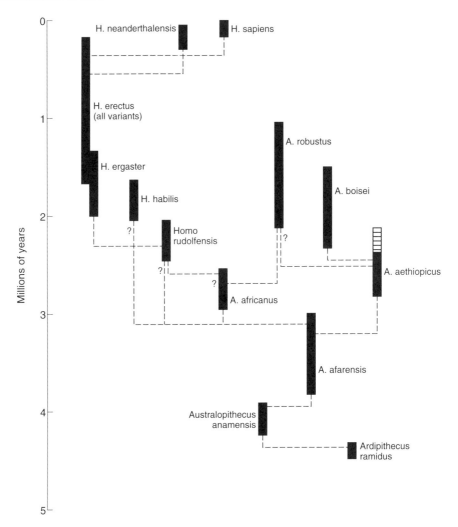

Figure 2.2 One view of the hominid evolutionary sequence in the last 5,000,000 years.

chimpanzees is in the reduced size of the canine teeth and the much larger size of australopithecine teeth in proportion to body size.

At the time of writing, at least six species of *Australopithecus* have been recognized. The earliest, *Australopithecus anamensis*, is dated between 3.9 and 4.2 million years ago (Leakey 1995; Leakey, Feibel, McDougall, and Walker 1995) and is found in northern Kenya. In the million years that followed, the only hominid fossils are those which can be attributed to the species *Australopithecus afarensis*, whose most famous representatives are the finds in the Afar region of Ethiopia, including "Lucy" and the "First Family" (Johanson and Edey 1981; Johanson and Edgar 1996). Although subsequent finds may eventually cloud the issue (such as the recent discovery of an

Australopithecus jaw in Chad, 2500 kilometers west of the Rift Valley which has been assigned to a new species and dated between 3 and 3.5 million years ago – Brunet et al. 1996), a reasonable case can be made for our ancestry running clearly through *A. afarensis*.

Between three and two million years ago, we now see a proliferation of hominid species, a much different picture from the simple linear progression model of only a few decades ago. *Australopithecus aethiopicus*, whose specimens date between 2.7 and 2.3 million years ago, has some distinctive anatomical characteristics which set it apart from its main contemporary, *A. africanus*. The question is what happened next. One possibility is that *A. aethiopicus* may have been the ancestor of the robust australopithecines, *A. robustus* and *A. boisei*, which persisted for nearly a million years themselves until they became extinct. *A. africanus*, then, would be a candidate to be a precursor of the genus *Homo*. Alternatively, *A. africanus* may have been the precursor of *A. robustus*, and thus was already headed down an evolutionary dead end, while early *Homo* may have sprung directly from *A. afarensis* or another of its descendants, hitherto undiscovered. Each of these evolutionary sequences has its adherents and detractors, and several other models are equally plausible.

Such confusion should not surprise us, and in fact the proliferation of hominid types during this period should be welcomed. We have a natural tendency to think of evolution as a ladder-like sequence in which taxa seamlessly evolve in response to various selective pressures. Robert Foley (1995) has pointed out the fallacy of this view, echoing the position of Stephen Jay Gould (1989) that the proper metaphor for evolution is not a ladder but rather a bush. Different species represent responses to different environmental conditions, and it is this variation that provides the raw material on which evolution acts. Between four and three million years ago, the bush appears to have been fairly thin, perhaps even a single stem, but between three and two million years ago, it was very dense as hominid species proliferated.

In Foley's view, two major specializations then crystallized, probably around 2.5 million years ago. The first involved the development of the massive dental apparatus, including large cheek teeth and powerful chewing muscles, which characterizes the robust australopithecines. The other is the progressive increase in brain size which marked the appearance of *Homo*. During the period between 2.5 and 1 million years ago, representatives of both types of hominid flourished in Africa, probably multiple species within each category. It was not necessarily a foregone conclusion which one would have persisted into the present, since only our intellectual hindsight and hubris see the advantages of a large brain over large teeth. Elizabeth Vrba (1996) has suggested that both of these changes were in response to global climatic cooling which created arid and open environments.

Let us focus the remainder of this story on the genus *Homo*. In the early 1960s, Louis Leakey had identified the fossils of a hominid whose cranial capacity exceeded that of known australopithecines and whose jaw and dentition were closer to that of *Homo* than to any other precursors. Geologically, it was clear that this species co-existed with *A. boisei* around 1.8 million years ago, but it was clearly not an australopithecine. Leakey christened this species *Homo habilis*, or "handy man," in reference to the association of these fossils with stone tools. Subsequent discoveries of *H. habilis* fossils later in the 1960s confirmed the validity of this nomenclature. The discovery of the postcranial remains of *H. habilis* in the 1980s indicated that its legs were surprisingly short and retained australopithecine characteristics, however.

In the early 1970s, Richard Leakey (son of Louis) discovered the cranium of a larger-brained hominid near Lake Turkana. He assigned this skull, known as "1470," to an indeterminate species of *Homo* rather than to *H. habilis*. Originally, this find caused a sensation, for it was believed that it came from a volcanic ash layer 2.6 million years old. Subsequent dating has revised that age to about 1.8 million years, the same as the date for *H. habilis*. Nonetheless, the 1470 skull is larger than those of *H. habilis*, and the current consensus is that it belongs to a different species, *H. rudolfensis*. Thus, even though australopithecines were out of the picture by this time, we now have two candidates to be the precursor of the remainder of the *Homo* lineage.

The third species of *Homo* from this period is clearly more advanced in the direction of later humans than the other two. Early *Homo erectus*, or *Homo ergaster* as some have argued these specimens should be called (Wood 1992), lived alongside *H. habilis*, *H. rudolfensis*, and even *Australopithecus boisei* in the area where its fossils have been discovered around Lake Turkana. *H. erectus/ H. ergaster* has a larger brain and a human-like postcranial skeleton with long legs. Perhaps the best-known representative of early *H. erectus/H. ergaster* is "Turkana Boy," a nine- or ten-year-old who died in an ancient swamp at Nariokotome, Kenya, about 1.6 million years ago where his corpse sank out of reach of scavengers leaving a nearly complete skeleton (Walker and Leakey 1993; Walker and Shipman 1996). If he had lived to adulthood, Turkana Boy would have been a tall man, with limb proportions resembling those of modern Africans living in the same region today.

The *H. ergaster* species nomenclature is not universally accepted, however, and many prefer to see these specimens as early representatives of *Homo erectus sensu stricto*. *H. erectus* emerged from the clutter of various *Homo* taxa by at least 1.6 million years ago, perhaps even earlier if the *H. ergaster* specimens are included, and persisted until 200,000 years ago or even later. *H. erectus* fossils have been found not only in Africa but also in Asia and Java, and later populations colonized Europe. The global expansion of *H. erectus* will be discussed further below, but it appears to have taken place remarkably quickly after the appearance of this large-brained hominid.

This review of human evolution collapses a complicated fossil sequence and controversial evolutionary relationships into a few paragraphs. Its purpose is to provide a summary of the major hominid species and their placement in the evolutionary scheme. It is also clear that the dating of the fossil record is sometimes out of sync with the dating of the archaeological record. Very early stone tools have been reported from the Hadar region of Ethiopia (Kimbel et al. 1996) dated to about 2.5 million years ago. What species made them? If we give credit to *Homo*, then this dating is several hundred thousand years in advance of the datings of *H. habilis* and *H. rudolfensis* fossils.

Moreover, early dates for stone tools from China are almost coincident with the dating of early *Homo* fossils from Africa. It is safe to say that the period between 2.5 and 2 million years ago has emerged as a crucial epoch for human evolution, both biological and cultural, and that in the decades to come there will be important fossil finds which will help clarify the relationships among the different hominid species.

Archaeology deals primarily with human culture and society, and much less with human biological evolution. The focus of this book is on archaeology and what it tells us about the prehistory of human culture. At this point it is necessary to mark a clean beginning point and arbitrarily eliminate some hominid species from further consideration. Any exhaustive discussion of the roots of human culture could take volumes, and in any event it would end "...to be continued!" It is probable that among the australopithecines there were some glimmers of human behavior, and there is no reason why there should not be. Tool use by australopithecines is entirely likely, for there is no anatomical reason why they could not have done so, but firm and unequivocal documentation for this is elusive. The prevailing assumption is that members of the evolving genus *Homo* made the earliest tools, even though there were remnant robust australopithecines in the same parts of Africa at the same time. Similarly, the evidence for concentrations of bones and stone artifacts which form the earliest traces of human activity cannot yet be reliably assigned to australopithecines, although the patterns of scavenging and even "home bases" discussed below did not appear out of thin air. For these reasons, and with apologies to the australopithecines and those who study them, the discussion of human culture and society in this book will begin with the earliest members of the genus *Homo*.

IMPORTANT EARLY AFRICAN SITES

Numerous sites throughout the Old World have yielded traces of early humans. A few localities stand out, however, as the places which have yielded data that have had the greatest impact on our understanding of human evolution and early society. Archaeologists and palaeoanthropologists keep returning to these localities because they are proven sources of well-preserved data in datable contexts. The huge investment of time, labor, and expertise in the recovery and analysis of the traces of early humans and their ancestors means that research projects at such sites may take years or even decades to complete. Moreover, discussion and debate about the interpretation of these finds often means that they are the subject of frequent re-examination.

For the understanding of early human biological and cultural evolution, the most important sites are located in eastern and southern Africa. In particular, the Rift Valley of northeastern Africa has been especially important in the last 50 years for the evidence it has provided. This concentration of sites does not mean that early hominids only occupied these regions. Rather, the geological activity in the Rift Valley and the formation of caves in the limestone breccias of southern Africa have resulted in the preservation and

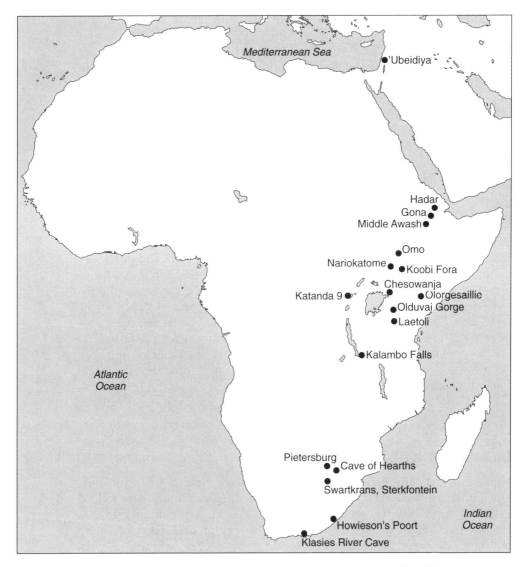

Figure 2.3 Map of Africa showing key early hominid sites mentioned in this chapter.

subsequent exposure of early hominid remains, which attracts palaeoanthro-pologists. The range of early hominids across the African grasslands was probably much larger than these limited localities would suggest.

Perhaps the best-known locality for the understanding of early hominids is Olduvai Gorge in northern Tanzania. Made famous through the work of Louis and Mary Leakey in the 1950s and 1960s, Olduvai is a 15-kilometer slice through 100 meters of Pleistocene lake deposits, which has exposed a two-million-year sequence of fossils and artifacts. A nearby volcano periodically deposited layers of volcanic ash, which enable a series of chronological checkpoints to be established using potassium-argon dating and which permit the definition of larger stratigraphic units called "beds." There are many different sites at Olduvai, designated by initials. A useful bit of archaeological trivia is that the "K" which ends each site designation stands for "*korongo*," Swahili for "gully."

Of the many sites at Olduvai, the most intensively studied is FLK ("Frida Leakey *korongo*," Frida having been Louis' first wife), where on July 17, 1959, Mary Leakey found the skull of *Zinjanthropus boisei* (now assigned to *Australopithecus boisei*), the first fossil hominid found at Olduvai after years of searching. Bed I at FLK is dated to about 1.8 million years ago, and since then remains of *Homo habilis* and *H. erectus* have been found in this unit, both at FLK and elsewhere at Olduvai (Potts 1988: 25). Of the excavations at FLK, the ones at the locality where *Zinjanthropus* was found, known as "FLK Zinj" has attracted the most attention from researchers, for in addition to Zinj and *H. habilis* ramains, it has also yielded a large sample of about 60,000 animal bones associated with about 2500 stone tools.

About 400 kilometers north of Olduvai in northern Kenya on the eastern side of Lake Turkana is an area known as Koobi Fora, a region of waterborne deposits mingled with a series of volcanic tuffs. One of these tuff layers, the KBS tuff, is dated to approximately 1.8 million years ago and provides the baseline for dating earlier and later materials in the region. As at Olduvai, significant associations of hominid fossils, stone tools, and animal bones have been found at a number of Koobi Fora sites, the result of both human and natural factors. One of the most intensively studied localities at Koobi Fora is the site known as FxJj50, dated to approximately 1.5 million years ago.

Northwest of Koobi Fora in southern Ethiopia is the valley of the Omo River, which cuts through several important geological formations. The most important of these is the Shungura Formation, which spans the period between 3.3 million and 800,000 years ago. The Omo deposits have yielded numerous early hominid fossils as well as a detailed record of the other animals which would have inhabited this region during the crucial periods for the emergence of humans. In addition, one of the key specimens for investigating the emergence of anatomically-modern humans has also been found at Omo.

Another key fossil locality in the Rift Valley is the Afar Depression in northeastern Ethiopia, which had been virtually unexplored by palaeoanthropologists prior to the 1970s. This area is most closely associated with a research program initiated by Donald Johanson and a number of American, European, and African collaborators in the Hadar region. The Hadar region is characterized by strong erosion which had created highly dissected badlands from which fossils are continually eroding. Such erosion resulted in the discovery of the first fossils of *Australopithecus afarensis* in the 1970s, including "Lucy." Datable ash layers and basalts bracket the fossil-bearing layers, indicating dates between about 2.8 and 3.4 million years ago. West of Hadar, the West Gona region has yielded stone tools that date to 2.6 million years ago, currently the oldest known (Semaw et al. 1997). Recent research in the Middle Awash valley, south of Hadar, has resulted in the discovery of a new hominid species, *Ardipithecus ramidus*, which may turn out to be an ancestor to australopithecines. Palaeoenvironmental research has shown that *A. ramidus* occupied a wooded habitat, rather than the open savannah inhabited by later hominids.

It would be wrong to conclude that all important early hominid sites lie in the Great Rift Valley. Some of the most important are found in southern Africa in the caves of limestone breccias in the Transvaal. Fossil hominids have been known from these sites since the 1920s, when Raymond Dart discovered the skull of a juvenile hominid which he named *Australopithecus*. At this time, the origins of humanity were thought to lie in the Far East, based on the finds of *Homo erectus* fossils in Java. Dart's discovery and subsequent finds in this region established the greater antiquity of the hominid line in Africa. Recent work at sites like Swartkrans and Sterkfontein has yielded important information on the grisly fate of many australopithecines as meals for hungry leopards (Brain 1981).

EARLIEST STONE TOOLS

The earliest artifacts which we can be certain were used by early humans for cutting, chopping, skinning, disarticulating, and otherwise modifying their circumstances are made of stone, thus beginning the use of stone as the fundamental raw material of toolmaking which persisted until only about 4000 years ago. Did hominids make tools of materials other than stone? Probably. Several decades ago, Raymond Dart (1957) floated the idea of the use of bone, teeth, and horn by the australopithecines of southern Africa, giving this industry the unwieldy name of "Osteodontokeratic." In Dart's view, animal skeletal parts were used as the earliest clubs and knives. Unfortunately, subsequent research by C. K. Brain (1981) showed how all the bone objects believed by Dart to be tools could have been produced naturally, primarily by carnivores and post-deposition forces. If there were any precursors to stone tools, it seems more likely that they were simple implements made expediently from wood, or unmodified stones used for pounding. Chimpanzees are clearly capable of using such basic implements, so it is probable that pre-*Homo* hominids did as well.

First appearing about 2.6 million years ago, the earliest stone tools do not look like much. In fact, if you were to dig one up today in your garden, you probably would not recognize it as having been modified. The identification of the earliest stone tools is a clear example of the importance in archaeology of context and pattern. While finding one cobble with a few flakes knocked off would be unremarkable, many similar objects, all modified in a consistently similar way, in association with each other and with other evidence such as fractured bones, take on archaeological significance. As more tools are recognized on the basis of such patterns and associations, they can be divided into different types based on their shape and pattern of flaking. The recognition of types clinches the fact that they were the products of human activity since they reflect a clear idea of what characteristics these tools should have to do their jobs. Finally, through experimentation, archaeologists have determined that the flaking of these stones is consistent with

Figure 2.4 A chopper/core from which sharp slivers of stone have been removed, found in Gona, Ethiopia and dated to 2.5 million years (photo courtesy of Professor J. W. K. Harris, Department of Anthropology, Rutgers University).

that which can be produced by a human hand rather than by natural impacts.

Early stone tools have been found at many sites in eastern Africa, but they were first collected in great numbers at Olduvai Gorge and studied by Mary Leakey. On the basis of her studies, Mrs Leakey was able to identify the major categories of early stone tools and their changes over time, and she applied the name "Oldowan" to this industry, or tool-making tradition. The Oldowan industry is based primarily on "core tools," in which a fresh piece of raw material has had flakes removed from it to form a cutting or chopping edge. The tool is the modified original block of stone, or "core," and the chipped-off flakes are generally by-products of the manufacturing process (although they may have been used to some limited extent). It was not until much later in prehistoric time that people gained the technical sophistication to reduce the block of raw material in such a way that the flakes, rather than the core, became the desired product.

Most of the Oldowan core tools appear to have been used as choppers, or at least this is the general function that their form suggests. In some cases, flakes were removed from one side of a flat, rounded cobble, along one edge, producing a "unifacial" chopper, whereas in others flakes are removed from opposing sides along one edge, producing a "bifacial" chopper. The finished tools are on the average a bit larger in diameter than a tennis ball, but flatter in cross section.

Some Oldowan core tools have flaking which suggests a scraping function, while others are flaked around more than one edge to produce "polyhedrons" and "discoids." For this discussion, any presumed functional differences among these tools are less important than the fact that they represent variations on a simple basic theme of a rock from which flakes have been removed to create sharp edges. In many cases, large flakes that were removed during the manufacture of these core tools were themselves chipped further or were used without further modification. An ongoing question among researchers is whether the large core tools really were the primary product of the Oldowan industry or whether they were incidental to the production of sharp flakes, which would have been more useful for skinning and dismembering. In any event, the core choppers can be considered the "signature" of an Oldowan industry, whether or not they were the most important item in the early hominid's toolbox.

Mary Leakey divided Oldowan assemblages into a basic Oldowan type with a high proportion of large core tools like choppers, discoids, and poly-hedrons, and "Developed Oldowan," with more altered and utilized flakes. It is unclear whether this distinction has any major significance, and it may simply reflect the function of sites, the size of collections, and especially raw material availability. Klein (1989: 167) emphasizes that we should not get the sense that Oldowan tools fall into such neat formal categories as the discussion above might suggest, and Toth (1985; also Schick and Toth 1993: 129) suggests that the shape of Oldowan tools was determined primarily by the initial piece of raw material and not by a clear model of the finished product in the maker's head.

The raw material for these tools at Olduvai and Koobi Fora are pieces of lava and igneous rock which had been rolled smooth by being in streams, whereas in the Omo region of Ethiopia, quartz pebbles were the material of choice. It is clear that there was conscious selection of raw material and that not just any rock would make an ideal Oldowan chopper or flake, and in some cases stone was acquired from a distance of up to 10 kilometers.

What would these early tools been used for? Schick and Toth (1993: 183–5) list several possible advantages that tools might have given their makers:

1 the ability to dismember large carcasses using the stone flakes and chop-pers in emulation of the large carnassial teeth of lions and leopards, thus beating such competitors to the best meat; this ability could be leveraged even further since the humans could carry away the meat to safer retreats;
2 ability to chop and pound could emulate carnivore jaws in splitting open bones for marrow;
3 pounding and cutting with stone hammers and flakes would also make opening nuts and fruits less tiresome;
4 digging sticks, which have not survived archaeologically, would give access to buried tubers, roots, and insects;
5 almost any stone, bone, or sharpened stick could have served as a useful weapon to drive away smaller competitors and at least have a fighting chance against larger ones;
6 tools used as levers and wedges to strip bark from trees would have pro-vided access to edible gums and insects.

In the view of Schick and Toth, the true advantage of early tools was to per-mit early humans to expand their ecological niche from the relatively narrow primate one into those occupied by many other species such as lions, hyae-nas, and warthogs.

These early tools did not need to be complicated to manufacture, nor did they need to undergo rapid refinement. Indeed, they can be considered relatively wasteful in their use of raw material, particularly the core choppers which sacrificed a large mass of material for a relatively small length of cutting edge. They got the job done, however. For about the next million years, until about 1.6–1.4 million years ago, they were quite adequate for the needs of early hominid life in many parts of Africa and Asia.

Beginning approximately 1.5–1.7 million years ago (as can be seen by the range of dates here and in the preceding paragraph, the transition was fluid), a technological advance over the Oldowan tools occurred with the development of larger bifacially-flaked implements known as handaxes, along with refinements to cleavers and flakes. The handaxes required much greater effort to produce than the Oldowan choppers and greater mastery and understanding of the flaking properties of stone. The payoff was an elongated, tapering tool which provided more cutting edge than before and a greater number of options in any working situation. If the user needed to pound something, the blunt thick end could be used, whereupon the tool could be turned around for chopping, cutting, and poking.

The handaxe industries from their earliest appearance to nearly 100,000 years ago, an enormous span of time, are known generically as "Acheulian" after the site of St-Acheul in the Somme Valley of northern France, where they were first recognized as prehistoric stone tools in the early nineteenth century (previously, stray finds of handaxes had been explained as "thunderbolts" or "lightning stones," the physical residue of a bolt of lightning). In the Eurocentric world of nineteenth- and early twentieth-century archaeology, the name "Acheulian" has been applied to all similar handaxe industries in Europe, Africa, and the Near East. The resemblance of a post-Oldowan quartzite biface from east Africa at 1.5 million years ago to a flint handaxe from southern England made 200,000 years ago is a bit of a stretch, although the heritage of the former is obvious in the latter.

As with in the Oldowan, raw material properties played a great role in determining the character of Acheulian assemblages. The quartzite and volcanic rocks of sub-Saharan Africa fracture differently from European flint. A major advance over the Oldowan by the Acheulian was in the initial reduction of the raw material. Whereas Oldowan tool-makers confined themselves to what they could make from cobbles and pebbles, the earliest Acheulian tool makers removed large flakes from boulders to form the cores for their handaxes and cleavers. This enabled them to have cores of relatively consistent shape with some ready-made sharp edges and permitted the final product to be thinner. The addition of this additional step is significant, for it clearly indicates that there was a conscious model of the final product in the minds of the makers. It also required a great amount of strength (Schick and Toth 1993: 237) to break the large flakes from their parent boulders.

Acheulian handaxe industries are widely distributed in the western Old World, but they appear to be largely absent east of peninsular India. Further east in Asia, handaxes are not found, and choppers reminiscent of the Oldowan are the dominant large tool type. Hallam Movius (1944) saw

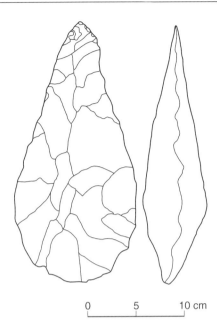

0   5   10 cm

Figure 2.5 A view and section of an Acheulian handaxe from Kalambo Falls, Zambia (after Schick and Toth 1993: 241).

this distinction as having been a great divide in the world of ancient humans, and the separation became known in the literature as the "Movius Line." With the passage of five decades, this division has become blurred, for there are now chopper and large flake industries known from Europe and some enigmatic sites with tools that look like handaxes have appeared in China and Korea. This frontier may be more functional than cultural, however. Since it is roughly coincident with the distribution of bamboo, the hypothesis has been advanced that with this excellent material for making knives and spears, stone tools were only needed for heavy-duty hacking. Differences in raw materials may also account for this frontier.

The lessons to be drawn from the study of early stone tools is that while they permitted a remarkable broadening of the human adaptive niche, thus enabling phenomena such as the dispersal of *Homo erectus* throughout the Old World, they did not develop any faster than humans needed them to. Oldowan industries persisted for a million years, and Acheulian industries even a bit longer. The earliest stone tools were made expediently, and generally the sharpest flake within reach that would get the job done was the tool of choice. With the advent of the Acheulian, we see the first glimmers of design and process, two key words used to characterize engineering today. In many respects, Acheulian handaxes might be said to have been engineered in a primitive sense rather than just being hastily modified pieces of raw material.

CULTURE OF THE EARLIEST HUMANS

SCAVENGING – FORAGING – HUNTING

For many years, the stone tools were the only real evidence of "culture" attached to the early hominid fossils. It was not until the 1970s that palaeoanthropologists began to examine the fossil animal bones which accompanied the hominid fossils and stone tools and the horizontal patterning of the remains. Inferring associations among these remains is tricky, for in the active geological environments of the Rift Valley it was very easy for things to be moved around by water and other agencies during the last two million years. A number of studies have been explicitly directed towards gauging the effect of these post-depositional factors on the patterning of archaeological remains (e.g., Behrensmeyer and Hill 1980; Nash and Petraglia 1987).

Until the 1970s, the prevailing assumption was the early hominids were hunters, coldly efficient killer apes which had gotten loose among the herbivores of the savanna. Hunting was a fairly familiar concept to modern humans, and thus "Man the Hunter" was not a particularly difficult model to extend backward, even two million years. Early humans were "hunter-gatherers," just as were many of their descendants in later prehistory and even still today. The cognitive skills needed for planning and executing the successful tracking and killing of prey were viewed as fundamental hallmarks of humanity.

The study of the faunal remains and patterning of hominid sites over the last 25 years has cast doubt on the hunting hypothesis and in doing so has brought early humans down a peg or two on the scale of heroic dominion over nature. It may come as a shock to some readers that the early hominids are widely believed now to have obtained much, if not all, of their meat from the scavenging of carcasses of savanna animals who had either died natural deaths or had been killed by big carnivores like lions and leopards. The extent of early human scavenging and the length of prehistoric time that this practice persisted as the primary means of subsistence are matters of considerable debate among palaeoanthropologists.

In order to understand the scavenging hypothesis, however, it is also necessary to understand the analytical approaches to early hominid sites. We cannot call them "campsites" at this time, since they lack evidence of long-term habitation which resulted in lasting structures and pattuuerns in the disposal of rubbish. Instead, they appear to have been locations of very short episodes of human activity or palimpsests of the traces of repeated visits to good locations, especially those bordering watercourses.

Early studies of early hominid archaeology (as opposed to the analyses of fossils and stone tools) interpreted the remains as somewhat simpler versions of a later hunter-gatherer way of life. Rather than being called "campsites" the larger and more complex concentrations of bones and tools were interpreted as "home bases" which were occupied for some duration by hominids who ate, slept, and met other members of their social group there.

Early human social life was organized around these localities, to which food was carried and shared. Other sites were seen as butchery locations, caches, and places for toolmaking. The late Glynn Isaac (1937–85) is most closely identified with the "home base" model, which represented one of the first attempts to understand how early hominids lived (Isaac 1978). Isaac subsequently (1981) took this model one step further and argued that the home bases reflected a sexual division of labor, with males provisioning females who focused on the responsibilities of child rearing. The implication of this model was that early hominids engaged in land use and social behavior which was more like that of extant hunter-gatherers than of non-human primate relatives.

Among the sites that had figured prominently in Isaac's formulation of his home-base model were those from Bed I at Olduvai, especially sites FLK and DK. DK, with its circle of stones evocative of a shelter or windbreak, appeared to be a natural representative of a home base, while several of the localities at the FLK site seemed to be butchering sites. FLK North-6, for example, is composed primarily of the remains of an elephant accompanied by stone tools. The natural conclusion was that these were locations in the landscape at which early hominid hunters carried out a clearly delineated set of activities which set them apart behaviorally from their primate ancestors.

At the same time, Lewis Binford (1981, 1987) had been studying how the human dismemberment and use of the animal carcass produces distinctive signatures in the archaeological record. Turning his eye to the early African hominid sites, particularly Olduvai, and comparing their animal bone assemblages to those produced by African predators like lions and hyaenas, he noticed no difference between the two. Both hominid sites and predator sites were composed primarily of bones which had little meat utility, and the bones at the hominid sites which had traces of modification were those which contained the most marrow. Binford concluded that early hominids did not actively hunt and carry meat back to base camps but rather scavenged bits of meat and marrow from carcasses which had already been picked over by the predators. In his view, sites with traces of early hominid activity were scavenging stations or locations where there were repeated opportunities for scavenging. Binford's model of early hominid scavengers at the mercy of carnivores contrasted sharply with Isaac's position.

Crucial to this discussion is the condition and composition of the assemblages of animal bones from the Olduvai sites, and subsequent studies have focused on them. The key question is how the animal bones got there. Based on their analysis of body-part representation, Henry Bunn and Ellen Kroll (1986) concluded that FLK was neither a kill or a butchery location. Rather, they argue that it was a location to which early hominids brought parts of carcasses from elsewhere, either from animals they had killed themselves or from carcasses which they were scavenging. Cuts and fractures on animal bones found at FLK Zinj suggest that hominids were skinning and dismembering animals using stone tools, as well as breaking open the bones to get at the marrow inside. Bunn and Kroll suggest that early hominids were either good at hunting or dominant scavengers, able to get to carcasses of dead herbivores before their competitors. Other researchers disagree, suggesting that early hominids were either scavengers plain and simple (Shipman 1986) or that the data reflect a complex interplay between hominid scavenging and butchery and the selective removal of anatomical elements by carnivores (Blumenschine and Marean 1993). However the animal bones reached these sites, it is clear that they are locations of hominid activity. Associated with them are many stone artifacts, some of which can be fitted together, which indicates that they were flaked on the site. Many of the stones were brought from several kilometers away, clearly as the result of intentional hominid behavior.

How can we now interpret the nature of these sites? Isaac's model was updated and modified by Kathy Schick (1987; Schick and Toth 1993) to suggest that these were favorable locations – by being safe, sheltered, and central – to which early hominids repaired after an episode of scavenging, hunting, and gathering. In Richard Potts' view (1988), the concentrations of stones found at these sites were caches gathered from across the landscape. When pieces of scavenged animal carcasses were brought to these locations, stone tools could be made expediently to dismember them. Recently, Lisa Rose and Fiona Marshall (1996) have proposed what they term a "resource defense model" for explaining these sites. In an environment of competition from carnivores for meat, early hominids would have transported hunted or scavenged animal carcasses to focal locations with immovable resources, such as water, fruit trees, and sleeping conditions. Such siege conditions would have promoted aspects of early human sociality such as food sharing. Others have developed the scavenging model still further. Robert Blumenschine and his colleagues have suggested that early hominids may have been particularly successful in scavenging big-cat kills in the trees along watercourses, as well as animals who died of disease and drowning (Blumenschine and Cavallo 1992). In their view, sites were refuges, possibly with climbable trees for safety and concealment (Blumenschine 1991).

We can be reasonably certain, however, that early hominid archaeological sites were not campsites of the sort observed in modern hunter-gatherers like the !Kung San. At site DK at Olduvai, a cluster of stones about four meters in diameter had been claimed to be the remains of a hut or a windbreak (Leakey 1971), although this interpretation is open to question. The identification of these stones as a shelter is based on their similarity to stone rings that support grass huts in southern Africa today. Richard Potts (1988: 257–8) has pointed out the problems with this interpretation, however. He notes that the basalt stones that make up the circle may represent the action of tree roots which have penetrated and broken up the bedrock, and in the absence of clear indicators of hominid activity, such a taphonomic explanation has equal credibility. Potts also points out that the DK stone circle is unique in the archaeological record, with the further indications of shelters not appearing until about 1.5 million years later at Terra Amata in southern France (and even these are problematic). He concludes that shelter-building was not a part of hominid behavior at Olduvai or elsewhere at this time.

HOMO ERECTUS COLONIZES EURASIA

With the origins of the genus *Homo* firmly established in Africa as a result of research in the 1960s and 1970s, a major question arose as to when humans dispersed out of Africa to Eurasia and the islands off Southeast Asia. "Peking Man" and "Java Man" had been known since before World War II. Although no method of establishing absolute dates for these specimens was available at the time of their discovery, they clearly established that *Homo erectus* had reached points which were very distant from eastern and southern Africa. In Europe and the Near East, sites like 'Ubeidiya and Terra Amata, along with the ubiquitous presence of handaxe industries associated with *H. erectus*, spoke to a widespread distribution of archaic hominids beyond their African heartland.

When did this breakout occur? Conventional wisdom over the last two decades placed it at a relatively recent date, generally between 1.1 million and 700,000 years ago (e.g., Klein 1989: 204). Such a view was consistent with the fact that most reliably dated sites were in Europe, where the earliest dates are younger than 700,000 years. Adding some time for the inevitable pushing-back of the Eurasian hominid sequence made 1.25 million years a fairly safe guess until about 1994 (as noted by Dean and Delson 1995: 472). In the mid-1990s, however, the dating of *H. erectus* finds in Georgia, Israel, and Java made it clear that the first hominid breakout from Africa was even earlier.

The Near East is a critical area for this discussion, since it forms the land bridge between Africa and Eurasia. 'Ubeidiya is located three kilometers south of the Sea of Galilee in the Jordan valley (Bar-Yosef 1994: 228) and has complex stratification. Some fragmentary hominid remains have been found but cannot be attributed to any species, although bones attributed to *H. erectus* have been found elsewhere in the Levant (Bar-Yosef 1994: 254). At 'Ubeidiya, several types of stone tools have been found, including an early core-chopper industry like that made by *H. erectus* in east Africa and a handaxe industry like that made by later *H. erectus*. The core-choppers and their associated animal bones have been dated through a variety of methods to between 1.2 and 1.4 million years.

In Georgia, at the site of Dmanisi, located southwest of Tbilisi, the lower jaw of a hominid identified as *H. erectus* was found in late 1991 (Gabunia and Vekua 1995). Three independent dating methods, including potassium-argon and palaeomagnetism, have placed the age of this jaw and its associated animal bones and Oldowan-like stone tools at 1.6 to 1.8 million years, although possibly as early as 1.4 million years. This dating established the Dmanisi find as the earliest securely dated trace of early hominids outside of Africa, at least for the time being.

As we will see throughout this book, new discoveries in archaeology have a tendency to move the dating of landmark events and processes progressively earlier. No sooner had the Dmanisi finds been reported when high-precision argon-argon dates for *H. erectus* from Modjokerto and Sangiran in Java were reported to be even earlier than the Georgian dates. An infant skullcap from Modjokerto produced a date of 1.81 million years, while two fossils from

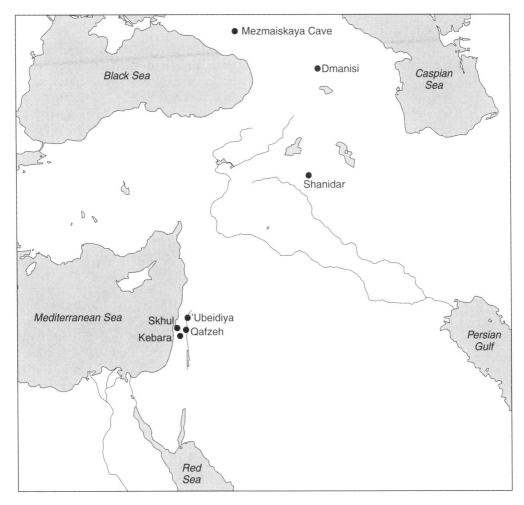

Figure 2.6 Map of the Near East showing key *Homo erectus* and Neanderthal sites mentioned in this chapter.

Sangiran were placed at 1.66 million years (Swisher et al. 1994). In order to reach Java, these hominids needed to traverse much of Asia, thus corroborating the Dmanisi dating. Even more recently, hominid teeth and jaw fragments from Longgupo in China have been dated by several methods to 1.78 to 1.96 million years (Larick and Ciochon 1996: 543).

It thus appears that *H. erectus* headed north by northeast out of Africa sometime just after 2 million years ago and turned right towards Asia rather than left towards Europe. Why did they leave Africa? Larick and Ciochon (1996: 551) propose that cool and arid climatic conditions drew them north, where their ability to adapt to many different sorts of environments enabled them to out-compete other species in landscapes with few barriers. *H. erectus* could have thus easily made it from Africa to east Asia in a few hundred thousand years, possibly less. Meanwhile, the more rugged terrain of southern

Europe may have required the development of more sophisticated methods of land use and tools like handaxes.

The dispersal of *H. erectus* from Africa was not an isolated occurrence, but surely the result of many sorties and even some returns. Recognition of an early date for this dispersal, however, has solved a nagging question in archaeology, namely why the early stone tool assemblages of eastern Asia were characterized exclusively by core-choppers, while from India westwards handaxes are the dominant tool type after about a million years ago. If *Homo erectus* populations broke out of Africa before handaxes had been developed, as the finds from early levels at 'Ubeidiya and Dmanisi suggest, then it was simply a matter of the East Asian hominids continuing the core-chopper tradition that their ancestors had carried all the way from Olduvai, Koobi Fora, and Omo (Schick and Dong 1993).

So when did *H. erectus* finally reach Europe? This is a matter of considerable debate and is further complicated by the presence of "tephrofacts," stones fractured by volcanic processes that produce forms that look like the work of humans (Raynal, Magoga, and Bindon 1995), and other pseudo-artifacts. The current consensus is that the first reliable traces of hominid activities in much of Europe are around 500,000 years old (Roebroeks and van Kolfschoten 1995: 297). Before this time, there are small contested primitive-looking stone assemblages, no human remains, and all finds have been selected from disturbed contexts. After about 500,000 years ago, there are large assemblages of tools and flakes from chipping localities in which many pieces can be fitted back together. These are clearly primary undisturbed contexts. Uncontested tool industries can be identified, including handaxes. Finally, human remains occur at many sites after this date. Recently discovered fossils and stone tools from Atapuerca in Spain may shift this date back to about 780,000 years ago if their initial dating is confirmed (Carbonell et al. 1995; Bermúdez de Castro et al. 1997). One possibility is that hominids from Africa and the Near East intermittently entered the Mediterranean perimeter of Europe prior to 500,000 years ago before eventually venturing further to settle the central and northern parts of the continent (Dennell and Roebroeks 1996).

By 500,000 years ago or shortly thereafter, hominids had reached the British Isles, as confirmed by a tibia from Boxgrove (Roberts, Gamble, and Bridgland 1995). This completed the initial settlement of most of the Old World. The remaining areas were penetrated slowly. Finds at Diring Yuriak 120 kilometers south of Yakutsk on the Lena river in Siberia are on an occupation surface which is dated between 366,000 and 268,000 years ago (Waters, Forman, and Pierson 1997). A marine barrier prevented the colonization of Australia until after *Homo erectus* times, a problem which is discussed extensively in the following chapter.

CONTROLLING AND MAKING FIRE

The ability to control and to make fire is one of the hallmarks of humanity. In many popular conceptions of early humans, the discovery of fire-making is treated as a momentous event which transformed society. The evidence for early fire use, however, is equivocal, and the earliest positive archaeological traces for it are probably much more recent than the date of its discovery by early humans.

Let us begin with the point on which until recently most archaeologists and palaeoanthropologists were in some measure of agreement: the evidence for fire and *Homo erectus* present at the same locality at apparently the same time at Zhoukoudian (also spelled in older literature "Chou-k'ou-tien"), Locality 1, in Hebei province, China, as early as 460,000 years ago. Excavations in the 1930s revealed darkened and discolored animal bones and lenses of soil, especially in Layer 10, which were considered to be the result of fires burning within the cave for extended periods. During the 1980s, this evidence was questioned (Binford and Ho 1985; Binford and Stone 1986), and many of the animal bones thought to be burnt were apparently manganese-stained. Recent analyses of the cave sediments which were thought to contain ash revealed that there was no evidence for the presence of wood ash in Layer 10, the darkened layer, although some of the bones were, in fact, burnt (Weiner et al. 1998). There is apparently no evidence for *in situ* burning in the Zhoukoudian cave, so the link between humans and the few burnt bones is very tenuous at the moment.

After about 400,000 years ago, the association between humans and fire becomes progressively stronger. At over a dozen European sites, there is evidence for burning of some sort before 100,000 years ago. These include Torralba and Ambrona in Spain, Vértesszőllős in Hungary, Swanscombe and Hoxne in England, and a number of sites in France. At Terra Amata, excavated in 1966 by Henry de Lumley, features interpreted as hearths were found within structures interpreted by the excavator as ephemeral brushwood shelters. The evidence for these shelters has been questioned (e.g., Gamble 1994a: 138), but the evidence for the association between human activity and fire is reasonably clear. The earliest dating for Terra Amata is about 380,000 years ago, but the direct dating of burnt flint produced a date of 230,000 years ago (Wintle and Aiken 1977). At Vértesszőllős, there is extensive evidence for burning in deposits dated by various uranium-series methods between 370,000 and 185,000 years ago. In a collapsed sea cave on the southern coast of Brittany called Menez-Drégan, Jean-Laurent Monnier has found concentrations of burnt pebbles and charcoal which have been dated to approximately 380,000 years ago, with other datings suggesting an even older date (Balter 1995).

Zhoukoudian and the European sites are all in northernly latitudes, where it makes considerable sense for early humans to have had some source of warmth beyond that of their bodies to survive. As Gamble notes (1994a: 140), the control of fire also would have enabled humans to use frozen animal carcasses that they had scavenged, which would give them a natural advantage over competing carnivores in the lean months of winter. The key question that confounds archaeologists, however, is whether these were true hearths which were tended and which were the focus for human social interaction or whether they were incidental cases of uncontrolled burning.

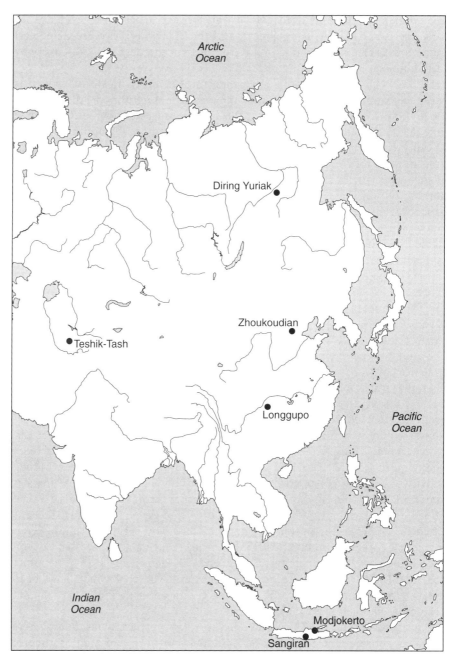

Figure 2.7 Map of eastern Asia showing key *Homo erectus* and Neanderthal sites mentioned in this chapter.

Prior to 400,000 years ago, the evidence for fire is even more controversial. A number of Chinese sites have produced some evidence for charcoal and burnt bone in association with *Homo erectus* remains, although the dating of these is highly variable (James 1989: 6). The high-latitude location of these sites makes it likely that fire would have been a requirement for human survival in the winter months, but the question of human control and its social implications is still unresolved.

Outside of Eurasia, early Pleistocene use of fire has been claimed from several sites in eastern Africa (Clark and Harris 1985). Of these, perhaps the best-known and most controversial is Chesowanja near Lake Baringo in Kenya. The evidence consists primarily of a concentration of stone artifacts, unmodified stones, and 51 lumps (or "clasts") of baked clay (Clark and Harris 1985: 10). These underlie a basalt stratum dated by potassium-argon to 1.42 million years ago. At Koobi Fora, site FxJj20 East, patches of reddish/orange sediments, caused by baking in antiquity at temperatures between 200°C and 400°C, were discovered in association with stone tools and flaking debris dated to 1.5 million years ago. Further north, in the Middle Awash region of Ethiopia, similar patches of fire-baked clay have been reported.

Since these sites lie in what had been open tropical savanna habitats, the possibility that these are traces of natural fires is even stronger. As James (1989: 4) points out, there are also such burnt concentrations in areas without archaeological remains, possibly rendering the association between stone tools and burnt clay fortuitous. In the absence of burnt bone or structured hearths, the most parsimonious explanation for these burnt patches lies in natural causes like brush fires. Yet the possibility of fire-conservation by early *Homo* or even late australopithecines should not be dismissed. About 270 burnt bones, from Member 3 in Swartkrans Cave in southern Africa, dated between 1.5 and 1.0 million years (Brain and Sillen 1988; Brain 1993; Brain 1995: 453), provide a tantalizing suggestion that fire was known at this early date, although no evidence of hearths has been found. Only *A. robustus* fossils are found in Member 3 (although *Homo* remains are found in an earlier deposit) and at least one of the burnt bones was from an australopithecine. One possibility is that captured fire was used to keep the leopards, who preyed on these hominids, at bay.

Later sites in Africa, particularly in the southern part of the continent, have yielded much more conclusive evidence for burning. At Kalambo Falls, charred logs were recovered from waterlogged deposits which also yielded Acheulian handaxes (Clark 1969; Clark and Harris 1985). Once believed to be relatively recent, these deposits are now dated to approximately 200,000 years ago. At the Cave of Hearths in Transvaal, it appears that the fires of humans ignited deposits of bat guano to create an enormous burnt deposit, sometime after 200,000 years ago. Much as in Eurasia, the earliest evidence for human use, control, and making of fire in Africa occurs towards the end of the Middle Pleistocene.

At the time of writing, there is only tenuous evidence that *Homo erectus* controlled and made fire. It is important to keep in mind, however, that archaeologists can never hope to identify the "earliest" instance of any technological development, and thus it is likely that humans before those at Zhoukoudian could have captured and used fire in some way whose archaeological traces have not yet been found. Although it might seem to the lay reader that it should be relatively easy, the documentation of early fire use between 1.5 million and 500,000 years ago has proven to be one of the most formidable challenges faced by palaeoanthropologists.

NEANDERTHALS IN EUROPE AND THE NEAR EAST

Neanderthals have always had a bad reputation. No sooner had they shed their identity as thick-skulled and thick-witted Ice Age brutes did their skeletal remains begin to frustrate attempts to see human biocultural development as a neat progression from *H. erectus* to anatomically-modern humans. Nonetheless, Neanderthals (or Neander*tal*s, as their name is sometimes spelled) were remarkable people who populated Europe and the Near East between about 100,000 (perhaps as early as 230,000) and 30,000 years ago. They lived in the cold world of the Middle and Late Pleistocene, and their archaeological remains are known almost exclusively from caves, perhaps an accident of preservation. Thus Neanderthals provide us with the cave-people of cartoons. Recently, however, they have figured prominently in a serious and often polarized scholarly debate concerning the transition from archaic humans, of which they represent the most recent variety, to anatomically-modern humans, which succeeded them. Rather than marking a clear stage in human biocultural evolution, Neanderthals are now considered to be a distinctive regional group of "late archaic" humans.

The Neanderthal world stretched over a broad part of Eurasia from Gibraltar in the west to Uzbekistan in the east and from the lower limit of the Würm ice sheets in the north to the Mediterranean coast. Of these boundaries, three are precise: the Atlantic, the ice margin, and the Mediterranean. The fuzzy one is in the east, in southwestern Asia, and is a result of the limits of archaeological research. In the Levant, it seems clear that Neanderthal remains do not extend south of the Jordan valley. The presence of several Neanderthal skeletons at Shanidar cave clearly places them in the Taurus-Zagros mountains. Far to the east, the Neanderthal child at Teshik-Tash provides the easternmost known evidence for them. Nothing is known of their penetration of the Iranian Plateau and north into unglaciated Siberia.

Throughout this area, Neanderthal skeletal remains are concentrated in a few areas, largely the result of the presence of caves which preserved the bones and the archaeological attention these have attracted. The caves and rock shelters of southwestern France have probably yielded the greatest number of Neanderthal remains, while others have been found in the karst regions of Slovenia and travertine caverns in Germany. Even if they have not yielded skeletal remains, hundreds of cave sites across Europe and southwestern Asia have Middle Palaeolithic assemblages which can be generally attributed to late archaic humans.

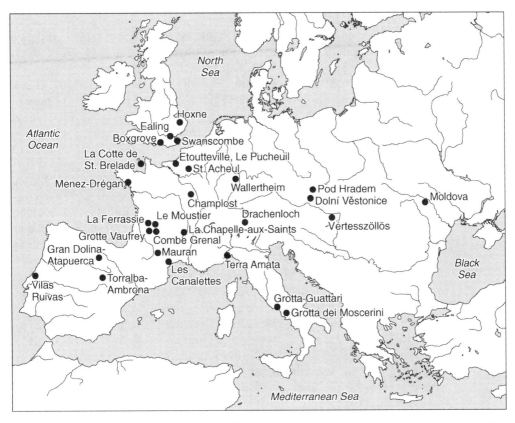

Figure 2.8 Map of Europe showing key *Homo erectus* and Neanderthal sites mentioned in this chapter.

Anatomically, what makes a Neanderthal? Typically, they exhibit a robust and powerful build, exhibited in the points of muscular attachment throughout their bodies, which suggests that they were very strong and probably able to accomplish physical tasks beyond the ability of most modern humans (Trinkaus and Shipman 1993: 412). Rather than seeing Neanderthals as simple brutes, a more constructive view would be that they had developed a distinctive set of biomechanical advantages. Yet their bodies were also adapted to the cold and dry Eurasian climate with large torsos and short limbs, fingers, and toes. Their brains were as large in proportion to their body size and as developed as those of modern humans, which was the culmination of the rapid increase in brain size observed in *Homo erectus* (Trinkaus and Shipman 1993: 418).

It is important to remember that there is no single "average" Neanderthal; like all hominid taxa they exhibit these characteristics over a range. Some are more robust, others less so. For a long time the elderly and pathological Neanderthal skeleton from La Chapelle-aux-Saints excavated at the beginning of the twentieth century was taken as evidence of Neanderthal anatomical primitiveness. This view has been offset by numerous subsequent discoveries which have provided a more complete picture of Neanderthal anatomy, although "healthy" Neanderthals are rare. Many exhibit evidence of trauma and lesions, attesting to a life of physical and dietary stress which led most of them not to make it to their fortieth birthday.

During their 70–200,000 year run, Neanderthals can be credited with a number of firsts, which have considerable relevance for the origins of human society. First, they clearly and consistently made their first in hearths, which implies that they were also cognizant of the social dimensions of having a fixed location for the fire in a band. Second, they were the first humans to bury their dead, as opposed to abandoning them for scavengers, which implies some sense of the human body as a social entity rather than simply another organism. Neanderthal burials were clearly deliberate acts, not simply accidental interments. Third, they developed techniques for making stone tools which represent significant advances over earlier industries and which formed the platform on which the subsequent Eurasian revolution in stone-tool technology developed.

Several recent volumes have done much to summarize the current state of research on Neanderthals (Stringer and Gamble 1993; Trinkaus and Shipman 1993; Mellars 1996, among others). This discussion will attempt to highlight the social and cultural accomplishments of Neanderthals as well as to situate them in the overall sweep of the human story. As with all points of controversy in human biocultural evolution, the status of Neanderthals may change significantly over the life of this book, so please supplement this text with a search for the latest authoritative scholarly positions. Many recent discussions have focused on the demise of Neanderthals (see p. 68–71 below) and scenarios for their replacement by anatomically-modern humans. Their place in the human lineage has been placed into doubt. Whatever their evolutionary status, it is clear that culturally Neanderthals were responsible for significant advances in human behavior, both technologically and socially.

TECHNOLOGY AND SUBSISTENCE

The archaeology of the Middle Palaeolithic, as the record of Eurasia in Neanderthal times is known, and the Middle Stone Age (MSA), the name given to the archaeological cultures of sub-Saharan Africa between about 100,000 and 40,000 years ago, continues to be dominated by stone tools. These happen to be much more interesting than the handaxes and choppers of the Lower Palaeolithic, since they involve greater sophistication in dealing with raw material and greater control over the final product. A series of steps can be observed in the production of many tools, not just whack-whack-whack…chopper. These developments are consistent with evidence for increases in brain size and mastery of the environment.

A general characterization of the Middle Palaeolithic/MSA is that core tools such as handaxes and choppers become markedly reduced in number and are replaced by an emphasis on flake tools. Of particular note is the length to which the core was shaped ("prepared") in order to determine the shape of the flake which was struck from it. Most Middle Palaeolithic/MSA assemblages are dominated by points, scrapers, and notched pieces. It is important to remember that although the names of these classes of tools suggest a function (e.g., scraping), studies of the edge damage caused by use indicate that their forms do not necessarily correspond to how the tools were actually used. In other words, just because a tool *looks* like it should have been used for scraping does not mean that it actually was.

Middle Palaeolithic/MSA tool assemblages go by a variety of names, which are mentioned here only to facilitate connection between this discussion and other literature. Perhaps the most common is the Mousterian complex, after the site of Le Moustier in France, which is applied to many of the Middle Palaeolithic tool assemblages of western and southern Europe, northeast Africa, and much of the Near East. For many researchers whose work is grounded in Europe, the Mousterian is seen as the tool industry of the Neanderthals. In northwestern Africa, the Middle Palaeolithic assemblages are characterized by a distinctive form of tanged point and are called the Aterian. In sub-Saharan Africa, the MSA assemblages are associated with anatomically-modern humans. Although they are not rigidly classified into industries, MSA assemblages are often characterized by reference to type sites such as Pietersburg and Howieson's Poort.

The way in which archaeologists look at stone tools has also evolved in the last three decades. For many years, archaeologists focused on the finished products that they found at sites and considered them to be the product of a clear "mental template" held by the prehistoric flintworker about what the finished tool should look like. There were finished tools, recognizable because they conformed to a typology of such artifacts, and there was chipping waste, known by its French name of *débitage*. Since the 1980s, there has been a change in how archaeologists look at stone tool technology, treating it as a process rather than an act. The manufacture of stone implements is essentially an exercise in the reduction of a block of raw material into useful pieces – cores, flakes, and blades – which can be refined further into various sorts of tools. Thus, the "reduction sequence" (called in French the *chaîne opératoire*) approach to the study of stone tools came into prominence. Such an analytical framework focuses on the way in which a piece of raw material changes form from one stage in the reduction sequence to another.

The view that stone tool types were discrete and reflected final products that were determined before flaking started gave rise to a major debate in Middle Palaeolithic archaeology during the 1960s and 1970s. François Bordes (1919–81), the towering figure of French Palaeolithic archaeology, defined five major groups of Mousterian assemblages – Mousterian of Acheulian Tradition A and B, Typical Mousterian, Denticulate Mousterian, and Charentian Mousterian – on the basis of the varying frequencies of hand-axes, scrapers, points, and other such types (Bordes 1961). Bordes interpreted this variation as being cultural and maintained that each such assemblage represented a different ethnic segment of Middle Palaeolithic society, something akin to a tribe. An alternative hypothesis was proposed by Lewis and Sally Binford (1966), who took the position that this variation was functional and related to the performance of different tasks such as butchering, cutting, and other hunter-gatherer activities. In their view, Mousterian assemblages were composed of constellations of artifacts representing different activities in varying proportions.

Dibble and Rolland (1992: 5) point out that "it is not so clear that the types recognized and defined by Bordes truly represent desired end-products that only reflect cultural norms or discrete functions." In fact, there is considerable evidence to the contrary. First, stone tools can be continually modified and reused. For example, Dibble (1987) has shown that the variability among the 17 types of scraper defined by Bordes can be explained by the continual resharpening of these tools, which reduced their size and changed their shape. A stone tool "type" just represents where the tool was in its life when it was last discarded, and it may be that many tool types really represent tools at the end of their useful lives. Second, the movement and compression of archaeological deposits can modify and break tools (Dibble and Holdaway 1993), producing tools that appear to have been deliberately chipped along their edges. Thus, most Middle Palaeolithic tool assemblages are continuously variable, and the discrete types on which archaeologists focused two decades ago have lost much of their interpretive power.

More likely determinants of the variation among Middle Palaeolithic assemblages appear in the form and quality of raw material and the intensity of occupation of settlement sites (Rolland and Dibble 1990; Dibble and Rolland 1992). Small nodules or pebbles of flint will produce different sorts of artifacts from those which originate with large nodules or blocks. Moreover, different sorts of flint were selected for different tools. For example, at some French sites, poorer quality local material was used to make notched tools, while scrapers were made from better-quality material brought from a distance (Dibble and Rolland 1992: 10). The imported flint was then conserved through resharpening, thus resulting in more diverse tools. Moreover, if Middle Palaeolithic people stayed at a site longer, the more prone they appear to have been to reuse and modify tools at hand, especially if they were using the tools for demanding tasks like butchering. Thus, during colder periods when people moved around less and ate more meat, assemblages appear to become more diverse due to continuous resharpening, while during warmer periods when they moved around more and ate more plants, tools were used less intensively, leading to less variability.

The reduction sequence approach to the study of Middle Palaeolithic stone tools recognizes several principal stages of production, use, and discard (Geneste 1985, cited in Mellars 1996): acquisition of raw material, preparation and production of primary flakes, shaping and retouching, utilization and resharpening, and discard. Each of these can be subdivided still further. For example, once the flint nodule has been acquired, the natural limestone coating must be removed, and the core shaped to provide striking platforms. Careful attention to core preparation is a hallmark of the Middle Palaeolithic. As flakes and blades were struck from the core, they would be selected for additional modification, and as they were used they would be sharpened or retouched still further.

One of the most distinctive aspects of Middle Palaeolithic stone tool manufacture is the so-called "Levallois technique" for producing a rounded core from which large, flat oval flakes could be struck (for details, see papers in Dibble and Bar-Yosef 1995). By varying how the edges of the core were shaped and by controlling the direction from which the large flakes were struck, a variety of shapes could be produced. In many cases, these Levallois flakes were directly usable as tools and points, but they could also be worked further. Mellars (1996: 88) points out that this technique must have involved five or six distinct stages which needed to be planned in advance.

It was once an article of faith among Palaeolithic archaeologists that the use of long, parallel-sided flakes known as blades did not become common until after about 40,000 years ago, but it has now become clear that the production of blades as primary tool forms took place in the Middle Palaeolithic as well. It is especially common in the Near East between 50,000 and 40,000 years ago, but it has also been recognized recently at many sites in northwestern Europe (Conard 1990; Révillion and Tuffreau 1994; Mellars 1996: 78) at a surprisingly early date around 90,000 years ago. Blade techniques allow much more efficient use of raw materials than do Levallois techniques, permitting the core to be reduced to a mere nub.

Middle Palaeolithic/MSA stone tool industries build on what was learned over the preceding two million years about flaking stone to produce an expanded range of shapes. Flake and blade tools markedly expanded the amount of cutting edge available from a volume of raw material and could be customized, resharpened, and reworked to be suited for a variety of special tasks. Humans' primary needs were still for cutting tools, but the appearance of points suggests some expanded needs in hunting and defense. A Levallois point among the bones of a mammoth at Ealing in England (Wymer 1968) provides some clear evidence in this direction, as do the traces of impact on Mousterian stone points from the Levant (Shea 1993, 1997).

Due to the excellent preservation of bone at most Middle Palaeolithic/MSA sites, we have a good idea of the meat component of the diet during this period. Plant remains are virtually unknown, largely because of the fact that there were few opportunities for them to be preserved. Eurasian Neanderthals and their African and East Asian contemporaries probably did not ignore plants, but berries, seeds, and nuts leave few good traces archaeologically. It is always important to remember that human diet is never reflected directly in the archaeological record, since bones are a natural by-product of meat consumption, while plant tissues are generally the parts that are being consumed.

The bones found at Middle Palaeolithic/MSA sites are typically those of medium and large herbivores, specifically ungulates like red deer, reindeer, wild cattle, bison, and horses. At several sites in western Europe and southern Russia, bison is the major species represented to the virtual exclusion of other taxa (Gaudzinski 1996), while others have more diverse faunal assemblages. In the Near East, gazelles and wild sheep and goats figured prominently among game species, while in Africa antelopes, zebras, and wild pigs were hunted. In Eurasia we know very little about the use of smaller animals, both terrestrial and aquatic. One hint that these taxa were not ignored comes from Grotta dei Moscerini, along the west-central Italian coast, where Neanderthals used marine shellfish and terrestrial and freshwater tortoises (Stiner 1993). At Katanda 9 in Zaire, numerous fish bones, particularly of large catfish, points toward the exploitation of freshwater resources by MSA peoples at a surprisingly early date – about 90,000 years ago (Yellen 1996). In southern Africa, MSA deposits at Klasies River Mouth have also revealed the use of intertidal molluscs, seals, and penguins, although fish and bird bones were conspicuously lacking in contrast with the numbers observed in deposits from later periods (Klein 1989: 321).

Until the 1980s, the general presumption was that the animals eaten by Middle Palaeolithic/MSA people had been acquired by hunting, but the emergence of the scavenging hypothesis and the apparent propensity of earlier hominids to rely on that method of acquiring meat led to the re-examination of the hunting assumption. A lively discussion of Middle Palaeolithic/MSA subsistence techniques has arisen (summarized in Mellars 1996). Important recent studies in Europe have included those by Philip Chase of the Middle Palaeolithic fauna from Combe Grenal in France (Chase 1986), by Lewis Binford of the bones from Grotte Vaufrey (Binford 1988), and by Mary Stiner of the Mousterian animal bones from several Italian sites (Stiner 1994). Binford also studied MSA faunal assemblages from the Klasies River Mouth in southern Africa (Binford 1984). More such detailed studies of Middle Palaeolithic/MSA subsistence will surely be forthcoming, although Mellars (1996: 194) has characterized this area as a "minefield of debate."

Despite differences in methodology and interpretive frameworks, the picture seems to be emerging that Middle Palaeolithic/MSA peoples practiced a combination of opportunistic scavenging and deliberate hunting, with the majority of researchers putting the stress on hunting. In his pioneering analysis of this issue, Chase regarded the data from Combe Grenal as primarily reflecting systematic hunting of the major large ungulate species. Binford interpreted the MSA faunal remains from Klasies River Mouth as reflecting the scavenging of large mammals, and the Mousterian materials from Grotte Vaufrey as having been introduced either by carnivores or by human scavengers. Richard Klein, on the other hand, has interpreted the large mammal data from Klasies River Mouth as indicating that the MSA people were hunters, albeit less adept and successful than their successors (summarized in Klein 1989: 323–7). Moreover, Binford's conclusions about scavenging by the inhabitants of Grotte Vaufrey have been challenged by Grayson and Delpech (1994), who argue that his assertions are without foundation.

Mary Stiner sees two contrasting patterns at several Mousterian sites in Italy. At some, the ungulates are represented primarily by head bones, the bones are largely those of old individuals, and the number of body parts per carcass which were brought to the site is low. Stiner interprets this as representing a scavenging pattern (although it is interesting that one of the sites with such ungulate bones was also the one mentioned above as having the tortoises and shellfish). Other sites have primarily bones which carry a large amount of meat, the animals represented are either prime individuals or reflect the structure of the living animal population, and many body parts per carcass were brought to the site. This is interpreted as reflecting the effects of ambush hunting. It is interesting to note that the sites with the scavenging pattern are earlier than 55,000 years ago, while those with the hunting pattern are later (Stiner 1994: 375).

Perhaps the most compelling faunal evidence that the Eurasian Neanderthals practiced deliberate hunting, however, comes from the sites where the animal bones are dominated by a single species, such as bison. Two such sites are Mauran in the foothills of the Pyrenees in southwestern France (Farizy and David 1992; Gaudzinski 1996), and Wallertheim near Mainz in Germany (Gaudzinski 1995). In addition to being dominated by a single species, these assemblages are also dominated by prime adult individuals. Human selection of bison to kill is clearly the most parsimonious explanation for the formation of such assemblages. Mauran and Wallertheim are both interpreted as kill sites where the primary butchery of the hunted animals took place. Such "focused" hunting of a particular species presages the specialized hunting strategies increasingly observed later in the Palaeolithic. Recently, the analysis of Mousterian faunal remains from Mezmaiskaya Cave in the Caucasus, where the sample is dominated by bison, sheep, and goat, has also pointed towards deliberate hunting as the sole means by which these large ungulates were brought into the cave (Baryshnikov, Hoffecker, and Burgess 1996).

HEARTHS AND HABITATIONS

The discussion of the first locations which can be identified with certainty as campsites is placed here more or less as the result of where the center of gravity of the evidence seems to fall. Placing it here does not mean that the evidence for earlier hearths and habitations is discounted, equivocal as it might be. It is simply the case that after 200,000 years ago, and certainly after 60,000 years ago, the evidence for campsites becomes much more compelling. Gamble (1994b: 25) identifies the following elements as the major characteristics of a campsite: built hearths, postholes, and rubbish-disposal areas. Burning by itself and a few enigmatic postholes do not define a campsite, which can be considered to be a location where humans lived for enough time to create a structured pattern of features and refuse.

The site of Terra Amata on the beach at Nice has already been mentioned, but a few more details about the huts are in order. As reconstructed by the excavator, Henry de Lumley, the shelters were built of bent saplings or branches, reinforced at their base by beach cobbles. The traces of such construction defined oval houses up to 15 meters long and up to 6 meters wide (dimensions mentioned in the literature vary considerably). De Lumley (1969) concluded that the site was repeatedly occupied seasonally, perhaps for a succession of 15 years, by people who engaged in beach fishing and gathering of shellfish. Pollen analyses suggest a late spring occupation. The neat layering of the sediments which led to the seasonal hypothesis has been called into question by Paola Villa (1983), who was able to fit back together flint tools and waste flakes from a number of the layers.

Terra Amata stands almost alone as a putative habitation site from 300,000 or more years ago. In the absence of corroborative evidence, it would appear at this point that *Homo erectus* was still highly mobile, perhaps with preferred locations in the landscape and seeking shelter in caves, but not *living* in a location for the duration and in the manner that produces a complex of features and zonation of debris. It is not until much later that we begin to see the first evidence of regular habitation in structured camps, generally associated with Mousterian stone tools and thus, by inference, with Neanderthals.

During the Middle Palaeolithic, a more consistent and systematic pattern of occupation of caves and rock shelters can be observed. Of course, the availability of caves was limited to those mountainous and dissected areas where they existed in geological formations and where their entrances were accessible. Yet where they existed, they came to be occupied repeatedly by people from Mousterian times onward, often in competition with other inhabitants such as bears and hyaenas. Indeed, the co-occurrence of stone tools, human bones, and cave bear remains at sites like the Drachenloch in Switzerland gave to the hypothesis of a Neanderthal cave bear cult (popularized in the novel by Jean Auel). Few archaeologists find merit in this idea, however. The evidence simply indicates that Neanderthals visited caves in which cave bears also lived and died. Indeed, it appears that many of the cave bears whose bones are found in great numbers at sites like Pod Hradem cave in the Czech Republic died during hibernation (Gargett 1996). Although they would have been justified in being terrified of these beasts, there is no evidence that Neanderthals engaged in ritual behavior with bear skulls.

Within cave and rock shelter sites, we start to see glimmers of evidence for spatial patterns of human behavior after about 200,000 years ago. At La Cotte de St Brelade on the Island of Jersey, two enigmatic piles of mammoth and wooly rhinoceros bones reflect deliberate human sorting and stacking for some unknown purpose (Scott 1986). Some limited and relatively unfocused patterning of human activities is indicated by analyses of the distribution of materials in Layer VIII at Grotte Vaufrey in the Dordogne (Rigaud and Geneste 1988; Rigaud and Simek 1991). It is clear, however, that the groups who visited this site were very small and were there for only short episodes, which served to blur the spatial distribution of various artifact types, and that wild carnivores then disturbed the remains of human occupations even further. After 100,000 years ago, the evidence for spatial patterning of human behavior comes into somewhat sharper focus. At the rock shelter of Les Canalettes in Languedoc, the remains of human activity are focused within a small part of the available surface of the site, and the distributions of flint tools and flakes and of animal bones are almost congruent (Meignen 1993). This distribution clearly conforms to our expectations of a single short-term campsite, in which the occupation area is small yet sharply defined.

Mellars (1996: 251) has made the following observations about the locations of Middle Palaeolithic cave sites in western Europe. The first is that they are usually located in well-sheltered locations, offer extensive wide-angle views of the valleys they overlook, and are near to sources of high-quality flint. The second is that they were well-situated to function not only as shelters but also as

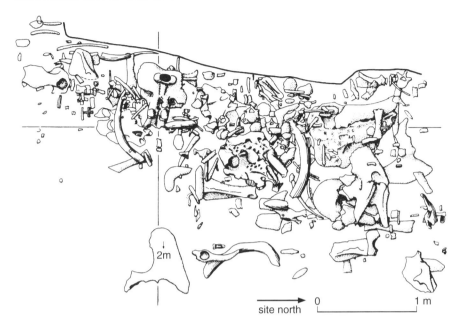

Figure 2.9   Bone heap at La Cotte de St Brelade (from Scott 1986, figure 18.3).

the focus of a wide range of economic and technological activities, with many resources available within a short radius. While these generalizations cannot yet be extended uncritically to Middle Palaeolithic sites in other areas, it seems that Neanderthals did have definite preferences about their choice of caves.

Outside of France, the evidence for spatial patterning of cave and rock shelter occupations also appears much more strongly after about 100,000 years ago. The numerous hearths in Shanidar Cave around 60,000 years ago lead Solecki (1995) to conclude that several fires were burning simultaneously and that these were the social foci of the inhabitants. Higher-resolution data are provided by the superimposed series of hearths and the distribution of stone and bone accumulations in Kebara Cave in the Levant, again dating from about 60,000 years ago (Bar-Yosef et al. 1992). The hearths were located in the middle of the living area, and stone debris was cleared away from around them. Meat-roasting and seed-parching seem to have been among the activities carried out at the hearths, whose ashes were then spread over a wider area, perhaps for bedding. Of particular note are the deposits of fragmented bones which occur at the back of the cave, which the excavators went to great pains to establish were the results of human, rather than carnivore, activity.

The study of Middle Palaeolithic open-air sites had begun only in the last couple of decades (Mellars 1996: 252), and the challenges to their systematic investigation are formidable. Yet they are numerous, both in France and in other parts of Europe, Asia, and Africa. Highway construction is one important means of discovery, as in the case of two recently excavated sites in Normandy, Le Pucheuil and Etoutteville (Delagnes and Ropars 1996).

Two good examples of open-air sites elsewhere in France are Mauran in the Pyrenees and Champlost in Burgundy (Farizy and David 1992). Mauran is interpreted as a kill site from which meaty portions of animals were transported away, while Champlost appears to be a camp to which the killed animals were brought and consumed. Accumulations of burnt bones and ash which can be interpreted as traces of hearths are also known from Champlost.

At Vilas Ruivas in Portugal, an open-air site with substantial hearths is dated to around 60,000 years ago (Gamble 1994b: 30). Perhaps the most convincing open-air habitation in Eurasia is found at Molodova in Ukraine, where a series of hearths is surrounded by large mammoth bones and reindeer antlers which are either structural elements in hide-covered houses, parts of windbreaks, or simply discarded debris. The circular arrangement of these bones and antlers clearly indicates a much more pronounced structuring of the living space than anything encountered at earlier sites.

In sub-Saharan Africa, the analysis of MSA open-air sites is only now getting underway. Katanda 9 is an important site in eastern Zaire which has been investigated by John Yellen (1996). Although the archaeological remains were displaced in various ways after deposition, two clearly defined clusters stand out. Yellen cautiously proposes that the patterning of remains at Katanda 9 conforms to the distribution that one might expect if the site were occupied by two nuclear family units.

RITUAL AND MORTUARY BEHAVIOR

Until very recently, it was an article of faith among most palaeoanthropologists that Neanderthals were the first humans to bury their dead in purposefully-excavated graves, which was taken as a marker of a symbolic and social advance, perhaps of religious beliefs. Furthermore, evidence for burial ritual, particularly the inclusion of grave offerings, could be viewed as a hint of human spirituality, or at least the emotions about life and death ascribed to modern humans. Yet, as with many orthodoxies, the evidence for Neanderthal burial and accompanying ritual has come under harsh critical scrutiny in the last two decades, and debate has ensued.

Neanderthal skeletal remains in pits have been known for nearly 100 years from sites in southwestern France. At La Chapelle-aux-Saints, the Neanderthal skeleton occurred in a clearly defined pit filled with soil different from the surrounding matrix, while at La Ferassie, the evidence is a bit more equivocal as to whether the seven Neanderthal skeletons were in deliberately-excavated pits or in natural depressions. One of the La Ferrassie skeletons was in a flexed position, however, which suggests human agency in arranging the corpse's final resting position. The Chapelle-aux-Saints find led to the first suggestions that Neanderthals buried their dead deliberately and thus had some form of "religion." Subsequent discoveries of Neanderthal skeletal remains which had apparently been buried deliberately further strengthened this view. At Teshik-Tash in Uzbekistan, A. P. Okladnikov excavated a burial of a Neanderthal child around which the horn cores of a Siberian mountain goat had been reportedly driven into the ground (Movius 1953).

Perhaps the most famous Neanderthal burials were excavated at Shanidar Cave in Iraq between 1957 and 1960 by Ralph and Rose Solecki (Solecki 1971; Trinkaus 1983). Four of the nine Neanderthals whose skeletons were found at Shanidar had apparently been killed by rock slabs falling from the cave's ceiling, but the other five seemed to have been deliberately buried. Soil samples taken from around Shanidar skeleton 4, that of an older man, revealed the presence of considerable amounts of wildflower pollen. The pollen analyst, Arlette Leroi-Gourhan (1975), took the position that the amount of pollen was more than could be accounted for by natural deposition or intrusion, which led to the suggestion that the individual was deliberately buried with flowers. Solecki developed this vision of Neanderthal humanity in his 1971 book, *Shanidar, the First Flower People* (which, I must note, was the first book on pre-history that I read and which sparked my interest in the topic).

Although the notion of deliberate Neanderthal burial made its way into prehistory textbooks and archaeologists sought to discern patterns and regularities in Neanderthal interment practices (e.g., Harrold 1980), it fell under critical scrutiny in the late 1980s. Perhaps the arguments against deliberate Neanderthal burial were articulated most strongly by Robert Gargett (1989), who took the position that the preservation of complete skeletons from Neanderthal times was simply due to the fact that natural processes had not had as much opportunity to disturb them and that the evidence for Neanderthal grave pits and grave offerings can be explained more economically by invoking natural processes rather than human activity and by a "discipline-wide naivete" about geological processes and taphonomy.

Attacking archaeologists of the early twentieth century for not using the precise methods of the late twentieth century is always a bit too easy, and only a few other palaeoanthropologists have espoused the position that Neanderthals did not deliberately bury their dead, usually with the qualification that the evidence is equivocal (e.g., Gamble 1994a: 166–7; Stringer and Gamble 1993: 158–60). In Stringer and Gamble's view, Neanderthals were simply disposing of corpses rather than practicing a spiritual custom (1993: 161), and that deliberate burial did not appear until much later, after ca. 35,000 years ago. On the other hand, Erik Trinkaus (1989: 184) has argued persuasively that the presence of so many well-preserved Neanderthal skeletons (see Smirnov 1989 for a comprehensive catalog) can only be explained through the action of an unusual process, such as intentional burial.

A reasonable middle ground has been sought by Paul Mellars (1996: 375–81), who finds that the evidence for Neanderthal burial is persuasive, but the evidence for rituals and symbolic offerings is weak. Lack of published documentation on the Teshik-Tash burial and its associated goat horns has long cast doubt on that find. The isolated Neanderthal skull from Grotta Guattari at Monte Circeo in Italy, found in 1939 among a ring of bones and held to be evidence of ritual activity, has been convincingly shown to be the result of hyaena activity (Stiner 1991). Chase and Dibble (1987) have argued that the few objects found in Neanderthal burials are mundane goods, such as stone tools and animal bones, which may have been accidental inclusions in the grave fill. Mellars' position of accepting Neanderthal burials but finding the evidence for ritual to be lacking seems sensible in light of the evidence currently available, although I believe that the argument for the inclusion of flowers in the Shanidar 4 burial cannot be dismissed.

Stronger evidence for burial ritual is found in the graves of early anatomically-modern humans from Qafzeh and Skhul caves in Israel (Vandermeersch 1989). At Qafzeh, dating to ca. 92,000 years ago, a contracted skeleton with a pair of fallow deer antlers placed over its shoulders was found, while at Shkul, where a dating between ca. 100,000 and 80,000 years ago seems likely, the skeleton of an adult male was found in a tightly contracted position with one hand apparently having held the jaw of a wild boar. Is this another example of Neanderthal deficiency when compared with anatomically-modern humans? At this point, such a conclusion is premature. It is true, however, that after 35,000 years ago, there is increasing evidence throughout Eurasia of burials in open sites, and cave burials also became more elaborate. More will be said about some of these finds in the following chapter, including the triple burial from Dolní Věstonice.

THE LANGUAGE PROBLEM

The ability to communicate verbally using words to represent both abstract and concrete phenomena which are related through a formal grammar is a uniquely human characteristic. Despite recent efforts to teach chimpanzees to communicate in sign language, no other species has developed a true language, not to mention the diversity and sophistication of human languages, as a system of cognition and communication. This ability to communicate lies at the root of all subsequent human cultural development. The key question concerns when humans acquired this ability, and this is a matter of debate among palaeoanthropologists. Most believe language to have been a relatively late development in evolutionary time, while others support an earlier emergence.

Several key lines of evidence are relevant in the debate about language origins. The first is the assessment of human cognitive capacity through the study of endocasts of hominid crania – in other words, trying to assess the growth and development of parts of the brain known to be associated with speech. Another is the analysis of the osteological evidence for the evolution of the human vocal tract, specifically the bones that border the larynx. Finally, attempts have been made to correlate various cultural remains, such as diversification of animal bone samples, burials, and art with a need for some verbal medium of communication.

Since most known crania from *Homo erectus* onward fall within the range of size variation of modern humans, the development of language was not simply a question of larger brain size (Mithen 1996: 140). Instead, the issue is the reorganization of the brain within the hominid skull. Terence Deacon (1992) has taken the position that the human brain is essentially a primate brain on which the major evolutionary restructuring influence has been the organization of language circuits in the prefrontal cortex (Deacon 1989, 1992). On the basis of his palaeoneurological research, Deacon has concluded that selection involving language began at least two million years ago, that this selection continued throughout the evolution of the genus *Homo*, and that the diversification of *Homo* into various lineages in the last 200,000 years did not result in additional neurological changes (Deacon 1989: 395). This view appears to be the current consensus on the basis of palaeoneurology, although there is some skepticism that endocasts can provide evidence for brain functions and organization (Gannon and Laitman 1993).

A somewhat different picture is presented by the study of the human vocal tract, where there is a clear change over time. Based on their study of the Neanderthal skeleton from La Chapelle, Philip Lieberman and Edmund Crelin argued that the position of the larynx in the neck would have limited the ability of Neanderthals to a narrow range of vocal sounds compared with those available to modern *Homo sapiens sapiens*. The Neanderthal configuration would have resembled that of a scaled-up newborn modern human rather than a modern adult. Houghton (1993) has re-examined Lieberman and Crelin's reconstruction and has differed with their conclusions, however.

As Lynne Schepartz (1993: 103, 110) has pointed out, the hypothesis of limited Neanderthal speech advocated by Philip Lieberman and others (1) implies that other archaic *Homo sapiens* lineages were capable of modern human speech and (2) does not rule out the possibility that pre-*sapiens* hominids were also capable of producing the range of sounds found in modern speech. For example, the part of the brain known as Broca's area, which is commonly associated with speech, appears to be well-developed on specimens of *Homo habilis* and *Homo erectus* (Mithen 1996: 141). Yet even if early hominids were *able* to produce a wide range of sounds, we do not know whether or not they organized them into the complex patterns of symbolic expression that we would consider to be a language or whether their sounds were confined to vocalization.

Archaeological evidence for language deals with the general areas of cognition (such as sequential thinking and planning) and symbolism (such as burial, art, and ornaments). As might be expected, these materialized considerably later than the palaeoneurological evidence cited above. Burial is discussed elsewhere in this chapter, and art and ornaments in the following one. It is important to understand that the archaeological evidence for language is indirect and inferential. For example, the late Pleistocene colonizations of Australia, Siberia, and the New World, discussed in the next chapter, are taken as evidence of a need for a sophisticated system of communication (Davidson and Noble 1989; Noble and Davidson 1996; Whallon 1989). The psychologist Michael Corballis (1992) has argued that prior to the late Pleistocene the primary mode of communication was by gesture, and the development of speech freed humans to use their hands to make a wider range of tools and ornaments. As Mithen (1996: 227) points out, however, the stone technology of the Middle Palaeolithic required as much manual dexterity as that of later periods.

The question of the emergence of language will remain unresolved for some time to come. Lynne Schepartz takes the position that

> Specifically, there are no data suggesting any major *qualitative* change in language abilities that corresponds to either 200,000–100,000 BP (the earliest date

for modern *Homo sapiens* origins proposed by single origin models) or 40,000–30,000 BP (the suggested date for the appearance of modern *Homo sapiens* in Western Europe).

The implication of this statement is that the capacity for language developed even earlier, among *Homo erectus* populations or even *Homo habilis*. Such a position finds support in Deacon's palaeoneurological studies (Deacon 1992) and in the case made by Leslie Aiello and Robin Dunbar (1993) that language emerged as a replacement for mutual grooming as a means of maintaining cohesion in hominid social groupings at least by about 250,000 years ago, perhaps much earlier. When, however, did humans begin to make full *use* of this capacity? It seems likely that as with many other aspects of human culture there was a progression from simple to complex. In this regard, Robin Dunbar's position (1993), echoed by Steven Mithen (1996), that there was a switch in language use from exchanging simple social information to communicating about many different topics, ranging from the concrete to the abstract, is an intriguing and promising way to examine this development. In Mithen's view (1996: 187), this transition took place between 150,000 and 50,000 years ago. Thus, while the capacity and ability to vocalize a wide range of sounds probably existed among early members of the genus *Homo*, it was probably somewhat more recently that archaic and early modern humans began to take full advantage of its potential for communication and management of information.

THE EMERGENCE OF MODERN HUMANS

DEBATES ABOUT PHYLOGENY

Until the 1980s, the sequence of later human evolution seemed to be fairly well understood. Modern *H. sapiens* was considered to have been a development from late *H. erectus* stock, after passing through a Neanderthal phase in Europe and the Near East and proceeding directly everywhere else. In other words, after the *H. erectus* dispersal, then believed to have occurred no more than a million years ago but now known to be nearly two million years old, human populations throughout the Old World continued to evolve locally. Given the generalized nature of human adaptation to many different habitats, it was no surprise that everyone ended up in basically the same shape.

Although discoveries in Africa during the 1960s and early 1970s focused on the earliest hominids, by the 1980s the fossil and archaeological record of the last million years in Africa was coming into sharper focus. A number of anatomically-modern specimens produced surprisingly early dates. So rather than being evolutionarily-retarded by having missed the Neanderthal stage, Africa suddenly came to be seen as an evolutionarily-progressive area by having skipped it. Louis Leakey had suggested this many years before, but the recovery of new specimens and improvements in dating led to a revival of this view. Thus, the emergence of anatomically-modern humans, which everyone had thought was fairly well understood in 1980, became a topic of heated and contentious scholarly debate in the decade that followed.

"OUT OF AFRICA II," OR THE RECENT AFRICAN
ORIGIN HYPOTHESIS

The 1980s revisionist view, which came to be widely accepted as the ortho-dox view of the 1990s, was that anatomically-modern humans first appeared in Africa about 100,000 years ago. From there, they spread throughout the Old World, and eventually to the New World (see chapter 3), replacing the indigenous archaic populations. Thus, the Neanderthals, once welcomed as our ancestors, were shunted off onto a siding, while the descendants of *H. erectus* in Asia never left the station. In its most extreme view, the Recent African Origin model does not allow for *any* hybridization between the new-comers and the locals, while more tempered versions accommodate some hybridization between the two populations (Aiello 1993: 73).

The palaeoanthropologist most identified with the Recent African Origin model is Christopher Stringer of the Natural History Museum in London. In numerous publications (e.g., Stringer 1994, 1995; Stringer and McKie 1996), Stringer, his collaborators, and other adherents of the Recent African Origin hypothesis (also sometimes called "Out of Africa II") have presented their case based on an accumulating corpus of early modern human remains in Africa and new techniques for comparing anatomy. Their work is very focused on the shape of the cranial vault and the face. Although it was not originally predicated on the genetic evidence discussed below, the Recent African Origin model resonates strongly with the hypotheses derived from the study of mitachondrial DNA about a recent African origin for all humans.

IN SITU EVOLUTION, OR THE MULTIREGIONAL EVOLUTION
HYPOTHESIS

In contrast to the Recent African Origin model, the traditional view of *in situ* evolution of modern human populations throughout the Old World contin-ues to have its staunch adherents. After having been the standard view until the 1980s, the Multiregional Evolution hypothesis has become eroded over the last decade, but there are enough difficulties and uncertainties associated with the Recent African Origin model that *in situ* evolution of modern humans remains a viable possibility. In essence, this model argues that mod-ern humans arose from indigenous stock throughout the Old World and that these populations were in contact such that genes flowed freely among them.

The most forceful proponents of the Multiregional Evolution model are Milford Wolpoff of the University of Michigan and Alan Thorne of the Australian National University (Wolpoff et al. 1994), although they are by no means alone. The processes which underlie the Multiregional Evolution model are far from simple, since they involve both the development of distinctive local characteristics by discrete human populations and these same populations having sufficient interaction to smooth out any radical differences among them. Improvements in technology permitted a global reduction in massive elements of functional anatomy, leading to the overall complex of gracile structures that characterize modern humans.

A hybrid between the Multiregional Evolution and Recent African Origin models has been proposed by Fred Smith and Erik Trinkaus (Smith 1992; Smith and Trinkaus 1992), who accept the idea of an African origin for anatomically-modern humans but believe that gene flow and selection rather than total population replacement resulted in the appearance of modern humans throughout the Old World. Unfortunately, this position does not appear to have attracted much attention outside of the specialists in this area, although it seems entirely plausible as a way of reconciling the two extremes.

THE AFRICAN EVE?

Until the late 1980s, the only data on the emergence of anatomically-modern humans came from fossil and sub-fossil bones. At that point, molecular biologists and population geneticists at the University of California at Berkeley who had been studying human mitachondrial DNA (mtDNA) entered the discussion. Allan Wilson, Rebecca Cann, Mark Stoneking, and colleagues reported that all mtDNA variation in living humans is derived from a single common female ancestor (Cann, Stoneking, and Wilson 1987), and moreover that this ancestor lived in Africa about 200,000 years ago. Mitachondrial DNA is inherited only from the maternal gamete, so the idea that all humans have a common female ancestor is not as earthshaking as newspapers and magazines portrayed it. All species with mtDNA have a common female ancestor somewhere in the past.

The novel and controversial part of the Cann, Stoneking, and Wilson paper and subsequent contributions was the identification of Africa as the heartland of modern human mtDNA and the dating of it to about 200,000 years ago. This suited the proponents of the "Out of Africa II" hypothesis just fine and was attacked by proponents of the multiregional model. It was impossible to miss the implications of their argument: when the bearers of modern mtDNA left Africa, they did not interbreed with the indigenous populations of Eurasia and instead replaced them. This position is even more extreme than that of the palaeontological proponents of "Out of Africa II," who were not adverse to the idea that a little interbreeding might have occurred.

Yet despite its laboratory-science foundation, the mtDNA approach has been criticized heavily. Cann, Stoneking, and Wilson's initial mtDNA analysis had some serious methodological flaws, which critics were quick to point out, although the Berkeley geneticists addressed these in subsequent analyses. Others have proposed alternative interpretations of the mtDNA data. Alan Templeton (1993), a geneticist, has argued that the genetic data indicate that the evidence for the geographical position of the common female ancestor is ambiguous, the time when this ancestor existed is likely to have been more than 200,000 years ago, and that Old World human populations had low but recurrent genetic contact for a substantial part of the last million years.

Other genetic evidence, however, continues to point towards a relatively recent African origin for modern humans. Studying a different segment of mtDNA from that used by the Berkeley researchers has led Maryellen Ruvolo (1996) at Harvard to propose that the modern human line began 222,000 years ago. Other recent studies of the Y chromosome have indicated that a male ancestor also existed in the last 200,000 years, and while nuclear DNA shows the most diversity in sub-Saharan Africa, it is relatively uniform in the rest of the globe (Tishkoff et al. 1996).

Although the "Mitachondrial Eve" captured the attention of the public, she is largely a journalistic invention. She was not "the one mother from whom all humans descend," but rather a mtDNA molecule (or the woman carrier of that molecule) from which all modern mtDNA molecules descend (Ayala 1995: 1933). This molecule was already in existence, and there were many other archaic humans living at this time whose genes we continue to carry as well. Since mtDNA is only 1/400,000 of the total DNA present in a person, all the rest was inherited from the contemporaries of this woman. For humans to have sustained the level of genetic diversity that we see in modern human populations, the population that produced the first modern humans would have had to have numbered at least 10,000 and possibly more than 50,000 (Ayala 1995: 1934). So rather than perpetuate the myth of the "Mitachondrial Eve," a more accurate statement is that genetic evidence indicates that modern humans developed relatively quickly from a founding population that lived in Africa about 200,000 years ago (Johnson and Edgar 1996: 42).

DISCUSSION

The emergence of anatomically-modern humans is probably far more complex than either the Recent African Origin (with total population replacement) or the Multiregional Evolution (with no population replacement) models depict. At the moment, the evidence does point towards the earlier development of anatomically-modern forms in Africa and the Levant than in Europe, but the evidence in Asia is very hazy (Aiello 1993: 89). Leslie Aiello has suggested a somewhat more complex model which would reconcile the evidence from fossils and genetics for an African origin of the main human stem but allow for some hybridization between moderns and Neanderthals in Europe and for the persistence of *H. erectus* forms in Asia. This model is graphically represented in figure 2.10.

Although the polarization of the supporters of the Recent African Origin model and adherents of Multiregional Evolution currently seems extreme, there is hope for the eventual resolution of the debate because these groups of scholars are looking at essentially the same corpus of fossil data and accept the same evolutionary forces. The genetic data are still inconclusive but also permit multiple interpretations (e.g., Ayala 1995). Smith and Harrold (1997) take an optimistic view that the existence of intermediate positions indicates that a continuum exists between the two poles which may permit their eventual reconciliation.

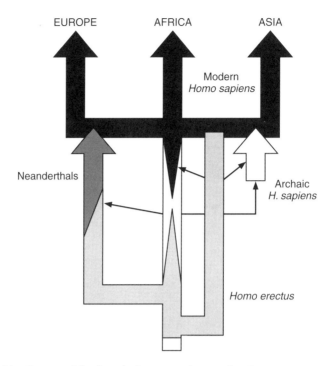

Figure 2.10 One model of evolutionary pathways for the emergence of modern *Homo sapiens* (after Aiello 1993, figure 5).

PLEISTOCENE BAND SOCIETY

Clive Gamble recently remarked that "as soon as we start discussing Palaeolithic society the pessimists come out to play" (1998: 426). This is indeed the case. Nowhere in the study of the archaeological record is there a prevailing sense of despair about understanding prehistoric social organization than in the study of the cultures of ancient humans. In a certain literal and empirical way, this pessimism is justified, especially if one regards archaeology as being a discipline devoid of imagination and in which inference and analogy are not to be acceptable tools of interpretation. It is also the case that the richness of the ethnographic record of hunter-gatherers can exert a heavy influence (characterized dramatically by Martin Wobst in 1978 as "tyranny") on archaeological interpretation and result in the uncritical projection of the behavior of modern hunter-gatherers into the past. So, the archaeologist seeking to understand the society of ancient humans has to tiptoe into a shadowy world of inference, conjecture, speculation, and carefully justified analogy.

Nonetheless, unless one wishes to confine the discussion to the arid categories of stone tools and subsistence, such forays are necessary. Archaeology necessarily involves the imaginative reconstruction of past society, and the fact that the evidence is so sparse does not mean that we should refrain from making some informed speculations, often grounded in the observed behavior of twentieth-century foraging societies. On the other hand, it is wrong to assume that modern-day hunter-gatherers are simply relics of ancient humans. Perhaps the most celebrated case of such an analogy was made by W. J. Sollas in the early twentieth century when he equated the aboriginal societies of Tasmania and Australia with the Lower and Middle Palaeolithic peoples of the Old World (Sollas 1911), although such parallels have been implicit in many subsequent studies. While extant foraging societies can give us some food for thought when it comes to reconstructing the culture of ancient humans, such one-to-one parallels have no reasonable foundation. After all, modern foragers are all members of *Homo sapiens*, so projecting their behavior back to earlier versions of *Homo* is fundamentally a risky, even flawed, exercise.

A few twentieth-century foraging societies have provided a significant amount of inspiration to archaeologists seeking insight into the culture of early *Homo*, however, despite the differences in species affiliation. Primary among these have been the people of the Kalahari Desert in Botswana known generally in the anthropological literature as the !Kung, or the !Kung San (although the ethnonym Ju/'hoansi is now appearing in anthropological literature to refer to largely the same people). The !Kung (anthropology students learn in their introductory course that the "!" represents a clicking sound) came to be seen as the "archaeologists' foragers" as a result of an intensive research program in the 1960s and 1970s which provided a wealth of primary data on subsistence and settlement patterns (e.g., Lee and DeVore 1976; Lee 1979). Unfortunately, since they live in an arid, resource-poor environment, the degree to which they could inform analyses of ancient life on the savannahs of east Africa, much less in the moister and colder regions of Eurasia, was severely limited. Moreover, recent revisionist views of the !Kung (e.g., Wilmsen 1989) have suggested that they are not nearly so pristine a foraging society as has been depicted earlier on, although a scholarly battle still rages on this issue.

Among other twentieth-century foragers who have provided anthropological archaeologists with ways of thinking about Palaeolithic society have been the Hadza of northern Tanzania, the Aché of eastern Paraguay, the Mbuti of eastern Zaire, the Negrito hunter-gatherers of the Philippines and the many aboriginal peoples of Australia, as well as other San neighbors of the !Kung in the Kalahari. As with the !Kung, archaeologists look to these peoples in order to generate hypotheses about the culture of early humans, although the rigor with which these hypotheses are tested varies from researcher to researcher.

At a fundamental level, we can be reasonably confident that early human society had the sort of sociocultural integration which anthropologists categorize as the "band," a flexible association without permanent membership. In many respects, hunting and gathering as an economic strategy is often equated with the band as a form of social organization. In the late 1960s and 1970s, it became common for anthropologists to characterize hunter-gatherer bands as "the original affluent society" (e.g., Sahlins 1972) in which small egalitarian groups of people did not have to work very hard to survive, did not defend fixed territories, and did not accumulate food or material goods. As Kelly (1995: 14–23) has pointed out, this model created a stereotype of band society which had "serious discrepancies between it and ethnographic reality."

As is usually the case, ethnographic reality is much more complicated. Anthropologists have come to recognize that there is a tremendous amount of variability among band societies. Some are highly territorial, others are not. They make conscious decisions about the foods that they hunt and gather and sometimes invest significant amounts of labor and energy in the pursuit of certain resources. Social relations among members of some hunter-gatherer bands are more complicated and asymmetrical than the egalitarian model presumes. This variability may be partly a product of adaptations over time to specific environmental conditions, and it may be partly an effect of the contact between extant hunter-gatherers and "outside" societies. Nonetheless, whatever variability may have also existed in the past, it is a reasonable assumption that until about 10,000 years ago humans lived in social units which would be recognizable by a modern ethnographer as fitting a consensus description of a band.

Having established this baseline for the discussion that follows, it is now important to return to first principles and look at characteristics of the archaeological record of early human societies which would have had an impact on band organization. Foremost among these is the demonstrable mobility of early members of the genus *Homo*. Not only did they have the capacity to disperse over long distances, they apparently moved around quite a bit on a local scale as well. While early hominids may have favored certain locations in the landscape for scavenging and safety, the fact that no evidence of habitations can be found until after 300,000 years ago, and probably later, reflects a degree of residential mobility which may not even be paralleled among extant hunter-gatherers.

Such mobility has important implications. First, it means that even more so than is the case today, hominid bands must have been flexible and fluid entities. This is an important distinction between ancient bands and the societies which followed them. Rather than being closed and fixed groups whose membership was clearly defined, we should think of them as collections of individuals whose affiliations can be defined in many different ways. Second, the role of specific locations would have been much different from that encountered in subsequent human societies. Rather than serving as the definitions of group identity and markers of exclusive territory, such locations would have held much less attachment for ancient mobile bands. Even though groups may have returned to particular spots at intervals, their composition may have been different each time, and it was also likely that the spot had been used by others in the meantime.

This is not to say that ancient hunter-gatherers would not have had a relationship with the land. In fact, they may have had a very complex view of themselves as a part of the landscape, and localities may have had spiritual or totemic significance. The difference between the band society of pre-modern humans and later social formations is that for the later, their domicile – a cave, a hut, a village – played a much greater role in defining one's social identity because it focused a web of affiliations which were much more difficult to alter or abandon.

Another critical aspect of the mobility of early humans was the fact that they did not accumulate material goods nor did they store things for any length of time. While it is possible that they did make some caches for later consumption, specialized storage facilities do not appear until much later in the archaeological record. For most of their existence, humans were what anthropologists would call "immediate-return hunter-gatherers" (Woodburn 1982). By this is meant that they consumed resources (primarily food) as soon as they acquired it. No surpluses were created, even though the techniques of storage and preservation may have been known.

One of the key characteristics of most hunter-gatherer groups, particularly of the immediate-return kind, is the institutionalized sharing of food. Hunter-gatherer sharing is more than a quaint custom done out of politeness. It seems to be a deeply-rooted element of the social fabric. A functionalist explanation for this practice would be that it distributes risk throughout the society, such that even though a hunter might return empty-handed one day and depend on another member of the band for his food, he may get lucky the next and be able to return the favor. Yet since hunting skill is not evenly distributed, some members of the band will always contribute more than others. Why should they continue to hunt if most of that they kill will be taken from them?

Sharing in many foraging societies takes the form of "tolerated theft" (Blurton Jones 1991), in which the giver provides resources to the communal stock not out of sheer altruism but because of social pressure and enforced reciprocity. Such demand sharing keeps any single member of the band, no matter how successful, from accumulating goods or food. In theory, everyone has equal access to food, but in reality some are more successful at procuring it than others. Enforced sharing, however, maintains a level of material equality, although social asymmetries by age and sex may persist.

The ubiquity of sharing among extant foragers worldwide, despite the fact that it takes many different forms, makes it a reasonable assumption that it was a part of early human band societies as well. If that is the case, then it would have been of profound significance in structuring social relationships. Each foraging society has its own way of organizing its patterns of sharing. These frequently extend beyond the spouse and offspring to include others, both relatives and non-relatives, with whom an individual has a sharing relationship. A foraging society, then, would be characterized by a network of such sharing partnerships. The strength of such sharing partnerships not only has a major role in defining the social landscape of a foraging community but also its physical structure, such as the proximity and arrangement of shelters.

Susan Kent (1995) has shown how in many foraging societies (with specific reference to the Kutse of Botswana) "friendship" is more the foundation of sharing networks than actual kinship. She points out that in highly egalitarian small-scale societies, everyone in the community may be considered to be related in some way, either biologically or fictively. Friendship and the sharing networks that grow from it often form a much more significant determinant of the intensity of social interaction among foragers than the degree of kinship. They may activate some kin relations and leave others dormant, but they also may extend beyond kinship and can be redefined with the passage of time. The relationships that emerge may have varying degrees of intensity and content.

It is hard to maintain such relationships over great distances, so another feature of foraging societies is what Nurit Bird-David (1994) calls "immediacy" to capture the sense of small scale, openness, and mutual connectivity of the community. Bird-David further proposes that this immediacy within band societies is expressed through "we relationships" which emphasize a sharing of space, time, and experiences. In many respects, the observable sharing of resources is a physical manifestation of a more abstract set of shared phenomena. In order to maintain such relationships, sustained physical proximity is necessary, for distance erodes immediacy.

Clive Gamble has recently taken a similar approach to the characterization of Palaeolithic society (Gamble 1996, 1998). In Gamble's model, the interactions of individuals produce networks of relationships at several levels: intimate, effective, extended, and global. The intimate network includes those interacting at the highest intensity with the individual, perhaps on the order of five, either relatives or very close friends. As noted above, friendship may be a stronger determinant of such relationships than kinship for many foragers. The effective network includes those people who provide an individual with "material and emotional assistance during the routines of daily life" (Gamble 1998: 434), perhaps on the order of between 15 and 30 friends and relatives. The extended network is composed of acquaintances and friends-of-friends of an individual, perhaps numbering in the hundreds. Finally, the global network is potentially unbounded, but in practical terms may reach into the thousands.

Gamble goes on to contrast what he calls "local hominid networks," which would have been composed primarily of the effective and intimate networks, with the "social landscape," which embraces extended and global networks. In his view (simplified here), prior to about 100,000 to 60,000 years ago, human sociality was confined effectively to local hominid networks, whereas the extended networks which form the social landscape supplemented (rather than replaced) the local hominid network around this time. A symptom of this transition is the fact that prior to this time, raw materials circulated within radii of no more than 100 kilometers, usually much less, whereas after this time, resource transfers on the order of hundreds of kilometers were common. Gamble characterizes this as a "release from proximity" in that humans had developed ways to conduct social relations without the need for sustained face-to-face contact. Language and speech would have been key factors in this transition, as would other forms of symbolic behavior, all of which may have been facilitated by increases in brain size among post-*erectus* humans.

The above perspectives on recent and ancient foraging societies converge to provide a working model of early human society, which could be called

"Pleistocene band society." Pleistocene bands were fluid associations of individuals whose affiliations were conditioned more by proximity and immediacy resulting in friendships among kin and non-kin than by any fixed set of biologically-determined relationships. These individuals shared many things, including food, space, and experiences. In the case of resources, the sharing was often done freely but also frequently in response to demand, or to anticipate demand, by other individuals. In such a society, settlements were places which provided shelter, safety, and conditions for "we relationships," not for privacy and the accumulation of material goods. They were locations of social inclusion, not of social demarcation and exclusion. Although asymmetries of status and power may have existed along lines of age and sex and in terms of skills in hunting and ritual, they were not expressed as material wealth. Common access to resources and an ethos of sharing enforced relative equality.

This was hardly the "original affluent society" celebrated in anthropology texts of the 1970s, however. Life was physically demanding, mobile, violent, and likely to be short. There was a good chance of winding up as a leopard's lunch or a rockfall sandwich. Scavenging carcasses for meat is hardly a romantic image of early humans, but a true one. The notion of affluence evokes images of leisure and accumulation, which continual foraging and enforced sharing norms would have certainly prevented. A member of a Pleistocene band, no matter how far down the road towards anatomical modernity, simply lived the rough life of a very social, tool-assisted higher primate.

Although the ability to conduct social relationships at a distance probably did have a profound effect on human society and may have played a significant role in the developments that are discussed in the next chapter, I believe that the above pattern of small and intimate Pleistocene bands, or something close to it, continued to be the dominant human social configuration for some time. Not until the global onset of sedentism at the end of the Pleistocene can we observe a radical and dramatic restructuring of human social relations. Nonetheless, if there was, as Gamble proposes, a "release from proximity" in the conduct of social relations, human societies would have taken yet another step to distinguish themselves from being simply a very successful primate.

FURTHER READING

Several good general-readership volumes have been produced recently that tell the story of human evolution. These include the large-format illustrated volumes *From Lucy to Language* by Donald Johanson and Blake Edgar (1996) with outstanding illustrations, *The Last Neanderthal: the Rise, Success, and Mysterious Extinction of Our Closest Human Relatives* (1995) by Ian Tattersall, and *The First Humans: Human Origins and History to 10,000 BC* under the general editorship of Göran Burenhult (1993). John Reader's *Missing Links* (1981) is a superb account of the search for human origins through 1980, which can be complemented by two recent volumes: *The Wisdom of the Bones* by Alan Walker and Pat Shipman (1996) and *The Neanderthals: Changing the Image of Mankind* by Erik Trinkaus and Pat Shipman (1992). *Humans before Humanity* by Robert Foley (1995) and *Humanity's Descent* by Rick Potts (1996) are excellent reflections on the ecological conditions and behavioral characteristics that shaped early hominids. The origins of technology are discussed in the lively volume by Kathy Schick and Nicholas Toth entitled *Making Silent Stones Speak* (1993). *In Search of Neanderthals* by Christopher Stringer and Clive Gamble (1993) is a readable treatment of the Neanderthal question in Eurasia, while *The Neanderthal Legacy: an Archaeological Perspective from Western Europe* by Paul Mellars (1996) covers the same territory in more academic detail. Human dispersals from Africa (the earlier one by *Homo erectus* and the presumed later one by anatomically-modern humans) are the topic of *Timewalkers* by Clive Gamble (1994) and *African Exodus: the Origins of Modern Humanity* by Christopher Stringer and Robin McKie (1996). One view of language origins is presented in *Human Evolution, Language and Mind* by William Noble and Iain Davidson (1996). Many journals carry technical scholarly articles about human evolution and the archaeology of early humans, including *Nature, Journal of Human Evolution, Journal of World Prehistory*, and *Journal of Evolutionary Anthropology*.

[3] *THE HUMAN DIASPORA*

THE FINAL BLAST OF THE ICE AGE

Around 50,000 years ago, the confused amalgam of ancient and modern humans depicted in the previous chapter was suddenly resolved. Anatomically-modern humans prevailed, and the debates about human phylogeny are no longer a central issue after this point. Previously confined to Africa and the southern edge of Eurasia, people moved northward and eastward, which brought them to several critical points on the rim of the Pacific basin. Beringia on the north and Sundaland on the south formed the jumping-off points for the colonization of the last two major land masses upon which humans had not yet trod, the New World and Greater Australia. Throughout this area, people spent much time articulating a vision of their world through their designs on cave walls and cliffs and the sculpting of figures.

One of the paradoxes of world prehistory is that the flowering of human technology and symbolic behavior took place during some of the most hostile climatic conditions ever encountered. For the first time, we can see consistent and regular patterns of social interaction over wide geographic areas. Archaeological occurrences cease to be unique and isolated and begin to form coherent and repetitive patterns as adventurous humans colonized far corners of the Old World and finally entered the New.

These were modern human beings, whose emergence into the world stage has been chronicled in the preceding chapter. We can relate easily to them, although we ourselves do not hunt mammoths or draw on cave walls. Their motivations and desires are understandable even after the millennia that separate us from them. These people are not the apelike australopithecines, the remote *Homo erectus*, or the peculiar Neanderthals. They are Moderns, whose direct descendants produced the cathedrals, the automobile, the airplane, and the computer.

The people of the late Pleistocene have been intensely studied by archaeologists for nearly two centuries. Much of this work has been concentrated in only a few regions, such as southwestern France, and on specific archaeological occurrences, such as the fluted-point cultures of North America. Recent work has led to a much more global picture, particularly as areas such as eastern Siberia and the Amazon Valley are penetrated by systematic archaeological research. Vast areas remain *terra incognita* in the study of late Ice Age life, however, so much exploration and fieldwork remains to be done.

BASIC GEOGRAPHY AND CLIMATIC CONDITIONS

In the late Ice Age world, water in both its liquid and solid phases played a major role in determining human activity. The distribution of ice masses and the relation of sea levels to the continental margins both posed impediments and created opportunities for people during the last 50,000 years. An understanding of the activity of members of the species *Homo sapiens* during this period is predicated on an understanding of the global distribution of water.

It may come as a surprise to some that the amount of water in the global ecosystem is relatively constant. The hydrological cycle transports water and redistributes it in various ways but in the grand scheme of things no new water is created. Thus, when there are large ice masses in the northern hemisphere, world wide sea levels drop, exposing continental margins. Similarly, the melting of these ice masses causes an inundation of the continental margins worldwide, a redistribution of water on the land surfaces adjacent to the ice front, and the ready evaporation of water to fall as rain elsewhere. The phase transition with which we are all familiar, the melting of an ice cube, has dramatic consequences when it occurs on a massive scale in time and space.

So where was the ice? The Fennoscandian ice sheet, which had made life cold for *Homo erectus* and Neanderthals during its previous advances, covered much of northern Europe. About 35,000 years ago, it began its most recent major advance southward after a period of relative warmth between 70,000 and 35,000 years ago. This advance reached its maximum southernly

Figure 3.1 Late Pleistocene Europe, showing location of Fennoscandian Ice Sheet (hatched area). Heavy line demarcates southern limit of tundra and permafrost, dotted lines indicate Late Pleistocene coastlines.

extent around 20,000 years ago near the Oder river in Silesia is what is now southwestern Poland. From this most southernly point, the ice front angled away sharply to the northwest through northern Germany and Denmark, across the North Sea to the British Isles. Ice covered much of northern England, Scotland, and about three-quarters of Ireland. East of Silesia, the ice front ran across central Poland and into European Russia along a line of approximately 53°N. Around the current headwaters of the Dniepr and Don rivers, the ice front began to angle sharply towards the northeast, finally reaching the Arctic ocean to the east of the White Sea. In the Alps and other mountain ranges of northern Eurasia, such as the Altai, smaller glaciers reached down to the neighboring plains.

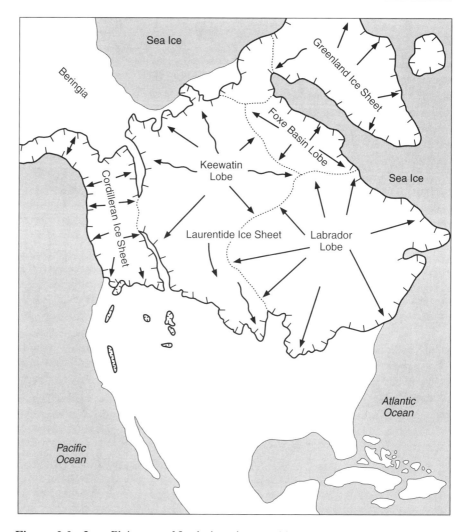

Figure 3.2 Late Pleistocene North America, ca. 20,000 years ago, showing extent of Laurentide and Cordilleran ice sheets (after Frison and Walker 1990, figure 17.2). The hypothesized "ice-free corridor" emerged when the Cordilleran and Laurentide sheets separated.

South and east of the Fennoscandian ice mass, a variety of periglacial environments could be found. Tundra and park-tundra along the ice front gave way to a massive steppe zone which stretched from southwestern Europe to northeastern Asia and across into Alaska. Guthrie (1990) has termed this area the "mammoth steppe" (about which more will be said below), a name which is appropriate both because of its enormous size and its most prominent mammal inhabitant. This region was harsh and cold, with mean January temperatures 10–20° colder than today (Soffer 1990: 233), yet productive enough to support human populations. Animal populations were substantial (Guthrie 1990) which also meant that humans could survive in this environment, despite the difficult conditions.

In North America, the pattern of glaciation was somewhat more complex than in Eurasia. Two major ice sheets covered the northern half of the continent, the Laurentide and the Cordilleran. The Cordilleran was a mountain glacier of the northern Rockies which extended west onto the Pacific coastal plain during periods of low sea levels or which dropped off into the Pacific when sea levels were high. It also extended across southern Alaska and out along the Aleutian Island chain. In the east, the Cordilleran glacier pushed east to touch, at points, the westernmost parts of the Laurentide ice sheet.

The Laurentide ice sheet was actually composed of three separate masses of ice. The Labrador ice mass covered the Maritime Provinces of Canada and the northeastern United States as well as the Great Lakes region and was responsible for the glaciated landscapes of New England and Ontario. The Keewatin ice sheet was the largest mass which extended from the base of the Rocky mountains and the Cordilleran glacier east to the Labrador mass. Finally, in the far north on Baffin Island, a third mass, known as Foxe Basin, filled a niche between the Labrador and Keewatin masses.

The behavior of the North American ice sheets paralleled that of the Eurasian ice masses, except that in addition to the major north–south axis of expansion and contraction there was also an east–west dimension. The expansion and contraction of the Cordilleran and Laurentide ice sheets produced the potential for them to be separated at various times in the last 50,000 years. The timing and extent of this separation is crucial for the understanding of the peopling of the New World, which will be discussed in greater detail below.

The thickness of the northern hemisphere ice sheets was astonishing, for in some places they reached 2500 meters. Along the ice front was a very active geomorphological environment. The advancing ice sheet pushed before it a mound of boulders and soil, which it then abandoned once it reached its maximum extent and began to retreat. Such terminal moraines are the way that the ebb and flow of the ice sheets can be documented. The retreating ice mass produced even more interesting effects. Massive torrents of meltwater sloughed off the ice front and tried to find their way to the nearest ocean. Blocks of ice from the retreating glacier were abandoned across the periglacial landscape, where they remained frozen for millennia and became covered by latter sediments. When these finally melted, they left hollows which became filled with water and form many of the lakelands of northern North America and Europe. Rivers blocked by the ice mass suddenly became undammed and gushed forward.

Did humans ever *see* the ice sheets? Very probably they did, especially during the summer as they followed herds of migratory mammals across the Eurasian tundra. During the maximum extent of the glaciation, the periglacial zone was probably not very hospitable, due largely to its dryness and the strong winds which carried massive amounts of soil from western Europe and deposited it as loess in eastern Europe and central Asia. As the ice sheet began to retreat, however, the winds would have abated and the melting ice would have resulted in much more moisture and, as a result, a more productive environment. Small shrubs and dwarf trees began to colonize the periglacial zone as the ice fronts retreated towards their central core areas. Herds of migratory animals such as reindeer adjusted their habitats in concert with the contraction (and periodic small-scale advances) of the ice sheet which began about 20,000 years ago, and humans followed animals across the periglacial steppe.

By 13,000 years ago, the average July temperature in northern Europe was about 18°C (Coope 1977), although sea levels were still much lower than today. Denmark and southern Sweden were connected, as were England and the whole coastline of northern continental Europe. The Baltic Sea was a vast ice-lake, dammed by the Denmark–Sweden land bridge, while the English Channel was only a large Atlantic Bay which ended at a land bridge between Dover and Calais. Thus the North European Plain extended practically from southern England to Russia and was covered by park tundra. Across this tundra, herds of reindeer roamed.

The end of the Ice Age, for the moment, is generally set at 10,000 years ago. By this time, the ice sheets had retreated to approximately their current locations, the land bridges were shrinking or already inundated, and the land which had been under the weight of millions of tons of ice had actually sprung upward (it later subsided). The climate warmed up in several fitful spurts called the Bølling and Allerød oscillations, separated by cold snaps and slight glacial advances. The most significant of these cold phases is called the Younger Dryas, after a shrub characteristic of periglacial habitats. Forests colonized open landscapes of Eurasia and North America, and the habitat for reindeer continued to shift northward. Ten thousand years ago, the world was still very much different from what it is like today, but the climatic changes of this era set in motion important changes in human society, which by then had settled virtually all of the world.

LAND BRIDGES AND WATER BARRIERS

In September 1931, the crew of the trawler *Colinda*, under the command of skipper Pilgrim Lockwood, dredged up a block of peat from the bed of the North Sea between the Leman and Ower banks. They had frequently brought up peat previously in this area between England and the Netherlands, and their usual procedure was to break up the chunk and toss the pieces back over the side. While breaking up this piece of "moorlog," as they called it, a barbed antler point fell out. Luckily, this find was called to the attention of archaeologists at Cambridge, who were able to identify it as being similar to known specimens from England and Denmark. Clearly, at this time, now known to be about 11,500 years ago, the southern part of the North Sea was a freshwater fen stretching from England to Germany and the Netherlands. England was at the western end of the North European Plain, while the Rhine and the Thames shared a common estuary, now inundated by the North Sea.

Over the following decades, the extent of the worldwide lowering of sea levels during the Pleistocene has become known. In addition to the land bridge between continental Europe and the British Isles, several other land bridges and one major water barrier played key roles in shaping the pattern of human movement in the later part of the Ice Age. Probably the most famous land bridge is the one between Asia and North America over the Bering Straits, since this is the route through which people first came to the New World. Another important land bridge existed between New Guinea and Australia, while yet another joined Tasmania to Australia. These three land masses together formed "Greater Australia," or "Sahul," which was separated from Southeast Asia and Indonesia, or "Sunda," by a water barrier which humans needed to cross.

The land bridge over the Bering Straits between Siberia and Alaska forms the central element of a much larger biotic, geological, and archaeological

Figure 3.3 Beringia, showing key Siberian and North American sites mentioned in this chapter.

entity known as "Beringia." The recognition that for much of the Pleistocene vast areas of the East Siberian Sea, Chukchi Sea and Bering Sea bordering Alaska and Siberia were also dry land has expanded the regional perspective from just the Bering Straits to a much larger province. West (1996a) defines Beringia as the area bounded on the east by the Mackenzie River in Canada and on the west by the Lena River in Siberia. Only vestiges of Beringia remain in the form of some islands in the Chukchi and East Siberian Seas in the north and the Kamchatka Peninsula in the south.

Beringia can be characterized as having been a vast plain punctuated in a few places by hills and mountain ranges, such as the Brooks Range in Alaska. It is clear from figure 3.3 that only a small part of this area was covered by ice during the Pleistocene, while the rest was relatively open. It was certainly cold, but as has been seen in Eurasia, late Pleistocene humans were quite at home in cold climates. The question of the vegetation in Beringia is the subject of heated debate among palaeoenvironmental researchers. Before the climate warmed up and permitted the growth of dwarf birch about 13,000 years ago, it certainly was treeless. Some, like Cwynar (1982), have characterized Pleistocene Beringia as a type of polar desert, with very few plants except for barren-land sages like *Artemisia. Artemisia*, the arctic sage, figures prominently in the pollen record of Beringia, and the key issue is its density of growth and the presence of other species of plants. Unfortunately, the Beringia pollen spectra have no modern analogs, which permits a number of different interpretations.

Others have attempted to characterize the flora of Beringia through the fauna. Guthrie (1990) has analyzed samples of Ice Age Beringian fauna which consist primarily of grazers that required large amounts of grass and their predators. On the basis of these collections, Guthrie has characterized Beringia as a vast grassland, what he called the "mammoth steppe," which was highly productive. Others, such as Ukraintseva, Agenbroad, and Mead (1996), have analyzed the stomach contents of frozen herbivore carcasses and shown that these animals, especially mammoths, were eating tundra plants. Tundra is a far less productive environment than grassland, which points to the need to account for the dietary requirements of large mammals. If Beringia was indeed mostly covered by tundra, then it must have been a more productive form of tundra habitat than those known today.

A drop in sea level of only 46 meters is all that would be required to expose a continuous land bridge across the Bering Straits. It is estimated, however, that at the Late Glacial Maximum sea levels were between 100 and 150 meters lower than at present, which would have created a very wide bridge across the dry continental shelves of northeastern Asia and Alaska. Although until recently it was believed that the Bering land bridge was drowned by rising sea levels as early as 14,000 years ago, new cores indicate that the connection between North America and Asia was not broken until after 10,000 years ago (Hopkins 1996).

As much as Asia was joined to North America by a land bridge, it was also separated from Sahul by a deep sea trough. This barrier was a significant impediment to the transfer of species from Asia to Australia and accounts for

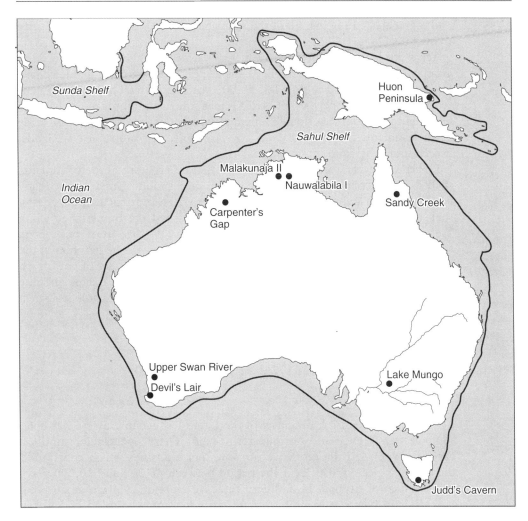

Figure 3.4 Map of Australia showing key sites mentioned in this chapter. Heavy line indicates approximate location of Late Pleistocene coastline.

the latter's distinctive fauna which evolved in isolation for millions of years. It also prevented humans from reaching Australia for a million or more years after they arrived in Southeast Asia and Java. On one side of this gap was the land mass of Sunda, consisting of Sumatra, Borneo, Java, Bali, and smaller southeast Asian islands, while on the other was Sahul, the supercontinent composed of New Guinea, Australia, and Tasmania.

The deepwater gap between Sunda and Sahul forms a province called "Wallacea," after the British naturalist Alfred Russel Wallace (1823–1913). It is a region of deep water, such as the Weber Trench and Timor Trough, and true oceanic islands, such as the Celebes. Although some species of mammals managed to hop the water barriers to a few of these islands, only mice and rats managed to cross all of the water barriers of Wallacea to Sahul prior to humans (Jones 1992).

Yet a sea level drop of only 30 meters creates land bridges joining New Guinea, Australia, and Tasmania. This region must be considered to have been one large unit during the last 50,000 years or more. Thus once humans reached the northwestern tip of New Guinea, they had unbroken dry land for 5000 km to the southern tip of Tasmania. Within this area was a diverse array of environments including tropical coastal plains, rich subtropical wetlands, deserts and oases, and mountain forests.

Lower sea levels worldwide also meant that much more of the continental shelf of every continent was exposed. The implication of this is that many late Pleistocene archaeological sites are under water. In particular, the coastal shelf along the eastern coast of North America and the Sunda shelf along Vietnam and Thailand were broad lowland plains that must have been attractive to many species of animals, including humans. The harpoon in the moorlog at the bottom of the North Sea is a poignant reminder of how much dry land on which humans once trod is now submerged. Perhaps at some future date, economical means will be developed to assess the archaeological potential of such areas.

SOCIAL COMPLEXITY IN WESTERN AND EASTERN EUROPE

For well over a century, the navel of the Late Pleistocene universe has been southwestern France and northwestern Spain. There, spectacular stratified cave sites provided the sequence of stone tool industries which constituted the chronological yardstick for the period between 40,000 and 10,000 years ago in much of Europe. In addition, the cave art and sculpture at sites like Lascaux and Niaux gave prehistorians a window into the mind of Ice Age people. The Dordogne Valley in particular has attracted vast numbers of pre-historians and continues to do so today. The sites are rich, the food is delicious, and the Bordeaux is usually having a good year. Towering figures in the field such as Dennis Peyrony, the Abbé Breuil, and François Bordes assured the primacy of southwestern France in the Palaeolithic World. European prehistory began in the caves of southwestern France and Cantabrian Spain.

The famous Franco-Cantabrian complex of stone tool industries – Perigordian, Aurignacian, Gravettian, Solutrean, Magdalenian – has come to dominate Late Pleistocene archaeology over much of Europe. The use of the term "Eastern Gravettian" to characterize the industries of the Russian Plain (e.g., Kozłowski 1986) highlights the role of southwestern France as a point of reference several thousand kilometers distant. More recently, however, the focus has begun to shift, and there are now numerous "hot spots" for the investigation of human existence during the last blast of the Ice Age and its aftermath. Many new sites have been found across Europe, from southern

Germany across southern Poland, the Czech lands, and into the Balkans. The Russian plain has emerged as a crucial area for the study of Late Pleistocene society.

The sequence of late Ice Age stone tool industries in Franco-Cantabria has been defined for many years. Although every attempt here will be made to avoid getting entangled in the details of this sequence, a brief and highly simplified summary is provided so the reader can connect it with the terminology used in the works cited here and elsewhere. The Upper Palaeolithic in Franco-Cantabria opened with the Lower Perigordian, about 35,000 years ago. Between about 33,000 and 21,000 years ago, the Aurignacian and the Upper Perigordian industries were interdigitated, in no clear chronological succession. Around 21,000 years ago, these were succeeded by the Solutrean, which lasted about 4,000 years. Finally, the Magdalenian occurred between 17,000 and 10,000 years ago. These industrial names have been applied very widely outside Franco-Cantabria. For example, the name "Aurignacian" has been used to characterize stone tool industries of the early Upper Palaeolithic as far afield as the Zagros Mountains in Iran, while late Ice Age industries across most of Europe are subsumed under the heading of "Magdalenian." "Solutrean," on the other hand, has a very localized usage due to the specific bifacial flaking technique of this industry. Contemporaneous assemblages in central and eastern Europe are generally assigned to the Gravettian complex.

This book is not the place for technical discussions such as what differentiates Aurignacian from Solutrean, although several decades ago a detailed exegesis of stone tool industries would have constituted most of the content of this chapter. Such material is better left to specialist volumes, especially since it is often highly subjective and contentious. There are more important issues to deal with in the limited space here. Of crucial importance is an understanding of the interplay between humans, their technology, and their environment. Cave sites, despite their usefulness as chronological indicators, have come to be supplemented by open-air sites to give a much fuller picture of Ice Age life. Animal bones have come to be recognized as important evidence of prehistoric diet seasonal activity. A key question is just how "complex" late Pleistocene society really was.

Caves and rock shelters have traditionally provided the richest information about late Pleistocene technology and culture change. Thus archaeologists have gravitated towards such sites over the last two centuries. Virtually no known cave in Europe has not been investigated for archaeological materials. New caves, such as the spectacular painted grotto known as Cosquer, are discovered only under exceptional circumstances (more on Cosquer below). Caves have several problems, however. The first is that prehistoric people were generally rather neat and did not allow vast amounts of rubbish to accumulate. They either threw it out the front or pushed it to the back. As a result, the layering of archaeological deposits in caves is usually not so even, and the layers are very thin. Moreover, a limited range of human activities seem to have taken place in caves. Humans seem to have spent as much time, or even more, living in the open air in shelters that they made from available materials without the rock over their heads. As a result, open-air

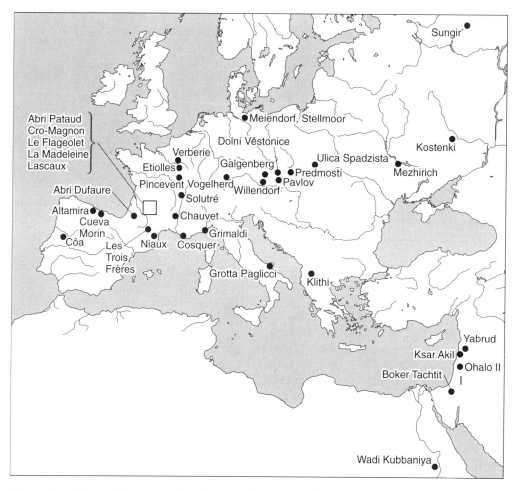

Figure 3.5 Map of Europe and the Levant showing key Upper Palaeolithic sites mentioned in this chapter.

sites have begun to assume greater importance for the study of late Pleistocene humans in recent decades.

The primacy of southwestern France in defining the development of human society in late Pleistocene Europe has also faded. A danger of overview volumes like this one, however, is that the reader may conclude that one central focus has been replaced by a number of regional foci, such as in Moravia and Ukraine. The fact is that important late Pleistocene sites are found throughout unglaciated Europe, and the reason that some sites and areas stand out in contrast to others is due to a concentration of archaeological activity or to particularly remarkable remains that seize the attention of archaeologists. The distribution of the intensity of archaeological research, in all periods, is uneven. A major determinant is the proximity of sites to towns in which archaeological research centers are located. In a sense, the shifting of attention away from southwestern France has been the result of the emergence of Brno, Kiev, Kraków, and Bonn as research centers alongside Bordeaux.

Following the flake technology of the European Middle Palaeolithic, the period after about 40,000 years ago saw progressive refinements in the ability to manipulate flint and other raw material. A special type of flake, called a "blade," is the basic element of this technology, which multiplied the amount of working edge that could be obtained from a given weight of raw material still further. Blades are simply flakes with long, parallel edges, with sides at least twice as long as the ends. Humans became very proficient at the use of bone or wood to knock off delicate flakes from blades to make a variety of specialized tools. Specialization of implements is a hallmark of the tool industries of this period. Whereas earlier technological traditions were characterized by the manufacture of generalized "Swiss Army Knife" tools, the people of late Pleistocene Europe believed in using the right tool for each job.

The reliance on tools made from blades rather than from flakes is a hallmark of most Upper Palaeolithic industries. General discussions of this transition have focused on the greater amount of working edge which could be obtained from a block of flint or the variety of specialized tools that blades permitted (e.g., Bordaz 1970; Schick and Toth 1993). Clearly these are important aspects of this development. Blade manufacture permits, conservatively estimated, a tenfold increase in the amount of working edge which a given mass of raw material can yield. At the same time, the resultant blade "blanks" have a consistent and regular form, so a standard series of stone tools can be based on them. Moreover, the blade blank is such a useful universal starting point that tools could be made which were suited for specific tasks. The right configuration of working edge and tool body could be used rather than some generalized flake which served a variety of purposes. This specialization opened the door for the increased use of antler, bone, and shell for both tools and ornaments, as well as the careful preparation of hides.

Perhaps the most significant aspect of the transition to blade tools came from a combination of the above two characteristics. Their simplicity and cheapness meant that tools could be quickly produced, various forms experimented with, and the successful ones replicated in mass quantities. In this way, blade technology constituted what could be called in modern terms a "platform industry" in which specialized applications can be rapidly and cheaply developed and put into production. A good analogy is to the microchip industry in the late twentieth century and how it contrasts with the earlier electronics industry. In the 1990s, a manufacturer wanting to add microprocessing capabilities to, for example, a washing machine, simply sends specifications to a chip manufacturer, which draws on a repertoire of standard logic devices and configurations to develop the desired microprocessor. A prototype can be made in a matter of days, if it has not already been developed, and within a very short time the microprocessor can go into production. Previously, each device had to be custom-designed and laboriously debugged, taking a very long time to go from conception to mass-production. In this way, the modern microchip industry can be called a "platform industry" which has permitted advances in many other aspects of technology.

It is possible to view Upper Palaeolithic blade technology in the same way. The Levallois tools of the Middle Palaeolithic are like early electronic devices, each one custom-designed using significant amounts of raw material and time between initial concept and final product. With the emergence of blade industries after ca. 40,000 years ago, stone tools could be configured into a remarkable range of forms and optimized for many different functions. This technological advance formed the foundation for almost all subsequent prehistoric stone tool manufacture.

Many have equated the apparent brilliance of blade technology with a significant human cognitive advance, and some have taken this even further to make it a hallmark of anatomically-modern humans which differentiates them from flake-using archaic humans. I would caution against making too much of this. Instead, I would view the emergence of blade technology in the Upper Palaeolithic as the inevitable maturing of a technological system which had its roots in earlier millennia. Humans did not suddenly become brighter to see that blades had considerable advantages over one-off flakes. While it took a certain degree of imagination and inventiveness to make the transition to blade technology, it did not require a sudden upward jump in intellect.

One of the reasons for this proliferation of tool types was the increased use of other sorts of raw materials, especially bone, ivory, and antler, to make tools and ornaments. Personal body ornaments made from bone, antler, and ivory assumed much greater importance, perhaps due to a need to communicate social identity (White 1993). Each of these contact materials required its own set of stone tools to work it best. In addition, the people of late Pleistocene Europe had to endure cold conditions not far from the glacial ice. Thus they needed to work hides in order to make clothes and shelters. As a result, they made and used a wide variety of perforating and scraping implements.

One of the most significant developments in late Pleistocene Europe was the development of fired-clay technology and of weaving, both of which are attested from Gravettian sites in the Moravian lowlands (Soffer et al.1993, 1999) between 28,000 and 24,000 years ago. The ability to produce ceramics was long believed to be a hallmark of the farming cultures of later prehistory, but recent research has demonstrated that humans had developed this technology much earlier. Weaving was similarly believed to have been a later development, but the use of baskets and netting appears to have made its way into the human repertoire in the late Pleistocene. At Dolní Věstonice and nearby sites, several thousand fragments of fired clay, including a number of figurines, made from local loess soils were fired at temperatures between 500° and 800°C in features that have been interpreted as primitive kilns. Several dozen of the baked-clay pieces show imprints of a textile or a finely-woven basket of plant fibers. Seven specific types of twining have been identified (Soffer et al. 1999), several of which suggest the manufacture of netting, perhaps for hunting of small and medium-sized animals.

Since the 1970s, the focus of archaeological investigations of late Ice Age people, especially in southwestern Europe, has shifted away from stone tools and technology to the study of human behavior across the landscape. Several lines of evidence converge, including site location studies, faunal studies, seasonality studies, and environmental studies. The rich Franco-Cantabrian animal bone assemblages and the numerous sites in this region have led to a great concentration of effort in this area, although such work has also been carried out in other parts of Europe as well. Much of this effort was stimulated by Lewis Binford's 1980 distinction between residential mobility, in which entire bands move their camps in search of resources, and logistical mobility, in which bands stay in relatively fixed locations and send out individuals or small task groups to bring back resources. Many archaeologists would like to see this distinction in evolutionary terms (although Binford did not intend this), with the dull residential mobility ascribed to the Neanderthals giving way to the sophisticated logistical organization of *Homo sapiens sapiens*.

Several different dimensions of variability complicate the study of this problem: time, geography, climate, culture, and seasonality. What people did one spring 33,000 years ago in the Périgord is not the same as what they did during a winter 26,000 years ago in Cantabria. The ice front in northern Europe moved in fits and spurts, creating regional minor warmings and coolings amidst the larger-scale continental advance and retreat. The Early Upper Palaeolithic Aurignacians may have had a different set of approaches to dealing with similar problems from those of the Late Upper Palaeolithic Magdalenians. At the moment, attempts to study late Ice Age hunting strategies and residential patterning are largely focused on specific sites and, with some greater ambition, regions. This produces a variety of positions which are all well-grounded in data but which appear to contradict each other.

For example, during the period between 33,000 and 23,000 years ago, the faunal record for most of southwestern France shows the exploitation of an assortment of species, suggesting diverse stocks of reindeer, mammoth, wooly rhino, ibex, red deer, aurochs, bison, and horse (Delpech 1983; Boyle 1990). The exception is the Dordogne region, where most sites from this period have faunal assemblages dominated by reindeer. What does this mean? Philip Chase (1989) has proposed that these sites were simply in locations where reindeer were abundant and thus represent one aspect of a very generalized hunting pattern. This would be consistent with Spiess' position that the reindeer at Abri Pataud were killed singly or in small groups, with no indication of mass slaughter (Spiess 1979). James Enloe, based on his analysis of the reindeer bones from a level about 26,000 years old at the Flageolet rock shelter, comes to a similar conclusion (Enole 1993). Randall White, on the other hand, has argued that the Dordogne sites of this period represent strategic decisions about site location and prey choice, with the Abri Pataud providing evidence of specialized migration hunting or reindeer (White 1989). As such, the sites in this region are more consistent with a model of logistical behavior requiring a more sophisticated level of organization than previously.

During and following the late glacial maximum, about 20,000 years ago, clear-cut evidence of increasing sophistication of hunting techniques and, by inference, of human behavioral organization, does appear. Straus (1993) has pointed out the use of topographic features to assist in hunting, such as corridors, canyons, and cul-de-sacs. For example, at the classic site of Solutré, Olsen (1995) has demonstrated how wild horses were diverted into a cul-de-sac at the base of the large cliff, where they were killed with spears and butchered (although earlier dramatic visions of the horses being driven off this cliff to their deaths do not stand up when the behavior of wild horses is considered and the animal bones are examined for evidence of trauma.) Elsewhere, gorges, sinkholes, and blind valleys were particularly attractive locations for humans to prey on large herbivores like reindeer and red deer. For example, at the Abri Dufaure around 14,500 years ago, Altuna and his colleagues (1991) have argued for the practice of specialized reindeer hunting, despite the deterioration of conditions favorable for this species, by taking advantage of the local topographical conditions. In contrast to the evidence for "encounter" hunting that Spiess found at the Abri Pataud, analysis of the Abri Dufaure age distribution indicates mass killing. Burke (1993) has argued for a complimentarity between horse hunting and reindeer hunting between 18,000 and 14,000 years ago in southwestern France, with horses filling the seasonal gaps between reindeer migrations.

For the Cantabrian Cordillera along the north coast of Spain, an elaborate logistical subsistence system has been proposed for Late Upper Palaeolithic groups by Laurence Straus (1986). In Straus' model, base camps were located along the glacial coastal plain of this region (which would have been somewhat broader than that which exists today). From these sites, their inhabitants could take advantage of the resources of the coast, the estuaries of the streams which drained across the coastal plain, the coastal plain itself, and the foothills of the Cordillera. In addition, special task parties could be sent out from these camps to stations up in the mountains, where they could hunt red deer and ibex. Although some have criticized this model for compressing 6,000 years of data to make a synchronous model (Rensink 1995), it does appear to be a reasonable approximation of the land use patterns in the numerous micro-habitats of this region during the late Ice Age.

It seems, then, that the onset of the deep freeze of the last glaciation between 24,000 and 20,000 years ago coincided with a clear shift towards increased human behavioral organization, or at least an acceleration of trends that began during the previous 10,000 years. Why? One possible explanation involves the deteriorating European climate and the concentration of population in a smaller area. In the mid-1980s, Michael Jochim advanced the hypothesis that as temperatures got colder in more northern and eastern parts of Europe around 25,000 years ago, people migrated southwestward to the very attractive habitats found in areas like the Dordogne valley and the Cantabrian cordillera (Jochim 1983, 1987). Thus at the deep freeze of the Late Glacial Maximum, southwestern Europe served as a refuge for people driven from other parts of the continent, especially north-central Europe.

If southwestern Europe did serve as a refuge, Jochim believes that this would have important consequences for human behavior which manifest themselves in the archaeological record. These would include increased specialization in hunting (with an increased focus on reindeer and horse), technological innovation to make hunting more efficient (the development of the spearthrower and perhaps the bow and arrow), elaboration of art (especially the elaboration of cave art) and exchange, and a proliferation of stone tool styles as people expressed their cultural diversity. The packing of people into a few circumscribed habitats led to increased stress and promoted the development of more complex social relationships. Once the climate began to warm up around 16,000 years ago, people sallied forth from southwestern Europe to recolonize northern Europe.

Specialized hunting strategies were also applied throughout southern Europe during the Upper Palaeolithic. In central and southern Italy, Graeme Barker (1975a, 1981) studied the animal bones from several Upper Palaeolithic sites at which red deer were the predominant prey species and found that the animals were killed either in their first year (perhaps for the best hides) or between four and eight years (at their prime body weight). This and other evidence led him to propose a logistical hunting system of base camps and hunting stations which were situated to intercept migration routes. Analysis of microscopic traces of wear on stone tools from Grotta Paglicci supported the identification of it as a hunting and butchery station rather than a residential site (Donahue 1988). Specialized hunting is also attested in Greece between 16,000 and 13,000 years ago at the meticulously analyzed site of Klithi in Epirus (Bailey 1997), where the primary activity appears to have been the killing and dismemberment of ibex (*Capra ibex*) and chamois (*Rupicapra rupicapra*).

Southern Europe was not the only part of Europe in which people lived during the last Ice Age, however. Late Pleistocene settlement in the uplands on both sides of the Carpathian arc and on the plains of eastern Europe has received considerably more attention in recent decades, despite the fact that it has been studied for over a century. Excavations at sites in Austria, Moravia, southern Poland, Ukraine, and the southern Russian Plain have yielded considerable new information on Ice Age life in these areas, and a broad picture is emerging over much of central and eastern Europe. The sites on the Russian Plain were previously considered in isolation, but they are now seen as part of a much broader cultural complex, generally referred to as the "Eastern Gravettian," over a period of about 18,000 years between approximately 28,000 and 10,000 years ago (Kozłowski 1990; Soffer 1993). Stone tool types, bone tool types, ornaments and figurines, and patterns of animal exploitation all seem to be relatively similar across this area.

Two features of Eastern Gravettian sites are ubiquitous across this territory: mammoth bones and female figurines. Perhaps the most widely-illustrated artifact of this period and region is the so-called "Venus of Willendorf," a tiny statuette of a buxom woman found in Austria in 1908. More will be said below about the Eastern Gravettian figurines in the context of late Pleistocene art. Large quantities of mammoth bones are found at virtually every major site (perhaps biasing the archaeological record in favor of such highly-visible remains) throughout this region, causing some early archaeologists to call this period "the Mammoth Age" (Maška 1886). At Predmostí in Moravia, the mammoth remains come from approximately 1000 individuals (Soffer 1993: 39), while at other sites individual counts ranging from several dozen to a hundred or more are common.

Perhaps the most remarkable sites of the Eastern Gravettian are those with dwellings which were constructed using the jaws, tusks, and long bones of mammoths as structural members for a frame on which skins and earth were placed. Across the treeless steppes of eastern Europe, mammoth bones constituted the most available building material, so their use is an ingenious adaptation of frigid Ice Age open conditions where caves and rock shelters were scarce. At Mezhirich near Kiev in Ukraine, at least four houses have been found, dated between 19,000 and 14,000 years ago. They consist of a circular arrangement of tusks, jaws, long bones, and scapulae between six and ten meters in diameter around a central hearth. Rubbish pits with butchered bone fragments and debris from the manufacture of stone tools are found near the houses. At Ulica Spadzista on a hill overlooking the modern city of Kraków in southern Poland, a Gravettian encampment with two or three similar arrangements of mammoth parts has been found (Kozłowski 1990: 212), dated to approximately 23,000 years ago.

The presence of so many mammoth bones that entire houses could be constructed from piles of jaws and long bones might lead one to conclude that the late Pleistocene hunters of eastern Europe were killing them right and left, which would have involved considerable human courage and appetite. A more realistic scenario has been presented by Olga Soffer (1993), who suggests that most of the bones were gathered from natural accumulations that may have been found in gullies and streambeds near the sites. Simulation studies by Mithen (1993) support Soffer's case that the majority of mammoth remains at the eastern Gravettian sites come from collecting rather than active hunting. The animals whose bones these were died of natural causes, although some of the bones used in building may have been from hunted animals as well. The bones show different degrees of weathering, and they generally lack cut marks indicating removal of meat with stone tools. In fact, it is possible that the locations of sites like Mezhirich and Ulica Spadzista were determined in part by the proximity of accumulations of building material. The mammoth mortality that produced these accumulations may have been the start of a progressive west-to-east pattern of extinction that eventually affected animals in the New World as well, which will be discussed further below.

Olga Soffer (1987, 1993) has made the case that eastern Europe formed a refuge as well during the last major advance of the Fennoscandian ice sheet. In fact, she has advanced the hypothesis that a significant population movement occurred over the course of 6000 years between about 24,000 and 18,000 years ago as the ice front bore down one last time upon central Europe. Prior to 24,000 years ago, substantial populations of foragers had lived in the Carpathian basin along the middle Danube, at sites like Dolní Věstonice, Willendorf, and Pavlov. In the millennia that followed these people may have shifted eastward, first to the Dniestr valley in Ukraine and subsequently to the Dnicpr and Don basins in southern Russia. Much of this shift, Soffer argues (1993), was driven by the concurrent shift in the natural resources on which these groups depended, with the Dniepr and Don valleys approximating similar grassland and riverine habitats to those found in the Carpathian Basin several millennia before. Another key resource which was also found on the Russian plain were the localized accumulations of mammoth bones.

Somewhat younger than the Polish, Czech, and Russian sites are the late Magdalenian sites of northern France and south-central Germany. By about 13,000 years ago, the ice sheets had retreated sufficiently to allow humans to move back into this region where so much settlement had occurred earlier in the Pleistocene. Over 50 Magdalenian sites in the Paris Basin are known, of which Pincevent, Verberie, and Etiolles are perhaps the best-studied, dating between 12,000 and 10,000 years ago. They were located on river terraces in an environment where the watersheds were still covered by cold steppe, while forests where found in the warmer valleys. Faunal remains from these sites consist primarily of reindeer and horse, although mammoth bones have also been found at Etiolles.

Pincevent and Verberie are best known for their evidence of the internal organization of late Pleistocene settlements. Hearths formed the foci of human activity, while areas with low densities of remains defined by arcs of debris have been interpreted as the traces of small circular tents (Leroi-Gourhan and Brézillon 1966). Nearby are concentrations of debris from the manufacture of stone tools. Pincevent appears to have been occupied from the spring to the early winter (Leroi-Gourhan and Brézillon 1972: 165), while Verberie appears to have been occupied at some point between March and November (Audouze 1987: 195).

During the last 20,000 years of the Ice Age, human mortuary practices come into sharper resolution across Eurasia. Upper Palaeolithic burials have been known since the early nineteenth century. Most date prior to the late glacial maximum, while relatively few are known from Magdalenian contexts. Perhaps greater human mobility in the very last millennia of the Ice Age resulted in many interments away from archaeologically-visible habitation sites. Since caves have formed the focus of archaeological research in southwestern Europe, that is where most of the late Pleistocene skeletons have been found, such as at Cro-Magnon in France, Cueva Morin in Spain, and the Grimaldi Caves on the Italian Riviera. In eastern Europe, Upper Palaeolithic burials have been excavated at a number of open sites, especially in Moravia and Russia.

Moravia has yielded the largest sample of burials known in Europe for the period between 25,000 and 30,000 years ago (Svoboda, Ložek, and Vlček 1996), many of them multiple interments. In 1894, Karel Maška excavated a mass grave at Predmostí, where a burial pit about 4 meters by 2.5 meters held the skeletons of over 20 individuals, 15 of whom were represented by complete skeletons (Svoboda, Ložek, and Vlček 1996: 226). Various animal bones, including a fox skull and two mammoth left shoulder blades, were among and over the bones. Another example of a Moravian multiple burial was found at Dolní Věstonice in 1986 (Klíma 1987). Three young adults were buried side by side in an extended position and covered with large quantities of red ocher. They wore necklaces of perforated fox teeth and small ivory pendants.

At Sungir', about 150 kilometers east of Moscow in Russia, several burials dated between 30,000 and 25,000 years have been interpreted as providing evidence of social hierarchization (White 1993; Dolukhanov 1996), although as we will see in the discussion of post-Pleistocene burials at Skateholm in chapter 4, the position is taken here that rich forager burials should not be equated directly with hierarchy. In one Sungir' burial, that of a male about 60 years old, grave goods included 20 thin ivory bracelets and about 3000 ivory beads, while a small boy had about 5000 beads, although these were smaller than those of the man, as well as over 250 canine teeth from arctic foxes. Lying alongside him was a massive ivory "spear" made from a straightened mammoth tusk. A presumed female child had over 5000 small ivory beads.

Dramatic changes appear to have happened between the Atlantic and the Urals beginning about 35,000 years ago. While it could be argued that this is simply an artifact of the concentration of archaeological research during the past century in Europe, it also seems clear that the marked climatic changes which occurred during the last onslaught of the Pleistocene ice sheets coupled with increased human sophistication about how to respond led to important advances in human culture. Rather than simply moving far away from the ice and cold, as they had done previously, the people of western Eurasia retreated a bit but then adapted to the opportunities that the cold climate provided. They ceased to be just another terrestrial mammal in the ecosystem and devised distinct cultural solutions to environmental challenges.

THE NEAR EAST AND AFRICA DURING THE LATE PLEISTOCENE

The role of the Near East as a bridge between Africa and Eurasia and its significance for the dispersal of anatomically-modern humans was discussed in the previous chapter. During the late Pleistocene, however, further significant developments took place in the Near East which set the stage for the emergence of sedentary agricultural societies. A discussion of these issues is deferred to the following chapter, but it is important here to signal that the Near East was not a cultural backwater during late glacial times. At the same time, as Marks (1990: 74) points out, its late glacial prehistory is different from contemporaneous developments in Europe. The heirs to the earliest modern humans who remained in Africa also developed new technologies beginning about 40,000 years ago, although much of the late Pleistocene archaeological record of this continent remains unknown. In both northeastern and southern Africa, however, research in recent decades has led to the recognition of important changes in human subsistence behavior beginning about 20,000 years ago.

In the Near East and Africa, rainfall appears to have played the role in shaping how humans occupied the landscape that cold and ice did in Eurasia. Many discussions of the late Pleistocene prehistory of these regions begin with an analysis of how the sites are located in relation to rainfall patterns suggested by climatic reconstruction. The Late Glacial Maximum between 22,000 and 16,000 years ago in particular was characterized by very dry conditions, with hyperaridity prevailing over much of the Near East and Africa, even in the tropical zones.

The indigenous development of Upper Palaeolithic industries in the Levant is documented at sites such as Ksar Akil and Boker Tachtit (Ohnuma and Bergman 1990; Marks 1990), although it is unclear what cultural changes accompanied this shift around 40,000 years ago. The industries from this period are characterized by small blades known as "bladelets" (Gilead 1991: 144). Around 32,000 years ago, a different type of industry appeared, in which the main tools are endscrapers and burins. The scrapers and some of the blades resemble the Aurignacian assemblages found in Europe at this time, so this industry is called the "Levantine Aurignacian." Gilead (1991: 144) believes that it represents an intrusion into the region from the north and notes that it coexisted with the bladelet industries for 16,000 years. The Kebaran industry, which came to dominate the Levant after about 18,000 years ago, apparently had its roots in the bladelet tradition rather than in the Levantine Aurignacian, however.

One of the more important Near Eastern sites during the late Pleistocene is the site of Ohalo II along the Sea of Galilee in Israel (Nadel et al. 1994). Exposed by a drop in water levels and investigated between 1989 and 1991, Ohalo II has provided a detailed picture of life in this region about 19,000 years ago. In the remains of a kidney-shaped hut about 4.5 meters wide, three successive floors were found along with fragments of mud walls containing wild grass stems, straw, and charcoal fragments. Numerous fish bones reflect a very poorly-known aspect of Upper Palaeolithic subsistence. Some of these fish bones were concentrated outside of the pits found on the site, and fragments of charred twisted fibers suggest the use of bags and nets for storage. In addition, about 30 species of plants were identified, including hundreds of grains of wild barley and wild wheat. About 130 *Dentalium* beads provide evidence for long-distance acquisition of marine shell. Among the habitation features was a burial of a 35-year-old man.

The acquisition of marine shells for personal ornamentation was particularly widespread in the Levant from about 32,000 years ago onward. They appear to have been transported distances of up to 100 kilometers (Gilead 1991: 142). Flakes of obsidian at Yabrud were acquired from a distance of 600–900 kilometers from sources in Anatolia. We can only speculate whether this transport reflects the wandering of Upper Palaeolithic bands or whether these materials passed from hand to hand in some sort of exchange network.

During much of the Pleistocene, northeast Africa was very similar to the way it is today: a hyper-arid desert interrupted by the moist and fertile Nile Valley.

The banks of the Nile, however, were home to significant Late Palaeolithic populations (Close 1996) who took advantage of the resources of this thin belt through the uninhabitable desert. Fish were a key resource, including Nile catfish and tilapia which appear to have been harvested seasonally as they were stranded in ponds following the annual flood. Close (1996: 49) suggests that some form of preservation and storage must have been employed, since such quantities could not be consumed all at once. Other river resources included the Nile oyster and waterfowl that were seasonal visitors to the area. Terrestrial animal resources included aurochs, hartebeest, and gazelle.

Of particular importance in the Nile Valley during the Late Palaeolithic were plant resources, especially wetland tubers. The most informative sites in this regard are found at Wadi Kubbaniya in upper Egypt, dating to approximately 18,000 years ago (Hillman 1989). Wadi Kubbaniya is a dry branch from the Nile Valley, and the sites are located about 3 kilometers from the river. During the Late Palaeolithic, the dunes on which these sites are located would have been flooded in late summer and for the rest of the year would have overlooked the swampy Nile floodplain. Botanical assemblages from these sites are dominated by tubers of wild nut-grass (*Cyperus rotundus*) and a variety of other tuberous species (claims for early grain cultivation made in the early 1980s based on preliminary findings at Wadi Kubbaniya have now been dismissed). It appears that the intensive collecting of wild tubers was an important seasonal complement to fishing during the Late Palaeolithic in the Nile Valley.

At the very end of the Pleistocene, a northward shift of the monsoon belt brought heavy seasonal rains to Upper Egypt (Close 1996). The net effect of this was to cause the Nile to behave wildly and unpredictably and to create large shallow playa lakes in the hitherto arid desert. People were drawn from the Nile floodplain out to these seasonal lakes and the wildlife that they attracted, including migratory waterfowl from Eurasia. This condition lasted for several millennia, whereupon the monsoon belt shifted southward again and the Eastern Desert returned to its familiar arid state.

South of the Sahara and north of the Limpopo River, the period between 40,000 years ago and 10,000 years ago is characterized by a number of sites and assemblages which are difficult to pin down in time, partly because many come from undated surface occurrences and disturbed sites and partly because stone tool industries span many millennia and are not so temporally specific as in much of Eurasia and the Near East. In this region, the Middle Stone Age (MSA), whose prepared-core technique was discussed in the previous chapter, grades into the Late Stone Age (LSA), in which tools are reduced significantly in size to small blades and fragments of blades called "microliths." The temporal boundary between the MSA and the LSA has never been clearly defined, however, and there appears to be a high degree of continuity between them (Phillipson 1993: 60).

The technological shift from MSA industries to the LSA in tropical Africa appears to have taken place between about 20,000 and 30,000 years ago (Brooks and Robertshaw 1990: 159). For the remainder of the Pleistocene, stone tool assemblages are increasingly characterized by microliths and small blades. There is some evidence to indicate that during the Late Glacial Maximum central Africa became progressively drier, which is consistent with the general trend towards aridity in low-latitude zones such as the Near East and Australia during this period. In many regions where the microlith technology emerged there is also a shift to the hunting of smaller animals rather than the large gregarious herbivores (Phillipson 1993: 100). There was also an increase in the use of small-scale resources such as snails and tortoises which parallels the broadening of the diet seen in the Near East during the last millennia of the Pleistocene (Brooks and Robertshaw 1990: 160).

South of the Limpopo River, the late Pleistocene archaeological record comes into much sharper resolution. After a fluid transition between the MSA and the LSA prior to 20,000 years ago, microlithic bladelet industries came to dominate the archaeological record. Faunal remains at LSA sites in southern Africa include migratory plains herbivores, including wildebeest, hartebeest, zebra, and eland, plus large species which became extinct at the end of the Pleistocene such as giant Cape horse and giant buffalo (Wadley 1993). Klein (1983, 1989) notes two significant subsistence developments during the late Pleistocene in southern Africa. The first is that LSA people took advantage of a broad range of resources, including fish, waterfowl, shellfish and tortoise, much like the pattern noted by Brooks and Robertshaw for central Africa. Wadley (1993) also notes that coastal sites become common after about 12,000 years ago with many marine species including seals and rock lobster. Second, LSA people increasingly took on animals which were far more dangerous to hunt than the plains herbivores, such as wild pig and buffalo. Klein interprets this development as the result of improvements in hunting technology.

The pattern observed in the Near East and Africa during the last millennia of the Pleistocene differs considerably from that observed in many parts of Eurasia. Whereas the Magdalenian and Ahrensburgian hunters of northern Europe, for example, specialized in the hunting of reindeer, the inhabitants of the Near East and Africa broadened their diet considerably to include many different species of terrestrial and aquatic resources. Although much of this difference has an environmental basis, and it also may be partially an artifact of archaeological recovery practices, it seems clear that in low-latitude parts of the Old World, the people of the late Pleistocene were engaging in what Flannery (1969) has called the "broad spectrum revolution," which will be seen in the chapters that follow to have had significant consequences.

PEOPLING OF NORTHERN EURASIA, THE AMERICAS, AND AUSTRALIA

Anatomically-modern humans have a very important behavioral characteristic: they liked to move about. Not only did they recolonize areas from which humans had been driven by the intense cold of the middle Pleistocene, but they went further to penetrate into North America and to cross water barriers to reach Australia. The diaspora between 60,000 and 10,000 years ago was unparalleled in human biogeography until the Age of Discovery began in the fifteenth century. Many factors constrained this process, and it is these constraints that provide important clues to the timing of human movements and to the challenges that people faced. The location of the ice sheets is a key determinant of when people could have moved northward in Eurasia and southward in North America. Land bridges permitted water barriers to be traversed, and we know that these existed only during particular phases of lowered sea levels.

The central debates concerning the colonizations of Australia and the New World are over the timing, specifically how early did it occur. In Australia, the earliest dates for human occupation have leapt backward at an astonishing pace, and the archaeologists there are generally peaceful about each re-setting of the clock. In the Americas, despite claims of great antiquity for a number of sites, the earliest secure dating remains stuck between 11,000 and 12,000 years ago, and archaeologists get into very heated arguments about backward shifts of a few centuries.

Improvements in dating techniques during the 1980s have played a crucial role in this discussion. AMS radiocarbon dating has made major contributions, although conventional radiocarbon dating has not been discarded. A relatively new dating technique known as "luminiscence dating" has played an important role in dating the appearance of the first humans in Australia, since this event appears to be outside the range of conventional radiocarbon dating. Luminescence dating includes two related techniques: thermoluminiscence (TL) and optically-stimulated luminescence (OSL). TL is the light which is emitted by a mineral upon heating, while OSL refers to the light emitted by a mineral when it is exposed to visible light. Luminescence dating can provide dates for sediments which have been exposed to sunlight before being buried. When a mineral is exposed to sunlight, the light-sensitive electrons in it escape to emit light of their own. The luminescence "clock" is thus reset to zero. Once the sediment is buried, the number of trapped light-sensitive electrons increases over time. When the sample is heated (as in TL dating) or illuminated (as in OSL dating) in the laboratory, the emitted light can be measured, and from this the amount of time since the sediment was buried can be calculated.

MEGAFAUNAL EXTINCTIONS

As in Eurasia, Australia and the Americas were the home to many species of large animals during the late Pleistocene. These are known collectively as "megafauna," defined as animals with a body weight of more than 44 kg. A better term for them, which will be used here, is "megamammals." Some elephant-sized Pleistocene megamammals of Eurasia and the Americas were over four tons, while the *Diprotodontidae* of Sahul were the size and shape of a rhinoceros. Although the megamammals of Eurasia had been in contact with humans for millennia, those of Australia and the Americas had never "peered down the shaft of a spear" (Meltzer 1993a) prior to the arrival of humans. Since 35 species of megamammals in the Americas and perhaps 50 such species in Sahul became extinct during the millennia that followed the arrival of humans, archaeologists and zoologists have wondered what role people played in this process.

Four principal causes of late Pleistocene extinctions have been proposed (Politis, Prado, and Beukens 1995):

1 the direct impact of man by hunting;
2 climatic and environmental changes;
3 ecological pressure: climatic changes, then human hunting;
4 indirect effects of human activity, such as gradual attrition, disruption of breeding pools.

Of these proposed causes, the two that represent the extremes – and have seized the attention of archaeologists – have been the first two. The proposition that the sudden arrival of hunters in the midst of naive and defenseless megamammal herds has been promoted vigorously over the last several decades by Paul Martin (1984) for North America and has been advocated by Tim Flannery (1990) for Australia. This model, formally known as "Pleistocene overkill" and informally referred to as the "Blitzkreig," envisions the first bands of hunters easily devastating the docile herds of mammoths and other megamammals. The large animals were slow breeders, so a heavy rate of predation would soon decimate the populations to the point where they could no longer reproduce. The result is that within a millennium or less the megamammals would be wiped out. Presumably such a number of mammoth carcasses rotting on the landscape would have resulted in a population explosion of carnivores, but these too would have dropped when the megamammals ran out.

Critics of the "Blitzkreig" model cogently argue that no human hunters, even the most bloodthirsty, could wreak such havoc on large mammal populations in such a short time (Grayson 1984). Instead, they move around from one territory to another, usually leaving well before the game are used up. Moreover, mammoths, even docile ones, were probably not very easy to kill with spears. Finally, if such a slaughter was perpetrated, then there should be kill sites everywhere in the Americas and Australia. Yet outside the High Plains of North America, kill sites of megamammals are very rare, and they are virtually nonexistent in Australia. Finally, it now appears that the extinctions did not happen simultaneously but rather at various times (Grayson 1987, 1991), which appears to further weaken the overkill hypothesis.

Regional studies of megamammal extinctions point to some period of coexistence between humans and the animals. For example, on the Pampas of South America, humans hunted at least four megamammal species (Politis, Prado, and Beukens 1995). In Australia, it also appears that the megamammals did not disappear until sometime after the humans arrived, although there is little evidence of human hunting of species like *Diprotodontidae* in the intervening period. Most archaeologists now concur that there was no mass slaughter of megamammals in either the Americas or Australia coincident with the arrival of humans and look more towards indirect results of human activity, climatic change, or a combination of human and natural factors.

One interesting hypothesis has been advanced by R. Dale Guthrie (1990), who has argued that in the arid grasslands of the northern latitudes during the late Pleistocene relatively long growing seasons were separated by short and harsh winters. The net effect of this pattern of seasons was that large mammals could subsist on the nutrients provided by the longer growing seasons, while the severe winters induced high mortality which reduced the competition for these nutrients. As the Ice Age ended, the growing seasons actually became shorter and the plant communities became more homogeneous. The large mammals could not adapt to these changes and thus became extinct. Guthrie's hypothesis depends on the reality of his hypothesized "Mammoth Steppe" across Eurasia and Beringia, although as noted above, its existence has not been demonstrated by pollen analysis. Moreover, it does not account for similar phenomena which took place in the vastly different environment of Australia.

At the moment, the causes of late Pleistocene extinctions in North America and Australia have not been completely determined. Nonetheless, it seems clear at this writing that human overkill was not the immediate cause in either area, although it may have been an accelerant to environmental factors. At the moment, the weight of scientific opinion favors climatic causes, although it is possible that these species were already at the end of their evolutionary rope and were well on the way to extinction in any event.

THE COLONIZATION OF SAHUL

The dating of the earliest humans in Greater Australia is a matter of some recent debate. One thing that is certain is that humans were present in Australia much earlier than anyone would have thought even as recently as 30 years ago. As recently as the early 1960s, the earliest humans were believed to have reached Australia no earlier than the early Holocene (Clark 1961), and one of the most dramatic advances of the radiocarbon revolution was to extend the record of Australia's past very rapidly backward (Jones 1973). By the early 1970s, there was convincing evidence from a number of sites which placed human antiquity in Australia close to 30,000 years ago.

A very important discovery in this early phase of the study of the earliest Australians was the find of a cremated human remains at Lake Mungo in New South Wales (Bowler et al. 1970) with associated stone tools, hearths with animal bones, and middens of freshwater mussel shells. The Lake Mungo remains are the earliest evidence of cremation anywhere in the world, dated to ca. 26,000 years ago. Subsequently, other freshwater shell middens in this region have provided dates in the range of 36–37,000 years ago (Bowler 1976) and additional human remains with ages of between 20,000 and 30,000 years have been found (Jones 1992).

Attention then shifted to the southwestern corner of Australia. Excavations in terraces of the Upper Swan River near Perth revealed artifacts whose associated charcoal was dated to approximately 38,000 years ago (Pearce and Barbetti 1981). Some of these artifacts were made with a distinctive form of chert whose source now lies some distance from the western coast of Australia and only would have been accessible during a period of low sea levels. South of Perth, excavations in a limestone cave called "Devil's Lair" produced secure dates directly associated with stone tools, burnt bones, and hearths of about 30–32,000 years ago, although lower levels which may possibly contain some small flakes have yielded dates of 35–37,000 years ago (Dortch 1984).

Finally, on the Huon peninsula on the northeastern coast of New Guinea, stone tools were found on a series of uplifted coral reefs behind which were lagoons (Groube et al. 1986). The tools were large axe-like implements, weighing up to 2.5 kilograms. The Huon peninsula finds are difficult to date. A conservative interpretation of the series of dates from the reefs and lagoon deposits would place them at ca. 40,000 years ago, although Jones (1992) suggests that they may be somewhat older.

Thus by the mid-1980s, it was quite clear that the antiquity of humans in Australia extended back well over 30,000 years ago, that secure radiocarbon dates placed the earliest traces of humans at nearly 40,000 years ago, and there were indications that even somewhat earlier dates were possible. These dates came from careful excavations in all parts of the continent, even Tasmania (Cosgrove 1989), and are supported by many slightly later dates which form a continuum of secure age determinations.

In the early 1990s, however, a certain degree of disagreement crept into the discussion, and two schools of thought emerged. One points to the fact that the dating of the earliest Australians, which had been so breathtakingly sent backwards in the late 1960s through the early 1980s, was stuck on the 40,000-year mark (Allen, J. 1989, 1994). The other points to the limitations of the conventional radiocarbon method and suggests that the 40,000 year "ceiling" may be an artifact of dating methods (Roberts, Jones, and Smith 1994) and that the appearance of humans in Australia may have been considerably earlier. The latter position was given impetus by luminescence dates on quartz sands from rockshelters in northern Australia which suggest human settlement between 53,000 and 60,000 years ago.

The rockshelters in question are Malakunaja II and Nauwalabila I in the Northern Territories of Australia along the East Alligator River (Jones 1990). During the late Pleistocene, these sites were about 350 kilometers inland. Layers below and above the oldest stone artifacts at Nauwalabila I have produced optically-stimulated luminescence dates of 60,000 and 53,000 years, which correspond to the thermoluminescence dates for the oldest tools from Malakunaja II. Some Australian archaeologists challenged these dates when they were first published, but by the mid-1990s a number of their colleagues have come to accept human presence in the northernmost part of Greater Australia by about 60,000 years ago.*

The debate in the late 1990s has shifted to the nature of the colonization of the rest of the continent. Two models have emerged. The first is advocated

---

* In late 1996, a thermoluminescence date of 116,000 BP for sediments associated with stone tools was announced from Jinmium rock shelter in the Northern Territories of Australia (Fullagar, Price, and Head 1996). Subsequent optical and radiocarbon dating of the same sediments (Roberts et al. 1998) has pointed towards a markedly younger age, leaving Malakunaja II and Nauwalabila I as the oldest dated Australian sites as this volume goes to press.

by Rhys Jones and Richard Roberts, who believe that the colonists who reached the Northern Territories about 60,000 or more years ago simply continued onward to settle the rest of the continent in the millennia that followed. In their view, the fact that sites older than 40,000 years have not been found in the rest of Australia and Tasmania is due to limitations of the radiocarbon dating method and the lack of preserved sites. Jones, Roberts, and Smith (1994) have characterized the period between 35,000 and 40,000 years ago as a "radiocarbon bottleneck" which has so far inhibited the dating of earlier sites.

A contrasting model has been advanced by Jim Allen and Simon Holdaway (1995). According to Allen and Holdaway, the 35–40,000 limit of the dating of human traces in most of Australia reflects a real condition of the absence of habitation rather than an artificial effect of dating techniques and preservation. In their view, two possibilities exist: (1) that humans arrived in tropical Australia at an early date and then did not go further until about 40,000 years ago, or (2) that two separate migrations from Sunda to Sahul occurred, the first at an earlier date which colonized only tropical Australia, and the second and larger one which spread as far as Tasmania by 35,000 years ago.

At the moment, there is no clear resolution as to whether one or the other of these two models accounts for the patterns seen in the Australian Pleistocene archaeological record. Further improvements in dating methods will be crucial, and there are still many sites which have not been investigated, particularly in the interior regions of the continent. It will come as no surprise if there are surprising revelations in the study of the earliest human settlement of Australia in the next decade which may totally revise even these sketchy outlines.

THE PENETRATION OF NORTHERN EURASIA

A paradox of the late Ice Age is that just when things were not very good climatically, people started to move northward in Eurasia. In European Russia, a slight climatic amelioration known as the Bryansk Interval between 30,000 and 24,000 years ago permitted settlement as far north as 64°N along the Pechora River (Velichko and Kurenkova 1990). Even after 23,000 years ago, when the deep freeze of the Late Glacial Maximum began to set in, people continued to roam the tundra north of 40° latitude, attracted by large herbivores. As these herbivores began to move north and northeast after 16,000 years ago, people followed them and settled the warmer parts of southern and northeastern Siberia.

Beginning in the 1960s, extensive archaeological reconnaissance and excavation between the Lena and the Aldan rivers in Siberia has permitted the delineation of a distinctive late Ice Age culture called the "Dyuktai," named after an important site in Dyuktai Cave. Although dating of Dyuktai sites has not been easy, it appears that most can be dated between 10,000 and 20,000 years ago, which would include the Late Glacial Maximum and the warming-up that followed. Characteristic Dyuktai artifacts include wedge-shaped microblade cores about 5–7 cm long from which long thin bladelets were struck and bifacially-chipped points.

Although concentrated in the Lena-Aldan area of central Siberia, Dyuktai sites are found further afield, for example at Ushki on Kamchatka (Dikov 1996). The stone tool assemblage at Ushki is characterized by small stemmed bifacial points but lacks microblades, and the lowest layer (dated between 14,000 and 13,000 years ago) had traces of dwellings and a burial pit with human bones and 800 perforated stone ornaments. The stemmed points are interesting, for they are very similar to bifacial stemmed points of northwestern North America.

Berelekh is the northernmost (71°N) Palaeolithic site in the world, located in northeastern Siberia near the mouth of the Indigirka River (Mochanov and Fedoseeva 1996). Although it was not expertly excavated, it does appear to be ca. 14,000–12,000 years old. A bone layer contains primarily mammoth bones (over 98 percent), plus bones of wooly rhinoceros, bison, horse, reindeer, cave lion, wolf, and hare. This bone bed may be a natural accumulation, of the sort proposed by Soffer on the Russian Plain, but Mochanov and Fedoseeva (1996: 221) suggest that it may be the remains of a mammoth-bone dwelling. The tools are characteristic Dyuktai bifaces and flakes, but again there is an absence of microblades. Pendants made from pierced pebbles reflect the penchant for personal ornamentation of late Ice Age people.

So, by about 14,000 years ago, people are present in eastern Siberia. How much earlier can we say with certainty that they were there? Twenty thousand years ago is certainly a possibility, but at the moment, it is very uncertain. The key to understanding the peopling of the New World lies in the peopling of eastern Siberia, and as David Meltzer (1993a: 95) says, "before we can speak of the peopling of Siberia, Siberia will have to be peopled by more archaeologists." Whenever they first arrived in Siberia, the first settlers' movements next took them further along the "Mammoth Steppe" into Beringia, and before they knew it, they were in the New World.

THE PEOPLING OF THE NEW WORLD

A few miles from where I write these words, but nearly 125 years removed in time, the physician Charles Conrad Abbott (1843–1919) began searching in the glacial gravels just south of Trenton, New Jersey, for stone tools which corresponded to those of the European Palaeolithic. His imagination and enthusiasm had been aroused by the establishment of the antiquity of European Palaeolithic artifacts and their association with Ice Age animal bones. Abbott soon found what he was looking for: "rude" stones which resembled in a vague way the famous Palaeolithic implements of France and England. He was able to enlist the assistance of Frederic Ward Putnam, who had founded the Peabody Museum at Harvard a few years before, and in September 1876 the two of them located more of what they believed were traces of Palaeolithic implements buried deep in the Trenton gravels.

If only I were a neighbor to a locality of such extraordinary antiquity and significance! Alas, the finds at the Abbott farm have been shown by investigations over the past century to be much more recent in age, and many of the "rude" palaeoliths do not seem to have been artifacts at all. Yet the controversy that they triggered over the antiquity of humans in the New World has not abated 125 years later nor shows any signs of imminent resolution. This controversy has been passionate and incendiary, perhaps out of proportion to the gravity of the matter. Yet the fundamental fact remains that after over a century of looking, the arrival of humans in the New World is still shrouded in the mists of conflicting data, extravagant claims, and fragile egos.

There is no dispute over the route taken by the first people to reach the New World, and it is certain that they came on foot, with dry feet, some time in the last 70,000 years. The key issue is one of timing, and current evidence points to a relatively late date, following the maximum advance of the last glaciation. Much of the case for this, however, is based on negative evidence, and the foregoing review of the establishment of human antiquity in Australia shows that negative evidence often does not stand the test of time.

Let us pick up the trail of the first arrivals from Eurasia who crossed from western to eastern Beringia, which would put them in what is now Alaska and the Yukon Territory. Several important sites shed light on the earliest people in the New World. Bluefish Caves I, II, and III are located in the Yukon Territory and have very complicated stratification. Although some radiocarbon dates (almost all of bone) are older than 20,000 years, other evidence points towards a dating of ca. 12,000–15,000 years ago (Cinq-Mars 1990). Fauna in the Bluefish Caves includes mammoth, horse, bison, elk, and reindeer, along with a variety of small mammals. Stone tools include wedge-shaped microblade cores and microblades. Another series of early sites is found in the Nenana Valley of Alaska (Powers and Hoffecker 1989). At Dry Creek, Moose Creek, and Walker Road, dated between 11,000 and 12,000 years ago, the stone tools consist primarily of bifacially-flaked points; wedge-shaped microblade cores and microblades are totally absent. Somewhat later, a second occupation at Dry Creek and at several nearby Nenana Valley sites did produce both microblades and their cores along with bifacial tools.

In the 1970s, a bone tool made from a reindeer tibia was found at Old Crow in the Yukon Territory, along with other bones which also bore traces of modification. Conventional radiocarbon dating of the reindeer tibia artifact produced a date of 27,000 years. Subsequent investigations, however, have shown that the modifications of the other Old Crow bones could have been produced naturally, and AMS dates on the reindeer tibia yielded a date of only 1350 years. Thus, Old Crow has fallen from scholarly favor as a site which provides any important information on the peopling of the New World.

The relationships among the sites in eastern Beringia and their connections with western Beringia are still being worked out. West (1996b) sees sites like the Bluefish Caves and the second occupation at Dry Creek as part of the "Denali Complex," which in his view is a direct derivative of the classic Dyuktai microblade-and-biface technological combination. On the other hand, the earlier Nenana Valley sites which lack microblades seem to represent something different, and perhaps derive from the biface-dominated tool-making tradition seen at sites like Berelekh and Ushki (West 1996b: 547).

The archaeological data from eastern Siberia, Alaska, and the Yukon Territory are only now beginning to fit together into coherent patterns, and the next two decades should see significant progress in unraveling the relationships among these various stone tool assemblages.

It is clear, however, that between 15,000 and 11,000 years ago, if not earlier, people with very similar stone tool technology moved from western to eastern Beringia and thus became the first people to set foot in the New World. What then? To the east, their progress was blocked by the Laurentide ice mass, to the south by the northern part of the Cordilleran ice sheet. Beringia was virtually a cul-de-sac – a very rich cul-de-sac with its abundant fauna – except for a tiny opening to the southeast between the two ice masses. Following the fauna into this opening led to the next great human migration, the colonization of North and South America.

Of crucial importance for the timing of the movement of people from Beringia to "sub-Laurentide" North America is the existence, width, and character of the corridor between the Cordilleran and Laurentide ice sheets. This topic has been the subject of lively debate among archaeologists and geomorphologists for several decades. In 1973, B. O. K. Reeves argued that except for a short local blockage between 20,000 and 18,000 years ago, when some lobes of the Cordilleran ice sheet contacted the Laurentide sheet, there was no ice barrier down the corridor between the two sheets. The implication was that there would have been no barrier to human movement, although it was unclear whether there would have been communities of animals and plants in the corridor to support human existence. Subsequent studies by Dyke and Prest (1987) indicated that at the Late Glacial Maximum, ca. 18,000 years ago, the two ice sheets were firmly together between about 50° and 60° N. By 14,000 years ago, the corridor was open for half this distance, while a millennium later the ice sheets were fully apart but the intervening area was filled with large lakes. Finally, by 12,000 years ago, Dyke and Prest argue, the ice sheets were far apart, but with many lakes remaining in the intervening zone.

Recent investigations suggest that the pulsations of the Cordilleran and Laurentide ice sheets were not synchronous, so the ice-free corridor was really a shifting zone rather than a static feature (Catto et al. 1996). Humans first had to find their way into this zone, thus conditions at the northern end in the Yukon and Northwest Territories were of crucial importance. Catto (1996) argues that no suitable entry points existed during the late Pleistocene until the ultimate deglaciation of this area about 12,400 years ago. Until then, the northern entrance to the corridor would have been blocked by ice or lakes. Once in the corridor, the bands of foragers would have needed to find the necessary biotic resources to survive, as well as suitable stone for making tools (unless they brought enough Yukon flint with them). Their campsites were probably ephemeral in terms of archaeological visibility, so it is not surprising that we do not have any traces of these groups as they moved south through Alberta.

As an alternative to the ice-free corridor model, Knut Fladmark (1979) proposed a coastal route from northeastern Asia to the unglaciated part of

North America which could have been used earlier in the Pleistocene. In such a model, human groups could have moved along an exposed coastal plain during a period of relatively mild climatic conditions before 40,000 years ago. The problem is that it depends on archaeological data that, if they exist, are now at the bottom of the Pacific Ocean off the coast of British Columbia and Alaska, as well as assumptions about human ability to cross fjords and outlet glaciers from the reduced Cordilleran sheet. Gruhn (1994) has recently restated the case for a coastal route of initial human entry to the New World based on linguistic evidence and ethnography analogy with the Yahgan people of coastal Tierra del Fuego. Nonetheless, most archaeologists dealing with the peopling of the New World continue to discount the coastal route as a viable alternative.

The model of human colonization of the New World through the corridor between the Cordilleran and Laurentide ice sheets essentially forces the event to have occurred some time after 18,000 years ago (more realistically 14,000 or fewer years ago) or before ca. 30,000 years ago. As Butzer (1991) points out, prior to 30,000 years ago, the path from Beringia down to more productive regions of North America was unimpeded, and the theoretical posssibility exists that people entered the New World during this period. He notes that the argument that there were no humans in the New World prior to ca. 12,000 years ago is based on negative evidence, and as has already been seen in the case of Australia, negative evidence can be subject to dramatic revision. Butzer also notes that the visibility of archaeological sites in the New World prior to 15,000 years ago would be very poor and suggests that we have not been looking in the right locations for them.

Michael Collins (1991) has pointed out that few caves and rockshelters in the New World have provided evidence for Pleistocene humans. This situation is in marked contrast to that of Eurasia, where caves and rockshelters have been primary sources of information on early human occupation. It is true that in the New World one rarely finds the limestone and travertine caves which are deep and often very stable. More frequently, caves and rockshelters in the New World are geologically dynamic and constantly being remodeled by collapse and erosion. Collins points out that New World archaeologists have generally investigated the Holocene strata in rockshelters but once their path is blocked by collapsed roofs and deep alluvial deposits, they do not dig deeper. On the other hand, Kelly and Todd (1988) have argued that rapidly moving hunting groups like the earliest Americans did not settle down in one location for very long and thus did not seek out such natural features for long-term habitation.

In examining the colonization of the New World, let us start from a baseline where there is no disagreement and then move backward to more controversial sites. Between 11,500 and 11,000 years ago, we find ample evidence for widespread human habitation throughout the New World. In the early 1930s, at Blackwater Draw, near Clovis, New Mexico, Edgar Howard of the Philadelphia Academy of Natural Sciences identified projectile points embedded in mammoth skeletons. On the basis of this find, Howard and his assistant, John Cotter, established conclusively that humans had been in

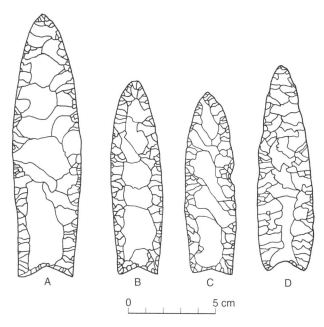

Figure 3.6 Clovis points from midcontinental North America (after Tankersley 1994, figure 6.1).

North America during the late Pleistocene. This was not the first find of points and Ice Age fauna together. In 1908, an African-American cowboy named George McJunkin had found bison bones eroding from a gully near Folsom, New Mexico; subsequent excavations in the 1920s revealed these to be the remains of *Bison antiquus*. Also discovered in association with the bones was a projectile point with a groove running up its base. The points which Howard found at Clovis a few years later had similar grooves, although somewhat less pronounced.

The Clovis and Folsom finds produced the first clear indication of late Pleistocene humans in North America, and archaeologists soon realized that they had been finding similar points over much of the continent. Sites with fluted points are found from central America to the Maritime Provinces of Canada. As with other North American projectile point types, many fluted points are found loose in plowed fields. Thus there are some counties in Ohio which have produced more Clovis points than some entire states or provinces. The wide dispersal and similarity of fluted points from many different parts of North America is truly remarkable. We now know that Clovis points are the earliest, dating between about 11,500 and 10,500 years ago, whereas Folsom points on the Great Plains and Dalton points further east date between 10,500 and 10,000 years ago.

Fluted-point habitation sites are widely distributed throughout eastern North America. Among the best-known are the Vail site in Maine (Gramly 1981), Bull Brook in Massachusetts (Byers 1954), Shawnee-Minisink and

Shoop in Pennsylvania (Witthoft 1952; McNett 1985), and the Flint Run complex in Virginia (Gardner 1977). Perhaps the most northeastern fluted-point site is at Debert in Nova Scotia, a long way from New Mexico. These sites consist characteristically of concentrations of artifacts around hearths. Reindeer are the primary game in the northeast, although as the climate warmed, boreal forest fauna such as red deer, moose, and beaver were also hunted. At the Vail site, specialized hunting of reindeer occurred on one side of the river, where the animals were butchered as well. On the other side of the river was the hunters' camp. It is clear that these sites were formed by the activities of the same people, for the broken upper parts of points found at the kill site fit broken bases found at the campsite (Gramly 1984). Raw materials were obtained from a distance at many eastern fluted-point sites, suggesting mobile populations.

In west-central North America, along the eastern slopes of the Rocky Mountains and on the High Plains of Texas, Oklahoma, and New Mexico, Clovis and Folsom kill sites are more common. At Murray Springs in Arizona, for example, a mammoth kill, a bison kill, and a campsite provide a vivid picture of an episode in Late Pleistocene life. A swath of mammoth tracks leads from a prehistoric water hole to a skeleton of a young female mammoth killed by Clovis hunters about 11,000 years ago (Haynes 1993). Eleven bison were killed nearby. Many of the western sites are the remains of kills that got away. For example, the Domebo mammoth in Oklahoma carried a number of projectile points from unsuccessful attempts to kill it but died a natural death.

For many years, archaeologists envisioned the fluted-point makers as specialized migratory hunters who followed the big game of North America. Robert Kelly and Lawrence Todd (1988) have given this concept some structure by characterizing these hunters as "high-technology foragers" who moved from place to place and from kill to kill leaving minimal evidence of their presence. They procured the best possible raw materials for their specialized hunting equipment, which emphasized a consistent reliable technology. Kelly and Todd's model of high residential mobility and search-and-encounter specialized hunting is markedly different from that proposed for Old World peoples of roughly the same general period, such as the Magdalenian and Ahrensburgian specialized hunters of Europe, who have been argued to have adopted a more logistical pattern of organization focused on specific localities.

David Meltzer has proposed that rather than being specialized hunters, the fluted-point makers were really more generalized foragers, particularly in the more southerly part of their range (1988, 1993b), which would have been the more sensible and stable strategy. He points out that there was considerable environmental variability across North America, and what was a successful way of life on the Great Plains would not necessarily have worked in the forests of the southeastern United States. Although the makers of Clovis points were certainly capable hunters of large terrestrial mammals, they did not ignore the other foods in the environment. At the Shawnee-Minisink site in Pennsylvania, for example, extensive sieving of deposits yielded the remains of many plant species (Dent and Kaufman 1985). In Meltzer's view

(1993b: 305), the fluted-point makers were opportunistic hunters of large animals and generalized hunters, collectors, and gatherers of other species of animals and plants.

An indication that the dietary breadth of some early New World hunters was somewhat broader than just big game comes from the site of Quebrada Jaguay on the Peruvian coast (Sandweiss et al. 1998), which is approximately the same age as the North American fluted-point sites. Slightly before 11,000 years ago (perhaps as early as 13,000 years ago, although this would get into issues discussed below), a group of hunter-gatherers relied on marine resources, including fish (primarily drum caught with nets), shellfish, and crustaceans. Obsidian used for tools indicates that the inhabitants of Quebrada Jaguay also had contact with nearby Andean highlands. It is possible that they spent part of the year on the coast and part of the year inland in the highlands.

The fundamental question in the peopling of the New World is: did the people who made the Clovis fluted points develop from a population of earlier immigrants or were they the initial population of migrants themselves? This debate has been waged passionately over the last several decades, and in the late 1990s the proponents and opponents of a pre-Clovis occupation of the New World are as divided as ever. Frison and Walker (1990) point out the fundamental dilemma facing archaeologists. If Clovis developed from earlier migrants, then there should be stratified sites with the older material. There are not. If Clovis is a recent immigration, then the trail should be traceable to northeastern Asia. The trail is very elusive – in fact, virtually invisible – despite the mammoth-hunting adaptations of Upper Palaeolithic peoples in northern Eurasia during the late Pleistocene, although admittedly the critical area of western Beringia has only been available for study by North American archaeologists since about 1990.

There is no shortage of sites in North America, and now increasingly in South America, which have been put forward as evidence for a pre-Clovis occupation of the New World. Many have formed the basis for extravagant claims of human antiquity. The Calico Hills site in southern California, whose claim to a dating of 50,000 to 80,000 years was supported by none other than L. S. B. Leakey, has been shown to be the result of natural formation processes. A similar evaluation has been made of the Tule Springs site in Nevada. The use of lignite for fuel at the Lewisville site in Texas produced anomalous radiocarbon dates of 37,000 years ago when the site was first studied in the 1950s.

The one site in North America which appears to be the most resilient in the face of critical scrutiny is the deeply-stratified Meadowcroft Rockshelter near Pittsburgh in western Pennsylvania. Excavations beginning in 1973 under the leadership of James Adovasio have revealed 5 meters of stratified deposits. Level IIa has yielded a number of traces of late Pleistocene occupation which have radiocarbon dates of between 12,800 and 16,175 years with an average of 14,250 years before the present. Somewhat deeper, a small fragment of woven basket or mat could be directly dated at $19,600 \pm 2,400$ years ago. This would make Meadowcroft the oldest site with a coherent series of radiocarbon dates in sub-Laurentide North America.

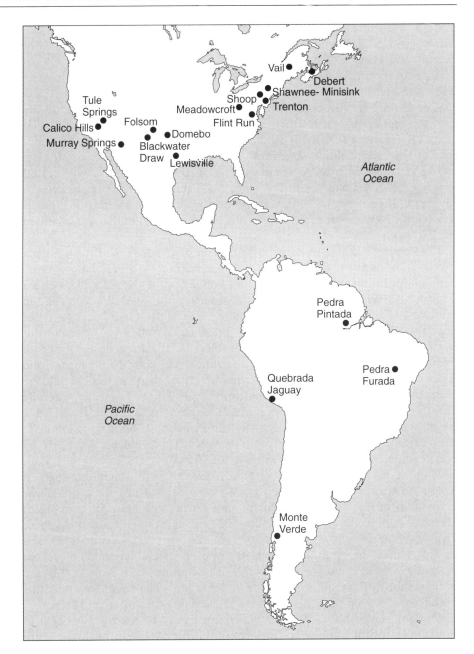

Figure 3.7 Map of North America south of the ice sheets and South America showing key localities (accepted, controversial, and spurious) mentioned in this chapter.

Yet there are question marks with the Meadowcroft data. Palaeobotanical data from Meadowcroft suggest a very non-glacial environment, despite the fact that during this period the southern edge of the Laurentide ice sheet would have been within 100 kilometers of the site. During this period,

Meadowcroft would have been in a zone of tundra and permafrost, as is indicated by pollen studies elsewhere in the Appalachian mountains (Mead 1980), yet the botanical and faunal evidence is characterized by deciduous trees and temperate forest fauna. The excavators (Adovasio et al. 1980) have defended this anomaly as a local characteristic based on the low elevation and southern exposure of the site.

C. Vance Haynes (1980, 1992) has been the most persistent critic of the Meadowcroft dating, arguing that the early dates are contaminated, perhaps by coal, but the nearest coal seam is 800 meters away. Moreover, Adovasio and his colleagues (1980) claim the contamination should have affected all the dates from Meadowcroft, not just those from Level IIa. At the moment, Meadowcroft stands alone in North America, and despite Adovasio's passionate advocacy of a late Pleistocene age for Level IIa, most archaeologists adopt the skeptical position exemplified by West (1996b: 540): the site was meticulously excavated, but the dating is too early. Time (and more AMS dating) will tell whether this view holds or whether Adovasio and his collaborators will be vindicated.

In the 1990s, an increasing number of claims for pre-Clovis occupation have come from South America, an even longer trek from the Bering land bridge but where there are no plausible alternative means for humans to arrive in the late Pleistocene. As in North America, there are some sites where the evidence for claims of great antiquity is of questionable validity if not spurious. For example, several rockshelters in eastern Brazil, such as Pedra Furada, have produced radiocarbon dates as old as 40,000 years, but the evidence for associated human tool industries is virtually invisible. Similarly, the earliest levels at the site of Monte Verde (Monte Verde I) in Chile, dated to about 33,000 years ago, have been shown not to have resulted from human activity. Two South American localities, however, have produced compelling evidence for pre-Clovis occupation: Monte Verde II in Chile and Pedra Pintada in the Amazon valley of Brazil.

About 800 kilometers south of Santiago in Chile, the site of Monte Verde II has produced some of the most tantalizing evidence for a pre-Clovis occupation of the New World (Dillehay 1989, 1997; Meltzer 1993a). Monte Verde II is unusual among late Pleistocene sites around the world in its preservation of organic remains such as wood, fruits, seeds, and pieces of animal hide. The animal bones are clearly late Pleistocene: mastodon and Pleistocene llama. Cords made from grass are still tied to wooden tent pegs, and the remains of 12 wooden huts surround a series of hearths. Next to one of the hearths are several human footprints. The stone tools, however, are fairly crude. Radiocarbon dates from Monte Verde II place the occupation between 12,500 and 13,500 years ago. Monte Verde II has been a very controversial site, and numerous archaeologists have tried to discount its evidence (e.g., Lynch 1990). As this is being written, however, a number of previously skeptical archaeologists have come to accept Monte Verde II as evidence of humans in the New World by at least 12,500 years ago.

At Pedra Pintada cave at Monte Alegre in the lower Amazon Valley, stratified late Pleistocene deposits have yielded an assemblage of finely-chipped stone tools which bear little resemblance to the fluted Clovis points (Roosevelt et al. 1996). Fifty-six radiocarbon dates and 13 luminescence dates place these deposits between ca. 11,200 and ca. 9800 years ago, corresponding to the *floruit* of Clovis and its successor, Folsom, in North America. A wide range of Amazonian forest and river animals and plants were eaten by the inhabitants of Pedra Pintada, and rock paintings believed to be contemporaneous with the Pleistocene deposits reflect a rich symbolic repertoire. The finds at Monte Alegre indicate that in the Amazon valley a population of foragers had developed a distinctive adaptation contemporaneous with the Clovis hunters of North America. This lends credence to the hypothesis that a pre-Clovis population reached Amazonia at a somewhat earlier date and adapted to the local habitats, although at the moment no traces of this population have been found.

Perhaps the most controversial late Pleistocene site in the New World is also located in Brazil. Excavated by the Brazilian-French archaeologist Nlède Guidon, the Pedra Furada rockshelter has five meters of deposits which have yielded extraordinarily early radiocarbon dates, including ones which suggest human occupation as early as 40,000 years ago. The sandstone walls of the Pedra Furada rockshelter were painted, and fragments of the painted walls flaked off and found their way into what are believed to be hearths. Radiocarbon samples from one hearth, containing a wall spall with two painted lines, are dated to 17,000 years. A few crude stone tools and a considerable amount of quartz flaking debris have been found.

Unfortunately, despite the fact that the Pedra Furada excavations began in 1973, very little has been published about the site, its stratigraphy, and its finds. The excavators' response to skeptical critics from the American archaeological community has been to accuse them of bias bordering on xenophobia. A recent visit to the site by a group of visiting archaeologists, reported in the press, apparently did not produce consensus. The key difference between Pedra Furada and Meadowcroft is that the latter is clearly a coherent corpus of archaeological data, published in detail, whereas the former remains an enigma as this is being written.

At the moment, the jury is still out on a pre-Clovis settlement of the New World. As the Australian example shows, however, our knowledge of the past can change over the course of a few decades, and despite the intensity of archaeological research in North America, there are still vast areas which have not been surveyed and late glacial deposits which have not been disturbed. It is almost certain that these will contain some surprises. South America is virtually *terra incognita* in the study of late Pleistocene humans. Anna Roosevelt's investigations in the lower Amazon valley and Tom Dillehay's results from Monte Verde point towards important discoveries yet to be made.

POST-GLACIAL RECOLONIZATION OF NORTHERN EUROPE

As the Fennoscandian ice sheet retreated in the millennia following the Late Glacial Maximum 18,000 years ago, humans in Europe were able to extend their range gradually to the north. Although people had already penetrated into these regions in warmer Middle Pleistocene times, the terminal Pleistocene saw the establishment of human settlement in England, northern continental Europe, and Scandinavia which continues uninterrupted to the present day. Between 13,000 and 10,000 years ago, pioneer foragers from the south moved northward as conditions permitted, pursuing migratory herd animals like reindeer on the tundra of the North European Plain. In England, most terminal Pleistocene sites that have been investigated are in caves, whereas in the lowlands of northern Germany and Poland, many open sites have been excavated.

The terminal Pleistocene peoples of northern Europe are characterized by tool kits specifically designed for life on the tundra. They are characterized specifically by distinctive tanged ("shouldered") projectile points in industries like the Hamburgian (ca. 13,000–12,000 BP) and Ahrensburgian and Swiderian (ca. 11,000–10,000 BP) and by backed blades and small "thumbnail" scrapers of the intervening "Federmesser," or Arch-Backed Blade industry (Schild 1996). Barbed antler harpoons came to be very important, perhaps as part of a fishing tool kit, during the Ahrensburgian and Swiderian (Price 1991). Of particular interest is the pattern of raw material procurement and movement across the North European Plain. In central Poland, a distinctive form of excellent flint, called "chocolate" flint, was mined from outcrops. About 12,000 years ago, it came to be used very heavily, and its use especially peaked after 11,000 years ago (Schild 1996). "Chocolate" flint dominates the assemblages of Swiderian sites up to about 200 kilometers from its source, with isolated examples found up to 750 kilometers away. The 200-kilometer radius suggests the extent of band movement as these groups ranged widely across the lowland plain.

A clear technological advance between the Hamburgian and the Ahrensburgian was from hunting with spears to the use of the bow and arrow (Bokelmann 1991; Eriksen 1996). Although the bow was probably invented at a number of locations in prehistory, on the North European Plain a very clear effect can be seen in its employment in hunting strategies. Both the Hamburgians and the Ahrensburgians practiced mass-killings of reindeer, although they were not (as once thought) specialized reindeer-hunters who lived on nothing else. Their settlements are frequently located astride reindeer migration routes across the lowland plains (e.g., Bokelmann 1991; Vang Petersen and Johansen 1991). Yet there are important differences in their technique. Analysis of sites such as Meiendorf and Stellmoor suggest that Hamburgian hunters stalked the reindeer, killed them with spears, and butchered the individual kills to make maximum use of the carcass. The later Ahrensburgian hunters, known also from Stellmoor and other sites, are argued to have practiced communal drive hunts of reindeer, killing many at once with arrows (Bokelmann 1991). Meat was so plentiful that only the best parts of each animal was used, with the rest abandoned with the carcass.

By about 12,000 years ago, the world was fully colonized save for Antarctica, Micronesia, Iceland, and various other isolated islands. There were still a few patches of ice in interior Scandinavia and other mountainous zones, and the environment of northern Eurasia and north America still had not yet warmed up completely, but humans could experience a range of new possibilities. A wide land bridge still existed between the British Isles and continental Europe over the southern North Sea, and the coastlines of North America and Australia were still substantially further out than they are today. These would be inundated in the millennia that followed. Once humans reached these locations, then, they were cut off and free to develop their own distinctive cultures, although local contact with watercraft was certainly possible after the land bridges were drowned.

CAVE AND PORTABLE ART IN GLOBAL CONTEXT

Perhaps the aspect of late Pleistocene society which has captured the imagination of the public has been the spectacular artistic creations which have been found throughout the world. The best known are perhaps the painted caves of southern France and northern Spain, but it is important to note that virtually everywhere that humans appeared in the late Pleistocene, they left some form of symbolic expression alongside their functional tools and discarded animal bones. Despite its visual appeal, Ice Age art forms a particularly challenging and difficult field of study for archaeologists interested in obtaining some insight into the mind of prehistoric people.

Before proceeding further, it is important to stress that the concept of "art" is particularly western and modern. It is used here as a convenient shorthand for the marks or images on rock faces or for the portable carvings of animals and people that prehistoric people made. As Flood (1996) points out, there is no word for "art" in any Aboriginal language in Australia today, and we have no way of knowing whether such a concept existed in any part of the prehistoric world. When we study Pleistocene art, we are trying to penetrate a symbolic system of which the physical consequences on rocks and in figurines are the only tangible traces which have survived. Tools, settlements, animal bones, and other such remains can be interpreted in a clear functional framework, although they too may have been imbued with symbolic content which is lost to us. Images on cave walls are a window into complex symbolic systems which have been so transformed over time that our interpretation of them will always be personal and emotive.

On the other hand, we should not be pessimistic that Pleistocene art is simply unfathomable. Indeed, regularities and themes can be observed wherever it is found. Through these recurring motifs, a framework of the ancient symbolic system can be constructed, although what should go in the interstices remains elusive. The study of Pleistocene art attracts a core group of dedicated scholars who, by and large, analyze it rigorously, despite the fact that each disagrees with most of the others about its interpretation.

It is important to note that there are two major categories of Pleistocene art: that which occurs on the walls of caves and rock shelters, and portable figurines, engravings, and ornaments. Portable art occurs throughout the Eurasian Upper Palaeolithic, from about 35,000 years ago onward. One of the earliest examples is the wooly mammoth carved from mammoth ivory found at Vogelherd in Germany. Another early example is the female figurine from Galgenberg in Austria (Bahn 1994). The "Venus" figurines of the Gravettian in central and eastern Europe have already been discussed above, but it should also be noted that such figurines also occur in contemporaneous sites in southwestern Europe as well. Most of the portable art in Europe, however, is dated to Magdalenian times, after the glacial maximum, and consists largely of very detailed naturalistic representations of animals carved on stone and bone or incorporated into the design of bone and antler artifacts like spear-throwers. One of the finest examples is the bison licking its side from La Madeleine rock shelter, which is about 14,000 years old.

Cave and rockshelter wall-art (often called "parietal" art) is a widespread phenomenon over much of the world colonized in the late Pleistocene. In southwestern Europe, it consists overwhelmingly of representations of herbivores of significant economic value like reindeer, horse, bison, aurochs, ibex, and mammoth and sometimes carnivores like lion, bear, and wolf. Human representations are virtually non-existent, except for the equivocal "sorcerer" at Les Trois Frères (and some stick figures at other caves). In the deep limestone caverns of Franco-Cantabria, the wall art frequently occurs in narrow passages far from the entrance. Another category of Ice Age cave art consists of abstract geometrical forms and silhouettes of human hands. Wherever people applied pigment to cave walls after about 35,000 years ago, someone inevitably made a stencil of his or her hand, usually by blowing pigment through a tube at the hand placed on the wall, leaving the outline for posterity.

Since the acceptance of the antiquity of Ice Age cave painting at the beginning of the twentieth century, many prehistorians and art historians have offered explanations for its motivation. Art historians have generally viewed it as the earliest awakening of some universal human impulse to decorate and depict features of their surroundings, and their analyses have tended to focus on identifying themes, style, and artistic vision (e.g., Giedion 1962; Mazonowicz 1975). Prehistorians, on the other hand, have generally sought "deeper" motivations, since it is clear that the frequent location of the art deep in the caves in narrow and often hardly accessible passages meant that it was clearly embedded in a complex cultural behavior. We can be very certain that this was not idle doodling to pass the time!

For the first half of the twentieth century, the canonical intepretation of Palaeolithic cave art was that of Abbé Breuil (1877–1961), who took the position that it was part of a system of hunting magic. Breuil interpreted the naturalistic depictions of animals, which frequently had spear wounds, as having been used in a form of "sympathetic magic," in which by capturing the likeness of an animal and then symbolically killing it, the hunter/artist/shaman ensured the success of the hunt. This interpretation of Palaeolithic cave art was accepted as dogma, perhaps due to its resonance with ethnographic accounts of similar behavior, until the 1960s, when it was challenged by André Leroi-Gourhan (1911–86). Leroi-Gourhan, influenced by structuralism in French ethnological theory, saw the art as an expression of some primeval binary opposition between the male and female components of society (Leroi-Gourhan 1968). He argued that the cave art was not haphazard in its placement on the walls, but rather that the space in the caverns was intentionally structured through the placement of different sorts of paintings. Abstract signs assume considerable importance, for Leroi-Gourhan believed that the line or arrow figures were male, while triangular designs and natural features like fissures were female. Animal species are either "male" (e.g., horse) or "female" (e.g., bison). Male motifs predominate in more peripheral chambers, while female ones occur in central galleries.

Although Leroi-Gourhan's interpretation still appears to be the orthodox view in France (e.g., Clottes and Courtin 1996), other recent treatments of Palaeolithic art have shifted away from symbolism to stress its value for conveying information about the environment and social context of its makers. One recent analysis of this sort is that of Mithen (1991), who argues that art facilitated the retrieval of information related to the tracking of large mammals and made possible the development of multiple scenarios for planned hunting activities. Mithen sees a correlation between the elaboration of art in the later Upper Palaeolithic and the development of specialized hunting strategies (1991: 112) in which the art acted as the stimulus for creative thought before carrying these out. Another view is to see Upper Palaeolithic art as the product of altered states of consciousness, by analogy with the way in which the San people of southern Africa in recent times have used rock paintings and engravings to harness supernatural power to enter trace states (Lewis-Williams and Dowson 1988; Lewis-Williams 1991).

Paul Mellars (1994) has sensibly pointed out that there seems to be almost no limit to the number of hypotheses that can be generated for the motivations behind Palaeolithic cave art and that virtually none of them can be rigorously tested in a systematic and controlled fashion. It seems more promising to try to situate Ice Age art in its broader technological, social, and economic context. Randall White (1992) has made the point that the emergence of representations is mirrored in other evidence for advances in non-verbal thought during the period between 35,000 and 10,000 years ago, for example in technological innovation. The manipulation of raw material to produce complex forms hitherto not made and the organization of seasonal and specialized hunting strategies are two examples of heightened cognitive ability which parallel the development of symbolic expression.

The many "classic" sites of Ice Age art in southwestern Europe have been described in many places. The bulls of Altamira and the "Chinese horses" of Lascaux have appeared in numerous volumes since they were discovered and authenticated. It is important to realize, however, that these sites are merely representative of a large corpus of cave paintings, rock engravings, and of portable carvings which Ice Age people made throughout this region. It is also important to realize that spectacular discoveries are continually being made, and it is likely that there are many more caves yet to be found which have equally important collections of Ice Age art.

One of the most dramatic discoveries of Pleistocene art in recent years occurred in 1991, when a French diver named Henri Cosquer discovered paintings and engravings in a cave which was accessible only through a

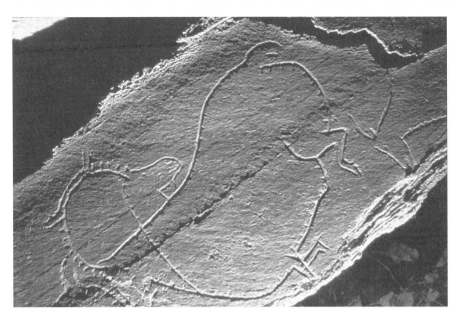

Figure 3.8 Upper Palaeolithic engravings at Foz Côa (photo courtesy of Dr João Zilhão, Instituto Português de Arqueologia, Lisbon).

passage whose entrance was about 36 meters below the surface of the Mediterranean. The Grotte Cosquer, as the cave has been named, was an unusual geological formation in which the tunnel, whose entrance was beneath the sea, angled upward over its length of 150 meters to open into a chamber whose sides were largely above the modern water level. Cosquer notified archaeologists of his discovery, and later that year he led archaeologist-divers on the first of several visits to the cave (Clottes and Courtin 1996).

Ice Age artists visited Cosquer on at least two occasions, first around 27,000 years ago and then around 18,500 years ago. During the first visit, the artists confined their work to stencils of hands and grooves in the soft lime-stone. During the second period, the walls were covered with animal paintings and engravings. By 1996, over 100 figures of animals had been recorded, mostly of horses, ibex, chamois, aurochs, bison, and deer. A distinctive fea-ture of the Cosquer art, no doubt due to its proximity to the sea, is the depic-tion of maritime fauna, including seals, fish, the great auk, and possibly jellyfish. The great auk depictions aroused some controversy, since in the ini-tial French reports they were called "pingouins," which was literally translated into English. This usage aroused doubts about the authenticity of the Cosquer art, since penguins are of course Antarctic species. D'Errico (1994) has shown convincingly that these are representations of great auks, the extinct penguin of the northern oceans, which is also called "pingouin" in French.

In 1994, a vast complex of Palaeolithic art was discovered on the walls of the Côa valley in northeastern Portugal – just in time, for the valley was scheduled to be inundated by a reservoir soon thereafter. Fourteen art sites, approximately 20,000 years old, have been identified along a 12-kilometer stretch of valley. Unlike the cave paintings of southern France, the Côa art occurs in the form of petroglyphs, or engravings, on the open schist faces of the valley, typically with an eastern exposure. They represent primarily animals (deer, ibex, horses, and aurochs), although there are some abstract figures and one possible human form. Petroglyph sites are relatively rare in the Ice Age art of southwestern Europe, although they are common elsewhere in Eurasia. The Côa sites are remarkable for their clear analogs to the painted cave art elsewhere in southwestern Europe and their concentration. At the time of writing, the hydroelectric project that was to have inundated the valley has been tabled, and the area is to be turned into an archaeological park.

Perhaps the most significant recent discovery of cave art, however, is the Chauvet cave at Vallon-Pont-d'Arc in the Ardèche region of France (Clottes 1996). Chauvet is significant for a number of reasons. First, there are abundant traces of human presence other than the painted walls, including hearths, flint tools, torches, and human footprints. Second, humans were not the only occupants of the cave; cave bears left behind their skeletons and lairs. Third, the approximately 300 representations of animals on the walls are both painted and engraved. In order of abundance, they include wooly rhinoceroses, lions, mammoths, horses, bison, bears, reindeer, aurochs, ibexes, giant Irish elk, red deer, and a panther. The range of beasts represented in this menagerie and the prominent attention to carnivores is unusual, for their proportions are markedly different from their representation in bone assemblages from habitation sites. Fourth, the Ardèche is well to the east and north of the classical centers of cave art in the Périgord, the Pyrenees, and Cantabrian Spain.

The most significant feature of the Chauvet paintings, however, is their dating. AMS radiocarbon dates on samples taken from charcoal drawings of rhinoceros and bison have given dates of about 31,000 years. Dating of soot from torches on a calcite layer which was deposited *over* one of the drawings gave a date of about 26,000 years. The dating of this art to the earlier part of the Upper Palaeolithic contradicts one of the conventional beliefs about Ice Age cave painting, that it is a feature primarily of the period after about 20,000 years ago. In the stylistic sequence defined by Leroi-Gourhan, only fairly crude paintings are supposed to accompany the accomplished portable art found at this time. The finding of sophisticated painted figures from such an early date will make it necessary to re-examine this sequence. As is frequently the case in archaeology, development of Ice Age art does not necessarily take the expected linear course.

It is very important that the spectacular Ice Age art of southwestern Europe not be seen in isolation, as some sort of local florescence. While it is vivid in its depiction of animals, it is part of a global pattern of human expression. Bednarik (1994), for example, points out that the Pleistocene art of Asia, particularly of Siberia, has been largely overlooked, perhaps due to the relatively low level of research intensity in this area (the same problem referred to by Meltzer in reference to finding the antecedents of the first

Americans). Although there are no painted caves, there are indeed two- and three-dimensional representations of mammoths and humans carved in bone from sites like Berelekh and Mal'ta, as well the head of an animal from Tolbaga carved on the vertebra of a wooly rhinoceros. The Tolbaga animal head has a date of about 35,000 years, about the same time that Aurignacian artists in western Europe were awakening to new possibilities.

The colonists of Australia also were inclined towards expressive behavior which led them to paint extensively on the walls of caves and rock shelters. Large pieces of red and yellow ocher were found at both the Malakunaja II and Nauwalabila I rock shelters, which date to about 60,000 years ago. Although it is unclear to what purpose this material was intended, Flood (1996: 10) identifies the options as the decoration of the inhabitants' own bodies, their artifacts, or the walls of the shelter, or possibly all three. The possibility also exists that human blood was used as a pigment (although human blood identification is a controversial biochemical issue). At Judd's Cavern in Tasmania, Thomas Loy has identified traces of blood which was mixed with red ocher and then applied to the cave walls in smears and hand stencils that can be dated to about 10,000 years ago.

The earliest undisputed date for an actual pictorial depiction in Australia (*at the time of writing*, it is important to note, for nothing in Australia seems to remain the "oldest" for very long!) is from the Sandy Creek rock shelter on Cape York Peninsula. Here, the carbon in a mineral layer which had formed over a pictograph was dated to about 25,000 years ago (Watchman 1993). Even older dates have been obtained for a fragment of a pictograph which appears to have fallen from the roof of the Carpenter's Gap rock shelter, which lies in a layer dated by AMS to about 40,000 years ago. Although controversial, some petroglyphs at Olary have also been dated using cation-ratio analysis of a bacterial crust called "desert varnish" to ca. 40,000 years (Nobbs and Dorn 1993) although many engravings at the site have much later dates.

In Arnhem Land, there is an extensive corpus of pictographic rock art which permits its analysis into characteristic manners of depiction and chronology (Taçon and Chippindale 1994), although the Pleistocene part of this sequence is still approximate. Although pigment use almost surely began earlier, the oldest painted art of Australia is of large animals depicted in a naturalistic style (some chronologies, such as that of Chaloupka [1984] place handprints and stencils earlier, but Taçon and Chippindale argue that these are not chronologically diagnostic). Some of these animals appear to represent Pleistocene fauna which became extinct in Australia about 15,000 years ago (Flood 1996: 13). The large naturalistic animals are followed by thousands of small figures of humans whose arms and legs are extended and active. They are running, carrying boomerangs, fighting, and throwing spears. These so-called "Dynamic Figures" are thought to be about 10,000 years old or older, based on an accumulating number of dates for silica films covering the art. Later styles carry the Australian tradition of rock art into the present.

In Africa, as in Australia, the practice of rock art which has continued into historical times in many places appears to have considerable antiquity. Perhaps the oldest securely dated Pleistocene rock art in Africa is found in Apollo 11 Cave in Namibia, where painted slabs bearing naturalistic depictions of animals had been exfoliated from the sites of the cavern and fallen into levels which could be dated to approximately 26,000 years ago (Lewis-Williams 1983). At the moment, however, the Apollo 11 find appears to stand alone, with a large chronological gap between it and the next appearance of art after about 10,000 years ago.

Finally, the discovery of late Pleistocene art in South America has extended evidence for this phenomenon to yet another continent. Meticulous excavations at the Pedra Pintada rock shelter in the Amazon valley, where the walls were painted in red and yellow geometric motifs, anthropomorphic figures, and handprints of adults and children, have permitted these paintings to be dated to the late Pleistocene (Roosevelt et al. 1996). When the walls were being painted, hundreds of drops and lumps of pigment fell on the cave floor and were incorporated into datable strata. AMS and luminescence dates date the levels with pigment to between 11,200 and 9800 years ago, while analysis of the elemental composition of the pigment from the late Pleistocene levels shows that it matches that used for the wall paintings.

BAND SOCIETY IN THE UPPER PLEISTOCENE

Despite their achievements in technology, art, and exploration, I believe that the people of the late Ice Age continued to be organized largely along the same social lines as their Neanderthal predecessors. In fact, the Neanderthal legacy of Pleistocene band organization was perhaps the most enduring feature of early human society. This is not meant to imply that early modern humans were stuck in a rut. Indeed, they were the ones who took the model of band society developed in Neanderthal times and made it a remarkably successful adaptive strategy throughout the world.

Perhaps this is most clearly seen in the development of specialized hunting strategies and of logistical behavior during the last 10,000 years of the Ice Age. Both required planning, foresight, assessments of risk and uncertainty, and a consensus among members of a band. It may also imply the development of techniques of preserving or storing meat, which also would presage important changes in human activity during the post-Ice Age world.

The organization of living space at the late Ice Age sites like Pincevent and Verberie in northern France, at Mezhirich in Ukraine, at Lake Ushki on Kamchatka, and at Monte Verde in Chile also reflects an important step in human social behavior. Once space is demarcated in some way it ceases to be completely communal, even if the general ethos of the society is one of sharing. At Middle Pleistocene sites like Shanidar, the hearth became a focus of human activity. In the Late Pleistocene, hearths became part of larger activity areas, including specific locations for flint working and discard.

For Ice Age mobile hunting societies, the band model of social organization, with its obligatory sharing of resources, was really the only way to live. The social distinctions introduced by the substitution of kinship for friendship and notions of private property would have fragmented these large adaptive units in such a way that they would have ceased to be viable as social entities. The vast reaches of unpopulated terrain provided limitless options for relocation and pursuit of mobile resources. Especially during the Late Glacial Maximum, the mobility of these bands allowed them to deal with staggering environmental challenges.

Thanks to this mobility, new continents were conquered. Sedentary farmers may never have found the New World or Australia! This is not so facetious as it sounds. Mobile hunters not only were mobile, but once they entered new territories they also tended to stay unless driven out by changing environmental conditions. Territories were large and shifting. Resources could be procured from a distance, and what mobility could not provide, exchange with neighbors could.

On the other hand, the symbolic depictions of animals and people do reflect an emergence of small-group and even individual identity, planning, ritual, and awareness of the complexity of the physical world. These characteristics cannot be underestimated, even if the underlying social substrate remained constant. Of these characteristics, I would rate the last as the key cognitive advance of this period. Humans ceased to be passive recipients of nature whose lives revolved around stone, animal carcasses, and fire. Early modern humans participated in a complex natural world which they were able to observe with increasingly finer resolution. These were thoughtful foragers rather than reflex-action hunters.

In 1972, Kent Flannery pointed out that the transformation of hunter-gatherers into agriculturalists was accompanied by a major social reorganization of society. It was characterized by a shift from groups of polygynous males, their wives, and children, living communally and serving as the primary unit of production, distribution, consumption, and reproduction, to communities of independent nuclear-family households. It is precisely this idea which is developed further in the remaining chapters of this volume, stressing the difference between the sharing norms of Pleistocene band society and self-interested household units. This transformation was the single most significant change in the history of anatomically-modern humans and provided the foundation for subsequent developments.

FURTHER READING

The "human revolution" of the Upper Palaeolithic and the colonization of Australia and the New World has seized the imagination of the public as well as having been a major focus of archaeological interest. The result is that there are a number of good books which can allow the reader to explore the topic further. Clive Gamble's 1994 book *Timewalkers: the Prehistory of Global Colonization* will continue the story from the previous chapter. The late Pleistocene prehistory of Eurasia is the topic of several essays in *The Pleistocene Old World*, edited by Olga Soffer (1987). Soffer and Gamble then teamed up to edit the two-volume anthology *The World at 18000 BP* (1990), which provides worldwide coverage of prehistoric societies at the Last Glacial Maximum. An important recent collection of essays dealing with the period after 18,000 years ago around the world is *Humans at the End of the Ice Age: The Archaeology of the Pleistocene–Holocene Transition*, edited by Lawrence Straus, Berit Ericksen, Jon Erlandson, and David Yesner (1996). Several regional studies provide coverage of many parts of Eurasia, including *Upper Pleistocene Prehistory of Western Eurasia* edited by Harold Dibble and Anta Montet-White

(1988), and *The Upper Palaeolithic of the Central Russian Plain* by Olga Soffer (1985). The essays in *Hunting and Animal Exploitation in the Late Palaeolithic and Mesolithic of Eurasia*, edited by Gail Larsen Peterkin, Harvey Bricker, and Paul Mellars (1993), focus specifically on hunting technology and techniques.

The colonization of the New World and Australia has been the topic of several recent works. A good general overview can be found in *Search for the First Americans* by David Meltzer (1993). Specific archaeological data is presented in *The First Americans: Search and Research*, edited by Tom Dillehay and David Meltzer (1991) and *American Beginnings: the Prehistory and Palaeoecology of Beringia*, edited by Frederick Hadleigh West (1996). The essays in *From Kostenki to Clovis. Upper Palaeolithic–Palaeo-Indian Adaptations*, edited by Olga Soffer and N. D. Praslov (1993), provide an interesting comparison between Eurasian and North American materials following the Last Glacial Maximum. Josephine Flood's review article, "Culture in early aboriginal Australia," in *Cambridge Archaeological Journal*, vol. 6, p. 3–36, is a useful baseline essay on the early settlement of Australia, although new data may revise this picture substantially.

Ice Age art is the topic of many books. A useful baseline volume is that of Paul Bahn and Jean Vertut entitled *Image of the Ice Age* (1998). Important recent sites include *Dawn of Art: the Chauvet Cave* by Jean Marie Chauvet, Eliette Brune Deschamps, and Christians Hillaire (1996), and *The Cave Beneath the Sea* by Jean Clottes and Jean Courtin (1996) which provides a detailed description of the remarkable Grotte Cosquer. The Coa Valley petroglyphs have been described in *Arte Rupestre e Pré-História do Vale do Côa* by João Zilhão (2nd edn., in Portuguese with extensive English summary, 1998).

[4]   AFTER THE ICE AGE

INTRODUCTION

A chapter title like "After the Ice Age" implies that we are now out of the woods so far as continental ice sheets are concerned. This is of course not entirely true, but since in our lifetime we will not have to confront the problem (if global conditions change so radically as to cause otherwise, the least of our worries will be the inundation of New York, London, and Los Angeles) it is not worth worrying about. Writing from the perspective of the present, we can look back and say that essentially modern climatic conditions have prevailed over most of the subtropical and temperate latitudes for the last 10,000 years. The Ice Age is in the past, and the modern human condition has been shaped in its final form under much the same climatic conditions which prevail today.

We now come to an important part of the human experience which is called the "Mesolithic" in much of Eurasia and the "Archaic" in the Americas. In sub-Saharan Africa, the picture is somewhat more complicated, since there is not such a clear unidirectional change in climate, flora, and fauna at the end of the Ice Age. There, the Late Stone Age foragers continued many of the patterns which characterized earlier periods, although there are important local variations. Our focus in this chapter is largely on the northern hemisphere.

For the first three-quarters of the twentieth century, the late foragers of the Mesolithic and the Archaic were considered a second-class topic for research. They did not seem to have a Big Problem associated with them. On the one hand, they followed the major developments of the Upper Pleistocene, such as cave art and the peopling of the Americas. On the other, they predated agriculture and the cultural developments that accompanied it. In some parts of the world, late foragers have been conspicuously ignored. In southeastern Europe, for example, their sites have never been considered worth locating, except when they are impossible to ignore, such as in the Iron Gates gorges of the Danube. In general, for archaeologists they were an arcane, acquired taste, best left to the second-rate students of local prehistory. There were, of course, a number of exceptions to this sweeping generalization. A few archaeologists, like Grahame Clark in England and Richard MacNeish in America, were able to build distinguished careers from these periods by taking advantage of the economic data which often accompanied them. Most archaeologists, however, were content to remain in the exotic remoteness of the earlier Stone Age cultures or to begin their personal quests for the past in the sturdier archaeological record of pottery-using agriculturalists.

Few periods in the archaeological record have gained such rapid respectability as the post-glacial foragers of North America and Eurasia. In the 1960s, there was a sudden recognition that post-glacial foragers were interesting in their own right, or at least because they eventually became farmers. Still, the overall sense was that the late foragers of the Mesolithic and Archaic were simply biding their time and waiting for agriculture. Some would eventually be lucky and discover agriculture themselves, while others would be the fortunate recipients of the new technology and lifestyle. In the meantime, they were the passive recipients of the bounty of nature, from woodlands, rivers, and oceans freed from the effects of the Ice Age.

In the 1970s and 1980s, however, it became clear that *without* the important adaptations that took place among the late foragers between 12,000 and 5000 years ago in many parts of the world, the subsequent development of human society would have been impossible. The Mesolithic and the Archaic came to be recognized as important periods in their own right, and the research that resulted from this realization is highlighted in this chapter. Archaeologists have tended to focus on the economic changes that resulted from the onset of new environmental conditions. In this chapter, I will try to take the discussion somewhat further by arguing that the new possibilities afforded by the post-glacial environment also caused important social changes which irrevocably moved human society from the Pleistocene bands to a point from which it could never again retreat.

THE ESTABLISHMENT OF MODERN CLIMATE, VEGETATION, AND FAUNA

The final retreat of the Pleistocene ice sheets in both hemispheres, beginning about 16,000 years ago and largely finished by 10,000 years ago, saw the establishment of climatic conditions, vegetation, and animal life which would be recognizable to us today. These changes were the most profound in the midlatitudes, between the Tropic of Cancer and the Arctic Circle in the northern hemisphere and between the Tropic of Capricorn and the Antarctic Circle in the southern hemisphere. A visitor from the twenty-first century who traveled back in time to this general period would not find the environs of Stuttgart or Cincinnati to be a barren periglacial wasteland but rather covered in forests with familiar tree species. In the Mexican highlands or the foothills of the Zagros mountains, our traveler would also find hospitable conditions. In all these cases, the modern environment is much different from that of 8–12,000 years ago, but that is largely the result of human activity in the intervening millennia.

Within the general agreement that the global climate ameliorated following the retreat of the ice sheets, there are many competing models of how this process actually occurred. For example, in the Near East, there are two main models, both based on the study of pollen and sediments. One model, championed by Donald Henry (1989), views the area as subject to alternating wet and dry conditions between about 15,000 and 10,000 years ago. These alternative cycles are time-transgressive from south to north as the storm patterns shifted northward due to the final retreat of the Scandinavian ice sheets. The other model, held by Ofer Bar-Yosef and his collaborators (e.g., Bar-Yosef and Belfer-Cohen 1989), also envisions alternating wet and dry cycles but with a different periodicity and timing. The key point is that the post-glacial warming-up was not a smooth progression from cold to warm and from dry to moist (or vice versa) but rather a series of phases with distinctive characteristics.

This variation is even more pronounced in what now could be called "temperate" latitudes, in north-central Europe and North America. Here, the landscape had actually been covered by ice, so the establishment of modern forests and fauna was truly a colonization of what had previously been windswept periglacial wastes or under hundreds of meters of ice. Rivers had to cut new channels, while ice-dammed lakes formed from the melting water and then were breached, sending immense amounts of water cascading towards the nearest ocean. Here, the glaciers were not far off, and every retreat, standstill, or short-lived advance was cause for climatic fluctuation. In Europe during the period known as the Allerød between 11,800 and 10,800 years ago, the climate was relatively warm, but during the Younger Dryas period which followed for the next 800 years, the cold conditions returned. Similar variations occurred in North America. Finally, about 10,000 years ago, the glaciers were well to the north, and the climate became progressively warmer.

As the climate ameliorated, the areas that had previously been covered by ice or tundra were colonized by shrubs and trees, while regions further to the south also experienced changes in vegetation. The vegetational sequence in northern continental Europe between about 50° and 60° north latitude is very well known. During the Ice Age, many species of trees had survived in refugia along the southern fringe of Europe, and these then spread northward as soon as conditions permitted. Beginning about 10,000 years ago, birch and pine woods became established across northern Europe. These were succeeded by a predominant vegetation of hazel, pine, and oak. By about 8000 years ago, the vegetation had reached a "climax" stage which is characterized by "mixed oak forest," a misnomer in which the dominant tree species was actually linden. Similar vegetation successions can be traced in North America as well.

In addition to tree species, the post-glacial forests had other important resources, many of which were very important for humans. The role of hazel in the human economies of this period in temperate latitudes will be discussed further below. Berries, tubers, roots, fungi, and rhizomes were all edible plants which provided important nutritional opportunities for people and which were now available in abundance in the new deciduous forests.

The post-glacial fauna that populated these forests were essentially those that we recognize today. The Pleistocene megafauna, whose disappearance was discussed in the previous chapter, were now truly absent. In northern Europe and North America, the reindeer (caribou) herds had moved north to their present-day ranges. In their place, red deer, roe deer, wild pig, and wild cattle, which had previously been found far to the south, now colonized the new temperate zone forests of Eurasia. In North America, white-tail deer, raccoon, and beaver extended their ranges northward.

The richness of the environments that the retreat of the glaciers now permitted is naturally reflected in the subsistence remains that are found at prehistoric sites. Archaeologists have tended to refer to such economies with the term "broad spectrum," but in light of the remarkable variety of edible plants and animals which were available, it is difficult to imagine people doing anything other than exploiting the environment fully. Even in maritime habitats where seafood was abundant, the variety of species used reflects an attempt to take advantage of every resource available.

In warmer latitudes, the retreat of the glaciers also produced significant effects. Rising sea levels created new wetland habitats in Southeast Asia and central America. Increased rainfall in the headwater region of the Nile starting around 13,000 years ago resulted in very high flow, which led the river to cut a deeper channel within a narrower floodplain. Around 11,000 years ago, there was a northward shift of the monsoon rainfall belts which caused the eastern Sahara to receive more moisture and make the desert temporarily available for human settlement. In general, more pronounced seasonality was introduced in many parts of the world where there had been previously a fairly constant climate, which in addition to the implications that it had for Pleistocene megafauna, also has great significance for the organization of human subsistence behavior.

BROAD-SPECTRUM POST-GLACIAL FORAGERS

Around the world, a number of post-glacial hunter-gatherer peoples have been brought into sharper focus through sustained archaeological research over the last 30 years. The case studies below are not meant to be a complete list, but one which provides a sense of the diversity of post-Pleistocene adaptations on one hand, and one which identifies a number of common characteristics on the other. They are not arranged in any chronological order. In general, those of the Old World are somewhat earlier than those of the New World. The lack of synchronicity indicates that the causes of the changes in human society after the Ice Ages were not due exclusively to climatic change, but rather that the changed environment offered new possibilities of which humans took advantage in different ways.

JOMON FORAGERS OF JAPAN

In Japan, post-glacial hunter-gatherers who practiced intensive maritime foraging are represented by the early stages of the Jomon culture. Jomon covers a remarkably long span of time; during its later phases, agriculture was introduced to Japan. Here, we are concerned with its earlier phases (Incipient, Initial, and Early – ca. 10,000 BC to 3500 BC) which saw a remarkable sedentary maritime adaptation which has much in common with Ertebølle (see below) in southern Scandinavia (Rowley-Conwy 1984). As in Denmark, many coastal Jomon sites take the form of shell middens, such as the one at Omori excavated in 1877 by Edward S. Morse who is credited with introducing modern archaeology to Japan.

"Jomon" means "cord marked," a reference to its later pottery. Yet, Jomon sites have also yielded some of the earliest pottery in the world, but it is not cord marked (Aikens 1995). Early ceramics have been found at Incipient Jomon sites, including Fukui Cave and Sempukuji Rockshelter on Kyushu dated about 10,700 BC and at Kamikuroiwa Rockshelter on Shikoku dated about 2000 years later. They reflect a need for storage containers, and hence indicate a marked re-orientation in subsistence practices from the generalized northeast Asian microblade industries that preceded Jomon.

Jomon settlements have yielded an extraordinary array of terrestrial and maritime species. For example, 34 species of shellfish, 17 species of marine fish, 11 species of mammals, and seven species of birds have been found at the Initial Jomon shell midden at Natsushima on Tokyo Bay (Aikens 1995: 14). At the Early Jomon site at Yagi on Hokkaido, which is not a shell midden, a large faunal assemblage reflected broad-spectrum littoral economy (Bleed et al. 1989). The major vertebrate taxa were sika deer and pinnipeds (seals, sea lions, and walruses). In addition, the Yagi faunal assemblage included fish (both cartilaginous and bony) and maritime waterfowl. The Jomon inhabitants of Yagi exploited all the environments around their community.

Torihama is an Early Jomon site in Fukui Prefecture not far from Kyoto. Here, waterlogged deposits have resulted in a remarkable level of preservation

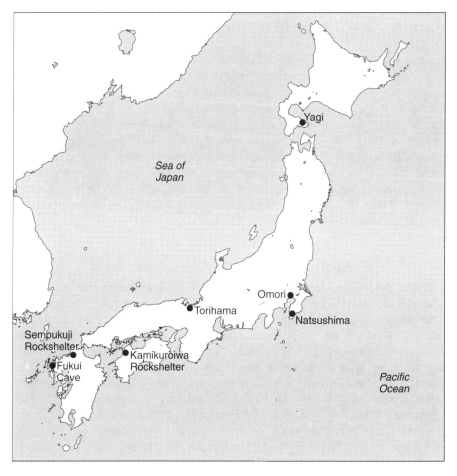

Figure 4.1 Map of Japan showing key Jomon sites mentioned in this chapter.

of wooden artifacts, including a dugout canoe, paddles, bows, tool handles, and bowls. Subsistence remains are also well-preserved. Gourds and beans from ca. 5000 to 3500 BC may reflect an incipient degree of horticulture in western Japan long before the appearance of rice agriculture, or it may be that the Jomon foraging adaptation featured patterns of harvesting of rich resources which mimicked or presaged agricultural patterns (Aikens 1995: 15).

Jomon communities lived in a littoral environment where a variety of habitats were within easy reach of any given site. Not only were there rich maritime resources, but the rugged Japanese topography provided a vertical heterogeneity in terrestrial resources. As a result, a remarkably stable and sustained foraging tradition persisted throughout the early part of the Holocene.

LATE FORAGERS OF SOUTHERN SCANDINAVIA

Along the coasts of Denmark, southern Sweden, northern Germany, and northern Poland, the late foragers of the western Baltic zone exploited the rich marine resources. Between 6000 and 4000 BC, these foragers, known as the "Ertebølle culture" after a site in northern Jutland, developed a complex maritime adaptation which represents the zenith of hunter-gatherer life in temperate Europe. Several different types of Ertebølle sites are known (Price and Gebauer 1992):

- coastal shell middens, the *køkkenmøddinger* or "kitchen middens," composed of the debris left behind during seasonal visits to the location;
- seasonal, special-purpose coastal sites for fishing, seal-hunting, or fowling;
- inland trapping stations at which fur-bearing mammals were skinned;
- possibly-perennial inland lakeside settlements.

The analysis of carbon isotopes from human bone collagen indicates the pronounced maritime orientation of the Ertebølle people. Terrestrial foods

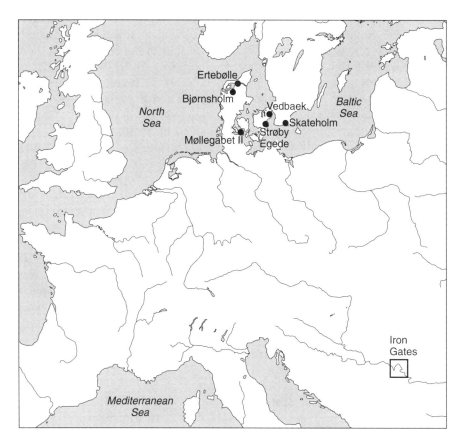

Figure 4.2 Map of Europe showing key Mesolithic sites mentioned in this chapter.

were simply a supplement to the rich marine resources such as fish, shellfish, whales, and seals. Clearly, these foragers had a deep-water capability, and dugout canoes up to 10 m long are known from waterlogged deposits.

An important *køkkenmødding* has recently (1985–92) been excavated at Bjørnsholm in northern Jutland, about 5 km south of the classic type-site at Ertebølle (Andersen 1991). Bjørnsholm is a large shell-mound about 325 m long, running NE–SW along the shore of a former fjord. It is a stratified deposit, with lower levels belonging to Ertebølle foragers covered by later layers left by early farmers. The mound appears to have functioned as a residential base for Ertebølle foragers who exploited the local maritime and terrestrial resources. Red deer, roe deer, and wild boar predominate among the land mammals (Bratlund 1991), while eel bones dominate the fish bone assemblage (Enghoff 1991), as at Ertebølle. The region of these two sites was famous for its eel fishing into the twentieth century, as it was 7000 years earlier. Of special note are the bones of fish species which occur today only in more southerly waters, indicating that the water temperatures in the region were warmer in Ertebølle times than at present.

Perhaps the most remarkable aspect of the late foragers of the western Baltic are their elaborate burials, which occur in cemeteries reminiscent of those of the Natufians in the Levant a few millennia earlier. Until the mid-1970s, only a few isolated graves were known, but in the last 20 years there has been an explosion of knowledge of Ertebølle burials. In 1975, a cemetery was discovered at Vedbæk (Bøgebakken) in Zealand. Investigation revealed 18 graves containing 22 individuals (Albrethsen and Brinch Petersen 1976). A copious amount of red ochre was sprinkled over the deceased in many of the graves, while red deer antlers were included in the graves of older individuals. Females frequently had necklaces and belts of beads made from shell and animal teeth. There were indications that the Vedbæk cemetery had once been larger, but part had been destroyed by road construction.

For several years, the Vedbæk cemetery stood as unique, but in the early 1980s several much larger cemeteries were found at the southern tip of Sweden at Skateholm (Larsson 1993) around what had been a lagoon in Ertebølle times. Skateholm I had at least 57 graves with the remains of 62 individuals; Skateholm II, less extensively excavated, yielded at least 22 graves, while several additional graves had been found at Skateholm III several decades earlier. The Skateholm burials reflect a remarkable diversity in burial rite. Three types of body positions – extended, seated, and contracted – occur in numerous variations. Cremations are also known. Many of the burials are accompanied by grave goods. As at Vedbæk, red deer antlers figure prominently in the burial rite, with full racks often placed over the deceased as if to restrain the individual in the grave. Elderly men and young women received the greatest amounts of grave goods.

Of particular interest at Skateholm are eight dog graves (Larsson 1990). These animals received the same sort of careful treatment as did human burials, and they are also often accompanied by antlers and grave goods and red ochre. Most of the dogs, however, lie some distance from the human burials in a distinct area.

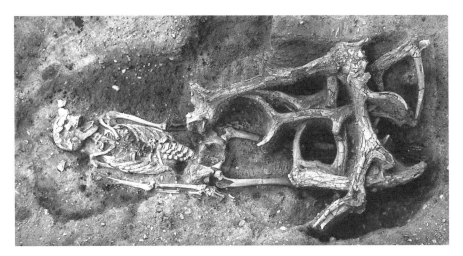

Figure 4.3 Mesolithic burial at Skateholm, showing red deer antlers which had been placed over the legs of the corpse (photo courtesy of Professor Lars Larsson, Department of Archaeology, University of Lund).

Since the excavations at Vedbæk and Skateholm, a number of other Ertebølle graves have been located in southern Scandinavia. At Strøby Egede in Jutland, a single grave containing the remains of eight individuals was found. In southern Denmark at Møllegabet, a submerged Ertebølle site yielded the remains of a dugout canoe which contained skeletal remains (Grøn and Skaarup 1991). The tradition of boat burials thus has a very long antiquity in Scandinavia!

By late Ertebølle times, farming communities were already established on the southern edge of the North European Plain. There is evidence for trade between the Ertebølle foragers and the farmers in the form of stone axes (Fischer 1982), ornaments, and knowledge of pottery production. Yet the late foragers of the western Baltic resisted agriculture for at least a millennium. The most parsimonious explanation is that they had no need for it. The maritime way of life provided adequately for their needs, and they were able to provide enough resources to support elaborate burial rituals and perennial settlements. Nonetheless, they were much different from the Palaeolithic hunter-gatherers who had inhabited Europe during the Ice Age.

HOABINHIAN PEOPLES OF SOUTHEAST ASIA

A long-term pattern of subsistence and settlement in Southeast Asia during the terminal Pleistocene and the early Holocene has been referred to in the literature since the 1920s as the Hoabinhian, after a region near Hanoi in Vietnam. Our knowledge of the Hoabinhian is hampered by the fact that before 6000 BC, sea waters inundated vast areas of the shallow Sunda continental shelf, particularly the Gulf of Siam and the Gulf of Tonkin, where

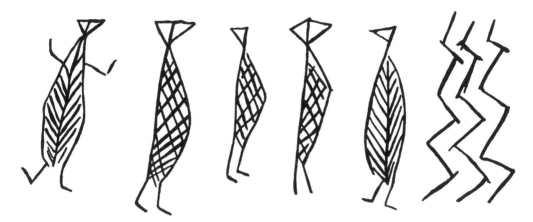

Figure 4.4 Schematic human figures, about 2–3 cm high, engraved on an aurochs bone from Rymarksgård, Denmark, often interpreted as a forager family near water (original specimen in National Museum of Denmark, Copenhagen).

many coastal Hoabinhian sites could have been expected to be found. A hint of the archaeological record which has been lost comes from late shell middens in Malaya and Sumatra which are also largely destroyed by their mining for lime. As a result, the Hoabinhian archaeological record is heavily skewed toward inland and upland rockshelters and caves.

What we know about Hoabinhian subsistence reflects an extraordinarily diverse resource base. The best-reported data come from Spirit Cave in Thailand, excavated in the 1960s and early 1970s. Spirit Cave was occupied by Hoabinhian foragers from about 11,000 to 7500 years ago. Excavations which paid close attention to subsistence remains revealed a variety of wild species, including candle nuts, butter nuts, canarium nuts, almonds, water chestnuts, cucumbers, lotus, and beans. Since many of these later became important in the diet of Southeast Asia, and since initial inspection indicated that many of the seeds were larger than would be expected of wild plants, it was suggested that the inhabitants of Spirit Cave had practiced a form of broad-spectrum horticulture that preceded rice farming (Solheim 1972). Subsequent analysis, however, revealed that the Spirit Cave plant remains were wild, gathered forms rather than domesticated (Yen 1977). Since then, however, no Hoabinhian site has provided such a wealth of subsistence data, although it is believed that Spirit Cave is representative of this culture. The inaccessibility of many parts of Southeast Asia to archaeological research and the drowning of the Sunda Shelf means that there will be an incomplete understanding of Hoabinhian subsistence for some time.

At the site of Khok Phanom Di on the Gulf of Thailand, pollen evidence indicates a long pattern of human interference with the environment before the site was actually occupied (Higham 1989a). Several burning episodes have been identified: 5800–4755 BC, 5300–4555 BC, and 4710–3960 BC. While it is possible that these episodes may be the result of natural conflagrations, it

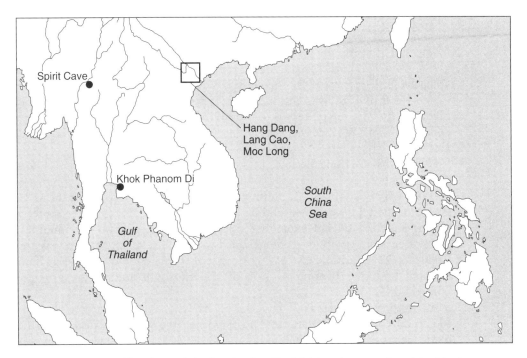

Figure 4.5 Map of Southeast Asia showing key Hoabinhian sites mentioned in this chapter.

seems more likely that they are the result of pre-agricultural interference with the vegetation, part of a global pattern discussed further below.

Hoabinhian burials are not well known. The best data comes from sites in Vietnam (Higham 1989a: 38–9). At Lang Cao, approximately 200 human crania were found in an area of about 25 square meters, without many other skeletal elements. Such a deposition suggests that the bodies were allowed to decay elsewhere and then the skulls were gathered up for burial. At the caves of Hang Dang and Moc Long, contracted burials covered in red ochre were found.

Much research remains to be done on the post-glacial foragers of Southeast Asia. The region provides a rich mosaic of food sources which might be presumed to inhibit specialization on any one plant or animal. As such, the Hoabinhian peoples are similar to the other "broad-spectrum" foragers described below and had a remarkably stable adaptation. There is even some evidence that Spirit Cave in northern Thailand was still occupied by foragers in the late first millennium AD, long after other parts of the region had adopted agriculture.

ARCHAIC PERIOD OF NORTH AMERICA

The term "Archaic" was introduced into the prehistory of the New World by William Ritchie, who used it to describe materials from the Lamoka Lake site in New York State (Ritchie 1932). These materials were clearly associated with a culture which derived its subsistence exclusively from hunting and collecting, yet existed under relatively modern forested conditions. Within the following ten years, the term became used to refer to North American postglacial foragers more broadly and eventually became formalized in the archaeological literature. By the early 1940s, the term was being applied to early sites in the midwestern and southeastern United States which clearly predated the use of pottery and agriculture. Indeed, the term was often defined in terms of what was *not* present: pottery, burial mounds, agriculture, and settled village life (Winters 1974).

Today, the "Archaic Period" in New World prehistory encompasses foragers from the Arctic to Patagonia. Under this rubric, one can find a remarkable diversity of adaptations, but in general the New World Archaic forms an analog to the Old World Mesolithic. In both cases one finds hunter-gatherer groups adapting to and exploiting essentially modern biotic communities. The discussion below will focus on two specific manifestations of the Archaic, the Maritime Archaic of eastern Canada and northern New England and the Riverine Archaic of the midsouth and midwest of the United States.

All Archaic cultures are characterized by what could be called "broad-spectrum" foraging adaptations. The breadth of the spectrum varies with the biotic richness of various habitats, but in every case the number of species exploited increased dramatically over that identified for previous periods, particularly in temperate latitudes. Again, the situation is analogous to that of the Eurasian Mesolithic and the Jomon foragers of Japan and comes as no surprise in light of the diversity and richness of Holocene habitats.

The Maritime Archaic and its Relatives: The Archaic occupation of northeastern North America received intensive scrutiny in the 1960s and 1970s by archaeologists such as William Fitzhugh, James Tuck, Bruce Bourque, David Sanger, and Arthur Spiess. In the early 1970s, Tuck defined what he called the "Maritime Archaic" of Labrador, the Canadian Maritimes, and northern New England, in which "the most important resources were in some way connected with the sea" (Tuck 1978: 32). Others would confine the Maritime Archaic *sensu Tuck* to Labrador and Newfoundland and emphasize the similarities of Archaic subsistence, technology, and settlement in New England to sites to the south and west instead (e.g., Sanger 1975). While archaeologists debate the geographical extent and variability of Archaic sites in northeastern North America, it is clear that this region supported substantial populations from very early in the Holocene, both along the Atlantic coast and in the interior.

The Maritime Archaic of Labrador and Newfoundland has a long existence, beginning about 7000 BC and lasting until about 1800 BC, a longevity reminiscent of the Jomon culture of Japan. It is best-known from several key settlements and burial sites, including L'Anse Amour, Port au Choix, Fowler, and EiBg-7. An important feature of these sites is the evidence for proficiency in exploiting the rich marine life of the cold Labrador and Newfoundland waters, especially in hunting of walrus and seals with harpoons. There is also evidence for whale hunting. Terrestrial resources, including reindeer and beaver, are clearly secondary in importance (Spiess 1993).

Maritime Archaic settlements are found along the numerous inlets and on the many small islets along the coasts of Newfoundland and Labrador. Early Maritime Archaic sites appear to be seasonal base camps and exploitation locations, with round pit-houses dug into boulder beaches. By the later part of this tradition longhouse (or long-tent) structures are found at sites like Nulliak and Alliik in northern Labrador, which appear to indicate year-round habitations. Some of the longhouses are 90–100 meters long and may have housed up to 100 people. Such concentrations of population attest to the productivity of the coastal marine-mammal hunting subsistence system.

Of particular importance in the Maritime Archaic are mortuary sites which indicate elaborate burial practices. At L'Anse Amour in southern Labrador, the burial of a child about twelve years old was found face down with a stone slab in its back beneath a low rock cairn about twelve meters in diameter. With the burial, dated to ca. 5500 BC, were a number of artifacts, including a toggling harpoon (one which twists inside its victim and prevents it from escaping). Walrus tusks and fish and bird bones reflect the maritime economy. The late Maritime Archaic cemetery at Port au Choix in Newfoundland, dating to ca. 2000–1500 BC, is a remarkable example of mortuary sophistication (Tuck 1976). Over 100 burials, many with red ochre, were accompanied by numerous grave goods. One burial of a young adult male had whalebone foreshafts of spears over each shoulder and a killer whale effigy made from stone on the chest. The number of whalebone artifacts in the Port au Choix graves indicates that the late Maritime Archaic people of Newfoundland were able to hunt large whales systematically (Spiess 1993). Numerous other antler, bone, slate, and ivory tools and ornaments, as well as inclusions of fur-bearing mammals, birds, and fish, in the Port au Choix burials not only provides rich data on Maritime Archaic technology and subsistence, but also reflects the investment in ritual made by this group.

Further south, along the Gulf of Maine, somewhat different subsistence patterns are found, as well as different technological affiliations. The Turner Farm site is located on an island in Penobscot Bay in Maine and has deposits which span 5000 years of prehistoric occupation (Bourque 1995). Of greatest interest here is Occupation 2, dated between 2500 and 2000 BC. Occupation 2 was a settlement of the people who were associated with the Red Paint cemeteries of Maine, which Bourque calls the "Moorehead Phase." Seasonal indicators among the faunal remains show that it was a year-round, or at least multiseasonal, occupation. Deer, shellfish, and marine fish such as cod, swordfish, and flounder were primary sources of dietary protein, and numerous bone fishhooks corroborate the importance of the marine resources. In contrast with the Maritime Archaic sites of Newfoundland and Labrador, however, seal and other marine mammals appear to have played a relatively minor role, although Spiess (1992) suggests that this was due to the fact that the Gulf of Maine supported relatively few seals during this period. Six dog burials were found at Turner Farm, including two with red ocher.

Figure 4.6 Map of North America and Mesoamerica showing key Archaic sites mentioned in this chapter.

Spiess (1993) and Bourque (1995) disassociate the Moorehead Phase from the Maritime Archaic described by Tuck and see it as part of a complex of interior, riverine, and coastal subsistence patterns. Numerous other Archaic sites in the northeast are found at the fall lines along major rivers. For example, at the Amoskeag Falls of the Merrimack River in Manchester, New Hampshire, a number of important Archaic sites have been found (Dincauze 1976; Robinson 1992), including a cemetery with ocher-stained cremation burials. It seems clear that further south in the more productive mixed or deciduous forests, the maritime focus becomes less pronounced in favor of varied strategies which took advantage of the diverse habitats available. Spiess (1992: 177) notes that this was "not because the coastal inhabitants were less competent maritime hunters, but because the interior offered richer alternatives in fish, small mammals, and reptiles."

The Riverine Archaic of the American Midwest: The onset of full Holocene biotic conditions in temperate latitudes in North America led to the proliferation of several important resources on which human populations came increasingly to depend. These included white-tailed deer (*Odocoileus virginianus*), mast-bearing trees such as oak and beech, and rapidly multiplying populations of freshwater mussels (both riverine and quietwater.) In the midwest (and the so-called "mid-South") of the United States, numerous sites have been excavated over the last century which were the settlements and burial locations of substantial populations who exploited these temperate-forest conditions.

The Early Archaic inhabitants of this region were heirs to the technological traditions of the Palaeo-Indians of late glacial and early post-glacial times (Meltzer and Smith 1986). Already, between 8000 and 6000 years ago, diversified patterns of subsistence were being pursued in the newly-established temperate forests. A classic site of this period is the Modoc Rockshelter in Illinois. Describing the subsistence remains in the lower levels, Joseph Caldwell (1965: 67) commented, "Everything that walked, flew, or crawled went down the alimentary tract into the inhabitants of Modoc at that time ..." At the same time, however, the Early Archaic levels at Modoc show relatively little use of aquatic resources (Styles, Ahler, and Fowler 1983: 289), despite its location not far from the Mississippi River. The gathering of nuts was also of great importance for the inhabitants of many sites. At the Icehouse Bottom site in Tennessee, hickory nuts and acorns were staple plant foods (Chapman 1985: 45).

Critical events appear to have happened between 5000 and 3500 BC throughout this region. Previously, Archaic foragers had lived in scattered campsites throughout the uplands and valleys as well as at riverine locations like Modoc. Now, however, semi-permanent settlements begin to appear at many sites, including Koster and Black Earth in Illinois, Eva in Tennessee, and Carlston Annis in Kentucky. Many of these sites appear at specific types of locations: point bars, stream and marsh edges, draws where secondary streams emerge into floodplains, and hilltops (Brown 1983: 9). Archaic foragers lived at these sites at least through the warm season and possibly throughout the year (Smith 1995b: 196).

Much of this change appears to have been correlated with a mid-Holocene amplification in the abundance of aquatic resources due to an unknown reason. The increase does not appear to have been completely simultaneous across this region. For example, at Modoc, the increase in aquatic resources appears about 5500 BC, whereas elsewhere it is perhaps a thousand years later. Such regional variation, however, might be expected as each river valley evolved along a different timescale to form sandbars and floodbasin lakes. In the Illinois River valley, there was an increase in the use of riverine mussels about 5300 BC, and about 3700 BC, the use of quietwater mussels and freshwater fish like bowfin and bullhead which are found in floodplain lakes became common (Styles 1986). Shell middens began to accumulate along many streams as human populations became increasingly "tethered" to the floodplains.

The valley base camps of the groups who exploited these aquatic resources contain storage pits and house floors, indicating significantly more commitment to particular settlement locations, although we still know relatively little about internal settlement organization. The deeply-stratified deposits at the Koster Site in Illinois provide a 6000-year record of human occupation, most of which occurred during the Archaic between 7000 and 1000 BC. The information from this site demonstrates that "significant steps toward sedentary life" took place in the Middle Archaic, beginning about 5000 BC (Brown and Vierra 1983: 166) and continued over the next 2000 years. A diversity of stone tool types reflects a variety of tasks that were performed on the site, and pit features relating to food preparation and perhaps storage are found. Of particular significance are a number of burials in two distinct plots found in Koster Horizon 6A, reflecting the emergence of formal areas for the disposal of the dead.

In addition to settlement burials such as those at Koster and Black Earth, specialized mortuary sites began to appear by about 4000 BC. Many of these are on higher parts of the landscape, where they would have been clearly visible (Charles and Buikstra 1983). Elsewhere, ceremonial mounds appear to have been constructed during the fourth millennium BC, such as the Watson Brake Mounds in Louisiana (Gibson 1994; Saunders et al. 1994; Russo 1996). Such mortuary and ceremonial sites are further evidence of the association of human groups with specific localities, much like Mesolithic burials like those at Skateholm reflect increasing sedentism in northern Europe.

The Late Archaic in midcontinental North America, between 3000 and 1000 BC, saw further elaboration of this sedentary exploitation of aquatic resources as well as an expanded degree of plant use which included local seed-bearing plants and perhaps tropical cultigens (Dye 1996). Along the Green River in Kentucky are large shell middens such as Carlston Annis (Watson 1985), which in addition to the residue of aquatic resources contained large quantities of hickory-nut shells. Not far away is the shell mound and mortuary site of Indian Knoll, where over 1100 burials have been found (Webb 1974 [1946]). Many of these burials were accompanied by exotic grave goods, such as stone tools made from non-local raw material and small amounts of marine shell and native copper. Some have interpreted this as a measure of social ranking (Boisvert 1979: 11), although Nan Rothschild (1979) has presented a compelling argument that the Indian Knoll population exhibits little variation in social status among its members. Twenty-one dog burials were also found at Indian Knoll, again a common feature of late forager mortuary sites in many parts of the world.

The end of the Archaic period saw the construction of one of the most remarkable prehistoric sites in North America, the earthworks at Poverty Point in northeastern Louisiana (Webb 1982; Gibson 1996, 1998). Built between 1730 and 1350 BC on a bluff overlooking a bayou, Poverty Point consists of six concentric ridges which enclose an open area of about 15 hectares, three small platform mounds, one large conical mound, and two mounds which appear to be the effigies of birds (Gibson 1998: 17). Gaps in the concentric ridges provide five aisles to the interior of the earthwork. Poverty Point has long been an enigma, although the discovery of earlier Archaic mounds at least provides some regional antecedents, and the debate has centered on its function. Over the last five decades, it has been alternatively proposed to have been a vacant ceremonial center serving the surrounding settlements, a large village, the seat of a theocratic chiefdom, and a vacant periodic meeting location. Despite the monumentality of the earthworks, the artifacts from Poverty Point are mundane, including an enormous number of fired clay balls that were used for boiling water after being heated. Midden deposits indicate sustained habitation. Jon Gibson's recent interpretation of Poverty Point appears to be the most reasonable: it was a special sacred place, home to a substantial number of people and a focus of ritual as well as of the long-distance exchange of stone of various types (Gibson 1996: 304). Yet following the decline of Poverty Point, no remotely comparable earthworks were built in North America for at least a millennium (Mainfort and Sullivan 1998: 2).

MESOAMERICAN HIGHLANDS AND LOWLANDS

Until very recently, much of what was known of the late foragers of Mesoamerica came from upland cave and rockshelter sites where there was good preservation of plant remains. At sites like Coxcatlán Cave and Guilá Naquitz rockshelter, Richard MacNeish and Kent Flannery conducted research in the 1960s, and these sites still provide the core of our data on late forager subsistence in the Mesoamerican uplands. Guilá Naquitz, a small rockshelter in Oaxaca, is a good example of one such site.

Flannery investigated the forager occupations which date between 8750 and 6670 BC in which a large variety of plant remains were preserved. These included acorns, maguey (a cactus-like plant in which the fleshy heart is consumed), mesquite seeds, and hackberries, as well as a small amount of squash and beans. Deer and rabbit bones were the most common animal remains found.

Flannery has proposed that Guilá Naquitz was occupied during the late summer and autumn by small bands, which MacNeish had earlier referred to as "microbands" to distinguish them from the larger groups which are believed to have been common during the Pleistocene. The actual composition of such a microband is unknown, but it is possible that it included a few nuclear families. Another possibility is that the archaeological remains at Guilá Naquitz were produced by repeated visits of even smaller, family-sized groups. In any event, it is clear that these were not fully sedentary people; rather, they occupied several sites in the course of their annual movements.

For the 20 years between 1970 and 1990, the dry cave sites in the southern Mexican uplands had produced virtually all the evidence for early Holocene foragers in Mesoamerica. Recent research in Mesoamerica supported by AMS radiocarbon dating, however, has refocused attention away from the dry upland caves towards the coastal lowlands along both the Gulf of Mexico and the Pacific Ocean. Although archaeologists have been excavating the aceramic coastal shell middens along the Pacific Coast for decades, only recently was it recognized that their basal layers all date to approximately 3000 BC. It is clear from these sites that shellfish collecting had become a major part of the subsistence by this time. Another resource, Barbara Voorhies (1976) has suggested, was shrimp, which could be collected in massive quantities and which when dried could be stored almost indefinitely. Along the Caribbean coast, by 3000 BC, swampland and estuarine habitats also were settled by hunter-gatherers. Here, a rise in sea level about this time seems to have resulted in a reorganization of the wetland habitats in a way that would have made them attractive for sustained human settlement.

Evidence for sedentism in Late Archaic Mesoamerica is elusive, however. A number of lowland sites associated with specific collecting tasks, such as shellfish gathering on the Chiapas coast or initial ventures in plant cultivation in Belize, appear to have been occupied for longer periods by about 3000 BC (Zeitlin and Zeitlin, in press). An important development, however, was the emergence of interregional trading links, particularly in obsidian and ornamental marine shells. For example, a perforated marine shell are found at the highland site of Cueva Blanca in Oaxaca came from the Pacific coast, 160 kilometers to the southeast (Marcus and Flannery 1996: 62). In addition, the Mesoamerican foragers had begun to experiment with a new carbohydrate-rich plant, maize, which could be stored for several weeks after its harvest. The implications of this will be taken up in the next chapter.

NATUFIANS IN THE LEVANT

The human reaction to the changed climatic conditions appeared most dramatically in the Near East, where – beginning about 15,000 years ago – foraging peoples underwent a series of changes. Archaeologically, these changes are represented in the Levant between 15,000 and 10,000 years ago by a variety of tool industries and cultures called the "Geometric Kebaran" and the "Natufian." The Natufian culture was discovered and named by Dorothy A. E. Garrod in 1928, but it is only in the last 25 years that it has received the systematic attention that it deserved. Although scholars disagree about many of the details of Natufian chronology and subsistence, it is clear that this period was crucial in the development of human society.

Bar-Yosef and Meadow (1995: 44) have presented a reconstruction of prehistoric climate in the Levant between 15,000 and 10,000 years ago which takes into account a variety of palaeoclimatic indicators. In their model, after cold and dry conditions, rainfall began to increase steadily from about 14,000 years ago and more rapidly after 13,000, to a peak around 11,500. Between 11,000 years ago and 10,000 years ago, there was a drier phase, after which moister conditions resumed. The dry spell between 11,000 and 10,000 is correlated with the Younger Dryas period at the end of the late glacial period in the northern hemisphere. All through this period, sea levels were rising, and Bar-Yosef and Meadow estimate that the 600 km Levantine coastal plain between Turkey and the Nile lost between 2 and 40 kilometers of its width. The terminal Pleistocene in the Levant, therefore, was characterized by the dynamic expansion and contraction of a variety of habitats, which in turn would have had an impact on foraging systems.

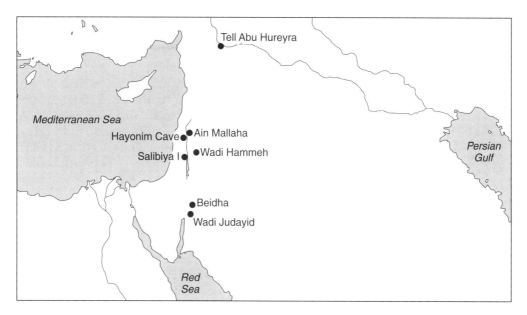

Figure 4.7 Map of the Near East showing key Epipalaeolithic and Natufian sites mentioned in this chapter.

The Geometric Kebaran industry, named after the site of Kebara Cave on Mt. Carmel, is derived directly from Upper Palaeolithic predecessors in the Levant. Its sites are found from the Mediterranean coastal zone of Israel to the Sinai peninsula and the Negev desert. There appears to have been an increase of sites in this period over preceding ones, suggesting population growth in response to post-glacial climatic amelioration. The size of Geometric Kebaran sites varies from between 15–25 m² to 600 m², with most falling into the smaller end of that range. Pounding tools, such as pestles, bowls, and cup-holes, are known from Geometric Kebaran sites in the Mediterranean coastal zone. Bar-Yosef and Belfer-Cohen (1989, 1992) interpret the Geometric Kebaran as representing small, mobile bands which experienced rapid population growth in the Mediterranean coastal zone. Regional variation in stone tools indicates constriction of local territories, which Bar-Yosef and Belfer-Cohen (1989: 487) regard as "semi-sedentary."

This constriction of territory, reduced mobility, and agglomeration of population continue and accelerate past ca. 13,000 years ago into the Natufian period. It is important at the outset to recognize that there are two Natufian phases, Early and Late, and Bar-Yosef and Belfer-Cohen (1992: 29) maintain that although many see the Natufian as a single entity, there are crucial differences between these two phases in the geography of settlement. Natufian sites are from the Euphrates to the Negev, with most in northern and central Israel and in northern Jordan. Early Natufians preferred the Mediterranean coastal and woodland zones, rarely the steppe areas further inland, whereas late Natufians established larger settlements in the steppe zone. Early Natufian sites are generally characterized by more substantial architecture, whereas the later sites have flimsier structures (Bar-Yosef and Meadow 1995).

Natufian sites include both open-air and cave settlements. An example of the former is Ain Mallaha, and of the latter, Hayonim Cave. At Mallaha, circular stone structures, varying from 4 to 9 meters in diameter, were built into the side of a terraced slope (Valla 1991). Each had a hearth, and interior postholes in some indicate the use of a wooden roof. Dispersed through the space among the houses were pits (interpreted as storage pits) and burials. Inside Hayonim Cave, similar circular structures are found (Bar-Yosef 1991). These were made of undressed stone, carried into the cave at great expenditure of energy and piled up to form rooms about 2–2.5 meters in diameter. Each such room has a hearth, indicating that its original use was probably as a habitation. Other Natufian sites in the Mediterranean zone have also yielded substantial structures.

Another type of Natufian site is found at Beidha, in the steppe zone of southern Jordan, where a campsite dating to ca. 10,500 BC has been found (Byrd 1991). Hearths and roasting areas are the only structural features found, although the variety of chipped stone tools indicates that a number of different activities were carried out on the site. Byrd interprets the Natufian

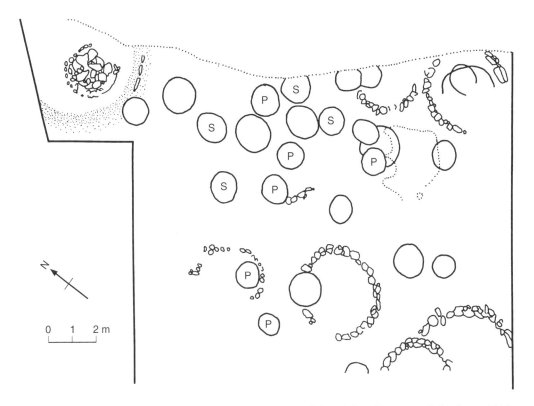

Figure 4.8 Natufian houses and burials at Ain Mallaha (after Perrot and Ladiray 1988, figure 6). P – primary (undisturbed) burials; S – secondary (reburied) burials.

encampment at Beidha as a mid-summer occupation, perhaps revisited repeatedly. At nearby Wadi Judayid (Hanry 1995), dated roughly the same as Beidha, settlement seems to have occurred during various seasons, perhaps over the better part of the year, based on the evidence from the cementum annuli in gazelle and goat teeth (Lieberman 1995).

Faunal remains at Natufian sites indicate the use of a broad range of species, which is not surprising in light of the numerous types of animals that inhabited the Levant in late glacial and early post-glacial times. The geographical setting of each site played a major role in determining the composition of its faunal assemblage, so there is no "typical" Natufian collection of animal bones. At Beidha, two species of caprines, wild goat and Nubian ibex, were the most hunted animals, followed by gazelle. At many other sites, gazelle was by far the most exploited species. This is particularly true in the coastal and woodland zones, where it often composes over 80 percent of the sample (for example, at Hayonim and Nahal Oren). At Ain Mallaha, the faunal assemblage is more diverse. Gazelle are still the most numerous, with 45 percent of the bones, but wild cattle, wild pig, red deer, roe deer, fallow deer and wild horse are also represented.

Even small Natufian sites have yielded an array of faunal species. At Salibiya I in the Lower Jordan Valley, besides the expected large number of gazelle bones, remains of wild pig, fallow deer, wild cattle, wild goat, fox, leopard, badger, hare, duck, tortoise, and raptorial birds were found (Crabtree et al. 1991). The carnivores were probably taken for their pelts, while the raptorial bird bones (primarily terminal phalanges) were possibly used for ornamentation. At Ain Mallaha, further up the Jordan Valley from Salibiya I, waterfowl and freshwater fish were heavily used (Bar-Yosef and Meadow 1995). There is some evidence for fishing in the coastal sites, although it is possible that earlier recovery techniques did not yield the small remains such as fish bones.

Considerable numbers of marine shells (either from the Mediterranean or from the Red Sea) were found at Salibiya I, often perforated to make beads. Of particular note are the eight species of marine shell found at Beidha, probably acquired from the Red Sea over 100 km away. Greenstone and malachite beads are also known (Bar-Yosef and Meadow 1995: 58). These modest finds indicate that the Natufians continued the Upper Palaeolithic tradition of personal ornamentation and also that they had contacts, either through exchange or expedition over a broad region of the Levant. On this latter note, Anatolian obsidian has been found at Ain Mallaha (Bar-Yosef and Meadow 1995: 58).

Natufian sites provide considerable evidence for the existence of formal burial areas, which can be taken as significant an indicator of sedentism as for the other late forager groups discussed above. At Ain Mallaha, for example, two types of burials have been found: individual burials under house floors and covered with stone slabs, and collective burials in larger pits outside the houses. Individual burials covered by stone slabs or in limestone cists have been found at Hayonim as well (Bar-Yosef 1991). There is little regularity in the position and orientation of the burials: some are extended, some are contracted, with heads pointing in various directions (Bar-Yosef and Meadow

1995). Some burials at Hayonim and Nahal Oren are missing their heads (Noy 1989; Bar-Yosef and Belfer-Cohen 1989: 473). Large Natufian sites typically have a large number of burials, whereas a number of the smaller sites have yielded a few burials each. The individuals appear to be largely in very good health (Belfer-Cohen, Schepartz, and Arensburg 1991), indicating that they were probably not experiencing dietary stress. Tooth size and dental disease patterns fall between those characteristic of hunter-gatherers and those of agriculturalists, probably due to Natufian use of larger amounts of ground cereals than their Palaeolithic predecessors (Smith 1991).

At Ain Mallaha and Hayonim, burials have been found in which a human and a domestic dog were buried together (Davis and Valla 1978; Bar-Yosef and Meadow 1995). The ritual interment of domestic dogs, of course, is characteristic of other late forager burials, such as those found at Skateholm and Indian Knoll. Clearly, the emergence of this species as an important part of late forager society occurred in many parts of the world at different times.

As noted above, the Natufian skeletal material suggests that large quantities of carbohydrates were consumed. How is this reflected in the subsistence remains? Unfortunately, only a few Natufian sites have yielded useful samples of botanical remains (Byrd 1989: 177). At Wadi Hammeh 27, wild barley and several species of legumes, including lentil, were recovered (Edwards et al. 1988). Hayonim Cave has also provided evidence of wild barley and legumes, as well as wild almonds (Hopf and Bar-Yosef 1987). Even at recent excavations, flotation at other Natufian sites in the coastal and woodland zones has failed to yield more than a few grains. Preservation is much better at sites further inland with deeper deposits.

Four hundred kilometers northeast of the Natufian core region, important changes took place during this period. Tell Abu Hureyra, a large multiperiod site in Syria on the Euphrates river with nearly 5 meters of deposits, was excavated in the early 1970s by a team led by A. M. T. Moore (Moore 1975, 1991; Moore, Hillman, and Legge 1999). Two major occupation phases have been distinguished. The earlier, Abu Hureyra 1, was established about 9500 BC by a group of foragers who lived in pit dwellings (the later occupation, Abu Hureyra 2, will be discussed in chapter 5). Extensive flotation of deposits at Abu Hureyra produced an enormous sample of plant remains, primarily wild einkorn wheat and wild rye, several other species of wild grasses, and several species of pulses including lentils (Hillman, Colledge, and Harris 1989). At first, all of these plants were phenotypically wild. There was a remarkable dietary diversity indicated by the carbonized seeds, which was in reality probably greater if the non-preserved tubers and rhizomes of the valley bottom are taken into account. Thus Abu Hureyra 1 can be considered to be a sedentary settlement of people practicing a particularly diverse strategy of plant collecting. This diversity can be contrasted with the faunal remains, which consist primarily of Persian gazelle (*Gazella subguturosa*). Legge and Rowley-Conwy (1987) have proposed that the gazelle were killed during their annual spring migration in mass drives, for Abu Hureyra lies at the point on the Euphrates where herds of Persian gazelle would cross. Moore (1991: 285) characterizes the focus on gazelle by the inhabitants of

Abu Hureyra as a very specialized mode of hunting. Both the plant-collecting and hunting strategies were intensive, but they represent two different types of intensity.

The onset of the Younger Dryas around 9000 BC is believed to have been the catalyst for important economic changes at Abu Hureyra (Moore, Hillman, and Legge 1999). The open park-woodland that had previously surrounded the site retreated away, leaving it in dryer open terrain. By this time, the inhabitants of Abu Hureyra 1 had graduated to timber and reed huts. They still hunted gazelle in considerable numbers and continued to gather many species of wild plants, but there is evidence now that they had begun to cultivate some species of grain, including wheat and rye in the final centuries of Abu Hureyra 1. One of the most important conclusions from the Abu Hureyra sequence is that it clearly indicates that sedentary settlement preceded the development of cultivation.

Back in the Natufian core area of the Levant, the case can be made that the large Natufian sites such as those at Hayonim and Ain Mallaha were also sedentary occupations. One indication is the amount of energy invested in the locality (Bar-Yosef and Belfer-Cohen 1989): leveling slopes to build houses on terraces; making plaster; carrying heavy stones into open and cave sites (e.g., at Hayonim) and the digging of subterranean storage pits (e.g., at Ain Mallaha). The burials also indicate sustained attachment to particular locations. Perhaps the most compelling evidence for human sedentism during this period is the sudden appearance of commensal species, particularly the house mouse (*Mus musculus*), in Natufian habitation sites (Tchernov 1991). Moreover, the mouse bones found in Natufian sites appear to have undergone rapid morphological changes from those known from pre-Natufian times, indicating adaptation to the different environment of long-term human settlement.

Bar-Yosef and Belfer-Cohen (1989: 473–4) differentiate between base camps and seasonal transitory camps in the core Natufian area, along with a continuation of the constriction of mobility which began in the earlier Kebaran complex. Natufian base camps are larger than any preceding settlements. Their broad-spectrum patterns of plant and animal exploitation and substantial architecture also differ from anything previously seen in this region. Radiating around the base camps were the seasonal transitory camps. Further inland, in the steppe and desert zones, seasonal movement appears to have been the norm (Byrd 1989), as sites like Beidha appear to blur the distinction between base camp and transitory camp.

Although there is still much to be done in the study of Natufian subsistence and settlement and its relationship with climatic change, it is clear that between ca. 13,000 and 10,000 years ago, substantial sedentary settlements, intensive hunting and gathering, and diverse patterns of land use came to characterize a particular core area of the Near East, in the woodlands along the Mediterranean and the adjacent steppes and desert. These people were foragers who lived by hunting and collecting, but they had abandoned mobility and settled down in particular locations. Of the groups in this chapter described as "late foragers," they represent the earliest case of sedentarization, yet perhaps the most consequential for subsequent developments described in the next chapter.

WAITING FOR AGRICULTURE, OR DYNAMIC ADAPTATIONS?

Although widely separated in time and space, the late foraging societies of the early and mid-Holocene (and in the case of the Natufians, the late Pleistocene) share some common characteristics. The first is that they exploited a far more diverse range of flora and fauna than their Pleistocene predecessors. The establishment of modern climatic and biotic conditions provided a wealth of new possibilities, and virtually everywhere in the world people took advantage of them. Second, their mobility was far more limited than previously, and a number of them could be considered fully sedentary or at least as having focal settlements where they spent large parts of the year. Third, and very important, is that for the first time on global scale we see mortuary behavior in which individuals either have a very high level of investment in the burial rite (e.g., the burial structure at L'Anse Amour or the Skateholm burials) as well as cemeteries where individuals are interred over time in relatively consistent ways. This is in sharp contrast with the largely ad hoc treatment of the dead in Pleistocene band societies. Although there are some Pleistocene examples of careful treatment of the dead (e.g., some of the Neanderthals at Shanidar or Kiik-Koba), the difference lies in the *consistency* in the manner by which dead late foragers were interred in their respective areas. Finally, the use of the dog for hunting and companionship occurred in very many parts of the world, and the role of dogs in human society is reflected in the mortuary treatment at late forager sites as widely separated in time and space as Hayonim, Skateholm, and Indian Knoll. When considered on a global scale, we see that many late foraging societies between 12,000 and 3000 years ago were doing very similar things.

All of these similar characteristics have considerable implications for the evolution of human society in many parts of the world. The remainder of this chapter will discuss these, particularly with regard to the transformation of Pleistocene band societies into a new kind of social configuration, which in turn laid the foundation for subsequent developments.

ATOMIZATION OF BAND SOCIETY

The late glacial and early post-glacial shifts in environment and subsistence practices in the northern mid-latitudes can be argued to have triggered a shift in human residence patterns and the organization of foraging behavior. Under these temperate climatic conditions, large bands operating collectively may not have been the optimal approach to the exploitation of diverse resources. Smaller, more flexible groups whose structural backbone was the family unit rather than an aggregation of mated pairs would have been able to forage more efficiently under the new conditions. Another factor that accelerated this trend may have been the more-pronounced seasonality of the post-glacial climate. This phenomenon has already been discussed in connection with the extinction of the Pleistocene megafauna. A heightened sense of seasonal rhythm and time would have established temporal limits to seasonal activity requiring cooperative behavior, such as game drives. As Glance and Huberman (1994) have pointed out, one factor in the degree to which individuals choose to collaborate in a group or to defect is their sense of how long a particular social interaction will last. A sense that after a certain point cooperation under the old band structure would not be in the self-interest of a family unit would have accelerated the atomization of the post-glacial foraging society.

Finally, the expectations and complex patterns of sharing, or "tolerated theft" (Blurton Jones 1991), which had built up among local populations over many millennia may simply have reached a breaking point. This might be expected under conditions of rapid local population growth, which the rich post-Pleistocene habitats may have encouraged. Under conditions of rapid population growth, one would also expect populations characterized by a large proportion of young individuals to emerge very quickly. This segment of society may simply not have been invested in the sharing ethos of their elders, and from one late forager community to another, younger people may have opted out of their communal expectations.

Perhaps the sharing ethos of Pleistocene band society may simply have ceased to be of much use in the new resource-rich modern environment. Indeed, the reason why band societies exist today in marginal environments may be that relative resource impoverishment encourages the continued adherence to sharing norms as a form of economic insurance. Low population densities do not overload the web of sharing obligations leading to hoarding and aggrandizement. Children continue to be liabilities in collecting because they get lost, tired, and thirsty (Blurton Jones, Hawkes, and Draper 1994), so there are disincentives to having them at shorter intervals. This is not to say that groups like the !Kung San are Pleistocene survivals, for there is some evidence that they have undergone substantial transformations of their own over time. The point is simply that once modern resource-rich environmental conditions were established in many parts of the world, the incentives for sharing diminished, as did the tolerance for contributing one's production to a common pool. There was more than enough for everyone.

PROTO-HOUSEHOLD AUTONOMY

The proposition that I would like to advance here is there was a significant transition in human organizational behavior during this period, beginning with the automization of Pleistocene foraging bands into smaller family-centered units and ending, in many regions, with autonomous co-residential groups with stable foci of residence. What can we call such autonomous residential groups? Some (e.g., MacNeish 1964; Flannery 1972) have used the term "microband," although this usage suggests that there was not a fundamental change in cooperative behavior from the earlier "macroband" organization of the Pleistocene. At the other end of the scale is the "household," which implies a sense of place in addition to a fixed co-residential group.

My own view falls towards the household end of the spectrum, although to many anthropologists, the notion of hunter-gatherer households may sound like an oxymoron. Yet the late forager societies around the world were not, like the !Kung San, living in a marginal environment. In every case mentioned above, and many more as well, they lived in the resource-rich, highly-productive habitats which appeared at the end of the Ice Age. Modern ethnographic analogs to the intensively hunting and collecting sedentary foragers of the early and mid-Holocene really do not exist today. The closest parallels would be the historically known Native American groups of the Northwest Coast of North America such as the Kwakiutl, Haida, and Tlingit. There is no question that the fundamental economic and social unit among the sedentary Northwest Coast maritime foragers was the household which occupied a single gable-roofed house (e.g., Matson 1996; Whitelaw 1991). In the ethnographic present, these groups are truly unusual, but in the early and mid-Holocene, such sedentary foragers were found in many different parts of the world. If it is possible to consider the Northwest Coast foragers as not being characterized by the band organization common among other extant foragers, but rather as household-based communities, then it is equally possible and likely that the Natufians of the Levant of the maritime and riverine foragers of North America were similarly organized.

In a spirit of compromise with skeptical anthropological colleagues, however, let me call the atomized units of late forager society "proto-households" to differentiate them from the developed households that characterized agricultural societies beginning a few millennia later. The term "proto-household" is preferable to anthropological jargon like "co-residential group" and conveys the sense that later developments were predicated on changes that took place prior to the onset of agriculture.

The most important consequence of a transition from cooperative bands to autonomous proto-households is that the behavior, success, and failure of the smaller group is clearly recognizable rather than being submerged and homogenized within the larger group. Such smaller units can exercise initiative and resourcefulness and take risks. Clearly the potential for failure exists as well, but the post-glacial environment may have offered so many new possibilities (and perhaps redundancies of resources) that for the first time in millennia the risk may have been relatively low or at least manageable. Again, the need to share in order to mitigate risk may have suddenly diminished in a number of key parts of the world between 12,000 and 3000 years ago.

Autonomous households freed of the sharing norms of Pleistocene band society also would have been free to experiment with new methods of plant and animal use. In a society where food must be shared, the incentive to produce more than one can consume is to yield the social benefits that come from sharing. Yet, there is little incentive to produce a whole lot more, since the social return will not be commensurate with the effort expended. If the sharing obligations were lessened or eliminated, a late forager proto-household for the first time could feel free to maximize its exploitation and to use it the way it saw fit for its own benefit. First, it might choose to make sure that its own dietary minima were met. Second, it might decide voluntarily to share some of it in the hope of some future reciprocity. Third, it might exchange it for a desirable commodity such as marine shell in the Levant or Ramah chert in the Canadian Maritimes. In short, the late forager residential group would have had more options for disposing of its bounty beyond a formulaic pattern of distribution as in Pleistocene band society.

SEDENTISM AND OPTIONS

A key characteristic of many late forager societies is sedentism. According to Kent (1989: 2), sedentism is the opposite of nomadism along a continuum of mobility. In other words, if nomadism represents the movement of a group on a landscape, sedentism is the lack of such mobility. Of course, no human group of community is entirely sedentary, just as none are absolutely nomadic. All fall between the two extremes on this continuum, although for classification purposes they can be characterized as one or the other depending on their state of mobility/non-mobility which is most prevalent.

For foraging societies, mobility provides a variety of options for adjusting conflicts and imbalances: in scheduling, in resource availability, in population, in social transactions. Increasing sedentism, or lack of mobility, implies that the options afforded by mobility would also decrease. Alternative structures need to be developed to resolve the same imbalances. These would include storage, exchange, social structure, ritual, and warfare. These factors, however, open the door to further challenges posed by increasing complexity in social and economic structures, which Johnson (1982) has called "scalar stress." One solution would be to invoke the remnants of the mobility option, as settlements fission and relocate. Another would be to elaborate extramural ways of addressing imbalances, such as trade and warfare.

Sedentism also represents a shift in the human approach to territoriality and time (Carlstein 1982). It also permits the accumulation of material possessions, allows the making of a new range of artifacts such as pottery, provides a stable place to find people for social contact and exchange, and enhances conditions for population growth. Higham and Maloney (1989) note that where food resources are predictable, sufficient, and storable, sedentary communities can expand their horizons, develop complex ranking behavior, and accumulate status and obligations. New demands are made on the creation of goods to signal such status.

Sedentary life, then, has its pros and cons. On one hand, it opens up a new conception of space and its ordering which permits a number of things which were suppressed in mobile society, such as accumulation and the manufacture of heavier artifacts. On the other hand, it places a great burden on band society and the sharing it demands. Overloaded sets of social obligations cannot be divested simply by moving away, and the options that a community has for resolving imbalances between resources and requirements are reduced.

A SENSE OF PLACE

Parkington and Mills (1991: 355) define place as "space given meaning," and argue that the settlements that people create "are not merely reflections of, but material manifestations of, the social formation." Pleistocene settlements consisted either of caves and rock shelters or of windbreaks in clearings (notable exceptions being the mammoth-bone dwellings in Ukraine). In both cases, the inhabitants adapted to a physical setting, but they did not make extensive physical alterations in the natural facilities. Parkington and Mills suggest that "custodianship" may be the appropriate term for such relationships to dwelling locations, and more broadly to land and resources, which are managed but not owned and not considered to be the property of any individual or family. This is consistent with the Pleistocene band ethos of sharing discussed in previous chapters.

In the sedentarization of the late foragers, this relationship changed dramatically. House structures were clearly the domain of a defined and bounded group of people. It is difficult to imagine the inhabitants of Ain Mallaha deciding to sleep in a different circular structure each night, with a different set of people. Rather, each structure was the domain of a residential group, and there is no difference between this dominion and actual ownership of the structure. These are not communal structures, as were the caves of the Ice Age or even the Kostenki longhouses. Rather, late forager buildings everywhere they are found are small and demarcated.

Parkington and Mills (1991: 365) argue that the way that people build structures and arrange them into settlements is not a passive reflection or symbol of social relationships. Rather, they make clear choices which "actively [organize] power relationships and the practice of social interaction." This is what was taking place in late forager societies around the world. People were making conscious decisions about how to organize their space within sedentary communities, and these decisions moved forward the atomization of band society.

The appropriation of space by a residential group is directly opposed to the band norm of sharing or "tolerated theft." In a sense, it is the hoarding of a resource just like food or stone for tools. Parkington and Mills (1991: 357) point out that !Kung San camps are very open with few boundaries, which "[guarantees] the evenness of resource acquisition and the relative egalitarianism of interpersonal relations." This is in contrast with the deep domestic structures at Hayonim Cave, oriented away from any central space and closed to the larger world.

ACCUMULATION, STORAGE, AND TRADE

A by-product of sedentism that is often overlooked is the opportunity that it provides for the accumulation of goods and the fixing of the position of the residential group so that it can engage in trade on a regular and systematic basis. Pleistocene bands generally travelled very lightly. While a good dry cave, if it could be found, or a mammoth-bone longhouse may have served some groups well, by and large they did not accumulate possessions that they needed to transport. Sedentism, on the other hand, promoted all sorts of accumulative behavior. Good-quality flint and shed red deer antler could be stockpiled for future use. Harvested wild seeds could be cached and fish could be dried for the winter. In short, a residential group could go from being devoid of more than the smallest portable items to being loaded down with baggage in the space of a few generations.

From accumulation, it is a short step to storage, whose development has a number of consequences (Testart 1982). Testart (1988: 172) makes some important observations on the economy of sedentary "storing hunter-gatherers," as he calls them. In many cases, the bountiful natural environment is also characterized by significant seasonal variations in the abundance of key resources. Mobile, non-storing foragers simply move about, but storage permits these seasonal variations to be damped. Yet what is substituted for seasonal variation in resource abundance is seasonal variation in *work*. The storing hunter-gatherers must work intensely during the peak seasons, and during the time of the year when they live off stored resources, they have much more free time. This pattern of seasonal variation in labor intensity, of course, parallels that which characterized agriculturalists, about which more will be said in chapter 6. Testart (1988: 173) argues that storage is *not* a way of coping with uncertainty in food supply, for the seasonal variation in abundance is perfectly predictable. In other words, it is not insurance but rather part of a calculated and planned economic strategy.

We see in storage another important shift from Pleistocene band society to late forager society: from economic strategies that function to prevent overall starvation and minimize risk to strategies which assume a certain amount of risk in the hopes of amplifying a group's ability to exploit rich but seasonally-variable resources. Moreover, the appearance of storage redefines the rights of residential groups or "proto-households" to subsistence resources. If in Pleistocene band society an animal was divided up and consumed immediately, there was no investment in the preservation of the meat for future use. The advent of storage meant that whatever residential group invested in the preservation of a resource and constructed a facility to keep it suddenly had a much greater investment in the resource by the time it was consumed. If there was any factor which "put the nail in the coffin" of Pleistocene band society, it may well have been this consequence of storage. Once a late forager group developed the ability to "time-shift" the abundance or resources in this way, there would be no going back to the enforced sharing and risk-minimization of Pleistocene band society.

Storage plus sedentism equals substantially increased opportunities for trade. The fact that a sedentary community is in a predictable and known location means that they can engage in trade in a much more sustained fashion than any previous exchange systems which depended on unpredictable encounters between mobile Pleistocene bands. People with something to trade can find the community, and if the community has access to a particular resource, others know where to find it. Trade, in turn, presents another opportunity for accumulation and another incentive for a residential group to produce beyond its nutritional minima.

MORTUARY RITUAL

The emergence of consistent, formalized burial ritual and of specific areas for the disposal of the dead is a significant development among late forager societies whose importance cannot be overstated. It is the beginning of a particularly human characteristic, treating the dead individual as an entity whose significance for the society lasted beyond the end of his or her life. No longer did people bury their dead and walk away from them. Instead, they had an attachment to the dead which played an important role in the lives of the survivors.

Why do we see this sudden change? A possible explanation lies in the replacement of friendship and putative kin bonds beyond the immediate family which characterized Pleistocene band society with an elaboration of the network of kinship and segmentation of society which presumably were a concomitant of sedentism. Lives ceased to be terminal, ephemeral, bounded existences. Suddenly it mattered who your grandparents, uncles, aunts, spouse(s), cousins, and children were. Residence defined your node in this network, and it was in your interest to mark your location in time and space by positioning yourself among your ancestors and relatives.

The notion of generations now takes on additional meaning, which will have consequences later on. Property and kinship must be passed from one generation to the next in some orderly and, from the perspective of the living, advantageous fashion. Mortuary ritual is one way of working out such transitions, as the living relatives come to grips with the departure of an individual not only from the physical life but also from the social life of the family and community.

Thus the sudden interest in mortuary ritual, I argue, is linked to this emerging sense of self-identity and its situation in a larger social setting across space and time. As such, it plays a role in the transgenerational perpetuation of the social order. I would not, however, like to overdraw this point and insist, as Foucault (1977: 24) has, that the body is invested with power relations. It simply is another aspect of the restructuring of society which took place in late forager times as part of a complex of changes triggered by sedentarization.

MANIPULATION OF THE ENVIRONMENT

There is ample evidence that foragers are open to the adoption of new behavioral patterns, and many are enthusiastic experimenters. The results of these experiments are incorporated into their practices as part of a system of knowledge about their environment. Griffin (1989: 69) notes that the Agta of the Philippines "are constantly experimenting with different emphases in food procurement." The nineteenth-century Kumeyaay of southern California had a complex understanding of plant biology and ecology that was acquired by experimentation and maintained over time (Shipek 1989: 165).

Such experimentation with their natural surroundings undoubtedly occurred among early Holocene foragers around the world. One possible stimulus to such experimentation would have been the breakdown of the sharing regimen of Pleistocene band society, with the result being that foraging households were motivated to explore new possibilities for increasing their subsistence yield. Households or groups of households could create opportunities for increasing yields of nuts, berries, and wild herbivores without the obligation to share these resources with minimal personal return. There would have been room for individual initiative and resourcefulness that had been hitherto suppressed by mandatory sharing.

One area where ecological knowledge is manifested regularly among modern foraging societies is their use of fire to create and maintain plant associations which are economically productive. Lewis (1991) has discussed the patterns of burning among aboriginal populations in the Northern Territories of Australia (as he did earlier with reference to the Native American populations of California and Alberta) as a reflection of a complex system of ecological knowledge. The Aborigines' knowledge, presumably gained over millennia of observation and experimentation, of the causes and effects of various patterns of burning enables them to manage a complex ecosystem to maximize a broad spectrum of resources.

Mills (1986) documented the practice of environmental manipulation by foragers through burning on a global scale. In her view, "it is clear that hunter-gatherer populations understand at least the effects of the successional process, if not the specific principles" (1986: 14). In most cases of temperate zone burning, increasing primary biotic production was the central goal of forager burning. Mills points out another important by-product of burning by temperate-zone foragers, namely that grasses and herbaceous plants may appear two to three weeks earlier on burned areas because the blackened soil absorbs and retains heat. In regions with marked seasonality and the short vernal florescence of herbaceous plants in the unaltered deciduous forest, such manipulation of the spring verdure would have had a direct effect on subsistence by shifting the productivity forward and increasing the duration of the productive understory growth. As was the case with storage, this is another example of the capacity of late foragers to "time-shift" the abundance of resources.

What effect would these burning disturbances have had on late forager subsistence? It is possible to presume that the benefits enumerated by Mellars (1976), particularly the spatial concentration of game, its increased biomass, and improved reproductive biology would be most appreciated by the foragers, as well as the production of economically useful herbaceous species, including hazel, for basketry and traps. There is also the possibility that such burned-over localities were dynamic habitats in which many things were possible. For example, by attracting herbivores to predictable locations, the foragers would have their pick of the herd rather than being satisified with animals killed on a chance "encounter" basis. Thus the herd could be systematically culled, while it was provided with a stable food supply, preventing the boom-and-bust cycles common among wild herbivore populations.

DECISIONS, DECISIONS

When visitors from eastern Europe came to the United States in the era of communist regimes, it was hard to resist not taking them to an American supermarket almost as soon as they had landed. A cousin from Poland remarked to me on one of these visits, "I don't know how I would manage in this sort of place. In Poland, when I want to buy toothpaste, I go to the store and buy the one tube marked 'Toothpaste' and pay the one set price. Here you have so many brands, so many sizes, and each a different price. I don't know how I would be able to decide what to buy!" My cousin now lives in Canada and manages just fine with these decisions, and people in eastern Europe now have the same decision-making challenges, but the anecdote illustrates an important point about the transition from glacial to post-glacial conditions in the northern hemisphere. The new richness of resources forced foragers to a level of sophistication about making decisions which they had never really faced before in such a widespread and sustained way.

If my argument that the primary organizational units of society became smaller entities which approximated households, then it is also likely that these units became the primary units of decision making. Inevitably, there was variability in their talent for doing this. Some chose to be safe and to avoid risk, while others may have been daring and accepted risks as a normal price of doing business. Some decisions would have been wise, while others would have been faulty. In some cases, smart decisions led to big payoffs, while in other cases the residential group's survival may have been placed in jeopardy.

The unequal or random distribution of intelligence, stupidity, bravery, foolhardiness, memory, dexterity, and intuition among such smaller social units would have had interesting consequences. Some groups would have been more successful in managing their affairs than others. Do the roots of social inequality lie herein? Perhaps they do in some very vague and diffuse sense. Yet it is difficult to perceive any evidence of institutionalized and self-perpetuating inequality at this time. Whatever may have existed due to the differential success of individual "proto-households" probably was ephemeral and transitory. In other words, the fortunes of a residential group may have been down one year and up the next, and no one in the larger community really remembered or cared about this variation over time. Other developments were necessary for inequality to become institutionalized, which will be addressed further in chapter 7.

CONCLUSION: THE GREAT TRANSITION

The restructuring of the subsistence infrastructure caused by the new post-glacial possibilities ultimately resulted in a fundamental restructuring of human society in many parts of the world between 12,000 and 3000 years ago. Such restructuring occurred along very different timescales in the Old World and the New World, but fundamentally many of the same processes occurred in many places widely separated in time and space. At the core of this transition were the possibilities afforded by the rich habitats that arose after the Ice Age. Such rich environments no doubt existed at earlier times, but they had not had such a profound impact on the nature of Pleistocene band society as they did later on. The resultant focusing of human subsistence activities on seasonally-abundant and storable resources led to sedentary life and a resultant atomization of the risk-averse Pleistocene bands into smaller units, which I have termed "proto-households."

Such a restructuring was an indispensable prerequisite for subsequent economic and social developments, such as agriculture, institutionalized inequality, and urbanism. To a large degree, modern humans crossed a very important threshold in their existence very recently, beginning about 12,000 years ago. The profound effects of this transition are only now coming to be realized. No longer can the Mesolithic of the Old World and the Archaic of the New World be seen as a static period of people in waiting. They were truly times of momentous change.

FURTHER READING

There are very few general volumes on post-Pleistocene foraging peoples. Instead, information must be gleaned from regional case-studies, site reports, and review articles. In addition, discussions of the origins of agriculture often contain information on pre-agricultural peoples; some good sources are listed at the end of the next chapter. A review article by T. Douglas Price (1991) entitled "The Mesolithic of Northern Europe" provides a good baseline of information about the post-glacial foragers of that region, although new information is continually forthcoming. Mesolithic burials at Skateholm and nearby sites are discussed in Lars Larsson's "The Skateholm Project: late Mesolithic coastal settlement in Southern Sweden" in Peter Bogucki's 1993 *Case Studies in European Prehistory* volume. Stanton Green and Marek Zvelebil describe post-glacial sites in Ireland in a piece in the same volume. In North America, Bruce Bourque's *Diversity and Complexity in Prehistoric Maritime Societies: a Gulf of Maine Perspective* (1995) provides a good case study of post-glacial foragers in the northeastern part of the continent. *Of Caves and Shell Mounds*, edited by Kenneth Carstens and Patty Jo Watson (1996), contains a number of papers which discuss foraging sites in the interior riverine area of North America. Natufian societies in the Near East and their congeners are discussed in Donald Henry's 1989 *From Foraging to Agriculture: the Levant at the End of the Ice Age,* while copious amounts of primary data are found in *The Natufian Culture in the Levant*, edited by Ofer Bar-Yosef and F. R. Valla (1991). A recent volume by Andrew M. T. Moore, Gordon Hillman, and A. J. Legge, entitled *Village on the Euphrates: The Excavation of Abu Hureyra* (1999) provides a comprehensive description of the important site of Tell Abu Hureyra. A picture of the Jomon foragers of Japan must be pieced together from a variety of sources, but a chapter by C. Melvin Aikens in *The Emergence of Pottery*, edited by William Barnett and John Hoopes (1995), provides an overview and a description of the earliest pottery. Very little general information is available in widely-available sources on the Hoabinhian foragers of Southeast Asia.

[5] SEEDS FOR CIVILIZATION

INTRODUCTION

One of the most extraordinary developments in the existence of the genus *Homo* was the successful shift from a subsistence economy based wholly on foraging to one based primarily on domestic plants and animals. For over two million years, human beings had obtained their food from scavenging, hunting, fishing, and collecting. Only within the last ten thousand years did markedly different subsistence economies based on cultivated plants and, in many areas, domesticated animals replace hunting and gathering around the world. When viewed from the long-term perspective taken in this book, the origin and dispersal of food production took place remarkably rapidly and very recently.

The origins and dispersal of food production has been a major focus of archaeological research for several decades, much of which has been concentrated on the areas and periods in which plants and animals were first domesticated from indigenous wild species. Considerably less research has been done on adoption of domesticated plants and animals and the techniques of agriculture and animal husbandry by populations who did not domesticate the species themselves, as well as the spread of populations practicing agriculture into areas where it had been hitherto unknown.

THE NATURE OF THE EVIDENCE

An extraordinary amount of research has occurred in the last 50 years to document the initial appearance of domesticated species of plants and animals. The techniques for the recovery, identification, analysis and interpretation of botanical and faunal remains have been improved markedly. In the late 1960s, there were only a handful of individuals around the world with expertise in seeds and bones. Today, a large expanded cohort of researchers have developed the necessary skills in identification and analysis. During the 1980s, the technique of radiocarbon dating using an accelerator mass spectrometer enabled the dating of very small (under 5 mg) samples, which in many cases correspond to the weight of individual seeds or small animal bones. Much of the evidence for early plant domestication in eastern North America, for instance, rests on AMS dating (Fritz and Smith 1988; Smith 1989).

The critical evidence for early domestication, as it always has been, remains the seeds and bones of the plants and livestock in question. There are several critical aspects to this evidence which enable researchers to differentiate between wild and domestic species. The first is metrical evidence, the sheer dimensions of the seeds or bones. In plants, the seed is usually the desired element for human consumption. Domestic seeds, then, tend to be generally larger than their wild counterparts. For example, modern marsh elder (*Iva annua*) achenes average 2.5 to 3.2 mm in length. A sample of 44 marsh elder achenes from the Napoleon Hollow site in Illinois dating to ca. 2000 BC averaged 4.2 mm and thus have been assessed as domesticated (Asch and Asch 1985). With animals, the issue is control, so domestic livestock are often smaller than their wild counterparts. In Neolithic Europe, for example, very large pig bones are taken to be the remains of wild boars, while smaller versions of the same bone are probably from their domesticated cousins.

Another crucial differentiating factor between wild and domestic elements is the morphology of certain diagnostic elements. In wheat and barley, the stem that connects the grain to the stalk is called the rachis. Wild wheat depends on a brittle rachis to shatter when the seed is ripe, which allows it to fall to the ground and propagate the stand of grain. For humans, the brittle rachis is not desirable, for it would result in the head of ripe wheat shattering when touched and individual grains falling to the ground, instead of staying intact to be harvested as a unit and then threshed. So, early human cultivators selected for a flexible instead of a brittle rachis, which can now be identified in the carbonized grain and chaff. The horncores of wild sheep and goat have different shapes and proportions than their domestic counterparts. Moreover, the confinement of livestock may be manifested as increased frequency of arthritic conditions, while the shift from wolves to domestic dogs is correlated with a greater frequency of dental cavities due to the increased amount of soft food in the diet.

Quantities of a species or proportions of different age groups in an archaeological assemblage which might be considered markedly different from what one might find in a wild population are also frequently taken as indicators of domestication. A few *Chenopodium* seeds on a site in the midwestern United States could be considered the accidental by-products of human gathering, while a bag with several thousand *Chenopodium* fruits could indicate intensive gathering or incipient cultivation (Fritz and Smith 1988). Faunal assemblages with large numbers of immature individuals are sometimes argued to reflect domestication, even if there is no other evidence. Gazelles in the Near East have sometimes been the subject of such debate (e.g., Legge 1972), but simulation studies by Hans-Peter Uerpmann (1979) have indicated that sustained hunting pressure will also eventually produce a kill population that is dominated by juveniles.

Finally, geography is an important indicator of domestication. Sheep and goat have no wild counterparts in temperate Europe, so when they appear on sites in that region there is no question of their domestic status. Similarly, when maize cobs appear on sites in woodland North America, there is no question that this tropical zone hybrid is domesticated. The interesting biogeographical issues occur on the margins of the zones where wild populations of plants and animals occur naturally. Presumably, a key aspect of domestication is the human movement of these species outward from their natural habitats to new zones where they do not occur. So, the seeds of a plant or bones of an animal found outside its natural habitat, even if they show no metrical or morphological effects of domestication, mean one of two things: either, that the prehistoric natural habitat was larger and encompassed that area as well, or that they are the remains of species in the very initial stages of human control and propagation. Such instances are usually occasions of intense debate among archaeologists, zoologists, and botanists.

ORIGINS AND DISPERALS

The study of the transition to agriculture encompasses two broad categories of processes: (1) the domestication of plants and animals within specific geographical regions, and (2) the dispersal of food production, in the form of agriculture or animal husbandry, outward from these core areas. Paul Minnis (1985: 309) has used the term "pristine domestication" to refer to situations in which the human control and manipulation of a species is sufficient to cause phenotypic changes for the first time. As can be seen from the discussion below, a number of such centers in which it appears that the concept of agriculture was independently developed have been identified in recent decades. Throughout the remainder of the globe, the techniques and, in many cases, biological raw materials for agriculture and stockherding were introduced from elsewhere. As Minnis points out, such cases have been more frequent and more widespread than the instances of pristine domestication, and he uses the term "primary crop acquisition" to describe them. Such a terminology reflects a New World perspective in which domestic animals are absent, and in many parts of the Old World a good case can be made for livestock having been the first domesticates to penetrate the frontier between foragers and farmers.

THE CENTERS OF INITIAL DOMESTICATION

In 1971, Jack Harlan, an American botanist, identified three main centers of pristine domestication within which the major complexes of domesticated plants and animals were first established: the Near East (emmer, einkorn, barley, peas, lentils, sheep, and goats), North China (millet and rice), and Mesoamerica (beans, chilies, maize, and gourds). As extensions of the Near Eastern center can be added Anatolia and the Indus Valley, where cattle (and pigs, in the case of Anatolia) were domesticated from local stocks. To Harlan's three localized centers of domestication can be added one more which has come to light in the last 15 years. In the inland river valleys of eastern North America, Smith (1989, 1992) has argued for the presence of an independently-developed complex of domesticates that includes squash, sumpweed or marsh elder, sunflower, and chenopod.

Figure 5.1 presents a simplified chronology of early domestication in these areas and several other regions discussed further below. A review of the literature available in 1999 reveals the degree to which this chronology is either still uncertain or can be revised very quickly by new finds. Moreover, in almost every area there are equivocal earlier finds which may or may not be evidence for domestication. Some researchers accept these, while others do not. As a result, the chart presented here reflects the earliest *secure* evidence for a particular domesticate in any given area.

THE NEAR EASTERN EVIDENCE

Although archaeologists know that such statements are risky, at the time of writing the earliest transition to agriculture in the world occurred in the Near East. More specifically, it took place in the arc which reaches from the southern Levant north into Anatolia and then east and southeast along the foothills of the Zagros mountains, known as the "Fertile Crescent." Exactly where in the Fertile Crescent this took place is still open to some discussion, for the geopolitical realities of the late twentieth century have steered the focus of research around the map. In the 1950s and 1960s, the foothills of

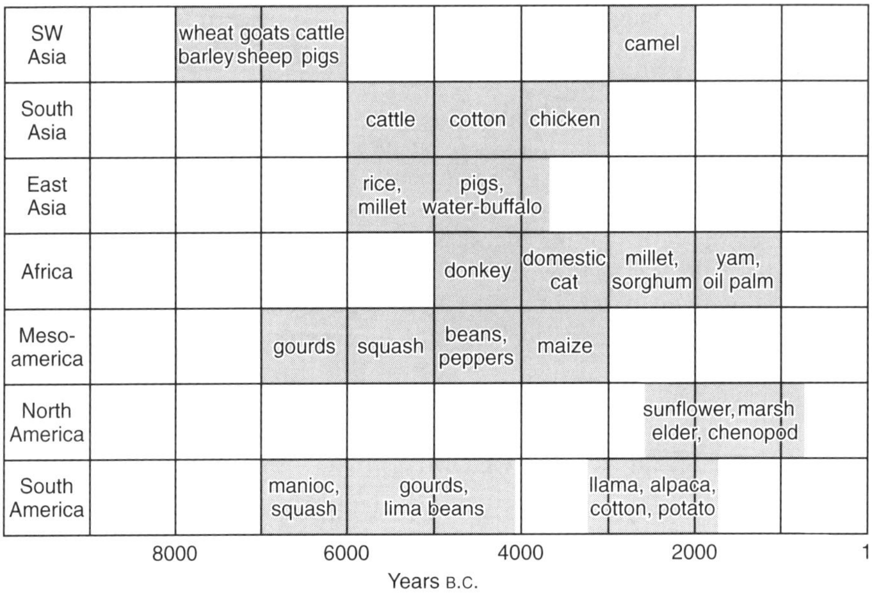

Region	8000–7000	7000–6000	6000–5000	5000–4000	4000–3000	3000–2000	2000–1000	1000–1
SW Asia	wheat barley goats sheep cattle pigs					camel		
South Asia			cattle	cotton	chicken			
East Asia			rice, millet	pigs, water-buffalo				
Africa				donkey	domestic cat	millet, sorghum	yam, oil palm	
Meso-america		gourds	squash	beans, peppers	maize			
North America							sunflower, marsh elder, chenopod	
South America		manioc, squash	gourds, lima beans			llama, alpaca, cotton, potato		

Years B.C. (axis: 8000 6000 4000 2000 1)

Figure 5.1 Schematic chronology of domestication in different world regions.

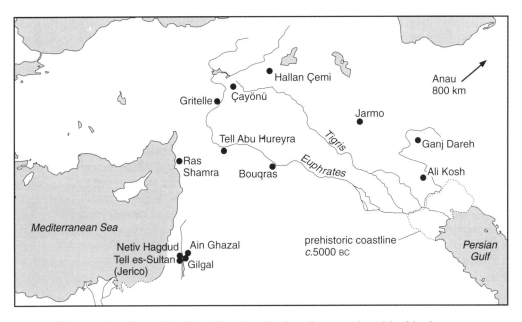

Figure 5.2 Map of the Near East showing key sites mentioned in this chapter.

the Zagros mountains in Iraqi Kurdistan and Khuzistan were the focus of research on the topic, at sites like Jarmo, Ganj Dareh, and Ali Kosh. In the early 1970s, sites on the upper Euphrates river in Syria were threatened by dam construction, resulting in the excavation of important settlements like

Tell Abu Hureyra. Until 1967, the Jordan Valley was the border between two states at war, but with the occupation of the West Bank, this region became available for archaeological research, leading eventually to excavations at Ain Ghazal and Netiv Hagdud. In 1980, however, the Iran–Iraq War turned the Hilly Flanks of the Zagros into a war zone, curtailing much of the study of agricultural origins in this area.

As this is being written in the late 1990s, the best available evidence indicates that the origins of Near Eastern agriculture occurred in a very limited area, which Ofer Bar-Yosef and Anna Belfer-Cohen (1992) have called "the Levantine Corridor." This inland zone, about 10 kilometers wide and 40 kilometers long, reaches from the Damascus Basin in Syria to the lower Jordan Valley. Ten thousand years ago, it would have been one of the moister parts of the Levant, with numerous lakes and springs and alluvial fans with high water table. If cereal cultivation were to begin anywhere in this region, the Levantine Corridor would be the prime location, for it included both stands of wild wheat and barley and the optimal habitats for early cultivation. The Natufian foragers who lived in this region had only to decide to make these two elements come together for cultivation to begin.

In the previous chapter, the late foragers of the Natufian culture were discussed, and the clear implication was that the origins of agriculture should be profitably sought among these communities. Actually, the identification of the Natufians as the earliest farmers was first made by Dorothy Garrod in 1932 and taken up by V. Gordon Childe in 1936, although at that time there was scant evidence of their subsistence practices. Nearly 70 years later, however, many archaeologists are not prepared to accept that the Natufians were farmers. Instead, the conventional wisdom is that they were intensive harvesters of wild cereals. Clearly, however, important changes in subsistence occurred somewhere at the end of the Natufian period, although there is an unfortunate lack of palaeobotanical evidence from this key moment. Somewhere in this period, about 10,000 years ago, the last hunters became the first farmers.

The first farmers who follow the Natufians are known by the technical name of "Pre-Pottery Neolithic A," or PPNA (although Uerpmann [1989] urges that this terminology be abandoned). It is generally accepted that PPNA people engaged in intentional cultivation, although the domesticated status of the grain finds from their sites is the subject of discussion. Hillman and Davies (1992) and Zohary (1992) believe that grain from a number of PPNA sites, including Jericho, Gilgal, and Netiv Hagdud, bears signs of domestication, whereas Kislev (1992) argues on the basis of experimental threshing evidence that the barley from Gilgal and Netiv Hagdud is still morphologically wild. At this point there is no sign of animal domestication, with the Natufian pattern of intensive gazelle exploitation continuing.

Emmer wheat, einkorn wheat, and barley are the three "founder crops" of Near Eastern agriculture (Zohary and Hopf 1993: 15). The principal marker of domestication in these plants lies in the rachis, or the stem which holds the grain to the ear. Other markers of domestication lie in the architecture of the spikelet, or the grain with its associated glumes and barbs, including a loss of features which enabled the grain to penetrate the ground on its own. How long might it have taken for this selection process to have yielded completely distinct populations of domestic cereals? Hillman and Davies (1992) believe that it could have occurred in about three centuries – 300 harvests and plantings. Cereal plants with tough rachises would not have been able to propagate themselves in wild stands with any reasonable degree of long-term success. But several centuries of human selection by cutting off heads of grain or pulling up whole plants on which the grains were held by tough rachises, then saving some of this grain for planting the following year, would have quickly produced plants dependent on humans for their propagation.

Perhaps the most famous PPNA site was that found at Tell es-Sultan, a place which has been identified securely as having been the biblical Jericho. Excavations by Kathleen Kenyon between 1952 and 1958 found a settlement of an early farming community surrounded by a substantial stone wall with a tower about 9 m in diameter at the base and about 8 m tall. Kenyon interpreted this site as a very early fortified town inhabited by several thousand people. As such it would be unique not only among PPNA sites but also for several subsequent millennia in the Near East. Bar-Yosef (1986) has presented an alternative interpretation in which the walls have a defensive function, but against water flowing from the copious spring at the Jericho oasis rather than people. Oval and circular houses with silos indicate a sedentary settlement, while numerous adult burials had their skulls removed, a typical PPNA practice. Unfortunately, subsistence remains were not recovered at Jericho in a way comparable with that of modern excavations.

A recently excavated PPNA site with good faunal and botanical remains is Netiv Hagdud in the lower Jordan valley, 13 km north of Jericho. Research conducted by Bar-Yosef and his collaborators in 1983–6 (Bar-Yosef et al. 1991) revealed a settlement with circular and oval structures and storage facilities. Two types of dwellings were identified: large oval structures 8–9 m long and smaller circular buildings 4–5 m in diameter. Their foundations were made of limestone slabs, upon which were built walls of unbaked mud bricks which were supported by wooden posts. The storage features also occurred in two forms: bins about 40 cm in diameter and 40–50 cm deep and clay silos about 1 m in diameter. Twenty-two burials at Netiv Hagdud occurred in a flexed position in shallow pits, both inside and outside houses. As at Jericho, adult crania had been removed, while those of children were left in place with the rest of the body.

Subsistence remains from Netiv Hagdud indicate that the environment of the lower Jordan Valley was completely different from that of today. It was clearly wetter, as shown by the many species of migratory waterfowl. Fish and eels were caught in a body of water nearby, as were freshwater mussels, snails, crabs, and frogs. Rodents and lizards were also part of the diet. The large mammal species that were exploited were gazelle and wild pig. A tremendous variety of wild plants, including nuts like figs, pistachios, almonds, and acorns, were consumed at Netiv Hagdud, but most importantly, thousands of barley fragments were recovered. As noted above, there is some discussion about the domesticated status of this barley. Bar-Yosef and his colleagues believe that it was cultivated, but had not yet undergone the morphological changes associated with domestication.

Four hundred kilometers to the northeast of Netiv Hagdud, the inhabitants of Tell Abu Hureyra (whom we last saw at the time of their initial venture into agriculture in chapter 4) also acquired greater experience with the cultivation of cereals and pulses during the ninth and eighth millennia BC (Moore, Hillman, and Legge 1999). Abu Hureyra 2, as this settlement is known archaeologically, was a cluster of mud-brick houses. When the inhabitants of these houses died, they were often buried under the house floor, and households appear to have occupied the same locations, as structures were rebuilt over time. During the early centuries of Abu Hureyra 2, Persian gazelle was still the main meat species, but in time, a new element was added to the economy: flocks of domesticated sheep and goat. The keeping of domestic livestock was perhaps a response to declining gazelle populations. By 6000 BC a mature mixed-farming economy was in place at Abu Hureyra, with cattle and pig added to the suite of domestic animals.

Just as emmer, einkorn, and barley were the "founder crops" of Near Eastern plant domestication, sheep and goat were the "founder animals" of ungulate domestication, with pig and cattle following about 500 years later. Goat domestication appears to have taken place earliest in the Zagros mountains. Hesse (1984) has used the population structure of the faunal assemblage from Ganj Dareh in western Iran to document goat herding there about 7000 BC, and the metrical analyses by Uerpmann and Helmer cited below support this position. The practice of herding goats then shifted to the western portion of the Fertile Crescent. Sites with the earliest evidence for early sheep cluster somewhat to the north of the Levantine Corridor in Syria and southern Turkey. Uerpmann (1987) and Helmer (1989) have documented the progressive size diminution in sheep bones from sites such as Bouqras, Çayönü, and Ras Shamra during the period between 6700 to 6200 BC.

The range of wild cattle and pigs is much larger than that of wild sheep and goats, and thus it has been more difficult to identify the core areas of early pig and cattle domestication. Rosenberg et al. (1995) have argued that the age profile of the pig bone assemblage from Hallan Çemi in Turkey shows evidence for domestication, or at least cultural control, about 8000 BC, which would make pig domestication earlier than that of sheep or goat. Metrical data are equivocal at this point in the analysis, however. Other analyses (e.g., Kusatman 1991) indicate that size diminution in pig may be evident at Çayönü in Turkey at the middle of the PPNB period (about 6500 BC) and at other Anatolian sites like Gritelle by late PPNB (about 6300–6200 BC). Cattle appear to have been domesticated last, with Grigson (1989) able to trace size diminution through a broad part of the Near East beginning about 6000 BC.

Between about 10,000 and 8000 years ago, agricultural economies took root in the Near East, specifically in the Fertile Crescent. Smith (1995a) has outlined a three-stage model of this process which is a useful way to summarize what we know about it in the late 1990s. The first stage is the experimental cultivation of cereals on well-watered areas in the Levantine Corridor, which triggered the morphological changes that mark the domestication of wheat and barley. Some communities incorporated farming into their subsistence, while others nearby continued their late forager lifestyle unabated. In the second stage, goats came under human control in the Zagros mountains, and roughly about the same time sheep are domesticated in the northern Euphrates valley. The various elements of a fully-agricultural economy began to fit together, with cereals and caprovines (sheep [*Ovis*] and goats [*Capra*]) complementing each other. In the third stage, numerous farming communities adapted the complex of plants and animals, with the addition of pigs and eventually cattle, to their local conditions, and a robust agricultural economy became the norm in many different Near Eastern habitats.

THE EAST ASIAN EVIDENCE

East Asia has its own distinctive pattern of agricultural development which has come into focus only in recent years. Despite the fact that early farming villages had been excavated in the 1920s at sites like Anyang, decades of geopolitical and ideological unrest have disrupted the study of early farming in this region. Nonetheless, Zhimin (1989) reports that between the 1950s and late 1980s, 7000 Neolithic sites were discovered in China, and hundreds of them were excavated. This evidence is making its way slowly into western journals and books, and a clearer picture is emerging of agricultural origins in East Asia.

It is clear that East Asia developed its agriculture independently from that of the Near East. From the evidence currently available, it appears that there were two separate foci of this change. One was on the Huanghe, or Yellow, River valley in northern China and its tributary the Wei, while the other was on the middle and lower drainage of the Yangzi River in southern China. Each region has its distinctive "founder crop." In the Huanghe basin, it is foxtail millet, *Setaria italica;* in the Yangzi valley, it is rice, *Oryza sativa.* Although rice domestication has attracted the most attention, due to the continuing role of this species in feeding a substantial portion of the world's population, the early millet farmers of northern China deserve attention as an outpost of early domestication.

The wild precursor of foxtail millet is green bristlegrass, *Setaria viridis,* a common Eurasian weed (Zhimin 1989; Zohary and Hopf 1993: 83). As with the Near Eastern wheats and barley, the wild and cultivated forms of foxtail millets differ in their methods of seed dispersal, with the wild form shattering and the domestic form retaining its grains. Foxtail millet is a warm-season cereal which does well in dry conditions and has a short growth cycle, making it very suitable for the environment of northern China. Deep deposits of loess, a dry but very fertile windblown soil, along the Huanghe River and its tributaries provided ideal growing conditions for this plant. Crawford (1992: 29) has pointed out that the north China environment at this time would have been very similar to that of the Near East at the time of early domestication there.

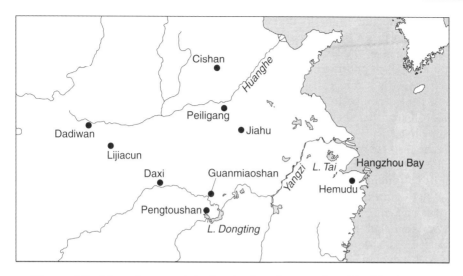

Figure 5.3   Map of eastern Asia showing key sites mentioned in this chapter.

The earliest farming culture of the Huanghe valley is called Peiligang, after the name of the site where it was first identified in Henan province (Harlan 1995: 146; Zhimin 1989; Higham 1995: 134). By now some 40 sites have been identified in several clusters, and an impression of their subsistence system, settlement form, and technology is now emerging. Peiligang, Cishan, Dadiwan, and Lijiacun are key sites, each reflecting a regional variant of this same early farming culture. Peiligang sites are small villages covering 1–2 hectares with small round houses 2–3 m in diameter. Storage pits are a very common feature, reminiscent of the storage pits and silos found in PPNA houses in the Near East. These have yielded plant remains, most commonly millet, and sickles and grain processing tools such as querns and rolling stones attest to the prominence of millet in the diet. Numerous burials are found on Peiligang sites as well, including 114 at Peiligang itself, with the heads generally pointing towards the south and with pottery, stone tools, and ornaments (Higham 1995: 136).

The animal bones from Peiligang sites have provided equivocal evidence for animal domestication. Domesticated pigs have been reported from Cishan (Smith 1995a), although the basis for their identification as domesticated is not known. Cishan has also yielded the remains of chicken (*Gallus gallus domesticus*), which would make it, at about 6000 BC, the earliest evidence for domestic fowl. The chicken, however, is believed with some confidence to have been derived from the red jungle fowl of Southeast Asia. In order to appear in north China by ca. 6000 BC, it must have moved northward from Vietnam through southern China at an earlier date in domestic form.

We do not know much about the antecedents to the Peiligang culture at this point, and it will be important to search for them. Just as wild wheat and barley were important food resources before being domesticated, it seems likely that green bristlegrass will be found to have been heavily used by the late foragers of the Huanghe valley. It will be especially interesting to see how these hitherto poorly-known hunter-gatherers of early Holocene China fit the pattern of late forager society discussed in the previous chapter. They may not necessarily be located on the dry loess deposits, however. I believe it is more likely that they will be found in wetland habitats such as those which appear to have existed to the east of the Peiligang area along the lower Huanghe (see map in Higham 1995: 135).

Six hundred kilometers to the south, in the Yangzi drainage, there are indeed wetland areas which have emerged in the last decade as a likely hearth of rice domestication. The middle and lower Yangzi valley has numerous lakes and marshes reaching from the inland Hubei basin to the coastal plain near Shanghai, and the known range of wild rice has been extended northward to include this area. Until very recently, the known range of wild rice was a belt extending from the foothills of the Himalayas in eastern India across northern Thailand and Burma into southern China and northern Vietnam, and many have argued that rice cultivation began in this area and spread north and south (e.g., Chang 1989). Recent work, however, has pointed directly to the Yangzi valley as the area where rice was probably first domesticated (Smith 1995a; Higham 1995; Underhill 1997). This picture may change, however, for rice remains earlier than 6000 BC have recently been reported from Jiahu in Henan in the Huanghe drainage, far to the north of any known distribution of wild rice (Chen and Jiang 1997).

In the Hubei basin, 800 kilometers inland, the Yangzi enters a lowland zone of lakes, wetlands, and meandering streams. A number of early farming settlements have been found in this region, as well as a number of equivocal sites which may represent either incipient agriculturalists or late foragers who were intensively collecting wild rice. Excavations at Pengtoushan revealed a large site with rectangular houses about 5–6 meters on a side and a midden deposit indicating several centuries of occupation. Radiocarbon dates place this settlement between 8500 and 7800 years ago. Rice was the only plant recovered, and on the basis of the sedentary nature of the community, it has been judged to be domesticated. In the absence of clear morphological signs of domestication in the rice remains themselves, I would urge caution on this point.

Whether the inhabitants of Pengtoushan and other early Yangzi sites were cultivators or gatherers of rice, however, it is clear that they were the forerunners of the rice-growing communities that followed them in the next two millennia. By about 6500 years ago, farming communities were well-established at sites like Daxi and Guanmiaoshan, living in houses very similar to those found at Pengtoushan. Whether or not they used domestic animals is unclear at this point, although if the chickens from Cishan in northern China are to be accepted, their precursors had to cross the Yangzi basin on the way north from Southeast Asia.

On the coastal plain south of Shanghai, 800 kilometers to the east of the Hubei basin, a series of sites have been found which also indicate early rice agriculture at this time. This region, south of the mouth of the Yangzi on either side of Hangzhou Bay, was another zone of marshes and lakes during the mid-Holocene, to which extensive peat deposits attest (Higham 1995: 136). Hemudu is the best-studied Neolithic settlement of this region, excavated over several seasons in the 1970s. At Hemudu several timber long-houses were built on piles which raised them above the wetlands where the settlement was located. The waterlogged deposits yielded large amounts of animal bones and seeds. Faunal remains included bones of domesticated dogs, pigs, and water buffalos, along with fish and waterfowl. Huge amounts of botanical material was recovered, including remains of water caltrop (*Trapa* sp.), fox nut (*Euryale ferox*), and especially of rice. The rice from Hemudu is undeniably domesticated on the basis of its sheer quantity and on morphological grounds (Higham 1995: 137). To the north, near Lake Tai, more pile-dwelling sites in wetland habitats have provided more evidence of early cultivation.

There is much work yet to be done on the origins of agriculture in East Asia (Underhill 1997). In particular, the study of the late foragers which preceded the first farmers in this region must be intensified. Nonetheless, the parallels with the Near Eastern evidence are striking in their focus on wetland or lacustrine habitats and the exploitation of a number of diverse species including fish and waterfowl. As in the Near East, animal domestication, first of pig and then of cattle, appears to have followed the earliest cultivation. At the moment, the evidence points towards north China as an independent center of millet domestication and the Yangzi valley as the location of rice domestication, which then spread south to the late forager communities of Southeast Asia, Indonesia, and the Philippines.

THE MESOAMERICAN EVIDENCE

For several decades, beginning in the 1960s, the origins of agriculture in Mesoamerica, and thus for all of the New World, were believed to lie in the dry upland caves of central Mexico. Sites in this region, particularly in the Tehuacán valley, yielded carbonized specimens of what appeared to be the earliest cobs of maize. Maize, *Zea mays*, is a peculiar species of hybrid plant whose origins are hotly debated by palaeobotanists. It belongs to a family of plants which also includes teosinte and *Tripsacum*, all of which have the same basic morphology *except* for that of the female ear. The relationships among these races of plants has been the subject of contentions and acrimonious debate among botanists.

Paul Mangelsdorf of Harvard, perhaps the grandfather of maize studies, maintained that teosinte had nothing to do with maize and the maize derived from a wild progenitor which later went extinct. George Beadle of the University of Chicago, on the other hand, maintained that teosinte was the ancestor of maize. This debate raged for many years, until relatively recently, when several researchers (Hugh Iltis of the University of Wisconsin, Bruce Benz of the University of Guadalajara, and John Doebley of the University of Minnesota) established fairly conclusively that wild populations of teosinte were the ancestors of modern domestic maize (Iltis 1983; Benz and Iltis 1990; Doebley 1990).

Doebley sought and found remote wild populations of teosinte in upland Mexico and examined their biochemistry. He found that teosinte populations which were most similar to maize were found in the central Balsas river valley, about 250 km west of Tehuacán. Little archaeological research has been done to look for early agricultural sites in this area, but it would appear that it would be important to at least identify sites where wild teosinte or teosinte in the process of being transformed into maize through the development of flexible rachis and other domesticated characteristics could be found. As yet, none have, so the Tehuacán record remains the baseline.

The problem is that the Tehuacan maize now does not appear to be as old as was once thought (Fritz 1994). Recent AMS radiocarbon dates negate, or at least call into question, the standard ca. 5500–4500 BC dating of the Coxcatlán phase from which the earliest cobs in the Tehuacan sequence come. These new dates indicate that the earliest maize at Tehuacan does not date any earlier than 3500 BC. Although it may be possible that there may be areas with earlier maize, such as the Balsas river valley mentioned above, it is unknown at this point how *much* older domesticated maize one might expect to find as opposed to undomesticated teosinte.

The revision of the dating of the emergence of agriculture in Mesoamerica actually resolves an anomaly which has existed in the global study of transitions to agriculture. As Gebauer and Price (1992: 8) note, evidence from Mesoamerica often has been raised as a major exception to the pattern seen in many other parts of the world of a rapid commitment to the use of domesticates once they become available. When the earliest maize was dated before 5000 BC, there followed a prolonged period in which the lives of the foraging peoples who adopted maize hardly changed. Villages of people dependent on agriculture and the other consequences that agriculture brings (discussed further in the next chapter) did not appear until about 2000 BC, so for about 3000 years it appeared that the extreme productivity of maize was hardly exploited. Such a difference from the other centers of domestication was not particularly troubling, for archaeologists expect differences which need to be explained, but the problem was that there appeared to be no reasonable explanation for the retarded impact of maize domestication. Now, with the time interval between incipient agriculture and maize-based village communities much shortened, the Mesoamerican situation is more in line with other major instances of plant domestication in the Near East and north China, in which changes occurred rapidly after the onset of domestication.

THE NORTH AMERICAN EVIDENCE

For decades, it was presumed that North America was not involved in early domestication. Maize, squash, and beans could be shown to have spread from Mesoamerica northward at a relatively slow pace, reaching the northern boundary of their prehistoric distribution in the woodlands of the northeastern United States and southern Canada about AD 1000. In the mid-1980s,

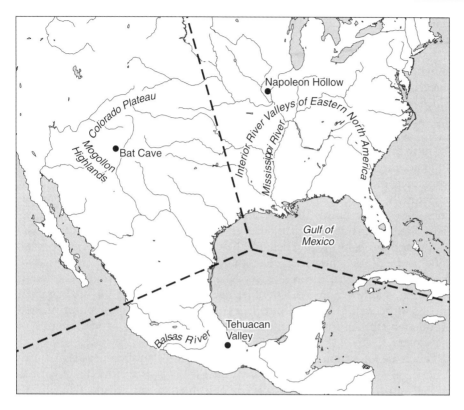

Figure 5.4 Map of North America and Mesoamerica showing key sites and regions mentioned in this chapter. Dotted lines divide chronologically distinct areas. Sites in Mesoamerica date to ca. 5000–3000 BC; sites in eastern North America date to ca. 2500–1000 BC; sites in western North America date to 1500–1000 BC.

however, the archaeologist Bruce D. Smith brought together a number of strands of domestication theory and new empirical evidence to propose what he calls the "floodplain-weed theory" of the domestication of four seed plants in the river valleys of eastern North America (Smith 1993, 1995a, 1995b). Although sunflower, squash, marsh elder, and chenopod did not form the basis for a monumental agriculturally-based civilization, Smith makes a convincing case that these four species were brought under cultivation between 2500 and 1500 BC in numerous disturbed habitats.

To a far greater degree than in the examples of pristine domestication reported above, Smith's model grows as much out of the theorizing of botanists about the circumstances of domestication as it is based on empirical evidence. Smith gives particular credit to the American botanist Edgar Anderson, who pointed out in the 1950s the importance of natural open habitats in providing niches in which plants could evolve into aggressively-growing forms which could be transplanted into anthropogenic open habitats and be manipulated by humans. He also notes the contribution of Jack

Harlan and J. M. J. de Wet in the 1970s, who described the consequences of intentional human intervention in the life cycle of plants on seed size (greater stored food reserves lead to increased seed size) and seed coat (reduced germination dormancy leads to thinner seed coat). This framework informed his analysis of samples of squash, marsh elder, sunflower, and chenopod seeds which had been accumulating for decades but which were recovered in increasing numbers through the use of techniques like flotation in the 1970s and 1980s.

Smith's "floodplain-weed theory" is essentially as follows: prior to about 5000 BC, foragers in eastern North America used a wide variety of plant and animal resources, including the marsh elder, chenopod, and squash that grew in naturally-disturbed habitats along rivers. After 5000 BC, human populations came to be drawn to these locations by rich riverine resources, especially shellfish (as described in chapter 4 above). They harvested these seed plants and brought them back to their settlements. Somewhere between 2500 and 1500 BC, however, clear morphological changes in the seeds of these plants, as well as in the seeds of sunflower, occurred. The seeds of squash, sunflower, and marsh elder became larger, while the seed coats of chenopod became thinner. Smith takes this to mark the clear onset of food production, rather than simply the intensive harvesting of wild stands of these plants.

The issue of whether or not there was wild squash in eastern North America is very interesting. For many years, wild squashes found along roads in the mid-south United States were presumed to be escapees from cultivation (i.e., of squashes which had been originally domesticated in Mesoamerica). Smith, however, has done extensive field surveys in this area which have produced good evidence for wild *Curcurbita pepo* populations along floodplains in isolated regions far from where they could have escaped from agriculture. He believes that squash was domesticated once in Mexico at an early date, and independently in eastern North America around 2500 BC at the same time that sunflower, marsh elder, and chenopod were domesticated and prior to the arrival of Mexican races of *C. pepo*.

"NON-CENTERS" OF DOMESTICATION

In addition to the focal points in which pristine domestication was part of a complex transformation of society, Harlan also identified three larger, non-localized regions in which domestication of a number of species of plants and animals also occurred. In South America, the potato and several camelid species became critical resources for highland populations, while in the lowlands manioc became a staple food. In the northern half of Africa, sorghum and possibly millet and cattle were early domesticates. Finally, in a broad region of Southeast Asia and Pacific islands, a complex of tree and root crops was managed, cultivated, and eventually domesticated.

In six of these areas, the crops and livestock which form the backbones of many different subsistence economies around the world were domesticated for the first time. The case of early domestication in eastern North America

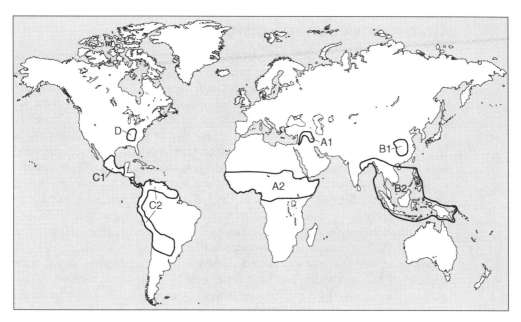

Figure 5.5 Map of centers and "non-centers" of pristine domestication. A1, B1, C1, and D are centers, while A2, B2, and C2 are larger regions in which initial domestication cannot be localized more precisely (A1–C2 after Harlan 1995, with addition of D after Smith 1992).

presents an example of a complex of plants which were superseded in later times by the Mesoamerican maize–beans–squash complex and which until their recent revival in health-food circles were not cultivated to any appreciable extent. Thus domestication is not a completely irreversible process, although had not the Mesoamerican domesticates been introduced it is likely that the use of indigenous domesticates would have persisted in North America.

Dolores Piperno and Deborah Pearsall have recently made a case for the early indigenous development of agriculture in the lowlands of Central America and northern South America at roughly the same time as it did in the Near East (Piperno and Pearsall 1998). In their interpretation of evidence from pollen and phytoliths (diagnostic silica structures formed in plant tissue), as well as starch grains embedded in grinding stones, Piperno and Pearsall propose that the cultivation of household gardens in which a variety of plants were grown arose in this area between 6000 and 7000 BC. After 5000 BC larger fields and tuber beds were prepared, leading to the pattern of agriculture known as "slash-and-burn" which characterizes rural cultivation in this area today. The principal crops involved were roots and tubers like manioc and arrowroot, squashes, and tree fruits like palm, as well as a primitive variety of maize. Although the evidence for maize cultivation is still equivocal (see Smith 1995a: 157–8 for a critique of the data), the evidence for early tuber and tree crop domestication is more compelling. New discoveries from the region in coming decades will surely be important for the study of pristine domestication in this large area.

GLOBAL AGRICULTURAL DISPERSAL

From these primary centers of domestication, food production spread outward. There are two fundamental processes in agricultural dispersals: movement of farming or pastoral peoples to settle new territory and the adoption of food production by indigenous people who had not previously done so. Although archaeologists are now reluctant to ascribe prehistoric change to movements of peoples (an explanation which had been applied uncritically in the early days of archaeology), it is clear that in some areas colonization occurred. The second process took place when local hunter-gatherer populations integrated elements of agricultural subsistence and technology, which eventually transformed or replaced their foraging lifestyle. Archaeologists must establish first which of these two processes prevailed in any given area before proceeding further with the study of how farming communities came to be established outside the core regions of pristine domestication. In some areas, these two processes occurred side-by-side, with the agricultural colonization of habitats which had been little-used by post-glacial foragers occurring in the vicinity of foraging populations who eventually came to adopt domestic plants (and in the Old World, animals).

Once a regional consensus is reached on whether colonization or local adoption was the dominant mechanism of agricultural dispersal (and in many places such a consensus has not been yet reached), further questions are posed. For example, in cases of colonization, it is crucial to understand what factors led prehistoric communities to relocate or disperse. When indigenous foragers adopted agriculture, archaeologists seek to determine why the prehistoric communities would forsake a reasonably comfortable way of life for the risk and uncertainty that agriculture entails and to examine the changes in social and economic organization which occurred as a result of this transition.

EUROPE

Agriculture came to Europe from the Near East beginning about 6000 BC. By about 3000 BC, agricultural communities had been established from the Aegean to the Orkneys and from the Dniepr to the Tagus. Europe presents an interesting case study in agricultural dispersals (Bogucki 1996a; see Whittle 1996 for a complementary view). The mechanisms of this dispersal varied. Several factors caused this variability: the climate, soils, and drainage of a particular region; the size and organization of pre-existing foraging populations; and the choices made by farming peoples about crops, livestock, and community organization. The resultant mosaic of agricultural communities persisted over many centuries. In some areas, agricultural peoples themselves dispersed, bringing a sedentary lifestyle, crops, and livestock. Elsewhere, indigenous populations which had previously lived by foraging gradually adopted agriculture.

The possibility of independent domestication of several key plants and animals in Europe can be safely excluded. Although wild einkorn wheat has

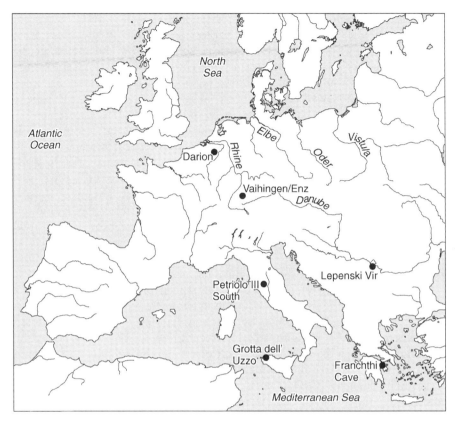

Figure 5.6   Map of Europe showing locations of sites mentioned in this chapter.

been claimed to occur in Greece and the Balkans, Zohary and Hopf (1993) suggest that these European habitats have a segetal or secondary character and that wild einkorn did not exist there prior to the opening of these areas for agriculture. More importantly, the wild distributions of the two principal Near Eastern founder crops, emmer wheat and barley, do not approach Europe. Similarly, wild sheep and goat do not occur in Europe, and thus no independent domestication could have occurred. On the other hand, wild cattle and wild pigs did occur in the European forests. Claims have been made for independent domestication in a variety of areas, such as Hungary (Bökönyi 1974) and northern Germany (Nobis 1975), but further analysis indicates that most of the specimens presented as evidence are probably small wild individuals (Rowley-Conwy 1995).

For the most part, then, the introduction of an agricultural economy to Europe involves the transport and propagation of species which were not only completely non-indigenous to the area but also adapted to considerably warmer and less seasonal climates. While the environment of Mediterranean Europe bears some resemblance to that of the Near East, temperate Europe to the north has landforms, soils, and climate hitherto not encountered by farmers of wheat and barley and where sheep and goats had never been seen. Yet within about 3000 years of the earliest agriculture in the Near East, Neolithic farming settlements had been established near the mouth of the Rhine. In another two millennia, nearly the entire continent – except for the boreal forests of Scandinavia, the Baltic region, and Russia – was occupied by farmers. When viewed in this light the achievements of the first European farmers at such northern latitudes are even more remarkable.

In light of the Near Eastern origins of wheat, barley, sheep, and goats, it is not surprising that the earliest European farming settlements are found in Greece. At this moment, there is little archaeological evidence of early farmers on either side of the Bosporus, although further fieldwork may revise this view. Van Andel and Runnels (1995) argue that the first farmers of Europe came via an island-hopping route through the Aegean. They then colonized the rich alluvial plains of Thessaly, which would have been the optimal energy-subsidized habitats for wheat and barley in this region. Other than at Franchthi Cave in southern Greece, there is relatively little evidence that indigenous foragers played a role in this first farming toehold in Europe.

For several hundred years, however, the spread of agriculture came to a standstill, while to the north of Greece indigenous foraging peoples still populated the Balkans. The method by which agriculture eventually continued its northern spread is a matter of some recent debate. For many years, the prevailing view was that it was the result of the continued spread of farming populations out of Anatolia (Van Andel and Runnels 1995) although it was occasionally challenged (e.g., Barker 1975b; Dennell 1984, 1992). Recently, Haskel Greenfield (1993) and Alasdair Whittle (1996) have also called the conventional view into question. Greenfield points out that the adoption of agriculture by indigenous farming peoples should produce a variety of local patterns, which he points out quite clearly in the patterns of animal use in the central Balkans. In his view, indigenous peoples may have played a much larger role than has been hitherto believed. At the same time, however, we can clearly see the adjustment made by farming peoples to the temperate conditions. Cattle and pig began to become more common than sheep and goat, while wheat and barley became summer (rather than winter) crops.

In the Iron Gates gorge on the border between Serbia and Romania, a group of late foragers flourished in the midst of the spreading tide of agriculture. Perhaps the best-known of their settlements is Lepenski Vir, excavated in the 1960s prior to inundation by a hydroelectric project (Srejović 1969). Located next to a whirlpool at a bend in the Danube, Lepenski Vir is a multi-period settlement with numerous trapezoidal-plan huts, each with a stone hearth and often with enigmatic stone sculptures with human-like faces but with fish-like mouths. Animal bones reflect an economy which relied on riverine resources, although bones of red deer and boar are also common in the early levels. In the latest layers, pottery and bones of domestic animals are found. One interpretation of Lepenski Vir and nearby sites is that they were settlements of hunters and fishers who resisted the adoption of agriculture through their successful foraging adaptation and only belatedly incorporated domestic plants, livestock, and pottery into their economy. Another

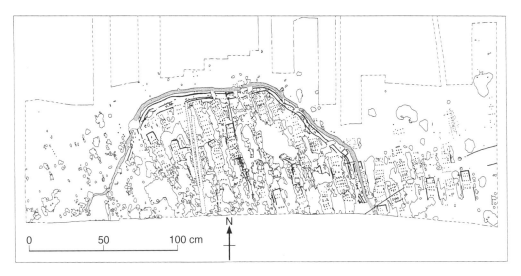

0   50   100 cm   N

Figure 5.7 Plan of part of the excavated area at the Linear Pottery settlement of Vaihingen/Enz in southwestern Germany, showing longhouses and boundary ditch (line drawing courtesy of Dr Rüdiger Krause, Landesdenkmalamt Baden Württemberg).

view is that they represent foraging communities which had already adopted a sedentary lifestyle prior to the appearance of agriculture and then very quickly adopted food production once it became available nearby.

North of the Balkans, farming societies underwent further transformations. As in Greece, there is good evidence to indicate that the alluvial soils of the major drainage systems of central Europe were colonized by farming peoples who spread rapidly from the central Danube region west to the Rhine, Maas, and Aisne valleys and north along the Elbe, Oder, and Vistula (Bogucki 1999). Not only are domesticated cereals, sheep, and goat not indigenous to this region, but also there is no pre-existing tradition of pottery manufacture or the construction of timber longhouses. Although Alasdair Whittle (1996) has argued recently that the settlements of the first farmers of central Europe were not as permanent as has been recently believed, the existence of fortification ditches at many sites (Keeley 1996: 137) indicates that significant commitments were made to particular residential locations. In central Europe, cattle predominate the animal bone samples which, along with the presence of ceramic sieves, has led me to argue that dairying was an important part of the Neolithic economy in this area (Bogucki 1984, 1986).

Yet again, however, the agricultural diaspora came to a halt, along a line running along the southern part of the North European Plain, the northern foothills of the Alps, and the Atlantic coastal regions of western Europe. Unlike the dry uplands of central Europe, these regions had been inhabited by large populations of indigenous foragers, who had no immediate need for agriculture. For about 1000 years, communities of farmers and foragers existed adjacent to and intermingled with each other. We can infer that relations between these two groups were mixed. In some areas and at some times, a placid multicultural mosaic existed, while elsewhere and at other times, the interaction was evidently hostile (as suggested by the fortification ditches at sites like Darion in Belgium and Vaihingen/Enz in Germany).

Eventually, however, domesticated plants and animals, along with pottery and stone tools, began to pass through the frontier between these two populations and had an impact on late forager society which had already undergone significant changes. I and others have argued (Davidson 1989; Bogucki 1995a) that feral domestic animals were the first taxa to pass through the agricultural frontier. In northern Europe, foragers' modifications to the landscape which created lush artificial glades may have provided these escaped cattle, sheep, and goat with excellent conditions for survival. They could have been incorporated into the Mesolithic diet first as new hunted species, then quickly reverted to domestic behavior when brought into the settlements. Crops and agricultural techniques could have been traded from farmers to foragers in exchange for forest products like furs, game, and honey. The clearest evidence for such semi-agrarian behavior comes from the Rhine-Maas delta in the Netherlands (Louwe Kooijmans 1993a), where foragers supplemented their hunting, fowling, and fishing with livestock and cereals.

At the same time, agricultural sites spread along the Mediterranean coast westward to Spain. Recent research has shown that this was a complex process, and there is no consensus whether it occurred through colonization or adoption of domesticates by late foragers. Much evidence supports a theory that indigenous foraging communities selectively adopted certain features of a food-producing economy nearly a millennium before sedentary agricultural settlements appear. In Tuscany, pottery at the site of Petriolo III South in levels from the late seventh millennium BC is unaccompanied by evidence for an agricultural economy. Evidence from the wave-damaged site of Grotta dell'Uzzo in Sicily suggests that by the early sixth millennium BC crops and livestock had made it this far to the west, although the diet of its inhabitants still consisted primarily of gathered wild terrestrial and marine species. Randolph Donohue (1992: 77) notes that "virtually all regions of the Mediterranean witnessed the appearance of domestic sheep and ceramics prior to the advent of sites with fully neolithic economy." João Zilhão (1993), however, argues that small groups of settlers brought the complex of domesticated plants and animals and pottery and eventually interacted with the indigenous foragers. He claims that mixing of deposits at many sites gives the impression that Neolithic technology and domesticates appeared piecemeal earlier than they actually did.

Adoptions of agriculture by foraging populations also occurred in southern Scandinavia, the Alpine Foreland, the Atlantic coastal zone of France, and the British Isles (Bogucki 1996a). In the case of the British Isles, some form of watercraft would have been necessary to transport domestic cattle, sheep, and goats as well as the seed from the Continent. Ireland, the ultimate western extension of Neolithic agriculture in Europe, has received very close scrutiny in recent years. Much recent evidence indicates that the last Irish foragers were the first Irish farmers (e.g., Green and Zvelebil 1993), but Cooney and Grogan (1994) have suggested that the colonization model not be completely discarded. They propose that small intrusions of farming groups from Britain brought a way of life which was an attractive alternative to foraging for the indigenous peoples of Ireland.

The introduction of agriculture to Europe was not a uniform process. In areas where alluvial habitats were sparsely populated by indigenous groups, such as in Greece and in central Europe, colonization by farming peoples from outside the region seems to have occurred. Where there were larger forager populations, agriculture was not so quick to be adopted, but it eventually insinuated itself into the existing subsistence economy of these peoples.

North American desert borderlands

Western North America was beyond the area of the wild distribution of the classic Mesoamerican domesticates of maize and beans, although as noted above there is evidence for indigenous wild squashes in some areas. Maize, as the cornerstone of a field crop subsistence system, had to be brought to far more northernly latitudes from its original subtropical heartland, thus encountering colder temperatures and greater seasonality. The Mogollon Highlands and the Colorado Plateau form the northern border of the Sonoran Desert of the southwestern United States and northern Mexico. Minnis (1992) terms this region the "Desert Borderlands" in order to avoid politically-based geographical terms, and this nomenclature will be used below. This region provides an important case study in the spread of cultigens to North America. As for most of the New World, domestic animals other than dogs are not in the picture, which is an important point of contrast between this and Old World examples of agricultural dispersals.

The prevailing weight of evidence is that maize, beans, and squashes were adopted by the indigenous populations of the Desert Borderlands and did not arrive there with a northward migration of peoples from Mesoamerica. Dissenting positions have been put forward by Berry (1982) and Matson (1991), but this view is contradicted on a number of grounds (Wills 1995). Despite the consensus on the fundamental process of agricultural dispersal to the Desert Borderlands, there are disagreements about the timing and impact of the introduction of domestic plants to this region (e.g., Wills 1995; Minnis 1992). In the long run, these may prove to be matters of scale than of substance.

The earliest appearance of maize in the Desert Borderlands can now be reliably dated no earlier than about 1500 BC in recalibrated radiocarbon years (conventionally listed as 3200 BP in unrecalibrated years), although there are some indications from pollen data that may push this back to about 2000 BC (Simmons 1986). Until recently, the earliest dates for maize in this region were believed to be much earlier, nearly back to 5000 BC (ca. 6000 BP unrecalibrated), based on radiocarbon dates made in the 1950s for materials from Bat Cave in New Mexico. Recent reinvestigation of Bat Cave and AMS dating of its corn cobs have produced substantially more recent dates (Wills 1992). Such a late dating has been confirmed by dates from other sites in the region, with most calibrations pointing towards between 1500 and 1000 BC. Beans appear to have entered the region a bit later than maize and squash, at some point in the first millennium BC.

Maize, squash, and beans appear to have been effortlessly integrated into the pre-existing late forager subsistence pattern in the Desert Borderlands, but it is not until the first millennium AD that people in this area became dependent on them for most of their food. Minnis (1992) characterizes the cultivation during the period between the first appearance of maize and the emergence of agriculturally-based communities as "casual agriculture" which was practiced as a "low cost, low effort way to increase the economic security of Archaic peoples." In Minnis' view, agriculture did not transform prehistoric society in the Desert Borderlands to any radical degree.

Wills, on the other hand (1992, 1995), notes the evidence for increased sedentism and complexity of resource use in late forager communities after the introduction of maize, and asks the question why would such peoples adopt a risky economic strategy in such seasonal northern latitudes? Wills believes that domesticates were so readily adopted by late foragers in the Desert Borderlands because they allowed these groups to sustain their hunting and gathering lifestyle. Their goal was not productivity but rather *predictability* or even greater control over their subsistence system. The addition of crops to their diet allowed the late foragers of this region to manage their production more effectively, which in turn permitted some groups to be more successful in their competition for key resource areas at the most productive times of the year.

The debate over the impact of maize agriculture in the Desert Borderlands echoes across North America throughout later prehistory. For example, McBride and Dewar (1981) have characterized the introduction of maize agriculture about AD 1000 to southern New England as a "non-event" which had little immediate impact on settlement patterns or subsistence practices. Yet subtle changes did occur eventually, once agriculture became the dominant practice. Wills' proposal that agriculture was adopted by late foragers because it initially allowed them to remain foragers is also attractive for its applicability to other parts of the world, such as northern Europe or the Nile Valley (Wetterstrom 1993), although it is less compelling as an explanation for the primary domestication of plants and animals.

THE MECHANICS OF DOMESTICATION

Many people outside the group of scholars who are interested in the transition to agriculture focus on what could be called "the mechanics of domestication," or the actual human behavior involved with planting the first seed or raising the first goat. Implicit in this focus is the belief that agriculture is so tremendous a development that it must have been a "discovery," or at least an innovation, behind which was one or more very insightful and creative foragers. They envision that one day long ago someone had the inspiration that putting a seed in the soil would cause it to sprout or that animals could be tamed and raised under human control. "Eureka!" (or something similar) this person presumably said, and thus agriculture was born.

From the outset, it is important to understand that the transition to agriculture did not at all involve a sudden discovery of the relationship between seeds and plants or a revelation about the behavioral characteristics of animal species. Prehistoric foragers certainly were keen observers of their natural surroundings. How else could they have developed such elaborate seasonally-scheduled strategies for obtaining their food? They were surely well aware of the relationship between seeds and their eventual sprouting and growth and of the relative suitability of animals of taming and control. As was noted in chapter 4, there is considerable evidence that late foragers engaged in the manipulation of biomass to increase their resources, again a reflection of considerable sophistication about plant and animal reproductive biology that exists among hunter-gatherers. It certainly did not take an observation of discarded seeds in a rubbish pile for foragers to learn about what happens when seeds are planted.

There is every reason to believe that humans may have planted seeds or kept animal pets well back in the Ice Age, although the mobility of the Pleistocene bands may have ensured that such activity was sporadic and had no lasting effect. Clearly, at certain key points, decisions were made to take advantage of the knowledge of plant and animal reproductive biology that had been acquired over the millennia. Yet the transition to agriculture involved no sudden discovery or flash of brilliance by a forager in the Levant or in the Mexican Highlands. Rather, it involved a complex set of motivations and consequences which emerged from the changes in band organization, sedentism, and household autonomy in late foraging society.

Describing the Agricultural Transition

When dealing with the transition to agriculture, it is also very easy to confuse a description of the process with reaching an understanding of *why* people really did it. Describing early domestication is easier than explaining it, since there is no compelling evidence either of a single global cause or that one local explanation is more compelling than one or more competitors. The question of explanation will be taken up in the following section, but let us first review some attempts to *characterize* the domestication process.

The late David Rindos (1984) proposed a typology of three kinds of domestication, which he called "incidental," "specialized," and "agricultural." This typology provides a good starting point from which to identify various aspects of human behavior associated with domestication. *Incidental domestication* occurs when humans remove a species from its native habitat, perhaps unintentionally, and protect and exploit it in its new setting. *Specialized domestication* takes incidental domestication one step further, when humans exhibit conscious behavior to propagate a species and to depend on it. Finally, *agricultural domestication* occurs when humans completely transform the relationship between the hitherto wild species and

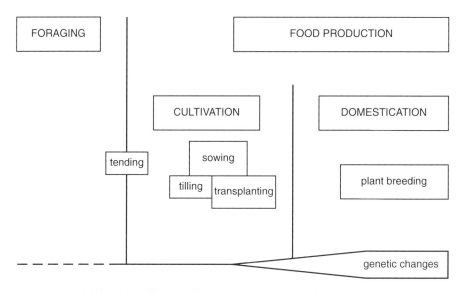

Figure 5.8 Richard Ford's model of the stages between foraging and food production, eventually leading to domestication (after Ford 1985, figure 1.1).

themselves by controlling its ecology and evolution. For example, in plant domestication, harvesting, seed selection and storage, weeding and removal of competitors, and tillage would also be characteristic of agricultural domestication. In Rindos' opinion, the critical transformation at the transition to agriculture is the change that humans effect in the ecosystem, specifically the relationships and interdependencies among plants, animals, and themselves.

Writing from the perspective of the prehistoric southwestern United States, Richard Ford (1985) took a somewhat different perspective, which is perhaps more characteristic of American evolutionary archaeology. Ford placed "foraging" and "food production" at the poles of the domestication progression and divided the latter into stages of "cultivation" and "domestication" (figure 5.8). A succession of methods provides landmarks in this sequence: "incipient agriculture," "gardening," and "field agriculture," and within these are human activities which become progressively more elaborate, beginning with tending, through tilling, transplanting and sowing, to plant breeding.

David Harris (1989) elaborated these descriptive schemes to include several thresholds at which the input of energy into food procurement and food production was increased (figure 5.9). Harris characterizes foraging as including activities such as the controlled burning of vegetation, gathering, and protective tending. In his view, food production begins when the first jump in energy input occurs, through sowing, weeding, harvesting, storage, and drainage/irrigation, even though plants at this stage are still phytogenetically wild. The next increase in energy input occurs when humans transform the environment through forest clearance and systematic tillage. A third step, also marked by another increase in energy investment, occurs when specific

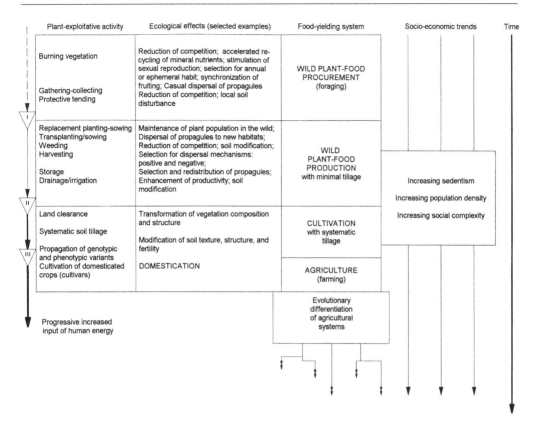

Plant-exploitative activity	Ecological effects (selected examples)	Food-yielding system	Socio-economic trends	Time
Burning vegetation Gathering-collecting Protective tending	Reduction of competition; accelerated re-cycling of mineral nutrients; stimulation of sexual reproduction; selection for annual or ephemeral habit; synchronization of fruiting; Casual dispersal of propagules Reduction of competition; local soil disturbance	WILD PLANT-FOOD PROCUREMENT (foraging)		
Replacement planting-sowing Transplanting/sowing Weeding Harvesting Storage Drainage/irrigation	Maintenance of plant population in the wild; Dispersal of propagules to new habitats; Reduction of competition; soil modification; Selection for dispersal mechanisms: positive and negative; Selection and redistribution of propagules; Enhancement of productivity; soil modification	WILD PLANT-FOOD PRODUCTION with minimal tillage	Increasing sedentism Increasing population density Increasing social complexity	
Land clearance Systematic soil tillage Propagation of genotypic and phenotypic variants Cultivation of domesticated crops (cultivars)	Transformation of vegetation composition and structure Modification of soil texture, structure, and fertility DOMESTICATION	CULTIVATION with systematic tillage AGRICULTURE (farming)		
Progressive increased input of human energy		Evolutionary differentiation of agricultural systems		

Figure 5.9 David Harris' model of the development of plant exploitation and its ecological and cultural effects (after Harris 1989, figure 1.1).

variants of the plants are propagated, the true domestication of the cultigens. The cumulative effect of this progression is the establishment of a true agroecosystem, at which point agriculture can be truly said to have begun, in Harris' view.

These descriptive sequences of the transition to food production generally concentrate on *plant* domestication, while animal domestication is either left out of the discussion (as would be appropriate in the New World, where domesticated animals played a minor dietary role) or assumed to follow along in step. Yet a crucial step in the development of animal domestication, which differentiates it sharply from plant domestication, is the shift in importance from the *dead animal* as only a source of meat to the *living animal* as a member of a breeding population (Meadow 1984). Human interaction with domesticated animals takes over the entire lives of the animals, whereas previously people observed them from a distance and interacted with them for a brief instant before killing them. Again, this change is marked by a leap in the energy invested in the many activities associated with stockbreeding.

It is difficult, however, to make broad generalizations about animal domestication, since the behavioral characteristics of the animals which were domesticated in prehistory vary widely. As a result, greater consideration is given to local patterns of animal domestication, as well as to models that emphasize the interplay between animal domestication and the local progression of plant domestication (e.g., Hole 1984). It is also important to note that the domestication of animals from their wild forms is only the first step towards their eventual exploitation for a variety of products, including milk and wool, which requires even further sophistication about animal behavior and greater patience in reaping the rewards of human effort.

EXPLAINING THE AGRICULTURAL TRANSITION

Although evolutionary sequences such as those presented above *describe* the progression of human cultural activities that culminate in domestication and agriculture, they do not illuminate the causal factors that move the process from one stage to the next. In other words, why did humans choose to add the work of weeding, harvesting, and storage to hunting and collecting and then proceed to clear land, till the soil, and propagate specific variants of edible plants? Why did they decide to control and breed herd animals like sheep and goats? Why did they assume the risk that agriculture entails? Archaeologists have proposed a number of different models to explain why human populations chose to rely on domesticated plants and animals. "Explanation" implies a search for causation, and the models that archaeologists develop to explain the transition to food production involve an attempt to identify factors which caused societies to make this change. Some models try to isolate single factors, while others propose an interplay of several.

Early prehistorians made relatively few attempts to try to explain the origins of agriculture. Most saw it as an inevitable development on the march of human progress. Given the focus of early prehistoric research on Europe and North America, where agriculture appeared to have shown up ready-made (and with Near Eastern and Mesoamerican research targeted on later, fully-agricultural societies), there was relatively little concern with the question of why agriculture began. A greater concern was documenting its initial appearance in any particular region, although Stone Age chronology was so elastic that the boundary between foragers and farmers was always somewhat fuzzy. One consequence of the greater precision in dating brought by radiocarbon was the stiffening of this boundary, which sharpened the contrast in archaeologists' minds between pre-agricultural and agricultural peoples.

V. Gordon Childe (1928) is often credited with the first attempt to seek causality in the transition to food production, although partial credit for this idea also is due to Rafael Pumpelly (1837–1923), an American geologist who led an interdisciplinary expedition to Anau in central Asia in 1904 (Pumpelly 1908). Following Pumpelly, Childe proposed that global warming and desiccation at the end of the last Ice Age led to the concentration of humans and animals in limited areas, such as desert oases in the Near East, and the sheer proximity of these species led to the establishment of human control over the eventual domesticates. The difficulty is that there is no evidence of widespread desiccation during the period in question between 15,000 and 10,000 years ago. Watson (1995) points out that Childe was referring primarily to animal domestication and did not deal explicitly with plant domestication, although many later discussions of Childe's theory attribute both to his model.

No archaeologists in the 1920s or 1930s appear to have introduced competing causal models, although this era saw considerable analytical thought from botanists (e.g., Vavilov 1926). In the late 1940s and 1950s, however, Robert Braidwood developed an alternative model on several lines of data. First, environmental evidence indicated that there is no basis for believing that there was widespread desiccation in the Near East after the Ice Age. Second, Braidwood thought that the best place to look for early domestication was where the habitats of the wild precursors of wheat, barley, sheep, and goats overlapped. With this goal, he excavated the early agricultural village of Jarmo in the foothills of the Zagros Mountains in Iraqi Kurdistan. Third, the application of radiocarbon dating to Jarmo and other early agricultural sites (like Jericho, although a classic disagreement arose between Braidwood and Kathleen Kenyon, the excavator of Jericho, over the validity and interpretation of certain dates) permitted the rise of agricultural economies to be traced chronologically with some precision.

With desiccation and other widespread climatic changes discounted as a proximal cause of agriculture, Braidwood sought an explanation in human behavior. He suggested that food production in the Old World emerged in certain "nuclear zones" in the arc of the Taurus and Zagros mountains of the Near East known as the Fertile Crescent. In these regions, increasing human familiarity with the behavior and reproductive biology of wheat, barley, sheep and goat would have led to the establishment of relations of control and manipulation which resulted in domestication. The advantages of domesticated plants and animals would have been so obvious that this would have become the dominant subsistence strategy in short order.

In the late 1960s, anthropological thinking shifted away from a belief in the inherent superiority and attractiveness of agriculture as an economic strategy (for a review of the evolution of anthropological thought about foragers, see Shott 1992). One catalytic event was the "Man the Hunter" conference held at the University of Chicago in 1967 (Lee and DeVore 1968), which resulted in an influential volume. A widespread view emerged that foragers enjoy an adequate standard of living with relatively little effort and that humans would not have taken on the drudgery and risks of agriculture unless they experienced some form of duress. Nonetheless, since it was clear that in the last 10,000 years virtually all the world's population had made this transition, the search for the factors which would have compelled humans to make it was intensified. In the spirit of the "New Archaeology," the hypotheses which were put forward stressed the identification of explicit causal factors rather than vague behavioral and cultural concepts such as "familiarity" and "sophistication."

Since the late 1960s, many different theories of the origins of food production have been proposed, and making sense of them can be very difficult. A very useful typology of models of agricultural origins was proposed by

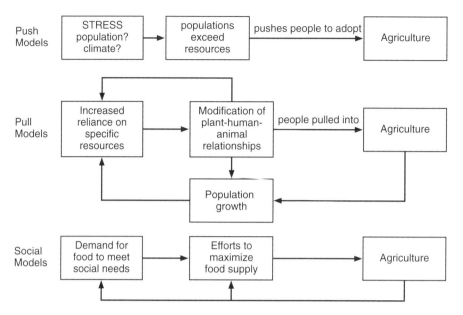

Figure 5.10 Schematic depiction of the relationships among various processes in "push," "pull," and "social" models to explain the origins of food production.

Barbara Stark (1986) in a review of the origins of food production in the New World. She identified three main types of models used by archaeologists to trace the transition to food production, which she terms "push" models, "pull" models and "social" models (figure 5.10). Although articulated for models in the New World, I believe that this typology describes the many attempts to explain agricultural origins in the Old World as well.

"Push" models can also be called "stress" models, because they focus on the presumed duress which would have forced people to abandon their secure and comfortable foraging existence for the drudgery and worry of food production. Stress models (e.g., Binford 1968; Flannery 1969; Cohen 1977) are usually based on imbalances between population and resources. Population growth is often argued to have been the "motor" which drove the sequence of causal relationships, with climatic change often playing the role of a trigger which introduces a sudden imbalance into the system. Other elements in such models are sedentism and the diversification of resource use among late foragers. Donald Henry (1989) notes that the main source of variation among "push" models is the sequence in which these three key elements are ordered. Such models are attractive because sedentism, resource diversification, and population growth can often be inferred from archaeological data.

Lewis Binford articulated one of the first "push" (or "stress") models in 1968. He proposed that populations living in coastal areas and relying on rich marine resources grew. At a certain point, they spilled over into adjacent inland zones which were not so richly provisioned. In these marginal zones, the spill over populations artificially increased their resource base by sowing wild wheat and barley taken from their native habitats. Binford's model is hypothetical and remains unsupported in its original formulation. Although there clearly were late forager maritime adaptations (some of which were discussed in chapter 4), there is no evidence of excessive late Pleistocene populations migrating inland. This model is important, however, because it introduced demographic pressure as a causal factor in the discussion of agricultural origins.

Somewhat later, Kent Flannery incorporated many elements of Binford's scheme in a model of agricultural origins in the Near East, yet reconciled it with archaeological evidence (Flannery 1969). He proposed that from about 20,000 BC onward, populations in the Near East broadened their subsistence base to include many hitherto underused plant and animal species. Flannery termed this a "broad spectrum" pattern. Human populations in certain optimal zones of the Fertile Crescent, which were also the natural habitats of wheat, barley, sheep, and goat, grew to the point where they exceeded the capacity of these regions to support them. At this point, which Flannery places about 8000 BC, they spilled over into adjacent marginal zones. Through cultivation, they attempted to produce artificial stands of cereals "as dense as those in the *heart* of the 'optimum' zone" (Flannery 1969: 81). At this point, phytogenetic changes in the cereals, such as the toughening of the rachis, occurred and reinforced the human manipulation of these plants. Harvests still would have been unpredictable, however, and the domestication of sheep and goat was undertaken to "bank" food to buffer the lean years.

Flannery's model, although to some degree almost as speculative as Binford's, was articulated clearly and persuasively, and it came to be the canonical hypothesis for origins of agriculture in the Near East. Population pressure remained the basis for the genre of "push" models of agricultural origins in southwestern Asia throughout the 1970s. Phillip Smith and T. Cuyler Young (1972) made the connection with the theories of the Danish agricultural geographer Ester Boserup (1965) on the relationship between population and intensification of subsistence activities. Further attempts to extend the population pressure hypothesis of agricultural origins worldwide (e.g., Cohen 1977) were frustrated by the absence of compelling evidence from many regions.

In the 1980s, dissatisfaction with single-factor "push" models emerged, particularly due to the fact that it proved to be very difficult to demonstrate "stress" or to infer it from population growth. Moreover, archaeologists realized that the earliest sites in the Levant with documented plant cultivation and animal husbandry were not in "marginal zones" but rather in the most productive areas. Recent multi-causal "push" models (e.g., Moore 1989; McCorriston and Hole 1991) analyze the interplay of several factors, including changing environments, demography, the foraging economy, settlement patterns, and social organization. Andrew Moore (1989), for instance, argues that the change to a more sedentary settlement increased pressure on local plant and animal resources. Joy McCorriston and Frank Hole (1991) stress the role of environmental change, as manifested in increased seasonal variation and the drying of lake basins.

"Pull" models of agricultural origins are somewhat rarer in the archaeological literature. In such models, the precursors of domesticated plants and animals are argued to have had certain attractive characteristics which drew human groups to rely increasingly on them. Reliance led to dependence to the point that it was impossible to return to the previous patterns of plant and animal exploitation. In such models, population growth is seen as a consequence of food production that prevents a group from reverting to its earlier pattern of resource use.

In 1968, Kent Flannery argued that the foraging bands of upland Mesoamerica practiced a tightly scheduled seasonal pattern of plant and animal exploitation. Subtle genetic changes in particular plants, especially beans and maize, made them more attractive to foragers, who then spent more time collecting them. This upset the tight schedule, leaving the foragers no option but to cultivate the plants on which they had focused in order to maintain their yields.

Donald Henry (1989) proposed a "pull" model for agricultural origins in the Near East. In his view, there were two key moments in the process of agricultural origins in the Levant. The first occurred around 10,500 BC when a global temperature increase promoted long-term settlement and necessitated a shift from what Henry calls "simple" foraging to "complex" foraging. A variety of high-yield resources, including wild cereals, were exploited, and restraints on population growth were relaxed. About 2000 years later, this complex foraging system collapsed, possibly as the result of a second climatic change, and the foragers had two options, depending on where they lived. In the highly-productive areas of the Levant, where the highest populations were, they began to cultivate cereals. In the marginal areas, people reverted to a simpler foraging system.

In the 1990s, social factors have begun to assume prominence in attempts to explain the origins of agriculture, although "push" and "pull" models still have considerable importance. Brian Hayden (1995a: 280) writes, "it now appears that neither deteriorating climate nor (extreme) population pressure of resource stress can be viewed as a convincing cause of domestication." Whether or not this position can be accepted universally, it is clear that there is dissatisfaction with the sorts of causal relationships that archaeologists have proposed since the late 1960s. As a result, some archaeologists have started to look for the causes of agricultural origins in social behavior such as competition, prestige, and trade.

In "social" models for the transition to agriculture, factors other than population growth produce the demand for resources which leads to the intensification of subsistence activity and to food production. Some human groups, it is hypothesized, needed to increase the amount of food available to meet social demands for feasting, exchange, bridewealth, and cementing alliances. The high productivity of certain potential domesticates led to a concentration on them for these social purposes and ultimately to their domestication. Evidence to support "social" models is often tenuous and requires crossing a wider inferential gap than for "push" and "pull" models (although as we have seen above the "push and "pull" models are also often built on weak evidence). Nonetheless, they should not be discounted simply because it is difficult to find direct support for them, and indeed they have considerable promise for advancing our understanding of how agriculture arose.

Brain Hayden (1992) has proposed a "social" model for the origins of food production which is based on competitive feasting. He notes that most hunter-gatherers occupying fluctuating environments share food, and hence there is no incentive to invest time and effort in producing extra since only others will benefit. In resource-rich areas with stable environments in which there was adequate food to relax such collective sharing, competition between ambitious individuals may have led to competitive feasts to gain control over labor and loyalty. Such competitive feasting has been observed ethnographically in many societies. The need to generate large amounts of desirable foods in order to stage such feasts stimulated cultivation, which was no great discovery for foragers who were well aware of seeds and their propagation. Hayden proposes his model without strict geographical reference, suggesting that it may be applicable to both the New World and Old World alike. Similarly, Runnels and van Andel (1988) have argued that in the eastern Mediterranean agriculture may have arisen as a result of a need to produce surplus commodities for trade or to support craftsmen.

In the last 30 years, archaeologists have made considerable progress towards understanding the origins of agriculture, but the question of *why* prehistoric people made the transition from foraging to farming is still elusive. There is an emerging consensus, however, that single-factor stress models are inadequate explanations by themselves and that any understanding of this process requires the incorporation of intentional human decisions (Watson 1995; Hayden 1995a). Since humans make choices and decisions within a social environment, it is important that this context be examined in order to understand how agriculture came about. The section that follows represents a modest attempt to place the origins of agriculture in the context of human society following its transformation at the end of the Ice Age.

THE TRANSFORMATION OF FORAGER SOCIETY AND AGRICULTURAL ORIGINS

Most models of agricultural origins assume, either implicitly or explicitly, that forager society had been relatively unchanged since the depths of the Ice Age. Yet, as was argued in the previous chapter, there is increasing evidence for pre-agricultural transformations of forager society. These changes are manifested in increased sedentism, smaller social units, individual domiciles, investment in burial ritual, and trade. Any unified theory of agricultural origins must take these changes into account.

While it may not satisfy those who seek a clear causal sequence for the transition to agriculture, I would like to propose that the domestication of plants and animals and the dispersal of food-producing economies is a part of the complex transformation of human society which began at the end of the Ice Age and continued into the Holocene. An extreme statement of this position is to suggest that agriculture is merely a "symptom" of parallel changes which took place at different times and rates in many parts of the world. At the least, however, I would like to argue that in order to understand the transition to agriculture, we need to consider the changes in band society which occurred in many different places during the millennia *prior* to the first use of domesticated plants and animals.

Whatever the proximal causes of the origins of domestication or the adoption of agriculture in any particular part of the world, these developments would not have been possible without a fundamental restructuring of Pleistocene band society. A sense of place and a sense of property were critical prerequisites for a society to take the risks associated with a commitment to agriculture. Most importantly, the critical transformation was the widespread defection from the sharing norms which had characterized Pleistocene band society for millennia.

WHY DIDN'T AGRICULTURE DEVELOP SOONER?

Although archaeologists have not stayed awake nights worrying especially about this question, a passing curiosity in the study of the transition to agriculture has been why did it not happen sooner, even back in the Palaeolithic? Clearly people were intelligent and knew the reproductive biology of plants in some detail. Moreover, the stresses invoked in the "push" models, such as population growth, surely occurred on a local scale at many earlier times. This would have especially been the case in areas such as parts of North America or Southeast Asia in the early Holocene, prior to the adoption of agriculture by late foragers. Why did people begin to cultivate so recently?

Robert Braidwood had an elegantly simple answer to this question in the 1950s. He said that human societies simply were not ready to make the transition to agriculture any time prior to the end of the Ice Age (Braidwood 1960: 134; Braidwood and Willey 1962: 342). It is possible to interpret this to mean that they had not acquired knowledge of plant reproductive biology and ecology to adapt to new environmental conditions. Actually, it is unclear what Braidwood meant by "ready," but the assumption was that he meant both intellectually and technologically ready.

Braidwood's "readiness" argument was ridiculed as simplistic by a number of New Archaeologists in the 1960s as they advanced "push" models based on human responses to stresses (e.g., Binford 1968). Yet left unquoted in these discussions was often the sentence which preceded the use of the word "ready." Braidwood wrote "the food-producing revolution seems to have occurred as the culmination of the ever increasing cultural differentiation and specialization of human communities" (1960: 134). Here is an intriguing and forgotten foundation of a "social" model of agricultural origins which I would like to expand in the sections below.

The position taken here is that prior to the end of the Ice Age human populations were indeed not ready for agriculture, not because they lacked the knowledge of plant reproductive biology or the technology to exploit it, but rather because the nature of Pleistocene band society impeded innovation and self-interested experimentation. We know that intellectually and technologically humans were ready for agriculture many millennia before. Yet they did not choose to develop cultivation. Climatic change, population growth, and other stresses occurred on a variety of geographical scales since the earliest hominids, yet people did not respond to these stresses as they are hypothesized to have done on a global scale at different times in the last 10,000 years. Something changed, yet it did not change with the world-wide synchrony that a major climatic event would have produced. Instead it was asynchronous, occurring first in the Near East and later in the Americas.

The change that occurred was in human society itself, as Pleistocene bands broke apart into smaller "proto-household" units. In order to understand this, it is crucial to examine the connection between sedentism and agriculture. Did one lead to the other, or are they both symptoms of a broader set of changes at the core of many different societies starting in the Near East about 10,000 years ago?

SEDENTISM, HOUSEHOLDS, AND DOMESTICATION

The role of sedentism in the development of agriculture was already highlighted by Flannery in the early 1970s (Flannery 1972, 1973). Subsequent authors have echoed this view (e.g., Miller 1992). The connection was fairly straightforward: the productivity of wild cereals permitted populations to settle down, whereupon population growth and plant domestication were linked in synergistic development. Sedentary peoples cultivated "to *ensure* a reliable food supply or to *increase* their food supply to satisfy growing social or dietary needs" (Miller 1992: 51). Sedentism was seen as a prerequisite to the development of agriculture as either providing the growing populations with "push" models required for stress or for the tethering to a single location which made it impossible for humans to revert to a mobile foraging way of life.

1 would like to propose that sedentism was not necessarily a direct cause of agriculture, but instead that both were consequences of the re-structuring of Pleistocene band society among late foragers. As I described the process in the previous chapter, hunter-gatherer bands were atomized into smaller units of decision making and production, which I characterized as "proto-households." Such a restructuring was a fundamental prerequisite for the emergence of food production. The argument for this is by necessity complex, but I believe that it explains the timing and pace of the transition in both situations of pristine domestication and of the adoption of agriculture by foragers on a global scale.

As was asserted above, the worldwide development of agriculture did not require great insights about the relationships between seeds and plants or about the propagation or transplantation of crop species. Instead, it required some form of *motivation* which caused people to *decide* to undertake this propagation on a large scale, to alter their existing subsistence strategies, and to repeat it annually. We have seen above, however, that models which require stresses or traps generally do not stand up to the evidence, and regional studies of initial food production generally reflect patchwork developments rather than uniform patterns. The motivations for food production, then, appear to be generated from *within* foraging societies, and their consequences vary considerably from locality to locality.

Band society, however, really provides no motivations for food production, especially when sharing norms are enforced. Food production, by definition, requires a much different approach to the timing of nutritional procurement than makes sense for a sharing band. A farmer at the time of the harvest has produced far more than is absolutely necessary at that moment. Obviously, the food must last for the year until the next harvest, as well as to provide seed grain for the next crop. In Pleistocene band societies, such a condition could probably not be tolerated. The investment of the farmer in the production of crops would be dissipated soon after the harvest if sharing was enforced. Why bother then?

The emergence of agriculture only makes sense if smaller societal units, tightly bounded and organized along explicit kin lines, formed the primary unit of production. The late forager "proto-households" would have provided such units, and thus emerges the rationale for food production. If the threat of having to share the fruits of one's labor with the entire community was lifted, there would be considerable motivation for such groups to invest time and work in propagating the wild precursors of domesticates. The absence of sharing within the band and the insurance it often provided would have been another powerful motivation to develop a reliable and abundant food supply. It would have been in the interest of late forager "proto-households" to try to maximize their production through all the methods they knew in order to store away as much as possible for the next year.

The self-reliance required on the part of each late forager "proto-household" to be responsible for its own subsistence would also have created the potential for innovation and creativity in techniques of cultivation. Instead of each person of the band trying to do just enough to be considered an adequate contributor to the common subsistence pool, individuals and their families would be free to experiment. The rewards of such experimentation and the risk it entailed now could be retained by those who undertook them. At the same time, such risk also contained the possibility for complete or partial failure. Such a calamity resulting from bad decisions or horticultural experiments gone awry, however, would have been confined to the individual "proto-household," while the larger community would have survived.

Social models for the origins of agriculture, such as those of Hayden (1992, 1995a) and Runnels and van Andel (1988) have emphasized the motivation for food production which would have stemmed from customs such as competitive feasting or trade. The notion that the emergence of sedentary "proto-households" was a crucial prerequisite for agriculture is very easy to reconcile with these models, for the emergence of such residential groups would have permitted several key developments. The first is a much more formal concept of kinship than can be presumed to have existed in Pleistocene bands. As Kent (1995) has pointed out, the notion of kinship has relatively little meaning in band society, since everyone is a kin of some sort. Instead, degrees of affinity are measured in fluid categories such as "friendship" and "sharing partners," which do not translate into transgenerational relationships easily. The second is the concept of ownership of productive resources by a single residential group or a group of them, but still bounded and defined by location of permanent residence. Tim Ingold distinguishes between *territoriality*, the demarcation of space practiced by many species, and *tenure*, the human "mode of appropriation, by which persons exert claims over resources dispersed in space" (Ingold 1987: 133). As people settled down, the nature of tenure would have changed considerably from that of mobile Pleistocene bands. As populations become less mobile and more sedentary, "land replaces animals as the material embodiment of the claims and counter claims that persons exert over one another" (1987: 170). Late forager groups such as the Natufians also can be presumed to have had close attachments between residential groups and specific productive tracts, adopting a tenure system measured in terms of area as opposed to herds, locations, and paths. Finally, sedentary households have new opportunities for accumulation and storage, which can easily translate into aggrandizing behavior. Having a fixed residence removes a major disincentive to accumulation.

The roots of competition among households and communities can easily be seen to lie in this suite of developments among late foragers. Such competition among residential groups will have continued significance well beyond the transition to agriculture. Despite the archaeological attention that has been focused on domestication and early agriculture, it may turn out to be only one manifestation of the transformation of Pleistocene band society into a household-based social order in the long run. It was a key development, to be sure, but one that did not occur in isolation from other changes.

THE CONSEQUENCES OF FOOD PRODUCTION

Since the 1950s, most archaeological research on the transition to agriculture has been focused on the narrow slice of time which marked the period of initial domestication of major cultigens. Yet the adoption of domesticated plants and animals did not complete the transition to fully agricultural societies; in fact, it was only the beginning of a much larger process. In many respects, the consequences of the transition to food production are as interesting as the reasons behind agricultural origins and dispersals, if not more so.

First, the domestication of plants and animals does not automatically lead to the immediate replacement of a foraging way of life. As was seen above in the discussion of the southwestern United States, foragers appear to have integrated maize and other cultigens into their subsistence in order to *continue* as foragers, and it was several centuries before agriculture became the dominant mode of subsistence. By contrast, in the Near East, cultivation displaced foraging very shortly after the initial domestication occurred, and agriculturally-based villages soon arose.

Second, the involvement of a society in agriculture, especially when it becomes their primary subsistence strategy, redefines how that group approaches its decision making and the conditions under which those decisions are made. Foraging societies have worked out various ways of dealing with environmental risks, but agriculture introduces a whole new set of considerations. Moreover, the risk cannot be spread over the entire band but is instead borne by individual household units. Such a redefinition will have important consequences for the developments that follow the establishment of agricultural societies in many parts of the world.

Finally, agriculture has an impact on the economic, social, and symbolic roles of men and women in society. The actual scope of these changes is very difficult to apprehend from a point several millennia in the future. We can infer, however, that the shift from Pleistocene bands, whose subsistence was derived in large measure from hunting, to agricultural societies changed the relative values attached to hunting proficiency (presumably a key source of male status in foraging society) and labor (an essential requirement in agricultural society). Whatever the relative status of men and women turned out to be in agricultural societies, it is clear that women now became important and vital elements in the production equation.

COMMITMENT TO AGRICULTURE

Welch (1991), paralleling Bronson's (1977) comparison of "cultivators" and "farmers," has made the crucial distinction between the initial use of domesticates, integrated into a subsistence economy similar in all other respects to the preceding one based on foraging, and the *commitment* to agriculture as reflected by the linkage of the full range of human behavior – economic, social, even ritual – with the maintenance of the agroecosystem and its production of reliable harvests. The commitment to agriculture represents the final step in the transition from one set of premises on which society is organized to another. Indeed, had this not occurred, we would not be as interested in the transition to agriculture as we are.

In the Levant, for instance, the domestication process itself and the onset of cultivation appears to have taken place relatively rapidly (Bar-Yosef and Belfer-Cohen 1992). On the other hand, the commitment to agriculture, with the establishment of communities that were specifically adapted to the maintenance of an agroecosystem, seems to have taken place more slowly over 2000 years (Byrd 1992). In the Desert Borderlands of North America, however, after a long period of practicing mixed horticulture (gardening, hunting, and collecting), communities suddenly made the transition to sedentary life structured around sustainable agriculture (Welch 1991).

Considerable archaeological research has been dedicated to the documentation of the initial appearance of cultigens and domestic animals, while much less has been devoted to the consequences of domestication. Yet committed agriculture is not simply the inevitable result of the initial use of domestic plants and animals. It is the product of a further set of choices, deci-sions, and responses which resulted in fundamental organizational changes in society. Prehistoric communities assumed constraints on their options, increased risk and uncertainty, and shifts in social roles as a result of their dependence on the new technology. Use of the term "commitment" is delib-erate; it implies that this was the result of intentional human behavior, as opposed to the passivity that a term like "dependence" would suggest.

In both regions of "pristine domestication" and of "primary crop acquisi-tion" all prehistoric populations eventually crossed the threshold of commit-ment to agriculture. The results were striking, and they underlie all the prehistoric developments discussed in the remainder of this book.

Risk and uncertainty

A key consequence of the commitment to agriculture would have been a change in the conditions under which decisions were made. As Hewitt (1983) has pointed out, the removal of domesticated plants from their origi-nal habitats increased their vulnerability to hazards. Since the subsistence system of agricultural peoples is based on an artificial association of plants and animals that can be maintained only through human intervention, it is inherently unstable. Moreover, it is prone to fluctuations of environmental conditions such as rainfall, sunlight, insects, diseases, as well as changes in the ability of human groups to invest the labor required to maintain fields and livestock. In order to understand early agricultural societies, it is impor-tant to remember that prehistoric farmers had to take these variables into account.

Hazards, and the varying degree to which their occurrence and severity can be anticipated, cause farmers to make decisions under two types of con-ditions: risk and uncertainty. This distinction was first made by the econo-mist Frank Knight in 1921, who differentiated between *risk*, in which probabilities could be assigned to a range of known outcomes, and *uncer-tainty*, in which an absence of information or predictive data made the range of outcomes unknowable. Some economic anthropologists have argued that this distinction is useful in dealing with small-scale agrarian societies. Cancian (1980) noted that there are differences between how farmers take account of known environmental variation such as rainfall in their decision making (which would be considered "risk") and how they deal with the unknown results of new technology (which could be termed "uncertainty"). Others have maintained that this distinction is artificial, for "probabilities of future events are never 'known' with complete certainty" (Berry 1980: 325).

The position taken here is that the distinction between risk and uncer-tainty can provide an important insight into different patterns of prehistoric agricultural behavior. Calavan (1984), for instance, points out that farmers in making production choices operate differently under these two conditions. Farmers producing a long-established crop with a familiar and traditional technology will obtain yields that will vary from year to year but within pre-dictable limits. Based on their observations of environmental conditions, they can allocate subjective, yet reasonably accurate, probabilities to these yields, and base their investment of labor and time accordingly. In such a circumstance, farmers operate under conditions of risk. On the other hand, farmers who are trying a new technology or a new crop, or who are colonizing new environmental zones, will find themselves in a situation where the yields cannot be predicted with confidence. While such innovation can pay off richly if the guess is correct, it can also be catastrophic if the farmer guesses wrong in allocating his resources. In this situation, the farmer operates under conditions of uncertainty. Such uncertainty can be turned into risk through experience and learning, although this may take several generations or more for knowledge of the range of possible outcomes to accumulate.

It is interesting to speculate whether the earliest farmers in any given region around the world operated more under conditions of uncertainty or more under risk. In the case of central Europe, for example, I have argued that the farmers of the Linear Pottery culture were coping with considerable uncertainty, and thus adopted a very conservative strategy towards settlement, animal husbandry, planting, and even the types of artifacts that they produced (Bogucki 1988, 1995b). On the other hand, foragers who integrated crops into their existing subsistence structure, such as in the Desert Borderlands (Wills 1988) or the Nile Valley (Wetterstrom 1993) may have been acting to mitigate risk in their foraging economies, although by making the investment in agriculture they added a new element of uncertainty. Subsequent established agricultural societies operated more under conditions of risk. As we will see in the next chapter, behavior under risk carries very important consequences for further divisions in society and the development of inequalities.

GENDER AND AGRICULTURE

The transformation of society which correlates with the transition to agriculture has led archaeologists to speculate on the relative roles of men and women in this process and the changes that resulted. From the outset, it is important to realize that the introduction of gender into the issue has been almost exclusively speculative, for men and women leave behind few gender-specific signatures in the archaeological record. As a result, there has been liberal use of ethnographic analogies of the sort which might have been derided by 1960s New Archaeologists several decades ago and the weaving of "stories" to enliven dry archaeological presentations. Nonetheless, this is an important issue if it can be subjected to objective analytical scrutiny.

The discussion of gender issues in the transition to agriculture has taken two forms in recent publications. The first is what Bruce Smith (1993) terms the "gender-credit critique" in response to his floodplain-weed theory of plant domestication in eastern North America (Watson and Kennedy 1991), while the second is represented by attempts to understand how the apportionment of activities between men and women changed with the onset of agriculture. Luckily, the gender-credit debate has been confined to a limited number of participants in a circumscribed region. The more substantive question of changing gender roles in the transition to agriculture, however, has relevance on a global scale.

The question of who actually did the domesticating of plants and animals, whether it was men or women, had not really occurred to most archaeologists concerned with the topic, particularly those who viewed the process as a societal transformation and not as a sudden discovery. It is true that in the 1950s and before many popular treatments of hunter-gatherer society relegated women to hearth, children, and gathering, but these are clearly patronizing in retrospect. Most recent hypothesis-generating essays are gender-blind, with the assumption that in various diverse ways men and women collectively participated in the process of domestication.

The issue of who should get "credit" for domestication in any particular part of the world only arose very recently in an essay by Patty Jo Watson and Mary C. Kennedy (1991) who were particularly critical of Bruce Smith's initial 1987 formulation of his floodplain-weed theory of domestication in eastern North America. Watson and Kennedy argue that Smith's model through its gender-neutral tone ignores the likely role of women as the innovators of plant domestication in this region and as such is androcentric. Smith (1993) replied that although his original formulation of the model did not take into account human intentionality and was rather faceless in general, he had envisioned the process as involving a number of small kinship-based social groupings (which I would term "proto-households" in this volume, although Smith avoids a specific characterization) in which women and men played active, if unspecified, roles. Rather than to deny women a role in domestication, Smith pointed out that his gender-neutral model was certainly not gender-biased.

The whole question of whether men or women should get "credit" for the innovation of agriculture in any particular region is rather irrelevant. First of all, it ignores the fact that plant and animal reproductive biology was well-known to people far back in the Pleistocene. Second, the successful *commitment* to agriculture is something that the entire society has to accept, and thus whether or not women took the first steps in its direction is irrelevant since men would have had to endorse this step as well. From the perspective of this book, the transition to agriculture can be viewed as part of a complex set of human societal transformations that followed the Ice Age, not an isolated development whose authorship can be attributed very precisely. Luckily, this debate has not been exported to key areas such as Mesoamerica or the Near East, and perhaps it has now been closed for good.

On the other hand, it is clear that the transition to agriculture was accompanied by dramatic changes in the economic and social roles of men and women. It is now taken as an article of faith that the onset of agriculture precipitated a change in apportionment of activities between men and women. Prevailing wisdom is that in a hunting and gathering society, men hunt and defend while women gather and cook and raise children. Indeed, this division is supported by many ethnographic accounts of foragers today. It may well have been a characteristic of foraging societies in the past. The transition to agriculture would have realigned these roles such that both sexes were involved in agricultural activity, which created a situation of relative gender equality or at least raised the social standing of women. Women would have played a larger role in the subsistence system and contributed more to the diet. The transition to agriculture, then, is seen as having been empowering to women in breaking down the rigid structures of male-dominated foraging society by enhancing the role of women.

If indeed most food procurement in Pleistocene band societies was in the hands of a small group of robust males, with gathering by women, children, and the elderly providing only a supplementary part of the diet, then presumably greater prestige would accrue to men, particularly the small group that did most of the hunting. Frost (1994) suggests that environmentally-induced mortality would have been much greater in hunting activities than in gathering. If these activities were indeed separated by sex, then one would expect that the sex ratio would decline steadily from younger to older groups. Moreover, a number of the adult men in any given band could be expected to be incapacitated in some way or simply incompetent hunters. Thus in many Pleistocene foraging societies which were dependent on hunting, the primary responsibility for food procurement would have been carried by a relatively small minority of fit adult men who were capable hunters. Such an asymmetry in the contribution to the diet of the band (even if it was diffused through enforced sharing) would have surely translated into social standing and prestige, ephemeral as these are among foragers.

With the onset of modern environmental conditions in subtropical and temperate regions at the end of the Ice Age, it is possible that such asymmetries might have been reduced. There was much more to gather in the open woodlands of the Levant or in the wetlands of coastal Mesoamerica. In addition, many of these new foods required considerable processing before consumption, such as hazelnuts. They could also be gathered, or even harvested, by all members of the group, including children, the elderly, and even the ambulatory incapacitated. Another likely side effect of the transformation of society from Pleistocene bands to late forager "proto-households" would have been a realignment of the relative contributions of men and women to the diet, which continued to shift as the transition to agriculture took place. Indeed, it is possible, as some have suggested (Peter Frost, personal communication), that agriculture entered foraging societies as a female activity, growing out of the earlier tradition of gathering. Men may have encouraged this activity, since it would have lightened their own burden.

When considering gender roles in small-scale agrarian societies, framing the question in terms of men's and women's role in subsistence procurement ignores the larger context of production and consumption. Our modern experience leads us to try to simplify the gender roles into static binary sets, while a more critical issue is the dynamic behavior of individual roles in household units. The transition to agriculture in both the Old World and the New World complicated the career paths of both men and women in ways that a simple male–female dichotomy obscures. At the root of this issue is the word *labor* both in its meaning of work and in its meaning of child-bearing.

In foraging bands, there is relatively little value attached to labor, since production is diffused through the group by sharing. Skill is everything, especially if it can produce sharable meat with as little effort and danger as possible. In agricultural households, labor is critical. Clearing fields, cultivating, planting, weeding, harvesting, and crop processing require temporally-concentrated human energy which cannot be redistributed over a longer time-scale. Moreover, at critical times during planting and harvesting, there may be "labor bottlenecks" where even the available labor supply may be insufficient and households may pool their resources. Once agriculture becomes the primary subsistence pursuit, individual skill at any one activity becomes a fairly trivial issue, whereas the generation of labor and the management of it over time becomes critical.

In farming societies, the forager desire to maximize birth spacing and to produce only as many offspring as can be reasonably supported by the efforts of the adult members of society is replaced by a natalist desire for offspring to fuel the requirements of the agricultural workforce. The children that women bear are no longer additional mouths to feed and hindrances to the band's mobility. Instead, they are the future of the agricultural household and its primary labor force starting a decade-and-a-half after they are born. Moreover, in most Neolithic societies, there are numerous other productive activities which were added to subsistence procurement. Central to these is pottery production, which has long been assumed to be a female pursuit. Although some have maintained that it would have been easy to add pottery production to the other responsibilities that women assumed (e.g., Brown 1989: 216), others have pointed out that this would have produced "a time management crisis for women" (Claassen 1991: 286).

Yet did these changes translate into any change in the relative standing of men and women? This is not yet possible to determine with any certainty. Perhaps the most favorable situations may have been those in which a community adopted agriculture as its almost exclusive source of nutrition and men toiled in the fields alongside women. One might imagine that in mixed foraging and horticultural societies, women received the worst deal, for men could still lay claim to their prestige as successful hunters whereas women not only continued their long-standing roles in gathering and child rearing but also were saddled with horticulture and pottery manufacture as well.

Some evidence may be sought in osteological evidence. Clark Larsen examined the skeletons of 269 foragers and 342 members of a mixed horticultural and foraging community on the Georgia coast (Larsen 1984). He found that the transition to agriculture affected women much more so than men, in the form of dental reduction, increased dental decay, and decreased skeletal and cranial size. Apparently, the last was due to disparities in the relative amounts of protein and carbohydrates consumed by men and women. The men, however, saw a reduction in the types of biomechanical bone stresses associated with hunting. Larsen's analysis suggests that men carried on their hunting and fishing after the adoption of agriculture, perhaps at a more leisurely rate, whereas women took on the taxing field and household chores.

Clearly the transition to agriculture would have had a profound impact on the sorts of activities taken by men and women to constitute their socially-constructed spheres of action. The transition from foraging to farming is really one from a society in which labor had little relevance as a critical concept to one in which the generation and mobilization of a workforce became a dominant concern.

THE FORAGING OPTION

In the 1960s and 1970s, there was a prevailing belief among archaeologists and anthropologists that once a society shifts to agriculture it cannot return. This position grew out of models of human cultural evolution in general and of the use of population growth as a causal factor in particular. The idea was that once population growth occurs as a result of the "improved" food supply brought about by food production, the society comes to depend more and more on its crops (e.g., Cassidy 1980). To put it into the terms being used here, full agricultural commitment was viewed as inevitable rather than simply being a likely possibility at some later point.

Yet all does not seem to be so simple. Long-term studies of a number of groups reveal fluctuations between foraging and farming with an annual or even longer periodicity. Moreover, there is little evidence to suggest that population growth is an automatic effect of the adoption of agriculture, and it appears that even among agricultural societies there are mechanisms that restrain population growth and fertility (see, for example, Englebrecht 1987 for a discussion of this among the Iroquois). It is entirely possible for societies at this boundary between foraging and farming to slide back and forth from one strategy to another, following one for a few years, then reverting to the other, and back again. For instance, the Agta in the Philippines, long thought to be prototypical hunter-gatherers (e.g., Peterson 1978a, b) living adjacent to agriculturalists, actually are opportunists who make use of the subsistence strategy that best suits the conditions of the moment (Griffin 1984).

These conditions can be determined by the natural environment but also by the sort of interactions that a group is having with agricultural neighbors at any given moment. In studying the dispersal of agriculture beyond areas of "pristine" domestication, archaeologists have begun to draw on comparative ethnological studies of forager-farmer interaction and to propose models for such interaction in prehistory (e.g., Gregg 1988). Often these involve the exchange of hunted or collected resources from the foragers for cultivated products of farmers, although the potential of forager populations for providing agricultural labor cannot be underestimated. The study of such forager–farmer interactions holds great promise for the understanding of the spread of food production, particularly in cases where foragers adopted domesticated plants and animals from nearby farming populations.

There is also increasing evidence that many populations viewed as having a "foraging" way of life, including those typically put forward as examples of "isolates," have really been in contact with neighboring agricultural societies for hundreds, if not thousands, of years (Headland and Reid 1989). Over this time, they have engaged in exchange relationships with agriculturalists, and, in many cases, practiced desultory food production themselves. Studies such as those of Bailey (1991) and his colleagues of the Ife of Zaire, Headland and Reid's (1991) of the Agta in the Philippines, and Wilmsen's (1989) of the San suggest that a common condition of foragers adjacent to farmers is long-term interaction *without* the full adoption of food-production by the foraging groups (Headland and Reid 1989)

The recognition that the universe is not divided into only foragers and farmers should bring greater clarity to the study both of primary domestication and to agricultural dispersals. For example, the possibility of the co-existence of foragers, farmers, and groups pursuing mixed strategies would explain the diversity of subsistence data from sites in the areas of primary domestication, particularly in the Near East. Rather than being anomalies to be reconciled with some universally-consistent model, the diverse subsistence data should indeed be expected during the period between initial cultivation and a regional commitment to agriculture. It would also accommodate the relative slowness of the dispersal of wheat and barley cultivation in northern Europe and of maize cultivation in the eastern United States.

SEEDS OF CIVILIZATION, ROOTS OF COMPLEXITY

What is the real significance of the transition to agriculture? More to the point, would hierarchically differentiated societies be possible without crops and livestock? It has been common in archaeology to point to the late prehistoric chiefdoms of the Pacific coast of North America and to other complex foragers around the world and argue that civilization is possible without agriculture and stockherding. Yet none of the civilizations of later prehistory and early history, and few of the non-state complex societies, were based on foraging. Moreover, as will be explained in the following chapter, it was not the crops and livestock themselves, but rather control over land, labor, and capital which resulted in social differentiation. Social, economic, and political complexity, therefore, would not have emerged without the existence of agriculture and (in the case of the Old World) of animal husbandry.

FURTHER READING

The transition from foraging to farming has been the topic of many books and articles in the last three decades, the result of the concentration of archaeological field research on this problem in the 1970s and 1980s. A highly readable single-author treatment of the subject is Bruce D. Smith's *The Emergence of Agriculture* (1995). Collections of papers which discuss the subject in greater detail can be found in volumes edited by Patty Jo Watson and C. Wesley Cowan (1992), by Anne Birgitte Gebauer and T. Douglas Price (1992), and by Price, Gebauer, and Keeley (1995). Barbara Stark's 1986 discussion of the models used to explain agricultural origins remains widely cited over a decade later. More comprehensive sources about the basic botanical and zoological data on domestication are volumes edited by David Harris and Gordon Hillman (1989) on general issues, Daniel Zohary and Maria Hopf (1993) on plants, and Juliet Clutton-Brock (1989) on animals. Jack Harlan's 1995 memoir, *The Living Fields*, is the story of a

remarkable botanical career which includes important reflections on the study of agricultural origins. Numerous regional studies of early farming societies have appeared in the last two decades.
Of note are Bruce Smith's 1992 *Rivers of Change* on eastern North America, W. H. Wills' 1988
Early Prehistoric Agriculture in the American Southwest, Graeme Barker's 1985 *Prehistoric Farming
in Europe*, and *Europe's First Farmers* edited by T. Douglas Price (1999). An up-to-date synthesis
of agricultural origins in Mesoamerica has yet to appear. A recent volume by Dolores Piperno
and Deborah Pearsall, *The Origins of Agriculture in the Lowland Neotropics* (1998), uses data from
phytoliths and pollen to argue for a very early origin of cultivation of a variety of species in the
lowlands of lower Central America and northern South America. Discussions of issues such as
labor, risk, and uncertainty in early farming societies are relatively rare, but examples include
Peter Bogucki's 1988 *Forest Farmers and Stockherders* regarding early European agriculture, and
papers in the volume edited by Joseph Tainter and Bonnie Bagley Tainter entitled *Evolving
Complexity and Environmental Risk in the Prehistoric Southwest* (1996).

[6]   *Pathways to Inequality*

INTRODUCTION

Within a millennium or two of the first domestication in the Levant, Mesoamerica, China, and eastern North America, people in these areas lived in sedentary communities that derived much of their diet from agriculture. With the dispersal of agriculture to other parts of the world, such communities arose in new regions, although the pace of their establishment varied. Where agriculture spread through colonization, as in central Europe, such communities appeared immediately, but where agriculture was adopted by indigenous peoples, there was usually a time lag while crops and, in the Old World, livestock were worked into the subsistence economy. Nonetheless, almost everywhere that agriculture appeared in prehistoric times, significant subsequent changes in society ensued within a short time.

These changes manifested themselves in different ways from one part of the world to another, but as in earlier times, numerous cross-cultural convergences suggest that similar processes occurred in many different places. Household-based communities in which social identity was defined through kinship emerged as the norm rather than the exception. Ceremonialism and ritual activity became elaborated to an unprecedented degree. Trade and exchange became especially prominent in the archaeological record. In the Old World, uses were found for domestic animals beyond their meat content. Complex technological processes such as fine pottery and metallurgy were developed and assumed a social prominence beyond their technological benefits. Social differentiation began to appear consistently in burials to the point where we can infer significant distinctions among individuals.

The basis for these changes lay in the household economy and social structure that accompanied the establishment of agrarian society. There would have been a number of dimensions to this phenomenon. One lay in the nature of the household developmental cycle, which would have provided a "metabolism" for the social order in its changes from one generation to the next. Another resulted from the competition among households for status, wealth, and leadership. A third was in the risk and uncertainty attached to agricultural decision making and the adoption of innovations by individual households. All of these played key roles in the next major global transition experienced by human society, specifically the emergence of differences in access to status, power, and wealth.

Just as agriculture provided the fundamental economic basis for modern human culture, the differentiation of society into haves and have-nots provides the basis for modern concepts of social relations and government. As with agriculture, this pattern has now spread globally, such that there are very few peoples (perhaps none) who can be said to be genuinely egalitarian. In the archaeological societies discussed in this chapter, which correspond to the Late Neolithic in the Old World and the Formative or Early Woodland periods in the Americas, these inequalities were probably not yet institutionalized and perpetuated across generations. Subsequently, social differences came to be fixed by lineages and kinship, and changing one's status in life was much more difficult.

The study of social differentiation and its emergence became one of the key issues of 1960s processual archaeology, perhaps due to the reaction of academics to hierarchy and authority in twentieth-century society. It was generally seen as part of the linear trajectory from simple to complex which fitted an evolutionary model of human society. As such, social differentiation was assumed to be more or less inevitable once agriculture tied people to territory and generated surpluses. Perhaps it is, but why? What is it about a sedentary and usually agrarian society which creates differences in access to status, power, and wealth?

Since the 1960s, archaeology has framed the answer to this question in terms of a variety of typological schemes, specifically those of Morton Fried (1967), Elman Service (1962), and others (summarized in figure 6.1). These schema tend to discuss inequality in one or two dimensions of variability.

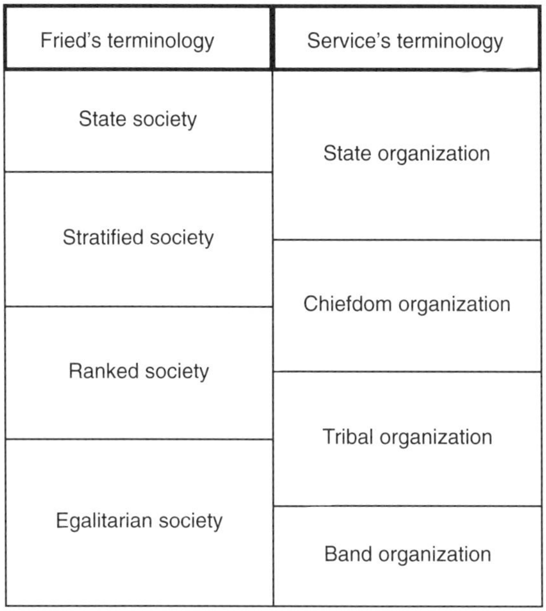

Fried's terminology	Service's terminology
State society	State organization
Stratified society	Chiefdom organization
Ranked society	Tribal organization
Egalitarian society	Band organization

Figure 6.1 Categories of social evolution according to Fried and Service, popular among archaeologists in the 1960s and 1970s.

Fried, for example, focused on political organization, so he laid out a progression from egalitarian, to ranked, to stratified societies. Service was more interested in functional organization and thus differentiated non-egalitarian chiefdoms from generally egalitarian tribes on the basis of centralized coordination of economic, religious, and social activities. "Coordination" over the years came to mean "control," and thus chiefs were the individuals who controlled access to resources. Yet, in a very important 1984 review of societies which have been characterized as either "tribes" or "chiefdoms," Gary Feinman and Jill Neitzel pointed out that variability among these societies occurs along many different axes (e.g., power, ownership, sedentism, wealth, etc.) and thus the formulation of ideal types was fraught with difficulty.

Another problem was that it was never entirely clear how society moved from one stage to another. Archaeologists frequently became hung up on trying to explain how inequality sprang from an initial condition of complete equality. As Price and Feinman (1995) note, however, inequality of some sort is ubiquitous in virtually all societies in some form or another. Price and Feinman note that the challenge for archaeologists is not necessarily to discover the roots of inequality but rather when it became institutionalized and formalized in society. In recent years, such a perspective has forced archaeologists to return to first principles in understanding the emergence of inequalities in prehistoric society.

This chapter will explore the process by which social inequalities became pronounced in a number of different prehistoric societies. First, a theoretical discussion will briefly address some conceptual issues concerning such societies and introduce the author's views on key factors in social differentiation. The position taken here is that only in the framework of a model of competing self-interested households can the roots of societal differentiation be understood. The general thesis is that as households compete for resources and emerge as successful in their domestic economy, some attract debtors, clients, and adherents which translate into status and power. At this early stage, these asymmetrical social arrangements are played out in a variety of arenas, which would include the affiliation of households into factions and their residential clustering into hamlets.

A number of prehistoric societies around the world which were in the process of the development of formalized inequalities will then be examined. This selective review includes Late Neolithic Europe, Halaf and 'Ubaid communities in the Tigris and Euphrates valleys, Formative Mesoamerica, Hopewell societies in the eastern United States, and Late Neolithic and early metal-using peoples of Southeast Asia. As seen in earlier chapters, similar processes can have significantly different consequences. Such varying outcomes substantiate the underlying assumption that small-scale decisions by individual agents, rather than inevitable processes, controlled the direction of societal development.

TRANSEGALITARIAN SOCIETIES

In general, the evidence for social hierarchy in prehistoric times tends to be exaggerated by archaeologists. Part of the problem lies in the conflation of "inequality" and "ranking." Identifying social ranking has been seen as a good thing which places the society that you study a bit higher up in the pecking order of prehistoric peoples. This was particularly true in the days of the New Archaeology, in which the progression from bands to tribes to chiefdoms elaborated by Service in 1962 became more than a heuristic device and served as a typology into which prehistoric societies were pigeon-holed. To get your prehistoric society to be a ranked chiefdom by identifying differing amounts of grave goods or rich child burials was an accomplishment. To characterize it as an egalitarian tribe was to admit defeat in your statistical analysis. O'Shea (1996: 5) notes "the imbalance of archaeological interest, and perhaps the added cachet of studying 'complex societies,' have led to a proliferation of supposed chiefly societies in the past, often based on the meagerest evidence of social inequality."

The focus on "chiefdom" as a type may be a hindrance in understanding what actually may have led to the emergence of political and economic structures beyond the household in later prehistory. Feinman and Neitzel (1984) reviewed the ethnographic literature on prehistoric groups which had been characterized as "tribes" and "chiefdoms" in the Americas and have pointed out the problems with an overly typological approach to this type of society. They found that there is not a clear distinction between egalitarian and ranked societies along a number of dimensions of variability, thus making it impossible to slot groups into neat categories. Rothman (1994) argues that the term "chiefdom" still has utility as a general concept to indicate multiple levels of organization and as a tool to facilitate cross-cultural comparison among societies of similar scale. Presumably a similar value could be found for the concept of "tribe."

The position taken here, however, is that the terms "tribe" and "chiefdom" are too laden with connotations to be useful in the sort of macro-level analysis attempted in this chapter. Moreover, I believe that most prehistoric societies moved more slowly towards political centralization and institutionalized ranking than many other archaeologists would prefer to believe. Such centralized, ranked societies did not truly emerge until somewhat later prehistory, and the argument will be made in the following chapter that such hierarchical pre-state societies would have been relatively unstable social formations which either moved on quickly to statehood or collapsed, due to either internal or external causes. During the period in prehistory covered in this chapter, however, societies around the world were simply moving in the general direction of institutionalized ranking but had not yet arrived at that point.

Clark and Blake (1994) and Hayden (1995b) use the term "transegalitarian" to describe societies which are neither egalitarian nor politically stratified, and I believe that this is the best characterization of societies like Late Neolithic Europe, Middle Woodland North America, Formative Mesoamerica, Halaflan and 'Ubaid settlements in the Near East, and early metal-using peoples in Southeast Asia (Hayden 1995b). It truly captures the sense that these societies were moving beyond the constraints of egalitarian households of late foragers and early farmers into a social environment of competition and differentiation. Yet the relationships among households over time were still fluid and had not become ossified into rigid hierarchical structures. "Leadership" had not yet become completely transformed into "power."

In such transegalitarian societies, however, the fuel of inequality had long been present and simply needed an engine of some sort to make it an active force. What could constitute such an engine? In an important hypothesis-generating essay, Hayden (1995b) identifies one key element: aggrandizive individuals, which could be expected to be present in any group of more than 50–100 individuals. Such aggrandizers, as the term is used by Clark and Blake (1994), are ambitious, enterprising, aggressive, accumulative people who achieve a dominant position in the community. They may control resources, labor, trade, or all three. Such people always existed, but in Pleistocene band society there were powerful social norms to keep them in check. The breakdown of band society which resulted in the major social transformations among late foragers and early farmers provided the incubator for such individuals to emerge as key factors once agrarian societies came to be firmly established.

Yet aggrandizers may represent only one part of the story. The other part, as is proposed below, would be demographic and economic factors which would lead certain segments of society to drop *down* in their access to resources and labor. If being an aggrandizer was the ticket to status, power, and wealth, then everyone would be an aggrandizer. Clearly that is never the case. Some other factors conspire against people and their kin to cause them to drop to second-class or third-class status. Just as a rocket in outer space does not move forward by pushing against the vacuum of space but rather by pushing against its own spent exhaust gases, so too do a few aggrandizers push themselves up in society against the other larger segment that is dropping further and further behind. The synergy between these two forces is the key to understanding transegalitarian societies.

THE DEMOGRAPHIC BASIS OF INEQUALITY

As was the case with the transition to agriculture, archaeologists have sought the origins of inequality and differential access to status, power, and wealth in terms of a number of "prime movers" which lent themselves to 1970s-style processual explanations. Among these, trade has figured prominently, the notion being that those who found themselves in control of key resources would enrich themselves sufficiently to emerge with high status and wealth. In some parts of the world, such as Mesopotamia, the argument was advanced that irrigation and the control and management of irrigation works required a class of individuals who had superordinated status. Craft specialization and metallurgy were two favorite causal factors in the Old World which also were argued to have led to the formation of elites.

Fundamental to these approaches was the belief that some single factor led to the emergence of an initial "petty elite" which was then able to concentrate wealth and power to progressively greater degrees. This process involves, either implicitly or explicitly, a quasi-Marxian view of class differentiation, in that the origins of inequality lie exclusively in the organization of production and exchange. Typically, this is seen as the effect of a novel technology or exotic material which caused a significant dislocation in society, either through the need to manage that technology or through greed. Unfortunately, these "prime-mover" explanations either break down shortly after they are introduced or are ethnologically specious. It is difficult to argue, for example, that exchange automatically leads to the production of elites. Indeed, there are exchange systems in many parts of the world which actually re-distribute wealth in a way that damps out social differentiation.

I would like to propose a different way of looking at this problem, by widening the discussion from an exclusive focus on the organization of production and exchange to include the organization of decision making and consumption under conditions of risk and uncertainty. Of particular importance are the primary units of decision making about the allocation of land and labor. In the societies under consideration below, this unit can be termed the "household." Although the discussion in the last few chapters has presaged this issue, the notion of households as primary units of production and consumption becomes especially germane here in understanding social processes for which "prime-mover" explanations are usually unsatisfactory.

Households

Within the larger context of social anthropology, the study of ethnographic households has been common for over thirty years. The initial use of the term in anthropological literature was more or less as a convenient way to describe the condition often encountered by ethnographers when ideal family types did not equate with what people actually did (Wilk and Netting 1984: 2). With time, the term took on more formal attributes, such as co-residence and collective economic interest. The expectation is that household members share cultural values and expectations and, by definition, live in similar physical and social environments. Economically, the household is a cooperating group that jointly makes production decisions (Barlett 1982). Socially, the household is the unit of reproduction and the focus of social interactions and obligations. In short, the household is viewed as a social grouping and an analytical unit of great relevance to studies of both subsistence farming and peasant societies today.

The use of the household as an analytical unit in archaeology has a particular justification, in that it provides a context in which settlement remains can be linked to a real social group with only a minimum of inference and assumption. While in other social sciences the exclusive focus on the household may reflect a conscious minimization of the role of other social structures, in archaeology it represents one of the few social structures that we can begin to isolate and compare in a meaningful way. For that reason, the analysis of settlement remains at the household level is more than just the use of a "convenient" unit of analysis but rather an attempt to structure the archaeological record so that we can begin to approach economic and political institutions beyond the household. In other words, the study of archaeological households affords us an opportunity to study prehistoric society "from the bottom up." As such, the goals of archaeologists who study households are different from those of researchers in allied social sciences who may exclusively focus on households to the exclusion of other relevant scales of inquiry.

Archaeologically, there has been increased interest in the last two decades in the identification of household units and the use of these as basic units of analysis (Ashmore and Wilk 1988). Yet it is very difficult, if not almost impossible, to identify actual households, and archaeologists must be content with proxy evidence for domestic groups. Distinct, yet essentially similar, modules consisting of houses and associated features within larger settlements or dispersed individually are generally taken as reflecting some sort of household structure, although multi-structure households are known from many societies and their presence in the archaeological record must also be taken into consideration. Although to equate single dwellings with single households is possibly an imposition of a western bias on the interpretation of the archaeological record, the dispersal of habitation units and discrete, recurring forms of houses and associated features suggest that in many archaeological remains we are indeed dealing with distinct decision-making units.

Tringham and Krstić (1990: 603) argue that

> It is not essential to be able to identify "households" in the historical and anthropological sense of the term. It is sufficient to be able to investigate changes in co-residence and cooperative activities of domestic groups on an archaeological site.

In their view, the term "household" functions as a concise way of saying "kin-based co-resident domestic group." They have developed this theme in considerable detail for the Late Neolithic and Eneolithic periods in southeastern Europe, arguing that there was a shift from larger corporate groups to smaller co-resident groups during this period. They note that competition among such units and the inequalities that are inherent in their developmental cycle over time would have formed the basis for the emergence of social differentiation during this period.

The position taken here is that there are several elements to the household's role in the emergence of social differentiation. The first is that households by their nature pursue strategies of accumulation in order to create wealth that can be passed from one generation to the next, thus ensuring the viability of offspring households. The second is that each household has its own developmental cycle, which progresses from their formation to their dissolution, as members are born, mature, and die. The third is that households will find themselves in asymmetrical social and economic relationships with each other depending where they are at different points in this developmental cycle. The question is, when do these asymmetrical relationships become institutionalized into permanent inequalities? This did not happen overnight, and it is suggested below that it may have been less a question of the emergence of elites but more the falling of more and more households into subordinate positions which resulted in what might be called "residual elites." Finally, leadership emerges first from successful management of the affairs of a household, which then permits the attraction of adherents and debtors, leading in turn to the growth of factions.

HOUSEHOLD ACCUMULATION STRATEGIES

Each household, as a self-interested economic unit, can be said to pursue a strategy of accumulation. This should not be equated with some sort of "primitive capitalism" but rather that each household looks out for opportunities to acquire resources, property, favors, and obligations that can provide economic and social security and possibly advancement. There may also be socially-instituted avenues for "decumulation," so the accumulative process is not necessarily linear. One major goal of the accumulation strategy is to acquire sufficient resources to be able to establish the households of offspring as viable economic units.

The fact that different households will have different degrees of success in the pursuit of their accumulation strategies does not automatically imply social inequality. Indeed, many societies have built-in levelling mechanisms that act to put a damper on excessive accumulation. Some households will take risks, while others will manage their resources conservatively. Hazards will have varying impacts on households of differing size, composition, holdings, and reserves. The mere fact of household level accumulation and competition for access to economic and social resources does not in itself lead to long-term permanent inequalities between households.

INTERHOUSEHOLD COMPETITION

Each household undergoes a developmental cycle, leading from its founding to its eventual dissolution. In his classic 1958 discussion of this process, Fortes describes five stages of development:

1 Establishment – the new household, possibly still dependent on its parental household(s), builds a house and establishes a farm;
2 Expansion – the new household becomes clearly independent and children are born;
3 Consolidation – the household expands to its fullest point;
4 Fission – children begin to marry and leave the parental household, perhaps associated with the relinquishment of control over household resources from the parental to the filial generation;
5 Decline – the final stage, which often contributes to the expansion stage of filial households, if the parental household becomes lodged in them.

Fortes' model assumes a two-generation structure of households and their filia. In many societies, these stages may not be so clear cut, especially if the development takes place over three generations as children remain in parental households after marriage and birth of their first children. In polygynous households, a single residential group may be going through several of these stages simultaneously in different subsections.

The important point here is that household structure is not static but rather is constantly changing. Similarly, the relationship between parental households and those of their offspring, as well as between them and other households into which they have entered into alliances through marriage and betrothal are constantly shifting. One effect of this process is to provide for the transfer of assets from the parental household to its filia. Such mechanisms for the transfer of capital resources across generations are routine in many societies in order to ensure the eventual establishment of new households as viable economic units.

Another effect of this process is that households in a settlement usually find themselves in some sort of asymmetrical relationship with each other, depending on where they are in the developmental cycle. These social and economic asymmetries could be characterized as "inequality" (e.g., Tringham and Krstić 1990: 606), except that they are not permanent and they are not cumulative. So long as the range of variation in the abilities of different households to accumulate and disperse assets falls within a very short range, each household can expect to find itself at different times on both the plus side and the minus side of this asymmetry. The crucial question, then, is when do these asymmetries become permanent (or, at least, lasting) and cumulative, in that the ability of households to accumulate commensurate with their peers is not simply a matter of the passage of time.

The developmental cycle and accumulation strategy of a household does not always behave as it ideally should, however. The human members of a household are prone to disease, accidents, and death. Animal populations are vulnerable to disease, predation, and theft. Bad decisions were probably just as much a reality of prehistoric life as they are today. Initiative, resourcefulness, and luck were as important 6000 years ago as they are today. While some households may consciously strive to get ahead, most are concerned more with staying afloat and not sinking below the status of their neighbors.

RESIDUAL ELITES

Archaeologists usually think about the origins of social differentiation in terms of the emergence of elites. Typically, the model is one of a smaller segment of society rising above the rest to a position of economic or social dominance or to attain greater authority. Movement is seen as invariably upward, towards the point of a progressively more exclusive pyramid of social hierarchy. Yet it should be remembered that we really do not know much about the process of social differentiation within previously "egalitarian" societies. Is it always that an elite group rises above the hitherto undifferentiated social norms of status and wealth or, possibly, is it the disadvantaged that fall below it? While these are two sides of the same coin, it may be possible to obtain some new perspectives on the emergence of social differentiation by taking the latter view. In other words, rather than some individuals or households emerging as an "elite" at the beginning of this process, perhaps this was an effect of a larger set of forces.

The model of elite formation which I would like to propose here differs from the way in which this process is envisioned by most anthropological archaeologists. Rather than conceiving of individuals as somehow suddenly rising above the rest of society in status, power, and wealth, I would like to suggest that the development of elites in a society at first took a reverse course, starting from an initial condition of roughly equal households in competition with each other. Of course, these households would never have been exactly equal, and some asymmetrical relationships would have always existed. Some factor would then have intervened which alters the abilities of individual households to accumulate prestige and property. At first, this differential accumulation may have had ephemeral effects, confined to a few months or years but able to be reversed easily. As asymmetries between households came to be more pronounced and to last longer, certain neolithic households would then begin to sink *below* existing norms of accumulation of property and prestige, while others might remain constant or even increase. Households would have sunk at differing rates, but eventually, those which had been able to resist finding themselves on the wrong side of social asymmetries would have remained at the top. Wise decision making and good luck would have played a critical role.

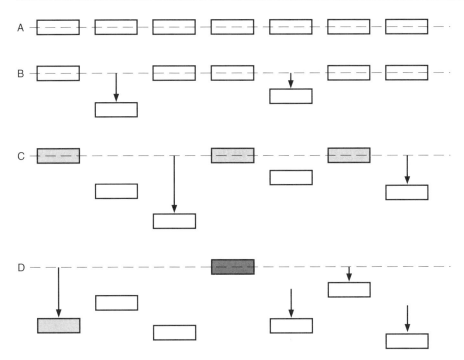

Figure 6.2 A model of downward social mobility among competing households. At time A, all households in the community are relatively equal along some baseline of accumulation; at time B, two households have fallen below this baseline; at time C, still more households have dropped below the earlier standard, leaving three that have retained their wealth; at time D, only one household remains at the earlier baseline of accumulation and wealth, while all others have fallen below to some degree.

Figure 6.2 depicts such a hypothesized sequence of household downward social mobility. Looking at the emergence of inequality from such a perspective has several advantages. First, it eliminates the need for an engine which causes some individuals suddenly to jump out in front of their neighbors. Second, it takes into account the fact that early farming households were always competitive to some degree. Finally, it forces us to look for social and economic factors which might have advanced this process. For example, in the case of Late Neolithic Europe described below, access to animal traction may have been one key element in causing certain households to flounder while others remained afloat. In other parts of the world, archaeologists may search for other factors which allowed households to accumulate at different rates or which amplified the effects of household demography.

The key transition came when these asymmetries were carried across generations and as the household demography changed over time. All households, both those of the residual elite and those of the households whose fortunes had declined, would fission, but since there would have been fewer households surviving on the top of the pile than would have sunk towards the bottom, within a few generations there would be relatively few of the households with wealth and prestige (and even they would have been in competition with each other) and many more descendants of the households which had moved downward. The rich might get richer in terms of wealth and prestige, but the poor as an aggregate might also get "richer" in terms of sheer numbers.

Under such a scenario, it is fairly easy to envision how within a very short time a society can be transformed from one of similar households jostling for position to one in which there are marked inequalities of status, power, and wealth. From this point, things can go in a variety of different directions. In some cases, the status differences may stabilize at a very shallow depth, particularly in situations where households may still have an easy route to acquire key productive resources and advance their position. In others, inequalities may increase exponentially and can be transmitted intact from one generation to the next, thus institutionalizing them. Once this generational barrier to the transmission of inequalities was broken, with children and even grandchildren responsible for the debts, social obligations, and clientage arrangements of their elders, then social inequalities would have been firmly woven into the fabric of society.

FACTIONS AND HAMLETS

Although a case can be made that households were the primary decision-making elements of early agrarian societies around the world, it is also clear that they affiliated into higher-order social units to varying degrees. Households did not exist in a social vacuum, and the arenas for their competition and alliances would have been social groupings consisting of a number of such units. Aspects of suprahousehold affiliation can be discussed under two rubrics: hamlets (Cancian 1996) and factions (Brumfiel 1994a). These are complementary concepts which have value for understanding the emergence of suprahousehold leadership in early agrarian societies.

Hamlets, as the term is used here, are institutionalized alliances of domestic groups (although more generally the term is often simply used as a synonym for village or collection of households), in which their affiliation is demonstrated through residential proximity. Cancian (1996) has noted several important characteristics of hamlets. First, they are "socially incomplete" and the social and public life of their residents extends beyond their boundaries. In other words, they are not self-contained entities, but each household has a set of external relations which reaches beyond the confines of the local group. Cancian cites Skinner's 1964 study of Chinese peasants whose social field was not the boundaries of their village but their "standard marketing area" for their products which extended beyond the village boundaries. Second, their public life is not formally organized. Relations with the outside world are conducted by many different people of all types of social standing. There is no single individual who speaks on behalf of all the component units of the hamlet. The result is that the hamlet as a whole functions as a social unit which "mediates" relations between the household and the larger society but which is still relatively small and informal.

Such social incompleteness and informality of hamlets is important for understanding how settlements function in transegalitarian societies. Archaeologists have traditionally placed a great emphasis on hierarchies of settlement size as an indicator of social ranking. Yet even a larger agglomeration of households may still be socially incomplete. Instead, it may simply be just that, an agglomeration of households, and remain so until some evidence of formal structure appears. The appearance of public architecture within a residential precinct in the form of temples or gathering areas, as well as the explicit patterning of open space in a settlement, can be seen as clear evidence that a community has moved beyond being a collection of households to a more complex entity.

Factions can also be characterized as institutionalized alliances of household groups, except that there is a clear purpose to them other than just forming a neighborhood of domestic units. Brumfiel (1994a) defines factions as "structurally and functionally similar groups which, by virtue of their similarity, compete for resources and positions of power and prestige," but which are not social classes or functionally-differentiated interest groups. Their members "hold similar ideas of what the world is like and what it should be like" (Brumfiel 1994a: 5), but so do members of other virtually identical groups. They have no common political goal other than obtaining an advantage for their own faction.

Factions form the arena in which leaders emerge (Clark and Blake 1994; Spencer 1993, 1994) thus allowing the formation of political structures beyond the household. As in the case of competition among households producing inequalities, competition among factions produces varying opportunities for leadership. In some cases, there may be several factional leaders in the community, each competing for authority, while in others one person may emerge as dominant, thus creating a centralized local structure. At the same time, as Spencer (1994: 33) notes, the tendency towards factionalism may inhibit the emergence of long-term authority, since no sooner has someone ascended to a position of leadership, then defectors may form a competing faction that undermines him. The key moment comes, in Spencer's view, when a local leader increases participation in inter societal contacts which allow him to control the external contacts of a community and also when the leader is able to extend his authority beyond a single community to include people in other communities.

Both hamlets and factions represent social entities which have limited organizational goals and which provide the arena for various forms of social interaction: alliances, clientship, competition. They are the realm of people who do not have the option to improve their lot or to resolve inter household conflicts simply by moving further together or away from each other. Yet they are loosely structured and informal. This informality is a crucial aspect of such entities. Their social structures and political organization has not become formalized into hereditary rankings and statuses. Leaders can emerge and disappear, and individual households can conduct business outside the bounds of the entity with impunity. Defense, trade, and other relations function within the context of "trusted networks" (Burns 1977) rather than as formal functions of a leadership elite.

Renfrew and Cherry (1986) have described such structurally similar, autonomous social groups as "peer polities," which is very much in the spirit of what is being discussed here. Yet to characterize hamlets and factions as "polities" would ascribe to them a greater degree of formality and organization than they actually warrant. Perhaps a better case is that hamlets and factions in early agrarian societies constitute forerunners or the elemental units from which "peer polities" eventually emerged in later prehistory. The key difference between hamlets and factions on one hand and "peer polities" on the other may lie in the degree of formality of the organization of public life.

Social entities such as hamlets and factions probably functioned among early agrarian societies and shaped their development, and it would be profitable for archaeologists trying to understand the development of social inequality to examine cultures around the world in these terms. Until now that has rarely been the case, since the identification of chiefdoms has been the paramount concern. Hamlets may be easier to discern in the archaeological record, while the argument for factions will be more complicated.

Nonetheless, analysis in this framework provides a useful approach for understanding how the atomized households of late foragers and early farmers became progressively organized into higher-order social entities.

CASE STUDIES IN SOCIAL DIFFERENTIATION

The emergence of social differentiation manifested itself in different ways in various parts of the world. Here, several instances will be examined in order to describe this process in detail. Late Neolithic temperate Europe is one area where there is good archaeological data to study this process, as is the Hopewell "tradition" of mid-continent North America. In Mesoamerica and the Near East, the archaeological data are somewhat more equivocal, due to the accelerated pace of societal development in these regions. Finally, in Southeast Asia, social differentiation appears now to predate the introduction of metallurgy, prompting new questions as to its causes.

LATE NEOLITHIC EUROPE

Agriculture was established throughout most of Europe, including the British Isles and southern Scandinavia, by 3000 BC. Only in the boreal forests of central and northern Scandinavia and northern Russia did foraging peoples persist until much later. Between 4000 and 2000 BC, prehistoric society in Europe underwent a remarkable transformation from late foragers and pioneer agriculturalists to transegalitarian communities which used metals and diverted significant amounts of effort to ceremonial architecture. At the same time, there was an important set of innovations which adjusted the relationship between people and livestock. People ceased to view their herds simply

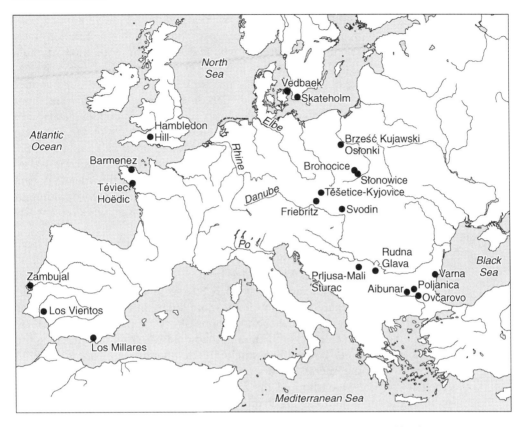

Figure 6.3   Map of Europe showing key sites mentioned in this chapter.

as tame sources of meat and saw them as providers of useful products while still alive, such as milk, wool, and power. The last was a crucial innovation which permitted the households with livestock to leverage their animal assets in the service of the household economy.

COPPER AND GOLD METALLURGY

Metallurgy, specifically the smelting of copper from ores like malachite, appears to have developed independently at several times and places in Europe and the Near East. By 5000 BC, there are clear traces of copper use in southeastern Europe (Whittle 1996: 117). Although copper artifacts soon became widespread in the Near East, it can be argued that the emergence of metallurgy had its most pronounced social and economic effect in Europe, and early copper metallurgy in Europe was perhaps more technically sophisticated than in southwestern Asia. Within a few centuries, copper came to figure very prominently in human ornamentation and in mortuary ritual and continued to do so until it came to be alloyed with tin to make bronze in the late third millennium BC.

Between 4500 and 3500 BC, copper use reached a remarkable apex in eastern Europe, with important implications for human society. Extraordinary measures were taken to procure copper, which become even more notable when one considers the extent to which copper was then taken *out* of circulation in living society through its use in mortuary ritual. Since pure copper would have been useless for making tools since it is so malleable and does not hold a cutting edge (what have been identified as copper "awls" are probably scrap from pounding the metal into ribbon to make the elaborate coiled artifacts), it is clearly a *social* metal, procured for its value as an exotic, bright, and attractive material. This period in southeastern Europe is frequently called the "Copper Age," since the appearance of this metal appears to correlate with a variety of changes in the archaeological record, although from a broader perspective, it can be seen that these were essentially Neolithic societies who came to use a novel technology.

During this period in southeastern Europe, as much energy seems to have gone into the procurement of copper as was being invested in megalithic tombs in western Europe. Mines have been discovered at several locations, including Rudna Glava and Prljusa-Mali Sturac in Serbia and Aibunar in Bulgaria, and there are probably many more such sites in the Carpathians and eastern Alps waiting to be found. Seams of copper ore were followed by miners who heated the rock and then dashed cold water on it to fracture the metal-bearing stone. It was then smelted at temperatures of about 1000°C to obtain the pure metal. At first, artifacts were made by hammering the smelted copper, which limited the range of forms, but later the practice of melting the metal and casting it into more complex forms emerged. By the early part of the fourth millennium BC, two-piece molds were in use to form axes and "hammer-axes" with shaft holes.

The demand for copper existed at a considerable distance from the copper sources. At Varna in northeastern Bulgaria, which will be discussed further below, copper was obtained from southern Bulgaria, a distance of about 200 kilometers. Even more remarkable is that the copper used in north-central Poland, at sites like Osłonki and Brześć Kujawski, was transported from as-yet-undetermined sources in the Carpathians, a distance of at least 500 and perhaps even 1000 kilometers (Bogucki 1996b). The transport costs of this heavy material, whether as ores, ingots, or finished products, would have been considerable. Even if transported on water by rafts or canoes, the direction of copper distribution is often against the prevailing current in the Danube drainage and there would have been occasions when it needed to be moved between watersheds and through mountain passes.

Copper ornaments and tools were clearly used in living society. At the end of the fourth millennium BC the famous "Iceman" found in 1991 in the Italo-Austrian Alps had a copper flanged axe with him (Barfield 1994). Nearly a millennium earlier, at Brześć Kujawski and Osłonki, copper ornaments are found in rubbish pits, presumably lost by their wearers as they moved about the settlement. Yet most commonly, archaeologists find the greatest amount of copper in hoards and graves, where it was deliberately buried. At some of the burials at Brześć Kujawski and Osłonki, thousands of copper beads, each

Figure 6.4 Burial XIII at Osłonki, Poland, close-up of skull, showing copper strips that had been wrapped around a perishable material like leather or cloth to form a diadem. This burial also contained five copper pendants and numerous copper beads (photo by Ryszard Grygiel, Museum of Archaeology and Ethnography, Łódz, Poland).

meticulously made, are found in belts and necklaces, and hoards of copper tools have been found throughout the Balkans. Copper artifacts are found in about a third of the graves at Varna, including the most spectacularly furnished ones.

Copper was not the only metal that received this sort of treatment. Gold also was keenly sought where it was available, especially in the Balkans. Again, Varna is the most spectacular occurrence of this metal, although simpler ornaments are known from graves and caches over a wider part of the Balkans. The metallurgical sophistication for working gold was less than for copper, but gold was less abundant and thus the acquisition costs would have been higher.

As Whittle (1996: 120) points out, copper and gold were acquired in Neolithic Europe to be used and displayed, not to be accumulated. In this connection, I would emphasize their role in mortuary ritual, which as will be seen in the following section, became significantly elaborated during this period. One could even say that gold and silver were acquired primarily to be disposed of in burials. Yet in Poland after about 4000 BC and in southeastern Europe after about 3000 BC the intensive use of copper abruptly appears to diminish – or is it simply the amount of copper which is being deliberately buried in graves and hoards? Not until closer to the end of the third millennium, and then on a continent-wide scale, is there a resurgence of metallurgy as the alloying of copper and tin to make bronze is discovered, with similarly profound implications for human society.

MORTUARY CEREMONIALISM

One of the defining characteristics of this period throughout Europe is what could be called (in terms borrowed from American archaeology) "mortuary ceremonialism." Such ceremonialism takes a variety of forms, from the earthen barrows and megalithic tombs of the Atlantic fringe to the elaborate cemeteries of southeastern Europe, most notably Varna. Archaeologists have tended not to see this as a single phenomenon, preferring to try to explain megalithic tombs or rich flat burials as separate problems. Yet there may be some value in stepping back and looking at Europe as a whole during the fifth and fourth millennia BC to see the larger pattern of transegalitarian societies in Europe.

Before going further, let me clarify the use of the term "ceremonialism." I am *not* advocating a return to the view of Childe and others in the 1940s and 1950s who wrote of a "megalithic religion" which spread from Iberia through the Atlantic façade of northwestern Europe. By "ceremonialism" I simply mean that the construction of massive monuments of large stones (the megaliths) and the furnishing of rich burials in barrows and cemeteries provided a context for elaborate ceremonial behavior. The impact of this behavior was to create a landscape which not only was altered for agriculture and habitation but was etched with large permanent monuments and formal cemeteries that persisted across generations and even millennia.

Megalithic mortuary monuments take a variety of forms and the archaeological literature is full of detailed discussions and typologies. Some forms, such as the so-called "court tombs" in Ireland appear to be very chronologically-sensitive, whereas the unchambered long barrows of France and England were constructed over many centuries. The number of megalithic tombs that survive today is astonishing (Daniel 1980: 81), and since many are known to have been destroyed in ancient and early modern times, we must confront the fact that a substantial diversion of labor into their prehistoric construction took place over the course of about a millennium. The dolmens, passage graves, and other tombs created a fantastic altered landscape rich in ceremonial significance.

Julian Thomas (1991: 32) has characterized this as an "inscribed landscape" in which people have created a countryside which conveys a variety of meanings, "continually altered, continually read and interpreted." Such a dynamic view has a certain logic to it which is more compelling than earlier single-function views of the megalithic phenomenon. For example, Colin Renfrew (1976) and Robert Chapman (1981, 1995) considered megalithic

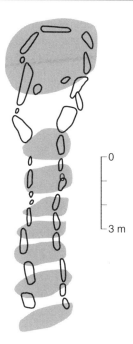

Figure 6.5 Plan of the megalithic tomb at Barmenez H in Brittany (after Patton 1993, figure 4.9c) showing upright stones that outline the passage and chamber and the capstones (hatched) that form the roof.

tombs to be symbols of a group's claim on land and resources, while Ian Hodder (1984, 1990) saw them as extensions of the structures of the living. These are all plausible hypotheses, but very difficult to test. We may never know the true symbolic "function" of the megaliths, but it is clear that they structured the landscape in a dramatic fashion.

Of greater interest here is the interrelationship between the megalithic structures and the organization of the society that built them. The prevailing assumption has been that the labor requirements of megalithic construction were so great that they represent the products of communal activities and corporate groups. This may well have been the case, but it is entirely compatible with a model of Neolithic society which is based on autonomous households. There is no reason why households, affiliated perhaps as a faction or a hamlet, cannot unite and cooperate to build structures that the community sees as important. Moreover, many smaller monuments, such as the dolmens, could easily have been the product of household labor over a very short time, particularly if animals were skillfully employed in hauling and erecting the slabs.

Andrew Sherratt (1990), in a review of the genesis and dispersal of megalithic construction, has pointed out the congruence between the areas of megalithic architecture and late foraging groups who had adopted agriculture. He makes the argument that megalithic architecture was essential for the creation of community among these ex-foraging peoples who needed permanent central foci among dispersed residential groupings. As Sherratt notes, "such monuments served their communities for many generations: as the burial places of founding ancestors, as communal ossuaries, and as a continuing focus for ritual" (149). He argues that on the loesslands of central Europe, settled by the Linear Pottery culture, the longhouse village served a similar purpose, whereas the megaliths were "surrogates for the living village."

Although dispersed farming households may well have been autonomous decision-making units, they still would have been interconnected in a web of relationships, especially as they came to affiliate into factions and hamlets. The ceremonialism associated with the construction and maintenance of megalithic architecture and the mortuary practices which occurred at these sites would have been a powerful integrative force among these atomized units. The late forager societies of northern and western Europe were already pre-disposed to elaborate mortuary ceremonialism, as seen in the cemeteries at Skateholm and Vedbaek in Scandinavia and Téviec and Hoëdic in Brittany. If we are to make the case that agriculture was adopted by these populations relatively seamlessly, albeit with some delay, then megalithic mortuary ceremonialism can be seen as an elaboration of pre-existing traditions, part of a general transformation of culture with the adoption of cultivation and domestic livestock.

On the other hand, ceremonialism centered on monumental architecture is not confined to the areas peripheral to the loess belt, as Sherratt suggests, and in Atlantic Europe there is considerable evidence for non-megalithic mortuary ceremonialism as well. In the loess zone, megaliths by definition could not be built, since there are no large stones of glacial origin. Contemporaneous with megalithic construction, and perhaps beginning even a bit earlier, non-megalithic monumental sites are indeed found in southern Poland, Bohemia, Moravia, Slovakia, and Austria. A number of sites, known as "rondels" are found in upland loess zones south of the Carpathians in Bohemia, Moravia, Slovakia, and Austria at sites like Těšetice-Kyjovice, Svodin, and Friebritz. These are circular ditched enclosures with causeways at four opposing points on the perimeter. Usually, there are few traces of settlement, so these appear to have served some form of non-habitation purpose, presumably ceremonial. In recent years, loessland analogues of monumental tombs have also been found. In 1996, for example, it was announced that at Słonowice near Kraków in southern Poland, a timber mortuary structure over 100 meters long had been excavated over the course of several seasons. Within a trapezoidal outline of timber posts, earth from ditches on either side had been heaped up over a primary burial dating to the fourth millennium BC.

Similar to the "rondels" of central Europe are the so-called "causewayed camps" of the British Isles, which would more appropriately be called "causewayed enclosures," for their role as locations of habitation is uncertain at best. About 40 such enclosures are known, largely on the chalk downs and river terraces of southern England. Often, they are associated with earthen long barrows of the first farmers of the British Isles. These sites have one or more courses of ditch, roughly circular in plan, interrupted at several points by unexcavated portions, which form the "causeways" into the interior. The existence of the causeways and the locations of the sites suggest that the earthworks did not fulfill a defensive function. Instead, they are most commonly interpreted as ceremonial or ritual sites. At a number of them, human remains have been found in the ditches and interiors.

Hambledon Hill in Dorset, England, is one of the better-known causewayed enclosures (actually a complex of two enclosures and several embankments over about 60 hectares.) The larger enclosure encompasses about 8 hectares with ditches that had been recut many times, while the smaller outer enclosure (the so-called Stapleton enclosure) has a more elaborate timber palisade. Both enclosures have evidence for some occupation in their interiors, although only in the form of pits, and ceremonial feasting. In the ditches of the main enclosure were an extraordinary number of human remains, about 70 individuals, even though only about a fifth of the whole ditch has been excavated. These human remains included isolated crania, disarticulated torsos, and occasional complete skeletons. Apparently, these remains had been exposed to the elements and largely defleshed prior to their deposition in the ditch. Some of the intact skeletons appear to have met a violent end, one with an arrowhead among the ribs. The interpretation of the site is as a mortuary center, to which deceased individuals were brought and left exposed to the elements, prior to the deposition of their remains in the ditch system.

In the southern part of the Iberian Peninsula, an unusual pattern of communal burial and nucleated fortified settlement appeared in the Copper Age. Perhaps the best-known site from this region is Los Millares, in southeastern Spain, which has been investigated for over a century. The complex at Los Millares consists of a fortified settlement surrounded by multiple stone walls, within which were small round houses. Just outside the settlement were over 80 megalithic tombs, which housed collective burials in their chambers and passages. Some contain exotic materials such as African ivory and ostrich shell. On surrounding hilltops were thirteen "forts." Other settlements in the region are also fortified, but on a smaller scale. A number of other sites in this region also have fortifications, but Los Millares is exceptional in its size and complexity. On the other side of the Iberian peninsula, fortified settlements with tomb complexes like Zambujal and Los Vientos share many characteristics with Los Millares.

Robert Chapman's analysis of the burial data from Los Millares leads him to conclude that some measure of social differentiation was already in effect, with higher-ranked groups being buried closer to the settlement than those of lower rank (Chapman 1990: 195). The differences, however, do not appear to be especially marked or based on hereditary status. Fernández Castro (1995: 32), in her recent review of later Iberian prehistory, appears to share this position. Such a view would be consistent with the concept of transegalitarian societies discussed in this chapter, in which individuals and households may achieve distinction but are not born to it. The complexity of the fortifications at Los Millares and similar sites suggests conflict among these communities, which probably approximated the definition of hamlets as used in this chapter.

Elsewhere in Europe, particularly in the Balkans, a different form of mortuary ceremonialism manifested itself roughly about the same time that monumental mortuary structures came to be built in northern and western Europe. Large cemeteries of several hundred burials have yielded graves which often contain copper and gold. Most archaeologists tend to see the monumental Atlantic mortuary structures and the rich Balkan burials as distinct phenomena, but they may also be considered to be different manifestations of a general trend towards mortuary ceremonialism throughout Europe in this period.

John Chapman (1991) has analyzed the emergence of mortuary ceremonialism in southeastern Europe in terms of competition among households and lineages. The cemeteries provided a social arena in which these entities could display their wealth and prestige to an extent not possible in the realm of the settlements. To recast the discussion into the framework proposed at the beginning of this chapter, the key actors in this setting can easily be envisioned to have been aggrandizive individuals who were able to pursue a successful household accumulation strategy. Again, the picture that emerged between 4500 and 3500 BC is one of a transegalitarian society in which households are competing for status and prestige. The differentiation among households became progressively greater and eventually can be observed in settlements such as Poljanica and Ovčarovo (Chapman 1991: 168), coeval with the cemetery at Varna.

Varna, in northeastern Bulgaria, provides the richest collection of burials of this period in eastern Europe. The nearly 300 graves are unique in their volume of gold, copper, and other luxury items, although one-fifth were "symbolic graves" or cenotaphs without actual human remains. Gold artifacts, which constitute the most distinctive aspect of the Varna cemetery, occur in 61 of the graves. Curiously, most of the gold is found in the cenotaphs, while only a few of the graves with skeletons were similarly furnished. Three of the cenotaphs – Graves 1, 4, and 36 – were extraordinarily rich. Grave 1 contained 216 gold objects which together weighed over a kilogram, while the 339 gold objects in Grave 4 weighed over 1.5 kg. Grave 36 had the most gold items – 857 – which together weighed 789 grams. Three other cenotaphs – Graves 2, 3, and 15 – contained gold-ornamented clay masks with male features.

Perhaps the richest burial at Varna was Grave 43, which contained the skeleton of a man who was about 40–50 years old and about 1.75 meters tall. Accompanying the skeleton were nearly a thousand gold objects weighing over 1.5 kg, along with other items made of copper, stone, clay, and *Spondylus* shell. One of the gold objects is termed a "scepter," in which a wooden handle had been sheathed with gold and topped with a stone macehead. The skeleton in Grave 43 also had large rings around the upper arms, numerous beads which had been strung together, and circles of gold sheet which ornamented the corpse's clothing.

While the gold artifacts are clearly the most memorable category of finds at Varna, it is important to remember that there are also significant numbers of copper, flint, and shell artifacts found in the burials as well. Many of the copper artifacts at Varna are hammer-axes, while others are pins, rings, and other ornaments. A variety of flint tools are found in the graves, made from long blades of high-quality material. Beads and arm-rings from the shells of the marine mussel *Spondylus* (probably from the Aegean Sea) were also found, particularly in the graves with the masks.

ANIMAL TRACTION

In a 1981 essay, Andrew Sherratt coined the term "Secondary Products Revolution" to characterize a major shift in the use of domestic animals. Until this point, Neolithic societies, Sherratt argued, had seen their livestock as providers of "primary products," namely meat and hides, which required the death of the animal. The purpose of raising the animal was for its death and the useful products that were then made available. "Secondary products," however, are renewable resources taken from living animals such as milk, wool, and animal traction. During the late fifth millennium BC and especially in the fourth millennium BC, Neolithic farmers in Europe (especially in east-central Europe) began to make much greater use of these secondary products. This shift is synchronized with a variety of social changes which are reflected in animal management. Although some (e.g., Chapman 1983; Bogucki 1984) disagreed with the "revolutionary" character of this concept by pointing to evidence for some elements, such as dairying, in earlier prehistoric periods, nonetheless it is clear that approaches to animal husbandry became progressively more complex during the Late Neolithic.

Sherratt (1981, 1983) and Greenfield (1988, 1989) have summarized the key data from prehistoric Europe for the Secondary Products Revolution: ceramic sieves and vessels presumed to have been used in milk handling; animal figurines; remains of wagons, wagon parts, and ploughs in burials and waterlogged deposits; wagon models and representations on pottery; rock-carvings of wagons; and plough-marks on fossil soils under barrows. Greenfield (1988, 1989) discussed a number of animal bone assemblages from southeastern Europe. Milisauskas and Kruk (1991) have presented evidence for secondary products use from Bronocice in southeastern Poland, dating to ca. 3500–3000 BC. Here, cattle form the major component of the faunal assemblage, with cows comprising just over half of the specimens that could be sexed and oxen – castrated males – accounting for about 20 percent. In addition, Bronocice has yielded a vessel with representations of what are almost certainly wagons. A horn core has furrows worn in it, possibly the results of yoking with a rope across the horns. Thus, for at least one major settlement complex in central Europe, a good case can be made for the use of animal traction between 3500 and 3000 BC.

I have focused on the use of animal traction as perhaps the most significant aspect of the Secondary Products Revolution (Bogucki 1993). Traction, as derived from oxen, would have been useful for two major innovations, ploughing and cartage, both of which appear about this time. Emphasizing products like milk and wool is a narrow view which loses its strength in the face of evidence that both were procured even earlier. Animal traction, however, is a

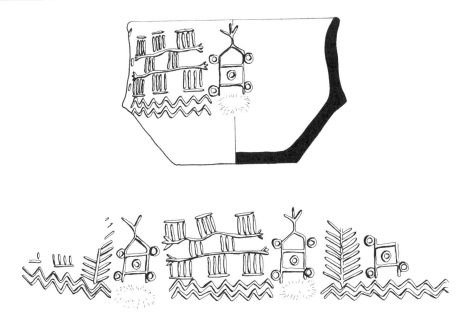

Figure 6.6 Depiction of a wagon on a vessel from Bronocice, Poland (after Milisauskas and Kruk 1982, figure 8).

truly revolutionary development which had significant implications for the household labor supply and the ability of individual households to manage their accumulation strategies. Perhaps the "Secondary Products Revolution" might be recast as the "*Animal Traction Revolution*" to capture the sense of the impact that this development had on prehistoric European society.

I have argued that animal traction enabled a Neolithic household to multiply its productive capacity well beyond that which its own human labor force can provide, particularly for two of the most labor-intensive aspects of an agrarian economy: the preparation of fields for cultivation and the transport of bulk materials from remote locations to the settlement (Bogucki 1993). Singh (1988) analyzed the economics of animal traction for plough agriculture in Burkina Faso in west Africa and found that households using animal traction are able to cultivate an area almost twice that of households not using animal traction. The use of animal traction was clearly a labor-saving technology, saving labor input by an average of 30–40 percent particularly for crops grown on heavier clay-based soils. Other African studies (e.g., Barrett et al. 1982; McCann 1984) support Singh's conclusions.

Oxen pulling wagons would also reduce household labor costs substantially. What would have been carted in the Neolithic? Although harvested crops would have been one type of load, it would have been a seasonal one and perhaps not the most important. Instead, a much more valuable use of carts would have been for bulk items that needed to be obtained regularly from locations at a distance from the settlement. Fodder would be one example, either as branches or as hay. Perhaps the most important material for carting, however, would have been wood for construction and for firewood. Studies of Third World economies have shown that firewood collection consumes significant amounts of time, particularly for women (e.g., Barnes, Ensminger, and O'Keefe 1984; Kumar and Hotchkiss 1988). Using draft animals and a wagon, a household could save significant amounts of time in procuring firewood.

Animal traction in Neolithic Europe transformed the role of domestic cattle from sources of nutrition to productive assets. In traction-using societies, cattle transform the labor dimension of the production equation and make it extremely elastic. The household that has control of draft animals is able to manage its labor in a way that is less constrained by its developmental cycle than the household without traction. Moreover, cattle for traction also allow less productive household members to channel their labor towards work in which they would otherwise not participate. For example, children may be very profitably occupied by the tending of traction animals and their offspring. Thus the use of animal traction can significantly alter the producer/consumer ratio that Chayanov viewed as the determinant of the economic success of a household (Chayanov 1986). Animal traction also would have permitted a Neolithic household to develop many other dimensions of its accumulation strategy, including increased crop yields, ownership of small stock like sheep and goats, and participation in other extractive and production activities, including metallurgy.

The emergence of cattle as a productive asset rather than as a subsistence resource altered the Neolithic household's long-term accumulation strategy. Since new households would have been limited in the number of cattle that they could possess, there must have been mechanisms for the loaning and borrowing of livestock between households. This is the case in many agro-pastoral societies today (Starr 1987). Such arrangements often involve households in their expansion and consolidation stage as lenders, and households in their establishment or decline stage as borrowers. Although an asymmetrical relationship may exist between borrower and lender, the developmental cycle of the new household and a successful accumulation strategy will make this a temporary situation. Once the household reaches its expansion and consolidation phase, participation in such a relationship may no longer be necessary.

Household developmental cycles and accumulation strategies do not always behave ideally, however. The human members of a household are prone to disease, accidents, and death, and livestock are vulnerable to disease, predation, and theft. Bad decisions occurred just as much during the Neolithic as today. The premature demise of prime breeding stock or draught oxen could disrupt a household's management of its livestock assets. Several such calamities could put a household into a downward spiral from which it would be difficult to recover simply by reallocating other resources. Livestock, especially cattle, were not "money in the bank" for the Neolithic household but rather an investment which carried some risk of failure.

As a result, if cattle turned into productive assets in Late Neolithic Europe, the potential existed for some households to find themselves in a downward economic spiral caused by hazards and mismanagement. They would also be limited in their ability to transfer assets to subsequent generations, creating a long-term pattern of economic stagnation or even impoverishment. At the same time, other households may have emerged with disproportionate control over livestock assets that could then be transferred to descendants or loaned to other households. Some of these households would have found themselves in an upward spiral of acquisition, particularly as livestock multiplied and wise management decisions continued.

This model, admittedly speculative, has implications for our understanding of the development of transegalitarian societies in temperate Europe during the Late Neolithic by providing a mechanism for the initial differentiation of households in a way that persisted across generations. With time, the number of cattle-poor households increased in number, while the number of cattle-rich households formed a progressively smaller proportion of society. The augmentation of this differentiation by trade for exotic metals and by mortuary ceremonialism would have constructed a society with marked inequality of wealth and perhaps status. But did this translate into power? It appears that it did not, for there is no evidence of a formal structure of public life which would suggest political power beyond factions and hamlet organization. Hierarchy would have to wait a few more centuries at least.

LATE FARMING VILLAGES IN SOUTHWEST ASIA

Somewhat before the European developments described above, transegalitarian societies emerged in the Tigris and Euphrates river valleys in Iraq, Turkey, and Syria. In the northern part of this area, these communities are known as "Halaf," while in the southern part they are known as "'Ubaid." It is possible that Halaf is an antecedent of 'Ubaid, but the relationship between these two complexes is still unclear. These communities had already been fully agricultural for a millennium or more, and during the sixth millennium BC they begin to exhibit signs of social differentiation and inequalities which formed the antecedents for urban civilization in this region.

Halaf and 'Ubaid sites were not the first manifestations of social complexity in southwestern Asia. That honor belongs to the settlement at Çatal Hüyük in central Anatolia several centuries earlier, which can be considered a precocious example of a transegalitarian community. Çatal Hüyük is a remarkable settlement covering over 13 hectares of agglomerated mudbrick dwellings. First excavated in the 1960s by James Mellaart and more recently by Ian Hodder, Çatal Hüyük is particularly notable for its size (which exceeds any contemporary settlement by a large margin), its prosperity (which can be attributed to its control of local obsidian sources which were then distributed over a large part of Anatolia and the Levant), and the evidence for ritual behavior (in the form of elaborately-decorated "shrines," in which bulls play a central role in the iconography). Yet Çatal Hüyük stands alone in its time, an oversized precursor of later developments in which trade and public architecture played a central role.

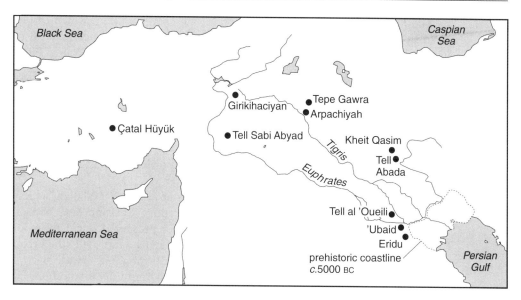

Figure 6.7 Map of Near East showing key sites mentioned in this chapter.

The roots of social inequality in the Tigris and Euphrates valleys lie in small farming communities, which are still very poorly-investigated in comparison with their European counterparts. These small communities were linked into regional trading networks which probably had their origins in the obsidian trade of previous millennia. Obsidian continued to be a major trade item (Campbell 1992). The widespread distribution of distinctive pottery types, particularly Halafian pottery, indicates that these communities were in constant communication with one another. For example, 30–40 percent of the pottery produced at Tepe Gawra was made at Arpachiyah (Davidson and McKerrall 1980).

Important recent excavations at Tell Sabi Abyad in northern Syria have shed light on Halaf origins (Akkermans and Verhoeven 1995). In pre-Halaf levels at Sabi Abyad, dating to the early sixth millennium BC, a complex of rectangular adobe buildings was accompanied by several round buildings. The circular buildings are known as "tholoi" (although they bear no connection to the later Mycenean tombs). Within the rectangular buildings were clay ovens. All of the buildings in this level were affected by an intense fire which destroyed the settlement. Of particular importance from these levels at Sabi Abyad are about 275 clay sealings with stamped impressions and small tokens. The sealings are lumps of clay which had been placed on the fastenings or openings of containers to secure them against unauthorized opening, then impressed with designs. Sealings of this sort are very common on archaeological sites throughout the Near East, and their discovery at Sabi Abyad is one of the earliest known. It indicated that the inhabitants of Sabi Abyad participated in exchange networks which contributed to the prosperity of the settlement.

The Halaf period was clearly built on a long local tradition, which can be seen in later sites. Girikihaciyan is a small Halafian mound near the headwaters of the Tigris river in southeastern Turkey (Watson and LeBlanc 1990). Stone foundations and adobe walls were the remains of tholoi about 2.25 to 4.5 meters in diameter, which constituted the majority of the buildings in the settlement. At Tell Sabi Abyad, the architecture of the Halafian levels includes a combination of multi-roomed rectangular house complexes and tholoi. Akkermans (1993) believes that the tholoi at Sabi Abyad functioned as granaries, whereas the rectangular buildings were the dwellings. At most Halafian sites, sheep and goats form the major portion of the faunal assemblage, supplemented by cattle and pigs.

There has been a continuing discussion about whether Halafian society was at the "chiefdom" level of social organization. LeBlanc and Watson (1973) argued that Halafian society may have represented a chiefdom or series of chiefdoms based on a number of characteristics, especially the broad distribution of the uniform Halafian pottery style throughout a wide part of the Near East, which was seen as a marker of intercommunity integration. By 1990, Watson and LeBlanc had retreated a bit from this position, characterizing Halaf as a "near chiefdom" or a "local, middle-range hierarchical society" (1990: 136). They point towards the extensive trade network in obsidian and other raw materials, differentiation in the size of settlements from 1–2 hectare to 8 hectare sites, and the distinctive burned building excavated by Max Mallowan in the 1930s at Arpachiyah which was structurally different from others and contained well-made artifacts (Campbell 1992). Watson and LeBlanc, however, admit that "the evidence for hierarchical organization of Halafian society is far from overwhelming, although there are some suggestive findings" (1990: 138). Akkermans (1993) takes a very different view and plays down the significance of the widespread ceramic distribution, suggesting that while it may point to increased regional integration, this does not necessarily imply hierarchical social organization. He also argues that the size differentiation of Halafian settlements was not so strongly developed but rather that it was a collection of small villages and hamlets. In Akkermans' view, the larger Halafian sites were probably "loose agglomerations of isolated farmsteads" rather than nucleated settlements.

As the Halafian settlements in northern Mesopotamia grew, 'Ubaid settlements with a different character emerged on the alluvial plains of southern Mesopotamia. This is a very resource-poor area which could only be made productive through irrigated field agriculture, fishing, and livestock. 'Ubaid sites clearly represent a colonization of the southern Mesopotamian alluvium, in keeping with the general Old World pattern of opportunistic agricultural colonization of uninhabited alluvial soils wherever possible, as in Greece and central Europe. Excavations at Tell al 'Oueili suggest that the initial settlement of this region may have occurred somewhat earlier than hitherto believed, perhaps as early as 6000 BC (Huot 1992). Numerous 'Ubaid sites are now known, although in recent decades much of southern Mesopotamia has become a war zone, so no new sites have been excavated since the late 1980s.

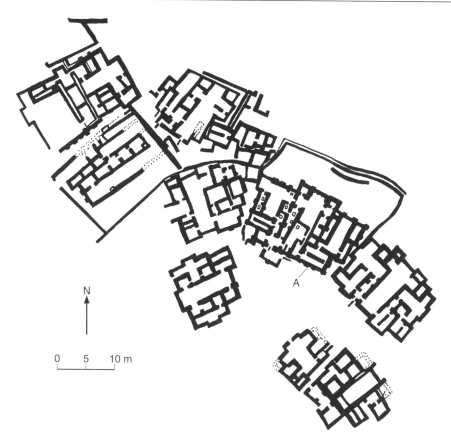

Figure 6.8 House plans in Level II at Tell Abada, with House A indicated (after Jasim 1985, figure 13).

'Ubaid settlements are characterized by multi-roomed rectangular houses built of mud bricks, known best from Tell Abada (Jasim 1985: 206) and Kheit Qasim (Forest-Foucault 1980) in the north, Eridu (Safar, Mustafa, and Lloyd 1981) and Tell el 'Oueili (Huot 1989, 1992, 1994) in the alluvial south. Houses had rooms that were grouped symmetrically on both sides of a large central hall, resulting in a tripartite floor plan of rooms–hall–rooms (figure 6.8). The central hall frequently has a smaller hall crossing it, to form a T-shape. Aside from this standard layout, 'Ubaid houses vary in size from about 70 square meters to 240 square meters (Jasim 1985: 207). Jasim has suggested that these houses were occupied by residential groups consisting of one or more families or an extended family household.

Some level of social differentiation appears to be indicated by some 'Ubaid domestic sites. For example, Building A at Tell Abada is larger, centrally-located, has gypsum-plastered walls, and has numerous child burials (57) beneath its floor in two phases (Hole 1989: 164). Jasim has suggested that this building held special status in the community. Along with two other large houses, Building A forms a group of buildings which have numerous child burials and artifacts from exotic raw materials. The other buildings on the site are smaller and lack the density of burials and exotic artifacts. Jasim speculates that Building A at Abada belonged to the head of the community, with the other large houses the dwellings of his relatives. Others (e.g., Forest 1987) have proposed that this is a community house, some rudimentary form of public architecture.

On the other hand, architecture at Tell el 'Oueili consists of complex structures – and at a surprisingly early date – but provides relatively little evidence of social differentiation (Huot 1992). Small amounts of obsidian and bitumen were imported, but otherwise the material remains are "remarkably homogeneous" (Huot 1994: 170). Pig and cattle are the dominant species among the animal bones, perhaps because the marshy environs of the site were poorly suited to sheep and goats. Clay sickles, which are very characteristic of 'Ubaid sites, are found in abundance.

Later in 'Ubaid, the practice of burying the dead within the architectural precincts ceased and large cemeteries became common (Hole 1989: 174). One of the best examples of these comes from Eridu, considered to be a "classic" 'Ubaid site, where a cemetery estimated to contain almost 1000 graves has been partially excavated. Most of the burials are in rectangular tombs built of mud bricks. The bodies are in an extended position, accompanied by ceramics and personal ornaments. Typically, three ceramic vessels accompanied each burial: an upright jar, a dish, and a cup (Hole 1989: 167). In some cases, the tombs were opened and the original corpse was disturbed when the second body was placed inside, reminiscent of the Hopewellian multiple use of burial crypts discussed below.

Eridu is important for another reason, in that it appears to have the remains of what has been interpreted as a ceremonial building or "temple" (figure 6.9). This structure begins as a small building with an "altar" and progresses into a series of large tripartite-plan structures on platforms, which resemble later Sumerian temples identified in texts. At the same time, however, these structures also resemble the classic tripartite T-shaped domestic structures found at sites like Tell Abada and Kheit Qasim. Some scholars (e.g., Forest 1987, Huot 1994) have challenged the interpretation of the Eridu buildings as a temple, arguing instead that they were an elite residence or audience halls.

However these buildings are interpreted, it seems clear that by late 'Ubaid we see developments which can be compared with what can be observed elsewhere in the world in similar contexts. As in examples from Formative Mesoamerica discussed below, structures can be identified which appear to have a public ceremonial or integrative purpose. The "temple" at Eridu or Building A at Abada stand out as public architecture within nucleated settlements. It appears that a sense of community emerged in 'Ubaid which resembles that seen in Formative Mesoamerica: large households, perhaps consisting of multiple family groups, and public architecture within the residential context, not as a separate destination.

Stein (1994) has analyzed the evidence for 'Ubaid social organization. He points out the fact that there is a clear two-level settlement hierarchy, with

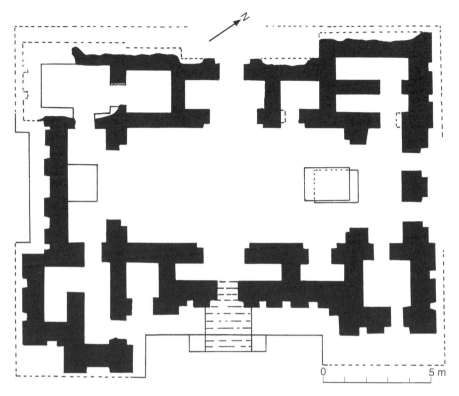

Figure 6.9 The "temple" in Level VII at Eridu (after Forest 1987, figure 8).

several large sites of 10 hectares or more (such as Eridu and Ur) and many small sites about 1 hectare in area which surround them. Stein believes that Building A at Abada is indeed a distinctive structure, more than three times the size of the smallest houses. Moreover, he notes, this architectural pattern persisted over all three occupation phases, suggesting an economic and status distinction that was passed from one generation to another. Finally, Stein notes the emergence of the public architecture interpreted as "temples." On the basis of this, Stein concludes that 'Ubaid consisted of a "series of ideologically linked chiefdoms."

On the other hand, 'Ubaid does not display the instability which often characterizes chiefdoms as they cycle between consolidation and collapse, nor are there fortifications, destruction layers, or depictions of weapons. Huot (1994) points out the "homogeneity" of settlements like Tell el 'Oueili and the relative lack of imported objects. 'Ubaid burials, as summarized by Hole (1989), display little variation, and exotic trade materials are also very scarce. Based on the "traditional" signature traits of chiefdoms, a very thin case can be made for such organization in 'Ubaid. Jasim, for example, argues that 'Ubaid was made up of small secular polities ruled by heads of kin groups, such as the personage who may have occupied House A at Abada (Jasim 1985: 213). In Jasim's view, 'Ubaid society could be more properly termed a "*shiekdom*" than a chiefdom. Stein, however, proposes that 'Ubaid elites emerged from large families who could mobilize consistent large amounts of agricultural labor on the basis of kinship, but who could also reach beyond their immediate households to mobilize additional labor, that which other non-elite households could spare. This is a very different view of the chiefdom from its usual construction as an organ of redistribution, and it allows 'Ubaid to be seen as a series of localized polities which have some form of emergent hierarchy.

The Halaf and 'Ubaid cultural complexes in the Tigris and Euphrates valleys provided the incubator from which later urban civilization in this region emerged. By the same token, ascribing to them the status of "chiefdoms," whether simple or complex, appears to be somewhat premature, in that they appear to lack political centralization and control. 'Ubaid presages later developments in this area, however, in its nascent formality in the organization of public life, while in Halaf interregional trade and exchange appears to have formed a lattice of communities in contact. The characterization of these societies as "transegalitarian" appears to be particularly appropriate.

FORMATIVE MESOAMERICA

In Mesoamerica, the two traditional foci of archaeological work since 1945 have been civilizations in the Mayan lowlands and the Mexican highlands on one hand and the search for agricultural origins on the other. The transegalitarian societies of the Formative period which fell between these two poles have remained relatively under-studied in comparison with earlier and later societies. Thus Kent Flannery could write in 1976 that "there is not a single published plan of a complete Early Formative house" (Flannery 1976: 13), although this situation has been remedied to some extent by research in the last two decades. In contrast to Europe and the Near East, societal differentiation progressed fairly rapidly in Mesoamerica, and by 1000 BC there is fairly clear evidence for marked inequality, which has typically been interpreted as representing chiefdoms. Formative Mesoamerica has long been dominated by the florescence of the Olmec "civilization," and this domination has had a profound effect on the archaeological interpretation of the emergence of transegalitarian societies in this region.

The geographical extent of Formative societies in Mesoamerica which are of interest here is large, ranging from the Valley of Mexico in the north, through Chiapas and Oaxaca in southwestern Mexico, down the Pacific coast to Costa Rica, and northward along the Gulf of Mexico to Veracruz and Tabasco. This area encompasses a remarkable variety of environmental zones, including the humid lowlands of the Gulf coast, the upland valleys of Oaxaca, the fertile coastal plain and alluvial fans of Chiapas, and the montane forests of interior Guatemala and El Salvador. Chronologically, the period of interest here corresponds to the years between ca. 1800 and 500 BC. In the Mesoamerican sequence, these are known as the Early and Middle Formative, although the term "Formative" is often used interchangeably with "PreClassic" in the developmental sequences of the major Mesoamerican civilizations.

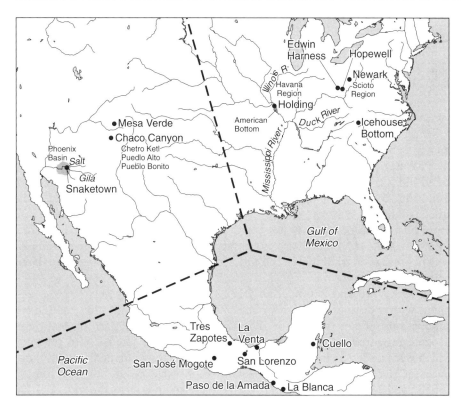

Figure 6.10 Map of North America and Mesoamerica showing key sites mentioned in this chapter. Dotted lines divide chronologically distinct areas. Sites in Mesoamerica date to ca. 1800–500 BC; sites in eastern North America date to ca. 500 BC–AD 200; sites in western North America date to AD 300–1300.

By the early part of the second millennium BC, agriculture based on the three key domesticates – corn, beans, and squash – had become firmly established throughout this region, and the discovery that the earliest domestic maize is apparently later than originally thought (see chapter 5) closes the gap between the first use of domesticates and the appearance of sedentary villages composed of farming households in the middle of the second millennium BC. Around this time, distinct pottery complexes appear in the central highlands of Mexico, Oaxaca, Chiapas, and El Salvador (Clark and Gosser 1995; Arroyo 1995), apparently independently of each other although all probably adopted from models derived originally from Central America and South America (Hoopes 1995). The emergence of these pottery complexes is regarded by Clark and Blake (1994) as particularly significant, especially those of the Barra phase along the Chiapas and Guatemala coast which are technologically and aesthetically sophisticated. They argue that ceramics were used by aggrandizive individuals to exhibit their status during displays of competitive feasting (Clark and Blake 1994: 25). Yet the same argument may be made for many other instances of early fine ceramics elsewhere in the world, and this may be jumping the gun a bit in the race to demonstrate social differentiation.

A number of Early Formative settlements have been investigated, but perhaps the best-known (on the basis of Flannery's classic 1976 volume, *The Early Mesoamerican Village*) is San José Mogote in the southern highlands of Mexico. San José Mogote consisted of a number of "household clusters" (Winter 1976) which consisted of a wattle-and-daub dwelling, ovens and hearths, storage features, and burials within an area of about 300 square meters. There is considerable evidence for trade in obsidian, which appears to have been conducted at the household level. A few buildings, however, stand out against the household clusters. These have a different orientation from the dwelling compounds, a crushed bedrock foundation and lime stucco floor (in contrast to the clay-and-sand floors of ordinary houses), more posts than ordinary houses, and are plastered with lime on the inside (Marcus 1989: 163). These are interpreted, persuasively, as "public buildings" which presage a tradition of public architecture that continues into later periods.

Between 1150 and 850 BC, San José Mogote grew into a very large settlement, with a distinct precinct for the public structures and other residential subdivisions. Trade increased. The inhabitants of one part of San José Mogote procured different types of iron ore and fabricated it into mirrors, which were traded as far as 250 kilometers away. Drums made from the carapaces of river turtles native to the Gulf of Mexico coast, stingray spines, conch shell horns, and armadillo shells made their way to the village. It is clear that the inhabitants of San José Mogote were participants in a trading network which extended over much of Mesoamerica.

Although San José Mogote is probably the most thoroughly investigated Formative village, it appears that similar developments may have occurred elsewhere in Mesoamerica. For example, at Paso de la Amada in Chiapas, a series of large structures in Mound 6 between 1350 and 1250 BC are distinctive among the other buildings at the site (Blake 1991). The floor area of this building increased with each reconstruction. Two possible explanations are put forth: (1) this was the home of an emergent chief; or (2) this was a public building like the one at San José Mogote. For a variety of reasons, Blake (1991: 43) argues that this is the residence of an elite household. At La Blanca in Guatemala, public architecture appears in the form of large mounds during the Middle Formative, although they are not arranged in a way which suggests formal structuring of space (Love 1991).

On the other side of Mesoamerica, at the site of Cuello in Belize, a small dispersed village was established beginning about 1200 BC (Hammond 1991). The lowland zone of eastern Mesoamerica, which later was the heartland of the Maya civilization, has yielded relatively few traces of Formative settlements, which has posed a problem in understanding the antecedents of later complex society in this area. Wilk and Wilhite (1991) have argued that the majority of the population in the Formative (Preclassic) phases at Cuello lived in perishable dwellings which did not leave behind architectural features. In the earlier Formative phases at Cuello, the community was a dispersed village, although one structure (Platform 34) emerges as a central sacred place which had a ritual and mortuary function. In contrast to the arguments for emergent chiefdoms made for western Mesoamerica, Hammond and his colleagues make the case that in these early phases Cuello was an egalitarian community (Hammond 1991: 246). Not until the later Formative periods (after ca. 400 BC) is there clear evidence for social differentiation. Some households occupied houses on large plastered platforms, while Platform 34 continued to develop as a ceremonial location.

The modest community at Cuello contrasts sharply with the precocious monumental architecture, iconography, and rich burials found at the key Olmec sites of San Lorenzo, La Venta, and Tres Zapotes in the coastal lowlands of Veracruz and Tabasco, 200 kilometers northeast across the Sierra Madre from San José Mogote. The remarkable public architecture and iconography of the major Olmec sites are really of a different order of magnitude from the transegalitarian Formative communities considered here, although the distinction is nonetheless arbitrary. Indeed, a first draft of this chapter considered Olmec at this very spot, but upon further reflection this block of text was shifted to the next chapter, which discusses the institutionalized and genealogically-based form of social differentiation commonly referred to as a "chiefdom."

When compared with the wealth of information on, for example, Late Neolithic Europe, knowledge of the Mesoamerican Formative is still very rudimentary. Nonetheless, there is a clear sense that this was a society in which the household was still a fundamental locus of activity and where differentiation occurs primarily at the household level. As such, it would appear that the model of social differentiation proposed at the beginning of this chapter may have applicability to developments in Mesoamerica, and the relative rapidity with which this differentiation took place would also suggest that household demography and competition were key factors.

HOPEWELL IN THE AMERICAN MIDCONTINENT

Beginning about 500 BC, a number of riverine societies characterized by elaborate mortuary ritual, monumental earthworks, and finely-crafted artifacts developed in the Eastern Woodlands of North America. These peoples are known collectively as "Hopewell" or the "Hopewell Tradition" and are distributed throughout the east-central part of the United States, in Ohio, Indiana, Illinois, Kentucky, and Tennessee, but also extending into Missouri, Michigan, Wisconsin, Georgia, Florida, and even New York. Their name comes from a farm in southern Ohio which was excavated to provide display artifacts for the 1893 Columbian Exposition in Chicago. A century later, the Ohio Hopewell remains the best-studied regional manifestation of this tradition. For many years, archaeologists focused their attention on the spectacular mortuary monuments, and not until recently did they turn their attention to settlements. Contrary to expectations, these were not large nucleated villages but rather single-household farmsteads consisting of one or two houses with their associated features. An important aspect of Hopewell societies is their long-distance trade, which spanned North America between the Rocky Mountains and the Appalachian Mountains and between the Great Lakes and the Gulf Coast.

The question of "just what is Hopewell?" has perplexed archaeologists for much of the twentieth century. It is clear that it is not a unified polity, nor does it have some form of ethnic identity. Many archaeologists eschew the word "Hopewell" completely, preferring the more-generic "Middle Woodland" terminology, especially when discussing subsistence and settlement separately from the spectacular mortuary and ceremonial remains. Some have defined Hopewell exclusively in terms of its exchange system, calling it the "Hopewell Interaction Sphere," although my view is that this limits the framework of analysis to the more spectacular aspects such as trade goods and burials. What is clear that as in Late Neolithic Europe, people of the central river systems of North America between 500 BC and AD 200 made significant investments in mortuary ritual and monumental construction, and more than any time previously, they accumulated materials and objects which had high costs of acquisition and production, which they then took out of societal circulation by burying them with their dead.

The two areas with the most intense manifestation of Hopewell are the Scioto River valley, a tributary of the upper Ohio River, and the Havana region of western Illinois bordering the Mississippi River, although other important foci are found in Tennessee and Alabama as well as along the Gulf of Mexico. In the Scioto region, where the type-site of Hopewell is located, the famous Hopewell mounds and earthworks are clustered in abundance. This is considered the "heartland" of Hopewell, although there is no evidence of population movements outward from this area. At the Hopewell site, a rectangular enclosure demarcates an area of 45 hectares, within which are 38 mounds. One of these, with over 250 burials, was 9 m high, 152 m long, and 55 m wide, making it the largest burial mound in North America (Fiedel 1987). Numerous other mound and earthwork sites are nearby. At Newark, Ohio, an earthwork complex of circles and other geometrical shapes was linked by earthen avenues over an area of 6.4 square km. Another southern Ohio mound runs along the ridge of a hilltop in the form of a snake. Such so-called "effigy" mounds support the notion that these were ceremonial rather than defensive structures. Ceremonial earthworks do not appear in the Havana region, although Hopewell burial mounds are also commonly found.

Two major categories of Hopewell burial structures can be identified: charnel houses and mortuary crypts (Brown 1979: 211), although overall there is considerable variability within Middle Woodland burial practices. Crypts, more common in Illinois Hopewell, are subterranean rectangular pits, often roofed with heavy timbers, in which corpses were placed with their grave goods. The roofs could be removed in order to place additional bodies in the tomb, although as Brown points out, relatively little ritual activity could actually take place in the opened chamber. The central crypts were then covered with earth to form a low burial mound. The primary burials are generally skeletons in an extended position, although there is evidence from a number of sites that the chamber was entered and the bones of the decomposed body gathered into a bundle which was then placed along the wall of the crypt (Brown 1979: 217). Charnel houses, by contrast, were aboveground facilities with doors in which burials and other mortuary activity occurred, particularly characteristic of Ohio Hopewell. They are generally identified by oval patterns of postholes or burned areas underlying burial mounds (Seeman 1979a), for they apparently were burnt down and covered with mounds once their usefulness had come to an end. There is considerable evidence for offerings and remains of feasts associated with these structures, and features identified as "cremation pits" provide additional evidence for the handling of the body prior to its interment. Ohio Hopewellians apparently dissected corpses before burning them in the small pits. In some cases, cremated bones appear to have been simply piled on the floor of the house. At the Edwin Harness Mound in Ohio, for example, 170 burials (mostly cremated but some skeletal), burnt and fragmented animal bones, and artifacts were found associated with structures which appear to have been mortuary structures that existed before being destroyed and covered with the large mound.

Hopewell burial, then, was a protracted affair, and the dead were certainly not "out of sight, out of mind." Some scholars have used the clinical term "processed" to describe how the Hopewellians treated their dead (Brown 1979). Indeed, it is very difficult to describe the dissection, excarnation, disarticulation, display, bundling, and other handling of the human remains in any different way. Again, a parallel raises itself with Late Neolithic Europe, particularly the excarnation and handling of human remains identified at sites like Hambledon Hill and the continual interment of corpses in megalithic crypts. Even so, the degree to which Hopewellians interacted with their dead to transform the bodies exceeds that seen in almost every other part of the world. Clearly it had profound symbolic import, although what it means can only be guessed.

Grave goods constitute perhaps the most distinctive element of the Hopewell phenomenon, for they include exotic raw materials from many parts of North America (Seeman 1979b: 291–308; Streuver and Houart 1972). In the last 30 years, the extent of this web of Middle Woodland resource procurement has been even further documented. The obsidian and grizzly bear teeth found in Hopewell graves came from the Yellowstone region of western Wyoming. Conch and turtle shells, shark and alligator teeth, and barracuda jaws came from Florida, while mica used in mirrors and chlorite came from the Appalachian Mountains of North Carolina. Hopewellians used native copper, hammered into breastplates, zoomorphic plaques, panpipes, and earspools, from the western end of Lake Superior. Galena came from the Ozarks, and chalcedony was obtained from the northern plains in North Dakota. Table 6.1 lists the major source areas and the primary raw materials that they yielded, as summarized by Brose (1990).

Joseph Caldwell coined the term "Hopewell Interaction Sphere" in 1958, and it was enshrined in the literature by an influential 1964 article by Stuart Streuver and a subsequent article by Streuver and Gail Houart (1972).

Table 6.1 Raw materials used by Hopewell peoples and the source areas from which they were procured (after Brose 1990).

Resource Catchment	Resources
Western Ranges	Obsidian, Knife River flint, grizzly bear canines and claws, bison bone
Upper Great Lakes	Copper, silver, specular hematite, iron pyrites
Western Side of Mississippi River	Galena, gypsum, quartz crystal, graphite, iron pyrites, novaculite, meteoric iron
Appalachian Highlands	Mica, steatite, quartz crystal, graphite, iron pyrites, greenstone
Gulf of Mexico coast	Marine shell, barracuda jaws, alligator and shark teeth (modern and fossil)
Ohio Valley	Pipestone, Flint Ridge chalcedony, cannel coal, calcite, gypsum, meteoric iron, iron pyrites

It refers to the concentration in several parts of mid-continental North America of the exotic raw materials noted above and the web of procurement activity that led to their distribution. Moreover, in Streuver and Houart's view, Hopewell trade took place among regularly spaced, hierarchically-organized transaction centers. Seeman (1979b) has argued that trade also took place in finished artifacts in addition to raw materials, but disagrees with the notion that it was organized to the degree that it occurred within a complex, hierarchically-structured network of sites. He concludes that the actual volume of Hopewell trade was relatively low in relation to the overall population and that the trading network was relatively unstructured. This may be an important contrast with the regular and sustained contact which has been argued to have occurred among transegalitarian communities in Mesopotamia and Mesoamerica.

The unresolved question is whether the raw materials or artifacts were obtained through "down-the-line" exchange (Renfrew 1975) or whether Hopewell prospecting and trading missions went out from the Scioto and Havana regions to distant locations. Brose (1990) has attempted to assess the relative "value" of the goods procured by Hopewell peoples based on the distance from the source of the exotic materials and the number of "hydrological adjustment points" (i.e., portages between drainage systems and around barriers like falls) that intervened. Although Brose's analysis is admittedly speculative and makes the fundamental assumption that most Middle Woodland long-distance travel was by dugout canoe, it suggests that by the time the raw materials reached the Scioto region in Ohio, most had acquired the highest values these materials had in any of the Hopewellian regions. The Gulf Coast is not far behind, particularly in the transport "cost" of Rocky Mountain obsidian and Great Lakes copper that made its way there.

Middle Woodland settlements associated with the Hopewell phenomenon are still poorly-known, due to the concentration of archaeologists on mortuary and ceremonial sites over the last two centuries. Only since the beginning of the 1980s has there been sustained attention paid to Middle Woodland

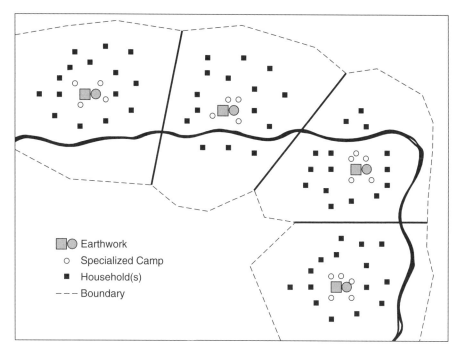

Figure 6.11 Schematic organization of Hopewellian communities along a river with households grouped around a ceremonial center (after Dancey and Pacheco 1997, figure 1.2). Note: Dancey and Pacheco use the term "hamlet" instead of the term "household" used here; the latter is consistent with the use of the term "household" in this chapter, where "hamlet" has a somewhat different meaning to refer to a larger community.

settlements both within the two core Hopewell areas and more broadly in midcontinent North America, and even then this work has not been widely reported. Smith (1992) has drawn together the available evidence from a variety of different sites. He points out that several alternative models of Hopewellian settlement have been proposed on the basis of the slim evidence: (1) permanent year-round villages composed of many household units whose inhabitants also used short-term special-purpose camps; (2) small hamlets of a few households occupied during the growing season and dispersed cold-season homesteads; and (3) dispersed year-round farmsteads whose inhabitants also used short-term seasonal camps.

Smith's analysis of the accumulating evidence, which I find persuasive, is that there is relatively little evidence for Hopewellian "villages" and points instead toward the existence of numerous dispersed settlements of one to three households. Such small farming settlements were distributed along the valleys of smaller streams, exhibiting some degree of concentration in the vicinity of the larger ceremonial centers. The best evidence for this comes from regional research programs in regions such as the Duck River Valley in Tennessee and the Illinois River valley and the American Bottom region in

Illinois, where numerous small dispersed sites have been found. A few, such as the Holding Site in the American Bottom (Fortier et al. 1989) seem to have had up to five clusters of household remains, but most are single-household habitations. In Smith's words (1992: 240), "almost all of the available evidence regarding Hopewellian farming settlements seems to indicate a largely independent and autonomous status for individual household units, and their consistent dispersal across the Middle Woodland landscape of the East." There is also some evidence, however, for short-term specialized Middle Woodland camps existing alongside the year-round household habitations (Farnsworth 1990).

Hopewell subsistence has been a hotly-debated topic even within the last decade. Fritz (1993: 41) reports that a discussant at the 1988 Society for American Archaeology meetings "warned that the use of the term 'Hopewell farmers' was 'incendiary'!" Hardly a decade later, there was compelling evidence to indicate that native seed plants constituted a significant portion of the Middle Woodland, including Hopewell, diet. These include the eastern domesticates described in chapter 5 – sunflower, chenopod, marsh elder, and squash – with the addition of erect knotweed (*Polygonum erectum*), maygrass (*Phalaris caroliniana*), and little barley (*Hordeum pusillum*). Substantial amounts of palaeobotanical data now support the argument that these starchy and oily seed plants were cultivated, and this cultivation increased substantially in the first millennium BC. By 500 BC, or the beginning of the Hopewell florescence, cultivation of native seed plants was so established that Middle Woodland peoples can very appropriately be called farmers (Smith 1992: 289–91). At the same time, they also collected substantial amounts of nuts, fruits, and other wild plants and hunted a variety of mammals.

Into this system of cultivation of starchy and oily seed plants, maize made its first appearance about 1BC or somewhat later. The earliest corn dated through the AMS method comes from the Holding site in Illinois (Fritz 1993: 52), while early Hopewell corn also is found at the Edwin Harness Mound in the Scioto region of Ohio and Icehouse Bottom in Tennessee. Yet, its introduction does not seem to have had a significant immediate effect on Middle Woodland subsistence, very similar to the situation in the Desert Borderlands region described in chapter 5. There is a time lag of 900 to 1000 years, long after the decline of the Hopewell tradition, before agricultural systems based fully on maize were found in eastern North America.

So what exactly is Hopewell? At one level, it represents a Middle Woodland trading system, the Hopewell Interaction Sphere, through which raw materials and perhaps finished products moved over remarkably long distances (just as was occurring at roughly the same time in the Roman Empire in the Old World). Yet such movement of raw materials would not have become apparent in the archaeological record without the elaborate mortuary ceremonialism of the charnel houses, crypts, and other complex burial practices. At their core, however, Hopewell societies were Middle Woodland communities composed primarily of distinct households or farmsteads sometimes clustered together into small hamlets. There were no large aggregations of population, nor is there evidence for chiefs or other institutionalized leadership. It is a classic transegalitarian society in which aggrandizive behavior took place in a relatively open and diffuse manner as households competed with each other for status and prestige.

LATE NEOLITHIC AND EARLY BRONZE AGE IN SOUTHEAST ASIA

Southeast Asia in later prehistoric times is only now coming into archaeological focus, after decades of disruption of research by war and politics. Unlike in Europe and the Near East, this region does not have a neat set of prehistoric cultures and phases to organize the archaeological discussion, and several key sites attract the most attention. The familiar elements of nascent social differentiation are present, however: complex mortuary behavior, exchange, metallurgy, and full commitment to agriculture. The problem is that there is very little known about settlement patterns and habitation in the last three millennia BC in this region, although perhaps this problem will be remedied shortly. Chronological chaos introduced by spurious early radiocarbon dates for the development of metallurgy has also confused the picture (see Higham 1996: 9–13 for an analysis and an attempt at "chronometric hygiene").

The crucial areas in the study of the Bronze Age in Southeast Asia include the Red River valley of North Vietnam and the Khorat Plateau and Bangkok Plain in Thailand. Rice cultivation had spread to the northern part of this area from the Yangzi valley in China by the third millennium BC, but it is unclear at what pace it proceeded further south and when it reached central Thailand. Phytolith and pollen data suggest very early dates in the fifth millennium BC, roughly contemporaneous with Hemudu on the coast of China (Higham 1989b: 275–6; Kealhofer 1996), but the earliest evidence from an archaeological context is approximately 2000 BC at Khok Phanom Di (Higham 1996: 251). Although coastal and upland foragers had existed in this region for many millennia and had an impact on the environment (see chapter 4), sedentary settlements were established in central Thailand only from the middle of the third millennium BC onward. The lower level of Nong Nor, located along what was once a bay but now several kilometers inland from the Gulf of Siam, is a shell midden with ash lenses, hearths, and other signs of burning. Although no evidence of rice was found (Higham 1996: 251), there was intensive use of marine resources.

Perhaps the most remarkable site excavated in this region in recent years is Khok Phanom Di, located on an estuary along the Gulf of Thailand southeast of Bangkok (Higham and Thosarat 1994). Excavated over several months in 1985, Khok Phanom Di is a mound rising about 12 meters above the surrounding floodplain. In an excavation 10 meters by 10 meters and 7 meters deep, a number of prehistoric strata revealed evidence of a community that lived along this estuary between 2000 and 1500 BC. The evidence consists primarily of burials, with no habitation traces as yet identified except at the very basal level of the mound. Presumably settlement occurred

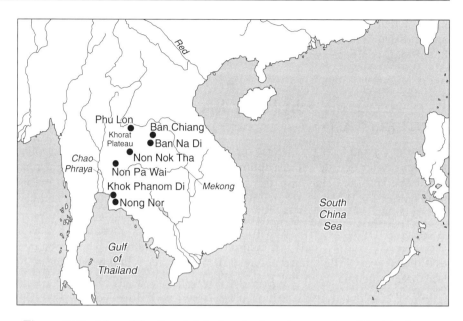

Figure 6.12 Map of Southeast Asia showing key sites mentioned in this chapter.

elsewhere on the mound or in its vicinity. In the 1985 excavation unit, which represents only a small fraction of the total area of the site, 154 burials were found.

The burials at Khok Phanom Di occur in several distinct clusters which retained their discrete character over the several centuries that the mound accumulated (Higham 1996: 252). Higham and his colleagues have been able to identify seven distinct mortuary phases, although in each successive phase the dead were buried over their ancestors, with later graves cutting into earlier ones. Thus in each of these clusters the graves are stratified one on top of the other, in some clusters to a depth of 5 m. Infants and adults occur together in these clusters, along with numerous pottery vessels, shell and stone ornaments, anvils and burnishing stones used for making pottery, and worked turtle carapaces. Mortuary structures were built over the graves or nearby.

Perhaps the most remarkable grave at Khok Phanom Di was number 15, "the Princess" (Higham and Thosarat 1994: 29). This woman, buried under a concentration of red ochre, had a remarkable profusion of shell ornaments, including 120,787 disk beads, and 950 elongated beads, along with a shell bracelet, two large shell disks at each side of the skull, and even larger shell disks with central hubs at her shoulders. Ceramic vessels lay across her legs, along with burnishing pebbles and a clay anvil nearby. Nearby is an infant grave with several thousand beads, a shell bracelet, similar pottery, and a burnishing stone and clay anvil. Additional wealthy graves were also nearby, but immediately to the side of "the Princess" was a headless burial of a young male with two simple pots.

Figure 6.13 The "princess," burial 15, at Khok Phanom Di (photo courtesy of Professor Charles Higham, University of Otago).

Higham and his colleagues interpret the Khok Phanom Di burial clusters as representing social units such as families (Higham 1996: 253–5). Cluster F, for example, can be traced through about 16 putative "generations," whereas other clusters seem to have been of shorter duration. Over time, the wealth reflected in the grave goods seems to have waxed and waned. In earlier burials, there seems to have been no visible difference in how men and women were treated, but in later phases, turtle carapace ornaments are frequently found with the men and clay anvils occur exclusively in female burials. Infants who survived for more than a few months were treated the same as adults, with numerous grave goods in the wealthy phases. Exotic shells and stone also make an appearance in later phases.

The people who lived and were buried at Khok Phanom Di did not appear to have known metallurgy. On the other hand, there is evidence for rice cultivation, along with the intensive use of maritime and estuarine resources. The overall picture is of a sedentary coastal community supported by rice agriculture and increasingly interested in the acquisition of exotic materials. Higham (1996: 258) makes the point that "the initial use of copper belongs in the context of communities keenly interested in exotic artifacts and who traded them within networks in which riverine and coastal transport were particularly effective." The remains of the community at Khok Phanom Di are certainly reminiscent of Hopewell sites in mid-continental North America, Late Neolithic Europe, and many other later prehistoric societies.

In the 1960s and 1970s, very early dates were claimed for bronze metallurgy in Southeast Asia which appeared to give this region the claim to be among the world's earliest centers of metal-working. The two key sites in this regard are Non Nok Tha (Solheim 1968) and Ban Chiang (Gorman and Charoenwongsa 1976), both in the northeastern part of Thailand. Radiocarbon dates from these sites appeared to push the earliest bronze metallurgy in this region back before 3000 BC. This information entered the archaeological literature, and it was widely accepted that the Southeast Asian Bronze Age predated that of comparable materials from China by a millennium or more. The paradox was that the societies that produced this bronze were nearly invisible at this date, in marked contrast to the abundant settlement remains from other parts of the Old World associated with early metallurgy. It seemed anomalous: sophisticated metallurgy in foraging or incipient agricultural societies.

Indeed it was the dates that are anomalous. Higham (1983) has pointed out that the Ban Chiang and Non Nok Tha dates are unreliable because they come from grave *fill* in which the charcoal might come from the layers through which the grave was dug. In light of the evidence for pre-agricultural burning from the Khok Phanom Di pollen cores, it seems likely that there was a lot of charcoal in the environment from a relatively early date near centers of human activity. The best evidence currently available indicates that metal-working in Southeast Asia began in the early part of the second millennium BC (Higham 1989a: 130) and around the middle of the second millennium BC on the Bangkok Plain (Higham 1989b: 257).

Two sites, Phu Lon on the Mekong River and Non Pa Wai in central Thailand, have yielded evidence for early copper smelting around 1500 BC (Pigott and Natapintu 1988; White and Pigott 1996). The Non Pa Wai copper smelting complex covers 5 hectares. Here, the copper ores were crushed, smelted, and cast into ingots, which were then sent into the exchange network which had previously been established (Higham 1996: 339). At Phu Lon, copper was mined – apparently seasonally – and processed on the site. Alloying of the copper with tin was developed shortly thereafter. Unlike in Europe, there was no protracted "Copper Age" to intervene between the early agriculturalists and the development of bronze metallurgy. This advanced metallurgy appears to have taken place further afield from the copper sources at sites like Ban Na Di.

The social impact of early metallurgy in Southeast Asia is difficult to assess. It does not appear to have had an immediate effect, in that the same range of variation in burial rite as was observed at Khok Phanom Di is observed in later cemeteries. The metal artifacts appear to have functioned alongside the other exotic materials in the trade network. For the moment, early Bronze Age Thailand appears to conform to our model of a transegalitarian society, in which certain aggrandizive individuals took steps to acquire wealth but where authority and prestige were transitory. Not until about the middle of the first millennium BC is it possible to describe Bronze Age society in Southeast Asia as clearly organized into chiefdoms.

TRANSEGALITARIAN FARMERS OF THE
NORTH AMERICAN DESERT BORDERLANDS

During the first millennium AD, three important cultural groups arose in the Desert Borderlands of southwestern North America, specifically in the states of Arizona, Colorado, and New Mexico. The Hohokam, Mogollon, and Anasazi were distinctive populations, each with its own developmental pathway. The Hohokam were found across the southern part of Arizona, the Mogollon in southern New Mexico, and the Anasazi in northern New Mexico and southern Colorado. These groups have been the subject of intense study by archaeologists since the late nineteenth century, and it will be very difficult to do justice to the rich scholarship of the last 100 years in a few pages here. The discussion below will focus on two of these groups: the Hohokam of southwestern Arizona and the Chaco Anasazi in northwestern New Mexico. These groups display many attributes of transegalitarian societies which correspond with the other prehistoric peoples discussed in this chapter.

Both the Anasazi and Hohokam have their roots in the local foragers and early farmers of the North American Desert Borderlands. By the first millennium AD, maize agriculture had become firmly established throughout this region and had become the foundation of the economy, despite constraints posed by soils, water, and – at higher elevations – growing season. Regional climatic fluctuations have had a documented effect on human societies as well (e.g., Dean et al. 1985). The agricultural economy, combined with hunting and wild plant gathering, permitted the growth of substantial populations in both the Hohokam and Chaco Anasazi regions (Vivian 1991; Masse 1991). The fundamental difference is that the Hohokam were desert farmers, while the Anasazi occupied moister upland terrain.

HOHOKAM: HOUSEHOLDS, BALLCOURTS, CANALS, AND
PLATFORM MOUNDS

The Hohokam peoples of southern Arizona have been the focus of archaeological research for over a century. During the mid-twentieth century, archaeological pioneers like Harold S. Gladwin and Emil W. Haury added considerably to our knowledge of the developmental sequence of prehistoric communities in the Phoenix basin. Much of the work on Hohokam sites has been rescue archaeology in the face of the rapid post-World War II expansion of the Phoenix and Tucson urban areas. As a result, the amount of archaeological data from these areas is very high in comparison with outlying Hohokam settlement.

During the first millennium AD, a distinctive Hohokam form of community organization developed. Several small pit-dwellings clustered around a courtyard or common area formed the basic household unit. Adjacent to the houses were ovens, trash mounds, and cemeteries. Each such "courtyard group" is estimated to have been the residence of approximately 16–20 people. Many display accretional growth over time. Although isolated courtyard groups appear to have functioned as individual farmsteads, larger sites are composed of aggregations of such groups, characterized as "hamlets" and "villages" (Gregory 1991: 162). Hohokam villages typically exhibit spatial patterning of clusters of courtyard groups around a central plaza, often ringed by ballcourts and small platform mounds.

Although there are changes in the sizes of Hohokam houses over time, there is relatively little evidence of marked differentiation in size or prosperity among them prior to about AD 1150. Instead, there appears to have been a great emphasis in early Hohokam society on communal activities, for which the ballcourt appears to have been one important focus. By about AD 1050, about 225 ballcourts had been built (Doyel 1991), with about 40 percent of them in the Hohokam core area in the Phoenix basin. Hohokam ballcourts are large oval depressions surrounded by earthen embankments. They appear to have been the setting for the playing of a version of the ceremonial ball game played at this time in Mesoamerica (Wilcox 1991: 264), but they also provided a context for community interaction which fostered trade and the sharing of ideas.

Snaketown is perhaps the largest single Hohokam site of the period before AD 1075 (Haury 1976; Wilcox, Maguire, and Sternberg 1981), excavated over many years by Gladwin and Haury and restudied by subsequent generations of archaeologists. Over about 900 years, it grew from a small cluster of pithouses to a large village consisting of numerous courtyard groups clustered around a central plaza. Snaketown's population at its maximum extent is estimated to have been between 300 (Wilcox 1991: 262) and 2000 (Haury 1976: 77) people living in an area of about a square kilometer. Its large ballcourt could accommodate 500 people on its embankments (Doyel 1991: 249). Snaketown's organization can be described as a concentric arrangement centered on the plaza. Around the plaza was an inner habitation zone which contained two concentrations of large houses and cemeteries. One house contained 60 ceramic vessels and 28 copper bells, the latter presumed to have come from northwestern Mesoamerica (Nelson 1986). This inner habitation area was ringed by a series of platform mounds, one of which was surrounded by a palisade. Beyond this circle of mounds was an outer habitation zone in which were located two ballcourts.

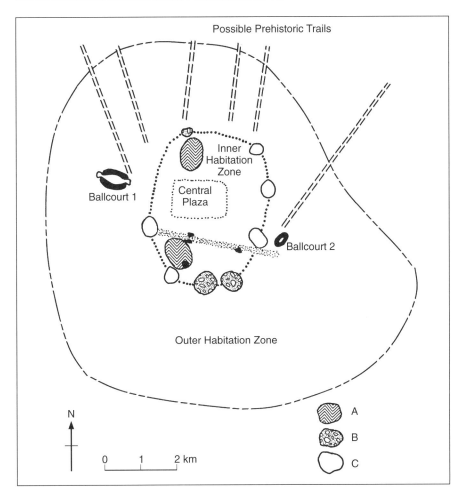

Figure 6.14 Snaketown site structure (after Wilcox, McGuire, and Sternberg 1981, figure 5.5). Key: A – house concentrations; B – mounds capped by *caliche*, a calcium carbonate crust; C – other mounds.

Relatively early in the Hohokam sequence large-scale canal irrigation began to be used to divert the desert rivers and expand the area available for cultivation. The Hohokam canal systems are fairly straightforward diversion channels of major desert rivers like the Gila and the Salt. First appearing around AD 600, the canal systems reached their maximum extent by about AD 1200 (Masse 1991: 220) and continued in use for several centuries thereafter. Initially, they were located close to the rivers, but over time they were expanded away from the floodplains to bring new areas into cultivation (Doyel 1991: 247). Neitzel (1991) has analyzed the labor requirements of Hohokam canal construction and argued that this work required leadership and organization structure to accomplish it on such a scale, although the construction methods used were relatively simple.

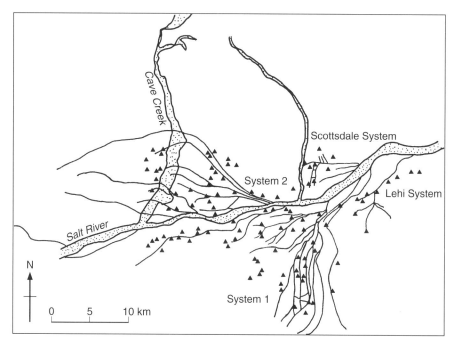

Figure 6.15 Hohokam canal systems in the Phoenix basin, and their relation to archaeological sites (after Abbott 1996, figure 18.4).

About AD 1150, a major reorganization of Hohokam society occurred. Peripheral areas were abandoned, and settlement was concentrated in a few core regions along the Gila, Salt, and Santa Cruz rivers. Ballcourts ceased to be built at the same rate as before, and interregional exchange networks became truncated and reorganized. While some people continued to live in pit houses, a number of residences were above-ground adobe structures organized into walled compounds. A village of this period might consist of between one and 20 such compounds. Platform mounds came to be a key form of public architecture and the foci of communities. After about AD 1200, almost all Hohokam platform mounds were surrounded by adobe walls. Eventually, residences came to be built on top of the platform mounds, apparently the dwellings of an elite group (Gregory 1987).

Archaeologists have reached no clear consensus about the degree of social differentiation in Hohokam society and whether differences in status, power, and wealth were institutionalized across generations. The construction of public works such as canals, platform mounds, and ballcourts is consistent with that seen in other transegalitarian societies discussed in this chapter, such as Hopewell and Late Neolithic Europe. With the ballcourts, there appears to be an emphasis on group ceremonialism similar to that seen in other societies discussed here, although in this case the ceremonialism is not linked to mortuary behavior but rather to community interaction. The emergence of walled adobe compounds and residences atop enclosed platform mounds testifies to a greater degree of differentiation among households after AD 1200, with an accompanying decline in community-oriented activity.

Most archaeologists view Hohokam as somewhere along a continuum from egalitarian to hierarchical (Gumerman 1991: 18), since although indicators of social complexity increase over time, they are diffuse. The canal systems and exchange networks reflect a high degree of regional integration, especially prior to AD 1200, while the restriction of access to mounds and the demarcation of residential locations reflects an increasing level of social differentiation in the centuries that follow. Yet the evidence for "vertical" hierarchical organization seems weak in comparison with that for "horizontal" community organization. To an outsider like myself, it appears that the Hohokam, at least before AD 1200, could well be another example of a transegalitarian society in which individual households competed for access to status, power, and wealth yet without a rigid genealogically-based division into elites and commoners.

CHACO ANASAZI: GREAT HOUSES, GREAT KIVAS, AND ROADS

Anasazi peoples lived in the Four Corners area where the states of Arizona, New Mexico, Colorado, and Utah converge. They have been the subject of archaeological research since the late nineteenth century, when explorers and pioneer ethnologists like John Wesley Powell and ranching families like the Wetherills took a close interest in the antiquities of this region. Perhaps the best-known Anasazi sites are the remarkable cliff dwellings of Mesa Verde in southwestern Colorado. These fall relatively late in the Anasazi sequence, however, and the focus here will be on a slightly earlier and spatially limited subset of Anasazi which is found primarily in northwestern New Mexico, focused on a small basin drained by the San Juan River known as Chaco Canyon.

Between AD 900 and 1150 in northwestern New Mexico the remarkable Chacoan phenomenon emerged, flourished, and declined. Use of the term "phenomenon" is actually common in the archaeological literature on Chaco, although the more technical characterization of it is as a "regional system" (Judge 1991). Chaco consists of a core area in Chaco Canyon where there is a dense concentration of settlement plus an extended distribution of sites over an area of nearly 70,000 square kilometers. Many outlying Chaco sites are connected to the core area by roads, whose traces can still be discerned today (Lekson 1991; Vivian 1997a, b). Major Chaco sites are defined by a central large masonry structure known as a "great house" with large rooms, which is generally surrounded by smaller houses. Associated with the "great houses" are large kivas, which are round subterranean ceremonial chambers up to 10 meters in diameter, and numerous smaller kivas. A dozen such great houses are known in Chaco Canyon itself, with about twenty other outliers in the surrounding countryside. Chaco sites have a much more formal appearance to their layout than other Anasazi communities outside this area, and the roads provide an additional distinctive element which integrated these communities into a regional entity.

The largest great house in Chaco Canyon is Pueblo Bonito, which was built in seven discernable stages over the course of two centuries (Lekson 1991). It consists of over 700 rooms, built in a D-shaped semi-circle, and at least 32 kivas, including two great kivas. The rooms are built up in terraces, and the tiers of rooms reach at least four deep along the back of the arc. Stephen Lekson (1984; Lekson et al. 1998) estimates that the construction of such a great house took 50 million building stones and 215,000 trees (which had to be brought from forests up to 75 kilometers away). Pueblo Bonito is a remarkable feat of prehistoric engineering and a sustained investment of labor and organization. Other nearby great house sites, such as Chetro Ketl and Pueblo Alto, exhibit similar investment, all during the same two-century construction boom, which is characterized by periodic bursts of activity separated by periods in which relatively little building occurred.

Although the "great houses" have dominated research on the Chaco Anasazi, they do not appear to have served as residences for the number of people that the many rooms might suggest. Instead, recent research supports the idea that they were public facilities (Lekson 1991; Lekson and Cameron 1995) which served some sort of formal, ceremonial function with only a small resident population. Most of the permanent residents of the Chaco region between AD 900 and 1150 lived in small clusters of domestic structures called "unit houses," consisting of seven to ten rooms and a small kiva. These appear to have been family dwellings – households – which were the basic residential units of Chacoan society. The basic "Chaco community" pattern, consisting of a great house, a great kiva, and a cluster of unit houses, is repeated throughout the Chaco region.

Connecting the outlying great houses with Chaco Canyon is a remarkable system of roads (Vivian 1997a). Chacoan roads, some still visible in the landscape today and others revealed with remote-sensing techniques, are long straight landscape features which extend for dozens of kilometers in different directions around Chaco Canyon and the outlying great houses. Eventually, the major segments converge on the Canyon. Chaco roads, like the great houses, display engineering skill. They are graded to run smoothly across uneven terrain and lined by earthen berms. One road, called the "Great North Road," runs true north out of Chaco Canyon for nearly 50 kilometers. The roads reach a width of nine meters closer to the great houses and become narrower as they get further away, much like the New Jersey Turnpike has additional lanes as it gets closer to New York City.

What purpose did the Chaco roads serve? Gwinn Vivian (1997b) identifies three possible purposes: economic, military, and integrative. The economic rationale suggests that the roads had a utilitarian purpose to move goods and supplies around the Chaco region. Large numbers of ceramic vessels were brought into the Canyon from distant points, while turquoise, ornaments of Pacific shell, and other exotic ornaments also were imported. It is not clear, however, what material objects came out of the Canyon (Lekson and Cameron 1995), or why roads were necessary for the movement of relatively light-weight goods other than the building materials used in the construction of great houses and kivas. The military explanation is equally tenuous, since there is little evidence of large groups of warriors enforcing Chaco authority in the outlying areas.

Vivian (1997b) suggests that regional integration appears to have been the most likely use of the roads. The patterning of the roads does not support the notion that they were controlled by a centralized authority. Instead, they facilitated communication among the various Chacoan communities to integrate them into a cohesive society. John Roney (1992) takes a slightly different view and points out that it is not entirely clear that the roads compose a coherent system of transportation corridors. With the exception of some major arteries, like the Great North Road mentioned above, most Chaco roads are short segments which emanate from an outlying great house and run off a few kilometers into the countryside. In Roney's view, Chaco roads are local phenomena, built for their symbolic value in conjunction with the great houses as shared labor projects to increase social solidarity.

There are differing views about the degree of Chaco social differentiation and hierarchy. In many publications the topic is avoided by characterizing Chaco as "a community of unprecedented complexity" (Lekson et al. 1988: 109) without a specific consideration of status, power, and wealth. Those who have addressed the topic directly appear to be polarized. Vivian (1991) views Chaco society as essentially egalitarian, with the differences between the great houses and the small sites explained by the presence of two groups with different cultural traditions. Lynne Sebastian, by contrast, characterizes Chaco as a stratified society with class distinctions based on access to productive land and control of religious knowledge (Sebastian 1991, 1992). In her view, the leaders lived in the great houses and the followers lived in the surrounding community. John Kantner (1996) also considers Chaco society to have been non-egalitarian, with competition among local leaders resulting in the formation of multi-village polities.

As with Hohokam, the indicators of differences in access to status, power, and wealth in Chaco society are diffuse. The great houses and kivas are certainly impressive, but if they were largely unoccupied, as Lekson and others suggest, then their attribution as the seats of the elite appears to be questionable. To a generalist outsider, the Chaco evidence is suggestive of the same sort of communal ceremonialism which characterized Late Neolithic Europe, Hopewellian North America, or Khok Phanom Di. Inequalities can be attributed to aggrandizive individuals and households acquiring transitory authority, without the institutionalized genealogically-based differentiation which characterizes more complex polities. Like the Hohokam, there appears to have been a greater emphasis on "horizontal" integration rather than "vertical" structure.

Whatever its degree of social differentiation, the Chaco system collapsed around the middle of the twelfth century AD. Construction of great houses ceased, perhaps due to droughts or other environmental factors, although they appeared to have been occupied for another few decades. Elsewhere in the Anasazi area, large communities continued to flourish for a short time longer, but they also eventually declined. By AD 1300 the prehistoric inhabitants of this region became virtually invisible in the archaeological record.

CONCLUSION: NOT MANY CHIEFS YET

A number of common threads occur throughout this discussion of transegalitarian societies. The first is that they exhibit a growing fascination with mortuary ceremonialism. Much of the acquisition of exotic materials, such as copper in Late Neolithic Europe and in Hopewell, occurred so that they could be disposed of in burials, even if they were first transformed into apparently useful objects like panpipes or hammer-axes. The second, and often related to the first, is the growth of trade as an activity to which considerable effort was devoted. Although the acquisition of exotic items was long a human pursuit prior to the last few millennia BC, in all these places people appear to have been willing to do whatever was necessary to obtain exotic materials and objects made from them. Third, there is often a desire to transform the landscape, to remake it in the vision of its human occupants, which had not manifested itself previously. The "inscribed landscape" of megalithic Europe and the Hopewell effigy mounds both seem to be part of a broader pattern. Finally, in some societies, the undifferentiated domestic architecture of individual households gives way to the appearance of a few buildings which reflect some public activity or different status of their occupants. Note how there is a similar difference of archaeological opinion about the unusual buildings in 'Ubaid and in Formative Mesoamerica. Were they residences of high-status individuals or public buildings such as temples?

Lest the reader fear that I am arguing for unilineal cultural evolution, let me hasten to point out that there are marked differences from one area to another as well. In Europe, and perhaps the Near East as well, the presence of domestic livestock provided an important "trigger" to the differentiation of households once their usefulness for traction and other secondary products was discovered. It would be useful for archaeologists to try to identify similar factors in areas in the New World where domestic livestock were not present.

The focus on chiefdoms by archaeologists has become a fundamental obstacle to our understanding of transegalitarian societies due to the conflation of "inequality" with "hierarchy." This is an artifact of the Service paradigm of band→tribe→chiefdom→state in which the term "chiefdom" has come to encompass every society lying between the egalitarian and the state. The concept of chiefdom, despite attempts by some (e.g., Earle 1991) to clarify it, has become in the eyes of many archaeologists a hallmark of a transegalitarian society. Almost any society which shows any degree of social differentiation is categorized as a chiefdom. As noted at the beginning of this chapter, having the society you study identified as a chiefdom is considered by archaeologists to be good, with the result being an aggressive interpretation of the data to find evidence, however tenuous, of chiefly characteristics. Much of the same evidence can be interpreted more conservatively as indicating transitory differences in status, prestige, talent, or even household size.

As an alternative to the prevailing interpretive framework which emphasizes progressively greater hierarchy, Crumley (1979, 1995) has introduced the concept of *heterarchy*. "Heterarchy" is defined as "the relations of elements to one another when they are unranked or when they possess the potential for being ranked in a number of different ways" (Crumley 1995: 3). In other words, heterarchy exists when there are many different axes along which differentiation can take place, rather than the pyramidal view of hierarchical organization implicit in the chiefdom concept. A heterarchy is more like a web or a lattice, with subordination and superordination between elements determined in situational and functional ways. Heterarchy does not equal egalitarian, but rather can exist in various ways in both egalitarian and non-egalitarian societies. It is not a necessary precursor to hierarchical organization but can represent an alternative configuration of social relations.

For the sorts of transegalitarian societies described here, the concept of heterarchy would appear to have considerable value, for it describes situations of increasing complexity without apparent centralized control. While it should not be applied uncritically to every transegalitarian society, the notion that there can be numerous axes along which asymmetrical social relationships can occur without necessarily being the vertical ranking found in chiefdoms would have great heuristic value. Indeed, the notion of heterarchical organization has been applied to the Southeast Asian Bronze Age societies described above (White 1995) and to Bronze Age society in Denmark which succeeded the Late Neolithic groups described in this chapter (Levy 1995) and which has frequently been characterized as fitting the chiefdom model (Kristiansen 1991; Earle 1991).

The notion of heterarchy would also accommodate the model of household differentiation proposed here better than one of hierarchy. The notion of households falling beneath some societal baseline as opposed to rising to the top of a societal pyramid would mean that the asymmetrical relationships among them would be situational and dynamic. The clustering of households into hamlets and their affiliation into factions would provide two more axes along which asymmetries could take place. Finally, the tension between the economic power of the successful households and the demographic power of the unsuccessful ones would further complicate the emergence of centralized authority and power. Thus, I would argue that heterarchy, no matter how it played itself out later on in prehistory, is an endemic condition of transegalitarian societies.

Despite attempts by archaeologists to discern chiefly rule in transegalitarian societies in the last few millennia BC, the position taken here is that the evidence for chiefdom-type institutionalized and hereditary social ranking and centralized authority is elusive at best in most Neolithic (and even Bronze Age) or Formative societies. Possible exceptions to this generalization are the 'Ubaid communities of Mesopotamia, as well as the immediate precursors to the Shang, Indus Valley, and Nile Valley civilizations discussed in the following chapter. Elsewhere in the world, it would be several more centuries or even millennia before one can truly speak of the emergence of chiefs and chiefly polities. Although aggrandizers and leaders of factions surely existed, in almost no case can we say that individuals had the sustained ability to claim control over a specific, bounded population, its internal social affairs, and its external economic relations. The authority and prestige of the nominal leaders of factions and hamlets grew from their ability as heads of households to pursue successful accumulation strategies and to hold other households in economic or social debt. Yet the business of social alliance and trade was still conducted largely at the household level, without central organization or control.

The emergence of transegalitarian societies in many parts of the world in the centuries following the establishment of agrarian communities suggests a clear connection. It is true that much later in prehistory transegalitarian societies emerged among late foragers, particularly on the Pacific Coast of North America, and the fully-agricultural status of Hopewell is still open to debate. Nonetheless, in most parts of the world, agriculture – and the self-interest and household organization which the agricultural economy entailed – were important prerequisites to the development of social differentiation. Systematic trade was also facilitated by food production, since now there was an elastic source of commodities which could be exchanged, if a group did not have access to some desired material.

In my view, a critical threshold was crossed when societies started to move beyond the domestic sphere into some formalized and structured public life. For this reason, the interpretation of the anomalous buildings in 'Ubaid Mesopotamia and in Formative Mesoamerica becomes very crucial. A conservative interpretation is that they were the residences of high-status individuals, yet with no indication that they exercised the authority of a chief, whereas a more aggressive interpretation would be that they were seats of chiefly power or temples. Indications of community planning would also be important in this connection. I would attach less significance as indicators of chiefdoms to the modification of the landscape, to trade in exotic materials (as opposed to the deliberate and systematic pursuit of finished products, as will be seen in Iron Age Europe in chapter 8), or to elaborate mortuary ritual. These can all occur, without much central direction, in communities of autonomous households, either acting on their own or affiliated into hamlets and factions.

This relatively conservative position (or perhaps it is radical, considering the archaeological tendency to find chiefs everywhere!) will contrast with the developments traced in the chapter that follows. In the last few millennia of prehistory, chiefs and kings came to populate the archaeological landscape throughout the world. The key difference between these later societies and the transegalitarian communities that preceded them lies in the formality of their public lives and in the sharper definition of suprahousehold affiliations.

FURTHER READING

Transegalitarian societies around the world have never been treated with the comprehensive approach taken in this chapter, so readers will need to supplement the discussion here with theoretical approaches on one hand and case studies dealing with specific sites on the other. Brian Hayden's chapter, "Pathways to power," in the volume edited by T. Douglas Price and Gary Feinman entitled *Foundations of Social Inequality* (1995), is a good place to start. The notion of heterarchy is introduced in *Heterarchy and the Analysis of Complex Societies*, edited by Robert Ehrenreich, Carole Crumley, and Janet Levy (1995). Animal traction and its possible consequences for the emergence of interhousehold inequality in Europe was the topic of a paper in the journal *Antiquity* by Peter Bogucki entitled "Animal traction and household economies in Neolithic Europe" (1993). A number of papers that deal with factions and competition appear in *Factional Competition and Political Development in the New World*, edited by Elizabeth Brumfiel and John W. Fox (1994). There are many regional case studies that deal with societies that have been considered in this chapter. *Europe in the Neolithic* by Alasdair Whittle (1996) and *An Ethnography of the Neolithic* by Christopher Tilley (1996) contain rich descriptions of the period discussed in this chapter, although their interpretations may diverge from the picture presented here. *Villages in the Steppe – Later Neolithic Settlement and Subsistence in Balikh Valley, Northern Syria* by Peter M. M. G. Akkermans (1993) provides an overview of basic data on some late Neolithic settlements in the Near East, and the December 1992 issue of *The Biblical Archaeologist* contains several short articles which deal with this same period. For Mesoamerica, the classic discussion of the Formative period is found in Kent Flannery's *The Early Mesoamerican Village* (1976), which has introduced several generations of students of early farming communities to the archaeology of the household, while Norman Hammond's *Cuello: an Early Maya Community in Belize* (1991) is a detailed site report and discussion of critical aspects of lowland Formative settlement. *Khok Phanom Di: Prehistoric Adaptation to the World's Richest Habitat* by Charles Higham and Rachanie Thosarat (1994) presents a case study of this remarkable site, which can be put into a broader context by consulting Higham's 1996 *The Bronze Age of Southeast Asia*. An up-to-date comprehensive treatment of the Hopewell phenomenon in mid-continental North America has yet to appear, but a good recent regional anthology is *Ohio Hopewell Community Organization*, edited by William Dancey and Paul Pacheco (1997). In contrast, there are many recent works dealing with the transegalitarian societies of the Desert Borderlands. Of note are *Chaco & Hohokam: Prehistoric Regional Systems in the American Southwest*, edited by Patricia Crown and W. James Judge (1991), *The Chaco Anasazi: Sociopolitical Evolution in the Prehistoric Southwest* by Lynne Sebastian, *Chaco Canyon: A Center and its World* by Mary Peck (1994), and *Exploring the Hohokam*, edited by George Gumerman (1991).

[7] ELITES AND COMMONERS

CHAPTER SYNOPSIS

BEYOND TRANSEGALITARIAN SOCIETIES: THE RISE OF ELITES

In the previous chapter, we encountered a number of societies around the world in the throes of some form of nascent social differentiation. Status, power, and wealth – hitherto widely but modestly distributed – began to be concentrated in the hands of a few households. Let us now fast-forward a few more centuries. We come to find societies in which the nascent inequalities have been perpetuated across generations to develop not just wealthy and powerful households but elite lineages whose head makes fundamental decisions for the larger society, which consists of many communities. These are not merely transegalitarian societies, but rather they display the social differentiation and political centralization characteristic of clearly inegalitarian social groupings.

Discussions of social differentiation and political centralization of pre-state societies lead inevitably to a consideration of polities known as "chiefdoms" and the economic, political, and ideological conditions that create and sustain them. Such societies take many different forms, and they are not inevitable developments from transegalitarian precursors. They should not be viewed as a "stage" through which the cultural development of each region passed. Nonetheless, they appeared in many parts of the works in later prehistoric times with an important common characteristic: genealogically-determined differences in access to status, power, and wealth. Prehistoric societies became composed of elites and commoners whose status was largely determined at birth.

The 1990s have seen extensive theoretical discussion of the economic, political, and ideological conditions which lead to the emergence of chiefdoms (e.g., Pauketat 1994; Muller 1997; Earle 1991, 1997). It is impossible to convey anything more than a superficial view of the richness and complexity of this discussion. After a brief introduction to some key issues, a number of prehistoric societies which appear to have had genealogically-based access to status, power, and wealth will be examined to understand how chiefdoms work in practice. Chosen for discussion here are early complex societies in temperate Europe, Mesoamerica, North and South America, China, and Polynesia. This list is not exhaustive but tries to include extensive geographical coverage and diversity in the archaeological record, especially where archaeologists have explicitly focused on the nature of pre-state polities in a region.

CHIEFDOMS AS AN ANALYTICAL CATEGORY

Many archaeologists have been fixated on chiefdoms since the rise of neo-evolutionary theory in the 1960s, which argued for a uniform cultural trajectory from bands through egalitarian tribes, then chiefdoms, and ultimately to states. Archaeologists like chiefdoms: they are nicely complex and not egalitarian, yet are not so complex and hierarchical as states; they provide a logical precursor to later, more complex social forms; they can be "easily" (perhaps too much so!) inferred from mortuary and architectural evidence; they give an archaeological community a certain cachet that lifts it above pedestrian precursors yet still renders it somewhat exotic and thus worthy of anthropological study. Yet it is also a concept that causes considerable discussion and debate in the field (e.g., Spencer 1987; Yoffee 1993) and as with many things that seemed so simple in the 1960s, by the 1990s the application of the concept of chiefdom is more complicated than could have been imagined.

A number of issues, which are often not clearly delineated in archaeological discussions, are involved in the study of prehistoric chiefdoms. Fundamental to the discussion is the justification of the concept itself: why is it important to study societies whose organization is based on hereditary, genealogically-determined status and have centralized leadership and authority? Do they form a valid analytical category? If they do, then what are their archaeological signatures? Finally, once chiefdoms are identified archaeologically, how do they behave? How do they emerge from previous conditions, develop their particular characteristics, change in response to internal and external forces, and eventually decline and disappear?

Chiefdoms represent the formalization of inherited differences in access to status, power, and wealth. After the emergence of chiefdoms and until the development of the modern democracy in the late eighteenth century, virtually all polities were governed in this manner. This fact alone makes the appearance of chiefdoms in the archaeological record significant. Moreover, the organization of society along hereditary lines explains much about the archaeological record in later prehistory. Elaborate monuments, differentiation among settlements, changes in subsistence, and evidence for feasting all take on considerable significance as the social order changes from one of households competing on a relatively level playing field to institutionalized differences between commoners and elites.

A critical issue for archaeologists and anthropologists has been the definition of "chiefdom," which has changed considerably since its formal introduction to anthropological thought in the 1950s (see Carniero 1981 for a discussion of the evolution of the concept). In the 1960s, Elman Service articulated his classical definition of a chiefdom as a society in which people are ranked according to genealogical proximity to the chief, who functions along with his retainers as the central agency of redistribution. "Redistribution" grabbed the attention of archaeologists, for it could explain the apparent generation of subsistence surpluses as well as the establishment of large central storage facilities. The prominence that Service gave to this concept was due to his use of Polynesian chiefdoms as the paradigm for the whole concept, following Sahlins' 1958 classic study. Unfortunately, it now appears that redistribution is not a common feature of societies which have genealogically-based access to status, power, and wealth. In a survey of prestate societies in the Americas, Feinman and Neitzel (1984: 56) observed "redistribution is clearly not the central function of leadership in prestate sedentary societies," a position echoed by others (e.g., Peebles and Kus 1977; Earle 1987).

As a result, there has been a trend towards a progressively more minimalist definition of what constitutes a chiefdom, which now focuses on its role as a political unit in which local autonomy has been surrendered to a central authority. Perhaps the most economical formulation is that used by Earle (1991: 1) who considers a chiefdom to be a "polity that organizes centrally a regional population in the thousands ... some degree of heritable social ranking and economic stratification is characteristically associated." I would link these two concepts somewhat more strongly by eliminating the "characteristically," since no truly egalitarian society is compatible with centralized control. The centralized control need not be a pyramidally-constructed hierarchy, but certainly a differentiation of the society into commoner and elite populations on the basis of hereditary status, not age, is fundamental. A chiefdom is not a gerontocracy in which status is achieved rather than ascribed, although skill and ability may enlarge this status and the power that accompanies it.

A very interesting question, which would not have occurred to many archaeologists in the 1970s, is whether the concept of "chiefdom" is a legitimate analytical category in the first place. Yoffee (1993) points out that the use of such an analytical category can be crippling to a true understanding of social change because such taxonomic exercises do not provide insight into how complexity emerges and how economic power is created. He criticizes those who see chiefdoms as an inevitable rung on the ladder of complexity towards statehood, and in fact suggests that chiefdoms may be incompatible with many of the social formations which later characterized states. These are serious and to a large degree valid criticisms, which will be taken into account in the discussion in this chapter. Nonetheless, we know from ethnohistoric accounts that chiefdom societies occurred in late prehistoric and early historic times in many parts of the world, and convincing cases can be made for their existence in certain deeper prehistoric instances as well.

Yet not every instance of complex prehistoric social organization inferred from mortuary remains or architecture should be called a "chiefdom," despite archaeologists' predisposition to do so. The emergence of centralized political authority and the differentiation of society into elites and commoners is not inevitable nor is it the only dimension of social complexity that is possible. Societies in which leadership is based on achievement and not on genealogy are clearly viable alternatives to chiefdoms and have been found in many later prehistoric contexts (e.g., in central Asia – see Lamberg-Karlovsky 1994). Yoffee (1993: 65) suggests that early states may be more reasonably derived from "achievement-oriented" societies than from "ascriptively determined" chiefdoms. This may indeed be possible, but the question under consideration here is not simply the road to statehood but rather the fact that it is indeed possible to document many cases of prehistoric societies in which status and power were ascriptively determined.

THE EMERGENCE OF CHIEFDOMS

How do chiefdoms emerge? As Earle (1991) points out, the "structural conditions for hierarchy" have to be present. A seminal structural condition

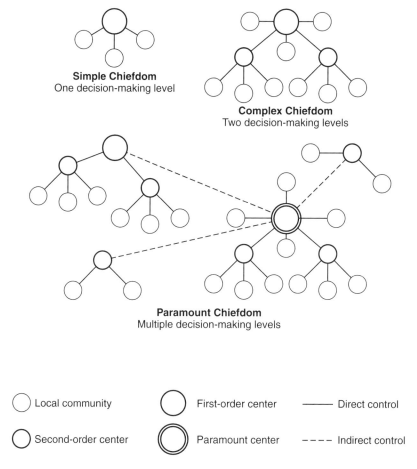

Figure 7.1 Schematic depiction of the structure of simple, complex, and paramount chiefdoms (after Anderson 1996, figure 10.1).

would be that a society must already acknowledge and engage in some form of social inequality based on factors other than age and sex. One such form of inequality would be the sort of differences among households in transegalitarian societies, described in the previous chapter, in which successful household acquisition strategies pursued by aggrandizive individuals resulted in differential household wealth and its transmission across generations. When this was coupled with the leadership of household heads in the organization of factions and hamlets, the seeds of some form of hereditary social differentiation clearly were present in many prehistoric societies.

In many respects, the sort of differentiation along genealogical lines that characterizes the emergence of chiefdoms is akin to the sort of variation that emerged among competitive agricultural households, just writ larger. Instead of individuals who aspire to greater things through successful management of a household and acquisition of additional wealth, now collections of related households act in concert to achieve and maintain their positions as an elite subgroup of the population. Differentiation is now on the community level, with the inhabitants of the chiefly residential center holding a higher social position than the commoners who lived in outlying hamlets. Social asymmetries among households are replaced, at least in part, by asymmetries among clearly delineated kin groups.

The emergence of centralized authority required what had been hitherto autonomous households comprising autonomous communities to surrender their authority and become subservient to the chiefly elite. How, then, does the authority of a small privileged elite come to be accepted and endorsed by the rest of the population? On this matter, there is little archaeological consensus. Allen (1996: 173) identifies three archaeological positions on what he calls "primal sources of power" in nascent chiefdoms: economic, ideological, and military. Some believe that leadership in warfare is what causes people to place their trust in an elite few (e.g., Carniero 1990; Price 1984). Others have taken the view that ideology is how elites persuade others to contribute labor to the maintenance of their status (e.g., Demarest 1989; Demarest and Conrad 1992). The third school of thought is that economic power could be usurped by elites and denied to other ambitious individuals and households (Arnold 1996; Allen 1996; Gilman 1995). In reality, some combination of these factors can probably be said to have been behind the emergence of most chiefdoms, but the foregoing discussion of the economic differentiation of households suggests that the root of power is some form of privilege in the access to wealth.

For many archaeologists, this debate is about the *character* of the chieftaincy. In the 1960s and 1970s, it became popular to stress the managerial role of chiefs, "public servants" of a sort. They were leaders in warfare and religion, they were bankers who collected surpluses and redistributed them, and – at a more abstract level – they were "risk managers" whose function was to make sure that everyone got enough to eat in lean years because they had collected tribute in the good years. According to Sahlins (1972: 140), "the chief creates a collective good beyond the conception and capacity of the society's domestic groups taken separately. He institutes a public economy greater than the sum of its household parts." Some things were just too big and important – like warfare, trade, religion – to be left to individuals and households.

The problem with this functionalist view, as Gilman (1991: 147) points out, is that it does not explain why the elites inherit their social position. Rather, he argues, chiefs are aggressive, aggrandizing bosses who pursue strategies to establish and maintain their elite status over time and cow the commoners into providing tribute. In Gilman's Marxian analysis, chiefs are exploitative folks who essentially run a protection racket, not benign regulators of exchange. A slightly more positive spin can be put on this view by suggesting that chiefs are hyper-successful individuals who have managed to secure the pre-eminent positions in society for themselves and their relatives through their skill, cunning, determination, prescience, charisma, and ability

to put others in their debt. The real question is the legitimacy of the inflic-
tion of debt: when does debt become tribute extracted by threat?

Here ideology enters the picture, for if the control was strictly economic
then too many opportunities would have existed for individual households to
opt out of the system. After all, these were still self-sufficient agrarian households with the capacity for sustaining themselves. Ideology and religion,
however, in the hands of an elite can serve a legitimizing function to establish
their right to primacy from one generation to the next. Again, although this
notion has its roots in Marxian analyses where it is assigned a primary role, it
is nonetheless an important consideration from the perspective taken in this
volume. It is clear that the commoner population needed to agree to be
indebted and to surrender its autonomy to the elite in perpetuity, and the
most powerful coercive force in a transegalitarian society would have been
the control and manipulation of the supernatural belief system.

The conflict between the "chief-as-manager" and "chief-as-despot" positions may also reflect genuine variability in types of chiefdoms. Renfrew
(1974) pointed out that chiefdoms may either reflect collective (what he
termed "group-oriented") or individual (what he termed "individualizing")
interests. In group-oriented chiefdoms, there was less lavish display of personal wealth and more emphasis on communal activity and group rituals to
integrate the population, with the chief serving as the coordinator and
master-of-ceremonies. In individualizing chiefdoms, there was a marked
emphasis on personal status and prestige, conspicuous disparity between the
elite and commoners, and less communal ritual and public construction.
Here the chief and his retinue were clearly the focus of attention. Although
Renfrew's focus was on prehistoric Europe, this distinction has been found
to have some utility in the study of prehistoric chiefdoms in the New World
as well (Feinman 1995: 267–8).

THE ECONOMIC FOUNDATION OF CHIEFDOMS

Another approach to the study of prehistoric chiefdoms has been to characterize the economic base of their political power. D'Altroy and Earle (1985)
and Brumfiel and Earle (1987) have identified two general categories
which they call "staple finance" and "wealth distribution." Staple finance
involves the generation of a surplus of staple crops such as corn or grain to
support the elite, while wealth distribution is the accumulation and distribution among the elite of exotic or expensive materials as symbols of power,
rewards, and barter for staples. Gilman (1987: 22) points out that these are
"partly alternative, partly complementary strategies by which elites in general
support their operations and life-styles." Each approach has its merits and its
problems.

Staple finance is fairly simple and direct: commoners intensify subsistence activities to produce surpluses for the elites. Storage and transportation costs, however, place constraints on the degree to which such systems
can expand. Moreover, staple-finance systems are fundamentally grounded
in coercion of the commoners by the elites. Gilman (1987: 22) calls them

"protection rackets." Although people can tolerate some degree of coercion, their tolerance is not infinitely elastic, and thus such systems cannot grow indefinitely. They can, however, sustain themselves at a moderate level of coercion and expropriation for some length of time. Elites engaging in wealth distribution can quickly expand their sphere of power and influence by forging new exchange relationships and concentrating their acquisitions into more and more prestigious goods. They are based on reliable procurement channels, however, since prestige goods must be acquired in progressively greater quantities. Gilman (1987: 22) likens wealth distribution systems to "Ponzi schemes." The rewards are high, but so also are the risks, as well as the vulnerability of the system to perturbations that disrupt the flow of prestige goods. Wealth-distribution systems are highly unstable; they either develop into higher-order polities like states or they collapse. Such systems are especially susceptible to the oscillations in chiefly power and prestige described below.

Gil Stein (1994: 40–1) has provided some archaeological correlates of these two types of chiefly economies. In a wealth-distribution chiefdom, the following characteristics would be expected: exotic goods as markers of status; centrally-located specialists in the production of prestige goods; pronounced differentiation of elites on the basis of their access to exotic goods and knowledge; and heightened levels of interregional competition and warfare. To this list I would add the cyclical florescences caused by the inherent instability of such systems. Staple-finance systems, on the other hand, lack the profusion of prestige goods but nonetheless exhibit economic differentiation, centralized staple storage, village craft production and local (rather than long-distance) exchange, and evidence for ritual, genealogical, or coercive modes of surplus mobilization.

Most archaeological chiefdoms, I would argue, fit the wealth-distribution model. Only in a few cases might one truly say that staple finance played the predominant role. Moreover, wealth-finance systems may still require some expropriation of staples from the population in order to support the acquisition of exotic raw materials. Perhaps the real issue is how quickly can a chiefdom make the transition from staple finance to wealth distribution. Brumfiel and Earle (1987: 7–8) appear to recognize this and proceed to identify two different types of wealth distribution. One involves the widespread distribution of prestige goods to retainers in return for loyalty, which would lead to their widespread occurrence in the community. The other restricts the ownership of prestige goods to the core of the elite which marks them as particularly privileged. It therefore seems that staple finance has limited value as an economic basis for power (as does any highly coercive system in the long run), and wealth distribution was the way to go for the chiefdom that was on the fast track to power and status.

THE INSTABILITY OF CHIEFDOMS

Once the first chiefdom emerges in a region, there is a compelling reason for neighboring polities to emulate it lest they risk losing their own autonomy and finding themselves to be the subjects of an alien chief. As a result, the simultaneous emergence of chiefdoms over large areas that can be observed in the archaeological record is hardly surprising, especially if the different subregions are roughly the same in agricultural productivity. Since chiefdoms require food surpluses, the natural productivity of a habitat is crucial. Moreover, since chiefdoms require communication between the central residence of the chief and the outlying communities, easy transportation routes in the form of rivers and roads are also important. In an area which is not circumscribed by oceans, mountains, or deserts people can move away if they prefer not to be subjugated to the chiefly elite, but in a region of high natural productivity which is bounded by natural barriers, complex social forms can emerge very quickly as high populations require multiple levels of administrative control.

The emergence of differences in status, power, and wealth which are based on genealogy carries with it, however, an inherent instability (Anderson 1996). A chief's supporters within his small group of kin are also his potential successors, and their ambition must be deflected and their patience rewarded. Not only was there always the possibility of a child or other relative deposing the chief, but his death even under natural circumstances would precipitate a period of social upheaval unless rules of succession were firmly established and enforced (which would be unlikely in pre-literate communities). There is an inherent organizational contradiction in chiefdoms: potential rivals have to be placed into positions of power in order to keep them happy, but at the same time these positions can be used as platforms from which to mount challenges to the authority of the chief and the succession upon his demise.

The instability of chiefdoms at times of leadership transition, or the replacement of a strong and wise chief by an incompetent successor, could cause a chiefdom to dissolve or to be subordinated to a stronger neighboring polity. By the same token, a skilled leader could bring other neighboring polities under his control to create a multi-tiered society, only to have this accomplishment collapse when he passed from the scene. This creates a phenomenon in chiefly societies which Anderson (1994, 1996) has called "cycling," the alternation between simple and complex states of chiefly authority and power. I would prefer to use the term "oscillation" here, largely for semantic reasons to provide a more vivid characterization of this process.

The oscillating character of chiefdoms has profound implications for the archaeological record. Elite centers begin small, rapidly grow to a maximum extent, then collapse and lose influence over their hinterlands. No single central residential site sustains its leading position for very long, although ritual locations may remain in long-term use. This is in contrast with the lengthy periods of growth and development seen at many earlier settlements. Moreover, the need for the elite to demonstrate its leadership through access to prestige goods typically results in very intense acquisition and consumption of such artifacts, which contributes to the archaeological "visibility" of chiefly residential and mortuary precincts.

The recognition that chiefdoms oscillate between states of greater and lesser organizational complexity indicates that societies do not, as strict evolutionary anthropologists would believe, move continually towards ever greater complexity. Such conditions of oscillation between complex but unstable and simple but stable have been recognized at even earlier periods in prehistory (e.g., Bogucki 1996b). With chiefdoms, however, the characteristic of oscillation is ingrained and takes place with a much shorter periodicity than it had previously, on the order of single generations or a few decades. It also accounts for spectacular florescences and sudden darkenings of the archaeological record, as chiefdoms emerge and are eclipsed.

The oscillations in many chiefdom societies, I would suggest, may also reflect a vacillation between episodes of robust, centralized, hierarchical structures and periods of heterarchy in which there is no clear centralized leadership, much as had prevailed in preceding times. Such would especially have been the case in transitional phases between transegalitarian societies and genealogically-based hierarchies. The prism of archaeology, however, tends to compress time and distort the archaeological record such that episodes of heterarchy sandwiched between episodes of hierarchy are overlooked. Since the archaeological record is naturally discontinuous, once a society provides some evidence of centralization and hierarchy, it is presumed to be unable to shift except along the vertical dimension of levels of decision-making. The notion that decision-making power may be concentrated at some times (at however many levels) and dispersed at other times is rarely considered. Gaps are attributed to incompleteness of data rather than to alternations between the two regimes. Hierarchical elites tend to leave more visible and spectacular remains (e.g., monuments and lavish burials) than heterarchical systems, hence the concentration of archaeological attention on the former.

It is important to remember that while the elite population amassed economic and ideological power, the commoner population retained an important trump card – demographic power. Due to their small size, elite populations would have increased at a much slower rate than the commoner population (Stuart and Gauthier 1988), even allowing for better nutrition and less taxing workload among the elite and higher mortality and shorter lifespan of commoners. Thus another destabilizing factor is introduced once disparities in status, power, and wealth become institutionalized. One way to offset this is to develop multiple levels of administrative control to retain the allegiance of rising commoner populations. Another is for the chiefdom to fragment into smaller politics, each of which can start the process anew.

The inherent instability of centralized, genealogically-based hierarchies means that conflict and warfare was endemic in chiefdom societies, perhaps to a greater degree than hitherto experienced in prehistory. Aspiring leaders would have sensed vulnerability in declining chiefly authority. Real and imagined social slights (such as during the division of food in feasting) could lead to feuds and revolts. Chiefs sought to extend their hegemony over resistant neighbors. The absence of a clear code of conduct among chiefly polities meant that most such societies were at war with someone during much of

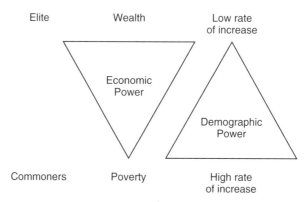

Figure 7.2 The economic power of the elite versus the demographic power of commoners, a key cause of the oscillations that characterize chiefdom systems (adapted from Stuart and Gauthier 1998, figure II.1).

their existence. Keeley (1996) argues that this is the expected result of many millennia of human interpersonal conflict, whereas others suggest that this is a new development with the emergence of marked social differentiation. The appearance of metal weapons in much of the Old World meant that people had a variety of new ways to kill each other, whereas the inhabitants of the New World relied on traditional stone-tipped spears and arrows.

The instability exhibited by chiefdoms, however, is precisely what makes them very interesting archaeologically and anthropologically. Once having reached this degree of organizational complexity, human societies could proceed in several possible directions. Some headed towards even greater complexity, forming states and empires. Others continued in the oscillation between simple and complex chiefdoms driven by the internal contradictions of power and succession. Still others entered into clientship relationships with more powerful entities nearby. These options for social complexity at the end of prehistory are discussed at greater length in the following chapter.

BRONZE METALLURGY IN THE OLD WORLD

In addition to the use of domestic livestock, the key element which distinguishes the prehistory of the Old World from that of the New is the development of the ability to alloy tin and copper to make bronze, which came into use during the last two millennia BC from the Atlantic coast of Europe to the Pacific coast of China. Although the ability to make bronze is predicated on the ability to smelt copper and tin, bronze metallurgy should not be considered to be the outcome of a simple evolution of pyrotechnology, although it is treated as such by many archaeologists. Rather, the development of the ability to make bronze and the demand for it as a material for tools and ornaments was the trigger for a number of changes in the organization of human society on a scale comparable to the onset of sedentism and agriculture several millennia earlier.

By itself, copper is a very soft metal, and its use during the early centuries of metallurgy was confined largely to ornaments or to semi-functional large tools. It did not keep an edge or a point well, nor could it be easily riveted together. Its acquisition, while requiring a sophistication in prospection and extraction, was fairly simple and very similar to the patterns of raw material acquisition which had been taking place for desirable forms of flint and obsidian since well back in the early Holocene. Bronze, however, adds another organizational layer to this process. Copper and tin, which do not typically occur together, must be transported from their sources and alloyed. Someone has to procure each of these metals, with some forethought and scientific knowledge for the tin by itself would not have produced a viable material under the manufacturing conditions of this period. There thus would have been a need for communication over significant distances and a coordination of the extraction and transport of the raw materials.

Clearly, interregional communication and interaction had begun to take place over much of Eurasia by the end of the third millennium BC. Horses had been domesticated (Anthony and Brown 1991), draft animals were in use for short distances, trackways were built across wetlands in northwestern Europe, and individuals such as the Iceman took part in arduous journeys across significant obstacles. The finding of 'Ubaid pottery on the Arabian Peninsula indicates the beginnings of maritime travel, although watercraft of some type must have been in use very early on. Alloying copper and tin, however, requires that this travel be sustained and directional, to the source and back, rather than sporadic and wandering.

It is not difficult to see why bronze was in such demand, for the possibilities offered by this metal are far more numerous than those available with copper or even gold. Very large and complex forms can be cast, strong sheets can be hammered and riveted, and weapons such as daggers and axes will not bend or dull as easily. Such artifacts were indeed useful in addition to being ornamental, even if the costs of acquiring raw materials and manufacturing the finished product were still steep. An explosion of metal-working occurs whenever bronze appears, and the effects on society were profound.

To be sure, some of these effects were only in the eyes of the archaeologists, for the elaboration in the archaeological record by the increase in metal objects is normally treated as a significant horizon. Yet the changes in societies carry through in other aspects of the archaeological record, such as in mortuary practices and in the elaboration of settlement, so these are not simply artificial transitions caused by the new material. Everywhere that bronze appears, evidence for markedly increased social organization soon follows. One possible explanation is that bronze, by virtue of the need to participate in interregional exchange to procure the raw materials and for specialized knowledge needed to alloy the metals, created a superb medium for the concentration of wealth. Bronze artifacts are often found as ingots, enormous unwearable armlets, or massive vessels which can only have served for conspicuous accumulation. In the New World, such a medium for wealth concentration and distribution was not available, so other factors assumed prominence in the course towards social differentiation.

CRAFT SPECIALIZATION

The topic of craft specialization has inspired a surprising amount of contention among the relatively small group of archaeologists with a passionate interest in it (e.g., Costin 1991; Clark 1995). Although these arguments may seem like a tempest in a teapot, they reflect the role that craft specialization is thought to have played in the emergence of social complexity. V. Gordon Childe was the first to draw attention to craft specialization. He considered one hallmark of urban civilization was the ability to divert a significant amount of labor from subsistence pursuits to the production of manufactured items. In the 1970s, Robert Evans refocused archaeological attention on craft specialization and gave it an explicit definition (Evans 1978). In Evans' view, craft specialization involved the manufacture of craft products by a small percentage of the total population in a community, the allocation of significant amounts of time by these individuals to craft production and the subtraction of that time from basic subsistence activities, and their resultant need to replace the lost subsistence production through the proceeds of the exchange of their craft products. The key difference between Childe and Evans was that Childe thought exclusively of full-time specialists, while Evans included the possibility of part-time specialization, which he then sought to identify in the Late Neolithic of southeastern Europe.

The concept of craft specialization was further amplified by Brumfiel and Earle in the 1980s to differentiate between "independent" and "attached" specialization (Brumfiel and Earle 1987). A general outline of this distinction is that the independent specialist makes goods for an open market in response to a demand whereas the attached specialist works under a closed arrangement to make specific products for a sponsoring person or institution. A current minor debate involves whether that arrangement necessarily involves social inequality. Brumfiel and Earle (1987), Costin (1991), and Arnold and Munns (1994) take the position that by definition attached specialization cannot exist prior to the emergence of elites, as it was a way for these groups to supply themselves with prestige goods such as weapons and ornaments. Clark and Parry (1990) downplay the difference between elite and general demand and focus on who has the rights to control and distribute the goods. In their view, if it is the maker then it is independent specialization, if it is the sponsor, then it is attached specialization.

Independent specialization, particularly at the household level, may well have emerged as another dimension of autonomous households competing with each other in a transegalitarian society. Some households may have found it advantageous to take advantage of craft skills as an alternative way of promoting their accumulation strategies. It is possible to imagine various sorts of independent household specialization (e.g., Clark and Parry 1990; Underhill 1991; Costin 1991) which involve domestic production or household-based workshops, either by individual households or by a consortium of several households. There is no need to assume any institutionalized social differentiation for independent craft specialization to exist. On the other hand, it is difficult to imagine attached craft specialization without some form of institutionalized social asymmetry. The key questions with attached specialization involve the location of the work (whether still in households of retainers or in elite precincts), the status of the artisans (whether still part-time or now full-time), and the scale.

On the theoretical end of the discussion, there appears to be a tendency towards the increasingly finer delineation of the different forms that special-ization can take (e.g., Costin 1991; Clark 1995). On the practical end, the problem is how to demonstrate the existence of specialization using archaeo-logical data and then to determine its specific role in the social system and economy. Some indicators of craft specialization include the identification of specific households and precincts in which manufacturing by-products are concentrated; nonrandom distribution of specific tools, such as borers used in bead production; homogeneity in some particular artifact characteristic, such as the thickness of ceramic vessel walls or decoration; and caches of identical artifacts which can be argued to have been produced by the same individual. Anomalous ratios of artifact classes are probably the most fre-quently cited indicator of craft specialization (Costin 1991: 21–2). Typically, the case for attached specialization is typically made after a society has been determined to have some measure of social differentiation by other means and the evidence for specialization has been found in association with an elite precinct.

Finally, there is the question of the role that craft specialization, when pre-sent, plays in the overall social and political structure of a given society. Under transegalitarian conditions, it can be considered as yet another strat-egy by which a household can try to obtain some competitive advantage and momentary wealth and prestige. In societies with hereditary social differenti-ation, however, the role of specialization is somewhat more difficult to pin down. Despite the Marxian position that specialization can be seen as a causal factor in social differentiation, it appears more likely that social differ-entiation stimulates the development of specialization (Muller 1987: 20). Clearly, attached specialization is another form of clientship, in that the pro-ducers depend on the continued demand for their product by the elite. Yet the elite also has a vested interest in taking good care of the specialists, for they produce the prestige goods which help substantiate authority and status, hence the frequent location of workshops in high-status precincts.

BRONZE AGE TEMPERATE EUROPE: WESSEX, STONEHENGE, ÚNĚTICE, THY

Between about 2500 and 1500 BC, the parts of Europe north of the Mediterranean zone – often called "temperate" Europe – saw the emergence of clear and pervasive social differentiation which was much more sustained and sharply defined than that seen in the Neolithic transegalitarian societies described in chapter 6. The period under consideration here spans the last centuries of the Neolithic and the first part of what is traditionally called the "Bronze Age." For the purpose of simplification, I will consider these societies under the general rubric of "Bronze Age," recognizing that in the British Isles and southern Scandinavia, many of the developments discussed are considered locally to have begun during the latest part of the Neolithic. This highlights a problem in European prehistoric nomenclature of which the reader should be aware, for rarely are developments neatly synchronous across the continent, nor are the chronological frameworks imposed on them by archaeologists.

The European Bronze Age is, according to Anthony Harding (1983: 1), regarded as "the most turgid and indigestible of the prehistoric periods ... by students and scholars alike" in Britain and North America whereas in continental Europe it is the object of fascination. Part of the problem appears to stem from the arbitrariness of its delineation from what precedes and follows it on the basis of the use of a single raw material, the alloy of tin and copper. Of course, copper was used much earlier in the Neolithic, so one cannot equate the Bronze Age with the innovation of metallurgy, and flint tools did not cease to be made, so the Bronze Age cannot be equated with the replacement of stone tools with metal ones. Late Neolithic groups with direct continuity into Bronze Age cultures can be identified as early as 2500 BC in most areas, the only difference being the moment of the first appearance of bronze artifacts. The Bronze Age is admittedly an arbitrary segment of a continuum, although as Coles and Harding (1979) point out, Europe during the second millennium BC saw particular economic, social, and technological developments which establish it as a valid framework for study.

It is clear that during the several centuries on either side of 2000 BC, the patterns of differential access to status, power, and wealth which had been brewing in transegalitarian Neolithic societies during the preceding millennium became an established part of the social order and an inescapable fact of life. Colin Renfrew was one of the first to import Service's concept of the chiefdom from American anthropology, first with reference to the Aegean (Renfrew 1972) but eventually to temperate Europe, specifically Late Neolithic and Early Bronze Age southern England (Renfrew 1974). In the following 25 years, archaeologists have generally accepted the view that some form of institutionalized and probably hereditary social differentiation became a characteristic of European society during the period. It is usually characterized as "social ranking" or "hierarchy," and "elite" is often used in order to avoid the use of the term "chief," but the general concept is the same. European chiefdoms, however, manifested themselves in a distinctive fashion which involved the exchange of prestigious materials and the construction of elaborate mortuary and ritual monuments.

BRONZE AGE SETTLEMENTS IN TEMPERATE EUROPE

A peculiar aspect of Early Bronze Age temperate Europe is the general absence of sites which can be considered the residences of chiefly elites, a marked contrast with the other chiefdoms considered in this chapter. Only in east-central Europe can we clearly identify fortified settlements which might be argued to have been the seats of chiefs and their retainers. Sites like Nitriansky Hrádok, Spišský Štvrtok, Boheimkirchen, and Barca

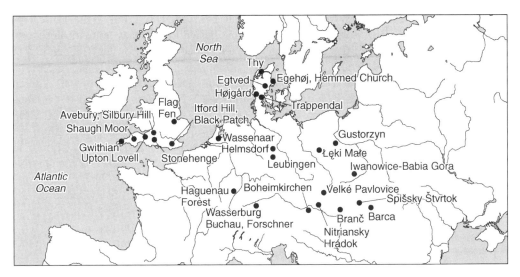

Figure 7.3 Map of temperate Europe showing key Bronze Age sites mentioned in this chapter.

controlled major trade routes in the Carpathians. Elsewhere, the population continued to live in hamlets of dispersed farmsteads much like their Neolithic predecessors.

One of the most thoroughly-studied Early Bronze Age settlements in central Europe is at Iwanowice-Babia Góra in southern Poland (Kadrow 1991, 1994). Between 2300 and 1600 BC, but particularly between ca. 2000 and 1800 BC, this hilltop site was occupied by a number of households of the Mierzanowice culture, an eastern neighbor of the better-known Únětice culture. In contrast with Únětice, however, Mierzanowice cemeteries and settlements have yielded relatively few bronze artifacts; almost all metal tools are made from copper (Hensel and Milisauskas 1985: 85). Iwanowice-Babia Góra was demarcated by a ditch on the western and southern sides of the hilltop, although its role as a fortification is unclear. Despite the absence of house outlines on the eroded loess, it has been possible to reconstruct the settlement plan on the basis of pit distribution. A number of bell-shaped pits have been identified by Kadrow as signatures of individual households, and the distribution of such pits over time indicates a shift from a concentrated group of households in the earlier phases to a more dispersed pattern in later occupations. An adjacent cemetery contains over 150 graves, although few have remarkable grave goods.

Before the 1970s, very few Bronze Age settlements were known in southern Scandinavia, but in the last several decades a number have been excavated (Jensen 1988). Continuity from Late Neolithic settlements is indicated by a continuation of earlier house types into the Early Bronze Age, particularly the "two-aisled" longhouse. Three such structures have been excavated at Egehøj in eastern Jutland (Boas 1983). All of the Egehøj houses were 6 meters wide and were 21, 18, and 19 meters long. The walls were built of irregularly-spaced posts, while in each case four larger posts down the center line of the house supported the roof ridge. Subsequently, three-aisled longhouses came into use during the middle of the Bronze Age, as exemplified by the house at Treppendal in south Jutland, whose 9-meter-wide outline was preserved under a large burial mound (Boysen and Anderson 1983). More three-aisled buildings are known from Højgård, where a number of houses 20–22 meters long and 8–9 meters wide have been excavated. The three-aisled house appears to have been used in southern Scandinavia throughout the remainder of the second millennium BC, as indicated by the well-preserved houses excavated at Hemmed Church in eastern Jutland (Boas 1991). These settlements were the remains of small farmsteads, the individual production units of Bronze Age society. These farmsteads appear to have existed in small groupings, but there is not evidence of any greater agglomeration of settlement. Their inhabitants practiced plough cultivation, primarily of barley, and kept domestic livestock, primarily cattle.

In the British Isles, Bronze Age settlements are also apparently the remains of small farmsteads. Circular houses, with approximately 100 square meters of floor area, are grouped in hamlets of two to ten houses. A good example is the Early Bronze Age house at Gwithian in Cornwall, where the walls consisted of a double-circle of stakes, with two massive posts at the entrance (Parker Pearson 1993: 95). In nearby Dartmoor, circular stone foundations of Bronze Age buildings at Shaugh Moor were enclosed by a stone wall. It appears that the largest building in this complex was the dwelling, while the others were animal pens and storage huts (Smith et al. 1981). Other important examples of Bronze Age houses in lowland Britain, although somewhat late in the second millennium BC, have been found at Itford Hill and Black Patch in Sussex, where small clusters of functionally-differentiated huts form household compounds (Drewett 1979).

Far to the south in southern Germany and Switzerland, the lakeside dwellings of the Bronze Age cannot be overlooked. These continue a tradition of lakeside settlement begun during the Neolithic (the so-called "Swiss Lake Dwellings") but become progressively more elaborate. For example, the Early Bronze Age Forschner site in the Federsee basin of southern Germany was occupied over several centuries between 1767 and 1480 BC (as determined by dendrochronology) and consisted of several houses surrounded by a palisade and a rampart (Billamboz et al. 1989). A later site in the same region, the Wasserburg Buchau, is located on an island in a moor and had two occupations. The first had 38 rectangular post structures, 37 of which were single-room buildings 4 meters by 4 meters while one was a larger two-roomed building. The second occupation had nine complexes of large, multi-roomed houses and assorted outbuildings. Both settlements were surrounded by a palisade.

Bronze Age settlement data in temperate Europe is still very meager in comparison to the rich burial record of the same period. While some of this is due to the focus of archaeologists on cemeteries, barrows, and monuments, much of this can be attributed to the relatively simple nature of these settlements. For the most part, they are not very visible archaeologically, especially when contrasted with the settlements of some of the other chiefly

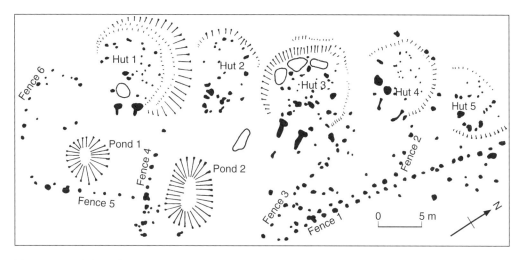

Figure 7.4 Plan of the Late Bronze Age settlement at Black Patch, Sussex, England, showing hut circles and associated boundary features (after Parker Pearson 1993, figure 98).

societies discussed in this chapter. Even where larger sites occur and can be considered the upper level of a settlement hierarchy, as in southwestern Slovakia, it is important not to make too much of this, as Shennan (1993: 151) notes, for even these are still relatively small.

THE RITUAL LANDSCAPE

A key element in the Early Bronze Age ritual landscape are mortuary monuments, which now are almost universally relatively small round mounds, referred to as "barrows" (Britain), "tumuli" (western Europe), or "kurhany" (eastern Europe). In Britain, much significance is attached to the transition from the communal burial ritual seen in the megalithic tombs to the practice of single burials under barrows. This is taken to reflect increased emphasis on the status of the individual (e.g., Barrett 1994: 49). Yet in central Europe, the practice of individual burials had been followed since the beginning of the Neolithic, with monuments such as the massive Kuyavian long barrows holding individual graves as early as 4000 BC (Midgley 1985). More significant, however, is the practice of individual burial of individuals accompanied by goods which took significant effort to acquire and produce under mounds whose *cumulative* effect was to produce a landscape of monuments to individual *ancestors*.

The ability to acknowledge individual ancestors would be especially important in a society in which status and prestige was determined by proximity to a specific genealogical line. The establishment of a barrow created a precise and discrete physical link with the past which could not be accomplished in a communal mortuary structure like a charnel house and not adequately in a cemetery of individual graves. The choice of a site carried significance. Surely it was made with reference to other elements of the land-scape which had symbolic significance, which would have included other monuments and perhaps natural features as well. This would have been an opportunity to demonstrate either social distance or proximity to lineages or totems. At the same time, the new barrow was distinct and fresh; Barrett (1994: 124) notes that to establish a grave could be "to lay claim to future obligations of veneration." Barrows simultaneously made reference to the ancestors but also marked themselves as requiring respect in their own right.

The most famous Early Bronze Age barrows are found in southern England. They are concentrated particularly in the Wessex region, which gives its name to the "Wessex culture" that has been traditionally defined on the basis of the grave goods from these barrows (Piggott 1938). Many Wessex barrows have been excavated, and many others remain intact, but one of the most famous was opened nearly 200 years ago. Located about a kilometer south of Stonehenge in Wiltshire, the Bush Barrow (formally known as "Wilsford G5") yielded the remains of a single individual (described as a "stout and tall man") lying on its back. Grave goods included a gold belt-fastener and breastplate, a copper dagger whose handle had been inlaid with thousands of tiny gold nails, a bronze dagger, and a bronze flanged axe (another bronze dagger was destroyed during excavation). Several carved bone bands and a stone macehead have been imaginatively reconstructed to form a scepter with an ornamented wooden handle, although there is some doubt as to whether these were part of the same arti-fact (Clarke, Cowie, and Foxon 1985: 280).

The Wessex barrows are those of an elite, whose international contacts were demonstrated through their access to gold (from Ireland), amber (from the Baltic), and the latest forms of continental weapons (especially from Brittany, where similar barrows are found). The technical proficiency of many of the artifacts in the Wessex barrows suggests that they may have been made by specialists under the patronage of the elite. Although the overall amount of gold is small (despite its domination of popular portrayals of the Wessex finds), the individuals who were able to amass such wealth were clearly part of a web of exchange which spanned the English Channel and the Irish Sea. Was this a commercial elite, whose wealth was due to success in the local agrarian economy? Or was it a coercive elite, perhaps immigrants from Brittany, who were able to demand tribute from commoners and con-vert it into prestige goods? At the moment, the most that can be concluded is that some individuals in Wessex society had far greater access to status, power, and wealth than did others.

At roughly the same time as the Early Bronze Age barrows were being con-structed in England, a number of others were being erected in northern cen-tral Europe over the elite graves of Únětice culture. The major Únětice barrows in eastern Germany and western Poland are remarkable architec-turally. At Łęki Małe in Poland, 14 tumuli have diameters between 24 and 42 meters (Jażdżewski 1981: 306). Skeletons of men in extended position lying on their backs are found in wooden-roofed burial chambers within a cairn of boulders. At Leubingen and Helmsdorf in southeastern Germany, the tall barrows (the one at Helmsdorf was 8.5 meters high when excavated in 1906) concealed mortuary structures with pitched roofs. In the Leubingen barrow, excavated in the mid-nineteenth century, the "main" interment, which was oriented along the axis of the structure, was an adult male, while lying perpendicularly across his pelvis was the skeleton of a young female, estimated to be about 10 years old. Assuming that the girl and the man were related, this suggests that status and privilege carried across generations and were not ascriptive properties of an elderly individual alone. Nearby was a variety of bronze and stone implements (including bronze chisels, daggers, axes, and halberds) and gold ornaments, including an armlet, beads, pins, and earrings.

Łęki Małe, Leubingen, and Helmsdorf stand out from among the barrows of this period in central Europe, although other less spectacular ones have also been investigated. Among other graves, found primarily in flat cemeteries, the differences are more subtle, although considerable effort was sometimes expended in such burials as well. For example, at Velké Pavlovice in Moravia, a Únětice cemetery of 20 graves containing 29 individuals was found (Stuchlík and Stuchlíkova 1996). A number of the graves had traces of wooden coffins with handles on their corners. Metal finds were fewer than in the classic barrows, but still included bronze ornaments.

To the east of the Únětice area at Branč in Slovakia, where about 300 graves were excavated, graves of both males and females in their twenties were especially well-furnished, and there were also a number of rich female children's graves (Shennan 1975). Thus, although the large tumuli may be the graves of exceptionally prominent individuals, additional gradations of status and wealth may have existed. Whether these are hereditary or vestiges of the transegalitarian milieu in which households could accumulate wealth regardless of their genealogical status is uncertain. After about 1800 BC, however, many more barrows – although not as remarkable as the ones mentioned above – are used for burial in central Europe, perhaps an outgrowth of the sort of internal differentiation observed by Shennan in the material from Branč.

Later in the Bronze Age, the ritual landscape of temperate Europe became dotted with barrows as membership in the elite broadened and more generations passed through the system. In the Middle Bronze Age of the Carpathian Basin, ca. 1800–1500 BC, tumulus burial became especially widespread, while additional barrows are scattered across southern Germany. In Alsace, the Haguenau Forest contains thousands of Bronze Age mounds, of which several hundred have been excavated.

Barrows in the Netherlands have revealed some very interesting trends from the Late Neolithic through the Middle Bronze Age (Lohof 1994). The largest mounds are known from the Early Bronze Age (ca. 2000–1800 BC) but in the Middle Bronze Age (ca. 1800–1500 BC) there is a marked increase in the number of mounds. In the Late Neolithic and Early Bronze Age, burial in barrows is almost exclusively the privilege of men, while in the Middle Bronze Age the number of women buried with grave goods under mounds increased, as did the reuse of mounds by adding additional fill to cover further interments. By the later part of the Middle Bronze Age (ca. 1500–1100 BC),

76 percent of the mounds have secondary interments (Lohof 1994: 103), and Lohof estimates that about 15 percent of the Middle Bronze Age population qualified for interment in or under a barrow.

Although Lohof explicitly does not interpret the Dutch barrow evidence within a model of social ranking, these data can be taken as an important complement to the emerging picture of Bronze Age chiefdom societies across Europe. As in Britain and Denmark, the focus on barrow interment has a long tradition. As with the German and Polish chiefly burials, the large Dutch barrows of the Early Bronze Age primarily hold the graves of men. As in the Carpathian Basin, the pattern of tumulus burial increases in the Middle Bronze Age. A key difference, however, as noted by Stephen Shennan (1994: 126), is that in Dutch evidence "a certain kind of male identity" is salient in the Early Bronze Age, whereas in the Carpathian Basin, female identity is prominent during the same period at sites like Branč. In the Netherlands, females apparently do not emerge with high social prominence until the Middle Bronze Age, perhaps consistent with the appearance of rich female barrow burials like Egtved in Denmark (see below) and Preshute 1a and Upton Lovell in England. I would also attach significance to the number of secondary burials in the Dutch barrows as evidence of increasing genealogically-based access to status and power, again suggesting the long-term institutionalization of differences between elites and commoners.

Between 1400 and 1100 BC, the practice of the burial of the elite under large mounds became especially common in southern Scandinavia, just as it had a short time before in central Europe. A distinctive feature of the Danish burials is the practice of burying the dead in coffins hollowed out from oak trunks. The oak coffins have resulted in remarkable preservation of organic material, such as the woolen clothing, textiles, hides, and even hair. The Egtved tomb is perhaps the most famous of these Bronze Age burials, for it presents a glimpse of a young woman about 20 years old, who died one summer (as indicated by a flower which had been placed in the coffin). She was wearing a woolen tunic and a short cord skirt, bound with a belt decorated by a large disk of engraved bronze. In the coffin with her was a birch-bark container in which there was the remains of a fermented beverage and a small bag with the burnt bones of a child about eight years old.

A somewhat more violent picture of Bronze Age life is presented by the finding of several mass graves datable to this period. At Gustorzyn in north-central Poland, 16 skeletons were found densely stacked like cordwood in a stone-lined burial pit datable to the Early Bronze Age (Grygiel, personal communication). Another large grave was found at Wassenaar in the coastal district of the Netherlands (Louwe Kooijmans 1993b), dating from the transition from the Early to the Middle Bronze Age, ca. 1600 BC. In this grave, 12 individuals, including males, females, adolescents, and infants were laid out in two opposed rows. Flint arrowheads and blow marks indicate a violent cause of death, which contradicts the traditional picture of peaceful agrarian society in the Dutch Bronze Age. Clearly conflict, sometimes violent, was a part of Bronze Age life.

The final centuries of the Bronze Age saw the continuation of the ceremonial tradition in a different form in eastern England. Several wetland sites dated to the final centuries of the second millennium BC indicate the role of bogs and fens as sacred locations. Such sites presage the role of bogs as the sites of ritual across northern Europe during the last millennium BC. One such site is Flag Fen near Peterborough in East Anglia, discovered in the 1980s (Pryor 1991). Several seasons of excavations revealed an immense waterlogged structure of about 50,000 posts upon which millions of planks and poles had been erected. It is estimated that over two million trees were felled to build the Flag Fen structure. The two major elements of the Flag Fen construction are a 10–12-meter wide swath of many posts running about a kilometer from the dryland fen margin into the center of the bog and an enormous timber platform supported on posts and covering about a hectare at the end of the alignments. The initial interpretation of this site was that the platform was a residential location in the middle of the bog, connected to shore by a causeway. Subsequent excavation and analysis revealed, however, that this was instead a ritual location where hundreds of bronze artifacts, many smashed and broken, had been thrown into the bog adjacent to the platform and post alignment. Flag Fen now appears to represent an elaborate local manifestation of a widespread practice of ceremonial activity at watery places in northern Europe.

STONEHENGE IN CONTEXT

Perhaps there is no archaeological site that is more famous than Stonehenge. Located on the Salisbury Plain in south-central England, this circular arrangement of massive stones has excited the imagination of antiquarians, archaeologists, and the general public for centuries. Although the construction of Stonehenge began in the Late Neolithic, it reached its final monumental form in the early part of the Bronze Age. Before proceeding further, it must be established for the non-archaeologist reader that Stonehenge has nothing to do with the Celtic priests commonly called "Druids." This romantic fantasy can be traced to the eighteenth-century antiquarian William Stukeley (Chippindale 1994: 83–7), but it persists today in popular culture. Nor has it anything to do with Egyptians, Greeks, or other peoples of the Mediterranean rim. Stonehenge is the product of an indigenous society in which ritual, power, and symbols converged to result in the long-term commitment of time and labor to the construction of this remarkable monument.

That Stonehenge was the result of an indigenous process is best demonstrated by the fact that it is relatively late in a series of prehistoric earth, timber, and stone enclosures built across southern England in the tradition of the megalithic tombs and causewayed camps discussed in chapter 6. Constructed somewhat earlier than the circle of upright stones at Stonehenge, the enormous ditched enclosure and complex of stone arrangements at Avebury, 30 kilometers to the north, is the most outstanding example of the early part of the "enclosure movement" of the third millennium BC. The ditch at Avebury encloses an area 365 meters in diameter, and in prehistoric times the vertical distance between the crest of the bank to the bottom of the ditch was nearly 20 meters. Since the bank is *outside* the ditch, the feature is clearly not a fortification. Along the inner margin of the ditch is a setting of undressed stones, a type of sandstone from the Marlborough Downs called "sarsen." From one of the entrances to the Avebury enclosure, an avenue defined by pairs of upright stones runs for about a kilometer to a smaller stone circle called "the Sanctuary." Nearby is mysterious Silbury Hill, the largest artificial mound of prehistoric Europe at 40 meters high and 160 meters in diameter, which also appears to have been built in the middle of the third millennium BC.

Stonehenge was built in a number of stages, which are best seen in figure 7.5. Stonehenge I was fairly unremarkable in the landscape of southern England, consisting of a round ditch with a single entryway, which had two stones erected just outside it, one of which is the Heel Stone. Inside the bank, 56 holes were dug and immediately filled in. These mysterious "Aubrey holes" have puzzled archaeologists for generations; no posts or stones appear to have been set in them, although perhaps they were intended for that purpose. The original Stonehenge persisted for a number of centuries between 3100 and 2300 BC. A further modification of Stonehenge, called Stonehenge II, began just before 2000 BC with a slight realignment of the entrance and setting of two more stones between the ditch and the Heel Stone. In the center of the enclosure, a double semi-circle of bluestones was erected only to be removed shortly thereafter and their holes filled in. Sometime in this general period, although not dated precisely, four small stones called Station Stones were set up inside the perimeter of the ditch to form a rectangular pattern.

The Stonehenge that we know today is actually the third remodelling of the site, which followed on the heels of the second. First, the massive upright sarsen stones and their lintels were erected in one of the great engineering feats of antiquity. The inner horseshoe consists of five pair of uprights and their lintels set up as discrete "trilithons," while the outer circle is a continuous ring of thirty uprights and thirty lintels. The uprights were carefully shaped so that their pointed bases slid easily into holes in the chalk. Various hypotheses exist for the method of erection of the lintels, but the most likely method was the construction of a system of scaffolding upon which the massive stones were levered upward the thickness of a log at a time, positioned over the uprights (so that the mortises in their undersides mated with the tenons on the uprights), and lowered into place. Over the next several centuries, minor additions were made to the site in the form of a circle of 20 bluestones within the inner horseshoe, a series of holes meant to hold stones (which were never set) outside the outer circle, and the resetting of the interior bluestones in two other circles within the outer sarsen circle.

The landscape surrounding Stonehenge is in many respects as interesting as the circular monument itself. In addition to numerous round burial mounds which were contemporary with the site, several major earthworks form the other elements of the Stonehenge complex. The most significant of these is "The Avenue," which consists of long parallel ditches, 30 meters apart, from which the earth had been thrown inwards to create a raised

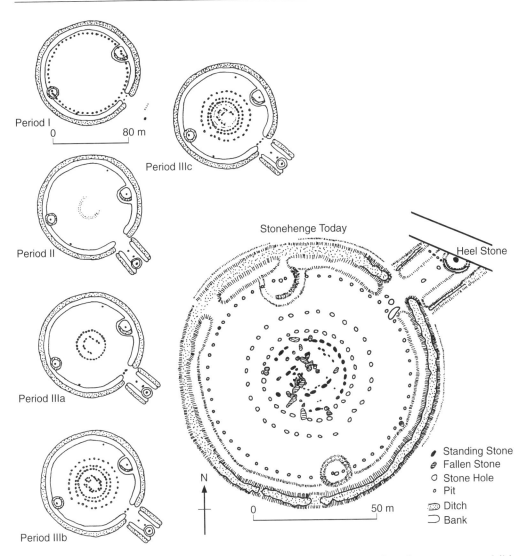

Figure 7.5 The stages in the development of Stonehenge. Note that the monument visible today is only the central part of a much larger and more complex structure.

pathway. The Avenue was begun during Stonehenge II, running about 500 meters to the northeast downhill from the entrance to the enclosure. Several centuries later, after 1500 BC, the Avenue was extended eastward for about 2 kilometers, indicating the continued significance of the Stonehenge complex several centuries after the monument itself had reached completion.

Judging from the construction sequence on the site itself and additional modifications to the landscape, Stonehenge was the focus of activity between about 3000 and 1000 BC, especially after about 2000 BC. What sort of activity was it? Clearly it was the product of a tremendous investment of labor. Clearly it was the focus of a modified landscape of non-utilitarian earthworks and mortuary monuments. Clearly it persisted over centuries, perhaps even millennia, as an important facility for the prehistoric inhabitants of this region, not simply a curiosity built in final form by forgotten ancestors.

One of the more arresting hypotheses to be advanced in the twentieth century for the function of Stonehenge was that it served as an astronomical observatory which permitted its users to predict solstices and lunar eclipses. These ideas were articulated by Gerald Hawkins and Fred Hoyle, both astronomers, and Alexander Thom, a Scottish mechanical engineer (Hawkins 1965; Hoyle 1977; Thom 1971). Their arguments are complex, divergent, and impossible to summarize in a paragraph, but they all stress the correlation between the geometry of chords drawn between various uprights and the positions of the sun and the moon. In doing this, however, they fell into the trap which catches many non-archaeologists who venture into the analysis of archaeological remains, in that while they make a strong case that Stonehenge *could* have been used for the purposes they describe, they are unable to prove that it ever actually functioned in this way. Moreover, by characterizing it as a "prehistoric computer," they have assumed that the goals and methods of modem science were also those of the inhabitants of the Salisbury Plain 4000 years ago.

Although it may not have had astronomical significance, Stonehenge can be argued compellingly to have had *cosmological* significance for Bronze Age people. Several of the stones clearly do line up on celestial events and the location was certainly carefully chosen. Rather than focus on the astronomical significance of this feature, it can better be seen as an aspect of the broader importance of the site as a ceremonial center. The rebuilding of the monument can also be considered to be a way in which the elite reiterated their authority and their association with the cosmological significance of the site. They must have been very powerful indeed to mobilize the labor "to demolish the great unfinished project of the old order, and institute an even more ambitious design" (Burgess 1980: 333).

CRAFT SPECIALIZATION IN BRONZE AGE EUROPE

Since prehistoric Europe was the main field of interest of V. Gordon Childe, it has been the area where craft specialization during the Bronze Age has long been seen as an element in the emergence of social differentiation. The discussion centers on bronze metallurgy, with other possible products of specialists, such as pottery, being largely ignored. The fundamental assumption has been that the alloying of tin and copper and the technical proficiency required to cast bronze was so complicated that such knowledge and skill could not have been possessed by everyone. Although this remains a large assumption, it is supported by hoard finds of identical weapons and ornaments made by the same production center, even by the same hand. Few actual workshops have been found, however, due to the relative lack of excavated settlement sites, so the evidence for craft specialization is indirect and tenuous.

In Childe's view, the development of bronze metallurgy represented a threshold in the evolution of European society, in which a cohort of smiths under the patronage of chiefs could turn away from subsistence production and be supported through the flow of tribute from commoners (Childe 1930, 1957). Childe was clearly thinking about full-time specialists, and it appears that in some formulations he saw them as independent entrepreneurs who wandered from community to community (Childe 1930: 44). Such a model verges on fantasy. There is no evidence for the existence of such behavior, and the limited geographical extent of bronze artifact styles indicates that metalworkers did not move around very much, if at all (Rønne 1986).

Michael Rowlands (1976) proposed a different picture of Bronze Age metal working from that imagined by Childe. In Rowlands' view, a heterogeneous mix of full-time and part-time specialists, some attached and some independent, produced metal artifacts in southern Britain during the Middle Bronze Age. He proposed a two-tiered hierarchy of smiths: a lower one of part-time, small-scale workers who traded locally and an upper one of highly-skilled, full-time specialists who produced for regional and long-distance exchange. According to Northover (1982), such a structure continued into the Late Bronze Age in Britain as well, although it appears to wane. Ehrenreich (1995: 36) sums up the situation as follows: in the Early and Middle Bronze Age in southern Britain, Rowlands' two-tiered hierarchy of specialists prevailed, while in the Late Bronze Age new technologies (sheet bronze and leaded bronze) that simplified the metalworking process caused the upper echelon of smiths to dissipate.

A third model has been proposed by Kristian Kristiansen (1987), based on data from Early Bronze Age Denmark. His position is that bronze working was superimposed on a tradition of craft specialization with roots in the fine flintwork of the Late Neolithic. The expense of bronze (southern Scandinavia has no natural copper or tin deposits, so all raw materials were imported) resulted in the need to concentrate the working of this material in the hands of only those who were skilled. Indeed, Kristiansen argues that it was bronze itself which provided a medium for the concentration of wealth that created pronounced social differentiation. Kristiansen does not explicitly say whether he viewed the Danish smiths as full-time attached specialists under the patronage of elites or as independent metallurgists.

Janet Levy (1991) argues that full-time specialists in Bronze Age Denmark would not have had enough work to support them. In her view, the elite was neither large nor powerful enough to require full-time specialists. She believes that a model similar to that proposed by Rowlands for Britain works best for Denmark as well, although without rigid distinction between the two levels. Only a handful of smiths had the skills to make the most complex and decorated metal objects, and these individuals may have been attached to elite households, perhaps "on call." Other smiths made everyday items for their local communities, but were also engaged in agricultural pursuits much of the time.

The range of skills and abilities possessed by any human population makes the relatively conservative position taken by Levy to appear to be the most realistic at this point. Some Bronze Age smiths may have served as attached specialists, but probably most remained as part-time local metalworkers.

It does seem logical, however, that the expense of producing bronze almost everywhere in Europe caused metalworking to be restricted somehow to individuals who were connected to interregional exchange networks in some sustained way. For someone to be an accomplished and recognized metalworker, he could not have simply had copper or tin come into his possession sporadically or intermittently. Presumably sustained access to raw material would require the patronage of an elite sponsor, although with time there may have been enough bronze in circulation for a smith to use melted-down artifacts of an earlier vintage, thus avoiding the need for long-distance procurement.

THE BRONZE AGE CHIEFDOMS OF THY

Relatively few attempts have been made to reconstruct Bronze Age polities in temperate Europe, in contrast with the other parts of the world discussed in this chapter. Recently, however, Timothy Earle (1997) has characterized Bronze Age society on the island of Thy, on the northwest coast of Denmark, on the basis of a long-term program of field research. Although settlement evidence is thin, one site at Bjerre has revealed a large three-aisled longhouse about 21 meters long, with other house locations nearby. Numerous Bronze Age barrows dot the island, with one especially large one at Bavnehøj which is over 10 meters high. Many of these barrows have yielded rich grave goods, particularly the finely-crafted swords found in male graves.

The relatively impoverished soils of Thy would have been a poor foundation for agricultural intensification. Instead, cattle appear to have formed the basis of the Bronze Age political economy, which would be a logical consequence of the argument made for transegalitarian Late Neolithic Europe made in the previous chapter. Wealth-in-cattle was transformed into wealth-in-prestige-goods, although this provided a relatively weak and decentralized structure to the economy. Ownership of grazing lands also would have been important, but the ability to convert animal wealth into metal was critical, since it provided both military and ideological power. Swords and daggers were the symbols of male chiefly status.

Although no mass graves like those at Wassenaar and Gustorzyn have been identified on Thy, the prevalence of weapons suggests that armed conflict was an unavoidable aspect of Bronze Age life. Earle believes that the diffuse distribution of resources on the landscape suggests that aggression took the form of raiding for cattle rather than competition for control of land. The construction of barrows created a vast ritual landscape which was owned and controlled by the chiefs, whose legitimacy rested in the visible traces of their dead ancestors. Artisans controlled as attached specialists made swords for the male elite and jewelry for the female elite.

The chiefly polities of Thy experienced the oscillation that is characteristic of such societies as they rose and collapsed. The elite, by its use of sword and weapon styles common to much of northern Europe, demonstrated their international connections just as those of Wessex did. To support this, livestock production was intensified, but as the grasslands were degraded, this economy would have faltered. Moreover, economic conditions beyond the horizon of the Thy chiefdoms could have cut off the flow of prestige goods on which the lords of Thy depended to demonstrate their status and power. As Earle notes (1997: 200), "trade is always a risky source of economic power, and leaders depending on it find their positions inherently unstable." In the long run, the chiefdoms of Thy were short-lived entities, although on a regional scale this oscillating system persisted over many centuries.

The Thy example is just one localized example of the development of a Bronze Age society in temperate Europe, and contemporaneous societies elsewhere in Europe exhibit considerable variation in the degree to which there appear to have been differences in status, power, and wealth. In some cases, such as Wessex, Únětice, and Denmark, the differences were pronounced from about 2000 BC onward. These societies can probably be characterized as chiefdoms without much difficulty. At the same time, somewhat less complex transegalitarian societies continued to develop, such as Mierzanowice in southern Poland and Maros in Hungary. These do not conform to expectations of chiefly society, although in the latter there is evidence for hereditary transmission of status and power (O'Shea 1996).

The question of community autonomy during the early part of the Bronze Age has rarely been addressed, yet it is crucial to the understanding of the development of complex polities. In the absence of good data on many settlements in particular regions, this issue will prove difficult. At the very least, it would be important to establish whether there was a hierarchy of settlement sizes, which archaeologists in other parts of the world often consider important evidence for social ranking. At the moment, such differences in settlement size do not appear until much later in the Bronze Age, ca. 1000 BC (Wells 1984).

The absence of settlement hierarchy does not mean that other evidence for differences in status, power, and wealth should be discounted – indeed, the mortuary data from Wessex, Únětice, and Denmark are compelling – but rather that perhaps these were societies which emphasized individual rank within local communities over political and economic control within a region.

EARLY COMPLEX SOCIETIES IN MESOAMERICA

In contrast with the European case, the emergence of a hierarchy of site sizes is one of the key pieces of evidence for the emergence of social complexity in Mesoamerica during the Middle and Late Formative period (ca. 800–100 BC) Although there was considerable variation from one region to the next, as there was in Europe, a consistent theme is the development of a few very large sites and the appearance of settlement hierarchies. Burials, particularly in western Mesoamerica, are found in and about domestic architecture, so unlike the disjointed situation in Bronze Age Europe of rich tombs, isolated ceremonial sites, and rather ordinary settlements, the study of emergent social complexity in Mesoamerica involves the convergence of elite architecture, rich burials, and ceremonial features.

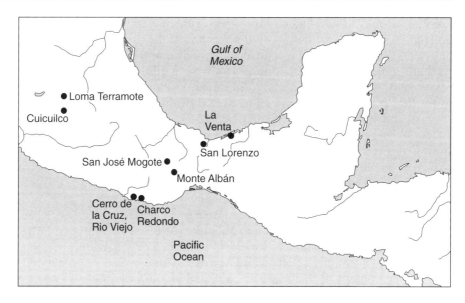

Figure 7.6 Map of Mesoamerica showing key sites mentioned in this chapter.

For example, in the Valley of Mexico, at least three, and perhaps even four levels of site size can be recognized during the period between 650 and 300 BC (Fiedel 1987: 272). The largest site in the region was Cuicuilco, whose population is estimated to have been 5–10,000. Five other sites in the Valley of Mexico formed the second tier of settlement sizes, estimated to have been between 1000 and 3500 inhabitants. One of these sites is Loma Terramote, which consisted of between 400 and 500 domestic compounds consisting of houses, patios, and storage pits (Santley 1993). Each compound had between three and six houses, each presumably the residence of a single family. Beneath the floors of the houses and patios were burials. The house compounds, in turn, were clustered into groups. One compound in each of the groups was typically larger and contained a more substantial dwelling.

Santley (1993: 81) proposes that the clusters of compounds at Loma Terramote were originally occupied by small, undifferentiated corporate groups or extended families, but over time, differences in status emerged as population levels grew. Relations among households grew increasingly asymmetrical, with some serving as patrons, while others were pushed into clientage. The patrons were those with greater access to productive land, while the clients were those who experienced more frequent economic shortfalls. The inhabitants of Compound A-1 in the area excavated by Santley's team, for example, would have been patrons of the surrounding compounds. Not only was their compound much larger and better-constructed than its neighbors, but access to it was restricted, while the neighboring compounds had interconnecting passageways.

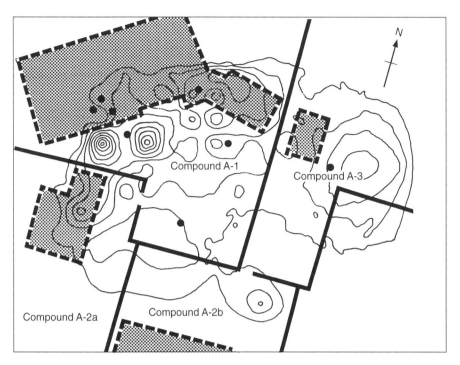

Figure 7.7 Compounds and houses in Zone A, Levels 3 and 4, at Loma Terramote in highland Mexico (after Santley 1993, figure 6).

EARLY SOCIAL COMPLEXITY IN OAXACA

Some of the highest-resolution regional data on the emergence of differences in status, power, and wealth comes from the Mexican states of Oaxaca and Puebla (Flannery and Marcus 1983a). The case of San José Mogote in the Valley of Oaxaca has already been discussed in the previous chapter. By about 850 BC, San José Mogote had emerged as a "first-order settlement" of about 60–70 hectares. Several other sites occupied about 3 hectares, while still more were in the 1–2 hectare range. Yet as Flannery and Marcus (1983b: 53) point out, there is reason to believe that this was not yet an administrative hierarchy. The household remains indicate a continuum from lower to higher status without true divisions, which I would formulate as a continuation of the transegalitarian pattern discussed in the previous chapter. During the next 300 years, San José Mogote continued to grow and took on the function of a ceremonial center for a group of about 20 villages. A complex of public buildings was built and an elite residential complex can be identified on the basis of the grave goods contained in their burials. Flannery and Marcus consider this to be evidence of a chiefdom (1983b: 60). Similar developments are observed in other parts of Oaxaca (Spencer and Redmond 1983), while adjacent regions lagged behind (Spores 1983). The overall impression is one of a number of competing small polities.

Shortly after 500 BC, however, the situation in the Valley of Oaxaca changed significantly. San José Mogote was eclipsed by a newly established center on a hill about 10 kilometers to the south – Monte Albán. The explosive growth of Monte Albán is one of the remarkable stories of prehistory, which culminated in the establishment of the Zapotec state by about 200 BC. For now, however, our focus is on the period between 500 and 300 BC (Monte Albán I), during which it appears to have been the seat of a powerful paramount chief whose domain included much of the valley. The evidence for hereditary social hierarchy is unambiguous.

There is almost no evidence of settlement on the Monte Albán promontory prior to 500 BC. Shortly after that date, however, three distinct residential areas were established over an area of about 65 hectares. The sudden appearance of such a large settlement at a previously uninhabited location has been the topic of some debate among archaeologists. One of the most persuasive explanations has been provided by Richard Blanton (1978), who has proposed that Monte Albán was established as a special-function administrative center by a confederation of elites in the Valley of Oaxaca, rather than serving as the seat of a powerful local chief. Such a neutral location would have been chosen to preclude undue power by any of the existing local polities, analogous to the selection of the site for the District of Columbia in the United States in 1790. Blanton sees this confederation as having had a military purpose, suggested by the iconography of about 140 carved figures (traditionally known as "*danzantes*" because they seemed to be dancing) which depict captive enemies undergoing torture or sacrifice. An alternative explanation for the rise of Monte Albán has been put forward by Roger Santley (1980) who argues that the site was established as a refuge from conflict over choice agricultural lands on the valley bottoms. In time, the richness of its own agricultural base made it a powerful polity which was able to dominate the political and economic order of the Valley of Oaxaca.

Over the next several centuries, Monte Albán grew rapidly, and by 200 BC it is estimated that some 17,000 people lived at or immediately around the site. They lived in small household units similar to those observed at earlier sites in the Valley of Oaxaca like San José Mogote. Several important public buildings were built, including the building on which the *danzantes* are depicted. Carved stelae adjacent to the *danzantes* gallery have calendric inscriptions as well as noncalendric glyphs, the oldest writing system in Mesoamerica (Marcus 1983a).

The story of Monte Albán will be taken up again in the following chapter, but many questions about its early stages remain unresolved. If it was the seat of a confederation of smaller polities rather than a single polity which came to dominate its neighbors, what then was the nature of leadership and the source of power of its elite inhabitants? When did it cease to be a neutral site and a locus of chiefly control? Fundamentally, when did the founding elites drawn from the outlying polities become the Lords of Monte Albán?

Simpler polities emerged elsewhere in Oaxaca between 400 and 100 BC. In the Rio Verde valley on the Pacific coast of Oaxaca, Arthur Joyce (1994) has identified a hierarchy of site sizes. Most sites were relatively small, on the order of 2–6 hectares. Some, however, were considerably larger. Charco Redondo was possibly as large as 100 hectares, while Río Viejo was about 25 hectares. Excavations at the small site of Cerro de la Cruz indicated a relatively low degree of social differentiation among various residences, although burials do appear to reflect genealogically-based inequalities. The overall pattern is one of simpler polities than those found in the interior Valley of Oaxaca, but nonetheless having a chiefdom form of social organization with hereditary elites.

THE OLMEC

The most remarkable, and perhaps even precocious indications of differences in access to status, power, and wealth in Formative Mesoamerica come from the states of Veracruz and Tabasco along the Gulf of Mexico. Almost a millennium earlier than the emergence of Monte Albán, this region saw the development of several spectacular centers with monumental architecture, rich burials, and other trappings of a high level of difference in status, power, and wealth. The Olmec, as these people are known, present archaeologists with an enigma: how did this arise, and why did it happen so early?

Much archaeological research and debate has gone into attempting to answer the question, "What is Olmec?" Several answers are forthcoming. Most generally, the term "Olmec" refers to the inhabitants of the southern Gulf Coast of Mexico between ca. 1500 and 500 BC. It also refers to the distinctive art style and iconography of these people. The Olmec display a number of characteristics of non-egalitarian societies (Diehl 1989), including clear social and economic distinctions, large construction projects of public buildings that required some form of authority for their planning and construction, long-distance trade in both utilitarian and luxury goods, and a complex religion in which certain individuals acted as mediators between the living and supernatural worlds. Of all the societies discussed in this chapter, the Olmec were perhaps the furthest down the road towards a higher-order complex society, yet their society evaporated after about 500 BC as other parts of Mesoamerica superseded them in importance.

The local precursors of the Olmec were small groups of ceramic-using sedentary peoples who had established themselves along the rivers that flow into the Gulf of Mexico prior to 1500 BC (Rust and Sharer 1988). Their predilection for monumental sculpture and large architecture developed relatively suddenly, however (Coe 1989). The center of San Lorenzo, a large nucleated village of about one square kilometer with a population estimated at about 1000, flourished between ca. 1200 and 900 BC. Two characteristics of San Lorenzo stand out. The first is the evidence for large-scale modification of the landscape. San Lorenzo is located on a natural plateau, which was reshaped by adding several spurs. On the plateau itself, earthen mounds for houses and temples were constructed, while the pits from which the mound fill was taken were turned into reservoirs or "lagunas" with drain systems to take away excess water. The second key characteristic of San Lorenzo is the monumental sculpture, particularly the famous Olmec heads but also many other carvings of people, jaguars, and other animals. Nine colossal heads, about 1.5 to 2.5 meters in height, are known from San Lorenzo, while seven more are known from other sites (Stuart 1993). Wherever they are found, they mark the initial Olmec horizon (Lowe 1989). In all, over 50 large stone sculptures were set up on the surface of the San Lorenzo plateau. The basalt for these sculptures was quarried over 70 kilometers away, but the carving was apparently done on site.

Around 900 BC, however, a traumatic change occurred at San Lorenzo. The monuments were deliberately defaced and then they were relocated in a line and buried. Settlement appears to come to an abrupt halt. Various hypotheses have been advanced to explain the demise of San Lorenzo. Michael Coe (1981) ascribes it to the work of outside invaders, but David Grove (1981) believes that the monuments were ritually defaced at the time of the death of the ruler they honored. Central to this hypothesis is the assumption that the colossal heads were those of leaders. Whatever the cause of the decline of San Lorenzo, over the course of the next century, primacy within the Olmec world shifted to the center at La Venta, about 100 kilometers to the northeast.

La Venta was even more sumptuous than San Lorenzo and had as its focal point an earthen pyramid over 30 meters high. Across the surface of the site, a number of low platforms are laid out symmetrically along a central axis. The inhabitants of La Venta, however, had a tendency to bury their most spectacular artistic achievements. Several of the platforms were built over mosaic pavements made from hundreds of blocks of serpentine. Another mosaic, which depicts a jaguar mask, was found at the bottom of a large pit about 7 meters deep in which serpentine blocks had been laid on a bed of tar, then covered immediately with layers of colored clay. Only a small section of La Venta has been investigated so far, but the finds indicate a community which diverted considerable labor to public construction and iconographic expression. La Venta flourished for several centuries before declining about 400 BC.

So who or what were the Olmec? Various scholars have offered their opinions, ranging from chiefdom to empire (as critically evaluated in Diehl 1989). There appears to be consensus that at a minimum, the Olmec were non-egalitarian and had a political organization that could be characterized as a chiefdom. Some individuals clearly enjoyed a higher status, and the large-scale earth-moving and sculpting are presumed to have required some central direction. Beyond that, however, the nature of Olmec social organization is poorly understood. Recent investigations in the La Venta region have shown that there was a large population in the countryside surrounding the site (Rust and Sharer 1988) which had occupied the area since the beginning of the second millennium BC. How this populace related to the residents of the major centers is unclear.

Since the first systematic research at Olmec sites in the 1940s by Matthew Stirling (1896–1975), the prevailing view among Mesoamerican archaeologists was that the Olmec were far more advanced in the direction of civilization than their Formative contemporaries. The appearance of Olmec-style objects in other parts of Mexico and adjoining countries was the result of waves of influence radiating out from the heartland along the Gulf Coast, spurred by the desire of the less-advanced peoples for the trappings of high civilization. The Olmec were considered to be the "mother culture" for all later developments, including the emergence of civilizations in the Maya lowlands and in highland Mexico.

In recent decades, this view has begun to change, since there has been more research outside the Olmec heartland since 1970 than there has been within it. Other Formative societies, particularly in the Valley of Oaxaca and the Chiapas coast, have come to be seen as also having made an important contribution to cultural development in Greater Mesoamerica. Each region has its own distinctive art style, and to attribute all developments to "Olmec influence" was clearly not warranted. At the same time, however, there is always the risk that more social complexity than the evidence supports may be attributed to garden-variety transegalitarian communities in an effort to place these other societies on a par with the spectacular Olmec evidence. It has become abundantly clear that trading networks in exotic and mundane items extended over a wide part of Mesoamerica, and the contact that this trade produced operated along many different axes and in both directions.

Arthur Demarest (1989) has proposed that rather than take an Olmec-centered view of Mesoamerica between 1500 and 500 BC, it is instead more appropriate to view this region as a lattice of continuously-interacting societies which were developing roughly in parallel. Communication among their elites and trade ensured that each of these societies (which Demarest characterizes as "evolving chiefdoms") would be "in the loop," so to speak, as they progressed towards social complexity. Demarest's model is reminiscent of the "peer polity" construction advocated by Renfrew and Cherry (1986), although I would again caution that calling these bodies "polities" may ascribe to them a greater formality of political organization than is appropriate.

SOUTH AMERICA: WEST COAST AND AMAZONIA

EARLY COMPLEX SOCIETIES IN WESTERN SOUTH AMERICA

The societies which flourished along the western edge of South America during the final two millennia BC confound attempts to make global generalizations about the emergence of differences in status, power, and wealth. Part of this is due to the unique geography of this region, with rich maritime resources adjacent to a fertile but arid coastal plain, through which rivers flow from mountain valleys. Major seismic and climatic events have caused radical environmental perturbations throughout the human occupation of the area, while the maritime winter moisture creates fog-dependent meadows called *lomas*. Part is the result of the early emergence of powerful ideological concepts embraced by communities, which led to immense monumental architecture even before the use of pottery. Another factor is the unique importance of "industrial" crops such as cotton, used for fishing nets and

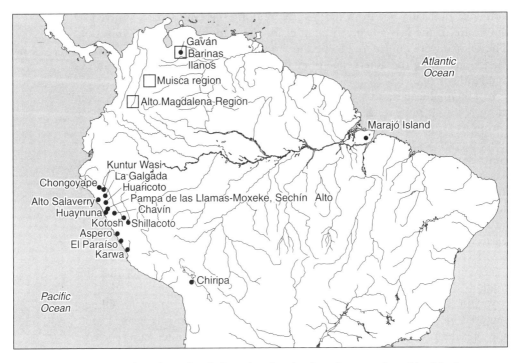

Figure 7.8 Map of northern South America showing key sites mentioned in this chapter.

textiles, and gourds, used for fishing floats, in the economy, along with a variety of animals such as llamas, alpacas, and guinea pigs.

An important consideration, however, is an intellectual tradition in the archaeology of the Andean region which promotes societies to statehood very rapidly, perhaps prematurely, following the initial appearance of sedentary communities. Quilter (1991: 431) has commented on "liberal" and "conservative" views of cultural development in this region, with the "liberal" interpretation of the evidence being to identify state-level societies at a very early date, with the "conservative" interpretation of the same data seeing a more gradual development of social differentiation. These differing interpretations come through very clearly in the archaeological literature of this area, often rendering it confusing and contradictory.

The appearance of monumental architecture has a profound impact on this discussion, since archaeologists begining with V. Gordon Childe have considered it a hallmark of a civilization. Moreover, the "chiefdom" category of complex societies was so believed to have been characterized by redistribution (now considered not to be a defining characteristic) that archaeologists of the 1970s largely passed over this concept in Andean South America except in a few cases. Transegalitarian social formations also were generally not considered. It appeared that one moment the coastal peoples were simple fisher-gatherers and the next they established complex polities with sophisticated ideology and administrative hierarchies.

In keeping with the spirit of this volume, the more gradual "conservative" approach to Andean cultural development will be endorsed here, although in the long run additional data may emerge to support the "liberal" position that very complex societies had appeared in coastal Peru by the beginning of the second millennium BC. When viewed in a global context, however, the gradualist view seems to be more persuasive. By many of the same criteria applied in Andean South America, Late Neolithic Wessex and Mississippian Cahokia could also be considered "states," whereas in those cases the "chiefdom" concept has more applicability. It is very difficult, however, to identify early chiefdoms along the Peruvian coast, nor are these units discussed widely by the archaeologists of this region. Indeed, the development of complex societies in this region may have been one of prolonged transegalitarian conditions in which investment in ritual and communal construction were alternatives to political centralization and the concentration of status, power, and wealth.

THE LATE PRECERAMIC AND THE MARITIME HYPOTHESIS

The origins of complex societies on the Peruvian coast can be traced to the Late Preceramic period (3000–2000 BC), which is sometimes called the "Cotton Preceramic" due to the fact that cotton is so common at sites of this period. During this period, the villages along the coast increased in size, and the first monumental construction occurs, in the form of pyramidal platforms. The explosive appearance of monumental construction and the populations that were needed to construct it is an issue which has attracted the attention of archaeologists for several decades. One key question is how this society was economically supported.

In the early 1970s, Michael Moseley proposed that the economic foundation of early Peruvian complex societies was maritime fishing (Moseley 1975). In Moseley's view, the rich marine resources due to the Humboldt Current enabled large permanent populations to live along the coast in the absence of agriculture. This view contradicted the conventional wisdom of the time that agriculture, especially irrigation agriculture, was a prerequisite for the development of social complexity. Moseley's "Maritime Hypothesis" considered Late Preceramic agriculture to have provided mostly "industrial" products which supported the fishing economy: cotton for nets and gourds for net floats. In fact, the anchovy schools alone could have sustained several million people with a rather boring and monotonous diet.

Moseley's model was formulated on somewhat limited data, due to the small scale of excavation at Late Preceramic sites prior to the mid-1970s. This hypothesis was controversial and was disputed on several grounds. One argument was advanced that the maritime resources of the Peruvian coasts would have been unstable due to the periodic perturbation known as "El Niño," in which warm incursions raise the water temperature and kill the phytoplankton on which the rich marine life depends (Raymond 1981). Yet the effects of El Niño are localized and would not cause widespread subsistence collapse. In some areas it may even drive the anchovies closer to

Figure 7.9 *Shicra*, stone-filled net bags, at El Paraíso, Chillon Valley, Peru (photo courtesy of Dr Jeffrey Quilter, Dumbarton Oaks, Washington, D.C.).

shore and make them easier to catch. Others have suggested that the terrestrial food crops, especially maize, were the real foundation of the Late Preceramic economy (Wilson 1981). There is virtually no evidence for maize at the large settlements with monumental architecture, and although other crop plants have been found, they appear to have contributed significantly less to the diet than the marine resources.

Excavations in the 1980s by Jeffrey Quilter at the monumental center of El Paraíso provided high-resolution data on Late Preceramic subsistence (Quilter et al. 1991; Quilter 1991). The El Paraíso rubbish middens yielded the remains of 30 animal taxa and 19 species of plants. Over 90 percent of the animals are bony fishes and molluscs like anchovies and mussels. Few land mammals were found. The plant remains include "industrial" taxa like gourds and cotton as well as dietary species like peppers, squash, beans, tree fruits, achira (*Canna edulis*), and jicama (*Pachyrrizus tuberosus*). The last two are root crops with high carbohydrate content. On the basis of evidence from El Paraíso and other sites, it appears that the real economic foundation of the Late Preceramic economy was the combination of marine animal protein and terrestrial plant carbohydrates. Despite the fact that maize appears to have been known in the Andes previously (Burger and van der Merwe 1990), it is conspicuously scarce at the Late Preceramic sites of the Peruvian coast (Quilter 1991: 400).

El Paraíso is an enormous site, covering over 50 hectares in the Chillón valley north of Lima, with eight or nine stone buildings. The smaller ones are three- or four-room structures, while the larger are enormous complexes of rooms 300 meters by 100 meters. The enormous size of El Paraíso has led some to conclude that it was the center of a significant polity. Moseley (1975: 97) suggested that El Paraíso was an administrative center with a small resident population because of an apparent lack of refuse deposits, while Wilson (1981) considered it to be a major political and ceremonial center. Quilter's excavations indicated that refuse had been burned and then buried, which led him to conclude that there was a larger resident population than previously believed (Quilter 1989; Quilter et al. 1991). Moreover, the absence of contemporaneous sites in the surrounding region and the small catchment from which resources were procured leads Quilter (1989: 474) to conclude that while El Paraíso has impressive architecture, it was a fairly simply organized community. There are no elite burials and no intensified staple production, and without satellite communities there was no one to administer who did not live at El Paraíso itself.

A much different picture is presented by Thomas and Shelia Pozorski and Robert Feldman based on research at Preceramic coastal sites including Alto Salaverry (S. Pozorski and T. Pozorski 1979), Huaynuná (S. Pozorski 1987; S. Pozorski and T. Pozorski 1987), and Aspero (Feldman 1987). These sites are also characterized by monumental architecture. At Aspero in the Supe valley, which is slightly earlier than El Paraíso, several large mounds consist of interconnected stone-walled rooms which were filled in to form the foundation for the next phase of construction. Much of the in-filling is in the form of *shicra*, or netted bags of rocks. Feldman (1987: 11) identified different levels of ceremonial space, with dedicatory caches in the larger rooms. In Feldman's view, this architecture was the product of a "corporate labor" force consisting of individuals from different households under the direction of an authoritative body. At Huaynuná in the Casma valley, a small nonresidential tiered platform on a hillside is viewed as a location from which prominent individuals could conduct public gatherings (S. Pozorski 1987: 18; S. Pozorski and T. Pozorski 1992), while at Alto Salaverry in the Moche valley, the presence of a sunken circular plaza in front of a mound marks an early appearance of this architectural form. Similar non-domestic structures are found at many other sites along the Peruvian coast.

There is no denying that prior to 2000 BC considerable effort was invested by the inhabitants of the Peruvian coast in the construction of monumental non-domestic architecture. The key question, then, is whether this construction can be interpreted as evidence for social differentiation. Feldman (1987) sees the Aspero mounds as evidence of the existence of a chiefdom, specifically one of Renfrew's "group-oriented" chiefdoms in which there is more attention given to public displays and less to personal prestige, and Shelia Pozorski (1987: 18) interprets the Huaynuná architecture in a similar vein. Quilter, on the other hand (1989: 475), cautions that "buildings alone cannot be used as evidence of a chiefdom or a state." Such different perspectives extend even to the interpretation of specific classes of finds, such as *shicra*. Feldman (1987) sees them as a form of labor tax in which the filling was part of rebuilding a structure to a more elevated position, with *shicra* used to keep a tally of loads carried; Quilter (1991: 423) just sees them as a convenient way to move stone on the kin-group level, without an authority giving orders.

We have seen earlier how groups of related households are capable of mobilizing labor, such as in the construction of megalithic tombs in Europe or the Hopewellian effigy mounds. Although some might consider these to be chiefdoms, the position taken in this volume is that they were the products of transegalitarian communities in which groups of households (characterized above as "hamlets") were competing for access to status and prestige. Such a view is echoed by Quilter (1991: 429) who writes, "it seems that the dynamics of social change in Late Preceramic Peru were centered in competition between kin groups rather than social classes." Rather than direct this competition toward the accumulation of personal wealth, it was channeled into the construction of public architecture (as suggested by Burger 1992: 37). Burger also stresses the role of ideology in motivating such collective efforts. From the perspective of an interested outsider to Peruvian archaeology, it appears that the monumental architecture can be explained by the convergence of ideology and the self-interest of collections of households.

The Preceramic emphasis on a communal ideology appears to have been even stronger in the Peruvian highlands, about 100 kilometers back from the coast. Away from the rich maritime resources, maize and guinea pigs were of greater importance in the highland diet, as were various species of deer (Burger 1992: 43). Several examples of substantial public architecture are known from sites like Huaricoto, La Galgada, and Kotosh. These sites are seen as ritual centers without large resident populations. At these sites, many small free-standing buildings with central firepits (often vented by subfloor flues) and with niches and benches around the walls are interpreted as ceremonial chambers in which people gathered around a fire and made offerings (Burger 1992: 45). From time to time, these sacral chambers were filled in and new ones erected. La Galgada is the only such site where residential features have been found alongside the ritual architecture. The open architecture of these highland sites is very different from the maze-like construction of the coastal sites, suggesting a different function and social organization. Collectively, they have been referred to as the "Kotosh Religious Tradition," a distinctive highland ideology which required a special sort of sacral structure.

CONTINUITY AND CHANGE IN THE INITIAL PERIOD

The introduction of irrigation agriculture and ceramics marks the transition from the Late Preceramic to the Initial Period (as it is known in the standard chronological scheme for the Peruvian Coast). During this period, between ca. 2000 and 900 BC, the settlement pattern shifted from the coastline to strategic points 10–20 km inland where the canal intakes were located along the small rivers draining from the highlands. Maritime resources continued to play a large role in subsistence, however. Woven textiles replaced twined ones, reflecting greater sophistication in the use of cotton.

As in the Late Preceramic, different views exist about the complexity of Initial Period society. The Pozorskis describe a "quantum jump" in sociopolitical complexity (S. Pozorski and T. Pozorski 1992: 845), whereas Quilter (1991: 429) suggests that the same Preceramic social system continued into the Initial Period, "with growing emphasis on public displays of authority... at monumental sites and, probably, monopolization of power by fewer kin groups than in the more open, fluid social dynamics of the Late Preceramic." Overall, there is clear movement in the direction of social complexity during the Initial Period, with the main question being whether it was dramatic or gradual.

One example of the major changes during the Initial Period can be found in the Casma Valley, where there is evidence for the growth of two large centers (S. Pozorski and T. Pozorski 1992): Pampa de las Llamas-Moxeke and Sechín Alto. Pampa de las Llamas-Moxeke covers about 220 hectares and has dozens of non-domestic platform mounds laid out in a deliberate pattern. The two largest mounds, Huaca A and Moxeke, are at opposite ends of an enormous plaza about 1.1 kilometers apart. Polychromed clay sculptures represent humans in elaborate clothing. Huaca A and Moxeke are very different structures, however. Moxeke is a 30-meter tall tiered pyramid, while Huaca A is a warren of 38 squarish room-units without common walls. The doorways into these room-units were made to hold wooden bars, which suggests a function as storerooms. The main mound at Sechín Alto was probably the largest man-made feature in the New World during the second millennium BC (Burger 1992: 80). The line of plazas and platform mounds at its base stretched out for 1.5 kilometers. Three of the plazas have sunken circular courts, the largest of which is 80 meters in diameter.

Pampa de las Llamas-Moxeke and Sechín Alto appear to be the seats of two distinct polities, which the Pozorskis declare to be "states" (1992: 862). The evidence for storage at Pampa de las Llamas-Moxeke and the existence of apparent satellite communities does suggest that these were complex polities of some sort, although Burger (1992: 88) points out that aside from the architecture there is little indication of internal differentiation within the settlements. Burger (1992: 87) suggests that these represent a patchwork of small "pre-state polities," each controlling an irrigation system and linked by marriages and shared ideology. Such small polities probably occurred in many other valleys along the Peruvian coast, where other smaller monumental complexes are found. Bawden (1996: 175) points out that the coexistence of several centers in a number of valleys suggests that none of them achieved dominant status, and the burials associated with these centers have none of the accumulation of prestige items which might be expected to indicate the presence of an elite class. As in the Preceramic, in Bawden's view, the community was unified by ideology which led it to construct such public architecture and which inhibited the emergence of a strong ruling elite.

In the highlands, the Kotosh Religious Tradition continued throughout the Initial Period. Ceremonial chambers like those of the late Preceramic are known from Shillacoto, La Galgada, and Huaricoto. La Galgada and Shillacoto are especially important for their large Initial Period stone-chambered tombs, which contain impressive grave goods (Greider et al. 1988). The appearance of rich burials in mortuary structures represents a new development in Andean prehistory and is substantially different from the simple pit graves found at the coastal sites. Gold, a metal which later figured prominently in Peruvian civilization, began to be worked for the first time. The intense emphasis on ceremonialism and ideology, however, obscures any evidence of increased social differentiation, although the rich burials are surely suggestive of a trend in this direction.

CHAVÍN AND THE EARLY HORIZON

The so-called "Early Horizon" (900–200 BC) is most closely associated with the florescence of a distinctive iconographic style, which includes representations of tropical forest animals, focused on the site of Chavín de Huántar in the central Peruvian highlands. The Chavín style has captured the attention of archaeologists interested in this period, and many have compared it with the Olmec florescence in Mexico at roughly the same time (e.g., Willey 1962). Whereas the Olmec appear almost from nowhere from a society of modest village agriculturalists, Chavín is the product of a millennium or longer of ideological elaboration and monumental architecture.

Chavín de Huántar is located over 3000 meters above sea level in the Peruvian highlands at the confluence of the Mosna and Huachecsa rivers. This location places it equidistant between the Peruvian coastal plain and the tropical forests of the eastern slopes of the Andes, where the Mosna river eventually leads. It is a complex site which developed in stages between 1000 and 200 BC (Burger 1992: 130–44). The oldest element in Chavín de Huántar is the structure known as the Old Temple, a U-shaped, four-story stone building which enclosed a sunken plaza. Inside and under this complex are galleries and rooms, including a cruciform-plan main chamber in which resides a large granite idol – a 4.5 meter tall stela carved to represent an anthropomorphic deity with a fanged mouth, claws for hands and feet, and snakes coming out of its head. This terrifying figure is believed to have been the supreme deity of the Chavín cult.

The Old Temple can be said to be the first "engineered" building in the New World, in that it required at least an intuitive sense of large-scale structural principles and the design skills required to incorporate a network of ventilation flues and drainage channels. Moreover, it incorporated directly into its architecture the remarkable Chavín iconography, in which felines, caymans, and other fantastic tropical creatures abound. The great Peruvian archaeologist Julio Tello argued that the iconography, and hence the Chavín phenomenon itself, originated in the tropical forest across the Andes. Richard Burger, however, has recently disagreed with Tello's position and argued that Chavín iconography and architecture owes at least as much to coastal predecessors as to the lowland forests. In Burger's view (1992: 156):

> ... the Chavín cult was created by fusing exotic tropical forest and coastal elements to forge a unique highland religion. The end product was a cosmopolitan ideology consonant with Chavín de Huántar's position at the crossroads of long-distance trade routes linking the highlands with the coast and the eastern lowlands.

The Old Temple functioned as the focus of Chavín ritual for over 500 years. After about 500 BC the population at Chavín de Huántar began to grow, and what had previously been a pilgrimage center developed into a larger settlement of several thousand inhabitants by about a century later. Long-distance exchange became a key element in Chavín life, with obsidian, ocean resources, and pottery being important trade goods. Burger (1992: 180) suggests that this is correlated with the development of the use of llama caravans for long-distance transport. There is also evidence for specialized production of shell ornaments. Additional ritual structures were built at Chavín de Huántar itself, while the Chavín style spread throughout the Andes.

Most Peruvianist archaeologists are in agreement that complex stratified polities were in existence in western South America during the Early Horizon. The debate continues as to whether these can be legitimately called "states," "chiefdoms," or just "complex polities," but there is ample evidence of differential access to status, power, and wealth at this time. Most significant are the lavishly provisioned burials, found at the highland sites beginning about 400 BC. At Kuntur Wasi, for example, several shaft tombs, each containing a single skeleton, were found in the site's rectangular sunken plaza. These burials had gold crowns, earspools, pectorals, and plaques decorated with Chavín motifs, as well as marine shells and fine pottery. On the floor of the burial of an elderly female were about 7000 shell and stone beads, perhaps elements of a garment (Burger 1992: 205). Other rich Chavín burials have been found at Chongoyape and Karwa.

Important evidence of social differentiation at the site of Chavín de Huántar itself has been documented by George Miller and Richard Burger through the study of the faunal remains (Miller and Burger 1995). They found that as the settlement grew, there was a shift to the almost exclusive consumption of domestic llamas. Llamas were also important as cargo-carriers and thus crucial to the participation of Chavín de Huántar in the interregional trade network. Some residents of Chavín de Huántar procured tender meat from young llamas, killed before they were able to provide a lifetime of service as pack animals, whereas most of the others had to eat the tough meat of the older animals. Moreover, many of the inhabitants of the core residential zones of Chavín de Huántar obtained choice cuts of llama meat, whereas the people living in more remote high-altitude settlements had to be content with heads and lower legs. The pattern that emerges is one like that proposed by Jackson and Scott (1995a, 1995b) for Mississippian sites in the southeastern United States, where outlying communities provisioned the elite who resided at ceremonial and political centers.

An earthquake at Chavín de Huántar about 200 BC appears to have been a major factor in the decline of the cult, although by this time complex societies were emerging in other regions as well. On the south coast of Peru, the Paracas culture was influenced by Chavín and sustained very high populations (Silverman 1996). The Paracas elite wore elaborately woven and embroidered textiles, which were then used as the wrappings for their mummified bodies after they died. In the Lake Titicaca basin, temple complexes appeared about 600 BC at sites like Chiripa (Mohr Chavez 1988) which had storage buildings around a sunken court. The art style on these buildings was different from that of Chavín, indicating a parallel local development.

CONCLUSION

The Peruvian evidence for the rise of complex societies is quite malleable, which permits different archaeologists to interpret it as having proceeded at either a faster or a slower pace. Jonathan Haas and Shelia and Thomas Pozorski see the development towards statehood as having proceeded at a rapid pace, with complex preceramic antecedents for the emergence of "theocratic" states in Initial Period, with an Initial Period site hierarchy in Casma valley of at least three levels (Haas 1987; S. Pozorski 1987; S. Pozorski and T. Pozorski 1992). Jeffrey Quilter and Richard Burger take a more conservative view: no secure evidence for the state until later in prehistory, not until 200 BC or later in the Early Intermediate Period (Quilter 1991; Burger 1992). The lack of evidence for high status burials, craft specialization, and uniform architectural styles in the Initial Period is compelling, albeit negative, evidence in support of a slower pace.

Yet where is the earliest appearance of some form of institutionalized differentiation in access to status, power, and wealth in Andean society? The evidence appears to converge on the Early Horizon, especially between 600 and 200 BC, although perhaps as early as 1000 BC. An unresolved question is the character of the elite. Were they high priests or secular chiefs? They clearly had power. As Burger (1992: 206) points out, the burials at Kuntur Wasi and Chongoyape convey a vivid message to the masses about the authority of the elite group. Whether they were a hereditary elite or priestly theocrats remains to be determined.

LATE PREHISTORIC CHIEFDOMS IN NORTHERN SOUTH AMERICA AND AMAZONIA

Although archaeologists of the Andean region are reluctant to characterize the polities of the Initial Period and Early Horizon as "chiefdoms," no such reticence is found in the lowlands of northern South America and Amazonia. During the first millennium AD (or, a millennium or more later than the emergence of complex society on the Peruvian coast), a number of distinct regional entities with settlement hierarchies and other trappings of chiefdoms emerged at a number of locations in this vast region (Roosevelt 1993; Spencer 1994; Drennan 1995). Adjacent areas of central America also supported chiefdom societies during the millennium prior to European contact.

Three key areas in northern South America are the headwaters of the Magdalena river in Colombia (Drennan 1991, 1996), the Muisca area in the Cordillera Oriental of Colombia (Langebaek 1995), and the lowland "llanos" in the Venezuelan state of Barinas (Spencer 1994; Redmond and Spencer 1994). All of these are slightly different in character. For example, chiefdoms in the highland Muisca region appear to be the result of a long developmental sequence, whereas those in lowland Barinas underwent a rapid florescence and decline.

In the Alto Magdalena area, population grew dramatically in the first centuries AD, reaching densities of 50–100 persons per kilometer (Drennan 1991: 276) by about AD 700. Yet settlement was very dispersed. Social differentiation is reflected in public works, including statues which depict humans and animals, and mortuary structures in the form of barrows. The architecture of some of the burials is very elaborate, which is regarded as evidence for social hierarchy, although the grave goods are not especially lavish. The statues and burials form complexes around which population congregated loosely, considered to represent small regional polities. Drennan (1991, 1995) proposes a model of several small, possibly competing, chiefdoms, each about 10 kilometers in radius. Although the elites used the public mortuary architecture to display their status, there appears to have been relatively little centralized control over production and accumulation of wealth. Around AD 800, the construction of elaborate mortuary architecture ceased, although the number of grave goods rose. Drennan (1995: 316) suggests that this represents a reorganization of Alto Magdalena elite society from one which emphasized ritual and ideology to one which was more concerned with the accumulation of wealth.

In contrast, the chiefdom in the lowland grasslands of the Barinas region developed and declined within a span of about 400 years, between about AD 600 and AD 1000 (Redmond and Spencer 1994; Spencer and Redmond 1992). Its three-tiered settlement hierarchy was focused on the 33-hectare site of Gaván, where two large mounds (10 and 12 meters high) are presumed to have had a ceremonial function. These mounds are found in an oval plaza surrounded by a raised causeway and palisade. Outside of this precinct were 130 smaller mounds on which residences were built. Causeways led from Gaván to five smaller centers with lower mounds, while in the hinterlands were 25 small villages with no mounds. Raised fields reflect the intensification of agricultural production, presumably mobilized by the elite inhabitants of Gaván and its supporting centers (Spencer 1994). The limited mortuary finds, however, are very modest. Gaván met its end around AD 1000, presumably at the hands of a neighboring polity, when it was attacked and burned.

In the Amazon Valley, some remarkable prehistoric chiefdoms flourished from approximately AD 500 until the arrival of Europeans in the 1500s (Roosevelt 1991, 1993). The discovery of these societies came as a bit of a surprise, for the conventional wisdom was that the Amazon valley was incapable of supporting complex societies, based on the assumption that Amazonian soils were poor and that the small and simply-organized modern indigenous societies were representative of the prehistoric pattern as well. Evidence for social complexity was dismissed as an ephemeral trans-Andean import (e.g., Meggers 1954). Ethnohistoric accounts from the sixteenth century (summarized, for example, in Palmatary 1965), however, indicate that large populations governed by chiefs lived along the banks of the Amazon and Orinoco rivers. These societies were expansionist and combative (Roosevelt

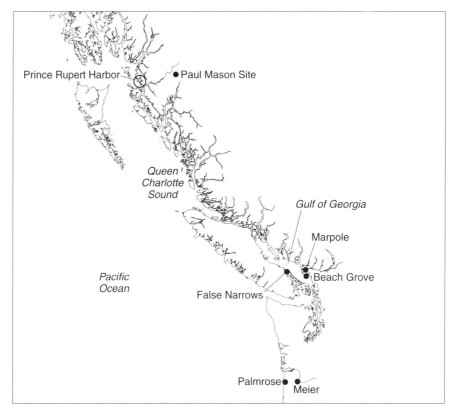

Figure 7.10   Map of Northwest Coast of North America showing key sites mentioned in this chapter.

1987: 154) and not only were divided into elites and commoners but also kept slaves. Archaeologically, they have left evidence that they existed for at least a millennium before European contact, during roughly the same period that the North American chiefdoms described below flourished.

The most spectacular evidence for prehistoric Amazonian chiefdoms comes from Marajó Island near the mouth of the Amazon, where the inhabitants built great clusters of mounds along the major watercourses (Roosevelt 1993). Similar mound clusters are known from the floodplains of the Bolivian Amazon, the middle Orinoco, and the Guyana coastal plain, all areas of fertile alluvial floodplains, but those on Marajó Island have been most closely examined. With an economy based on maize, small-seed floodplain grasses, and fish (which differs markedly from current indigenous subsistence in which root crops dominate), the Marajoara chiefdoms lived in large settlements with special-purpose craft areas, ceremonial areas, defensive earthworks, cemeteries, and substantial domestic structures (Roosevelt 1993: 273). As with Near Eastern *tells*, the Amazonian mounds represent centuries of accumulation of architectural debris and refuse. Marajó Island cemeteries have been the focus of archaeological research for nearly a century

(Palmatary 1950) because of the practice of interment of the bodies in enormous urns. Great variation exists in the type and decoration of these urns, the treatment of the body, and the grave goods included in the burials. Marajoara society, in Roosevelt's reconstruction, was one of many separate, warring, complex chiefdoms with large populations divided into several social ranks which developed from indigenous precursors.

NORTH AMERICA: NORTHWEST AND SOUTHEAST

North America has provided several classic examples of chiefdoms in later prehistory, between about 500 BC and the time of European conquest. At two corners of the continent, very different sorts of complex societies emerged which appear to have been organized as simple and complex chiefdoms. Perhaps the most vivid insight into prehistoric chiefly society comes from the southeast, where there is marked social differentiation among communities. In the northwest, stratified societies without agriculture provide a caveat to the assumption that food production is a prerequisite for complex society.

STRATIFIED SOCIETIES ON THE NORTHWEST COAST

As with the Peruvian Preceramic, the Northwest Coast of North America provides evidence that agriculture is not an absolute prerequisite for the emergence of differences in access to status, power, and wealth. The appearance of social complexity in the area between southeastern Alaska and northern California is thought to have been about 2500 years ago, initiating a way of life which continued relatively unchanged until contact with European explorers in the eighteenth century AD. Throughout this period, no agriculture at all was practiced in this area. Maize cultivation reached no closer than parts of the Great Basin in prehistory, so the Northwest Coast peoples relied exclusively on maritime, riverine, and forest resources.

As with the other regions discussed in this chapter, the appearance of hereditary elites along the Northwest Coast was preceded by a period of autonomous transegalitarian communities composed of a number of households. In this case, however, the households are believed, on the basis of ethnographic evidence, to have been composed of several family groups. One explanation for this may be the nature of the Northwest Coast resource base. Hayden and Cannon (1982) argue that multi-family households are likely to exist where there is competition for access to key resources, while Wilk and Rathje (1982) suggest that such households may occur where there are a large number of economic tasks to be performed concurrently, such as when there are seasonally-abundant resources. Such conditions may have been particularly acute in parts of the Northwest Coast, where the best locations for catching sea mammals and migratory fish would have been limited, and where it was important to mobilize many people at one time during salmon season.

One important early village which does not have evidence of social ranking is the Paul Mason site in northern British Columbia (Coupland 1996). Ten uniform depressions in two rows mark the sites of rectangular houses approximately 3000 years old. Excavation of several depressions revealed internal features such as hearths and benches. Absent, however, are types of artifacts which in later periods in the Northwest are taken to be markers of social status, such as native copper, obsidian, jet, amber, and *Dentalium* shell (Matson and Coupland 1995: 187). Due to the uniform dimensions of the houses and the lack of "wealth artifacts," the Paul Mason site is considered to represent an egalitarian community, although I would suggest that if there was competition among households for resource access, then perhaps the characterization of "transegalitarian" would be more appropriate.

Within the next 500 years, however, evidence for social ranking appears in burials from the Prince Rupert Harbor area in northern British Columbia and the Gulf of Georgia in southern British Columbia. In the latter region, cemeteries of the Marpole phase contain a number of burials of adolescents and children with abundant grave goods (Moss and Erlandson 1995: 24). Moreover, some adolescents are buried in stone cists under cairns up to 6 meters in diameter and 2 meters high (Matson and Coupland 1995: 209). Another indication of social differentiation is the deliberate deformation of the skulls of certain individuals carried out in infancy, which is another indication of a group with a different status. Matson and Coupland (1995) conclude that this evidence points towards the existence of inherited social inequality. Near Prince Rupert Harbor, one particularly elaborate burial of an adult male has copper bracelets, sticks wrapped with copper, and a variety of weapons, including clubs made from a killer whale jaw and whalebone. The whalebone club is decorated with a carved human effigy at the base of the handle.

Increasing evidence of violence is found during this period, particularly in burials from Prince Rupert Harbor. A number of the skeletons show evidence for violent trauma. Trophy skulls are found in a number of the graves, while other burials are headless. Jerome Cybulski (1992) noted a high incidence of forearm fractures, which he characterized as "parry fractures" as the arm was raised to block a blow. Some skulls have depressions caused by blows of stone clubs. Bone clubs, like those in the burial mentioned above, also reflect a capacity for violence.

In the Gulf of Georgia region, Marpole phase villages (such as those at False Narrows, Beach Grove, and Marpole itself) are characterized by larger house depressions. The postholes are very large, probably from the frames of cedar-plank walls, just as are known from historic-period houses. The smallest houses at Beach Grove, out of about ten overall, are estimated to be about 10×13 meters (Matson and Coupland 1995: 208), substantially larger than the earlier houses at the Paul Mason site. Other houses are considerably larger. Unfortunately, many houses have not been excavated in the Prince Rupert Harbor area where graves have yielded such evidence for social inequality. These settlements are interpreted as formal winter villages based on analogy with the historic pattern of settlement and on limited study of seasonal indicators such as layers in clam shells.

A distinctive Northwest Coast art style emerged with the Marpole phase which shows continuity into historic times. Birds, snakes, and people are the most common motifs. Basketry which reflects the same complex plaiting techniques used during historic periods has been recovered from sites with good preservation in the Prince Rupert Harbor area (Croes 1989).

Faunal remains from this period reflect a reliance on salmon at many of the larger settlement sites, which was probably caught in large numbers and then preserved and stored over the winter. A good indicator of salmon storage is an overwhemingly high ratio of body elements to head elements (Matson and Coupland 1995: 223). The increased harvesting of salmon for preservation and storage may have accelerated the growth of multi-family households. At other sites, there is an abundance of smaller fish, such as herring, which would have required netting and still further cooperation among those participating in this activity.

It is unclear how far to the south this pattern of emergent social complexity reached. The Palmrose site, near the mouth of the Columbia River, yielded evidence of a large planked house about 2000 years old. Faunal remains consisted primarily of salmon bones, along with a number of sea mammals, which would be consistent with the stored-salmon hypothesis noted above. Analysis of seasonal layers in clam shells points toward a late winter/early spring occupation. Such evidence is consistent with the model of social complexity developed for regions further north (Matson and Coupland 1995: 228–9).

It is clear that by 2000 years ago, much of the Northwest Coast of North America was inhabited by societies which had some degree of hereditary social ranking. Progressively larger households formed in response to the labor requirements of tasks which required "all hands on deck" during a short period. Ames (1996) has pointed out how long these households probably persisted through time, since a large cedar-plank house could have been used for several hundred years. Such permanence and investment in settlement locations would have led to very powerful local attachments.

The first European explorers in this region encountered powerful chiefs and highly stratified societies, in which the lowest members were effectively slaves of the elite. A number of polities were distributed along the coast in permanent villages of enormous cedar-plank houses. Some late prehistoric houses, like the one excavated at the Meier site on the Columbia River, could hold perhaps 60 people. This house was occupied for perhaps 400 years, and eventually required between 400,000 and 1,000,000 board feet of red-cedar lumber to build and maintain it (Ames 1996: 141). Clearly these were complex groups, composed of elite, commoners, and slaves, perhaps all living under the same roof in different parts of the house. Such communities, however, represent the culmination of a developmental trajectory that began three millennia earlier.

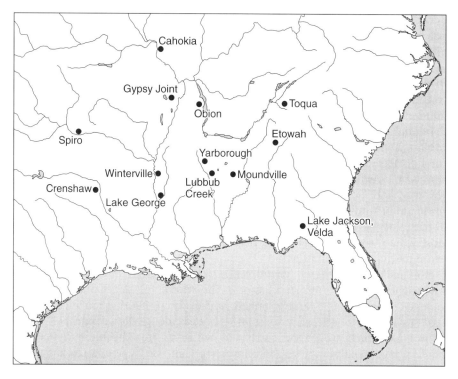

Figure 7.11 Map of southeastern North America showing key Mississippian sites mentioned in this chapter.

CHIEFDOMS IN THE LATE PREHISTORIC SOUTHEAST

In the south-central and southeastern United States, between AD 750 and 1600, many chiefdom societies flourished. These chiefdoms are collectively known as "Mississippian" societies, a term applied by W. H. Holmes in the late nineteenth century, although they are really a collection of distinctive polities which emerged from Late Woodland societies throughout southeastern North America. A historical point of connection with Mississippian societies exists, for in the sixteenth century, Spanish explorers traveled through this region. From the accounts of these explorers, we can clearly recognize chiefdom societies, and in fact, it is possible to match certain archaeological sites with settlements visited by De Soto and others (Brain, Toth, and Rodriguez-Buckingham 1974; Hally, Smith, and Langford 1990; Hudson 1990). From this historical baseline, Mississippian chiefdom society can be traced backwards in time until about AD 750. In contrast to the Hopewellian transegalitarian florescence several centuries earlier, it is possible to identify Mississippian polities and their centers, to obtain a general idea of their territorial size, and to trace their rise and fall. With some certainty, archaeologists characterize them as having hereditary elites and multiple levels of decision-making authority.

The two Mississippian chiefdoms which have received the most archaeo-logical attention in the last two decades are one on the American Bottom region of Illinois with its center at Cahokia and the one in the Black Warrior River valley of Alabama with its center at Moundville. In fact, from a cursory survey of the archaeological literature the reader might conclude that these were the only two Mississippian chiefdoms in existence, which is certainly *not* the case. Other regional polities have been identified in many parts of the southeast, from east Texas to the Atlantic and from the Ohio valley to the Gulf of Mexico (Smith 1990). They range in size from small collections of a few hamlets to the enormous Coosa paramount chiefdom, visited by the De Soto, De Luna, and Pardo expeditions of the sixteenth century, which extended for 500 kilometers from Alabama through Georgia and into Tennessee (Anderson 1994: 151).

Mississippian society was the direct outgrowth from Late Woodland soci-ety following the Hopewellian florescence several centuries before. It was an "independent pristine process of social transformation, uninfluenced by Mesoamerican state-level societies" (Smith 1990: 1) which flourished around the same time (see chapter 8). Around AD 750, in many river valleys of the eastern woodlands, chiefdoms emerged from local transegalitarian communi-ties. They were linked by exchange and communication networks and also held similar beliefs and ritual practices that are manifested archaeologically in a complex of traits called the "Southeastern Ceremonial Complex." In recent decades, we have come to know considerably more about Mississippian settlements, especially the smaller farmsteads occupied by one or two house-holds, and subsistence, based in large measure on corn, which had become fully established in eastern North America by the first centuries AD.

MISSISSIPPIAN SETTLEMENTS AND CEREMONIAL CENTERS

Until the late 1970s, the best-studied Mississippian sites were the large cen-tral settlements with one or more mounds. Etowah in Georgia, Spiro in east-ern Oklahoma, Moundville in Alabama, Toltec in Arkansas, and Cahokia in Illinois are the best-known and are mentioned most frequently in the litera-ture, but many other Mississippian mound sites are found across the southeast. Dozens of Mississippian mound sites are known throughout the southeastern United States. Some are large complexes, but most are small sites consisting of a handful of mounds, often situated around a plaza, and associated features like ditches and palisades. The larger the site, the more archaeological attention it has attracted over the last century.

One example of a Mississippian mound center is the Lake Jackson site in northern Florida, which has been studied by archaeologists since the 1940s (Payne 1994). The Lake Jackson site covers about 27 hectares, with a cere-monial core consisting of six mounds, the largest of which is nearly 8 meters high (Jones 1994; Scarry 1996). One of the smaller mounds, Mound 3, yielded the most interesting evidence of elite society. Twelve successive building floors formed the footings for the buildings erected on the mound.

Figure 7.12 The main burial from Mound 72 at Cahokia on a bed of shell beads (photo courtesy of Dr Melvin L. Fowler, University of Wisconsin at Milwaukee; the assistance of Dr Thomas E. Emerson, Illinois Transportation Archaeology Research Program, University of Illinois at Urbana-Champaign in obtaining this photo is gratefully acknowledged).

In the mound were over 25 burials (many had been quarried away before systematic excavation). These were primarily of adult males, but several of the women and children also had impressive grave goods of copper, mica, shell, and stone. Most remarkable were the "hawk-man-dancer" copper breastplates found lying on top of several of the skeletons, often with fabric patterns preserved by the copper oxide (Jones 1994). Radiocarbon dates indicate that Lake Jackson flourished between AD 1250 and 1500.

Many other Mississippian centers are considerably smaller, although in comparison with most other archaeological sites they would still be considered very large. For example, Lake George in Mississippi was located adjacent to an oxbow lake which was once a channel of the Mississippi river (Williams and Brain 1983). A bank enclosed an area of about 22 hectares, within which were 25 surviving mounds, mostly small house platforms. The mounds are arranged around two plazas, which are separated by a large central mound (a similar arrangement is noted at Winterville, about 80 kilometers to the north). In northern Tennessee, the Obion site is surrounded by a palisade about a kilometer in circumference (Garland 1992, 1996). Within this area are seven mounds, on which there is evidence for ceremonial activity. Hundreds of other such sites dot the southeastern United States, creating ritual landscapes comparable to the Salisbury Plain of England at the time of Stonehenge.

At the upper end of the Mississippian spectrum is Cahokia, the most enormous Mississippian site known, which covers 13 square kilometers just across the Mississippi River from St Louis (Milner 1996; Pauketat and

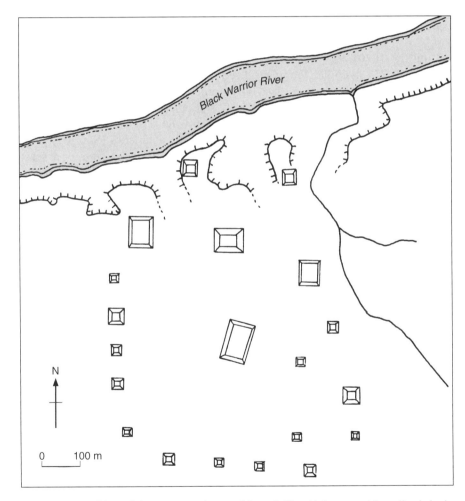

Figure 7.13 Plan of the core precinct at Moundville, Alabama, with stylized depictions of mounds.

Emerson 1997b). Despite its size, Cahokia is only one of many mound centers in this area, known as the "American Bottom." About 100 mounds form the core area of Cahokia, which is enclosed by a palisade of massive logs. It is dominated by the Monks Mound (so named because it was the residence of a group of Trappist monks when first visited by antiquarians early in the nineteenth century). Monks Mound is a flat-topped series of terraces about 30 meters high and about 300 meters by 240 meters at the base. The pits from which the seven million cubic meters of earth were dug to construct the mound are clearly visible nearby. On top of the mound was a large building, presumably the residence of the paramount chief. Monks Mound formed one end of a large quadrangle surrounded by 17 smaller mounds, also topped by residences, presumably those of the lesser elite. Other mounds were used for burials. For example, Mound 72 contained over 250 skeletons, mostly of young women, apparently sacrificial victims. One individual in Mound 72, a male, was buried on a bed of 20,000 shell beads. Alongside were the disarticulated remains of several other individuals, artifacts of sheet copper and mica, plus a cache of superbly crafted stone points.

Until the 1970s, very little was known of the small sites in which much of the general Mississippian populace lived. In the two decades following the excavation and publication of the Gypsy Joint site in Arkansas (Smith 1978), several dozen more small Mississippian settlements have been excavated, many in the course of the FAI-270 salvage project east of St Louis. These sites are generally comparable in size and their characteristics (Smith 1995c). In general, they have provided evidence for year-round occupation, or at least during most of the year. On some, including Gypsy Joint itself, paired structures have been interpreted as seasonal habitations, with one having served as a warm-weather residence, the other as the winter house (Smith 1978: 151; Pauketat 1989: 302), although at others the houses appear to have been occupied by separate households. The duration of occupation of these sites appears generally to have been less than a decade (Smith 1995c: 241).

A fairly typical small Mississippian settlement is the Velda site in northern Florida (J. Scarry 1995). Here, traces of two houses and a third structure define a courtyard area, forming a compound of about 0.15 hectare. The houses are round post-built structures, 5.5 and 7.5 meters in diameter, with posts set at about one-meter intervals. Several interior posts supported the roof. The third structure, which does not have such a regular outline of posts, is interpreted as a granary or corn-crib, as have been mentioned in ethnohistoric accounts. In the surrounding countryside, more one- or two-household homesteads have been found, either relatively isolated or loosely grouped into hamlets.

In most Mississippian polities, a clear settlement hierarchy has been distinguished. At the bottom are the farmsteads of one or two households. Many of these are clustered to form hamlets, although they remain dispersed rather than nucleated. Next are the central settlements with single mounds, which are interpreted as the residential and ritual centers of the elite and local leaders. Finally, in most of the Mississippian polities, there is one site with multiple mounds, which is interpreted as the seat of the paramount chief for the entire region. Over time, these settlement systems developed and declined. Each has a unique pattern and chronology, despite the common elements.

The Moundville chiefdom provides a notable example of the changes in a Mississippian settlement system over time (Scarry and Steponaitis 1997), although each polity had its own developmental trajectory. Prior to AD 1050, settlement in the Black Warrior River valley in Alabama was composed of autonomous villages with no mounds and no elaborate burials. No evidence for social differentiation has been identified in this region before AD 1050. Between AD 1050 and 1250, single pyramidal mounds appeared at several of the villages, while most of the others were abandoned in favor of one- or two-household farmsteads. The mound sites became the centers of political, economic, and ritual life. There is thus a centripetal tendency, which has been noted in other Mississippian polities as well (e.g., Mehrer 1995; Pauketat 1997b in the American Bottom area around Cahokia), after AD 1000 in which some of the large sites got larger and the smaller sites became progressively more dispersed and isolated. About AD 1150, Moundville itself gained clear political ascendancy over this region with the construction of a 100-hectare civic and ceremonial precinct with 20 pyramidal mounds around a rectangular plaza, all enclosed by a massive palisade with defensive bastions. The palisade was rebuilt at least three times, using a minimum of 10,000 logs each time. The Moundville complex has clear signs of a deliberate layout, much as was the case of the Olmec sites at La Venta and San Lorenzo nearly 2000 years earlier. Until about AD 1550, Moundville was the center of politics and ritual for the Black Warrior River region, after which the polity collapsed and there was a return to village settlements similar to those which had been common over 500 years earlier.

MISSISSIPPIAN SUBSISTENCE

Although indigenous agricultural systems had existed in eastern North America for several millennia (see chapter 5), the introduction of maize transformed the subsistence economy of this region. Seed plants such as chenopod and sunflower remained important contributors to the diet, but maize had several advantages. It was highly productive, especially on the fertile bottomlands of the eastern rivers, and it could be easily stored. Its productivity enabled it to support higher population densities, and its storage potential allowed it to finance chiefly elites and their operations, provided commoners could be induced to grow more than for their basic dietary needs. Indeed, maize agriculture was a prerequisite for the Mississippian emergence.

Margaret Scarry (1993b; Scarry and Steponaitis 1997) has traced the transformation of the subsistence system at Moundville as the polity formed between AD 900 and 1250. There was a significant increase in corn production between the pre-chiefdom phase of village settlement and the emergence of the Moundville polity, while there is a dramatic drop in hickory nut shell at the same time. It appears that the outlying farmsteads especially began producing considerably more corn at the onset of Moundville chiefly society, much more so than their village-living predecessors *and* more so than the inhabitants of Moundville itself, as reflected in the amounts of corn cupules recovered from the outlying sites. Scarry and Steponaitis interpret this evidence as indicating that corn was raised in the outlying farmsteads, possibly in fields belonging to the chiefly elite, and then shelled before transport to the center at Moundville.

Mississippian animal use has only recently begun to be studied as a reflection of social organization. Arthur Bogan (1983) was one of the first to correlate different patterns of animal use with segments of chiefly society at the Toqua site in Tennessee, where he identified unequal distributions of anatomical elements and even species in elite and non-elite precincts. More recently, H. Edwin Jackson and Susan Scott (1995a, 1995b) have studied faunal patterning at several Mississippian sites, including the Crenshaw ceremonial center in southwestern Arkansas, the Lubbub Creek mound complex in Alabama, and the Yarborough farmstead in Mississippi. At Crenshaw and Lubbub Creek, Jackson and Scott identified what they interpret as the provisioning of meat to the elites inhabiting these centers. Anatomical elements, especially from white-tailed deer (*Odocoileus virginianus*), with high meat content were well-represented at these elite settlements. Moreover, at Crenshaw, there is a marked underrepresentation of the bones of the lower leg, which do not bear much meat (Jackson and Scott 1995a: 110–1). By contrast, many different anatomical elements were represented at Yarborough, suggesting that primary butchery of deer took place at this outlying site. Deer lower leg bones are well-represented in the Yarborough sample, as are skull bones, while the representation of upper hind limbs, where the most meat can be found, is significantly lower than at Lubbub Creek or Crenshaw.

MISSISSIPPIAN CRAFT PRODUCTION AND EXCHANGE

A difference of opinion exists concerning the nature of Mississippian craft production. The key issue is whether full-time craft specialization, either independent or attached, existed or whether the elites acquired prestige artifacts produced by a diffuse network of non-specialist artisans. Underlying this is a debate over the nature of the economic infrastructure of Mississippian society. Was it a highly integrated interregional production and exchange system managed by the elites or was it a relatively simple organization in which elites acquired locally-produced symbols of status and prestige, which were then exhibited and distributed locally as well?

A case for Mississippian craft specialization was made by Peebles and Kus (1977: 442; see also Welch 1996: 80–3) with specific reference to Moundville. They argued that concentrations of finished shell beads, unworked shell, and beadworking tools in one part of the site, hide processing equipment in another, and pottery materials in yet a third location was suggestive of craft specialization, as was low variability in ceramic forms. Since Moundville is an elite center, these concentrations were interpreted as indications of resident craft specialists. Brumfiel and Earle had not yet articulated the concept of "attached specialization," but the Moundville data were viewed in a similar light. In the 1980s, Guy Prentice argued for the presence of household-based "cottage industries" in the American Bottom region around Cahokia which produced goods for trade (1983). Later, he took this idea a step further and suggested that various Mississippian farm-steads specialized in particular productive activities (Prentice 1985). Yerkes (1989, 1991) also characterized microlith and shell-bead production in the American Bottom as having been a household specialization.

A contrasting position has been taken by Jon Muller (1987), who argued that although there were some localized production centers for shell and chert artifacts, calling this "specialization" is an overstatement. This view is echoed by Timothy Pauketat (1987, 1997a) and George Milner (1990, 1996). Milner (1996: 38) writes, "although some well-made items generally fashioned from nonlocal materials were produced by unusually skilled indi-viduals, there is no indication that a great number of artisans spent their lives laboring away on precious objects." Pauketat (1997a) proposes that instead of conceptualizing this productive activity as "specialization," it should be viewed as a dimension of an overall centralization of political life which encouraged the production of valuable objects as "legitimating symbols" of authority.

A larger issue is the nature of exchange, especially of exotic and finely-crafted objects in Mississippian society. James Brown, Richard Kerber, and Howard Winters (1990) maintain that Mississippian elites depended on their control of access to objects which enhanced their prestige. Interregional trade played a major role in obtaining these objects, and local craft production was also stimulated to feed this "prestige-goods economy." Knight (1997: 238) identifies the components of this trade: exotic chert, mica, galena, copper, pigments, fine-grained rocks, and marine shell. Some archaeologists, such as Kelly (1991) and Peregrine (1992) have stressed the interregional inter-action promoted by such exchange. Yet – as Muller (1987), Milner (1996), and Pauketat and Emerson (1997) point out – the characterization of Mississippian centers like Cahokia as mercantile emporia able to project their economic power over large areas is a considerable exaggeration.

Welch (1996) proposes a direct link between the economic and the politi-cal structure of the Moundville polity, based on the ability of the elite to con-trol the local production of axes (necessary for the clearance of agricultural fields) and the importation and distribution of non-local prestige goods. In Welch's view, the chief's ability to acquire and control prestige goods affected his standing within the polity by legitimating his elite status. Pauketat (1997a: 11) takes a similar view of production and exchange at Cahokia, proposing that the control of production by the political elite at the site was their way of appropriating cultural symbols and their meanings, which fostered their political interests. These symbols acquired meaning largely on the local scale, where relatively mundane objects like stone hoes and axe-heads acquired prestige through their association with the sponsors of their manufacture.

It is clear that Mississippian production and exchange cannot be studied in isolation, but instead must be viewed as a part of the fabric of society. At the moment, there is little support for an elaborately organized system of specialized production and interregional mercantile exchange. Rather, most indications point towards local stimulation of production, perhaps with some part-time or small-scale specialization, under the sponsorship of the elite populations. The valuables which were thus generated enabled the chief and his retainers to maintain their support within the polity as symbols of their efficacy.

THE SOUTHEASTERN CEREMONIAL COMPLEX

An important dimension of Mississippian craft specialization and long-distance exchange is the phenomenon known as the Southeastern Ceremonial Complex. Often characterized somewhat inappropriately as the "Southern Cult," it is a complex of decorative motifs and artifact types which is widely distributed throughout the southeast between AD 1200 and AD 1300 (Waring and Holder 1945; Brown 1976; Galloway 1989). The Southeastern Ceremonial Complex was not a "cult" in the true sense of the word (meaning a religious system focused on a single deity or object) but rather a widespread appropriation of symbols and prestige goods intended to legitimize the authority of the Mississippian elite. Central to this phenomenon was the participation of the Mississippian elites in exchange networks which brought them exotic raw materials and fine finished goods. This institution linked together many of the Mississippian chiefdoms in a limited fashion, contributing to the impression of greater integration than is probably the case.

The characteristic artifacts of the Southeastern Ceremonial Complex include engraved marine shells, sheets of native copper embossed with a variety of designs, stone palettes, stone figurines, and painted pottery. These objects are typically found in graves, and often appear to have served as parts of costumes or body ornaments, suggesting that they were badges of elite status. Most of the symbols on them relate to warfare or to mythical beings. Depictions of weapons, such as maces, and gruesome depictions of mutilated victims suggest a preoccupation with conflict and violence. Mythical beings appear as fantastic animals, including horned and winged serpents, raptorial birds, and panthers.

The convergence of exotic raw materials and rich iconography, as well as the fact that these objects were concentrated at elite ceremonial precincts such as Moundville, Etowah, and Spiro, contributed to the original conception of them as the material manifestation of a religious cult. This view has been considerably altered in recent years. Current thinking is that they served for the social reproduction of elite status (King and Freer 1995) or as markers of chiefly legitimation (Brown 1976; Muller 1989; Rogers 1996). Yet they are not completely secular, in that a case can be made that they do involve supernatural power (Knight 1986). Thus the manufacture and exchange of prestige goods during the thirteenth century AD appears to have been a point of articulation between the political and ideological dimensions of Mississippian society.

MISSISSIPPIAN CHIEFDOMS

On the basis of this rich archaeological record, combined with ethnohistoric data from contact with European explorers, it has been possible to characterize Mississippian polities with a degree of precision not possible in many other parts of the world. In addition to addressing questions of the size and duration of Mississippian chiefdoms, it is also important to examine the variability among them. In such syntheses it is easy to fall into the trap of "one size fits all," but this would be a mistake in considering Mississippian chiefdoms. Cahokia is very different from Moundville, which in turn differs from smaller polities from Oklahoma to North Carolina. Part of the variation is simply in size, but structural differences also apparently existed among various regions.

How much territory did the Mississippian polities control? Many different estimates have been published. Size estimates for the Moundville chiefdom range from 200 kilometers in maximum dimension down to 28 kilometers. Jon Muller (1986: 187) suggests that one chiefdom extended for over 120 kilometers in the Lower Ohio River valley, while Scarry and Payne (1986) believe that the polity centered on Lake Jackson was about 90 kilometers in diameter. Cahokia, on the other hand, appears to have been much more compact, about 40 kilometers along the Mississippi river. Based on an analysis of Mississippian centers in northern Georgia, David Hally (1993) argues that lower size ranges are more realistic and that simple Mississippian chiefdoms rarely exceeded 40 kilometers in maximum dimension and were usually much smaller. Anything larger would have taxed the ability of individual chiefs to control it. Hally (1993: 163) suggests that a key limiting factor may have been the ability to travel round-trip between the administrative center and the most remote outlying community in a single day. Some Mississippian chiefdoms defy this generalization, however. Complex chiefdoms such as Moundville and Etowah appear to have had control over somewhat larger areas, while paramount chiefdoms such as Coosa embraced as many as six subordinate chiefdoms along a distance of about 500 kilometers at the time of the first Spanish contact.

On the basis of his study of platform mound construction at sites in northern Georgia, David Hally (1996) has attempted to understand the rise and fall of Mississippian chiefdoms. The office of the chief was closely related to the construction of such mounds, since his divinity was attested by the bones of the ancestors stored in the mortuary temple on the mound. Hally suggests that additional layers of soil were added to mounds at the times of chiefly succession. From his analysis of such construction stages, Hally concludes that almost all Mississippian chiefdoms in this area lasted less than 100 years, often considerably shorter, with only one lasting more than 200 years. He found, however, that where a chiefdom rose and fell early in the Mississippian sequence, another often followed it 100–200 years later on the same spot, often using the same mounds. In Hally's view, rather than being of long duration and oscillating between higher and lower levels of decision making, the Mississippian polities of this region were simple two-tiered entities which cycled "between birth and death" (Hally 1996: 125). Elsewhere, however, sites appear to have been occupied continuously for much longer. The 12 building episodes at Mound 3 at Lake Jackson in Florida suggest a sequence of chiefly succession of several centuries. Clearly there were major, long-lasting polities and minor ephemeral ones.

Vincas Steponaitis (1991) has stressed the considerable variability in Mississippian polities. At one extreme is Moundville, whose developmental history has already been summarized above, and the other large centers like Etowah, Cahokia, Lake Jackson, Lake George, and Spiro. At the other are many smaller polities, many of which are still poorly known. These may have been simpler chiefdoms (Steponaitis suggests that some might not have attained chiefdom status at all). For example, in the Pocahontas region of Mississippi, about 50 kilometers southeast of Lake George, the mound centers are on a much smaller scale and the degree of differentiation among sites is considerably less. In fact, after AD 1200 the amount of exotic materials in graves drops off, suggesting that the elites in the smaller polities could no longer engage in the procurement network, or that the chiefdom had to pay tribute to a more powerful polity. No further centralization occurred.

It may be that the emergence of some complex chiefdoms during the thirteenth century AD in the interior southeast precluded the ascendance of many others, as Steponaitis suggests. For the preceding five centuries, most of the chiefdoms of this area were very similar polities, with small centers and localized settlement hierarchies. They all seemed to participate relatively equally in the exchange network that provided the socially prestigious exotic goods. After the thirteenth century, a number of chiefdoms blossomed into more elaborate entities with progressively more levels of settlement hierarchy, more mounds in their social and ceremonial centers, and more access to exotic products. Why did this happen? Steponaitis suggests some possibilities: larger populations from which the chief could mobilize the labor for construction or generation of surpluses; location on prime communication routes; or just random factors such as having an unusually charismatic or skilled leader at the right time. Whatever the cause of this acceleration, the other smaller chiefdoms simply could not catch up, and thus remained at about the same relatively simple level of organization for the next several centuries.

The "big bang" seen in the Mississippian Midsouth in the thirteenth century AD appears to have taken place at Cahokia 400 kilometers to the north approximately two centuries earlier (Pauketat 1997b; Anderson 1997). About AD 1000, the American Bottom was the scene of an emergent Mississippian polity after centuries of steady population increase (Kelly 1990). The organization of villages suggests that authority centered on hereditary lineage heads was in effect by this time. Long-distance trade in exotic materials was already established. In the middle of the eleventh century AD, there was "an abrupt and large-scale transformation of community order" (Pauketat 1997b: 32) which altered the social landscape of the American Bottom. The large villages in the region were replaced by centers with mounds and plazas on one hand and dispersed farmsteads on the other, anticipating the developments seen somewhat later further to the southeast. Cahokia itself became the central settlement in a three-tiered settlement hierarchy and its inhabitants embarked on an intense episode of mound construction. "Downtown Cahokia" was completely redeveloped using new construction techniques and concepts of the organization of public and domestic space (Dalan 1997), which created an inscribed landscape that defined the social dimensions of the community. Between AD 1050 and 1100, the population of Cahokia increased five to tenfold (Pauketat and Lopinot 1997).

Over the course of the next century, Cahokia was the capital of a concentrated polity, clearly a complex chiefdom with multiple levels of authority. Other chiefdoms, both simple and complex, appear to have been under its direct or indirect control (Anderson 1997: 248). The political elite, who inhabited Cahokia's central "political-administrative complex" (Pauketat 1997b: 37) were able to mobilize craft production to generate a set of local symbols of their power and resided in progressively larger houses to reflect their social prominence. Some archaeologists have characterized Cahokian chiefship during this period as "divine," due to the appearance of ceramic types decorated with cosmological motifs and construction of circles of posts which perhaps have some celestial orientation (Pauketat and Emerson 1997: 271). At the same time, Cahokia's connections extended throughout mid-continental North America, probably through a radiating series of down-the-line transactions that solidified social relations among lesser polities (Anderson 1997: 255; Milner 1996: 46). The influence and authority of its rulers, however, appears to have remained confined to the American Bottom and immediately adjacent areas.

After about AD 1200, however, the Cahokia polity began to dissolve. About this time, the defensive palisade was erected around the political-administrative core area. The population began to slip away from Cahokia towards the outlying areas (Milner 1996: 47). For a while, the elite tried to hold on to their trappings of power, prestige, and wealth, and Cahokia maintained its prominence through its "inertia…as a sacred place" (Pauketat 1997b: 49). Eventually, however, residential structures were built in areas which had previously been reserved for public architecture (Milner 1996: 49). Evidence for long-distance exchange also declines. By AD 1350, Cahokia and many of the other centers in the American Bottom had been abandoned, which Anderson (1996: 248) characterizes as "an organizational collapse that is itself as unprecedented in scale as the emergence of this society in the first place."

The Mississippian chiefdoms of southeastern North America are classic examples of the instability of chiefdom societies. It appears that the larger they became the quicker their cycle of florescence, dominance, and decline. Critical thresholds of population and area combined with limitations on the personal leadership qualities of the elites and the stability of exchange networks to create limits to the longevity of a chiefdom polity. We cannot blame the demise of Mississippian chiefdoms on the arrival of European colonists, for many of the major polities had collapsed centuries before. Had the indigenous societies not been eradicated by conquest and disease, it is likely that this oscillating pattern of chiefdom organization would have continued indefinitely.

STATUS DIFFERENTIATION IN LONGSHAN CHINA

Following the establishment of farming communities in the Huanghe and Yangzi valleys (see chapter 5), the period between 5000 and 2500 BC is characterized by a progressive consolidation of settled agricultural life and proficiency in pottery manufacture. Throughout much of northern China, particularly the central plains of Shanxi and Henan, many small villages belonging to the Yangshao culture are found. Yangshao villages, much like their counterparts elsewhere in the world, appear to have been composed of autonomous households with little evidence for social differentiation. At sites like Banpo and Jiangzhai, a large house is surrounded by several smaller ones, suggesting the emergence of a wealthier or more prosperous household. Nonetheless, Fung (1994: 55) notes that "if there were people of high status in Yangshao culture, they did not display their wealth of position very prominently." It would appear that the "transegalitarian" condition of competing households described in chapter 6 would more appropriately apply to the Yangshao Neolithic communities.

Two areas in northern China do exhibit somewhat greater tendencies toward more pronounced differences in wealth and status after about 4000 BC. In Liaoning in northeastern China, the Hongshan culture exhibits some rather precocious evidence of social differentiation (Nelson 1995), while in Shandong along the lower Huanghe, the communities of the Dawenkou culture developed sophisticated ceramic technology which enabled the production of very delicate fine pottery. In both cultures, the mortuary rites take on characteristics reminiscent of the transegalitarian Hopewell communities of

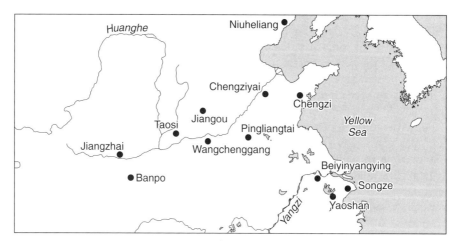

Figure 7.14   Map of China showing key sites mentioned in this chapter.

North America. At the Hongshan site of Niuheliang, a mortuary structure known as the "Goddess Temple" (Nelson 1991, 1995) contained a life-sized clay figure and smaller figurines of humans and pigs. Hongshan jade carvings are especially elaborate, and there is some evidence for metallurgy (Nelson 1995: 15). Dawenkou cemeteries have yielded evidence of mortuary structures built of timber chambers filled with many grave goods, including delicate black and white ceramics in many different forms which sugggest elaborate serving and drinking rituals (Fung 1994: 5). At Chengziyai, a Dawenkou cemetery contained graves of 11 people in wooden coffins accompanied by grave goods, 17 graves without coffins but with some grave goods, and 54 burials without any grave goods (Nelson 1996: 138).

The area of the Dawenkou culture in Shandong province continues to provide the clearest evidence for the emergence of hereditary social differentiation and centralized authority in the Huanghe Valley, where progressively more elaborate sites are found between ca. 2500 and 2000 BC. The name "Longshan" is applied to this period, which appears to both refer to an archaeological culture along the lower Huanghe but also to subsume other cultures as well, such as the Qijia located further upstream (Liu 1996; Higham 1996) and other regional variants (Chang 1986, 1994). Longshan cemeteries and settlements both reflect significant structural changes in social organization from the preceding Neolithic periods, as well as the initial evidence for metallurgy in the Huanghe basin.

Longshan cemeteries provide very clear evidence for social differentiation. At Chengzi in Shandong province, 87 graves were organized into three clusters (Chang 1994; Higham 1996). Within these clusters, several rich graves (which feature a ledge of soil around the coffin on which grave offerings were displayed) are surrounded by a number of poorer ones. The richest graves contain both tall-stemmed cups and pig jaws, while the next richest class of burials, also with ledges, only sometimes includes pig jaws and tall-stemmed cups as well. The poorest graves, which are in the majority, have no ledges and few grave goods. At Taosi, in Shanxi province, over 1000 graves, each in its own grave pit with the head pointing toward the southeast, have been excavated. Here again significant differentiation in mortuary wealth is found. Nine graves at Taosi stand out as exceptionally rich and contain wooden chambers, jade rings and axeheads, sets of musical instruments (one of which is a wooden drum with a crocodile-skin cover) and high-quality painted pottery (Pearson and Underhill 1987; Underhill 1991). Eighty others are moderately furnished and hundreds of others have few, if any grave goods. The cemetery also appears to be divided into sections, each with rich, middling, and poor burials. Chang (1994: 64–5) considers the Taosi evidence as an indication that wealth was concentrated in the hands of a few. Based on early Chinese texts, he proposes that it reflects a lineage system in which status, both within and between lineages, was determined by proximity to the line of descent from the founder to the current chief.

Longshan settlement patterns are dominated by large settlements with packed-earth walls. Pingliangtai is located on an elevated flat mound of 5 hectares and 3–5 meters above the surrounding plain (Chang 1986: 262).

The core of the settlement is a walled enclosure 185 meters square (Higham 1996: 51) oriented along the four cardinal directions. This example of public architecture had gates on the northern and southern sides and a drainage system of pottery pipes. Another walled settlement is Wangchenggang in Henan, where human skeletons were found in the packed-earth foundations of houses in the central area. Chang (1986: 274) proposes that these are elite residences. At Chengziyai, the packed-earth wall was estimated to be about 6 meters high and about 9 meters thick (Fung 1994), a remarkable investment of labor.

The earliest evidence for cast-bronze metalworking in China comes from Wangchenggang in the form of a fragment of a bronze vessel composed of an alloy of copper, tin, and lead (Chang 1986: 274). The dating of this artifact suggests that bronze casting was known in China by at least 2000 BC. At Meishan, crucible fragments with metal analyzed to be 95 percent copper still adhering to the interior surface are also dated to the late third millennium BC (Higham 1996: 52). Qijia sites further up the Huanghe have yielded many metal artifacts, including bronze mirrors.

Longshan pottery appears to have been produced in limited areas within settlements, and kilns have been identified on several sites. Anne Underhill's analysis of ceramics and settlement remains suggests that a "complex household industry" mode of specialized ceramic production prevailed (Underhill 1991). In her view, Longshan pottery production took place in a limited set of houses, since there is considerable variability in size, shape, and decoration rather than the standardization that would be expected from wares produced in workshops. Individual families specialized in production of utilitarian pottery, whereas the finer wares such as the delicate "eggshell" cups may have been made by independent craftsmen. Such a structure is reminiscent of the two-tiered form of craft specialization which Rowlands (1976) and Levy (1991) suggested for Bronze Age Europe.

The most recent and most detailed analysis of Longshan settlement organization has been carried out by Liu (1996) in southern Shanxi and Henan. Liu found that Longshan settlements in this area consisted of three very large sites (greater than 200 hectares), three large sites (70–199 hectares), 22 medium-sized sites (20–69 hectares), and 641 small sites (19 hectares or smaller). Moreover, a number of site clusters were identified, within which different patterns of site distribution and site hierarchy suggested variations in social organization. Liu interprets these data as indicating different forms of chiefdoms: "centripetal" polities in geographically-circumscribed regions (Taosi and Sanliquiao), interpreted as the most complex chiefdoms; "centrifugal" polities in semi-circumscribed regions (valleys of the Yi-Luo and Qin rivers), interpreted as somewhat less integrated chiefdoms; and decentralized polities in non-circumscribed regions (northern and central Henan), interpreted as weakly-integrated chiefdoms in which competition was rife.

Both Liu (1996: 278) and Chang (1994: 65) stress the evidence for intergroup conflict between the various Longshan polities as a factor in the emergence of further forms of social complexity. Indeed, Liu argues that the subsequent state-level polities in northern China emerged not in the regions of centralized chiefdoms but in the areas of decentralized chiefdom systems in northern and central Henan. Larger and heavier spearpoints and arrowheads are found, which it has been suggested were designed to kill people rather than animals (Fung 1994: 59). At Jiangou in Hebei province, a water well was filled with five layers of human skeletons, some of which had been decapitated and others which showed signs of struggling after having been buried alive (Chang 1986: 270). Elsewhere at this site, several skulls with evidence of scalping were found. Such evidence, along with the packed-earth fortification walls, suggests that inter-group violence was endemic in the Huanghe valley in Longshan times.

Even more important than the control of weapons, Chang suggests (1994: 65–6), was the elite monopoly on ritual paraphernalia during this period, which would have provided exclusive access to the supernatural world by the chiefs and thus the ideological basis for authority. The musical instruments in the rich Taosi graves provide one indication of this. Similarly, the *cong*, or decorated jade square tubes, which are found in elite graves at Longshan sites like Taosi and at cemeteries of the Longshan-related Liangzhu culture along the lower Yangzi at sites like Yaoshan, Songze, and Beiyinyangying, are decorated with cosmological symbols. *Cong* are known from later Shang times to have been used as ritual paraphernalia in which heaven is represented by the round interior and earth by the square exterior (Nelson 1996: 138).

Many features of the Longshan period in northern China point toward increasing social differentiation and the concentration of economic and ideological authority in the hands of a limited portion of the population. The scale and nature of chiefly authority is still unclear, but the towns with packed-earth ramparts were probably the seats of the chiefs and their retainers who ruled the surrounding polity. Limited evidence for metallurgy and other crafts suggests that the elites sponsored craftsmen at the protected settlements (Underhill 1996: 145). As in the Mississippian case, the most complex Longshan chiefdoms were those with the greatest centripetal tendencies, but it appears that there was greater competition and conflict among the smaller polities. Subsequent developments (discussed in the next chapter) appear to stem from the latter rather than from the former.

COMPLEX POLITIES IN THE PACIFIC ISLANDS

In many respects, the "classic" examples of chiefdoms which form the basis for archaeological models of such societies are the late prehistoric and historic island polities of Polynesia. Indeed, studies of such chiefdoms by ethnologists Firth (1959) and Sahlins (1958) have provided analogs for prehistoric ranked societies around the world. The key difference between Polynesian chiefdoms and their European Bronze Age or Mississippian counterparts is the fact that they arose in circumscribed island habitats and not in continental settings. Competition among small polities was often very intense, yet the topography of many islands inhibited expansion and consolidation into larger units.

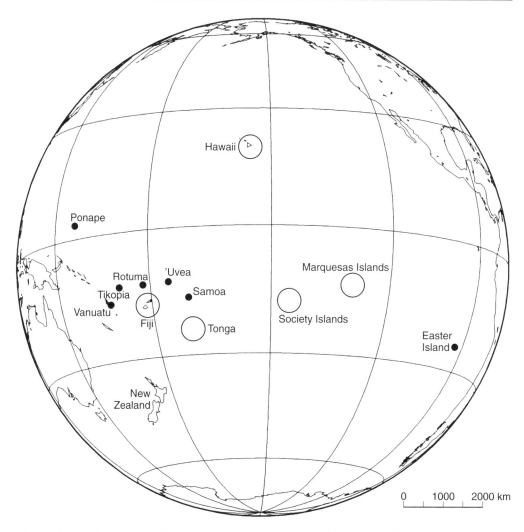

Figure 7.15 Map of South Pacific showing locations of key islands and island chains mentioned in this chapter.

The settlement of the Pacific Islands between 3000 and 1000 years ago was the final element in the prehistoric human diaspora which colonized the entire globe except for remote oceanic islands and the polar ice caps. Shortly after 2000 BC, makers of a pottery type known as Lapita ware began to undertake open-water voyages from their original homeland in Melanesia (Kirch 1997). It seems clear that these voyages were not accidental but rather were the result of deliberate upwind navigation using double-hulled sailing canoes (Irwin 1992). Between 1600 and 100 BC, Lapita makers settled western Polynesia and established settlements on Vanuatu, Fiji, Tonga, and Samoa. Lapita peoples brought a complex economy which included maritime resources, indigenous island trees, domestic pigs and chickens, and imported root and tree crops like breadfruit, taro, and yams. They transformed the landscapes of the Pacific islands and introduced commensal species like the Pacific rat, geckos, and skinks (Kirch 1997: 218–19). Extensive exchange systems in obsidian, ceramics, oven stones, and shell ornaments linked Lapita communities throughout western Polynesia.

Subsequently, Micronesia and eastern Polynesia were settled by the descendants of the Lapita peoples, with the Marquesas occupied about AD 1 and Hawaii by about AD 400 (Irwin 1992: 89). Despite claims by the Norwegian adventurer Thor Heyerdahl that it was settled by voyagers from South America, the archaeological record of Easter Island clearly indicates that it was colonized by people from Polynesia during the first centuries AD. New Zealand, due to its location downwind from the major axes of navigation across Polynesia, was settled relatively late, between AD 1000 and 1200.

Following the establishment of small communities on the Pacific islands, steady population growth led to the emergence of increasingly stratified polities. Earle (1997) traces the development of chiefdoms in Hawaii, probably the most populous of the Polynesian island groups. After a period of relatively slow demographic increase between AD 400 and 1200, population grew rapidly and reached a peak of 160,000 or more by about AD 1500, whereupon it stabilized or even declined slightly. At the same time, the Hawaiian landscape was transformed as the native forests were cleared and irrigated pond-fields for taro, orchards, fish-ponds, and gardens were established. Monumental stone-walled enclosures known as *heiau* were built, which required considerable labor and resulted in the construction of a sacred landscape (Kolb 1994). Similar developments, although with considerable variation, can be observed in other Polynesian archipelagos. For example, the stone *marae* of Tahiti and the Society Islands are the analogs of the Hawaiian *heiau* (Graves and Sweeney 1993).

Polynesian social organization has been characterized as a "conical clan" in which rank is measured as distance from a central line of descent through primogeniture (Sahlins 1958). The early settlers of Polynesia are believed to have arrived with moderate ranking and the concept of a chief, but the descendants of the original settlers on each island or island group developed chiefdoms with their own particular characteristics. In general, the larger the island the more elaborate the social and political organization. On smaller islands, such as Tikopia, the elite were not strongly differentiated from commoners (Firth 1959), whereas in larger islands, such as Hawaii, paramount chieftaincies emerged after about AD 1200. Archaeological indicators of status differences include the construction of mortuary structures and ceremonial structures like *heiau* and *marae* and the establishment of land divisions running between inland points and the coast.

Competition between chiefly polities appears to have been widespread and some appear to have had territorial designs on the land occupied by their neighbors and even on nearby islands. One example is the Tongan maritime chiefdom, which attempted to extend its political control to other islands (Sand 1993). One of these islands was 'Uvea, about 800 kilometers to the north. After Tongan chiefs arrived on 'Uvea shortly after AD 1400, they created a strong centralized political system and constructed fortifications and monumental buildings. They also introduced the practice of large burial mounds in which the elite were interred.

On a number of islands, some integration above the level of the chief occurred. Thegn Ladefoged (1993) has examined the chiefly polities of Rotuma, an isolated island about 485 kilometers north of Fiji. In protohistoric times, the island was divided into seven districts of varying productivity, each of which was led by a chief. Several island-wide leadership positions also existed: the *fakpure* or secular ruler and the *sau* or sacred ruler of the chiefs. The *sau* and his entourage moved around the island from district to district. The interesting aspect of Rotuman *sau* was that they were more likely to come from districts which had relatively low resource productivity, which is somewhat counterintuitive. Ladefoged explains this by suggesting that they had greater motivation to attain and maintain their positions than did chiefs from the more productive districts, who could be content with expressing their powers locally.

Perhaps the most complex polities in prehistoric Polynesia were those of Tonga and Hawaii. They differ considerably in their environmental settings. In the Tongan archipelago, the islands are small, yet permitted significant populations to build up; in Hawaii, the main islands are larger, yet still heavily populated. The Tongan islands lack permanent watercourses, so irrigation is impossible, but in Hawaii, the diversion of streams permitted the development of large (but relatively simple) irrigation systems. Finally, Tonga is subject to major environmental catastrophes, such as cyclones and drought, whereas the Hawaiian islands are less prone to such events. Tonga is situated among other archipelagoes, whereas Hawaii is relatively distant from other major island groups. Tonga was settled several millennia earlier than Hawaii, and thus social structures had a longer time to develop there.

Yet despite these underlying differences, Hawaii and Tonga developed relatively similar structures of political organization (Kirch 1984: 262–3; Kirch 1994; Earle 1997: 210). In both cases, there were both sacred and secular chiefly offices, although in Tonga this structure is somewhat more formalized. Administrative and decision-making structures were also very similar. In both cases, annual tribute was paid to the ruling elite. The key contrasts lie in the foundations of the chiefly power. The Tonga polity was a centralized "maritime chiefdom" which was based on the acquisition and control of prestige goods and the demand for tribute from the outlying islands which it dominated (Kirch 1984: 241). In Hawaii, by contrast, the chiefs controlled an intensive terrestrial subsistence system based on irrigation, dryland terrace farming, and fishponds which formed the core of a staple-finance economy (Kirch 1994; Earle 1997: 210). The surplus from this economy could then be used to finance military and ceremonial activities which amplified the power and prestige of the chiefs.

TERMINAL AND TRANSIENT CHIEFDOMS

This quick tour through several prehistoric societies in which hereditary differences in status, power, and wealth emerged and persisted has shown the considerable global variation in how such differences are manifested archaeologically. In some parts of the world, mortuary remains are the primary evidence for social differentiation, while elsewhere the modification of the landscape and the construction of monumental buildings is the hallmark of power. Hierarchies of site sizes are important in some regions, while in others these are nonexistent. Within regions there is also variation. Rich Únĕtice exists adjacent to middle-class Mierzanowice in central Europe, while not far from Monte Albán are the simple chiefdoms of the Rio Verde.

Yet there are also many similarities. For example, control and manipulation of access to the supernatural world seems to be one common way for elites to display and maintain their power. The Lords of Cahokia may have had quite a bit in common with the Lords of Stonehenge and the Lords of Chavín, although separated by oceans and millennia. Creation of a ritual *landscape*, not just one or two buildings, was critical to this. Stonehenge makes no sense without the hundreds of barrows and the Avenue, but when viewed as a visible element of such a complex of human ceremonial activity, its significance becomes clearer. The instability of individual chiefdoms is nearly universal, despite the long-term persistence of such pre-state societies in some regions. Even where such societies persisted, such as in Europe, different areas wax and wane in their wealth and prestige. Elsewhere, this instability became the foundation for the further development of states.

Thus, we can identify two trajectories of these societies which we have loosely characterized here as chiefdoms. In North America, Europe and the Pacific, despite the oscillations in which individual polities developed and collapsed, the overall system was very durable and probably would have persisted almost indefinitely. As we will see in the next chapter, contact with external states can actually amplify the power of chiefs, until those states actually decide to encroach territorially on the chiefdoms. Elsewhere, as in Mesoamerica, Andean South America and China, this pre-state era of nascent social inequality was transitory and lasted only a few centuries, spinning out of control into progressively denser concentrations of population, more elaborate administrative hierarchies, and expansionary militarism. Elsewhere, in cases discussed in the next chapter, chiefs were hardly in evidence at all, with states established almost overnight (in archaeological time) on the basis of transegalitarian autonomous villages.

A final note in this general consideration of emergent differences in status, power, and wealth is that these attributes of the elite may not always be what they seem. Archaeologists, as do many other social scientists, have tended to assume that power and status in such societies are absolute, that they are pervasive, and that they are often greater than what is generally acknowledged by the society and what is perceptable archaeologically. We are reminded, however, of the limits of status and power by the ethnographic studies of Glenn Petersen on the island of Ponape (Petersen 1982, 1993), who found that there was a difference between the hierarchical principles of political organization and what actually happened in practice. On Ponape, members of a community may express egalitarian values in one context and hierarchical ones in another (Petersen 1993: 338). Polities fission as a result of internal strains, and a leader's power may be fragile. In this case, and probably in many prehistoric ones as well, status and power of the elite is *less* than what the societal ideology recognizes. Thus we should not get carried away in treating prehistoric ranked societies as anything more than small-scale polities in which there may have been multiple pathways to status, power, and wealth and in which leadership was often tenuous.

FURTHER READING

Societies which have hereditary differences in status, power, and wealth have received consider-able anthropological and archaeological attention since the 1960s. A highly readable recent volume which discusses several of them in comparative perspective is *How Chiefs Come to Power: the Political Economy in Prehistory* by Timothy Earle (1997). An earlier, but highly influential anthology of papers on chiefly societies is *Specialization, Exchange, and Complex Societies*, edited by Elizabeth Brumfiel and Timothy Earle (1987). Earle also edited *Chiefdoms: Power, Economy, and Ideology* (1991), another important collection of papers. The 1995 *Foundations of Social Inequality* volume edited by T. Douglas Price and Gary Feinman, cited in the previous chapter, is also relevant to this discussion. Craft specialization was the focus of a 1995 volume edited by Bernard Wailes entitled *Craft Specialization and Social Evolution*. Early metallurgy is more often discussed from a scientific rather than a social perspective, and the reader wishing to learn more should consult R. F. Tylecote's 1987 *The Early History of Metallurgy in Europe*.

Regional studies of the archaeology of early ranked societies are too numerous to catalog com-prehensively, so the following list is simply a sample of what is available. For Europe, the authoritative volume remains *The Bronze Age in Europe* by John Coles and Anthony Harding (1979), although an updated edition would be welcome. For an overview of developments in the British Isles, Michael Parker Pearson's 1993 *English Heritage Book of Bronze Age Britain* is a good place to start, complemented by John Barrett's *Fragments from Antiquity: An Archaeology of Social Life in Britain, 2900–1200 BC* (1994). For interior continental Europe, the reader should consult the review article "Settlement and social change in central Europe, 3500–1500 BC" by Stephen Shennan, which appeared in the *Journal of World Prehistory*, vol. 7, pp. 121–61 (1993a). John O'Shea's *Villagers of the Maros* (1996) is an important case study in this area. An important vol-ume on southwestern Europe, a region not discussed at length in this book, is *Emerging Complexity: the Later Prehistory of South-east Spain, Iberia, and the West Mediterranean* by Robert Chapman (1990).

Two important collections of papers on the emergence of social ranking in Mesoamerica are *The Cloud People: Divergent Evolution of the Zapotec and Mixtec Civilizations* edited by Kent Flannery and Joyce Marcus (1983), and *Regional Perspectives on the Olmec* edited by Robert Sharer and David Grove (1989). Further south, Robert Drennan's 1995 review article, "Chiefdoms in northern South America," appeared in the *Journal of World Prehistory*, vol. 9, pp. 301–40.

Discussions of the emergence of differences in status, power, and wealth in Andean South America are clouded by the fact that some scholars promote societies rapidly to the level of states while others see developments in more gradual terms. *Early Settlement and Subsistence in the Casma Valley* by Shelia and Thomas Pozorski (1987), *Life and Death at Paloma. Society and Mortuary Practices in a Preceramic Peruvian Village* by Jeffrey Quilter (1989), *and Chavín and the Origins of Andean Civilization* by Richard Burger (1992) will give the reader the flavor of the issues involved.

A detailed discussion of the emergence of complex societies on the northwestern coast of North America can be found in *The Prehistory of the Northwest Coast* by R. G. Matson and Gary Coupland. Turning to the southeastern part of the continent, the last decade has seen an explo-sion of monographs and edited volumes on Mississippian chiefly societies. The early develop-ment of Mississippian society is treated by the papers in Bruce D. Smith's *The Mississippian*

Emergence (1990). Peter Peregrine's *Mississippian Evolution: a World-System Perspective* (1992) presents another view of Mississippian development, while David Anderson's *The Savannah River Chiefdoms* contains a valuable discussion of the oscillation of power in chiefly societies. *Political Structure and Change in the Prehistoric Southeastern United States* edited by John Scarry (1996) contains a series of important baseline essays on Mississippian society in various regions, while the chapters in *Mississippian Communities and Households* edited by J. Daniel Rodgers and Bruce D. Smith (1995) characterize Mississippian settlements. Jon Muller's *Mississippian Political Economy* (1997) provides in-depth discussion of Mississippian trade and production. Papers in *The Southeastern Ceremonial Complex: Artifacts and Analysis* edited by Patricia Galloway (1989) discuss this enigmatic phenomenon, while James A. Brown's recent volume *The Spiro Ceremonial Center* (1996) treats the ceremonial features and artifacts from the extreme western edge of the Mississippian realm. Volumes on individual Mississippian sites are too numerous to catalog here. Cahokia has been the subject of two important recent books: *Cahokia: Domination and Ideology in the Mississippian World*, edited by Timothy Pauketat and Thomas Emerson (1997) and *Cahokia and the Archaeology of Power*, also by Thomas Emerson (1997). *Excavations at the Lake George Site, Yazoo County, Mississippi, 1958–1960* by Stephen Williams and Jeffrey Brain (1983) places a smaller Mississippian center in its regional context, while *Moundville's Economy* is the title and subject of a 1991 book by Paul Welch. By the time this book appears, additional volumes on Mississippian archaeology will surely have appeared.

Kwang-Chih Chang's *The Archaeology of Ancient China* (3rd edn, 1986) still provides the authoritative archaeological discussion of the emergence of complex society in eastern Asia. It can be complemented by important recent articles by Li Liu, "Settlement patterns, chiefdom variability, and the development of early states in North China," *Journal, of Anthropological Archaeology*, vol. 15, pp. 237–88 (1996), and by Anne Underhill, "Variation in settlements during the Longshan Period in northern China, *Asian Perspectives*, vol. 33, pp. 197–228 (1994).

There are many volumes on the emergence of chiefly societies in Polynesia, from prehistory to the present. *The Evolution of the Polynesian Chiefdoms* by Patrick Vinton Kirch (1984) provides a good baseline, while the essays in *The Evolution and Organization of Prehistoric Society in Polynesia* edited by M. W. Graves and R. C. Green (1993) give additional archaeological detail.

[8] EARLY STATES AND CHIEFDOMS IN THE SHADOW OF STATES

CHAPTER SYNOPSIS

INTRODUCTION

The final chapter of prehistory in many parts of the world saw the emergence of a variety of new configurations of human society. For most readers of this volume, even though some may study simpler societies, the state is the organizational structure with which they have the most direct familiarity. A companion volume in this series (*The Beginnings of Civilization*, by Robert

Wenke) will discuss the rise of states in greater detail, so the focus in this chapter will be to situate this development in the context of the overall sweep of prehistory and to describe several cases of complex chiefdom societies which functioned in the shadow of states. In these latter cases, the proximity of the states triggered interesting structural developments in the economic and political structure of neighboring areas.

STATES, CIVILIZATION, URBANISM, AND WRITING

In this chapter, I will discuss societies with a level of organizational complexity and cultural sophistication beyond the transegalitarian societies and chiefdoms which were described earlier. To characterize them, archaeologists have used a variety of overlapping and complementary concepts, and before proceeding it will be necessary to unravel them. Such concepts include "the state," "civilization," and "urbanism." Another term widely used in modern archaeology in an effort to avoid endless debates over whether or not a particular society is a state or has cities is "complex society," although it is an obvious redundancy, for there is no society from Pleistocene bands onward which is not complex in some way. It will be avoided here as much as possible.

CIVILIZATION

"Civilization" is a cultural term, which has a long and distinguished history of use among archaeologists. It identifies a society which has emerged, by virtue of some suite of characteristics, as belonging to a small group of archaeologically-visible and spatially-extensive peoples of later prehistory who had produced some degree of monumental construction and sophisticated culture. Unfortunately, there is no consensus about what actually constitutes a civilization. In the early 1950s, V. Gordon Childe identified ten characteristics of a civilization which for many years provided a checklist for archaeologists. Childe's criteria included permanent settlement in dense aggregations, nonagricultural specialists, taxation and wealth accumulation, monumental public buildings, a ruling class, writing techniques, predictive science, artistic expression, trade for vital materials, and a decline in the importance of kinship. As we have seen in preceding chapters, many of these traits – such as trade, craft specialization, and wealth accumulation – are often associated with societies which we would consider not to be civilizations but rather smaller-scale polities or transegalitarian communities. Others are virtually impossible to document, such as predictive science. Many of the rest are vague concepts, such as ruling class and artistic expression, which also have precursors deep in prehistory. Finally, writing is a key trait, but not all civilizations were literate.

An archaeological focus on civilizations is understandable. After all, most people in the twentieth century do live under some form of civilized society, or at least one which has the organizational complexity of a state, and it is natural to try to understand the factors that result in the formation of such societies. Classical archaeology and ancient history have had an almost exclusive focus, by definition, on literate civilizations, so there is a large segment of the archaeological community which has chosen to concentrate on the states of later antiquity. Nonetheless, the fascination with civilizations needs to be tempered by an understanding that they reflect only recent configurations of long prehistoric sequences of development, and a conscious consideration of the biases that leak in as a result of such a focus is necessary. Ruth Tringham (1974) discussed these biases inherent in the notion of "civilization" with specific reference to Europe, but I believe that these concerns can be generalized globally.

The classification of a society as "civilized" implies that it is in contrast to other societies that are not. In an objective analytical framework, there is nothing wrong with this, but too often the vision of archaeologists becomes clouded with enhancing the status of the people they study. They become like the ancient Greeks and Romans, who described their societies as civilized in contrast to the barbarians of temperate Europe. Such an approach tends to exaggerate the differences between civilizations and their uncivilized neighbors and obscures the similarities. In reality, civilizations and their neighbors may have more in common than might be apparent from their own ancient writings or from the view of the modern archaeologists who study them.

Archaeologists rarely use the word "progress" explicitly, but it is implicit in many analytical frameworks, including quite possibly the one taken in this book. Taken uncritically, however, the notion of progress encourages value judgements that favor civilizations and assumes that barbarians would be keen to adopt innovations which would bring them closer to that state. There is a prevailing notion of "high" and "low" cultures, with the high ones having more to offer the low ones than vice versa. As we will see below, non-civilized societies in proximity to states often eagerly adopted the superficial trappings of fine objects and architectural styles, but made a conscious choice not to adopt complex social and political structures until they were compelled to do so either by invasion or by local developments. At the same time, representatives of states who lived among these non-civilized groups often became "barbarized," rather than having the opposite effect of "civilizing" the natives.

Finally, some scholars seem to feel that societies which were not civilized are less interesting than those who achieved civilization and statehood. A corollary to this is that developments on the pathway to civilization are often considered to be more interesting than those which were off the path. Such a bias surely has skewed regional patterns of archaeological research. For example, South American archaeology has been weighted heavily towards a small segment of the Andean coast and highlands, and the complex chiefdoms of Amazonia and northern South America are only now coming to be recognized as significant also. It is essential to realize that it is as important to understand why the people of a particular region elected *not* to develop more complex organizational forms as it is to study the development of states and civilizations.

When subjected to archaeological study, the interactions between civilizations and their barbarian neighbors turn out to have been remarkably complex. Frontiers between societies were unexpectedly open and porous, and people and information passed freely back and forth. There was often technological parity between civilizations and their neighbors, with the key difference being not only organizational structures on a societal scale but also smaller-scale organization and authority. The crucial areas in which these organizational differences are manifested are in commerce and in warfare. A merchant who has ready access to supplies of goods and who has sufficient knowledge to predict demands has a great advantage over the trader who operates on the periphery of the economic system. An army organized into disciplined sub-units under unquestioned authority has a clear advantage in a campaign of conquest over a disorganized group with ineffective leadership. These factors were often decisive in the long-range outcome of interactions between civilizations and their barbarian neighbors.

Defining "civilization" has proven so elusive, however, that archaeologists have tried to focus on organizational characteristics. Two particular ones which deserve attention are urbanism and the notion of a state. Again, these pose difficulties, for not all states are urban, and it is unclear whether some early urban societies can truly be called states.

URBANISM AND ITS ALTERNATIVES

Urbanism means having cities which are functionally more than simply agglomerations of people. Although it may appear intuitively obvious, there is little consensus as to what actually constitutes a "city." In English, the term tends to be used relatively loosely, with no clear separation between it and "town," whereas in other languages there are very clear meanings attached to "Stadt" and "cité," for example. In archaeology, there have been attempts to generate useful generalized definitions of cities, which almost always end up becoming conflated with the criteria for civilizations outlined above. For example, Clyde Kluckhohn defined a city as a settlement with over 5000 inhabitants with a written language and monumental ceremonial centers. George Erdosy (1988: 5) has defined cities as "containers of institutions that are required for the maintenance of increasingly complex and inegalitarian societies."

With a nod towards Childe's criteria for civilization, Coningham (1995) states that a city "consist(s) of (1) a large settlement with (2) a degree of internal planning and (3) public architecture (4) at the top of a settlement hierarchy and (5) encircled by defences. Its inhabitants should have access to (6) a script, (7) craft specialization, (8) long-distance trade and (9) a subsistence strategy capable of raising the carrying capacity of the surrounding area in order to support (10) the increasing population." I would propose to eliminate the references to defenses, craft specialization, and long-distance trade from the above definition, since all those are present clearly in antecedent and clearly non-urban peoples around the world. Reference to a "script" also complicates things, because if enforced rigorously, it would eliminate the later Andean civilizations who built such cities as Cuzco.

It is important to have a clear, yet generalizable, definition of a city in order to facilitate archaeological discourse. Yet these traits did not exist in a societal vacuum. For a society to be considered truly "urban," the agglomerations of population must play a clear role in an interaction with a much larger territory and must be sustainable over a period of more than a few generations. Archaeologists frequently attempt to extend the concept to embrace settlements in societies which were certainly *not* urban in character. For example, Mississippian Cahokia has been termed a "city" (Fowler 1975) or even a "capital" of a state (O'Brien 1989, 1991), but despite the colloquial use of the term "downtown" for the central precinct of the site by archaeologists, it really was neither a city or a capital of a state polity (Emerson 1997). Perhaps it might have become one, had the unstable chiefdom form of political organization not doomed it to collapse within a relatively short time.

THE STATE

Societies are characterized as states almost exclusively on their organizational properties, to the extent that these can be inferred from the archaeological record. Elizabeth Brumfiel (1994b: 1) defines states as

> powerful, complex, institutionalized hierarchies of public decision-making and control. They are created to implement the relations of production in stratified societies and to mediate conflict between diverse economic interest groups. Maintaining economic organization is a primary function of all state hierarchies, and this function is the key to political power for state personnel.

She differentiates between tributary states and capitalist states. In the former, elites use their coercive power to extract goods and services from their subjects, while in the latter markets determine how wealth is generated and accumulated. In tributary states, the personnel of the state are directly involved in the extraction and accumulation of surplus goods and services, while in the capitalist state, firms and other such enterprises provide the means for generating wealth and state personnel are more involved in resolving conflicts and regulating competition.

Most early states fall into the category of tributary states, which is logical since this can be seen as an extension of the chiefdom form of political economy discussed in the previous chapter. In the pre-state societies households are persuaded, coerced, or manipulated into producing extra to support elites, but their allegiances can wane and shift, producing the oscillatory character of chiefdoms described earlier. In tributary states, however, state personnel directly intervene in the household economy and extract surplus production through overt means such as taxation and corveé, backed by force.

Archaeological discussions of state formation tend to focus on the same sorts of forces that attend the emergence of elites in chiefdoms and similar societies: population growth, trade and craft specialization, centralization of decision making, and leadership in warfare. If this was all there was to it, then states would simply have been larger-scale chiefdoms. At some point in state formation a transition occurs from the ephemeral sort of access to power and wealth that characterize chiefdoms to the development of a powerful elite sustained by the administrative and bureaucratic apparatus that runs the economy, plans the cities, marshals the armies, and promotes an ideology. This transition has received inadequate archaeological attention, but it is the key to understanding how states emerge from antecedent societies.

More archaeological attention has been focused on the *collapse* of states, since a few spectacular examples are known from prehistory (e.g., Tainter 1988; Yoffee and Cowgill 1988). Catastrophes or other, less spectacular, environmental calamities are popular explanations, but these usually do not stand up to critical scrutiny. Depletion of key resources is also often invoked, essentially a humanly-induced environmental calamity. Invasion by barbarians and internal conflicts have their proponents, especially since such factors have played a role in the decline of historically-known civilizations. In most cases, however, the collapse of states can be attributed to a complex set of factors, often beginning with economic stresses and fissures which lead the society to be vulnerable to external threats and internal malaise. Just as states can be defined primarily as economic organizations, the central role of economic issues in their collapse is perhaps the most promising framework for analysis (Tainter 1988).

THE ARCHAEOLOGY OF LITERACY

The archaeology of many civilizations and states is the archaeology of literacy and the effects of literacy. There are exceptions to this, Peru and the early states of sub-Sahara Africa being the most notable, but one of the defining characteristics which separates many states from their neighbors is a readable language recorded using a consistent notation system. The ability to write is also the foundation of history, so the emergence of written sources begins the end of prehistory. It is not a sharp division, however, for until recently the only people whose history was recorded were the elite. Commoner society was less adequately recorded, and some groups who were even worse off (for example, African slaves in ante bellum southeastern United States) remained essentially prehistoric in their lack of recorded history.

The earliest formal writing systems appeared in Mesopotamia about 3300 BC in the form of pictographic signs on clay tablets. These had been preceeded by "proto-writing" systems which involved clay "tokens" that probably served some accounting purpose (Schmandt-Besserat 1978, 1992). The Sumerian tokens are small geometrical shapes such as discs, half-moons, and cones, which were often incised and frequently found in clay pouches, or "envelopes." On the envelopes are impressions, often made by the tokens themselves. Some scholars, particularly Denise Schmandt-Besserat, see these impressions as the roots of later Sumerian writing, whereas it is also possible to take the position that these are merely tallies or package-tracking devices whose development accompanied the earliest pictographs on clay tablets (Robinson 1995).

Writing systems subsequently emerged in many other parts of the world, but there is no evidence to suggest that other systems were derived in any way from the Mesopotamian cuneiform script. Each has a distinctive set of signs, media, and initial purposes. In Mesopotamia, and probably in the Indus valley, the initial purpose of the script was economic, to record trans- actions and track goods. Only later did Mesopotamian texts evolve into what can be considered literature and to record non-economic activity. Egyptian writing was hieroglyphic, consisting of a vocabulary of pictograms and signs organized into syllables. It appears on many different portable and stationary objects, and from the beginning it was used to document a variety of reli- gious rituals, historical and quasi-historical events, and personal lives of the elite. In the New World, Maya writing was also hieroglyphic and syllabic, but totally unlike that of Egypt. Mayan writing focused on political events, docu- menting the achievements of rulers and tracking time through an elaborate calendrical notation.

Writing and literacy have dramatic effects on a society (Goody 1986: 171–85). One of the most significant is that they transform the ephemeral character of transactions conducted on an oral basis to ones which are docu- mented. While administratively this may be desirable, socially such docu- mentation can have dramatic consequences, since no longer can the facts of a matter be manipulated, changed, and forgotten to accommodate particular circumstances. Tradition and customs become laws and regulations, while memory and sentiments are discounted in favor of authoritative written evidence. Such authority and institutional memory can serve as the platform for rapid organizational change.

Yet authoritative written evidence can also be manipulated, and it is pre- cisely because it is authoritative that such manipulation can have significant social consequences. For example, the hieroglyphic writing of the early Mesoamerican states consisted almost exclusively of "political information set in a calendrical framework" (Marcus 1976: 43). Each leader would dis- play inscriptions advertising his accomplishments, presumably aware that his successor would conduct the same exercise. The goal was not so much to create history for the future but instead to produce propaganda for the present. Such authoritative presentation of the ruler's accomplishments amplified his authority beyond anything possible in a pre-literate society.

Literacy is also a vehicle for the further differentiation of society, perhaps even an accelerant in this process. The ability of some members of the elite to read and to write enabled them to play an even more important role in the management of complex economic and administrative transactions. Literacy, especially when combined with elite genealogy, would render an individual particularly powerful. Yet it also may have provided a way for commoners who could somehow acquire mastery of written communication to join the elite classes, thus providing a way for individuals not born to elite lineages to obtain the privileges and benefits of elite membership.

A key question, which remains unanswered, concerns the extent of literacy in early state societies. Just how many people could read and write? Were there only a few who were fully literate and a larger number which could recognize certain signs and glyphs in order to comprehend basic information? Or were there a small number of scribes who handled all the writing and reading on behalf of the elite? Such questions may be beyond the ability of archaeologists to answer, but they must be taken into account when models of the role of literacy in the development of early states are advanced.

EARLY STATES AND THEIR ROOTS

Many volumes have been devoted to the emergence of civilization and early state societies, and it is impossible to discuss them adequately in a few pages below. The purpose of including them here is to gain some closure in the discussion of the prehistoric record of many parts of the world and to point towards recent literature which might be reliably consulted for further information. The focus here will be on the prehistoric roots of these historical and proto-historical states rather than a synopsis of their history.

Unfortunately, limitations on space preclude a discussion of early Mediterranean civilizations of the last two millennia BC. The Greek and Roman civilizations are well known historically, but their roots are prehistoric. They are sometimes viewed as not being "pristine" civilizations, since they were preceded by developments along the Nile and in the Near East, but they would not have developed as they did without a local foundation of complex chiefly polities. Ancient Greece is rooted in the Bronze Age polities of the Aegean and Crete, and ancient Rome owes as much to its local Iron Age precursors as it does to the Greeks. Valuable discussions of the prehistoric roots of Mediterranean civilizations have recently been published by Dickinson (1994), Castleden (1990), Bietti Sestieri (1997), Barker and Rasmussen (1998), and the authors of papers in the volume edited by Mathers and Stoddart (1994). The impact of these civilizations on the later prehistoric chiefdoms of temperate Europe is discussed below.

THE CITIES OF MESOPOTAMIA

Mesopotamia, the land between the Tigris and Euphrates rivers, lays claim to the title of the world's first urban civilization. The literature on Mesopotamian civilization and its neighbors could easily fill several libraries, so the brief review here is intended simply to provide a general characterization of early urban centers, their economic and social structure, and the impact of this civilization on its neighbors to the east and west. Study of early Mesopotamian civilization has been impeded severely since 1979, first with the exclusion of western scholars from Iran and subsequently with the battlefield conditions in southern Iraq. Prior to this period, however, there had been extensive excavations throughout this region, which have provided copious material for analysis when fieldwork has not been possible.

We last considered this region in chapter 6, in the discussion of Halafian settlements in the north and the 'Ubaid settlements in southern Mesopotamia (or Sumeria) during the sixth and early fifth millennia BC.

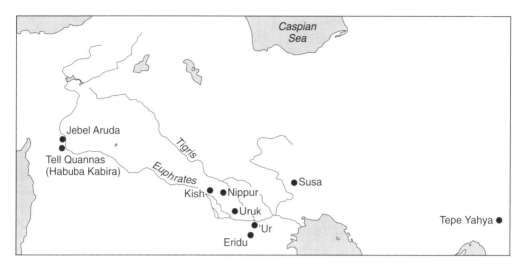

Figure 8.1 Map of Mesopotamia and Iranian Plateau showing key sites mentioned in this chapter.

These communities were characterized as "transegalitarian," suggesting that there were few, if any, indications of hereditary differences in access to status, power, and wealth. In the 'Ubaid settlement of Eridu, however, a series of structures appears to represent the beginnings of public architecture and formal public life.

During the late fifth millennium BC and continuing through the fourth millennium in southern Mesopotamia, there was a growing trend towards social differentiation and concentration of population in towns. Within about 1500 years there was a transition from many small autonomous farming hamlets to a few large urban polities. The period between about 4600 and 3200 BC is known as the Uruk period (calibrated dating, based on table 1 in Hole 1994; many researchers use uncalibrated dating, often showing this period as beginning much later), after the major site in southern Mesopotamia which will be discussed further below. Of greatest interest here is the Late Uruk period, from about 3600 BC onward. It is followed by the relatively short Jemdet Nasr period, which marks the transition to full-blown literate civilization and eventual dynastic rule. Shortly after 3000 BC, recorded history emerged from the mists of prehistory with the Sumerian King Lists that document dynastic lineages at several Mesopotamian cities.

THE DEVELOPMENT OF URBAN SOCIETY IN SUMERIA

The most striking feature of the archaeology of the fourth millennium BC in Sumeria is the number of new settlements on the alluvium of southern Mesopotamia, followed by the apparent depopulation of the countryside and the concentration of the population into a small number of villages and towns by the early part of the third millennium. This phenomenon was documented vividly by Robert M. Adams and Hans Nissen (1972) in their study

The Uruk Countryside and by other research. Many of these towns exhibit continuity from earlier settlements, as at Eridu, although others were new foundations. Natural population growth cannot account for such a rapid increase in population. Populations appear to have been drawn from a fairly large catchment, including northern Mesopotamia and from the plains of southwestern Iran. Regional nomadic populations may also have settled down in or near these towns. What drew all these people to the towns is unclear. Recently, Frank Hole (1994) has proposed that a series of environmental changes caused dislocations in 'Ubaid society which resulted in some displaced segments of the population becoming nomadic and others coalescing to form larger agglomerations on the alluvium of southern Mesopotamia.

By the second half of the fourth millennium BC, it is possible to speak of true cities and states in Mesopotamia and surrounding regions. Five stand out as principal centers: Uruk, Eridu, Ur, Nippur, and Kish. Unlike many of the other civilizations discussed in this chapter, in which the cities are the political and religious centers of large regional hinterlands, in Mesopotamia the borders between cities and the states they commanded are not widely separated. The early Mesopotamian state was a city-state, rather than an integrated pan-regional polity with a single capital and a number of subsidiary centers of political administration. Instead, the administration appears to have been concentrated in a multi-level hierarchy.

At the apex of this hierarchy appear to have been individuals with a mixture of religious and secular authority. The centrality of the temple, usually placed on a stepped pyramid known as a *ziggurat*, and its eventual enclosure by walls at many sites indicate that these were clearly precincts of the elite. The *ziggurats* and the temples on them were frequently rebuilt, such that over the course of the fourth millennium BC they towered over the urban centers in several of the larger sites. In addition to their ceremonial function, it appears that these temples served as storerooms and administrative centers for the accumulation and redistribution of agricultural goods and the oversight of craftsmen, construction projects, and trade. Until the advent of writing in Late Uruk and Jemdet Nasr times, however, it is very difficult to get to know the people involved in this administrative system. Susan Pollock (1992) notes that "fourth millennium *societies* have been credited with impressive achievements, but the *people* who constitute these societies have not."

THE GREAT CITY OF URUK

Uruk (whose modern name is Warka) occupies a special position in the study of early Mesopotamian cities. Quite a bit is known about the site, since German archaeologists have conducted research more or less continuously (except in wartime) on the site for a century. Uruk is by far the largest of the early Mesopotamian cities. The earliest settlement on the site took place in 'Ubaid times and through the fifth and fourth millennia BC continued to grow. By about 3200 BC, Uruk occupied an area of about 100 hectares, and the city continued to grow still more during the centuries that followed, reaching its maximum extent of about 400 hectares early in the third millennium BC.

The focal point of the early city of Uruk was its *ziggurat*, topped with a temple believed to have been dedicated to Anu, the sky god, on the basis of tenuous evidence from later periods. The White Temple, as it is called because of the gypsum plaster coating on its walls, was a large hall with two rows of rooms on each side and an altar at one end. By about 3000 BC, the *ziggurat* had reached a height of about 13 meters, and the temple at its top was clearly a shrine of major importance.

About half a kilometer to the east of the *ziggurat* was the precinct known as Eanna, which contains several monumental public structures laid out in a much different fashion. Although they were not raised on platforms, some of these buildings appear also to have been temples, one of which was built on a base of limestone blocks. The Eanna precinct was separated from the rest of the city by a wall (Nissen 1995: 799), and buildings here were torn down and rebuilt frequently.

In the refuse and demolition debris in the Eanna precinct, several thousand clay tablets with pictographs, the precursor of cuneiform writing, were found. These are economic tablets, not true texts. The pictographs that appear on them are a shorthand notation that records transactions by showing numbers, units of measurements, the product measured, accounting periods, names of officials, and similar information. Different materials and products appear to have had different counting systems. For example, a dot might mean ten when associated with sheep, six when associated with barley, and 18 when associated with fields (Robinson 1995: 65). The Uruk proto-writing deals with mundane numbers and quantities, not with beliefs, emotions, and great events.

The practice of making small clay tokens and sealing them in a clay envelope, along with the use of cylinder seals to mark these and other clay surfaces, became additional instruments of economic activity. Hans Nissen (1988, 1995) notes the rapid development of tablets, cylinder seals, and tokens in the last centuries of the fourth millennium BC and argues that these were the instruments of a highly bureaucratized administrative system. He also interprets the beveled-rim bowls that were mass-produced in Late Uruk times as being the product of a tightly-organized production system. In Nissen's view, the evidence reflects a hierarchically-structured economy whose roots lie early in Uruk times.

Central to this system was writing, which quickly moved around 3000 BC from the accounting pictographs described above to archaic texts. One important such text from the Jemdet Nasr period is a list of titles and professions in order of status, sometimes with three or four ranks in each job title (Nissen 1988: 80, 1995: 797). Over the next several centuries, this list was repeatedly copied, so it provides an important way for tracing the development of writing. The writing on the earliest versions was not yet the cuneiform script of later Mesopotamian history, but it was clearly a step beyond the economic tablets of Late Uruk times and closer to literacy as we conceive it today.

INTERNATIONAL CONTACTS OF EARLY SUMERIAN CIVILIZATION

The urban society which developed on the southern Mesopotamian alluvium did so in an environment which was amply supplied with clay, salt, water, and bitumen, but lacking in stone, timber, and metal deposits (Moorey 1993: 31). The Sumerians needed to sustain existing exchange systems and develop new ones if they were to have access to these materials. The axes of these systems ran north and west to Syria and Turkey, east to the plains and highlands of Iran, and southeast to the Persian Gulf. Of these, the principal direction from which these materials were procured was from the east, from Iran and eventually from as far as the Indus valley.

Documenting this trade is relatively straightforward, since the sources of raw materials are fairly easy to trace and Sumerian archaeological material is found at places distant from southern Mesopotamia. For example, Late Uruk material is found in northern Mesopotamia at sites which might be considered Sumerian colonies along the bend of the Euphrates (Potts 1994: 53; Algaze 1993: 23). These include Tell Quannas/Habuba Kabira and Jebel Aruda, which appear to have been urban-scale enclaves that served as "gateway communities" at critical nodes in communication routes and exchange networks (Algaze 1993: 61). Materials imported into Sumeria from these northern regions included timber, metals, flint, semiprecious stones, and common stones like basalt and limestone. Lapis lazuli found at Jebel Aruda came from sources on the Iran/Afghanistan border, attesting to the international character of this trade and the links of Uruk to the distant east (Postgate 1992: 208).

Sumer enjoyed particularly close connections with the neighboring emergent state of Susa in southwestern Iran. For much of the fourth millennium BC, in Middle and Late Uruk times, Susa was closely integrated with southern Mesopotamia. Yet in Jemdet Nasr times, there was a break with Mesopotamia and Susa went its own way to develop its own non-Sumerian written language and culture, known as Proto-Elamite, and to establish a trade route with the east, passing through Tepe Yahya in southeastern Iran. In the region of Tepe Yahya, carved chlorite vessels were produced for export to western markets by the middle of the third millennium BC (Kohl 1975).

There is also evidence of Sumerian activity on the Arabian peninsula during the fourth and third millennia BC (Potts 1993). Omani copper was supplied to Mesopotamia, which accounts for the finds of Mesopotamian imported pottery throughout the southern edge of the Persian Gulf and the Straits of Hormuz. Somewhere in this area was the legendary "Dilmun" to which there are numerous textual references in Sumerian documents.

HISTORY BEGINS AT SUMER?

Thus was titled a classic 1959 book by Samuel Noah Kramer but without the question mark. It is indeed true that history, as a written record of human affairs, has its roots in the late fourth millennium in southern Mesopotamia. The rich archaeological and textual evidence over the next several millennia has led to a focus on this region as the cradle of civilization. Yet to concentrate on Sumer at the expense of the rest of the still prehistoric Near East during the late fourth and early third millennia BC is to ignore other paths towards urban life which remain prehistoric, at least for a few centuries longer. The Sumerian model of very large, very nucleated cities during this period does not hold elsewhere in this region.

There is a tendency, as noted by Potts (1993: 201), to regard the areas located at a distance from the Tigris and Euphrates as peripheral to the sweep of history. From an archaeological perspective, however, Sumer is simply another example of a complex society, albeit the one which developed writing and thus is privileged by historians. Yet the Near East in the fourth millennium BC was a complicated mosaic of cultures. Even though there is evidence for contact among them, recent work has made clear that contact or proximity does not in itself mean that what is seen outside of Mesopotamia is derivative or secondary.

While large concentrated cities like Uruk were developing in the fourth millennium BC, a patchwork of urban and rural settlement systems developed to the west in the Levant (Falconer and Savage 1995). The period beginning about 3400 BC is traditionally taken as the start of the "Bronze Age," although bronze did not appear in this area until much later. During the millennium that followed, small-scale urbanism occurred primarily along the Mediterranean coastal plain, while further inland, small towns and villages independently followed their own courses of development. The urbanism seen in this area owes little, if anything, to the emergence of cities in Mesopotamia but rather has a distinctive local character of a number of small coastal towns interacting with villages in the uplands (Falconer and Savage 1995: 55). Despite contacts with Egypt and even direct Egyptian colonization in the southern Levant during the late fourth millennium BC, it appears that there was relatively little impact of these contacts on this region. Instead, it appears that a pattern of oscillations began in which the dominant roles shifted back and forth from rural to urban society (Joffe 1993: 92).

MESOAMERICAN CIVILIZATIONS

After the eclipse of the Olmec in the latter part of the first millennium BC, urban states emerged in three key areas in Mesoamerica: central Mexico, Oaxaca, and the Maya lowlands. This period is traditionally known as the "Classic" period, although new archaeological data continually points towards the fact that many of the characteristics of complex Mesoamerican societies had their antecedents in the Preclassic. Thus, the reader must keep in mind that these are convenient archaeological periodizations, not landmark advances in human cultural development. The beginning of the Classic period is conventionally considered to have been about AD 100 for central Mexico and Oaxaca, and AD 300 for the Maya area, although recent work has established that this is an artificial threshold and that Mesoamerican urbanism began several centuries earlier.

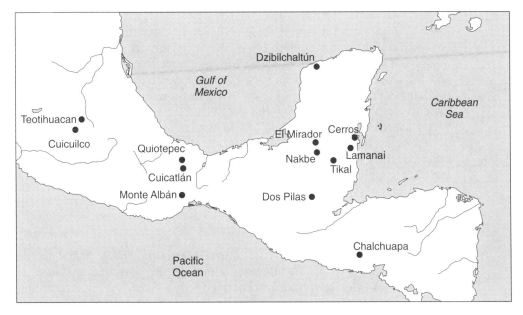

Figure 8.2 Map of Mesoamerica showing key sites mentioned in this chapter.

Such a chronology would imply that developments were somewhat later in the lowlands of Yucatán, Guatemala, and Belize than in the highland basins of Oaxaca and central Mexico. Indeed, many Mesoamerican archaeologists have taken this point of view (e.g., Sanders and Price 1968). Much of this perspective, however, can be attributed to the relatively limited knowledge about the Preclassic in the Maya lowlands, which has been remedied to some extent in recent years by investigations at sites like Cuello (Hammond 1991), Komchén (Andrew et al. 1984), and the discovery that the earliest architectural complexes at sites like El Mirador and Tikal were begun during the last few decades BC. At the larger sites, the Late Preclassic evidence is often buried under later construction, so archaeologists must dig deeply to find it.

Another key difference between the highlands and the lowlands is that in the former, the focus of urban society is on a single enormous site in each region – Teotihuacan in central Mexico and Monte Albán in Oaxaca – which dominates the archaeological record, while in the Maya region, there were many large sites of roughly equivalent size and importance, and many smaller sites in a variety of size ranges. This difference, and the fact that the Maya built their domestic structures out of relatively perishable materials, contributed to a view that the highland societies had an urban character and that the Maya were an anomalous non-urban civilization, with large monumental ceremonial centers and a dispersed rural population. Only recently has more detailed research shown that there were significant concentrations of population around the larger Maya sites which certainly place them in the category of "urban."

Although an important research problem, a detailed consideration of the question of why these civilizations eventually collapsed is beyond the scope of this volume. It is possible that the use of the term "collapse" is too dramatic. What is certain is that these civilizations flourished until the period between AD 700 and 800, whereupon they experienced significant transformations which resulted in the eclipse in importance of the major Classic sites and the emergence of new, and usually smaller, urban centers. In fact, the resultant polities that emerged from this transformation were even larger in their geographical extent than the previous Classic states, and have often been characterized as "empires." Even within regions, the transformation from Classic to Postclassic did not occur all at once, suggesting that the causes of the changes were internal, gradual, and local rather than external and catastrophic.

THE PLACE OF THE GODS

The emergence of state society in central Mexico is closely linked to the fortunes of the city of Teotihuacan, although the surrounding basin of the Valley of Mexico certainly contained other sites. At its maximum, Teotihuacan was simply the largest settlement in the New World, and it had political and economic ties throughout Mesoamerica. There are two major dimensions to Teotihuacan: the central ceremonial district and the surrounding residential compounds. At its center was the enormous "Pyramid of the Sun," 64 meters high and 210 meters square at the base. In front of the Pyramid of the Sun runs the major north–south axis of the city, the so-called "Avenue of the Dead," lined with tombs and ending at the Pyramid of the Moon, a very large structure in its own right. About 2000 residential compounds are known, each housing up to 100 people in a complex walled off from the adjoining street. Multiplying these figures provides the standard maximum population estimate of Classic period Teotihuacan of about 200,000 individuals (although this assumes full occupancy and the actual figure was probably closer to 150,000).

Teotihuacan was planned from the outset. Around 200 BC, the Valley of Mexico had many small villages in addition to the center of Cuicuilco (discussed above in chapter 7). By AD 1, Cuicuilco had been eclipsed, the villages depopulated, and Teotihuacan had emerged as the major center in the region (Pasztory 1997: 77). At this time, the Avenue of the Dead was laid out and the pyramids as well. All public buildings and residential compounds are laid out along the grid whose axis is formed by the Avenue of the Dead. Somewhat later, between AD 100 and 200, a rectangular enclosure known as the "Citadel" was built at the southern end of the Street of the Dead. Access to this enclosure was restricted, and two compounds called "palaces" were built inside it, along with the Pyramid of the Feathered Serpent. The interpretation of this complex is that it was the residence of a ruler and an administrative center (Pasztory 1997: 109). Excavations at this pyramid have revealed evidence of human sacrifice (primarily of young male warriors) and some very rich burials (Cowgill 1992: 211), suggesting that a powerful ruler occupied this compound (Pasztory 1997: 120).

An important feature of the residential compound districts are the craft workshops, many of which specialized in the manufacture of obsidian blades and ceramics. The obsidian artifacts were traded throughout Mesoamerica, as far as Yucatán and Guatemala. We also know that people from all over Mesoamerica traveled to Teotihuacan. For example, one group of compounds was occupied by traders from Oaxaca, who built their own tombs in the style of Monte Albán (Pasztory 1997: 101). Another neighborhood, the "Merchant's Barrio," was probably occupied by people from the Gulf of Mexico coast in Veracruz, who lived in round houses and brought with them their local pottery as well as Maya ceramics (Manzanilla 1997: 120–1).

At its peak, about half the population of the Valley of Mexico lived in Teotihuacan (Manzanilla 1997: 111). It was a planned community with the multiplicity of functions of a modern city: manufacturing center, political capital, spiritual center. Yet around AD 700, it collapsed and was destroyed, largely by fire. The reasons for the destruction remain mysterious. Millon (1988) offers a convincing functional explanation: bad administration and inefficient bureaucracy. Cowgill (1997: 156–7) suggests that a combination of belligerent neighbors and unhappy insiders could have caused the demise of the weakened and poorly-led city. Whatever the cause, the New World's largest city became a shadow of its former self within a few decades.

MONTE ALBÁN

We have already discussed the emergence of a society with marked differences in status and power in the Valley of Oaxaca in previous chapters. The logical consequence of this was its emergence as the center of a civilization known as the Zapotecs during the first millennium AD. As in the Valley of Mexico, Zapotec civilization was centered on a single very large site, Monte Albán, which appears to have functioned as the capital of a confederacy of chiefdoms at first, then assumed paramount power and authority and also extended its influence beyond the valley during the first centuries AD. Monte Albán never grew as large as Teotihuacan, having at its largest extent about AD 700 somewhere around 25,000 inhabitants (some estimates run higher). Nonetheless, it was certainly an impressive city with all the public construction, elite residences, and temples which characterize most of the early states discussed in this chapter.

Around the central plaza of Monte Albán, which measures 300 by 200 meters, are 20 pyramid platforms on which were built temples and elite residences. The rulers of Monte Albán probably lived in the residences on the north side of the plaza, built on a massive platform. In the plaza is a small structure, Building J, with an unusual heart-shaped (some say "arrow-shaped") ground plan, built sometime between 200 BC and AD 100. The walls of Building J are lined with about 50 stone panels, many of which had symbols for place-names and inverted human heads. Joyce Marcus (1983: 108, 1992) has suggested that these celebrate the conquest of localities in the hinterland of the Zapotec realm. An even larger single structure was the platform at the south side of the plaza which was built sometime after AD 300.

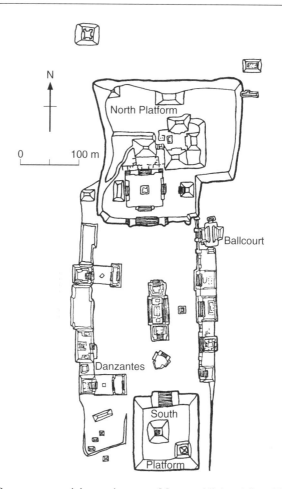

Figure 8.3 Core ceremonial precinct at Monte Albán (after Flannery 1983, figure 4.12).

Unlike Teotihuacan, the residential precincts of Monte Albán were not organized on a grid. Instead, the inhabitants lived on over 2000 terraces, each holding a few households, on the hillsides below the central plaza and on neighboring slopes. Fourteen "neighborhoods" have been identified through survey and excavation. Each of these consists of a group of mounds and plazas, presumably the residences of the lesser elite and ceremonial structures, around which are terraces on which the commoners lived (Blanton 1983: 129).

Early in the first millennium AD, the Zapotec lords of Monte Albán extended their influence and control over a large territory outside the valley. Exactly how far their territory reached is difficult to say. At Cuicatlán Cañada, a canyon about 80 kilometers north of Monte Albán, Redmond and Spencer (1983: 119) found large amounts of pottery similar to the characteristic Monte Albán ware, whereas 7 kilometers further north the pottery was characteristic of sites to the north. The fortified site of Quiotepec possibly marked the Monte Albán frontier in this region, at least until about AD 200.

The collapse of Monte Albán around AD 700 is still unexplained, although it was probably part of the general syndrome of the transformation of Mesoamerican society during this period. Specific local factors may have included overpopulation or the implosion of the fragile political system. After this time, a small resident population remained at Monte Albán, but political power shifted to a variety of smaller competing centers elsewhere in the valley.

THE LORDS OF THE JUNGLE

For decades, the prevailing view of Maya civilization was very romantic: a peaceful non-urban society of farmers presided over by priests who ruled from the great ceremonial centers between AD 300 and 800. The economic basis of Maya civilization was thought to be slash-and-burn agriculture, in which the jungle was cleared for short periods, then allowed to lie fallow for a much longer period to restore its fertility. Farmers from the rural hinterlands brought their produce to markets at the larger sites. The priests formed a benevolent theocracy, engaging in science and art. This idyllic New Age utopia was isolated from external influences and threats by the tropical rainforest.

We now know that this characterization of the ancient Maya was almost entirely wrong. The modern image of Maya civilization is far more secular and warlike. Their agricultural system was far more intensive, and the large sites are now known to have been the locations of substantial permanent settlement. The rainforest did not cut off trade among the Maya and with other parts of Mesoamerica. We also now know that Maya civilization emerged several centuries earlier than previously thought, during the final centuries BC. Several large sites with monumental public architecture appear to have developed and declined between 200 BC and AD 200, during the Late Preclassic period. These include El Mirador and Nakbe in Guatemala, Dzibilchaltún in Yucatán, Cerros and Lamanai in Belize, and Chalchuapa in El Salvador.

Several advances in archaeological research have contributed to this revision of our views of the Maya. First, surveys and excavations at the large ceremonial centers revealed substantial evidence of small domestic structures built from perishable materials which had not been previously recorded when archaeological attention focused on the pyramids and other large stone structures. These surveys have also identified fortification systems. Second, additional surveys and investigations using airborne, satellite, and space shuttle imagery have identified irrigated raised-field systems which fed these concentrations of people. What had been previously thought to be "plazas" have been revealed to have been garden plots. Third, advances in the decipherment of Maya glyphs have permitted the identification of specific rulers and the correlation of events with the Maya calendar. Finally, large-scale monumental complexes dating to the Late Preclassic have been exposed in the depths of the jungle, and the pyramids, temples, and ballcourts at these sites exhibit architectural sophistication similar to that found at later ruins.

One of the most important of these Late Preclassic centers is El Mirador, which was archaeologically unknown until the late 1960s due to its inaccessible location in the Petén jungle of Guatemala. In an area of about 16 square kilometers are several enormous architectural complexes and causeways (known as *sacbés*). At the core of the site are two clusters of architectural complexes, the West Group and the East Group, located about a kilometer apart. The largest architectural complex in the West Group, referred to as El Tigre, consists of a pyramid 55 meters high with three temples on top and other temples nearby. On one of the temples in the El Tigre complex are giant stucco masks with human and jaguar features that depict Mayan deities. In the East Group, the Danta complex was built on top of a natural hill, which gave it a total height of 70 meters. From the top of the Danta pyramid, one can look over the jungle canopy for a distance of 40 kilometers. From this central core, six causeways radiated out, which would have been important access routes during the summer rainy season. That such monumental complexes could have existed as early as they did would have been unthinkable 30 years ago. At the nearby site of Nakbé, monumental structures appear to have been built even earlier, so the jungle may hold still more secrets about the earliest Maya cities.

One of the major advances in Maya research has been the identification of early trading networks, since the procurement of status goods such as jadeite, marine shell, quetzal feathers, and obsidian was linked with the emergence of elites. The site of Cerros, on the Caribbean coast of Belize, is particularly significant (Robertson and Friedel 1986). It lies on Chetumal Bay near the mouths of the New River and Rio Hondo, which lead into the interior of Belize. Not only was it well-suited to engage in coastal trade between the salt-producing areas of Yucatán to the north and the source area of obsidian and jade in Guatemala and El Salvador to the south, but from this location goods could also move into the interior of Belize and northern Guatemala. Between 50 BC and AD 200, Cerros reached its maximum size, including a 5-hectare precinct of sophisticated monumental architecture located directly on the coast. The core settlement area was delimited by a canal-like depression which functioned as a reservoir, and a complex system of water management consisting of smaller ditches and depressions has been identified (Scarborough 1994: 190).

By the end of the second century AD, urban centers had been established throughout the lowlands of eastern Mesoamerica. They were the centers of small kingdoms whose ruling dynasties were based on patrilinear succession and which were closely identified with individual cities. A stela dated to AD 199 displays the first clear depiction of a Maya king performing the shamanic rituals of his office (Friedel 1992: 119). Maya rulers practiced ritual self-mutilation, often using sting-ray spines to pierce their tongues and foreskins, as they mediated between the supernatural world and their subjects. The commoners in Maya society lived in small household groups. Nearby were their kitchen gardens, while further away were the fields. The Maya landscape was intensively inhabited and used, particularly in the vicinity of the major centers.

As time went on, these Maya polities grew in size. For example, by the eighth century AD, Dos Pilas exercised hegemony over an area of nearly 4000 square kilometers in northwestern Guatemala (Demarest 1993). Yet an elaborate system of fortification ditches could not save the rulers of Dos Pilas from a revolt by their vassals, and internecine warfare ravaged the kingdom for the next century. Fortifications have come to light at many Maya sites, and the glyphs tell stories of conquest and sacrifice of captives. Yet Arthur Demarest (1992: 144) points out that defeat in warfare did not result in the political domination or territorial control of the loser by the winner. For example, after Tikal was defeated by Dos Pilas in AD 678, the next ruler of Tikal was not a vassal of the king of Dos Pilas, although the prestige of the latter was greatly enhanced.

During the final centuries of the first millennium AD, Maya society experienced the same transformation that befell the states in central Mexico and Oaxaca. Much effort was expended in the 1970s to try to explain the Maya collapse (see papers in Culbert 1973, for example). More recent work has highlighted the variability in the decline of the various Maya urban centers. For example, as centers in the south were collapsing, many in Yucatán were experiencing a renaissance. No single factor accounts for the demise of many of the great Maya cities, although a combination of military and political upheavals and environmental stresses appear to have played key roles.

EARLY CIVILIZATIONS OF THE ANDES

Following the decline of the widespread Chavín "phenomenon," Andean South America saw the emergence of a number of regional polities which bear many of the hallmarks of state societies. The period between 200 BC and AD 600 in Andean prehistory is known as the "Early Intermediate" and has attracted the attention of archaeologists (and, unfortunately, collectors and grave-robbers) with spectacular coastal mortuary remains which include remarkable gold artifacts. During this period, two important societies emerged in coastal Peru: the Moche on the north coast and the Nasca on the south coast. At the same time in the highlands, the Tiwanaku state which ultimately came to dominate the southern Andes began to take shape. The short discussion here cannot hope to provide any more than a brief introduction to these remarkable societies.

MOCHE AND THE CHIMU

The origins of the Moche state lie on the north coast of Peru between the Chicama and Casma valleys, where the seats of local polities like Pampa de las Llamas-Moxeke and Sechín Alto flourished a millennium earlier (see chapter 7 above). The Moche valley, from which this civilization takes its name, lies among this group of small rivers which drain the arid coastal plain. During the final centuries BC, this stretch of coast saw the emergence

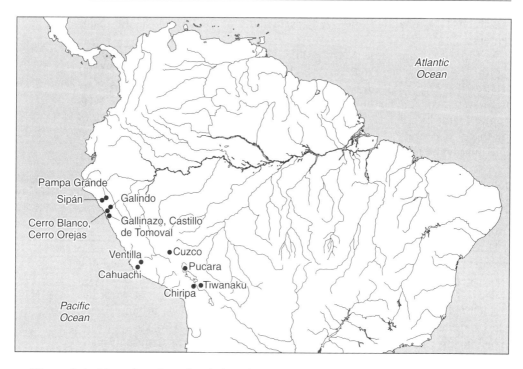

Figure 8.4   Map of northern South America showing key sites mentioned in this chapter.

of centers with elite residences, expansion of irrigation and road networks, and corrals for llama (which became a significant domesticate several centuries earlier in Chavín times). Clearly these represent elaborations of the pattern of small local polities in individual valleys which had begun much earlier. The challenge for archaeologists is to determine when the political power and religious authority of one of these local polities spilled over into neighboring valleys up and down the coast.

At the moment, the best candidate for this is the "Gallinazo culture," which flourished between about 200 BC and the first century AD and was centered on the Virú valley. In this small valley, a number of fortified sites were built on hilltops, including the Castillo de Tomoval, while elsewhere large adobe platforms were built of slabs of tempered mud and, later, mold-made mud bricks (Bawden 1996: 188–9). In the next valley to the north, the Moche, the large terraced site of Cerro Orejas was built about 25 kilometers inland, while closer to the coast the site of Cerro Blanco was founded. Similar developments occurred in neighboring valleys. Yet perhaps the most important site was found on the coastal plain of the Virú valley, the so-called Gallinazo Group. Bawden (1996: 191) characterizes the Gallinazo Group as an enormous town that covered over eight square kilometers in which clusters of houses were separated by courtyards and streets. Distributed throughout were platforms used by the administrators and their retainers for public functions, adjacent to elaborate residential complexes which contained rich burials. This site is believed by many to represent the capital of the first North Coast multi-valley state (Fogel 1993; Bawden 1996).

The action soon shifted north to the Moche valley, however. The connections between the Gallinazo and Moche cultures are unclear. Bawden (1996: 197) makes the argument that Moche culture was distinct from Gallinazo and developed in parallel to eclipse it by about AD 100. Yet Moche continues many of the characteristics of Gallinazo, especially the use of sun-dried mud bricks to build massive platforms which dominate dispersed clusters of residences. Continuity in ceramic design is also apparent (Fogel 1993). For the moment, what is clear is that the Moche elite – whatever their lineage – came to dominate the neighboring valleys and eventually expand their control along 600 kilometers of the Peruvian coast.

Located in this valley is the site of Cerro Blanco, which had been established in Gallinazo times. Located about 6 kilometers inland, the Moche people chose Cerro Blanco as their capital and built some remarkable structures, notably enormous flat-topped pyramids. The fancifully named Huaca del Sol (or "Shrine of the Sun," not to be confused with the pyramid of similar name at Teotihuacan in Mexico) is the largest mud-brick pyramid in the New World. It was built in eight stages, using over 140 million adobe bricks (Bawden 1996: 229), and currently covers an area of 160 by 340 meters (only a fraction of the original mound, eroded away by attempts to loot it by diverting a river in 1602) to a height of 40 meters. About 500 meters to the east is the smaller Huaca de la Luna ("Shrine of the Moon"), a somewhat more complicated structure of rooms, courts, and platforms about 25 meters high, using "only" about 50 million bricks. Charles Hastings and Michael Moseley (1975) have pointed out that the Huaca del Sol and Huaca de la Luna were built in segments from bricks marked with impressions denoting their makers. They believe that this system reflects a labor tax imposed by the Moche lords by which outlying communities were obligated to contribute work brigades, each of which made its own bricks, to building the structure. Such a practice of corveé continued throughout later Andean prehistory.

What purpose did the Huaca del Sol and Huaca de la Luna serve? They were clearly imposing public monuments which must have been dazzling in their prime. The Huaca del Sol had been covered with red plaster, while polychrome murals adorn the Huaca de la Luna. Modern architects distinguish between "foreground" and "background" buildings, the former which jump out at the beholder and the latter which blend in nicely with their surroundings. The two major structures at Cerro Blanco are certainly *foreground* buildings! Bawden (1996: 233) paints a picture of these platforms having been stages for various ceremonies which proclaimed the power of the elite. Their elite character is stressed by the presence in the areas between them of elite residences, courtyards, administrative platforms and structures, and burial chambers. In addition, on the terraces of the Huaca del Sol are traces of elite residences (and their rubbish) and wealthy burials. Bawden (1996: 233) points out that such domestic and mortuary use of the pyramid suggests that "it was the focus of the everyday activities of community integration, not merely a dominant symbol of power." Theresa Topic (1982: 268) suggests, however, that the highest elite actually lived in the brightly-painted rooms of the Huaca de la Luna complex.

Similar pyramid complexes were built throughout the north coast as Moche power spread south to the Huarmey valley and north to the Piura valley. Everywhere the Moche lords demonstrated their power and wealth in spectacular, even ostentatious, ways. At Sipán, in the Lambayeque valley, a remarkable tomb was discovered in 1987 (Alva and Donnan 1993). Two additional tombs eventually came to light, all within a complex of pyramids and platforms, a typical Moche administrative and elite residential complex which overlooked the river and the fields it irrigated. Tombs 1 and 2 are dated to ca. AD 250, while the third is somewhat earlier. Tombs 1 and 2 were those of adult males who had been buried in wooden coffins, while the male in Tomb 3 was wrapped in a mat and textiles. Each tomb contained one or more additional individuals and sacrificed llamas, along with astonishing amounts of gold, silver, and copper artifacts, and numerous Moche pots (hundreds, in the case of Tomb 1). These burials were those of members of the royal theocracy that ruled the Lambayeque valley on behalf of the Moche state.

The Moche state reached its zenith between AD 200 and 400, when it controlled most of the north coast of Peru, with administrative centers in each valley. After about AD 500, however, things began to unravel. Control was lost over the valleys south of the Moche, the Huaca del Sol and Huaca de la Luna fell into disuse, and the center of power shifted north to Pampa Grande in the Lambayeque valley (Shimada 1994). Pampa Grande displays a degree of formal urban planning which had not been seen at the Moche Valley capital. The central precinct is a complex of walled enclosures with elite residences and specialized craft workshops that surrounded the enormous main pyramid, the Huaca Fortaleza. Unlike the Huaca del Sol, the Huaca Fortaleza and its surrounding architecture appear to have been built very quickly using a modular construction which eliminated the need for so many adobe bricks. Around these landmarks were dense residential zones, which contrast with the dispersed residential clusters at Cerro Blanco.

In the Moche Valley itself, a new center, also with a degree of formal planning, was established at Galindo, inland from the earlier capital at Cerro Blanco which was by now largely unoccupied. Galindo represents the last gasp of Moche statehood. Garth Bawden (1996: 304) stresses the degree to which Galindo was divided strictly into residential precincts for the elite and the non-elite by tall walls which dominated the site. It was a very large town, covering 5 square kilometers, but very different in character from the earlier Moche centers where the ceremonial and administrative activity was meant to be seen. At Galindo, the late Moche rulers secluded themselves in the walled compounds.

By AD 700, the Moche state had effectively collapsed, perhaps the result of environmental factors like a succession of El Niño events, perhaps as a result of internal instabilities. It was eclipsed by the short-lived Huari empire which had originated in the central highland zone. Later North Coast polities, including the Sicán state and the Chimu empire, had strikingly different urban forms in which the main settlements were exclusively for the elite and their retainers. These later polities are beyond the scope of this volume, but the residue of Moche political and religious concepts can be traced throughout later Peruvian prehistory (Bawden 1996: 332–7).

NASCA

A brief discussion of Nasca society on the South Coast of Peru is important here as a contrast to the Moche, with which it is roughly contemporaneous. Unlike the Moche, Nasca society was not that of a state. Instead, it was a society of small villages, perhaps organized into small chiefly polities, whose inhabitants made some of the most remarkable pottery and textiles in the ancient New World. The agricultural potential of the South Coast is limited by the lack of rainfall and the dependence on the flow of water from the distant Andes. To make the best of this situation, Nasca people devised clever irrigation systems that included a system of underground aqueducts to capture groundwater.

Cahuachi is the best-known Nasca site, but in contrast with the large administrative centers of the North Coast, it is very clearly not a town even though it covers 150 hectares (Silverman 1993). The lack of domestic refuse and its inhospitable location in the midst of an arid plain suggest that there was little, if any, resident population. Instead, Cahuachi appears to have been a ceremonial or pilgrimage center, with 40 mounds and terraced hills. Later, extensive cemeteries were established there, indicating a changed function from a pilgrimage center to a burial ground.

Twenty kilometers away is the large town of Ventilla, perhaps the largest Nasca site known. Discovered in the late 1980s, it covers about 200 hectares along the Rio Ingenio at the edge of the desert plain. Based on limited investigation, Silverman (1993: 326) proposes that Ventilla was the Nasca urban center that Cahuachi was not, perhaps with Cahuachi as a religious capital and Ventilla a secular capital. Further research will be needed to clarify the relationship between these two major sites.

Nasca society is best known for its "geoglyphs," or immense desert markings made by scraping away the reddish-brown surface pebbles to expose the lighter subsoil. The "Nasca Lines," as they are called, cover 200 square kilometers of desert. Thousands have been identified by aerial surveying and photography. Only a few represent human or animal figures (such as monkeys, spiders, and killer whales), and the majority are geometric figures, primarily trapezoids. We know more of what the Nasca lines are not than what they are. They are certainly not the work of aliens, as popularized in the 1970s by Ehrich von Däniken (1970). Recent work has also demonstrated that they were not aligned to celestial bodies and that they did not represent a calendrical system. The best explanation for them is that they served as ritual pathways which linked sacred places (Aveni 1990). Many of the lines converge on Cahuachi, while others radiate outward from small hills which have been found to have small shrines on them. This would be consistent with the role of Cahuachi as a ceremonial center and with the pervasive role of religion in Nasca society.

TIWANAKU ORIGINS

As the Moche state was emerging on the Peruvian north coast and the Nasca chiefdoms flourished on the south coast, the *altiplano* surrounding Lake Titicaca saw the emergence of urban civilization. Lake Titicaca provided rich aquatic resources which complemented the highly productive farming and herding economy of the highlands. Large villages with evidence of public architecture and organized layout appeared in the first millennium BC. At Chiripa, a sunken court was surrounded by sixteen meticulously-arranged buildings (Mohr Chávez 1988; Conklin 1991). Stelae with serpent, animal, and human motifs were erected in the sunken court, and additional carved stone plaques lined its walls.

Two early urban centers came to be established at either end of the Lake Titicaca basin. The earlier, Pucara, about 75 kilometers northwest of the lake, had a central religious and administrative complex on an artificial terrace. The main enclosure in this complex echoes the layout at Chiripa, with rectangular rooms arranged around a sunken court on three sides. These buildings had foundations of dressed stone blocks on which adobe walls were erected. Stone-carving at Pucara is more sophisticated than that seen earlier at Chiripa, and the motifs carved in stone are repeated in the distinctive Pucara polychrome ceramics. These include felines, birds, fish, and serpents, along with realistic depictions of humans holding trophy heads. Surrounding the elite core precinct at Pucara is an urban agglomeration which is frequently described in the literature as "sprawling" over an area of 4 square kilometers. Pucara flourished between 200 BC and AD 200, and at its peak it dominated the surrounding area in which the inhabitants of smaller towns and villages engaged in farming, herding, and fishing (Kolata 1993: 71). It was soon eclipsed, however, by Tiwanaku.

At the southeastern end of Lake Titicaca, the city of Tiwanaku (also frequently seen spelled as "Tiahuanaco") arose early in the first millennium AD. Within a few centuries, it came to cover 6 square kilometers and was the capital of an empire which dominated the *altiplano*. The roots of the Tiwanaku state lie clearly in the tradition of Chiripa and Pucara, but the origins of the capital site of Tiwanaku are only recently starting to be understood (Kolata 1993, 1996). From its beginnings as a small farming village established in the late first millennium BC, Tiwanaku began to be transformed around AD 100 by the construction of a large ceremonial and administrative core dominated by a terraced pyramid known as the Akapana and surrounded by a ceremonial moat. From this center, the Tiwanaku elite expanded their control over the Titicaca basin and subsequently beyond. A key to this expansion was the mobilization of agricultural production using a raised-bed technique which produced remarkable yields (Erickson 1988; Kolata 1991).

An extensive discussion of the Tiwanaku empire and other Andean states and empires is beyond the scope of this volume. The important point, however, is that the Inca whom the Spanish encountered in the sixteenth century AD were only the latest, albeit perhaps the most intriguing and complicated, of a series of states and empires which had existed in Peru and Bolivia during the previous two millennia. Our knowledge of these polities has been handicapped by the fact that they did not leave us a written language and by the widespread looting of their sites for the antiquities market. Yet they provide a remarkable record of human organizational and symbolic achievement.

EGYPT AND NUBIA

Civilization in Egypt arose ca. 3000 BC, but it followed a long sequence of early agricultural settlements. The striking feature of Egyptian civilization is that it appears relatively suddenly, compared with other parts of the world where there is a protracted run-up to the state through varying degrees of social differentiation. In order to understand the Predynastic developmental sequence in Egypt, it is important to understand the geography of the Nile Valley. Unlike the other Old World river valleys in which early states developed, the Nile valley consists of a very narrow strip of fertile and moist land along the river, beyond which is inhospitable desert. Following the onset of modern climatic conditions by about 7000 BC, only a few oases such as the Fayum Depression could support agriculture. The northward flow of the Nile determines the geographical nomenclature of Egypt and its southern neighbor, Nubia. Lower Egypt consists of the Nile delta and a short stretch of the main course of the Nile in the general vicinity of Cairo, whereas Upper Egypt runs from there south to Aswan. Lower and Upper Nubia continue south along the Nile down to Khartoum in the Sudan.

Agricultural settlements appeared in the Fayum Depression about 5300 BC (Hassan 1988; Close and Wendorf 1992; Wetterstrom 1993). Their wheat and barley clearly originated in the Levant and were brought in as a complex (Wetterstrom 1993), as did their domestic animals, but their inhabitants were indigenous foragers who continued to hunt elephant, hippopotamus, and gazelle and to catch fish in the large lakes of the depression. Somewhat later, between 4800 and 4300 BC at the western edge of the Nile delta, the inhabitants of Merimde beni-Salama established a large settlement covering 24 hectares. Lightweight round or oval structures 2–3 meters in diameter in the early phases were supplemented by oval mud semi-subterranean structures up to 4 meters in diameter in the later phases. The mud structures may have been special-function buildings, perhaps for storage (Eiwanger 1982: 68). Buried baskets were also used for storage later in the Merimde sequence. The increased emphasis on storage and the use of more substantial buildings as the Merimde occupation wore on suggests a progressively greater reliance on agriculture. Although the faunal sample consists largely of domestic sheep (Gautier 1987), there was continued use of fish and hunting of river animals like crocodile, hippo, and turtle. Similar features were found at El Omari, south of Cairo (Wetterstrom 1993: 214).

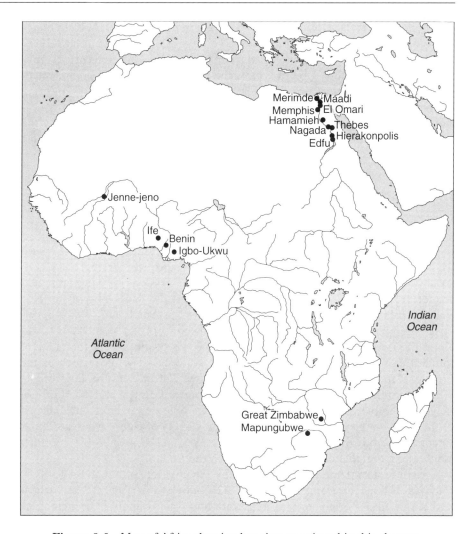

Figure 8.5 Map of Africa showing key sites mentioned in this chapter.

In Upper Egypt, the Predynastic sequence is better known, through the classic sequence of cultures – Badarian, Amratian, Gerzean – established by Flinders Petrie on the basis of burial finds (Petrie 1920). The sequence begins around 4500 BC, perhaps slightly earlier, in the Badari region, whose inhabitants produced a distinctive thin-walled reddish-brown pottery with blackened rims. At Hamamieh, one of the few known settlements with Badarian deposits, sparse evidence suggests lightweight surface structures and a few basket-lined subterranean storage pits (Wetterstrom 1993: 218). Subsequent Amratian habitations at this site, after about 3900 BC, produced more substantial above-ground structures, including circular mud-walled huts up to 2.3 meters in diameter, roofed over with straw and reeds. Numerous Badarian and Amratian graves are known, and the differentiation in grave goods in later Amratian times suggests that some element of competition for status and wealth had begun by the middle of the fourth millennium BC.

The Gerzean and its congeners, beginning about 3600 BC, saw the appearance of a new type of house that replaced the earlier lightweight oval shelters. A good example was investigated by Hoffman (1980) at Hierakonpolis 29. A rectangular pit was dug into the Nile silt with its sides plastered with mud. Mud bricks were used to build walls around the pit, and the roof was supported by eight posts. Similar mudbrick houses are known from later Dynastic times, reflecting continuity in residential architecture. Numerous Gerzean graves have been found in a number of localities in Upper Egypt, some of which are very elaborate. One, excavated at Edfu a century ago, was a 2×5 meter pit lined with mud brick which had been plastered and then painted with scenes of people and boats. Simpler graves consist only of small pits in which the deceased was placed with a few grave goods.

The Hierakonpolis area, where over 50 settlements and cemeteries have been discovered, was a large population center during the second half of the fourth millennium BC, while further downstream at Nagada, large cemeteries and settlements also indicate another center of substantial population. Hassan (1988: 161) suggests that the population of Hierakonpolis was about 2000, while two large settlements at Nagada each had 800–900 inhabitants. These settlements have been called "towns" and reflect an increasing nucleation of population, but they also were probably the seats of local polities in which the elite demonstrated their status and wealth by lavish burial practices (Hassan 1988: 163–9). Such polities generally appear to fit a chiefdom model of political economy, and over the next several centuries a distinct hierarchy of local and paramount chiefs appears to have emerged (Hassan 1988: 172).

At the same time in Lower Egypt, evidence for long-distance trade has been found at the site of Maadi, south of Cairo (Hassan 1988: 160; Bard 1997: 72–3). Maadi is a large settlement and cemetery complex. Although the subterranean pit houses at Maadi are less substantial than those found in Upper Egypt, many large grinding stones and storage pits attest to the importance of the agricultural economy. It appears, however, that the site was divided into a central residential precinct surrounded by storage facilities (Hassan 1988: 160). The graves were also simpler, without many grave goods (Bard 1997: 73). Although the pottery is different from that found in Upper Egypt, there are many imports such as slate palettes and diorite jars which reached Maadi by boat from upstream. In addition, Maadi had strong connections with communities in Palestine, the Negev, and beyond (Caneva, Frangipane, and Palmieri 1989), attested by Syro-Palestinian vessels and copper objects.

The roots of Egyptian civilization are found in the late Predynastic communities of Upper and Lower Egypt. Until recently, the focus has been on the elite towns of Upper Egypt, such as Hierakonpolis and Nagada, assumed to have formed the core of the nascent Egyptian state. Here are all the trappings of complex chieftaincies, along with the public architecture and incipient urbanism that characterize state polities. Yet Maadi and similar localities in Lower Egypt (where important sites may lie buried beneath the silts of the Nile Delta) also signal complex economic behavior, almost commercial in nature. These will also need to be taken into account as understanding of the origins of Egyptian civilization develops.

Hassan (1988) has offered a model for the formation of the Egyptian state. The emergence of chiefly polities strung along the Nile and linked by river and land transport in the Nile corridor led to competition among these polities and eventually systematic warfare, while alliances and consolidation of chiefdoms resulted in a hierarchy of chiefs. Each of these chiefs adopted an iconography of both religious and secular power. Over time, these chiefdoms came to be integrated into progressively larger polities. Chiefs used imported and locally-made prestige goods to enhance their status, which also benefited from success in warfare. The linear arrangement of these chiefdoms along the Nile and their circumscribed agricultural area may have amplified the effects of such conflict.

This mixed pattern of conflict and alliance within the narrow Nile corridor led to the eventual political integration of both Upper and Lower Egypt, an event which is linked to the mythical King Narmer but which may have been the result of the complex social processes that began in the last centuries of the fourth millennium BC. Kemp (1989) has described a "proto-kingdom" in Upper Egypt which expanded northward to absorb the less complex societies of Lower Egypt and southward into Nubia. It is unclear, and a matter of debate, whether this unification resulted from a military conquest of Lower Egypt or from the cumulative effects of alliances and warfare over many generations. Current consensus (reflected in Bard 1997: 78) appears to favor a gradual process. What is clear, however, is that by about 3000 BC Egypt was unified into a single state which extended about 1300 kilometers along the Nile.

For many years, it was an article of faith that ancient Egypt was a "civilization without cities" (Wilson 1960), since the agglomerations of population consisted primarily of farmers who went out every day to their fields, while the pharaohs lived in isolated palaces. Yet there is increasing evidence that Egypt did have cities and towns. Memphis and Thebes were Dynastic capitals, while the local seats of the late Predynastic chiefs developed into the administrative centers of the *nomes*, or local bureaucratic units. Hassan (1993) has traced the connections between the development of the earliest Egyptian towns and the development of the Egyptian state. The *nome* capitals were the centers of political and religious power as well as centers for economic activity such as craft production and distribution. Their size is limited by the narrowness of the Nile floodplain, for they could not grow beyond the ability of their inhabitants to be supplied by an agricultural hinterland. Yet they were, according to Hassan (1993: 567), "key links in the chain by which Egypt was integrated." Thus the Egyptian state was able to exist over a much larger area than the contemporaneous, but much smaller city-states in southern Mesopotamia, despite the fact that most people continued to live in small farming villages.

A detailed description of Egyptian Dynastic civilization lies beyond the scope of this volume. The most important conclusion to be drawn from the discussion here is that the roots of the Egyptian state are indigenous and not the result of influence from Mesopotamia or elsewhere, despite the fact that trade can be documented between Lower Egypt and southwest Asia. As was the case in other parts of the world, however, competition between small-scale polities produced a syndrome of conquest and alliance which led to progressively greater political integration. This integration occurred over a remarkably long but very narrow area, within which local administrative centers played a key role in administering the state bureaucracy.

THE INDUS CIVILIZATION

The prehistory of South Asia east of the Iranian Plateau and west of Thailand has not been discussed previously in this volume, save for passing references in the discussion of early hominid dispersals. A conscious decision was made to do this, primarily because the prehistory of this region is dominated by the Indus Valley civilization of the third millennium BC. The flourishing of this civilization between 2500 and 2000 BC provides a central point of reference for the later prehistory of this region. Rather than scattering the discussion of its precursors through the preceding chapters, it makes more sense to treat the roots of the Indus, or Harappan, civilization here as part of the story of this remarkable prehistoric development.

Although it is centered on the Indus Valley, where the two great urban sites of Harappa and Mohenjo-Daro are located, the Indus civilization extended over a very large area of Pakistan and northwestern India. It was completely unknown in historical literature and tradition until its discovery by British and Indian archaeologists in the 1920s. Even today, it remains mysterious. The Indus script remains undeciphered, despite claims to the contrary. Antecedent sites do not provide a smooth and gradual developmental sequence. The demise of the civilization remains unexplained as well.

Just as the story of the Indus civilization is dominated by its two major sites of Harappa and Mohenjo-Daro, the record of the five millennia leading up to the establishment of these cities is defined by a single site, Mehrgarh, in north-central Pakistan (Jarrige and Meadow 1980). The aceramic earliest levels of this remarkable site indicate that agriculture and village life reached this area very quickly after its development in the Fertile Crescent, at least by 6500 BC, and provide some of the earliest evidence of the herding of zebu cattle, *Bos indicus* (Meadow 1993). Chaff-tempered pottery began to be produced by 5500 BC, and pottery technology was progressively refined in the centuries that followed. Eventually, Mehrgarh came to cover 75 hectares in the late fifth millennium BC. At this time, craft production became especially important. Wheel-made painted pottery and beads of steatite and shell were made for local consumption and for trade (Kenoyer 1992; Wright 1989), and copper metallurgy was also important. Mehrgarh provides the baseline sequence for Indus Valley prehistory prior to 4000 BC, although several other

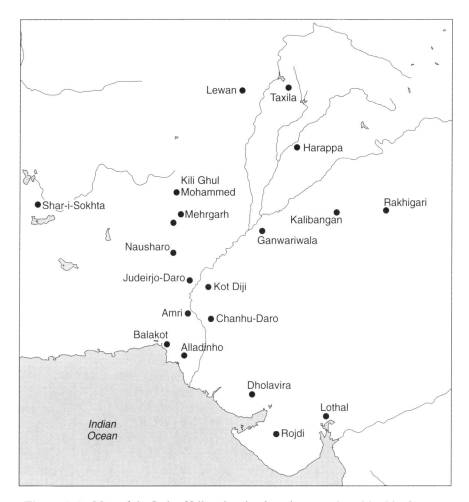

Figure 8.6   Map of the Indus Valley showing key sites mentioned in this chapter.

agricultural communities from the fifth millennium BC, such as Kili Ghul Mohammed, have been identified in Pakistan.

During the fourth millennium BC, many small farming villages connected by regional networks of interaction and exchange were distributed along the rivers of the Indus system and along the Makran coast of Pakistan towards the Iranian Plateau. Inland, an important trade route ran through southern Iran in the direction of Mesopotamia, while others reached north into central Asia (Kenoyer 1991: 344). The potters, bead-makers, and metal-workers at Mehrgarh continued to refine their crafts. Even at a small site like Lewan, in northern Pakistan, the inhabitants appear to have specialized in the manufacture of stone tools in the late fourth millennium BC (Allchin and Allchin 1993). A number of sites came to have substantial mud-brick or stone walls.

All this, however, was a prelude to the main event, the appearance of large, arguably urban settlements during the third millennium BC. Two contrasting views concerning the character of Indus urbanization are current among archaeologists. One position sees it as the outcome of a gradual progressive nucleation of settlement (e.g., Mughal 1990) while the other sees it as a rapid, almost discontinuous transformation from small villages to large urban sites (e.g., Possehl 1990). At the moment, it seems unlikely that this difference in views can be resolved completely, although in archeological time and in global perspective the emergence of Indus urban sites within a mass of agricultural villages was certainly quick. Unlike other regions where the precursors of nucleated settlements, public architecture, and pronounced social differentiation can be traced back through a long developmental sequence, such clear precursors of Indus civilization are elusive.

Against this background, it is easier to say what *did not* cause the development of Indus civilization than what did. It is clear, for example, that it was not the result of colonization or even influence from Mesopotamia, although trade with the Iranian Plateau and with the Persian Gulf was indeed important. The usual factors which are invoked to explain the rise of urban civilization – warfare, ideology, irrigation, population pressure – are either absent or impossible to document. In the Indus Valley villages and towns of the late fourth and early third millennia, there is ample evidence for intensive craft production and local exchange, and perhaps the political and economic system that these supported experienced a complex transformation in which minor changes were suddenly amplified. The emergence of Indus civilization may belong to a such a category of complex self-organizing phenomena.

Whatever its roots, a four-tiered hierarchy of sites appeared in the Indus valley around 2600 BC (Kenoyer 1991: 351). At the top, larger than 50 hectares, are the classic sites of Harappa and Mohenjo-Daro, along with another large settlement, Ganwariwala, and possibly a fourth at Rakhigarhi. Such large sites can be considered to be "cities." A second tier of regional centers, between 10 and 50 hectares, included sites such as Kalibangan, Dholavira, and Judeirjo-Daro. A series of large villages of between 5 and 10 hectares includes Amri, Lothal, Chanhu-Daro, and Rojdi, while a fourth level of small villages of between 1 and 5 hectares includes important sites like Allahdino, Kot Diji, Balakot, and Nausharo. In addition, there are many localities which appear to have been pastoral camps or short-term production sites.

Indus cities and towns are remarkably similar. Their street plans are very regular and rectilinear, their buildings modular, and their sanitation systems integrated into the urban construction. They are more reminiscent of the Minoan and Mycenaean palace-cities than the less-organized layouts of the Mesopotamian towns. Parts of the settlements were built on giant mud-brick platforms which resulted in variations in height. For example, one part of Mohenjo-Daro, known traditionally as "the citadel," was laid out atop a 200 by 400 meter platform 12 meters high and contained a variety of architectural features which have been speculatively and fancifully termed "the Great Bath," the "Granary," and "the College." Archaeologists have no good idea of how these spaces were actually used, however. Similar public structures have been found at Harappa and other Indus cities and towns. Residential districts are composed of compounds of houses and workshops along a network of streets. Covered drains ran from the houses into central sewers. At Mohenjo-Daro, about 700 wells have been identified, each of which served a group of households.

The inhabitants of these cities and towns, along with the outlying villages, were supported by an agricultural and pastoral economy, supplemented by hunting and fishing. The principal crops were barley and wheat, sown in the fall, although the use of numerous other plants, both domesticated and wild, has been documented (Weber 1992). Cattle were especially important, both the humped *Bos indicus* and the non-humped *Bos taurus*, as were water buffalo (*Bubalus bubalus*), sheep, and goat (Meadow 1989). Domestic chicken make an early appearance at Mohenjo-Daro. A wide variety of wild bovids and cervids, along with smaller game, were hunted. In light of its riverine setting, it is not surprising that there is considerable evidence for the use of fish at Harappa, primarily catfish and carp (Belcher 1991).

It is clear that the people of the Indus civilization engaged in both local and long-distance trade. Of particular importance is the long-distance commerce, both maritime and overland. Indus trade routes stretched into Afghanistan (Francfort 1992) and to Mesopotamia (Potts 1990). From Afghanistan came lapis lazuli, copper, and tin (Stech and Pigott 1986), while a variety of commodities probably traveled along the sea and land routes between the Indus and the Euphrates. On the Iranian Plateau, trade in steatite and turquoise led to the development of important centers at Tepe Yahya and Shahr-i-Sokhta. Trade with Mesopotamia can be documented by the presence of Indus-produced objects such as seals and beads at Mesopotamian sites, although almost no Mesopotamian artifacts have been found in Indus sites. Mention of the land of "Meluhha" in Mesopotamian texts is taken to refer to the Indus region.

We know virtually nothing about Indus social and political organization. Despite the large scale of the urban architecture, there are no clear major religious buildings or palaces, so the identification of a religious, economic, or political elite is elusive. Fairservis (1986) has suggested that the Indus polities were simply overblown chiefdoms, but even in chiefdoms one expects to find more evidence of social differentiation and ideology than is seen in the Indus. Possehl (1996: 13) characterizes the Indus civilization as "a faceless culture without the aggrandizement of individuals," which aptly sums up much of what we can tell at the moment about this society. Although the basic structural principles of Indus civilization were completely different from those of Mesopotamia, Egypt, China, or any of the New World civilizations discussed here, the city planning, writing, long-distance trade, and organization of craft production all testify to a high level of economic and political organization which remains invisible at the moment.

The Indus civilization independently developed a writing system, although it has not been deciphered despite over 50 claims to the contrary (Kenoyer 1991: 362; Possehl 1996). It consists of short texts on seals, amulets, and ceramic vessels. Each text consists of about five hieroglyphic signs chosen from a repertoire of several hundred symbols. The uses of the text on seals and pottery and the shortness of the inscriptions suggest that its primary purpose was for identification, accounting, and package tracking. No long texts or inscriptions on architecture are known. It frequently appears on square stamp seals, along with a depiction of an animal.

At its peak in the second half of the third millennium BC, the Indus civilization embraced an area of 800,000 square kilometers. Yet almost as quickly as it emerged, Indus civilization went into decline after 2000 BC. Harappa, Mohenjo-Daro, and many other large sites in the core area were effectively abandoned around this time, although in other regions like Punjab, Rajastan, and the Gujarat there is evidence that the civilization continued to flourish. Many hypotheses to account for the collapse of the Indus civilization have been advanced, including Aryan invasions and catastrophic flooding, but these do not survive careful scrutiny.

For much of the next two millennia, south Asia reverted to its pre-urban configuration of villages primarily concerned with agriculture, herding, and craft production, although there are a number of continuities from earlier periods (Coningham 1995: 69). It was not until the second half of the first millennium BC that a new pattern of settlement nucleation can be observed in several parts of south Asia, presaged by the emergence of social and political complexity more in line with that observed in other parts of the world, including chiefdoms, warfare, and prestige goods (Erdosy 1988, 1995). This culminated in the rise of city-states throughout northern India and Pakistan, such as Taxila, and eventually the Mauryan state which encompassed much of south Asia in the final centuries BC.

Can we call the Indus civilization a state as well? Possehl (1996: 14) urges caution in admitting it to this category of society. Given the absence of evidence for a self-aggrandizing elite, it certainly does not conform to our expectations of early states or even their chiefdom precursors. For the moment, the Indus civilization remains an anomaly, a complex urban "non-state" which appears to have spontaneously self-organized itself from a society of transegalitarian villages 4500 years ago and to have collapsed equally spontaneously five centuries later, leaving behind remarkable architecture and an undeciphered script.

XIA AND SHANG CIVILIZATIONS IN CHINA

The archaeological study of Chinese civilization developed much differently from that of the other early civilizations discussed in this chapter. Few investigations were conducted prior to the 1930s, and World War II and the onset of communism effectively closed China off from western scholarship for decades. Much of what was known was based on artifacts which had made their way to art museums and which were devoid of archaeological context. Until the opening of China in the 1970s, only a small group of scholars had an interest in the emergence of early Chinese civilization as an anthropological problem. Prominent among them was the Chinese-born American archaeologist Kwang-Chih Chang, whose contribution in bringing the results of Chinese investigations of the 1950s and 1960s through political and

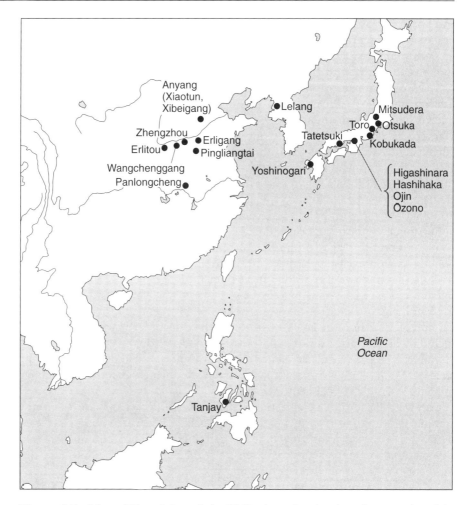

Figure 8.7 Map of East Asia and the Philippines showing key sites mentioned in this chapter.

language barriers must be acknowledged here. Through his efforts and those of a growing number of Chinese and western scholars in the last two decades, the origins of Chinese civilization are becoming better understood.

In the previous chapter, the emergence of chiefdom societies in the Longshan Late Neolithic and its congeners was discussed, and it appears that during the centuries that followed the process of social stratification accelerated. Liu (1996) has pointed towards areas with decentralized and competing chiefdoms in northern and central Henan as the heartland in which states subsequently developed. Early Longshan towns like Wangchenggang and Pingliangtai exhibited the *hangtu* technique of rammed-earth wall and platform construction which is elaborated in later periods (Wieshieu 1997).

Just before 2000 BC, the archaeological record begins to converge with the historical evidence even though the latter is more based on legend than fact

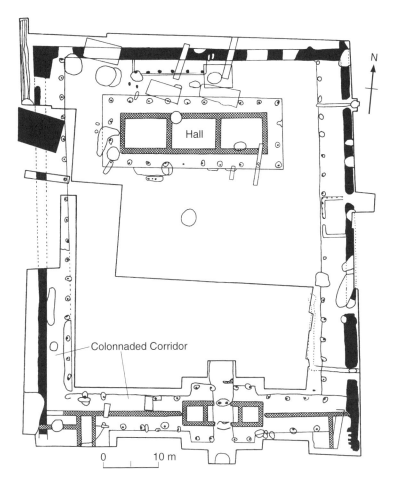

Figure 8.8 Palatial structure at Erlitou set on a platform with a timber hall and courtyard surrounded by a colonnaded corridor (after Chang 1986, figure 262).

initially. The beginning of the three sequential dynasties of the *San dai* – the Xia, Shang, and Zhou – is traditionally guessed to be about 2200 BC on the basis of legends, although such historical dating is not viewed as reliable (Chang 1986: 306). The Xia (Hsia) dynasty was long considered to be legendary. During the 1950s and 1960s, excavations at the site of Erlitou in Henan have pointed towards its reality, leading to the identification of a regional archaeological culture named after the site (Chang 1983). Although it was a matter of considerable disagreement during the 1970s, most archaeologists now accept the identification of Erlitou with Xia.

Erlitou sites are characterized by distinctive tripod ceramic vessels, jade ornaments (including *cong* tubes), and bronze cups, tools, and weapons. The bronze vessels are among the earliest in China and were used for wine. Of considerable interest are the structural remains at Erlitou, where a wall enclosed houses of various sizes. Within the enclosure, a terrace built of *hangtu* rammed earth about 100 meters square was surrounded by its own wall, within which ran a corridor delimited by posts. On it were built large timber buildings, including a hall about 30 meters long raised on a low platform. About 150 meters away from this compound, another walled platform compound also contained a raised hall, in roughly the same position as the first. Adjacent to the hall was a pit grave, which had been robbed but in which fragments of a lacquered coffin and dog skeleton suggest that it contained a rich burial. The walled-platform compounds at Erlitou are characteristically referred to as "palaces" and, in Chang's (1986: 314) view, suggest the presence of a powerful and wealthy elite at a higher level than the Longshan chiefs.

About 100 kilometers to the east of Erlitou is the city of Zhengzhou, where the district of Erligang has yielded traces of an early Shang capital (An 1986), either Ao or Bo, both of which are mentioned in inscriptions on oracle bones. The central precinct of this city covers an area of about 3.5 square kilometers and dates to the middle of the second millennium BC. It was surrounded by a roughly rectangular *hangtu* wall which survives in places up to a height of 9 meters and was 22 meters thick at the base. Large palace compounds, some 300 meters by 150 meters, are built on *hangtu* platforms and have traces of enormous timber posts. The jade and copper artifacts, along with sacrificial burials found in their foundations support the identification of these structures as palaces. Of considerable interest at Erligang is the evidence for craft production outside this central zone. In one area, fourteen kilns, associated with dense concentrations of broken vessels and decorating tools, indicate a pottery factory. At another location, the scrap from bone implement manufacture included as much human bone as it did animal bone. Bronze foundries contained clay moulds for the mass production of weapons such as arrow points and vessels.

Erligang is identical in organization and layout, albeit on a smaller scale, to the later site of Anyang, to which the Shang capital was relocated several centuries later. Anyang, located about 150 kilometers north of Erligang, has been the focus of intense archaeological interest since the 1920s, when excavations were begun by Li Chi, often considered the founder of modern Chinese archaeology. It is an enormous site, covering 24 square kilometers, and it runs for nearly 6 kilometers along both sides of the Huan river. Between 1300 and 1050 BC, this city was the capital of the late Shang state, known in the historical accounts as Yin, or Yinxu (the "ruins of Yin"), where 12 kings ruled for 273 years.

Anyang consists of a complex of sites, which include the palace complex at Xiaotun, the royal shaft graves at Xibeigang, many other residential and workshop sites, and caches of oracle bones. The Xiaotun palace complex contained 53 large *hangtu* platforms on which were built large halls, the largest of which measured 70 by 40 meters. The foundations of these buildings contain hundreds of human sacrifices, often decapitated. Outside this central precinct, as at Erligang, were the residences of commoners and workshops, again specializing in bronze casting, pottery manufacture, bone working, and jade carving. Nearby, the royal burial complex at Xibeigang consists of a number of complex subterranean structures consisting of a central shaft which held the royal personage in a wooden chamber surrounded by ledges on which were buried sacrificed retainers. Most of these graves were looted in antiquity, but one which was excavated in 1976 was intact. Identified as the grave of the royal consort Fu Hao, it contained 1600 artifacts, including 440 bronze ritual objects and weapons, 590 jades, and 560 bone artifacts, along with 7000 cowrie shells.

Of particular importance at Anyang are the inscribed oracle bones, of which over 100,000 have been found. They are flat bones, usually the cleaned and polished shoulder blades of cattle and water buffalo or the plastrons (lower shells) of turtles, many of which were carved with archaic forms of Chinese characters. Pits were bored on the surface of the bone and a hot poker was applied to the pit, causing cracks to appear on the opposite surface. These cracks were then interpreted as answers to divination questions. Many topics were the subjects of divination: the weather, military campaigns, the harvest, tribute payments, and pregnancies, to name a few. On particularly auspicious oracle bones, the questions and answers to the divination were inscribed, along with the date and the name of the diviner. Divination was the exclusive domain of the literate royal elite, and we know the names of over 120 diviners who served the Shang kings (Keightley 1994: 73). As a result of these numerous inscriptions, we know quite a bit about the Shang rulers and their numerous concerns.

The Shang kings were considered to be divine, and power flowed from them to a complex hierarchy of local officials, who ruled over their own territories in a fairly autonomous fashion. Just how much territory was under the control of the Shang ruler is unclear. Shang artifacts are distributed over a relatively wide past of northern and central China, but it is possible that direct political control was confined to a fairly small area along the Huanghe river. Panlongcheng in Hubei province, a walled town of 7.5 hectares, is thought to be a southern outpost of the Shang political system.

By the time that the Shang state was conquered by the Zhou, Chinese civilization had fully entered the realm of history, and the development of the later Chinese states and empires lies well beyond the scope of this volume. Of crucial significance, however, is the fact that the archaeology of early Chinese civilization reflects many long-term continuities from the Longshan Neolithic and even earlier, with the progressive addition of bronze metallurgy, oracle bone inscriptions, and truly urban centers with elite palaces and burials. Although archaeological research has been concentrated on a few large sites, it will be important to investigate the vast number of smaller villages and towns that date between 2200 and 1000 BC in order to understand more fully the nature of Xia and Shang polities.

KINGDOMS OF SUB-SAHARAN AFRICA

A little-known aspect of the archaeology of sub-Saharan Africa is the emergence of kingdoms and states in the first millennium AD. These were relatively small polities, but archaeological research in recent decades has demonstrated that they were complex urban societies. They sprang up in many parts of the continent, on the basis of local Iron Age chiefdoms. Space permits the mention here of only a few of these polities and others remain to be discovered. These are almost entirely indigenous developments, not primarily the results of contact with the Muslim and European worlds as was once believed.

In West Africa, the site of Jenne-jeno ("ancient Jenné") forms a mound in the Inland Delta of the Niger river (McIntosh and McIntosh 1993; McIntosh 1995). By AD 300, the settlement had reached 25 hectares in area, and over the next few centuries it grew to 33 hectares (41 hectares, if the adjoining site of Hambarketolo is taken into account) and was surrounded by a wall. By AD 800, the site had become a center of craft specialization in metalworking, pottery, grindstones, and ornaments and was part of a well-developed trading network, which included gold and copper. Survey in the surrounding area has revealed a cluster of 25 satellite sites within a one-kilometer radius and many others beyond that which form a hierarchy of site sizes (McIntosh and McIntosh 1993: 634–8). At its zenith in the late first millennium AD, Jenne-jeno was an urban center whose wealth was based on its favorable position for trade and the rich economic potential of the Niger floodplain.

Fifteen hundred kilometers to the southeast, the finds at Igbo-Ukwu in Nigeria hint at the differentiation in access to status, power, and wealth during the first millennium AD that preceded the establishment of the Ife and Benin kingdoms several centuries later. Excavations by Thurstan Shaw (1970) uncovered the burial chamber of a high-status individual, sitting on a stool, with all the trappings of his office. These included a fly-whisk with a bronze handle, three elephant tusks, numerous other copper and bronze objects (685 in all) and over 100,000 glass and carnelian beads. India was the probable source of the carnelian, indicating the extent of the trade network in which this community participated (McIntosh and McIntosh 1988: 119). Many of the larger bronzes, including vases with detailed decoration, were cast by the "lost-wax" method. Although they have no known local antecedents, the Igbo-Ukwu bronzes are believed to have been manufactured locally (Phillipson 1993: 179). Radiocarbon dates indicate that the Igbo-Ukwu burial dates to the ninth century AD, which apparently aroused some skepticism when first reported but which is now generally accepted (Connah 1987: 138).

Although nothing is known of the settlements associated with the Igbo-Ukwu burial, such a concentration of wealth suggests that complex trading networks and craft specialization preceded the establishment of the Ife state around AD 1100. Settlement at Ife began late in the first millennium AD, but it soon rose to prominence because of its control of local trade in ivory, gold, pepper, and kola nuts. By AD 1300, it was the walled capital of a state whose artisans were known for their bronze work and their manufacture of naturalistic terracotta heads. Two centuries later, Ife declined and power shifted to Benin, famous for its bronze working and with whom the first Europeans to visit the area made contact. Research by Darling (1984) has revealed the presence of elaborate linear earthworks which apparently began to be

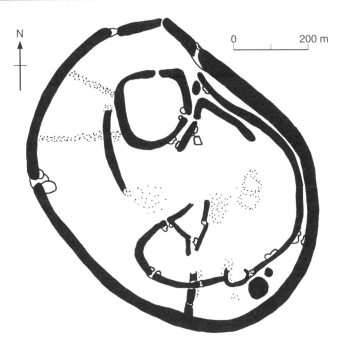

Figure 8.9 Plan of the Great Enclosure at Great Zimbabwe, showing major stone walls standing today.

constructed late in the first millennium AD, and a cistern from the mid thirteenth century AD contains a mass burial of 41 young women, indicating that Benin was a center of ritual and political activity long before its zenith.

Perhaps the best-known early state in sub-Saharan Africa is centered on Great Zimbabwe, located in the country which has taken its name (perhaps the only country named after an archaeological site!). Prior to the emergence of Zimbabwe around AD 1250, the dominant polity in this region was that of Mapungubwe in the Limpopo valley, where extreme differences in status, power, and wealth emerged on the basis of cattle ownership and trade with the coast (Huffman 1986). The rise to prominence of Great Zimbabwe perhaps represents a northward movement of the rulers of this polity. At Great Zimbabwe, the most distinctive features are the high drystone walls which form an elaborate complex of enclosures with towers. These were probably elite residential and ceremonial precincts, while most of the populace lived in pole-and-mud houses. The entire site covers about 78 hectares, and its population has been estimated at about 18,000 (Huffman 1986). Participation in international trade is reflected in finds of imported Chinese stoneware and glass, cloth, and other products from countries around the Indian Ocean.

Apart from its large size, Great Zimbabwe is not unique, and a number of similar enclosures are known from elsewhere in Zimbabwe and neighboring Mozambique (Barker 1988; Sinclair et al. 1993). These regional centers appear to have been the seats of elites who were subordinate to the rulers of

Great Zimbabwe. Barker (1988) and Garlake (1978) have pointed out the critical role of cattle-keeping for the location of the regional centers and for creating marked disparities in wealth and status. On this pastoralist system was superimposed the control of the mineral resources of interior southeastern Africa and the engagement in coastal trade.

The distinguishing feature of the early African states appears to have been the interplay of local and long-distance trade with high local subsistence productivity to create disparities in status and wealth, which in turn became translated into political and ideological power. Rulers of what were relatively small polities in the first millennium AD were able to extend their authority over progressively larger areas. The later prehistory of sub-Saharan Africa is still poorly-known in comparison with that of the rest of the world, and there is much that is still to be discovered about the early chiefdoms and states of this region.

CHIEFDOMS IN THE SHADOW OF STATES

The societies discussed here are frequently glossed over by anthropological archaeologists and left to historians. As a result, they are rarely considered from the perspective of the broad sweep of human prehistory taken in this volume. A significant amount of space is accorded them here because (1) they are prehistoric, despite references to them by authors in the neighboring literate civilizations, and (2) they represent organizational alternatives to state organizations which were robust in their own right and which persisted for centuries. Indeed, it was their contact with neighboring states which may have enabled their elites to resist the pressures which contribute to the rapid developmental oscillations of the chiefdoms described in the previous chapter. The presence of nearby states directly affected their political and economic development, despite the fact that they remained in a pre-state form for centuries. Regions which are particularly worthy of consideration in this regard include Eurasia from the Atlantic to Mongolia, Southeast Asia, Japan, and the Philippines.

EURASIAN IRON AGE CHIEFDOMS

The Iron Age cultures of Eurasia are typically examined in isolation. Those of Europe are considered to be a separate entity from those of the steppes of eastern Europe and central Asia. While such an approach may make sense for regional archaeological analyses, the purpose here is to examine them as a broader example of complex chiefly polities in contact with states. Clearly the sedentary farmers of temperate Europe had a different way of life from that of the nomadic horse-riding pastoralists of south Russian steppes and the high pastures of the Altai. Yet there were important commonalities. One was the engagement in trans-regional exchange networks which were far more robust than those of the Bronze Age. Rather than reflecting the intermittent and sporadic flow of scarce metals and handicrafts, the Iron Age

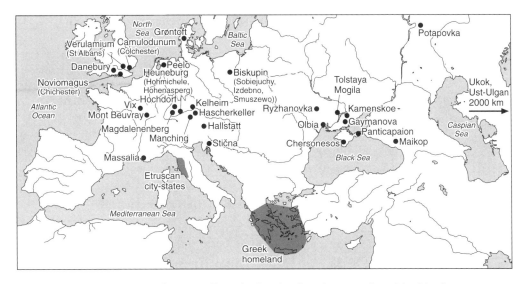

Figure 8.10 Map of western Eurasia showing key sites mentioned in this chapter.

exchange networks of Eurasia had a clear commercial character and indicate a sustained flow of raw materials and manufactured goods across long distances. These commercial exchange systems were tied in to those of the neighboring states, but among the barbarians they functioned in political economies which were essentially continuations of the Bronze Age chiefdoms. The result was the generation and accumulation of enormous wealth by the elites. This wealth is reflected in the extraordinarily lavish "royal" burials which dot the landscape from France to Siberia.

In this section, I would like to consider three Eurasian societies of the first millennium BC: the Hallstatt and LaTène peoples of temperate Europe, the Scythians of the Ukrainian and south Russian steppes, and the unnamed pastoralists of the Altai highlands on the borders of China and Mongolia. The last group is sometimes considered as very similar to the Scythians and is given the name of "Pazyryk," which is simply the local name for a burial mound. While both peoples were horse-riding pastoralists, several thousand kilometers separate them, and they interacted with different neighboring states. Terminological confusion is generated by the conflation of archaeological names and ethnic labels assigned by Classical writers. "Hallstatt" and "LaTène" are terms for archaeological periods and decorative styles derived from sites in Austria and Switzerland. When Romans encountered LaTène peoples and their congeners in western Europe, they became the Gauls, Britons, and Germans of history. In the case of the Scythians, archaeologists simply adopted Herodotus' term for these peoples.

A digression is in order here to discuss the concept of "ethnicity," the legacy of which plagues the world today. The notion of the existence of different ethnic groups in Eurasia can largely be traced back to the categorization of the barbarian peoples undertaken by Greek geographers in the first millennium BC, who divided the inhabitants of temperate Europe into Celts and Scythians. Yet, as Colin Renfrew (1993: 23) notes, we have no evidence that these people ever thought of themselves as single ethnic entities or ever called themselves "Celts" or "Scythians." As inhabitants of nation-states in the late twentieth century, we tend to assume that the world is divided into groups that have different languages, cultures, and coherent self-identities. In the Iron Age world of the final millennium BC, there were probably broad distinctions based on geography, economy, and political affiliations, but these probably did not coincide neatly with the ethnic labels assigned by Classical writers.

IRON AGE COMMERCIAL CHIEFDOMS IN CENTRAL EUROPE

Europe during the early part of the first millennium BC was still a world of farmsteads and villages, much as it had been in the Bronze Age. A typical site in central Europe is Hascherkeller in Bavaria, which consisted of three enclosed farmsteads (Wells 1983, 1993), each inhabited by a household of 6–12 people. A range of productive activities – including pottery manufacture, weaving, and bronze-working – took place at the site. Trade brought glass beads, bronze, and graphite to the small hamlet.

Against this backdrop of farmsteads and hamlets, presumably organized into simple chiefly polities as in the preceding Bronze Age, trade took on a new dimension. During the Bronze Age, the primary substances exchanged were exotic materials: copper and tin to make bronze, along with small quantities of amber, jet, and other rare items. Early in the first millennium BC, some communities, particularly in the Alpine zone, began to prosper because of their extraction and processing of mundane commodities like iron and salt. Hallstatt, high in the Austrian Alps, emerged as a major salt-mining center around 800 BC. The cemetery adjacent to the salt mines has yielded remarkably rich cremation and skeleton burials. Although most items originated within a 30 kilometer radius, amber was obtained from the Baltic coast and ivory came from Africa by way of Italy (Wells 1984: 85). South of the Alps in Slovenia, Stična emerged as a commercial center based on the smelting and forging of iron, which it traded for luxury goods from Italy. Although Hallstatt and Stična were unusual for their time, they reflected a greater interest in entrepreneurial behavior and the existence of a well-developed network for exchange which reached far north into temperate Europe.

This pattern of chiefdoms with a robust infrastructure for the extraction of raw materials and manufacturing provided the springboard for the next major development in central European prehistory – the generation of extraordinary wealth during the period between 600 and 400 BC in the parts of this region which were easily accessible from the Mediterranean world. The key factors in this development were the demand by the Mediterranean peoples for the forest products of central Europe, the appetite of the central European chiefs for exotic prestige goods (especially those associated with wine and wine-drinking), community-level specialization in the extraction of raw materials and production of finished products, and the existence of an internal network for the commercial exchange of materials and products. When the Mediterranean demand for forest products was mated with the barbarian demand for exotic products, the combination produced remarkable concentrations of wealth in the hands of the elite individuals who controlled this exchange.

The Rhône river figures prominently in this discussion, since it was the autobahn on which the forest products heading south and the prestige goods going north passed. Of course, central Europe had been in contact with the Mediterranean world for millennia through a variety of routes. The frozen body of the Late Neolithic "Iceman" indicates that drastic measures were sometimes taken to cross natural barriers like the Alps. It is simply not practical, however, to drag bulk items across high Alpine passes, so the Rhône became the access corridor to interior central Europe. The developments described here are directly associated with this access, for their traces are found along the headwaters of the Rhône or across short drainage divides on the headwaters of the Rhine and the Danube. In other parts of temperate Europe, life continued much as it had during the Bronze Age, although local developments unrelated to Mediterranean contact presaged subsequent changes.

A trading colony was established by Greeks from Phocaea in Asia Minor at Massalia at the mouth of the Rhône about 600 BC (Wells 1984: 104). This event had an immediate and dramatic effect on the chiefdoms of west-central Europe, along the headwaters of the Rhône, Rhine, Danube, and Seine. The elites of these polities were able to control the flow of trade goods which were sent north from Massalia, presumably in turn for securing the local products which were given in return from the subjects and vassals. It is unclear exactly what commodities were traded southward. Hides, furs, and forest foods are obvious candidates, as were metals, salt, and slaves. The barbarian aristocrats who profited from this trade were clearly powerful enough to procure these goods from their subjects without sharing the wealth. Almost no Mediterranean goods are known from commoner settlements or from areas beyond the headwater zone identified above.

The rich Hallstatt-period elites in west-central Europe manifested their wealth in two ways: building fortified hilltop settlements which served as their seats and burying their dead nearby with opulent collections of exotic objects. In both instances, they showed off their connections with the Mediterranean world and their familiarity with Mediterranean behavior, particularly the drinking of wine. This was clearly a "prestige-goods economy," but unlike that seen in Mississippian North America, it was triggered by the external connections and a desire to demonstrate familiarity with the exotic and unusual. Peter Wells (1984) has characterized the western Hallstatt fortified settlements as "towns" which had a clearly commercial function, whereas Arnold (1995: 47) has suggested that they were more symbolic in their function. The term "seat" seems to characterize them best, for they were clearly the foci of chiefly polities.

The Heuneburg is a particularly important example of a seat of a Hallstatt chief. Located on a hilltop overlooking the headwaters of the Danube in

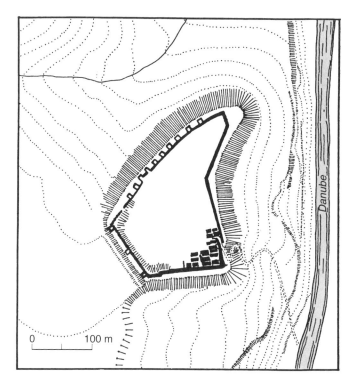

Figure 8.11 The Heuneburg in southwestern Germany, showing mud-brick fortification system, excavated structures in southeast corner, and location overlooking the Danube River (after Wells 1984, figure 31).

southwestern Germany, the Heuneburg's ramparts enclosed an area of about 3 hectares. The fortifications were renewed in several phases between about 650 and 450 BC. For the most part, they consisted of stone-filled timber cribs, but in one phase they were constructed from sun-dried mud bricks on a Mediterranean plan, with closely-spaced projecting bastions. Mud bricks, of course, are a highly unsuitable material for permanent construction in damp central Europe, although a coating of lime plaster and a wooden walkway at the top protected the bricks from rain. Clearly the idea for such a wall must have come from the Mediterranean world, presumably by a *nouveau riche* entrepreneur who decided to exhibit his foreign connections very conspicuously after returning from a trip south. Other evidence at the Heuneburg for trade with the Mediterranean world takes the form of amphorae from Massalia, black-figured vases, silk, domestic chicken bones, and coral. Inside the wall, closely-spaced timber structures suggest a substantial resident population and workshops, while outside the walls an unfortified settlement, with exceptionally large houses, also was occupied for some time.

The wealth accumulated by the elite who controlled the trade with the Mediterranean is reflected in a number of spectacular burials in southern Germany and eastern France, usually found near one of the major chiefly centers. One such burial is located at Eberdingen-Hochdorf in Baden-Württemburg and is dated between 550 and 500 BC, contemporaneous with the nearby center of Hohenasperg. Estimated to have been 6 meters high, 60 meters in diameter, and containing 7000 cubic meters of soil in its original state, the tumulus contained a central burial shaft, 11×11 meters and about 2.5 meters deep. Inside this shaft were two wooden structures, one within the other, and each covered with a timber roof. The outer one was constructed of oak timbers and formed a box 7.5 meters square and about 1.5 meters deep. Inside this was another oak box, 4.7 meters square and 1 meter deep. Within the inner box was the burial and all its associated offerings. At the north side of the mound, low stone walls had formed a gate into the central burial chamber. These were then covered over by the mound, which contained residues from the working of gold, bronze, and iron, indicating that there were workshops near the tomb which probably produced many of the grave goods.

The individual buried in the Hochdorf mound was a man about 6 feet tall and between 30 and 40 years old. He wore a conical birchbark hat. Around his neck was a gold hoop and on his chest was a small bag with a wooden comb, an iron razor, five amber beads, and three iron fishhooks. Gold ornaments, including fibulae, cuffs, and bands of hammered gold, decorated his clothes and even his shoes. The corpse had been placed on a bronze recliner which has no known parallel in Celtic Europe. It was upholstered in furs and textiles and was supported by bronze figures of eight women with upstretched arms. Scenes of wagons and dancers are embossed on the large bronze surfaces of the back and sides of the couch. At the foot of the recliner was a large bronze kettle, probably made in a Greek colony in southern Italy, which was decorated with three lions. In the kettle was residue from mead, which played a large role in Celtic ritual. On the other side of the burial chamber was a four-wheeled wagon with harnesses for two horses. Its light construction, however, indicates that it was only suitable for ceremonial use.

The Hochdorf tomb, and others like it at Vix, Grafenbühl, Hohmichele, and Magdalenenberg provide additional evidence of the strength of the Mediterranean contacts. At Vix, located near the chiefly center of Mont Lassois, an enormous wine-mixing vessel 1.64 meters tall and weighing over 200 kilograms dominates the grave finds. It is the largest metal vessel known from the ancient world and was apparently made in a Greek workshop in southern Italy. A similar source is attributed to the pair of carved-bone sphinxes from the Grafenbühl tumulus, located near Hohenasperg and Hochdorf, which were decorated with amber faces and bronze rivets. Such objects have been interpreted as political gifts from the Greeks to the local elites to cement the trading relationships, although it is also possible that they were commissioned by wealthy entrepreneurs who wanted to show off their wealth conspicuously (Wells 1984: 114).

By 400 BC, however, the late Hallstatt florescence in west-central Europe had come to an end. The hilltop fortified settlements were abandoned, and the opulent tumulus burials ceased. Such a collapse is consistent with the oscillations seen in chiefly polities, discussed in the previous chapter. Although contact with the Mediterranean did not come to a complete halt, the decline in importance of Massalia (perhaps due to a simultaneous increase in importance of the Greek colonies along the Black Sea, described below) and heightened competition among polities in central Europe are likely factors in this decline. Imported Mediterranean goods are rarely found in central Europe after 400 BC.

EARLY NUCLEATED SETTLEMENTS IN NORTHERN POLAND

Northern Europe lay largely beyond the influence of the Mediterranean economies during the first millennium BC. It was largely a world which was little-changed from that of previous millennium, except that iron permitted the manufacture of useful metal tools for the agrarian economy. Clusters of farmsteads, such as those known from Peelo in Holland (Kooi 1996) and Grøntoft in Denmark (Hedeager 1992: 193–200), continued to be the dominant settlement type. Houses were of the three-aisled type in which two rows of interior posts support the roof. One end of the longhouse was used for the stalling of cattle, the other for human habitation.

Far beyond the areas of direct Mediterranean influence on the Hallstatt world, a few precocious nucleated settlements are found on the lowlands of northern Poland. The best-known of these sites is Biskupin, although there are several other similar settlements nearby, found on islands and peninsulas on the many small lakes that dot the region. The sites at Sobiejuchy, Izdebno, Kruszwica, and Smuszewo have also been investigated, although not nearly as extensively as Biskupin, and have a similar layout and use of timber construction. All were waterlogged, which preserved the settlement plans in remarkable detail along with many wooden artifacts and even textiles. Rising lake levels about 500 BC forced their abandonment and concealed them until their discovery in the twentieth century AD.

The early Iron Age settlement at Biskupin covered about 2 hectares, surrounded by a rampart about 4 meters thick built from timber cribs filled with sand and stones and plastered with clay, which was protected from wave erosion by a breakwater of oak logs. A single gate controlled access to the settlement. Thirteen rows of houses, each about 10 by 7 meters with walls preserved to a height of nearly 4 feet, formed the core of the settlement. The houses had party walls and consisted of a uniform module of an anteroom beside the door and a central area with a stone hearth. About 100 such houses could be identified. Between the rows of houses were eleven parallel streets paved with logs, while just within the walls ran a perimeter street. Various dating methods, including carbon-14 and dendrochronology, now point towards a 100-year occupation somewhere between 650 and 500 BC (Miklaszewska-Balcer 1991; Pazdur et al. 1991).

The inhabitants of Biskupin grew millet, wheat, barley, rye, and beans. Animal bones indicated that pigs were important food animals, but cattle were kept for milk and as draft animals as well as for meat. The waterlogged deposits permitted the recovery of an extraordinary range of products made from wood, bone, and cloth, in addition to grindstones and metal ornaments and tools. The huge amount of wood used in the construction and maintenance of the settlement, as well as for cooking and for working metals, must have had a significant impact on the local forest cover. When inhabitants of Biskupin and Sobiejuchy died, their cremated bones were buried in an urn in a nearby cemetery.

Biskupin and its congeners present a bit of an enigma. Although there is evidence for the nucleation of late Bronze Age settlement at sites such as the Wasserburg-Buchau site discussed in the previous chapter, the prevailing patterns of early Iron Age settlement in central Europe were still based on dispersed farmsteads, like the one at Hascherkeller described above. The uniformity of the Biskupin houses suggests that, for some reason, a number of households chose to agglomerate their habitations and work at fields outside the ramparts of these settlements. Was this due to some localized pattern of conflict or part of some larger political development?

The proximity of these sites and their apparent contemporaneity makes it difficult to argue that each was the seat of its own polity. Moreover, there does not appear to have been a clear division of society into an elite who lived in the fortified settlements like Biskupin and Sobiejuchy and commoners who lived in the rural hinterlands, for there seem to be no differences in wealth among these sites. The only difference lies in the centrality and planning that are apparent in the fortified centers. The populations of the fortified sites may have been relatively small, perhaps on the order of several hundred individuals at most (despite much higher estimates made by the early excavators of Biskupin). In short, Biskupin and its congeners appear to be farming towns, much different from the elite Hallstatt centers which arose several hundred kilometers to the southwest.

OPPIDA AND THE END OF EUROPEAN PREHISTORY

During the second century BC, a new category of settlement emerged in western and central Europe. In the accounts of his campaigns in Gaul in 58–51 BC, Caesar used the term *oppidum* (plural *oppida*) to refer to a fortified native town of the sort that he encountered throughout the region. Similar sites are found to the east of Gaul in Bavaria and Bohemia. *Oppida* are different from the late Hallstatt princely seats like the Heuneburg in their wider distribution and in the array of residential, commercial, industrial, and administrative activities that took place at them. They also differ from the hillforts that are found throughout the British Isles at this time, again in the range of functions and in their sizes. *Oppida* are massive, typically over 30 hectares (the walls at the Heuneburg, by contrast, enclosed an area of 3.2 hectares).

Although there is no "typical" *oppidum*, Mont Beuvray in central France is a good example (Collis 1984), encountered by Caesar in 58 BC as Bibracte, the capital of the Aedui. It was investigated in the nineteenth century, prior to the development of modern excavation techniques, but it has the main archaeological features usually encountered at *oppida*. The ramparts at Mont

Beuvray, constructed in the *murus gallicus* timber-laced style, enclosed 135 hectares, with gates formed where the walls turned inward. Near the main gateway are many small workshops, apparently an industrial quarter, while in the interior of the site are residential precincts. A small square enclosure is interpreted as a sanctuary. Streams running through the ramparts and springs provided the interior of Bibracte with fresh water.

In Bavaria, enormous sites like Manching and Kelheim have been systematically investigated in recent decades, although only a small fraction of their areas can ever possibly be excavated. Manching, on the Paar river near its confluence with the Danube, has walls enclosing 380 hectares, of which about 7 hectares have been excavated. These excavations have yielded thousands of pits, postholes, house outlines, and other features, and hundreds of thousands of artifacts and animal bones. Besides being the scene of extensive iron smelting and craft production, Manching also appears to have been a center for commerce in the region. It grew rapidly after about 150 BC but appears to have met a violent end around 50 BC. Over 300 skeletons, many with injuries inflicted by metal weapons, were found scattered around the settlement, along with fragments of iron weapons.

In the British Isles, the development of central places followed a different path during the second half of the first millennium BC. Beginning in the sixth century BC, a number of sites known as hillforts appeared throughout southern Britain, a continuation of a pattern of the enclosure of elite settlements that had its roots in the late Bronze Age. The Iron Age hillforts have earthworks that enclose an area generally between 5 and 15 hectares. A classic example of a hill-fort is Danebury, excavated over many seasons by Barry Cunliffe (1993). Within the walls of Danebury, a dense concentration of round houses and rectangular storage buildings, along with pits cut into the underlying chalk for grain storage, were found. Streets ran through the settlement, separating rows of structures. During the period between 600 and 100 BC, the layout of the site was revised several times. There does not seem to be a qualitative difference between the artifacts found at Danebury and smaller outlying farming settlements, but as Cunliffe (1993: 283) notes, "The fort is so redolent of power and the desire to display it that it would be perverse to suggest that the elite were not, in some way, involved."

During the first century BC, many of the hillforts were abandoned, the result of either some indigenous change in the social order or a halo effect from the Roman activity across the English Channel. They were supplanted by a smaller number of sites at which complex earthwork systems delimit large interior areas. These are true *oppida* on the scale of their continental counterparts. At some, the area enclosed by the earthwork is clearly defined, such as at Silchester in Hampshire which was to become the Roman town of Calleva. Elsewhere, the banks and ditches carry on for long distances to roughly delimit a territory within which are habitation areas, industrial areas, burials, and defended locations. The earthworks at the *oppidum* known to the Romans as Camulodunum (now Colchester in Essex) defined an area of about 16 square kilometers (Cunliffe 1995: 70). Most Iron Age *oppida* like Camulodunum, Verulamium (St Albans in Herfordshire), and Noviomagus

(Chichester in Sussex) later became the sites of Roman towns after the Claudian invasion of AD 43.

SCYTHIAN NOMADS OF THE PONTIC STEPPES

North of the Black Sea, the steppes of southern Russia and the Ukraine had been inhabited by horse-riding peoples for several millennia. Horses had been domesticated in this region about 4000 BC (Anthony and Brown 1991) and Bronze Age burial mounds in this region contain lavish burial goods and horse sacrifices. At Potapovka, a burial dated to approximately 2000 BC contained a decapitated human who had been buried with a horse's head replacing his (Brown and Anthony 1996: 1). These peoples were also among the first speakers of proto-Indo-European, the mother tongue of the languages of northern India, Iran, and most of Europe (Anthony 1995). They had been largely sedentary, combining stockherding and agriculture, and buried their dead in subterranean timber chambers covered by mounds (Dolukhanov 1996: 117).

The pattern of nomadic pastoralism on the steppes north of the Black Sea was established early in the first millennium BC. Unlike settled agrarian societies in which wealth was derived from land and labor, pastoralist wealth lies in animals. Since livestock require extensive pastures on which to graze, pastoralist societies are of necessity mobile as their herds consume grass. Their equipment is light and moveable, consisting of carts and wagons for transport of domestic goods and tents for shelter. It now appears that during the seventh and eighth centuries BC, pastoralist nomads from points to the east and southeast migrated to the lands north of the Black Sea and established themselves in several areas which were most suitable for raising livestock (Marčenko and Vinogradov 1989: 806). There they mingled with the indigenous populations and constituted the society which is known from Greek accounts as the Scythians.

The pastoralist societies who migrated into southern Russia were no strangers to other complex forms of social organization. Already during the third millennium BC evidence for contacts with Near Eastern societies is apparent in the rich burials at Maikop in the Caucasus. Later, there is documentary evidence of conflict between nomads and northern Near Eastern kingdoms such as Urartu in the early part of the first millennium BC, prior to their migration to the Pontic steppes.

Beginning in the late seventh century BC, the Greeks from Asia Minor established trading colonies along the north coast of the Black Sea, just as they did at the same time at the other end of the Classical World at sites like Massalia. Particularly prominent among these were Olbia at the mouth of the Bug river, Chersonesos on the tip of Crimea, and Panticapaion at the entrance to the Sea of Azov. These colonies appear to have had cordial relations with the local peoples and there are documented examples of intermarriage between Greeks and Scythians, such as the mother of Demosthenes (Rolle 1989: 13). The Greek colonies developed into substantial towns with multicultural hinterlands inhabited by Greeks, Scythians, and other local peoples. Over the next three centuries, trade links, cemented by gift exchange and tribute, bound the Greeks and the Scythians economically and politically.

Contact with the Greeks had a decisive effect on pastoralist society north of the Black Sea. For the first time, they have an identity through the ethnic label assigned by the Greeks, *Scytoi*. The Scythian label has expanded to include all the pastoralists of the late first millenium north of the Black Sea (Dolukhanov 1996), although the direct association between the people described by Herodotus and specific archaeological remains is often tenuous. As new pastoralist groups migrated into the region, they also were subsumed under the "Scythian" ethnonym.

In the eyes of art historians and the general public, the Scythians are best known for their appetite for gold and silver objects. As a result, Scythian burials have been plundered with regularity since antiquity, and we know much more about the fine grave goods which the Scythians acquired and buried than about their everyday lives, for which the accounts of Herodotus remain the primary source. Herodotus' visit to Scythia appears to have occurred in the middle of the fifth century BC, and although he is known to have reached Olbia on the southern edge of the Scythian realm, it is unclear how much further he actually travelled into the Scythian heartland. Much of his accounts of Scythian customs are clearly based on hearsay, so archaeology provides an important check on his description.

Scythian gold and silver ornaments and vessels are frequently decorated with representations of animals or of humans engaged in typical daily scenes like battle or milking. Wild animals and battling warriors are two prominent themes, but some motifs are more placid. For example, a silver bowl excavated in the Gaymanova tomb was decorated with a gold-plated frieze in which two elderly warriors wearing typical Scythian tunics of fur-trimmed leather are engaged in relaxed conversation. The gold pectoral from Tolstaya Mogila depicts a child milking a sheep and two men making a hide garment.

Like the "royal" burials of the Hallstatt commercial elite, the Scythians also concentrated an enormous amount of wealth in the burials of their chiefs, as well as investing considerable labor in the construction of impressive mortuary monuments. Scythian tombs typically have a central shaft, 10–15 meters deep. At its base, a tunnel leads into a hollowed-out burial chamber, often reinforced with massive timbers. The grave shafts were then filled with earth and rocks, and the burial mound, which could reach a height of 20 meters, was heaped up over the top of the shaft by scraping up the black topsoil for some distance around. Additional burials were sometimes added by digging adjacent shafts and either tunneling into the original burial chamber or hollowing out another.

Tolstaya Mogila is a classic example of a Scythian tomb. Although it is not one of the largest at 8.6 meters in height (some Scythian barrows range up to 20 meters tall), it is a good example of tomb architecture and grave goods. The Tolstaya Mogila main grave, that of a male about 50 years old, had been robbed in antiquity, but an untouched secondary burial shaft, which did not connect with the main grave, was found intact. The side grave contained five burials: a young woman and infant laid side-by-side with rich burial goods, a young man with a bow and arrow, a young woman next to a niche with food offerings, and a male associated with a complete wagon and several horses. Tolstaya Mogila has been interpreted as a mausoleum for an elite Scythian family (Rolle 1989: 29). First the "prince" died and was buried in the main grave. Shortly afterwards, the woman died and was buried in the side grave. After that was filled, the child died, so yet another entrance to the side grave was dug and the child was laid to the right of the young woman. A ditch around the perimeter of the mound contained the bones of 35 horses, 14 boar, and two stags, as well as shards of wine vessels, presumably the remains of a funeral feast.

Although the central grave at Tolstaya Mogila had been robbed, the thieves had missed a sword in a gold scabbard and a gold pectoral. The latter is perhaps the finest example of goldwork found in the Scythian lands. As with many of the Scythian gold artifacts, it was the product of a Greek colonial workshop, in which Scythian themes were interpreted by Greek artisans. The Tolstaya Mogila pectoral is a complex piece, but the overall theme is a contrast between the domestic pursuits of Scythians and the wildness outside their encampments. The upper register depicts foals and calves suckling, while the lower band shows griffins attacking horses and lions attacking deer. In the side burial, both the young woman and the child had similar grave goods, including gold fingerrings and armrings. Even one of the horses had a gold frontlet depicting a woman whose legs terminate in snake-heads.

Despite the presumed nomadism of the Scythians, their contact with the Greeks led to the emergence of their own permanent settlements. Elizavetovka, on an island at the mouth of the Don, developed into a center of craft production and trade in the second half of the fourth century BC (Marčenko and Vinogradov 1989: 810; Dolukhanov 1996: 124). It was surrounded by fortification walls and ditches. Another large settlement in Scythia is the fortress of Kamenskoe on the lower Dniepr (Rolle 1989: 120–1), which covers an area of 12 square kilometers. Kamenskoe is reminiscent of the *oppida* of western Europe, on the scale of Manching in Bavaria. Like Manching, Kamenskoe has yielded abundant evidence for iron-working; almost every house yielded traces of smelting or forging (Dolukhanov 1996: 123). Beyond these sites, however, evidence for Scythian settlements is very slim.

Relations between the Scythians and the Greeks were not completely peaceful, however. In 339 BC, the Scythians were defeated by Philip II of Macedonia, which caused their decline in the area immediately along the Black Sea. North of this region, however, they continued to flourish and perhaps adopted a more sedentary lifestyle. In 1996, a team of Polish and Ukrainian archaeologists excavated a remarkable unrobbed late Scythian tomb at Ryzhanovka, south of Kiev (Chochorowski and Skoryi 1997). The layout of the tomb resembles that of a two-room house. One chamber is analogous to a kitchen with a mock hearth containing bronze kettles with boiled horse and lamb bones. The other is like a bedroom, in which the chief's body lay on a wooden platform. Around his neck was a gold torc with lion-head finials. Nearby were 34 gold medallions and over a hundred appliques which had decorated a headdress. Two silver cups, decorated by griffins attacking a bull and a deer, were found in a tightly sealed bronze bucket. Outside the entrance to the burial chamber was the body of the chief's retainer, who was probably killed at the time of burial in order to guard the chief in death, as well as the skeleton of the retainer's horse. The "domestic" nature of this grave and its late date has led to the hypothesis that the late Scythians were in transition from nomadic to settled life (Chochorowski and Skoryi 1997: 32).

The Scythians present an example of a nomadic society with social ranks which came into contact with the expanding Greek state. Like the Iron Age chiefdoms of central Europe, they used prestige goods produced in colonial workshops to demonstrate their access to the larger world. The colonial Greeks and the Scythians entered into a symbiotic relationship in which each became dependent on the other, the Greeks for steppe and forest products and the Scythians for Greek luxury goods. The importance of this relationship for the Scythians is demonstrated by the fact that the Greek colonies along the Black Sea were essentially defenseless, but they were allowed to exist so long as the Scythians were in power.

FROZEN TOMBS OF THE ALTAI

During the first millennium BC, the Altai Mountains on the border of Russia with China and Mongolia were the home of pastoralists who buried the members of their aristocracy in lavish tombs. These people have no commonly-accepted archaeological name but are frequently referred to as the "Pazyryk," which is actually the local name for "burial mound." Like the Scythians 4000 kilometers to the west, and most of the Iron Age peoples in between, they were horse-riding nomads. In fact, they are often treated as the eastern cousins of the Scythians in many archaeological discussions, which is as great a stretch as calling the Anasazi the cousins of the Mississippians because they both grew corn (and were separated by only 2000 kilometers) in North America! Although they share many similarities, enough to be considered together here, their external relationships were significantly different from those of the Scythians.

Virtually all we know about the Pazyryk people comes from their burial mounds. The contents of many of these tombs were literally "frozen in time" and contain not only superbly-preserved bodies of people and horses, but also exceptional textile and leather objects. Such finds not only provide a wealth of information about the Iron Age societies of this remote region but also the peoples with whom they had contact, notably China and Persia. The Altai tombs appear on the surface as low earthen mounds covered with stones, up to 46 meters in diameter. Each large mound conceals a central tomb shaft between 4 and 5 meters deep, which must have been dug during the warm season, since the ground was frozen during the rest of the year. Within the shafts were nested timber chambers which contained the primary burial and grave goods. Above these, layers of logs and stones filled the shaft up to the base of the mound. The water vapor that remained in the chambers after their construction condensed on the stones in the grave fill, trickled back down into the grave, saturated the corpses and the accompanying grave goods, and then froze during the Siberian winter. The mounds above insulated the frozen tombs, and thus the bodies and grave goods remained refrigerated for over two thousand years.

In Barrow 2 at Ust Ulagan the burial chamber was lined with felt wall-hangings. Within it, the embalmed bodies of a man and a woman, wrapped in a woolen rug, had been placed in a coffin made from a larch trunk. On the man's body were remarkable tattoos depicting imaginary and real animals, including griffins, rams, birds, snakes, and deer. Elsewhere in the burial chamber were more clothing and textiles, leather objects, wooden furniture, gold and silver ornaments, and mirrors.

As in the Scythian tombs, numerous horses were also buried with the royal dead on the Altai. Typically between seven and 14 are found per tomb, off to one side from the main burial chambers. In some cases, the horse bodies were preserved along with extraordinary furnishings including bridles, saddles, and cloth horse-coats. Among the horses in one barrow was a large four-wheeled wagon, with a felt canopy ornamented with appliqued figures of swans.

In the summer of 1993, the Russian archaeologist Natalya Polosmak found another important frozen tomb at Ukok. The barrow was excavated carefully to reveal an unlooted frozen tomb with the elegantly tattooed body of a woman about 25 years old in a long larch-log coffin, with textiles and leather items, and wooden plates bearing cuts of mutton and horsemeat. Just outside the burial chamber were six horses, each killed with a blow to the head, with their chestnut-brown manes and felt saddle-covers preserved in extraordinary detail. The woman in the Ukok tomb was clearly a person of high status in her own right, not the wife or concubine of a male chief.

The clothes of the Ukok woman were exceptionally well-preserved. She wore a large hair-and-felt headdress decorated with gold-covered carved cats, a silk blouse with maroon piping, a woolen dress, and felt boots. The silk blouse has particular significance. The silk in the Pazyryk tombs was long presumed to have come from China, but there is some evidence from the fibers of the Ukok blouse to suggest that it may have come from elsewhere, possibly India. This would suggest that the trade connections of the Pazyryk people were more extensive than hitherto expected.

YAYOI AND KOFUN JAPAN

The Jomon maritime foraging adaptation described in chapter 4 above was surprisingly durable. In fact, during its later stages, it provided a foundation for the emergence of transegalitarian societies much like those which about the same time appeared on the northwestern coast of North America as the precursors of the complex chiefdoms found there in later prehistory. Although the Jomon people appear to have done some small-scale gardening of dry rice, millet, and barnyard grass (*Echinochloa*) from about 2000 BC onward, the transition to a wet-rice-based economy does not appear to have taken place until the second half of the first millennium BC (Crawford 1992). This transition is associated with the arrival of immigrants from the Asian mainland in the fourth and fifth centuries BC.

The time between the fifth century BC and the third century AD in Japanese prehistory is known as the Yayoi period. It is characterized by four major developments (Imamura 1996: 127):

1 the establishment of wet-rice cultivation as the backbone of the agricultural system;
2 the procurement and manufacture of bronze and iron tools, which appeared simultaneously;
3 interaction – in the form of migration, trade and diplomacy – with Korea and China;
4 the emergence of differences in access to status, power, and wealth and the establishment of polities which later formed the basis for the early Japanese state.

All these developments are related, since wet-rice cultivation was introduced from the Asian mainland, alongside metallurgy. Metal objects were prestige items, and the procurement of these items and the participation in foreign trade and diplomacy enhanced the prestige of the emergent elite.

Wet-rice cultivation spread quickly across Japan, and with it the use of iron agricultural tools. Farming settlements were located adjacent to the paddies. One such settlement is Toro, in Shizuoka prefecture in central Honshu, which was located on a levee in a floodplain along the Abe river. Twelve sub-rectangular (i.e., rectangular with rounded corners) houses with four major posts and surrounded by a banked enclosure were found. Numerous wooden tools were preserved, including shovels, fire-making mortars and bows, spading forks, and a footstool. Not far away, the larger site of Otsuka had several dozen houses and was surrounded by a fortification ditch, unlike Toro. Such evidence for conflict is corroborated by a number of burials throughout Japan in which iron, bronze, and stone arrowheads are embedded among the bones.

Another fortified Yayoi site is Yoshinogari in northern Kyushu, the part of Japan which is closest to Korea. A large outer ditch encloses an irregular area about 1000 meters by 450 meters, while within this area are several additional ditched enclosures about 150 meters in diameter. Over 2000 jar burials were found, as well as traces of a bronze-making workshop and storehouses. Two burial mounds, called *funkyobo*, cover jar burials which have bronze swords and glass beads. *Funkyobo* mounds are considered to be the burials of high-status individuals (Makoto 1992; Imamura 1996: 191). The Yoshinogari complex represents a site which is considerably more elaborate than the farming settlements like Toro and Otsuka, suggesting that it was the fortified seat of an individual who might be considered a chief.

Bronze mirrors imported from China figured prominently in Yayoi elite circles. They can be correlated very closely with the chronology of the mainland. Initially, the bronze mirrors and other bronze artifacts were imported from Korea and China (Imamura 1996: 170). Han Chinese bronze mirrors passed through many generations over a couple of centuries in Japan before being buried in tombs. Local bronze and iron foundries arose in a number of parts of Japan, making copies of the Chinese mirrors, bronze spears, iron axes, and ceremonial copper bells called *dotaku*. The *dotaku* cast at Higashinara, where molds for them have been found, have been found at several sites in neighboring prefectures. Hoards of bronze tools and *dotaku*, reminiscent of the deposits found in Europe from the second millennium BC, are common in southwestern Japan (Imamura 1996: 174).

Burial evidence points towards an increasing differentiation between the elite and the commoners. In some areas this took the form of *funkyobo* burial mounds in the midst of public cemeteries, whereas elsewhere the elite had their own special burial precincts (Imamura 1996: 182). Progressively larger *funkyobo* point towards an increased emphasis on elite display. One of the largest, Tatetsuki in Okayama prefecture, is 40 meters in diameter and 5 meters high (Hiroshi 1992: 66). *Funkyobo* also have distinct local forms. Some are square or rectangular in plan, sometimes with extensions at the corners, while in other areas the mounds are round with two lateral extensions.

In general, the Yayoi period is one of increasing social differentiation and access to the prestige goods which were both imported from across the Korea Strait and produced locally. Han Chinese accounts report that there were "more than 100 polities" in Japan, some of which sent delegations to the Chinese provincial capital in Korea (Imamura 1996: 185). The primary point of contact between the Yayoi and the Han was the Lelang Commandery, a Han outpost near modern Pyongyang. Through Lelang, Han court gifts were passed along to the Yayoi, while raw materials were procured for Han court use. The situation is very reminiscent of the Greek trading colony at Massalia and the contact it facilitated between the Mediterranean world and Iron Age polities in central Europe. The variation in the *funkyobo* burial mounds also points towards the existence of a number of smaller polities, each with its distinctive way of marking the burials of its elite.

During the third century AD, a dramatic increase in the size of the burial mounds can be observed. Moreover, they came to exhibit a common keyhole-shaped plan, in which a round burial mound has a trapezoidal extension to appear in plan like the keyhole for an old-fashioned skeleton key. These keyhole tombs are known as *kofun*, from which the name of the period between AD 300 and 700 is taken. The Kofun period is associated with the rise of polities which have been labeled "states," but which might also be seen as complex commercial chiefdoms.

The standardization of *kofun* tombs is evidence for the interregional integration of the elite. Kondo (1983) interprets this standardization as the establishment of symbolic kinship among the elite, by demonstrating links to common ancestors through common mortuary ritual. One of the earliest *kofun* is the large mound of Hashihaka on the Yamato Plain in the Kyoto-Osaka region. It dates to the late third century AD and is nearly 300 meters long and 30 meters high at the top of the circular part. Hashihaka is dated through a fragment of a *haniwa* moulded clay sculpture found on its surface. The practice of placing statues on tombs was another practice imported to

Japan from the Chinese court and the *haniwa* styles have sufficient variability to be very sensitive chronological indicators. Like the other *kofun*, Hashihaka was built with a series of steps along each side, creating a terraced effect. Pebbles covered the surface of the mound.

Since most of the *kofun* are in the custody of the Imperial Household Agency because they are believed to be the tombs of the earliest emperors, excavation of them has begun only very recently, usually in conjunction with repairs (Edwards 1997). The rounded portions of them certainly cover burial chambers, while the trapezoidal extensions are often interpreted as platforms for mortuary rites. Deposited in the burial chambers were large quantities of prestige goods, including bronze mirrors.

Imported Wei dynasty Chinese mirrors played an extremely important role in early Kofun Japan (Tanaka, Sasaki, and Sagawa 1998). Many of these mirrors were cast from the same molds, yet are found in widely-separated parts of southern Japan. These mirrors were between 20 and 25 centimeters in diameter and had a thick rim. Inscriptions along the rim allow them to be dated accurately. The elites of the various districts exchanged Chinese bronze mirrors to cement their political links. Sasaki (1992) has proposed that the paramount chiefs, such as those buried in the large *kofun*, distributed duplicate mirrors to the local elites who owed loyalty to them.

Relatively little is known of Kofun residential sites. Hiroshi (1992: 80–1) describes the establishment of chiefly residential compounds, separate from the rest of the population. At Mitsudera, there was a central area with large post structures, separated from an area with pit houses by a fence. The latter area is presumed to be the workshops of craft specialists or houses of retainers (Hiroshi 1992: 81) The Ōzono site contains only post structures and is interpreted as the residence of a minor chief or a powerful farmer. On the other hand, the Kobukada site is a collection of pit houses and is interpreted as a village of commoner farmers.

Over time, the size of the *kofun* keyhole tombs continued to grow. Although, as Edwards (1997: 42) points out, reliable assignment of tombs to specific historical personages is not possible, *kofun* near Osaka attributed to the emperor Ojin and his son Nintoku are the largest known, dating to the fifth century AD. The Ojin keyhole tomb is 415 meters long, while that attributed to Nintoku is the largest in Japan at 485 meters, with a volume similar to that of the Egyptian pyramids. By this time, it appears that the polities of Honshu had been united into a centralized state ruled from the Yamato region.

It is significant that the initial state society in Japan did not arise in the Kyushu region directly across from the Korean peninsula, where the most complex Yayoi sites are found and where these were the strongest connections with the Han empire. Instead, the largest *kofun* and the seat of the emergent Yamato state are located several hundred kilometers east on Honshu. Despite its indigenous character, the Yamato state maintained close relations with the Chinese court and contemporaneous kingdoms in Korea. Korean immigrants to Japan introduced a distinctive gray unglazed stoneware known as *sue*, which is found in keyhole tombs of this period.

Japan provides an interesting case study of the effect of a nearby powerful state on a society organized into small competing polities. When it is finally possible to excavate more of the *kofun* tombs, as Edwards (1997) suggests will be forthcoming despite calls for restraint (Imamura 1996: 194), more details on the formation of early state polities in Japan will emerge. Of particular interest will be the patterns of royal gifting, traced through artifacts such as the bronze mirrors, which will demonstrate the progressive integration of the elite among the various polities.

COMMERCIAL CHIEFDOMS IN THE PHILIPPINES

Like Japan, the chiefdoms in mainland Southeast Asia and the offshore islands were greatly affected by the presence of the Chinese state. As in Europe, the relationship went both ways. The state had a demand for non-local materials and products, while the chiefs had the means of extracting these materials from their sources and concentrating them for trade. It was in the interest of the state not only to promote the status of the chiefs but also to foster competition among them. The result, as in Europe, was the accumulation of fantastic wealth by the elites in places far distant from the destination of their trade goods.

For about a millennium prior to European contact in the sixteenth century AD, the Philippine Islands were inhabited by a number of complex stratified societies which have been characterized as "chiefdoms" (Junker 1993, 1994). These societies are known from ethnohistoric accounts by Chinese and Spanish writers and, increasingly, from archaeology. The Philippine chiefdoms were primarily lowland coastal polities, while the island interior uplands were occupied by simpler agriculturalists and foragers. The Philippine coastal chiefdoms first appeared around the sixth century AD, but from the tenth century onward they engaged in vigorous long-distance exchange with mainland Asia, especially with China. This exchange intensified even more in the fifteenth and sixteenth centuries AD, immediately prior to European contact. There is even evidence during this period of "trade missions" from Philippine polities to cement exchange relationships (Junker 1994: 241).

The Philippine chiefdoms were centered on large coastal settlements which were the seats of the chief and his retainers. One such center is located at Tanjay, on the eastern coast of Negros Island (Junker 1993, 1994; Junker, Mudar and Schwaller 1994). Excavations revealed that during the fifteenth and sixteenth centuries, two distinct residential zones existed. In one, three large houses were surrounded by ditch and palisade fortifications. Around these houses were higher densities of Chinese porcelain, bronze and iron objects, and glass beads than in the other residential zone with simpler architecture. Similar patterns of residential differences in wealth can be traced back to the eleventh century at Tanjay.

Surveys of the area around Tanjay indicate that a two-tiered regional settlement hierarchy began in the second half of the first millennium AD. In the fifteenth century, it was transformed into a three-tiered structure, in which secondary centers were evenly spaced along riverine trade routes leading into the interior. Apparently, the elite control of exchange between the upland interior and the coastal lowlands was a crucial factor in permitting the acquisition of large quantities of foreign prestige goods. Increasing standardization of lowland-produced pottery in the fifteenth and sixteenth century suggests specialist production (Junker 1993). These pottery vessels were traded inland in exchange for metal ores and forest products, including rattan, beeswax, honey, tree resins, tropical hardwoods, and spices (Junker 1994: 235). The chiefs could then export these items in exchange for luxury goods from the Asian mainland. Acquisition of Chinese porcelains had begun already in the tenth century AD, but it remained at a relatively low level for about five centuries (Junker 1993: 26). The reorganization of the settlement structure in the fifteenth century was apparently driven by an intensification of the external prestige-goods trade.

Ethnohistoric data also indicate that Philippine chiefs engaged in displays of wealth which enhanced their status and prestige. There is also evidence that the elite at Tanjay had access to the best cuts of meat. Rubbish deposits at the chiefly compounds have higher proportions of water buffalo, pig, and other animals known from ethnohistoric accounts to have had greater prestige (Junker, Mudar, and Schwaller 1994). Moreover, the high-status compounds at Tanjay have more high-meat-value faunal elements in comparison with the lower-status residences. One likely possibility is that this is the result of the ceremonial division of animal carcasses that would have occurred during competitive feasting (Junker, Mudar, and Schwaller 1994: 350).

There is also considerable archaeological and ethnohistoric evidence for interpolity conflict during the fifteenth and sixteenth centuries. A mass grave of nine individuals at Tanjay included four detached skulls with evidence for violent deaths. One possibility is that individual polities were trying to disrupt the foreign trade of their competitors and thus gain an advantage in the access to prestige goods (Junker 1994: 235). In fact, the increase in interpolity competition in this period is accompanied by the territorial expansion of a number of the Philippine chiefdoms.

As in Iron Age Eurasia, the Philippine chiefdoms, particularly in the fifteenth and sixteenth centuries AD, provide an example of complex polities in which external trade was the catalyst for the extreme concentration of wealth and the restructuring of the local economic system. In fact, the Philippines may represent an even more robust case of this syndrome than, for example, Europe. Whereas in Europe the foreign prestige goods were relatively rare and focused on wine and wine-drinking, the Chinese trade goods in the Philippines occur largely in elite domestic contexts but also permeated in small quantities to other segments of society (Junker 1994: 242). In the Tanjay region, they appear to have circulated locally in networks of exchange and redistribution. Thus, while the chiefs of Hallstatt Europe largely held on to their exotic acquisitions, the Philippine chiefs fed some of them back into the local network of exchange.

CONCLUSION

Prehistory ends with human societies organized in many different ways around the world. Perhaps the greatest diversity among human societies existed between 1000 BC and AD 1000 and has declined steadily in the last thousand years as traditional cultures have given up their ancient ways either voluntarily or by conquest. Such a loss of cultural diversity is an inevitable by-product of literate civilization, which propels human society towards increasing commonality in language and values, and of technological developments in communications and travel. History, therefore, documents a progressive loss of cultural diversity, whose full extent is known only through archaeology.

No sane reader of this volume would wish a return to prehistoric times, of course. Through archaeology we can visit past societies, but we would not want to live in them. Yet the study of such societies can teach us many important lessons about human adaptability, about human resourcefulness, about human motivations, and about the consequences of human decisions. Are these important lessons? In a strictly utilitarian sense, perhaps not. Most decisions about the world today are made in complete ignorance of any precedents in antiquity. In a broader sense, however, it is impossible to appreciate the achievements of modern humans without some understanding of the complex path they have followed. Technologically, it is a record of sustained accomplishment. Politically, it is a record of short-term success and long-term failure. Spiritually and artistically, it is a record of how essential these qualities are to being human. Only with knowledge about the 100,000 generations of humans who have preceded us can we fully appreciate what it means to be alive.

FURTHER READING

The rise of civilizations and states is the aspect of prehistoric archaeology that does not fail to engage the interest of people outside the field. The emphasis in this chapter has been on the prehistoric roots of the classic civilizations, as well as the societies on their margins that flourished in their shadows. A much fuller treatment of early civilizations through their development, apex, and decline can be found in the following volume in this series, *The Beginnings of Civilization* by Robert Wenke.

Urbanism and writing are two important characteristics of early civilizations. *First Cities* by Anthony Andrews (1995) is a short, readable, and comprehensive overview of the development of cities. A case study treatment of specific cities can be found in *Emergence and Change in Early Urban Societies*, edited by Linda Manzanilia (1997). Early writing systems and their precursors are discussed by Denise Schmandt-Besserat in *Before Writing: From Counting to Cuneiform* (1992) and by Andrew Robinson in *The Story of Writing* (1995).

Hans Nissen's *The Early History of the Ancient Near East 9000–2000 BC* (1988) provides the basic overview of the emergence of Mesopotamian civilization. Entries in *Civilization of the Ancient Near East*, edited by Jack M. Sasson (1995), provide updated information. *The Uruk Countryside* by Robert M. Adams and Hans Nissen (1972) remains the classic study of the changes in settlement that accompanied urbanism in lower Mesopotamia. Daniel T. Potts discusses the artifacts found at Mesopotamian sites in *Mesopotamian Civilization: The Material Foundations* (1997), while J. N. Postgate takes a more historical view in *Early Mesopotamia: Society and Economy at the Dawn of History* (1992). The crucial Uruk and Jemdet Nasr periods are discussed by Susan Pollock in "Bureaucrats and managers, peasants and pastoralists, imperialists and traders: research on the Uruk and Jemdet Nasr periods in Mesopotamia," in *Journal of World Prehistory*, vol. 6, pp. 297–336 (1992). Foreign connections between early Mesopotamian sites and the Iranian Plateau are described by Timothy Potts in *Mesopotamia and the East: An Archaeological and Historical Study of Foreign Relations, ca. 3400–2000 BC* (1994).

The emergence of Harappan civilization is described by Gregory Possehl in a review article entitled "Revolution in the urban revolution: the emergence of Indus urbanism," in the *Annual Review of Anthropology*, vol. 19, pp. 261–82 (1990) and by Jonathan Mark Kenoyer in "The Indus Valley tradition of Pakistan and Western India," *Journal of World Prehistory*, vol. 5, pp. 331–85 (1991). Additional archaeological information can be found in *Harappan Civilization: A Recent Perspective*, edited by Possehl (1993) and *The Archaeology of Eary Historic South Asia: The Emergence of Cities and States*, edited by F. R. Allchin (1995). Possehl discusses the Indus script in *Indus Age: The Writing System* (1996).

K. C. Chang's 1986 *The Archaeology of Ancient China* (3rd edn) remains the canonical reference for the origins of Chinese cities and states.

The roots of Egyptian civilization are described by Barry Kemp in *Ancient Egypt: Anatomy of a Civilization* (1989), which can be supplemented by articles by Robert Wenke, "The evolution of early Egyptian civilization: issues and evidence," in *Journal of World Prehistory*, vol. 5, pp. 279–329 (1991) and Fekri Hassan, "The Predynastic of Egypt," *Journal of World Prehistory*, vol. 2, pp. 135–85.

Early urban societies in sub-Saharan Africa are described in a number of the chapters in *The Archaeology of Africa: Food, Metals, and Towns*, edited by Thurstan Shaw, Paul Sinclair, Bassey Andah, and Alex Okpoko (1993). David W. Phillipson's *African Archaeology* (2nd edn, 1993) and Graham Connah's 1987 *African Civilizations. Precolonial Cities and States in Tropical Africa: an Archaeological Perspective* are also important sources.

The literature base for Mesoamerican civilization is enormous, and only a handful of the important general works can be mentioned here. For the Valley of Mexico and the site of Teotihuacan, Esther Pasztory's *Teotihuacan: An Experiment in Living* (1997) can be complemented by the review article by George Cowgill entitled "State and society at Teotihuacan, Mexico," in *Annual Review of Antliropology*, vol. 26, pp. 129–61 (1997). For Oaxaca, the key sources are *Monte Albán: Settlement Patterns at the Ancient Zapotec Capital* by Richard Blanton (1978) and *The Cloud People: Divergent Evolution of the Zapotec and Mixtec Civilizations*, edited by Kent Flannery and Joyce Marcus (1983). The Maya realm has an enormous amount of literature. Some good general overviews include *The Ancient Maya* by Robert Sharer (5th edn, 1994), *Daily Life in Maya Civilizaion*, also by Sharer (1996), *The New Archaeology and the Ancient Maya* by Jeremy Sabloff (1994), and *Ancient Maya Civilization* by Norman Hammond (1982). These works can be supplemented by books focused on individual sites. Among these are *Scribes, Warriors, and Kings: the City of Copan and the Ancient Maya* by William Fash (1991) and *Hieroglyphs and History at Dos Pilas: Dynastic Politics of the Classic Maya* by Stephen Houston (1992). Mesoamerican hieroglyphs are discussed by Joyce Marcus in *Mesoamerican Writing Systems: Propaganda, Myth, and History in Four Ancient Civilizations* (1992), while "Maya writing," by David Stuart and Stephen Houston, appeared in *Scientific American*, vol. 261, no. 2, pp. 82–9. *War and Society in Ancient Mesoamerica* by Ross Hassig (1992) focuses on competition and conflict throughout the region in prehistory.

Andean civilization has a similar copious body of literature. An excellent overview is *People of the Andes* by James B. Richardson III (1994), while *Peruvian Prehistory. An Overview of Pre-Inca and Inca Society*, edited by Richard Keatinge (1988), goes into greater archaeological detail. Beyond such overviews, the early stages of Andean civilization are best examined locally. The Moche peoples of the north coast of Peru are the topic of *The Moche* by Garth Bawden (1996), which can be supplemented by *Royal Tombs of Sipán* by Walter Alva and Christopher Donnan (1993) and *Pampa Grande and the Mochica Culture* by Izumi Shimada (1994). Cahuachi, the important ceremonial site of the south coast, is described in detail by Helaine Silverman in *Cahuachi in the Ancient Nasca World* (1993), while the Nazca lines are discussed in the essays in *The Lines of Nazca*, edited by Anthony Aveni (1990). Alan Kolata has written two recent books on the highland civilization of Tiwanaku, including *The Tiwanaku: Portrait of an Andean Civilization* (1993) and *Tiwanaku and its Hinterland: Archaeology and Palaeoecology of an Andean Civilization* (1996).

A number of important volumes have discussed the complex societies which existed alongside states. For Europe, the best overview can be found in *Farms, Villages, and Cities: Commerce and Urban Origins in Late Prehistoric Europe* by Peter Wells (1984), which can be supplemented by *Towns, Villages, and Countryside of Celtic Europe from the Beginning of the Second Millennium to the End of the First Century BC* by Françoise Audouze and Olivier Büchsenschütz (1992) and the essays in *Celtic Chiefdom, Celtic State*, edited by Bettina Arnold and D. Blair Gibson (1995). Iron Age societies in Britain are the specific topic of *English Heritage Book of Iron Age Britain* (1995) and *English Heritage Book of Danebury* (1993), both by Barry Cunliffe. A similar overview is provided for southern Scandinavia by Lotte Hedeager in *Iron-Age Societies: From Tribe to State in Northern Europe, 500 BC to AD 700* (1992). Scythian culture is described in *The World of the Scythians* by Renate Rolle (1989). The fundamental volume on the early excavations of Pazyryk barrows is Sergei Rudenko's *Frozen Tombs of Siberia* (1970), while Natalya Polosmak's 1994 article in *National Geographic*, vol. 186, no. 4, pp. 80–103 entitled "A mummy unearthed from the Pastures of Heaven" provides initial information on recent research. Turning to east Asia, *Prehistoric Japan: New Perspectives on Insular East Asia* by Keiji Imamura (1996) provides a needed overview of Japanese prehistory in English. The late prehistoric chiefdoms of the Philippines are the topic of a number of articles by Laura Lee Junker, such as "Trade competition, conflict, and political transformations in sixth- to sixteenth-century Philippine chiefdoms," in *Asian Perspectives*, vol. 33, pp. 229–60.

BIBLIOGRAPHY

Abbott, David R. 1996. Ceramic exchange and a strategy for reconstructing organizational developments among the Hohokam. *Interpreting Southwestern Diversity: Underlying Principles and Overarching Patterns*, P. R. Fish and J. J. Reid (eds), pp. 147–58. Tucson: Arizona State University (Anthropological Research Papers 48).

Ackerman, Robert E. 1996. Bluefish Caves. *American Beginnings. The Prehistory and Palaeoecology of Beringia*, F. H. West (ed.), pp. 511–13. Chicago: University of Chicago Press.

Adams, Robert M., and Hans T. Nissen 1972. *The Uruk Countryside.* Chicago: University of Chicago Press.

Adovasio, James M. 1993. The ones that will not go away. A biased view of pre-Clovis populations in the New World. *From Kostenki to Clovis. Upper Palaeolithic – Palaeo-Indian Adaptations*, O. Soffer and N. D. Praslov (eds), pp. 199–218. New York: Plenum Press.

——, J. D. Gunn, J. Donahue, R. Stuckenrath, J. E. Guilday, K. Volman 1980. Yes, Virginia, it really is that ofld: reply to Haynes and Mead. *American Antiquity* 45: 588–95.

Agnew, Neville, and Martha Demas 1998. Preserving the Laetoli footprints. *Scientific American* 279: 44–55.

Aiello, Leslie C. 1993. Fossil evidence for modern human origins in Africa: a revised view. *American Anthropologist* 95: 73–96.

——, and R. I. M. Dunbar 1993. Neocortex size, group size, and the evolution of language. *Current Anthropology* 34: 184–93.

Aikens, C. Melvin 1995. First in the world: the Jomon pottery of early Japan. *The Emergence of Pottery*, W. K. Barnett and J. Hoopes (eds), pp. 11–21. Washington: Smithsonian Institution Press.

Akkermans, Peter M. M. G. 1993. *Villages in the Steppe – Later Neolithic Settlement and Subsistence in the Balikh Valley, Northern Syria.* Ann Arbor: International Monographs in Prehistory.

——, and Marc Verhoeven 1995. An image of complexity: the burnt village at late Neolithic Sabi Abyad, Syria. *American Journal of Archaeology* 99: 5–32.

Albrethsen, Svend E., and Erik Brinch Petersen 1976. Excavation of a mesolithic cemetery at Vedbæk, Denmark. *Acta Archaeologica* 47: 1–28.

Algaze, Guillermo 1993. *The Uruk World System. The Dynamics of Expansion of Early Mesopotamian Civilization.* Chicago: University of Chicago Press.

Allchin, Bridget, and Raymond Allchin 1993. Lewan – a stone tool factory of the fourth to third millennium BC. *Harappan Civilization. A Recent Perspective*, G. L. Possehl (ed.), pp. 521–53. New Delhi: Oxford and IBH Publishing.

Allchin, F. R. 1995. *The Archaeology of Early Historic South Asia. The Emergence of Cities and States.* Cambridge: Cambridge University Press.

Allen, Jim 1989. When did humans first colonise Australia? *Search* 20: 149–54.

—— 1994. Radiocarbon determinations, luminescence dating and Australian archaeology. *Antiquity* 68: 339–43.

——, and Simon Holdaway 1995. Contamination of Pleistocene radiocarbon determinations in Australia. *Antiquity* 69: 101–12.

Allen, Mark W. 1996. Pathways to economic power in Maori chiefdoms: ecology and warfare in prehistoric Hawke's Bay. *Research in Economic Anthropology* 17: 171–225.

Allen, Michael J., Michael Morris, and R. H. Clark 1996. Food for the living: a reassessment of a Bronze Age barrow at Buckskin, Basingstoke, Hampshire. *Proceedings of the Prehistoric Society* 61: 157–89.

Altuna, Jesus, Anne Eastham, Koro Mariezkurrena, Arthur Spiess, Lawrence Straus 1991. Magdalenian and Azilian hunting at the Abri Dufaure, SW France. *ArchaeoZoologia* 4: 87–108.

Alva, Walter, and Christopher B. Donnan 1993. *Royal Tombs of Sipán.* Los Angeles: Fowler Museum of Cultural History.

Ambrose, Stanley H., and Karl G. Lorenz 1990. Social and ecological models for the Middle Stone Age in southern Africa. *The Emergence of Modern Humans. An Archaeological Perspective*, Paul Mellars (ed.), pp. 3–33. Ithaca: Cornell University Press.

Ames, Kenneth M. 1996. Life in the big house: household labor and dwelling size on the Northwest Coast. *People Who Lived in Big Houses. Archaeological Perspectives on Large Domestic Structures*, G. Coupland and E. B. Banning (eds), pp. 131–50. Madison: Prehistory Press.

Amiet, Pierre 1993. The period of Irano-Mesopotamian contacts 3500–1600 BC. *Early Mesopotamia and Iran: Contact and Conflict 3500–1600 BC*, John Curtis (ed.), pp. 23–30. London: British Museum Press.

An Chin-huai 1986. The Shang city at Cheng-Chou and related problems. *Studies of Shang Archaeology*, K. C. Chang (ed.), pp. 15–48. New Haven: Yale University Press.

Andersen, Søren H., and Kaare Lund Rasmussen 1991. Bjørnsholm: a stratified Køkkenmødding on the central Limfjord, North Jutland. *Journal of Danish Archaeology* 10: 59–96.

Anderson, David G. 1994. *The Savannah River Chiefdoms: Political Change in the Late Prehistoric Southeast.* Tuscaloosa: University of Alabama Press.

——1996. Fluctuations between simple and complex chiefdoms in the late prehistoric Southeast. *Political Structure and Change in the Prehistoric Southeastern United States*, J. F. Scarry (ed.), pp. 231–52. Gainesville: University Press of Florida.

Anderson, David G. 1997. The role of Cahokia in the evolution of Southeastern Mississippian society. *Cahokia. Domination and Ideology in the Mississippian World*, T. R. Pauketat and T. E. Emerson (eds), pp. 248–68. Lincoln: University of Nebraska Press.

Anderson, Patricia C. 1991. Harvesting of wild cereals during the Natufian as seen from experimental cultivation and harvest of wild einkorn wheat and microwear analysis of stone tools. *The Natufian Culture in the Levant*, O. Bar-Yosef and F. R. Valla (eds), pp. 521–56. Ann Arbor: International Monographs in Prehistory.

Andrews, Anthony 1995. *First Cities*. Montreal: St. Remy Press.

Andrews, V., E. Wyllys, William M. Ringle III, Philip J. Barnes, Alfredo Barrera Rubio, and Tomás Gallereta Negron 1984. Komchén: an early Maya community in northwest Yucatán. *Investigaciones Recientes en el Area Maya, vol. 1*, pp. 73–92. Mexico City: Sociedad Mexicana de Antropología.

Anthony, David 1995. Horse, wagon & chariot: Indo-European languages and archaeology. *Antiquity* 69: 554–65.

——, Dimitri Y. Telegin, and Dorcas Brown 1991. The origin of horseback riding. *Scientific American* 265: 94–100.

Arnold, Bettina 1995. The material culture of social structure: rank and status in early Iron Age Europe. *Celtic Chiefdom, Celtic State*, B. Arnold and D. B. Gibson (eds), pp. 43–52. Cambridge: Cambridge University Press.

Arnold, Jeanne E. 1996. Organizational transformations: power and labor among complex hunter-gatherers and other intermediate societies. *Emergent Complexity. The Evolution of Intermediate Societies*, J. E. Arnold (ed.), pp. 59–73. Ann Arbor: International Monographs in Prehistory.

——, and Ann Munns 1994. Independent or attached specialization: the organization of shell bead production in California. *Journal of Field Archaeology* 21: 473–89.

Arroyo, Barbara 1995. Early ceramics from El Salvador. The El Carmen site. *The Emergence of Pottery. Technology and Innovation in Ancient Societies*, W. K. Barnett and J. W. Hoopes (eds), pp. 199–208. Washington: Smithsonian Institution Press.

Asch, David L., and Nancy B. Asch 1985. Prehistoric plant cultivation in west-central Illinois. *Prehistoric Food Production in North America*, R. I. Ford (ed.), pp. 149–204. Ann Arbor: Museum of Anthropology (Anthropological Papers 75).

Ashmore, Wendy, and Richard R. Wilk 1988. Household and community in the Mesoamerican past. *Household and Community in the Mesoamerican Past*, R. R. Wilk and W. Ashmore (eds), pp. 1–27. Albuqerque: University of New Mexico Press.

Audouze, Françoise 1987. The Paris Basin in Magdalenian times. *The Pleistocene Old World*, O. Soffer (ed.), pp. 183–200. New York: Plenum Press.

——, and Olivier Büchsenschütz 1992. *Towns, Villages and Countryside of Celtic Europe from the Beginning of the Second Millennium to the End of the First Century BC*. Batsford: London.

——, and James Enloe 1997. High resolution archaeology at Verberie: limits and interpretations. *World Archaeology* 29: 195–207.

Aveni, Anthony (ed.) 1990. *The Lines of Nazca*. Philadelphia: American Philosophical Society.

Ayala, Francisco J. 1995. The myth of Eve: molecular biology and human origins. *Science* 270: 1930–6.

Bahn, Paul G. 1991. Pleistocene images outside Europe. *Proceedings of the Prehistoric Society* 57: 91–102.

—— 1994. New advances in the field of Ice Age art. *Origins of Anatomically Modern Humans*, M. H. Nitecki and D. V. Nitecki (eds), pp. 121–32. New York: Plenum Press.

—— (ed.) 1996. *The Cambridge Illustrated History of Archaeology*. Cambridge: Cambridge University Press.

—— and Jean Vertut 1988. *Images of the Ice Age*. New York: Facts on File.

Bailey, Geoff (ed.) 1997. *Klithi: Palaeolithic Settlement and Quaternary Landscapes in Northwest Greece*. Cambridge: McDonald Institute for Archaeological Research.

Bailey, Robert, Genevieve Hear, Mark Jenike, Bruce Owen, Robert Rechtman, and Elżbieta Zechenter 1989. Hunting and gathering in tropical rain forest: is it possible? *American Anthropologist* 91: 59–82.

Balter, Michael 1995. Did *Homo erectus* tame fire first? *Science* 268: 1570–1.

Bar-Yosef, Ofer 1986. The walls of Jericho: an alternative interpretation. *Current Anthropology* 27: 157–62.

—— 1991. The archaeology of the Natufian layer at Hayonim Cave. *The Natufian Culture in the Levant*, O. Bar-Yosef and F. R. Valla (eds), pp. 81–92. Ann Arbor: International Monographs in Prehistory.

—— 1994. The Lower Paleolithic of the Near East. *Journal of World Prehistory* 8: 211–65.

——, and Anna Belfer-Cohen 1989. The origins of sedentism and farming communities in the Levant. *Journal of World Prehistory* 3: 447–98.

——, and Anna Belfer-Cohen 1992. From foraging to farming in the Mediterranean Levant. *Transitions to Agriculture in Prehistory*, A. B. Gebauer and T. D. Price (eds), pp. 21–48. Madison: Prehistory Press.

——, and Avi Gopher (eds) 1997. *An Early Neolithic Village in the Jordan Valley. Part I: The Archaeology of Netiv Hagdud*. Cambridge: Peabody Museum of Archaeology and Ethnology (American School of Prehistoric Research Bulletin 43).

——, and Richard Meadow 1995. The origins of agriculture in the Near East. *Last Hunters, First Farmers. New Perspectives on the Prehistoric Transition to Agriculture*, T. D. Price and A. B. Gebauer (eds), pp. 39–94. Santa Fe: School of American Research Press.

——, Avi Gopher, Eitan Tchernov, and Mordechai E. Kislev 1991. Netiv Hagdud: an Early Neolithic village site in the Jordan Valley. *Journal of Field Archaeology* 18: 405–24.

——, B. Vermeersch, B. Arensburg, A. Belfer-Cohen, P. Goldberg, H. Laville, L. Meignen, Y. Rak, J. D. Speth, E. Tchernov, A.-M. Tillier, and S. Weiner 1992. The Excavations in Kebara Cave. Mt. Carmel. *Current Anthropology* 33: 497–550.

Bard, Kathryn A. 1997. Urbanism and the rise of complex society and the early state in Egypt. *Emergence and Change in Early Urban Societies*, L. Manzanilla (ed.), pp. 59–86. New York: Plenum Press.

Barfield, Lawrence 1994. The Iceman reviewed. *Antiquity* 68: 10–26.

Barker, Graeme 1975a. Prehistoric territories and economies in central Italy. *Palaeoeconomy*, E. S. Higgs (ed.), pp. 111–75. Cambridge: Cambridge University Press.

—— 1975b. Early Neolithic land use in Yugoslavia. *Proceedings of the Prehistoric Society* 41: 85–104.

—— 1981. *Landscape and Society. Prehistoric Central Italy*. London: Academic Press.

—— 1985. *Prehistoric Farming in Europe*. Cambridge: Cambridge University Press.

—— 1988. Cows and kings: models for zimbabwes. *Proceedings of the Prehistoric Society* 54: 223–40.

—— (ed.) 1999. *The Routledge Companion Encyclopedia of Archaeology*. London: Routledge.

——, and Tom Rasmussen 1998. *The Etruscans*. Oxford: Blackwell.

Barlett, Peggy (ed.) 1982. *Agricultural Choice and Change. Anthropological Contributions to Rural Development*. New Brunswick: Rutgers University Press.

Barnes, Carolyn, Jean Ensminger, and Phil O'Keefe 1984. *Wood, Energy and Households. Perspectives on Rural Kenya*. Stockholm: The Beijer Institute.

Barnett, William K. 1995. Putting the pot before the horse: earliest ceramics and the Neolithic transition in the western Mediterranean. *The Emergence of Pottery: Technology and Innovation in Ancient Societies*, W. K. Barnett and J. W. Hoopes (eds), pp. 79–88. Washington: Smithsonian Institution Press.

Barrett, John C. 1994. *Fragments from Antiquity. An Archaeology of Social Life in Britain, 2900–1200 BC*. Oxford: Blackwell.

Barrett, V., G. Lassiter, D. Wilcock, D. Baker, and E. Crawford 1982. *Animal Traction in Eastern Upper Volta: a Technical, Economic, and Institutional Analysis*. East Lansing, Michigan: Department of Agricultural Economics, Michigan State University.

Baryshnikov, Gennady, John F. Hoffecker, and Robin L. Burgess 1996. Palaeontology and zooarchaeology of Mezmaiskaya cave (Northwestern Caucasus, Russia). *Journal of Archaeological Science* 23: 313–35.

Bawden, Garth 1996. *The Moche*. Oxford: Blackwell.

Bednarik, Robert G. 1994. The Pleistocene art of Asia. *Journal of World Prehistory* 8: 351–75.

Behrensmeyer, Anna K., and Andrew P. Hill (eds) 1980. *Fossils in the Making: Vertebrate Taphonomy and Paleoecology*. Chicago: University of Chicago Press.

Belcher, William R. 1991. Fish resources in an early urban context at Harappa. *Harappa Excavations 1986–1990. A Multidisciplinary Approach to Third Millennium Urbanism*, R. H. Meadow (ed.), pp. 107–20. Madison: Prehistory Press.

Belfer-Cohen, A., L. A. Schepartz, and B. Arensburg 1991. New biological data for the Natufian populations in Israel. *The Natufian Culture in the Levant*, O. Bar-Yosef and F. R. Valla (eds), pp. 411–24. Ann Arbor: International Monographs in Prehistory.

Benz, Bruce F., and Hugh H. Iltis 1990. Studies in archaeological maize I: the "wild" maize from San Marcos Cave reexamined. *American Antiquity* 55: 500–11.

Bermúdez de Castro, J. M., J. L. Arsuaga, E. Carbonell, A. Rosas, I. Martínez, and M. Mosquera 1997. A hominid from the Lower Pleistocene of Atapuerca, Spain: Possible ancestor to Neandertals and modern humans. *Science* 276: 1392–5.

Berry, Michael S. 1982. *Time, Space, and Transition in Anasazi Prehistory.* Salt Lake City: University of Utah Press.

Berry, Sara 1980. Decision making and policy making in rural development. *Agricultural Decision Making. Anthropological Contributions to Rural Development*, P. Barlett (ed.), pp. 321–35. New York: Academic Press.

Biel, Jörg 1985. *Der Keltenfürst von Hochdorf.* Stuttgart: Konrad Thesis.

Bietti Sestieri, Anna Maria 1997. Italy in Europe in the Early Iron Age. *Proceedings of the Prehistoric Society* 63: 371–402.

Binford, Lewis R. 1967. Smudge pits and hide smoking: the use of analogy in archaeological reasoning. *American Antiquity* 32: 1–12.

—— 1968. Post-Pleistocene adaptations. *New Perspectives in Archaeology*, S. Binford and L. Binford (eds), pp. 313–41. Chicago: Aldine.

—— 1980. Willow smoke and dogs' tails: hunter-gatherer site systems and archaeological site formation. *American Antiquity* 45: 4–20.

—— 1981. *Bones: Ancient Men and Modern Myths.* New York: Academic Press.

—— 1984. *Faunal Remains of Klasies River Mouth.* New York: Academic Press.

—— 1987. Searching for camps and missing the evidence? Another look at the Lower Palaeolithic. *The Pleistocene Old World*, O. Soffer (ed.), pp. 17–32. New York: Plenum Press.

—— 1988. Étude taphonomique des restes fauniques de la Grotte Vaufrey, couche VIII. *La Grotte Vaufrey: Paléoenvironment, Chronologie, Activités Humaines*, J. P. Rigaud (ed.), pp. 535–63. Paris: Éditions du CNRS (Memoires de la Societé Préhistorique Française 19).

——, and Sally R. Binford 1966. A preliminary analysis of functional variability in the Mousterian of Levallois facies. *American Anthropologist* 68: 238–95.

——, and Chuan-Kun Ho 1985. Taphonomy at a distance: Zhoukoudian, "The cave home of Beijing man"? *Current Anthropology* 26: 413–42.

——, and Nancy M. Stone 1986. Zhoukoudian: a closer look. *Current Anthropology* 27: 453–75.

Bird-David, Nurit 1994. Sociality and immediacy: or, past and present conversations on bands. *Man* 29: 583–603.

Blake, Michael 1991. Emerging Early Formative chiefdom at Paso de la Amada, Chiapas, Mexico. *Formation of Complex Society in Southeastern Mesoamerica*, W. R. Fowler, Jr. (ed.), pp. 27–46. Boca Raton: CRC Press.

Blanton, Richard E. 1978. *Monte Albán: Settlement Patterns at the Ancient Zapotec Capital*. New York: Academic Press.

—— 1983. Urban Monte Albán during Period III. *The Cloud People. Divergent evolution of the Zapotec and Mixtec Civilizations*, K. V. Flannery and J. Marcus (eds), pp. 128–31. New York: Academic Press.

Bleed, Peter, Carl Falk, Ann Bleed, and Akira Matsui 1989. Between the mountains and the sea: optimal hunting patterns and faunal remains at Yagi, an early Jomon community in southwestern Hokkaido. *Arctic Anthropology* 26: 107–26.

Blitz, John H. 1993. *Ancient Chiefdoms of the Tombigbee*. Tuscaloosa: University of Alabama Press.

Blumenschine, Robert J. 1991. Hominid carnivory and foraging strategies, and the socio-economic function of early archaeological sites. *Philosophical Transactions of the Royal Society of London B* 334: 211–21.

——, and John A. Cavallo 1992. Scavenging and human evolution. *Scientific American* 267: 90–6.

——, and Curtis W. Marean 1993. A carnivore's view of archaeological bone assemblages. *From Bones to Behavior: Ethnoarchaeological and Experimental Contributions to the Interpretation of Faunal Remains*, J. Hudson (ed.), pp. 273–300. Carbondale: Center for Archaeological Investigations.

Blurton Jones, Nicholas G. 1991. Tolerated theft: suggestions about the ecology and evolution of sharing, hoarding, and scrounging. *Primate Politics*, G. Schubert and R. D. Masters (eds), pp. 170–87. Carbondale: Southern Illinois University Press.

——, Kristen Hawkes, and Patricia Draper 1994. Foraging returns of !Kung adults and children: why didn't !Kung children forage? *Journal of Anthropological Research* 50: 217–48.

Boas, Niels Axel 1983. Egehøj: a settlement from the early Bronze Age in East Jutland. *Journal of Danish Archaeology* 2: 90–101.

—— 1991. Bronze Age houses at Hemmed Church, east Jutland. *Journal of Danish Archaeology* 8: 88–107.

—— 1993. Late Neolithic and Bronze Age settlements at Hemmed Church and Hemmed Plantation, east Jutland. *Journal of Danish Archaeology* 10: 119–35.

Bogan, Arthur E. 1983. Evidence for faunal resource partitioning in an eastern North American chiefdom. *Animals and archaeology: 1. Hunters and their Prey*, J. Clutton-Brock and C. Grigson (eds), pp. 305–24. Oxford: British Archaeological Reports (BAR International Series 163).

Bogucki, Peter 1984. Linear Pottery ceramic sieves and their economic implications. *Oxford Journal of Archaeology* 3: 15–30.

—— 1986. The antiquity of dairying in temperate Europe. *Expedition* 28: 51–8.

—— 1988. *Forest Farmers and Stockherders. Early Agriculture and Its Consequences in North-Central Europe*. Cambridge: Cambridge University Press.

—— 1993. Animal traction and household economies in Neolithic Europe. *Antiquity* 67: 492–503.

—— 1995a. Prelude to agriculture in north-central Europe. *Before Farming: Hunter-Gatherer Society and Subsistence*, D. V. Campana (ed.), pp. 105–16. Philadelphia: University Museum, MASCA (MASCA Research Papers in Science and Archaeology 12, Supplement).

—— 1995b. The Linear Pottery Culture: conservative colonists? *The Emergence of Pottery*, W. K. Barnett and J. W. Hoopes (eds), pp. 89–97. Washington: Smithsonian Institution Press.

—— 1996a. The spread of early farming in Europe. *American Scientist* 84: 242–53.

—— 1996b. Sustainable and unsustainable adaptations by early farming communities of northern Poland. *Journal of Anthropological Archaeology* 15: 289–311.

—— 1999. How agriculture came to north-central Europe. *Europe's First Farmers*, T. D. Price (ed.), in press. Cambridge: Cambridge University Press.

——, and Ryszard Grygiel 1993. The first farmers of north-central Europe. *Journal of Field Archaeology* 20: 399–426.

Boisvert, Richard 1979. Mortuary practices, modes of exchange and cultural change: archaeological evidence from the Lower Ohio Valley. *Kentucky Archaeological Association Bulletin* 12: 1–16.

Bokelmann, Klaus 1991. Some new thoughts on old data on humans and reindeer in the Ahrensburgian tunnel valley in Schleswig-Holstein, Germany. *Late Glacial in North-West Europe: Human Adaptation and Environmental Change at the End of the Pleistocene*, N. Barton, A. J. Roberts, and D. A. Roe (eds), pp. 72–81. London: Council for British Archaeology (CBA Research Report 77).

Bökönyi, Sándor 1974. *The History of Domestic Animals in Central and Eastern Europe*. Budapest: Akadémiai Kiadó.

Bordaz, Jacques 1970. *Tools of the Old and New Stone Age*. Garden City: Natural History Press.

Bordes, François 1961. *Typologie du Paléolithique Ancien et Moyen*. Paris: Éditions du CNRS.

Boserup, Ester 1965. *The Conditions of Agricultural Growth*. Chicago: Aldine.

Bourque, Bruce J. 1995. *Diversity and Complexity in Prehistoric Maritime Societies. A Gulf of Maine Perspective*. New York: Plenum Press.

Bowler, J. M. 1976. Recent developments in reconstructing late Quaternary environments in Australia. *The Origin of the Australians*, R. L. Kirk and A. G. Thorne (eds), pp. 55–77. Canberra: Australian Institute of Aboriginal Studies.

——, R. Jones, H. R. Allen, and A. G. Thorne 1970. Pleistocene human remains from Australia: a living site and human cremation from Lake Mungo. *World Archaeology* 2: 39–60.

Boyle, Katherine V. 1990. *Upper Palaeolithic Faunas from South-West France. A Zoogeographic Perspective*. Oxford: British Archaeological Reports (BAR International Series 557).

Boysen, Aage, and Steen Wulff Anderson 1983. Trappendal: barrow and house from the early Bronze Age. *Journal of Danish Archaeology* 2: 118–26.

Braidwood, Robert J. 1960. The agricultural revolution. *Scientific American* 203: 130–41.

——, and Gordon R. Willey (eds) 1962. *Courses toward Urban Life; Archaeological Considerations of Some Cultural Alternates*. Chicago: Aldine.

Brain, C. K. 1981. *The Hunters or the Hunted? An Introduction to African Cave Taphonomy*. Chicago: University of Chicago Press.

—— 1993. The occurrence of burnt bones at Swartkrans and their implications for the control of fire by early hominids. *Swartkrans: a Cave's Chronicle of Early Man*, C. K. Brain (ed.), pp. 229–42. Praetoria: Transvaal Museum.

—— 1995. The influence of climatic changes on the completeness of the early hominid record in southern African caves, with particular reference to Swartkrans. *Palaeoclimate and Evolution, with Emphasis on Human Origins*, E. S. Vrba, G. H. Denton, T. C. Partridge, and L. H. Burckle (eds), pp. 451–8. New Haven: Yale University Press.

——, and A. Sillen 1988. Evidence from the Swartkrans cave for the earliest use of fire. *Nature* 336: 464–6.

Brain, Jeffrey P., Alan Toth, and Antonio Rodriguez-Buckingham 1974. Ethnohistoric archaeology and the de Soto Entrada into the Lower Mississippi Valley. *Conference on Historic Site Archaeology Papers* 7: 232–89.

Bratlund, Bodil 1991. Bone remains of mammals and birds from the Bjørnsholm shell-mound: a preliminary report. *Journal of Danish Archaeology* 10: 97–104.

—— 1996. Hunting strategies in the Late Glacial of northern Europe: a survey of the faunal evidence. *Journal of World Prehistory* 10: 1–48.

Briard, Jacques 1979. *The Bronze Age in Barbarian Europe. From the Megaliths to the Celts*. London: Book Club Associates.

Bronson, Bennett 1977. The earliest farming: demography as a cause and consequence. *The Origins of Agriculture*, Charles Reed (ed.), pp. 23–48. The Hague: Mouton.

Brooks, Alison S., and Peter Robertshaw 1990. The glacial maximum in tropical Africa: 22,000 to 14,000 BP. *The World at 18 000 BP. Volume Two, Low Latitudes*, C. Gamble and O. Soffer (eds), pp. 121–69. London: Unwin Hyman.

Brose, David S. 1990. Toward a model of exchange values for the eastern Woodlands. *MCJA: Midcontinental Journal of Archaeology* 15: 100–36.

Brown, Dorcas, and David Anthony 1996. Excavations in Russia. *Institute for Ancient Equestrian Studies Newsletter* 3, Fall, pp. 1, 3.

Brown, James A. 1976. The Southern Cult reconsidered. *MCJA: Midcontinental Journal of Archaeology* 1: 115–35.

—— 1979. Charnel houses and mortuary crypts: disposal of the dead in the Middle Woodland period. *Hopewell Archaeology*, D. S. Brose and N. Greber (eds), pp. 211–19. Kent, Ohio: Kent State University Press.

—— 1983. Summary. *Archaic Hunters and Gatherers in the American Midwest*, J. L. Phillips and J. A. Brown (eds), pp. 5–10. New York: Academic Press.

—— 1989. The beginnings of pottery as an economic process. *What's New? A Closer Look at the Process of Innovation*, S. E. van der Leeuw and R. Torrence (eds), pp. 203–24. London: Unwin Hyman.

—— 1996. *The Spiro Ceremonial Center: the Archaeology of Arkansas Valley Caddoan Culture in Eastern Oklahoma.* Ann Arbor: Museum of Anthropology.

——, and Robert K. Vierra 1983. What happened in the Middle Archaic? Introduction to an ecological approach to Koster Site archaeology. *Archaic Hunters and Gatherers in the American Midwest,* J. L. Phillips and J. A. Brown (eds), pp. 165–95. New York: Academic Press.

——, Richard A. Kerber, and Howard D. Winters 1990. Trade and the evolution of exchange relations at the beginning of the Mississippian period. *The Mississippian Emergence,* B. D. Smith (ed.), pp. 251–80. Washington: Smithsonian Institution Press.

Brumfiel, Elizabeth 1994a. Factional competition and political development in the New World: an introduction. *Factional Competition and Political Development in the New World,* E. M. Brumfiel and J. W. Fox (eds), pp. 3–13. Cambridge: Cambridge University Press.

—— 1994b. Introduction. *The Economic Anthropology of the State,* E. M. Brumfiel (ed.), pp. 1–16. Lanham: University Press of America.

——, and Timothy K. Earle 1987. Specialization, exchange, and complex societies: an introduction. *Specialization, Exchange, and Complex Societies,* E. M. Brumfiel and T. K. Earle (eds), pp. 1–9. Cambridge: Cambridge University Press.

Brunet, M., A. Beauvillain, Y. Coppens, E. Heintz, A. H. E. Moutaye, and D. Pilbeam 1996. *Australopithecus bahrelghazali,* une nouvelle espèce d'Hominidé ancien de la région de Koro Toro (Tchad). *Comptes Rendus des Séances de l'Academie des Sciences (Paris)* 322: 907–13.

Büchsenschutz, Olivier 1995. The significance of major settlements in European Iron Age society. *Celtic Chiefdom, Celtic State. The Evolution of Complex Social Systems in Prehistoric Europe,* B. Arnold and D. B. Gibson (eds), pp. 53–63. Cambridge: Cambridge University Press.

Burenhult, Göran (ed.) 1993. *The First Humans: Human Origins and History to 10,000 BC.* New York: HarperCollins.

Bunn, Henry T., and Ellen Kroll 1986. Systematic butchery by Plio/Pleistocene hominids at Olduvai Gorge, Tanzania. *Current Anthropology* 27: 431–52.

Burger, Richard L. 1988. Unity and heterogeneity within the Chavín horizon. *Peruvian Prehistory,* R. W. Keatinge (ed.), pp. 99–144. Cambridge: Cambridge University Press.

—— 1992. *Chavín and the Origins of Andean Civilization.* London: Thames and Hudson.

——, and Lucy Salazar-Burger 1986. Early organizational diversity in the Peruvian Highlands: Huaricoto and Kotosh. *Andean Archaeology. Papers in Memory of Clifford Evans,* M. Ramiro Matos, S. A. Turpin, and H. H. Eling, Jr. (eds), pp. 65–82. Los Angeles: Institute of Archaeology.

——, and Nikolaas J. van der Merwe 1990. Maize and the origin of highland Chavín civilization: an isotopic perspective. *American Anthropologist* 92: 85–95.

Burgess, Colin 1980. *The Age of Stonehenge.* London: Dent.

Burke, Ariane 1993. Applied skeletochronology: the horse as human prey during the Pleniglacial in southwestern France. *Hunting and Animal Exploitation in the Later Palaeolithic and Mesolithic of Eurasia*, G. L. Peterkin, H. M. Bricker, and P. Mellars (eds), pp. 145–50. Washington: American Anthropological Association.

Burl, Aubrey 1987. *The Stonehenge People*. London: J. M. Dent and Sons.

Burns, J. Joseph 1977. *The Management of Risk: Social factors in the Development of Exchange Relations among the Rubber Traders of North Sumatra*. Unpublished doctoral dissertation, Yale University.

Butzer, Karl W. 1991. An Old World perspective on potential Mid-Wisconsinan settlement of the Americas. *The First Americans: Search and Research*, T. D. Dillehay and D. J. Meltzer (eds), pp. 137–56. Boca Raton: CRC Press.

Byers, Douglas S. 1954. Bull Brook – a fluted point site in Ipswich, Massachusetts. *American Antiquity* 19: 343–51.

Byrd, Brian F. 1989. The Natufian: settlement variability and economic adaptations in the Levant at the end of the Pleistocene. *Journal of World Prehistory* 3: 159–98.

—— 1991. Beidha: an early Natufian encampment in southern Jordan. *The Natufian Culture in the Levant*, O. Bar-Yosef and F. R. Valla (eds), pp. 245–64. Ann Arbor: International Monographs in Prehistory.

—— 1992. The dispersal of food production across the Levant. *Transitions to Agriculture in Prehistory*, A. B. Gebauer and T. D. Price (eds), pp. 49–61. Madison: Prehistory Press.

Calavan, Michael M. 1984. Prospects for a probabilistic reinterpretation of Chayanovian theory: an exploratory discussion. *Chayanov, Peasants, and Economic Anthropology*, E. Paul Durrenberger (ed.), pp. 51–69. Orlando: Academic Press.

Caldwell, Joseph R. 1958. *Trend and Tradition in the Prehistory of the Eastern United States*. Washington: American Anthropological Association (Memoir 88).

—— 1965. Primary forest efficiency. *Southeastern Archaeological Conference Proceedings (Southeastern Archaeological Conference, Bulletin no. 3)*: 66–9.

Campbell, Stuart 1992. The Halaf Period in Iraq: old sites and new. *Biblical Archaeologist* December: 182–7.

Cancian, Frank 1980. Risk and uncertainty in agricultural decision making. *Agricultural Decision Making: Anthropological Contributions to Rural Development*, P. Barlett (ed.), pp. 161–76. Orlando: Academic Press.

—— 1996. The hamlet as mediator. *Ethnology* 35: 215–28.

Caneva, Isabella, M. Frangipane, and A. Palmieri 1989. Recent excavations at Maadi. *Late Prehistory of the Nile Basin and Sahara*, L. Krzyzaniak and M. Kobusiewicz (eds), pp. 287–93. Poznań: Museum of Archaeology.

Cann, Rebecca L., Mark Stoneking, and Allan C. Wilson 1987. Mitochondrial DNA and human evolution. *Nature* 325: 31–6.

Carbonell, E., J. M. Bermúdez de Castro, J. L. Arsuaga, J. C. Diez, A. Rosas, G. Cuenca-Bescós, R. Sala, M. Mosquera, X. P. Rodríguez 1995. Lower Pleistocene hominids and artifacts from Atapuerca-TD6 (Spain). *Science* 269: 826–30.

Carlstein, Tommy 1982. *Time Resources, Society, and Ecology: on the Capacity for Human Interaction in Space and Time*. Boston: Allen & Unwin.

Carniero, Robert L. 1981. The chiefdom: precursor of the state. *The Transition to Statehood in the New World*, G. D. Jones and R. R. Kautz (eds), pp. 37–75. Cambridge: Cambridge University Press.

—— 1990. Chiefdom-level warfare as exemplified in Fiji and the Causa valley. *The Anthropology of War*, J. Haas (ed.), pp. 190–211. Cambridge: Cambridge University Press.

Carstens, Kenneth, and Patty Jo Watson (eds) 1996. *Of Caves and Shell Mounds*. Tuscaloosa: University of Alabama Press.

Cassidy, Claire M. 1980. Nutrition and health in agriculturalists and hunter-gatherers: a case study of two prehistoric populations. *Nutritional Anthropology. Contemporary Approaches to Diet and Culture*, N. W. Jerome, R. F. Kandel, and G. H. Pelto (eds), pp. 117–45. Pleasantville, NY: Redgrave Publishing Co.

Castleden, Rodney 1990. *Minoans: Life in Bronze Age Crete*. London: Routledge.

Catto, Norm R. 1996. Richardson Mountains, Yukon-Northwest Territories: the northern portal of the postulated "Ice-Free Corridor." *Quaternary International* 32: 3–19.

——, David G. E. Liverman, Peter T. Bobrowsky, and Nat Rutter 1996. Laurentide, cordilleran, and montane glaciations in the western Peace River – Grande Prairie region, Alberta and British Columbia, Canada. *Quaternary International* 32: 21–32.

Chaloupka, George 1984. *From Palaeoart to Casual Paintings*. Darwin: Northern Territory Museum of Arts and Sciences.

Chang, Kwang Chih 1983. Origin of Shang and the problem of Xia in Chinese archaeology. *The Great Bronze Age of China*, G. Kuwayama (ed.), pp. 10–15. Los Angeles: Los Angeles County Museum.

—— 1986. *The Archaeology of Ancient China*. New Haven: Yale University Press.

—— 1994. Ritual and power. *China. Ancient Culture, Modern Land*, R. E. Murowchick (ed.), pp. 61–9. Norman: University of Oklahoma Press.

Chang, T. T. 1989. Domestication and the spread of the cultivated rices. *Foraging and Farming. The Evolution of Plant Exploitation*, D. R. Harris and G. C. Hillman (eds), pp. 408–17. London: Unwin Hyman.

Chapman, Jefferson 1985. *Tellico Archaeology: 12,000 Years of Native American History*. Knoxville: Department of Anthropology University of Tennessee.

Chapman, John C. 1983. "Secondary products revolution" and the limitations of the Neolithic. *Bulletin, Institute of Archaeology, London* 19: 107–22.

—— 1990. Social inequality on Bulgarian tells and the Varna problem. *The Social Archaeology of Houses*, R. Samson (ed.), pp. 49–92. Edinburgh: Edinburgh University Press.

—— 1991. Creation of social arenas in the Neolithic and Copper age of S. E. Europe: the case of Varna. *Sacred and Profane: Proceedings of a Conference on Archaeology, Ritual and Religion, Oxford, 1989*, P. Garwood, et al. (eds), pp. 152–71. Oxford: Oxford University Committee for Archaeology.

Chapman, Robert 1981. The emergence of formal disposal areas and the "problem" of megalithic tombs in prehistoric Europe. *The Archaeology of Death*, R. Chapman, I. Kinnes, and K. Randsborg (eds), pp. 71–81. Cambridge: Cambridge University Press.

—— 1990. *Emerging Complexity: the Later Prehistory of South-East Spain, Iberia, and the West Mediterranean.* Cambridge: Cambridge University Press.

—— 1995. Ten years after – megaliths, mortuary practices, and the territorial model. *Regional Approaches to Mortuary Analysis*, L. A. Beck (ed.), pp. 29–51. New York: Plenum Press.

Charles, Douglas K., and Jane E. Buikstra 1983. Archaic mortuary sites in the central Mississippi drainage: distribution, structure, and behavioral implications. *Archaic Hunters and Gatherers in the American Midwest*, J. L. Phillips and J. A. Brown (eds), pp. 117–45. New York: Academic Press.

Chase, Philip G. 1986. *The Hunters of Combe Grenal. Approaches to Middle Paleolithic Subsistence in Europe.* Oxford: British Archaeological Reports (BAR International Series 286).

—— 1989. How different was Middle Palaeolithic subsistence? A zooarchaeological perspective on the Middle to Upper Palaeolithic transition. *The Human Revolution*, P. Mellars and C. Stringer (eds), pp. 21–337. Princeton: Princeton University Press.

——, and Harold L. Dibble 1987. Middle Paleolithic symbolism: a review of current evidence and interpretations. *Journal of Anthropological Archaeology* 6: 263–96.

Chauvet, Jean Marie, Eliette Brunel Deschamps, and Christian Hillaire 1996. *Dawn of Art: the Chauvet Cave.* New York: Harry N. Abrams.

Chayanov, A. V. 1986. *The Theory of Peasant Economy.* Madison: University of Wisconsin Press.

Chen, Baozhang, and Qinhua Jiang 1997. Antiquity of the earliest cultivated rice in central China and its implications. *Economic Botany* 51 (3): 307–10.

Childe, V. Gordon 1928. *The Most Ancient East.* London: Routledge and Kegan Paul.

—— 1929. *The Danube in Prehistory.* Oxford: Clarendon Press.

—— 1930. *The Bronze Age.* Cambridge: Cambridge University Press.

—— 1957. *The Dawn of European Civilization*, 6th edn. London: Routledge and Kegan Paul.

Chippindale, Christopher 1988. Invention of words for the idea of "Prehistory." *Proceedings of the Prehistoric Society* 54: 303–14.

—— 1994. *Stonehenge Complete.* Revised edition. London: Thames and Hudson.

Chochorowski, Jan, and Sergei Skoryi 1997. Prince of the Great Kurgan. *Archaeology* 50 September/October: 32–9.

Cinq-Mars, Jacques 1990. La place des grottes du Poisson-Bleu dans la préhistoire beringienne. *Revista de Arquelogía Americana* 1: 9–32.

Claassen, Cheryl P. 1991. Gender, shellfishing and the Shell Mound Archaic. *Engendering Archaeology: Women and Prehistory*, J. Gero and M. Conkey (eds), pp. 276–300. Oxford: Blackwell.

Clark, Geoffrey A., and Lawrence G. Straus 1983. Late Pleistocene hunter-gatherer adaptations in Cantabrian Spain. *Hunter-Gatherer Economy in Prehistory: A European Perspective*, G. Bailey (ed.), pp. 131–48. Cambridge: Cambridge University Press.

Clark, Grahame 1961. *World Prehistory, an Outline*. Cambridge: Cambridge University Press.

Clark, J. Desmond 1969. *Kalambo Falls Prehistoric Site, Volume I*. Cambridge: Cambridge University Press.

——, and J. W. K. Harris 1985. Fire and its role in early hominid lifeways. *African Archaeological Review* 3: 3–27.

Clark, John E. 1995. Craft specialization as an archaeological category. *Research in Economic Anthropology*, B. L. Isaac (ed.), vol. 16, pp. 267–94. Greenwich: JAI Press.

——, and Michael Blake 1994. The power of prestige: competitive generosity and the emergence of rank societies in lowland Mesoamerica. *Factional Competition and Political Development in the New World*, E. M. Brumfiel and J. W. Fox (eds), pp. 17–30. Cambridge: Cambridge University Press.

——, and Dennis Gosser 1995. Reinventing Mesoamerica's first pottery. *The Emergence of Pottery. Technology and Innovation in Ancient Societies*, W. K. Barnett and J. W. Hoopes (eds), pp. 209–21. Washington: Smithsonian Institution Press.

——, and William J. Parry 1990. Craft specialization and cultural complexity. *Research in Economic Anthropology*, B. L. Isaac (ed.), vol. 12, pp. 289–346. Greenwich: RAI Press.

Clarke, D. V., T. G. Cowie, and Andrew Foxon 1985. *Symbols of Power at the Time of Stonehenge*. Edinburgh: National Museum of Antiquities of Scotland.

Clay, R. Berle 1992. Chiefs, Big Men, or what? Economy, settlement patterns, and their bearing on Adena political models. *Cultural Variability in Context. Woodland Settlements of the Mid-Ohio Valley*, M. F. Seeman (ed.), pp. 77–80. Kent: Kent State University Press (MCJA Special Paper 7).

Close, Angela E. 1996. Plus ça change. The Pleistocene–Holocene transition in northeast Africa. *Humans at the End of the Ice Age: the Archaeology of the Pleistocene-Holocene Transition*, L. G. Straus, B. V. Eriksen, J. M. Erlandson, and D. R. Yesner (eds), pp. 43–60. New York: Plenum Press.

——, and Fred Wendorf 1992. The beginnings of food production in the Eastern Sahara. *Transitions to Agriculture in Prehistory*, A. B. Gebauer and T. D. Price (eds), pp. 63–72. Madison: Prehistory Press.

Clottes, Jean 1996. Thematic changes in Upper Palaeolithic art: a view from the Grotte Chauvet. *Antiquity* 70: 276–88.

——, and Jean Courtin 1996. *The Cave Beneath the Sea. Paleolithic Images at Cosquer*. New York: Henry N. Abrams, Inc.

Clutton-Brock, Juliet (ed.) 1989. *The Walking Larder: Patterns of Domestication, Pastoralism and Predation*. London: Unwin Hyman.

Coe, Michael D. 1981. Gift of the river: ecology of the San Lorenzo Olmec. *The Olmec and their Neighbors. Essays in Honor of Matthew W. Stirling*, E. P. Benson (ed.), pp. 15–19. Washington: Dumbarton Oaks.

Coe, Michael D. 1989. The Olmec heartland: evolution of ideology. *Regional Perspectives on the Olmec*, R. J. Sharer and D. C. Grove (eds), pp. 68–82. Cambridge: Cambridge University Press.

Cohen, Mark N. 1977. *The Food Crisis in Prehistory*. New Haven: Yale University Press.

Coles, J. M., and A. F. Harding 1979. *The Bronze Age in Europe*. London: Methuen.

Collins, Michael B. 1991. Rockshelters and the early archaeological records in the Americas. *The First Americans: Search and Research*, T. D. Dillehay and D. J. Meltzer (eds), pp. 157–82. Boca Raton: CRC Press.

Collis, John 1984. *Oppida. Earliest Towns North of the Alps*. Sheffield: Department of Prehistory and Archaeology.

Conard, Nicholas J. 1990. Laminar lithic assemblages from the last inter-glacial complex in northwestern Europe. *Journal of Anthropological Research* 46: 243–62.

Coningham, R. A. E. 1995. Dark Age or continuum? An archaeological analysis of the second emergence of urbanism in South Asia. *The Archaeology of Early Historic South Asia. The Emergence of Cities and States*, F. R. Allchin (ed.), pp. 54–72. Cambridge: Cambridge University Press.

Conklin, William J. 1991. Tiahuanaco and Huari: architectural comparisons and interpretations. *Huari Administrative Structure. Prehistoric Monumental Architecture and State Government*, W. H. Isbell and G. F. McEwan (eds), pp. 281–91. Washington: Dumbarton Oaks.

Connah, Graham 1987. *African Civilizations. Precolonial Cities and States in Tropical Africa: an Archaeological Perspective*. Cambridge: Cambridge University Press.

Cooney, Gabriel, and Eoin Grogan 1994. *Irish Prehistory: A Social Perspective*. Dublin: Wordwell.

Coope, G. R. 1977. Fossil coleopteran assemblages as sensitive indicators of climatic changes during the Devensian (Last) Cold Stage. *Philosophical Transactions of the Royal Society of London*, series B, 280: 313–40.

Corballis, Michael C. 1992. *The Lopsided Ape: Evolution of the Generative Mind*. New York: Oxford University Press.

Cosgrove, Richard 1989. Thirty thousand years of human colonization in Tasmania: new Pleistocene dates. *Science* 243: 1703–5.

Costin, Cathy Lynne 1991. Craft specialization: issues in defining, docu-menting, and explaining the organization of production. *Archaeological Method and Theory*, M. B. Schiffer (ed.), vol. 3, pp. 1–56. Tucson: University of Arizona Press.

Coupland, Gary 1996. The evolution of multi-family houses on the Northwest Coast of North America. *People Who Lived in Big Houses. Archaeological Perspectives on Large Domestic Structures*, G. Coupland and E. B. Banning (eds), pp. 121–30. Madison: Prehistory Press.

Cowan, C. Wesley, and Patty Jo Watson (eds) 1992. *The Origins of Agriculture: an International Perspective*. Washington: Smithsonian Institu-tion Press.

Cowgill, George L. 1992. Social differentiation at Teotihuacan. *Mesoamerican Elites. An Archaeological Assessment*, D. Z. Chase and A. F. Chase (eds), pp. 206–20. Norman: University of Oklahoma Press.

—— 1997. State and society at Teotihuacan, Mexico. *Annual Review of Anthropology* 26: 129–61.

Crabtree, Pam J., Douglas V. Campana, Anna Belfer-Cohen, and Daniella E. Bar-Yosef 1991. First results of the excavations at Salibiya I, Lower Jordan Valley. *The Natufian Culture in the Levant*, O. Bar-Yosef and F. R. Valla (eds), pp. 161–72. Ann Arbor: International Monographs in Prehistory.

Crawford, Gary W. 1992. The transitions to agriculture in Japan. *Transitions to Agriculture in Prehistory*, A. B. Gebauer and T. D. Price (eds), pp. 117–32. Madison: Prehistory Press.

Croes, Dale R. 1989. Prehistoric ethnicity on the Northwest Coast of North America: an evaluation of style in basketry and lithics. *Journal of Anthropological Archaeology* 8: 101–30.

Crumley, Carole L. 1979. Three locational models: an epistemological assessment of anthropology and archaeology. *Advances in Archaeological Method and Theory*, M. B. Schiffer (ed.), vol. 2, pp. 141–73. New York: Academic Press.

—— 1995. Heterarchy and the analysis of complex societies. *Heterarchy and the Analysis of Complex Societies*, R. M. Ehrenreich, C. L. Crumley, and J. E. Levy (eds), pp. 1–6. Washington: American Anthropological Association.

Culbert, T. Patrick 1973. *The Classic Maya Collapse*. Albuquerque: University of New Mexico Press.

Cunliffe, Barry 1993. *English Heritage Book of Danebury*. London: Batsford/English Heritage.

—— 1995. *English Heritage Book of Iron Age Britain*. London: Batsford/English Heritage.

Cwynar, Les C. 1982. A late Quaternary vegetation history from Hanging Lake, northern Yukon. *Ecological Monographs* 52: 1–24.

Cybulski, Jerome S. 1992. *A Greenville Burial Ground: Human Remains and Mortuary Elements in British Columbia Coast Prehistory*. Hull, Quebec: Canadian Museum of Civilization (Archaeological Survey of Canada Mercury Series 146).

D'Altroy, Terence, and Timothy K. Earle 1985. Staple finance, wealth finance, and storage in the Inka political economy. *Current Anthropology* 26: 187–206.

D'Errico, Francesco 1994. Birds of the Grotte Cosquer: the Great Auk and Palaeolithic prehistory. *Antiquity* 68: 39–47.

Dalan, Rinita A. 1997. The construction of Mississippian Cahokia. *Cahokia. Domination and Ideology in the Mississippian World*, T. R. Pauketat and T. E. Emerson (eds), pp. 89–102. Lincoln: University of Nebraska Press.

Dancey, William S., and Paul J. Pacheco (eds) 1997. *Ohio Hopewell Community Organization*. Kent: Kent State University Press.

Daniel, Glyn 1964. *The Idea of Prehistory*. Baltimore: Penguin Books.

—— 1980. Megalithic monuments. *Scientific American* 243 (1): 78–90.

Darling, P. J. 1984. *Archaeology and History in Southern Nigeria: the Ancient Linear Earthworks of Benin and Ishan*. Oxford: British Archaeological Reports (BAR International Series 215).

Dart, Raymond A. 1957. *The Osteodontokeratic Culture of* Australopithecus prometheus. Praetoria: Transvaal Museum.

Davidson, Iain 1989. Escaped domestic animals and the introduction of agriculture to Spain. *The Walking Larder: Patterns of Domestication, Pastoralism, and Predation*, J. Clutton-Brock (ed.), pp. 59–71. London: Unwin Hyman.

——, and William Noble 1989. The archaeology of perception. *Current Anthropology* 30: 125–55.

Davidson, Thomas E., and Hugh McKerrell 1980. The neutron activation analysis of Halaf and 'Ubaid pottery from Tell Arpachiyah and Tepe Gawra. *Iraq* 42: 155–67.

Davis, S. J. M., and F. Valla 1978. Evidence for domestication of the dog 12,000 years ago in the Natufian of Israel. *Nature* 276: 608–10.

Deacon, Terrence W. 1989. The neural circuitry underlying primate calls and human language. *Human Evolution* 4: 367–401.

—— 1992. Biological aspects of language. *The Cambridge Encyclopedia of Human Evolution*, S. Jones, R. Martin, D. Pilbeam (eds), pp. 128–33. Cambridge: Cambridge University Press.

Dean, David, and Eric Delson 1995. *Homo* at the gates of Europe. *Nature* 373: 472–3.

Dean, Jeffrey S., Robert C. Euler, George J. Gumerman, Fred Plog, Richard H. Hevley, and Thor N. V. Karlstrom 1985. Human behavior, demography, and palaeoenvironment on the Colorado Plateaus. *American Antiquity* 50: 537–54.

Deetz, James 1965. *The Dynamics of Stylistic Change in Arikara Ceramics*. Urbana: University of Illinois Press.

Delagnes, Anne, and Anne Ropars 1996. *Paléolithique Moyen en Pays de Caux (Haute-Normandie). Le Pucheuil, Etoutteville: Deux Gisements de Plein Air en Milieu Loessique*. Paris: Éditions de la Maison des Sciences de l'Homme.

Delpech, Françoise 1983. *Les Faunes du Paléolithique Supérieur dans le Sud-Ouest de la France*. Paris: Éditions du CNRS (Cahiers du Quaternaire 6).

Demarest, Arthur A. 1989. The Olmec and the rise of civilization in eastern Mesoamerica. *Regional Perspectives on the Olmec*, R. J. Sharer and D. C. Grove (eds), pp. 303–44. Cambridge: Cambridge University Press.

—— 1992. Ideology in ancient Maya cultural evolution: the dynamics of galactic polities. *Ideology and Pre-Columbian Civilizations*, A. A. Demarest and G. W. Conrad (eds), pp. 135–57. Santa Fe: School of American Research Press.

—— 1993. Violent saga of a Maya kingdom. *National Geographic* 183: 94–111.

——, and Geoffrey W. Conrad (eds) 1992. *Ideology and Pre-Columbian Civilizations*. Santa Fe: School of American Research Press.

Dennell, Robin 1984. The expansion of exogenous-based economies across Europe: the Balkans and central Europe. *Exploring the Limits: Frontiers and Boundaries in Prehistory*, S. P. de Atley and F. J. Findlow (eds), pp. 93–116. Oxford: British Archaeological Reports.

—— 1992. The origins of crop agriculture in Europe. *The Origins of Agriculture: an International Perspective*, C. W. Cowan and P. J. Watson (eds), pp. 71–100. Washington: Smithsonian Institution Press.

——, and Wil Roebroeks 1996. The earliest colonization of Europe: the short chronology revisited. *Antiquity* 70: 535–42.

Dent, Richard J. 1995. *Chesapeake Prehistory. Old Traditions, New Directions*. New York: Plenum Press.

——, and Barbara E. Kauffman 1985. Aboriginal subsistence and site ecology as interpreted from microfloral and faunal remains. *Shawnee Minisink*, C. W. McNett (ed.), pp. 55–79. Orlando: Academic Press.

Dibble, Harold L. 1987. The interpretation of Middle Palaeolithic scraper morphology. *American Anthropologist* 52: 109–17.

——, and Ofer Bar-Yosef (eds) 1995. *The Definition and Interpretation of Levallois Technology*. Madison: Prehistory Press.

——, and Simon Holdaway 1993. The Middle Palaeolithic industries of Warwasi. *The Palaeolithic Prehistory of the Zagros-Taurus*, D. I. Olszewski and H. L. Dibble (eds), pp. 75–99. Philadelphia: University Museum.

——, and Anta Montet-White (eds) 1988. *Upper Pleistocene Prehistory of Western Eurasia*. Philadelphia: University Museum of Archaeology and Anthropology.

——, and Nicolas Rolland 1992. On assemblage variability in the Middle Palaeolithic of western Europe: history, perspectives, and a new synthesis. *The Middle Palaeolithic: Adaptation, Behavior, and Variability*, H. L. Dibble and P. Mellars (eds), pp. 1–28. Philadelphia: University Museum.

Dickinson, Oliver 1994. *The Aegean Bronze Age*. Cambridge: Cambridge University Press.

Diehl, Richard 1989. Olmec archaeology: what we know and what we wish we knew. *Regional Perspectives on the Olmec*, R. J. Sharer and D. C. Grove (eds), pp. 17–32. Cambridge: Cambridge University Press.

Dietler, Michael 1995. Early "Celtic" socio-political relations: ideological representation and social competition in dynamic comparative perspective. *Celtic Chiefdom, Celtic State. The Evolution of Complex Social Systems in Prehistoric Europe*, B. Arnold and D. B. Gibson (eds), pp. 64–71. Cambridge: Cambridge University Press.

Dikov, Nikolai N. 1996. The Ushki sites, Kamchatka Peninsula. *American Beginnings. The Prehistory and Palaeoecology of Beringia*, F. H. West (ed.), pp. 244–50. Chicago: University of Chicago Press.

Dillehay, Thomas D. 1989. *Monte Verde. A Late Pleistocene Settlement in Chile*. Washington: Smithsonian Institution Press.

—— 1997. The battle of Monte Verde. *The Sciences* 37: 28–33.

Dincauze, Dena F. 1976. *The Neville Site: 8,000 Years at Amoskeag, Manchester, New Hampshire*. Cambridge: Peabody Museum of Archaeology and Ethnology.

—— 1993. Fluted points in the eastern forests. *From Kostenki to Clovis. Upper Palaeolithic – Palaeo-Indian Adaptations*, O. Soffer and N. D. Praslov (eds), pp. 279–92. New York: Plenum Press.

Doebley, John 1990. Molecular evidence and the evolution of maize. *New Perspectives on the Origin and Evolution of New World Domesticated Plants*,

P. K. Bretting (ed.), pp. 6–28. New York: New York Botanical Garden (Economic Botany 44).

Dolukhanov, Paul 1996. *The Early Slavs: Eastern Europe from the Initial Settlement to the Kievan Rus*. London: Longman.

Donahue, Randoph E. 1988. Microwear analysis and site function of Paglicci Cave, level 4A. *World Archaeology* 19: 357–75.

—— 1992. Desperately seeking Ceres: a critical examination of current models for the transition to agriculture in Mediterranean Europe. *Transitions to Agriculture in Prehistory*, A. B. Gebauer and T. D. Price (eds), pp. 73–80. Madison: Prehistory Press.

Dortch, Charles 1984. *Devil's Lair: a Study in Prehistory*. Perth: Western Australian Museum.

Doyel, David E. 1991. Hohokam cultural evolution in the Phoenix Basin. *Exploring the Hohokam. Prehistoric Desert Peoples of the American Southwest*, G. J. Gumerman (ed.), pp. 231–78. Dragoon, Arizona: Amerind Foundation.

Drennan, Robert D. 1991. Pre-Hispanic chiefdom trajectories in Mesoamerica, Central America, and northern South America. *Chiefdoms: Power, Economy, and Ideology*, T. K. Earle (ed.), pp. 263–87. Cambridge: Cambridge University Press.

—— 1995. Chiefdoms in northern South America. *Journal of World Prehistory* 9: 301–40.

—— 1996. Betwixt and between in the Intermediate Area. *Journal of Archaeological Research* 4: 95–132.

Drewett, Peter 1979. New evidence for the structure and function of Middle Bronze Age round houses in Sussex. *Archaeological Journal* 136: 3–11.

Driesch, Angela von den, and Joachim Boessneck 1985. *Die Tierknochenfunde aus der neolithischen Siedlung von Merimde-Benisalame am westlichen Nildelta*. Munich: Institut für Palaeoanatomie, Domestikationsforschung und Geschichte der Tiermedizin.

Dunbar, Robin 1993. Co-evolution of neocortex size, group size, and language in humans. *Behavioral and Brain Sciences* 16: 681–735.

—— 1996. On the evolution of language and kinship. *The Archaeology of Human Ancestry. Power, Sex and Tradition*, J. Steele and S. Shennan (eds), pp. 30–96. London: Routledge.

Dye, David H. 1996. Riverine adaptation in the Midsouth. *Of Caves and Shellmounds*, K. C. Carstens and P. J. Watson (eds), pp. 140–58. Tuscaloosa: University of Alabama Press.

Dyke, A. S., and V. K. Prest 1987. Late Wisconsinan and Holocene history of the Laurentide Ice Sheet. *Geographie Physique et Quaternaire* 41: 237–64. Montreal: Les Presses de L'Université de Montreal.

Earle, Timothy K. 1987. Chiefdoms in archaeological and ethnohistorical perspective. *Annual Review of Anthropology* 16: 279–308.

—— 1991. The evolution of chiefdoms. *Chiefdoms: Power, Economy, and Ideology*, T. K. Earle (ed.), pp. 1–15. Cambridge: Cambridge University Press.

—— 1997. *How Chiefs Come to Power: the Political Economy in Prehistory.* Stanford: Stanford University Press.

Edwards, P. P., S. J. Bourke, S. M. Colledge, J. Head, and P. G. Macumber 1988. Late Pleistocene prehistory in the Wadi al-Hammeh, Jordan Valley. *The Prehistory of Jordan: the State of Research in 1986*, A. N. Garrard and H. G. Gebel (eds), pp. 525–65. Oxford: British Archaeological Reports (BAR International Series 396).

Edwards, Walter 1997. Japan's new past. *Archaeology* March/April: 32–42.

Ehrenreich, Robert M. 1995. Early metalworking: a heterarchical analysis of industrial organization. *Heterarchy and the Analysis of Complex Societies*, R. M. Ehrenreich, C. L. Crumley, and J. E. Levy (eds), pp. 33–9. Washington: American Anthropological Association.

Eiwanger, Josef 1982. Die neolithische Siedlung von Merimde-Benisalame: vierter Bericht. *Mitteilungen des Deutschen Archäologischen Institut, Abteilung Kairo* 38: 67-82.

Emerson, Thomas E. 1997a. Reflections from the countryside on Cahokian hegemony. *Cahokia. Domination and Ideology in the Mississippian World*, T. R. Pauketat and T. E. Emerson (eds), pp. 167–89. Lincoln: University of Nebraska Press.

—— 1997b. *Cahokia and the Archaeology of Power.* Tuscaloosa: University of Alabama Press.

Enghoff, Inge Bødker 1991. Mesolithic eel-fishing at Bjørnsholm, Denmark, spiced with exotic species. *Journal of Danish Archaeology* 10: 105–18.

Englebrecht, William 1987. Factors maintaining low population density among the prehistoric New York Iroquois. *American Antiquity* 52: 13–27.

Enloe, James G. 1993. Subsistence organization in the early Upper Palaeolithic: reindeer hunters of the Abri du Flageolet, Couche V. *Before Lascaux. The Complex Record of the Early Upper Palaeolithic*, H. Knecht, A. Pike-Tay, and R. White (eds), pp. 101–15. Boca Raton: CRC Press.

Erdosy, George 1988. *Urbanization in Early Historic India.* Oxford: British Archaeological Reports (BAR International Series 430).

—— 1995. The prelude to urbanization: ethnicity and the rise of Late Vedic chiefdoms. *The Archaeology of Early Historic South Asia. The Emergence of Cities and States*, F. R. Allchin (ed.), pp. 75–98. Cambridge: Cambridge University Press.

Erickson, Clark 1988. Raised field agriculture in the Lake Titicaca basin: putting ancient Andean agriculture back to work. *Expedition* 30: 8–16.

Eriksen, Berit Valentin 1996. Resource exploitation, subsistence strategies, and adaptiveness in late Pleistocene–early Holocene northwest Europe. *Humans at the End of the Ice Age. The Archaeology of the Pleistocene–Holocene Transition*, L. G. Straus, B. V. Eriksen, J. M. Erlandson, and D. R. Yesner (eds), pp. 101–28. New York: Plenum Press.

Evans, Robert K. 1978. Early craft specialization: an example from the Balkan Chalcolithic. *Social Archaeology: Beyond Subsistence and Dating*, C. L. Redman, M. J. Berman, E. V. Curtin, W. T. Langhorne, Jr., N. M. Versaggi, and J. C. Wanser (eds), pp. 113–29. New York: Academic Press.

Fairservis, Walter A. 1986. Cattle and the Harappan chiefdoms of the Indus Valley. *Expedition* 28: 43–50.

Falconer, Steven E., and Stephen H. Savage 1995. Heartlands and hinterlands: alternative trajectories of early urbanization in Mesopotamia and the southern Levant. *American Antiquity* 60: 37–58.

Farizy, Catherine, and Francine David 1992. Subsistence and behavioral patterns of some Middle Palaeolithic local groups. *The Middle Palaeolithic: Adaptation, Behavior, and Variability*, H. L. Dibble and P. Mellars (eds), pp. 87–96. Philadelphia: University Museum.

Farnsworth, Kenneth B. 1990. The evidence for specialized Middle Woodland camps in western Illinois. *Illinois Archaeology* 2: 109–32.

Fash, William L. 1991. *Scribes, Warriors, and Kings: the City of Copan and the Ancient Maya*. London: Thames and Hudson.

Feibel, C. S., N. Agnew, B. Latimer, M. Demas, F. Marshall, S. A. C. Waane, and P. Schmid 1995. The Laetoli hominid footprints – preliminary report on the conservation and scientific restudy. *Evolutionary Anthropology* 4: 149–54.

Feinman, Gary M. 1995. The emergence of inequality. A focus on strategies and processes. *Foundations of Social Inequality*, T. D. Price and G. M. Feinman (eds), pp. 255–79. New York: Plenum Press.

——, and Jill Neitzel 1984. Too many types: an overview of prestate societies in the Americas. *Advances in Archaeological Method and Theory*, vol. 7, M. B. Schiffer (ed.), pp. 39–102. Orlando: Academic Press.

Feldman, Robert A. 1987. Architectural evidence for the development of nonegalitarian social systems in coastal Peru. *The Origins and Development of the Andean State*, J. Haas, S. Pozorski, and T. Pozorski (eds), pp. 9–14. Cambridge: Cambridge University Press.

Fernández Castro, and María Cruz 1995. *Iberia in Prehistory*. Oxford: Blackwell.

Fiedel, Stuart J. 1987. *Prehistory of the Americas*. Cambridge: Cambridge University Press.

Firth, Raymond W. 1959. *Social Change in Tikopia: Re-study of a Polynesian Community after a Generation*. London: Allen & Unwin.

Fischer, Anders 1982. Trade in Danubian shaft-hole axes and the introduction of Neolithic economy in Denmark. *Journal of Danish Archaeology* 1: 7–12.

Fischer, Franz 1995. The early Celts of west central Europe: the semantics of social structure. *Celtic Chiefdom, Celtic State. The Evolution of Complex Social Systems in Prehistoric Europe*, B. Arnold and D. B. Gibson (eds), pp. 34–40. Cambridge: Cambridge University Press.

Fladmark, Knut R. 1979. Routes: alternate migration corridors for early man in America. *American Antiquity* 44: 55–69.

Flannery, Kent V. 1968. Archaeological systems theory and early Mesoamerica. *Anthropological Archaeology in the Americas*, B. J. Meggers (ed.), pp. 67–87. Washington: Anthropological Society of Washington.

—— 1969. Origins and ecological effects of early domestication in Iran and the Near East. *The Domestication and Exploitation of Plants and Animals*, P. Ucko and G. W. Dimbleby (eds), pp. 73–100. London: Duckworth.

—— 1972. The origins of the village as a settlement type in Mesoamerica and the Near East: a comparative study. *Man, Settlement and Urbanism,* P. J. Ucko, R. Tringham, and G. W. Dimbleby (eds), pp. 25–53. London: Duckworth.

—— 1973. The origins of agriculture. *The Annual Review of Anthropology* 2: 271–310.

—— (ed.) 1976. *The Early Mesoamerican Village.* New York: Academic Press.

—— 1983. The development of Monte Albán's main plaza in Period II. *The Cloud People. Divergent Evolution of the Zapotec and Mixtec Civilizations,* K. V. Flannery and J. Marcus (eds), pp. 102–4. New York: Academic Press.

——, and Joyce Marcus 1983a. The earliest public buildings, tombs, and monuments of Monte Albán, with notes on the internal chronology of Period I. *The Cloud People. Divergent Evolution of the Zapotec and Mixtec Civilizations,* K. V. Flannery and J. Marcus (eds), pp. 87–91. New York: Academic Press.

——, and Joyce Marcus 1983b. The growth of site hierarchies in the Valley of Oaxaca, Part I. *The Cloud People. Divergent Evolution of the Zapotec and Mixtec Civilizations,* K. V. Flannery and J. Marcus (eds), pp. 53–64. New York: Academic Press.

Flannery, Tim 1990. Pleistocene faunal loss: implications of the aftershock for Australia's past and future. *Archaeology in Oceania* 25: 45–67.

Flood, Josephine 1996. Culture in early aboriginal Australia. *Cambridge Archaeological Journal* 6: 3–36.

Fogel, Heidy P. 1993. *Settlements in Time: a Study of Social and Political Development during the Gallinazo Occupation of the North Coast of Peru.* Ann Arbor: UMI Dissertation Services.

Foley, Robert 1995. *Humans Before Humanity.* Oxford: Blackwell.

Ford, Richard I. 1985. The processes of plant food production in prehistoric North America. *Prehistoric Food Production in North America,* R. I. Ford (ed.), pp. 1–18. Ann Arbor: Museum of Anthropology, University of Michigan (Anthropological Papers 75).

Forest, Jean-Daniel 1987. La grande architecture obeidienne, sa forme et sa fonction. *Préhistoire de la Mésopotamie,* J.-L. Huot (ed.), pp. 385–423. Paris: Éditions du CNRS.

Forest-Foucault, Chantal 1980. Rapport sur les fouilles de Kheit-Qasim III, Hamrin. *Paléorient* 6: 221–4.

Fortes, Meyer 1958. Introduction. *The Developmental Cycle in Domestic Groups,* J. Goody (ed.), pp. 1–14. Cambridge: Cambridge University Press.

Fortier, Andrew C., Thomas O. Maher, Joyce A. Williams, Michael C. Meinkoth, Kathryn E. Parker, and Lucretia S. Kelly 1989. *The Holding Site: A Hopewell Community in the American Bottom (11-Ms-118).* Urbana and Chicago: University of Illinois Press.

Foucault, Michel 1977. *Discipline and Punish. The Birth of the Prison.* Translated by Alan Sheridan. New York: Pantheon Books.

Fowler, Melvin L. 1975. A Pre-Columbian urban center on the Mississippi. *Scientific American* 233: 92–101.

Francfort, Henri-Paul 1992. New data illustrating the early contacts between Central Asia and the north-west of the subcontinent. *South Asian Archaeology 1989: Papers from the Tenth International Conference of South Asian Archaeologists in Western Europe, Musée National des Arts Asiatiques – Guimet, Paris, France, 3–7 July 1989*, C. Jarrige (ed.), pp. 97–102. Madison: Prehistory Press.

Freidel, David A. 1992. The Trees of life: *Ahau* as idea and artifact in Classic lowland Maya civilization. *Ideology and Pre-Columbian Civilizations*, A. A. Demarest and G. W. Conrad (eds), pp. 115–33. Santa Fe: School of American Research Press.

Fried, Morton 1967. *The Evolution of Political Society: an Essay in Political Anthropology*. New York: Random House.

Frison, George C., and Danny N. Walker 1990. New World palaeoecology at the Last Glacial Maximum and the implications for New World prehistory. *The World at 18 000 BP. Volume I. High Latitudes*, O. Soffer and C. Gamble (eds), pp. 312–30. London: Unwin Hyman.

Fritz, Gayle J. 1993. Early and Middle Woodland period palaeoethnobotany. *Foraging and Farming in the Eastern Woodlands*, C. M. Scarry (ed.), pp. 39–56. Gainesville: University Press of Florida.

—— 1994. Are the first American farmers getting younger? *Current Anthropology* 35: 305–9.

——, and Bruce D. Smith 1988. Old collections and new technology: documenting the domestication of Chenopodium in eastern North America. *MCJA: Midcontinental Journal of Archaeology* 13: 3–27.

Frost, Peter 1994. Geographic distribution of human skin colour: selective compromise between natural selection and sexual selection? *Human Evolution* 9: 141–53.

Fullagar, R. L. K., D. M. Price, L. M. Head 1996. Early human occupation of northern Australia: archaeology and thermoluminescence dating of Jinmium rock-shelter, Northern Territory. *Antiquity* 70: 751–74.

Fung, Christopher 1994. The beginnings of settled life. *China. Ancient Culture, Modern Land*, R. E. Murowchick (ed.), pp. 51–9. Norman: University of Oklahoma Press.

Gabunia, L., and A. Vekua 1995. A Plio-Pleistocene hominid from Dmanisi, East Georgia, Caucasus. *Nature* 373: 509–12.

Galloway, Patricia (ed.) 1989. *The Southeastern Ceremonial Complex: Artifacts and Analysis. The Cottonlandia Conference*. Lincoln: University of Nebraska Press.

Gamble, Clive 1983. Culture and society in the Upper Palaeolithic of Europe. *Hunter-Gatherer Economy in Prehistory: A European Perspective*, G. Bailey (ed.), pp. 201–11. Cambridge: Cambridge University Press.

—— 1991. The social context for European Palaeolithic art. *Proceedings of the Prehistoric Society* 57: 3–15.

—— 1993. The center at the edge. *From Kostenki to Clovis. Upper Palaeolithic – Palaeo-Indian Adaptations*, O. Soffer and N. D. Praslov (eds), pp. 313–21. New York: Plenum Press.

—— 1994a. *Timewalkers: the Prehistory of Global Colonization*. Harvard: Harvard University Press.

—— 1994b. The peopling of Europe 700,000–40,000 years before the present. *The Oxford Illustrated Prehistory of Europe*, B. Cunliffe (ed.), pp. 5–41. Oxford: Oxford University Press.

—— 1996. Making tracks. Hominid networks and the evolution of the social landscape. *The Archaeology of Human Ancestry. Power, Sex, and Tradition*, J. Steele and S. Shennan (eds), pp. 253–77. London: Routledge.

—— 1998. Palaeolithic society and the release from proximity: a network approach to intimate relations. *World Archaeology* 29: 426–49.

——, and Olga Soffer (eds) 1990. *The World at 18 000 BP. Volume II: Low Latitudes*. London: Unwin Hyman.

Gannon, Patrick J., and Jeffrey T. Laitman 1993. Can we see language areas on hominid endocasts? *American Journal of Physical Anthropology* supplement 16: 91.

Gardner, William M. 1977. Flint Run Paleoindian complex and its implications for eastern North American prehistory. *Amerinds and their Paleoenvironments in Northeastern North America (Annals of the New York Academy of Sciences 288)*, pp. 257–63. New York: New York Academy of Sciences.

Gargett, Robert H. 1989. Grave shortcomings: the evidence for Neandertal burial. *Current Anthropology* 30: 157–90.

—— 1996. *Cave Bears and Modern Human Origins. The Spatial Taphonomy of Pod Hradem Cave, Czech Republic*. Lanham: University Press of America.

Garlake, Peter S. 1978. Pastoralism and Zimbabwe. *Journal of African History* 19: 479–93.

Garland, Elizabeth B. 1992. *The Obion Site: an Early Mississippian Center in Western Tennessee*. Starkville, Mississippi: Cobb Institute of Archaeology (Report of Investigations 7).

—— 1996. Some observations on ceremonialism at the Obion Site. *Mounds, Embankments, and Ceremonialism in the Midsouth*, R. C. Mainfort and R. Walling (eds), pp. 44–9. Fayetteville: Arkansas Archaeological Survey.

Gaudzinski, Sabine 1995. Wallertheim revisited: a re-analysis of the fauna from the Middle Palaeolithic site of Wallertheim (Rheinhessen/Germany). *Journal of Archaeological Science* 22: 51–66.

—— 1996. On bovid assemblages and their consequences for the knowledge of subsistence patterns in the Middle Palaeolithic. *Proceedings of the Prehistoric Society* 62: 19–39.

Gebauer, Anne Birgitte, and T. Douglas Price (eds) 1992. *Transitions to Agriculture in Prehistory*. Madison: Prehistory Press.

Geneste, Jean-Michel 1985. *Analyse Lithique d'Industries Moustériennes du Périgord: une Approche Technologique du Comportement des Groupes Humains au Paléolithique Moyen*. Doctoral dissertation, University of Bordeaux I (cited in Dibble and Rolland 1992 and Mellars 1996).

Gibson, Jon L. 1994. Before their time? Early mounds in the lower Mississippi Valley. *Southeastern Archaeology* 13: 162–86.

—— 1996. Poverty Point and greater Southeastern prehistory. The culture that did not fit. *Archaeology of the Mid-Holocene Southeast*, K. E. Sassaman and D. G. Anderson (eds), pp. 288–303. Gainesville: University Press of Florida.

Gibson, Jon L. 1998. Broken circles, owl monsters, and black earth midden. Separating sacred and secular at Poverty Point. *Ancient Earthen Enclosures of the Eastern Woodlands*, R. C. Mainfort and L. P. Sullivan (eds), pp. 17–30. Gainesville: University Press of Florida.

Giedion, S. 1962. *The Eternal Present. A Contribution on Constancy and Change*. New York: The Bollingen Foundation.

Gilead, Isaac 1991. Upper Paleolithic Period in the Levant. *Journal of World Prehistory* 5: 105–54.

Gilman, Antonio 1987. Unequal development in Copper Age Iberia. *Specialization, Exchange, and Complex Societies*, E. M. Brumfiel and T. K. Earle (eds), pp. 22–9. Cambridge: Cambridge University Press.

—— 1991. Trajectories towards social complexity in the later prehistory of the Mediterranean. *Chiefdoms: Power, Economy, and Ideology*, T. K. Earle (ed.), pp. 146–68. Cambridge: Cambridge University Press.

—— 1995. Prehistoric European chiefdoms: rethinking "Germanic" societies. *Foundations of Social Inequality*, T. D. Price and G. M. Feinman (eds), pp. 235–51. New York: Plenum Press.

Gimbutas, Marija 1965. *Bronze Age Cultures in Central and Eastern Europe*. The Hague: Mouton.

Glance, Natalie S., and B. A. Huberman 1994. The dynamics of social dilemmas. *Scientific. American* 270: 76–81.

Goody, Jack 1986. *The Logic of Writing and the Organization of Society*. Cambridge: Cambridge University Press.

Gorman, Chester F., and Pisit Charoenwongsa 1976. Ban Chiang: a mosaic of impressions from the first two years. *Expedition* 18: 14–26.

Gould, Stephen Jay 1989. *Wonderful Life*. New York: W. W. Norton.

Gramly, Richard Michael 1981. Eleven thousand years in Maine. *Archaeology* 34: 32–9.

—— 1984. Kill sites, killing ground and fluted points at the Vail site. *Archaeology of Eastern North America* 12: 110–21.

Graves, Michael W., and Maria Sweeney 1993. Ritual behavior and ceremonial structures in eastern Polynesia: changing perspectives on archaeological variability. *The Evolution and Organisation of Prehistoric Society in Polynesia*, M. W. Graves and R. C. Green (eds), pp. 106–25. Auckland: New Zealand Archaeological Association (Monograph 19).

Grayson, Donald K. 1984. Explaining Pleistocene extinctions: thoughts on the structure of a debate. *Quaternary Extinctions*, P. S. Martin and R. G. Klein (eds), pp. 807–23. Tucson: University of Arizona Press.

—— 1987. Analysis of the chronology of late Pleistocene mammalian extinctions in North America. *Quaternary Research* 28: 281–9.

—— 1991. Late Pleistocene mammalian extinctions in North America: taxonomy, chronology, and explanations. *Journal of World Prehistory* 5: 193–231.

——, and Françoise Delpech 1994. The Evidence for Middle Palaeolithic scavenging from Couche VIII, Grotte Vaufrey (Dordogne, France). *Journal of Archaeological Science* 21: 359–75.

Green, Stanton W., and Marek Zvelebil 1993. Interpreting Ireland's prehistoric landscape: The Bally Lough Archaeological Project. *Case Studies in European Prehistory*, P. Bogucki (ed.), pp. 1–29. Boca Raton: CRC Press.

Greenfield, Haskel J. 1988. Origins of milk and wool production in the Old World: a zooarchaeological perspective from the central Balkans. *Current Anthropology* 29: 573–93.

—— 1989. Zooarchaeology and aspects of the secondary products revolution: a central Balkan perspective. *ArchaeoZoologia* 3: 191–200.

—— 1993. Zooarchaeology, taphonomy, and the origin of food production in the central Balkans. *Culture and Environment: a Fragile Coexistence*, R. W. Jamieson, S. Abonyi, and N. A. Mirau (eds), pp. 111–17. Calgary: University of Calgary Archaeological Association.

Gregg, Susan Alling 1988. *Foragers and Farmers. Population Interaction and Agricultural Expansion in Prehistoric Europe*. Chicago: University of Chicago Press.

Gregory, David A. 1987. The morphology of platform mounds and the structure of Classic Period Hohokam sites. *The Hohokam Village: Site Structure and Organization*, D. E. Doyel (ed.), pp. 183–210. Glenwood Springs, Colorado: Southwestern and Rocky Mountain Division, AAAS.

—— 1991. Form and variation in Hohokam settlement patterns. *Chaco & Hohokam. Prehistoric Regional Systems in the American Southwest*, P. L. Crown and W. J. Judge (eds), pp. 159–93. Santa Fe: School of American Research Press.

Grieder, Terence, A. Bueno Mendoza, C. E. Smith, Jr., and R. M. Malina 1988. *La Galgada, Peru: a Preceramic Culture in Transition*. Austin: University of Texas Press.

Griffin, P. Bion 1984. Forager resource and land use in the humid tropics: the Agta of northeastern Luzon, the Philippines. *Past and Present in Hunter-Gatherer Studies*, C. Schrire (ed.), pp. 95–121. Orlando: Academic Press.

—— 1989. Hunting, farming, and sedentism in a rain forest foraging society. *Farmers as Hunters: the Implications of Sedentism*, S. Kent (ed.), pp. 60–70. Cambridge: Cambridge University Press.

Grigson, Caroline 1989. Size and sex: evidence for the domestication of cattle in the Near East. *The Beginnings of Agriculture*, A. Miles, D. Williams, and N. Gardner (eds), pp. 77–109. Oxford: British Archaeological Reports (BAR International Series 496).

Grøn, Ole, and Jørgen Skaarup 1991. Møllegabet II – a submerged Mesolithic site and a "boat burial" from Aerø. *Journal of Danish Archaeology* 10: 38–50.

Groube, L., J. Chappell, J. Muke, and D. Price 1986. A 40,000 year-old human occupation site at Huon Peninsula, Papua New Guinea. *Nature* 324: 453–5.

Grove, David C. 1981. Olmec monuments: mutilation as a clue to meaning. *The Olmec and their Neighbors. Essays in Honor of Matthew W. Stirling*, E. P. Benson (ed.), pp. 49–68. Washington: Dumbarton Oaks.

——, and Susan D. Gillespie 1992. Ideology and evolution at the pre-state level: Formative Period Mesoamerica. *Ideology and Pre-Columbian*

Civilizations, A. A. Demarest and G. W. Conrad (eds), pp. 15–36. Santa Fe: School of American Research Press.

Gruhn, Ruth 1994. The Pacific Coast route of initial entry: an overview. *Method and Theory for Investigating the Peopling of the Americas*, R. Bonnichsen and D. G. Steele (eds), pp. 249–56. Corvallis (Oregon): Center for the Study of the First Americans.

Grygiel, Ryszard, and Peter Bogucki 1997. Early farmers in north-central Europe: 1989–1994 excavations at Osłonki, Poland. *Journal of Field Archaeology* 24: 161–78.

Guilday, John E. 1971. *Biological and Archaeological Analysis of Bones from a 17th Century Indian Village (46-Pu-31), Putnam County, West Virginia*. Morgantown: West Virginia Geological and Economic Survey.

Gumerman, George J. 1991. Understanding the Hohokam. *Exploring the Hohokam. Prehistoric Desert Peoples of the American Southwest*, G. J. Gumerman (ed.), pp. 1–27. Dragoon, Arizona: Amerind Foundation.

Guthrie, R. Dale 1990. *Frozen Fauna of the Mammoth Steppe: the Story of Blue Babe*. Chicago: University of Chicago Press.

Haas, Jonathan 1987. The exercise of power in early Andean state development. *The Origins and Development of the Andean State*, J. Haas, S. Pozorski, and T. Pozorski (eds), pp. 32–5. Cambridge: Cambridge University Press.

Hally, David J. 1993. The territorial size of Mississippian chiefdoms. *Archaeology of Eastern North America. Papers in Honor of Stephen Williams*, J. B. Stoltman (ed.), pp. 143–68. Jackson, Mississippi: Mississippi Department of Archives and History.

—— 1996. Platform-mound construction and the instability of Mississippian chiefdoms. *Political Structure and Change in the Prehistoric Southeastern United States*, J. F. Scarry (ed.), pp. 92–127. Gainesville: University Press of Florida.

——, Marvin T. Smith, and James B. Langford, Jr. 1990. The archaeological reality of De Soto's Coosa. *Columbian Consequences II: Archaeological and Historical Perspectives on the Spanish Borderlands East*, D. H. Thomas (ed.), pp. 121–38. Washington: Smithsonian Institution Press.

Hammond, Norman 1982. *Ancient Maya Civilization*. New Brunswick: Rutgers University Press.

—— (ed.) 1991. *Cuello: an Early Maya Community in Belize*. Cambridge: Cambridge University Press.

Harding, Anthony F. 1983. Bronze Age in central and eastern Europe: advances and prospects. *Advances in World Archaeology* 2: 1–50. New York: Academic Press.

Harlan, Jack 1971. Agricultural origins: centers and non-centers. *Science* 174: 468–74.

—— 1995. *The Living Fields. Our Agricultural Heritage*. Cambridge: Cambridge University Press.

Harris, David R. 1989. An evolutionary continuum of people–plant interaction. *Foraging and Farming. The Evolution of Plant Exploitation*, D. R. Harris and G. C. Hillman (eds), pp. 11–26. London: Unwin Hyman.

Harrold, Francis B. 1980. A comparative analysis of Eurasian Palaeolithic burials. *World Archaeology* 12: 195–211.

Hassan, Fekri A. 1988. The Predynastic of Egypt. *Journal of World Prehistory* 2: 135–85.

—— 1993. Town and village in ancient Egypt: ecology, society, and urbanization. *The Archaeology of Africa. Food, Metals, and Towns*, T. Shaw, P. Sinclair, B. Andah, and A. Okpoko (eds), pp. 551–89. London: Routledge.

Hassig, Ross 1992. *War and Society in Ancient Mesoamerica*. Berkeley: University of California Press.

Hastings, C. Mansfield, and Michael Edward Moseley 1975. The adobes of Huaca del Sol and Huaca de la Luna. *American Antiquity* 40: 196–203.

Hastorf, Christine A. 1993. *Agriculture and the Onset of Political Inequality before the Inka*. Cambridge: Cambridge University Press.

Haury, Emil W. 1976. *The Hohokam: Desert Farmers and Craftsmen*. Tucson: University of Arizona Press.

Hawkes, Kristen 1993. Why hunter-gatherers work. An ancient version of the problem of public goods. *Current Anthropology* 34: 341–61.

Hawkins, Gerald S. 1965. *Stonehenge Decoded*. Garden City (NY): Doubleday.

Hayden, Brian 1992. Models of domestication. *Transitions to Agriculture in Prehistory*, A. B. Gebauer and T. D. Price (eds), pp. 11–19. Madison: Prehistory Press.

—— 1995a. A new overview of domestication. *Last Hunters, First Farmers. New Perspectives on the Prehistoric Transition to Agriculture*, T. D. Price and A. B. Gebauer (eds), pp. 273–99. Santa Fe: School of American Research Press.

—— 1995b. Pathways to power. Principles for creating socioeconomic inequalities. *Foundations of Social Inequality*, T. D. Price and G. M. Feinman (eds), pp. 15–86. New York: Plenum Press.

——, and Aubrey Cannon 1982. The corporate group as an archaeological unit. *Journal of Anthropological Archaeology* 1: 132–58.

Haynes, C. Vance, Jr. 1980. Paleoindian charcoal from Meadowcroft Rockshelter: is contamination a problem? *American Antiquity* 45: 582–7.

—— 1992. Contributions of radiocarbon dating to the geochronology of the peopling of the New World. *Radiocarbon After Four Decades*, R. E. Taylor and R. S. Kra (eds), pp. 355–74. New York: Springer-Verlag.

—— 1993. Clovis-Folsom geochronology and climatic change. *From Kostenki to Clovis. Upper Palaeolithic – Palaeo-Indian Adaptations*, O. Soffer and N. D. Praslov (eds), pp. 219–36. New York: Plenum Press.

Hays, J. D., J. Imbrie, and N. J. Shackleton 1976. Variations in the Earth's orbit: pacemaker of the ice ages. *Science* 194: 1121–32.

Helmer, Daniel 1989. Développement de la domestication au Proche-Orient de 9500 à 7500 BP: les nouvelles données d'El Kowm et de Ras Shamra. *Paléorient* 15: 111–21.

Headland, Thomas N., and Lawrence A. Reid 1989. Hunter-gatherers and their neighbors from prehistory to the present. *Current Anthropology* 30: 43–66.

Headland, Thomas N., and Lawrence A. Reid 1991. Holocene foragers and interethnic trade: a critique of the myth of isolated independent hunter-gatherers. *Between Bands and States*, S. A. Gregg (ed.), pp. 333–40. Carbondale, Illinois: Center for Archaeological Investigations.

Hedeager, Lotte 1992. *Iron-Age Societies. From Tribe to State in Northern Europe, 500 BC to AD 700.* Oxford: Blackwell.

Henry, Donald O. 1989. *From Foraging to Agriculture: the Levant at the End of the Ice Age.* Philadelphia: University of Pennsylvania Press.

—— 1995. *Prehistoric Cultural Ecology and Evolution: Insights from Southern Jordan.* New York: Plenum Press.

Hensel, Witold, and Sarunas Milisauskas 1985. *Excavations of Neolithic and Early Bronze Age Sites in Southeastern Poland.* Wrocław: Ossolineum.

Hesse, Brian 1984. These are our goats: the origins of herding in west-central Iran. *Animals and Archaeology 3: Early Herders and their Flocks*, J. Clutton-Brock and C. Grigson (eds), pp. 243–64. Oxford: British Archaeological Reports (BAR International Series 202).

Hewitt, Kenneth 1983. Interpreting the role of hazards in agriculture. *Interpretations of Calamity from the Viewpoint of Human Ecology*, K. Hewitt (ed.), pp. 123–39. Boston: Allen and Unwin.

Higham, Charles 1983. The Ban Chiang culture in wider perspective. *Proceedings of the British Academy* 69: 229–61.

—— 1989a. *The Archaeology of Mainland Southeast Asia from 10,000 BC to the Fall of Angkor.* Cambridge: Cambridge University Press.

—— 1989b. The later prehistory of mainland Southeast Asia. *Journal of World Prehistory* 3: 235–82.

—— 1995. The transition to rice cultivation in Southeast Asia. *Last Hunters, First Farmers. New Perspectives on the Prehistoric Transition to Agriculture*, T. D. Price and A. B. Gebauer (eds), pp. 127–55. Santa Fe: School of American Research Press.

—— 1996. *The Bronze Age of Southeast Asia.* Cambridge: Cambridge University Press.

——, and Bernard Maloney 1989. Coastal adaptation, sedentism, and domestication: a model for socioeconomic intensification in prehistoric Southeast Asia. *Foraging and Farming. The Evolution of Plant Exploitation*, D. R. Harris and G. C. Hillman (eds), pp. 650–66. London: Unwin Hyman.

——, and Rachanie Thosarat 1994. *Khok Phanom Di: Prehistoric Adaptation to the World's Richest Habitat.* Fort Worth: Harcourt Brace.

Hill, James N. 1970. Broken K Pueblo. *Prehistoric Social Organization in the American Southwest.* Tucson: University of Arizona Press.

Hillman, Gordon C. 1989. Late Palaeolithic plant foods from Wadi Kubbaniya in Upper Egypt: dietary diversity, infant weaning, and seasonality in a riverine environment. *Foraging and Farming. The Evolution of Plant Exploitation*, D. R. Harris and G. C. Hillman (eds), pp. 207–39. London: Unwin Hyman.

——, and M. S. Davies 1992. Domestication rates in wild wheats and barley under primitive cultivation: preliminary results and archaeological implications of field measurements of selection coefficient. *Préhistoire de l'Agriculture: Nouvelles Approches Expérimentales et Ethnographiques*, P. C. Anderson (ed.), pp. 113–58. Paris: Éditions du CNRS.

——, Susan M. Colledge, and David R. Harris 1989. Plant-food economy during the Epipalaeolithic period at Tell Abu Hureyra, Syria: dietary diversity, seasonality, and modes of exploitation. *Foraging and Farming. The Evolution of Plant Exploitation*, D. R. Harris and G. C. Hillman (eds), pp. 240–68. London: Unwin Hyman.

Hiroshi, Tsude 1992. Kofun period and state formation. *Acta Asiatica* 63: 64–86.

Hodder, Ian 1984. Burials, houses, women and men in the European neolithic. *Ideology, Power and Prehistory*, D. Miller and C. Tilley (eds), pp. 51–68. Cambridge: Cambridge University Press.

—— 1990. *The Domestication of Europe*. Oxford: Blackwell.

Hoffman, Michael A. 1980. A rectangular Amratian house from Hierakonpolis. *Journal of Near Eastern Studies* 39: 119–37.

Hole, Frank 1984. A reassessment of the Neolithic Revolution. *Paléorient* 10: 49–60.

—— 1989. Patterns of burial in the Fifth Millennium. *Upon this Foundation – the 'Ubaid Reconsidered*, E. F. Henrickson and I. Thuesen (eds), pp. 149–80. Copenhagen: Carsten Niebuhr Institute.

—— 1994. Environmental instabilities and urban origins. *Chiefdoms and Early States in the Near East: the Organizational Dynamics of Complexity*, G. Stein and M. S. Rothman (eds), pp. 121–51. Madison: Prehistory Press.

Hoopes, John W. 1995. Interaction in hunting and gathering societies as a context for the emergence of pottery in the Central American isthmus. *The Emergence of Pottery. Technology and Innovation in Ancient Societies*, W. K. Barnett and J. W. Hoopes (eds), pp. 185–98. Washington: Smithsonian Institution Press.

Hopf, Maria, and Ofer Bar-Yosef 1987. Plant remains from Hayonim Cave, western Galilee. *Paléorient* 13: 117–20.

Hopkins, David M. 1996. Introduction: the concept of Beringia. *American Beginnings. The Prehistory and Palaeoecology of Beringia*, F. H. West (ed.), pp. xvii–xxi. Chicago: University of Chicago Press.

Houghton, Philip 1993. Neandertal supralaryngeal vocal tract. *American Journal of Physical Anthropology* 90: 139–46.

Houston, Stephen D. 1992. *Hieroglyphs and History at Dos Pilas: Dynastic Politics of the Classic Maya*. Austin: University of Texas Press.

Hoyle, Fred 1977. *On Stonehenge*. San Francisco: W. H. Freeman.

Hudson, Charles M. 1990. *The Juan Pardo Expeditions.. Explorations of the Carolinas and Tennessee, 1566–1568*. Washington: Smithsonian Institution Press.

Huffman, Thomas N. 1986. Iron Age settlement patterns and the origins of class distinction in southern Africa. *Advances in World Archaeology*, vol. 5, F. Wendorf and A. E. Close (eds), pp. 291–338. New York: Academic Press.

Huot, Jean-Louis 1989. 'Ubaidian villages of lower Mesopotamia: perma-
nence and evolution from 'Ubaid 0 to 'Ubaid 4 as seen from Tell el 'Oueili.
Upon this Foundation – the 'Ubaid Reconsidered, E. F. Henrickson and
I. Thuesen (eds), pp. 19–42. Copenhagen: Carsten Niebuhr Foundation.

—— 1992. The first farmers at Oueili. *Biblical Archaeologist* December:
pp. 188–95.

—— 1994. *Les Premiers Villageois de Mésopotamie. Du Village á la Ville*, Paris:
Armand Colin.

Iltis, Hugh H. 1983. From teosinte to maize: the catastrophic sexual transformation. *Science* 222: 886–94.

Imamura, Keiji 1996. *Prehistoric Japan. New Perspectives on Insular East Asia.*
Honolulu: University of Hawaii Press.

Ingold, Tim 1984. Time, social relationships, and the exploitations of animals: anthropological reflections on prehistory. *Animals and Archaeology:
3. Early Herders and their Flocks*, J. Clutton-Brock and C. Grigson (eds),
pp. 3–12. Oxford: British Archaeological Reports (BAR International
Series 202).

—— 1987. *The Appropriation of Nature: Essays on Human Ecology and Social
Relations*. Iowa City: University of Iowa Press.

Irwin, Geoffrey 1992. *The Prehistoric Exploration and Colonisation of the
Pacific*. Cambridge: Cambridge University Press.

Isaac, Glynn L. 1978. The food-sharing behavior of protohuman hominids.
Scientific American 238: 90–108.

—— 1981. Stone age visiting cards: approaches to the study of early land use
patterns. *Pattern of the Past: Studies in Honour of David Clarke*, I. Hodder,
G. Isaac, and N. Hammond (eds), pp. 131–55. Cambridge: Cambridge
University Press.

Jackson, H. Edwin, and Susan L. Scott 1995a. The faunal record of the
southeastern elite: the implications of economy, social relations, and ideology. *Southeastern Archaeology* 14: 103–19.

——, and —— 1995b. Mississippian homestead and village subsistence organization. Contrasts in large-mammal remains from two sites in the
Tombigbee valley. *Mississippian Households and Communities*, J. D. Rogers
and B. D. Smith (eds), pp. 181–200. Tuscaloosa: University of Alabama
Press.

James, Steven R. 1989. Hominid use of fire in the Lower and Middle
Pleistocene: a review of the evidence. *Current Anthropology* 30: 1–26.

Jarrige, Jean François, and Richard H. Meadow 1980. The antecedents of
civilization in the Indus Valley. *Scientific American* 243: 122–33.

Jasim, Sabah Abboud 1985. *The Ubaid Period in Iraq: Recent Excavations in
the Hamrin Region*. Oxford: British Archaeological Reports (BAR
International Series 267).

Jażdżewski, Konrad 1981. *Pradzieje Europy Środkowej*. Wrocław: Ossolineum.

Jelinek, Arthur J. 1992. Perspectives from the Old World on the habitation of
the New. *American Antiquity* 57: 345–7.

Jensen, Jørgen 1988. Bronze Age research in Denmark 1970–1985. *Journal of
Danish Archaeology* 6: 155–74.

Jochim, Michael 1983. Palaeolithic cave art in ecological perspective. *Hunter-Gatherer Economy in Prehistory: A European Perspective*, G. Bailey (ed.), pp. 212–19. Cambridge: Cambridge University Press.

—— 1987. Late Pleistocene refugia in Europe. *The Pleistocene Old World*, O. Soffer (ed.), pp. 317–31. New York: Plenum Press.

Joffe, Alexander H. 1993. *Settlement and Society in the Early Bronze Age I and II, Southern Levant: Complementarity and Contradiction in a Small-Scale Complex Society*. Sheffield: Sheffield Academic Press.

Johanson, Donald, and Maitland A. Edey 1981. *Lucy: the Beginnings of Humankind*. New York: Simon & Schuster.

——, and Blake Edgar 1996. *From Lucy to Language*. New York: Simon & Schuster.

Johnson, Gregory A. 1982. Organizational structure and scalar stress. *Theory and Explanation in Archaeology*, C. Renfrew, M. J. Rowlands, B. A. Segraves (eds), pp. 389–421. New York: Academic Press.

Jones, B. Calvin 1994. The Lake Jackson mound complex (8LE1): stability and change in Fort Walton culture. *The Florida Anthropologist* 47: 120–46.

Jones, Rhys 1973. Emerging picture of Pleistocene Australians. *Nature* 246: 278–81.

—— 1990. From Kakadu to Kutikina: the southern continent at 18,000 years ago. *The World at 18 000 BP. Volume Two. Low Latitudes*, C. Gamble and O. Soffer (eds), pp. 264–95. London: Unwin Hyman.

—— 1992. Human colonisation of the Australian continent. *Continuity or Replacement: Controversies in Homo sapiens Evolution*, G. Bräuer and F. H. Smith (eds), pp. 289-301. Rotterdam: A. A. Balkema.

Joyce, Arthur A. 1994. Late Formative community organization and social complexity on the Oaxaca coast. *Journal of Field Archaeology* 21: 147–68.

Judge, W. James 1991. Chaco: current views of prehistory and the regional system. *Chaco & Hohokam. Prehistoric Regional Systems in the American Southwest*, P. L. Crown and W. J. Judge (eds), pp. 11–30. Santa Fe: School of American Research Press.

Junker, Laura Lee 1993. Craft goods specialization and prestige goods exchange in Philippine chiefdoms of the fifteenth and sixteenth centuries. *Asian Perspectives* 32: 1–35.

—— 1994. Trade competition, conflict, and political transformations in sixth- to sixteenth-century Philippine chiefdoms. *Asian Perspectives* 33: 229–60.

——, Karen Mudar, and Marla Schwaller 1994. Social stratification, house-hold wealth, and competitive feasting in 15th- and 16th-century Philippine chiefdoms. *Research in Economic Anthropology*, vol. 15, B. L. Isaac (ed.), pp. 307–58. Greenwich: JAI Press.

Kadrow, Sławomir 1991. Iwanowice, Babia Góra site: spatial evolution of an Early Bronze Age Mierzanowice culture settlement (2300–1600 BC). *Antiquity* 65: 640–50.

—— 1994. Social structures and social evolution among early-Bronze-Age communities in south-eastern Poland. *Journal of European Archaeology* 2: 229–48.

Kantner, John 1996. Political competition among the Chaco Anasazi of the American Southwest. *Journal of Anthropological Archaeology* 15: 41–105.

Kealhofer, Lisa 1996. The human environment during the terminal Pleistocene and Holocene in northeastern Thailand: phytolith evidence from Lake Kumphawapi. *Asian Perspectives* 35: 229–54.

Keatinge, Richard W. (ed.) 1988. *Peruvian Prehistory. An Overview of Pre-Inca and Inca Society.* Cambridge: Cambridge University Press.

Keefer, Erwin 1990. "Siedlung Forschner" am Federsee und ihre mittel-bronzezeitlichen Funde. *Bericht der Römisch-Germanischen Kommission des Deutschen Archäologischen Instituts* 71: 38–51.

Keeley, Lawrence H. 1996. *War Before Civilization.* New York: Oxford University Press.

Keightley, David N. 1994. Sacred Characters. *China. Ancient Culture, Modern Land*, R. E. Murowchick (ed.), pp. 71–9. Norman: University of Oklahoma Press.

Kelly, John E. 1990. The emergence of Mississippian culture in the American Bottom region. *The Mississippian Emergence*, B. D. Smith (ed.), pp. 113–52. Washington: Smithsonian Institution Press.

—— 1991. Cahokia and its role as a gateway center in interregional exchange. *Cahokia and the Hinterlands: Middle Mississippian Cultures of the Midwest*, T. E. Emerson and R. B. Lewis (eds), pp. 61–80. Urbana: University of Illinois Press.

Kelly, Robert L. 1995. *The Foraging Spectrum. Diversity in Hunter-Gatherer Lifeways.* Washington: Smithsonian Institution Press.

——, and Lawrence C. Todd 1988. Coming into the country: early Paleoindian hunting and mobility. *American Antiquity* 53: 231–44.

Kemp, Barry J. 1989. *Ancient Egypt. Anatomy of a Civilization.* London: Routledge.

Kenoyer, Jonathan Mark 1991. The Indus Valley Tradition of Pakistan and Western India. *Journal of World Prehistory* 5: 331–85.

—— 1992. Harappan craft specialization and the question of urban segregation and stratification. *Eastern Anthropologist* 45: 39–54.

Kent, Susan 1989. Cross-cultural perceptions of farmers as hunters and the value of meat. *Farmers as Hunters: the Implications of Sedentism*, S. Kent (ed.), pp. 1–17. Cambridge: Cambridge University Press.

—— 1995. Unstable households in a stable Kalahari community in Botswana. *American Anthropologist* 97: 297–312.

Kimbel, W. H., R. C. Walter, D. C. Johanson, K. E. Reed, J. L. Aronson, Z. Assefa, C. W. Marean, G. G. Eck, R. Bobe, E. Hovers, Y. Rak, C. Vondra, T. Yemane, D. York, Y. Chen, N. M. Evensen, and P. E. Smith 1996. Late Pliocene *Homo* and Oldowan Tools from the Hadar Formation (Kada Hadar Member), Ethiopia. *Journal of Human Evolution* 31: 549–61.

King, Adam, and Jennifer A. Freer 1995. Mississippian Southeast: a world-systems perspective. *Native American Interactions. Multiscalar Analyses and Interpretations in the Eastern Woodlands*, M. S. Nassaney and K. E. Sassaman (eds), pp. 266–88. Knoxville: University of Tennessee Press.

Kipp, Rita Smith, and Edward M. Schortman 1989. The political impact of trade in chiefdoms. *American Anthropologist* 91: 370–84.

Kirch, Patrick Vinton 1984. *The Evolution of the Polynesian Chiefdoms*. Cambridge: Cambridge University Press.

——— 1994. *The Wet and the Dry: Irrigation and Agricultural Intensification in Polynesia*. Chicago: University of Chicago Press.

——— 1997. *The Lapita Peoples. Ancestors of the Oceanic World*. Oxford: Blackwell.

Kislev, Mordechai 1992. Agriculture in the Near East in the seventh millennium BC. *Préhistoire de l'Agriculture: Nouvelles Approches Expérimentales et Ethnographiques*, P. C. Anderson (ed.), pp. 87–93. Paris: Éditions du CNRS.

Klein, Richard G. 1983. Stone Age prehistory of southern Africa. *Annual Review of Anthropology* 12: 25–48.

——— 1989. *The Human Career: Human Biological and Cultural Origins*. Chicago: University of Chicago Press.

Klima, Bohuslav 1987. Triple burial from the Upper Paleolithic of Dolní Věstonice, Czechoslovakia. *Journal of Human Evolution* 16: 831–5.

Knight, Frank H. 1921. *Risk, Uncertainty, and Profit*. Boston: Houghton Mifflin Company.

Knight, Vernon James, Jr. 1986. The institutional organization of Mississippian religion. *American Antiquity* 51: 675–87.

——— 1990. Social organization and the evolution of hierachy in southeastern chiefdoms. *Journal of Anthropological Research* 46: 1–23.

——— 1997. Some developmental parallels between Cahokia and Moundville. *Cahokia. Domination and Ideology in the Mississippian World*, T. R. Pauketat and T. E. Emerson (eds), pp. 229–47. Lincoln: University of Nebraska Press.

Kohl, Philip L. 1975. Carved chlorite vessels: a trade in finished commodities in the mid-third millennium. *Expedition* 18: 18–31.

Kolata, Alan L. 1991. Technology and organization of agricultural production in the Tiwanaku state. *Latin American Antiquity* 2: 99–125.

——— 1993. *The Tiwanaku: Portrait of an Andean Civilization*. Oxford: Blackwell.

——— 1996. *Tiwanaku and its Hinterland: Archaeology and Paleoecology of an Andean Civilization*. Washington: Smithsonian Institution Press.

Kolb, Michael J. 1994. Monumentality and the rise of religious authority in precontact Hawaii. *Current Anthropology* 35: 521–48.

Kondo, Yoshiro 1983. *The Age of the Keyhole-Shaped Tombs* (in Japanese). Tokyo: Iwanami Shoten.

Kooi, P. B. 1996. Het Project Peelo. Het onderzoek van her Kleuvenveld (1983, 1984), het Burchtterrein (1980) en het Nijland (1980) met enige kanttekeningen bij de resultaten van het project. *Palaeohistoria* 37/38: 417–79.

Kozłowski, Janusz K. 1986. The Gravettian in central and eastern Europe. *Advances in World Archaeology, Vol. 5*, F. Wendorf and A. Close, (eds), pp. 131–200. Orlando: Academic Press.

Kozłowski, Janusz K. 1990. Northern Central Europe c. 18000 BP. *The World at 18000 BP. Volume One. High Latitudes*, O. Soffer and C. Gamble (eds), pp. 204–27. London: Unwin Hyman.

Kristiansen, Kristian 1987. From stone to bronze: the evolution of social complexity in Northern Europe. *Specialization, Exchange, and Complex Societies*, E. M. Brumfiel and T. K. Earle (eds), pp. 30–51. Cambridge: Cambridge University Press.

—— 1991. Chiefdoms, states, and systems of evolution. *Chiefdoms: Power, Economy, and Ideology*, T. K. Earle (ed.), pp. 16–43. Cambridge: Cambridge University Press.

Kumar, Shubh K., and David Hotchkiss 1988. *Consequences of Deforestation for Women's Time Allocation, Agricultural Production, and Nutrition in Hill Areas of Nepal.* Washington: International Food Policy Research Institute.

Kusatman, B. 1991. *The Origins of Pig Domestication with Particular Reference to the Near East.* Unpublished doctoral dissertation, Institute of Archaeology, University of London (cited in Bar-Yosef and Meadow 1995).

Ladefoged, Thegn N. 1993. The impact of resource diversity on the sociopolitical structure of Rotuma: a geographic information system analysis. *The Evolution and Organization of prehistoric Society in Polynesia*, M. W. Graves and R. C. Green (eds), pp. 64–71. Auckland: New Zealand Archaeological Association (Monograph 19).

Lamberg-Karlovsky, C. C. 1994. Bronze Age khanates of Central Asia. *Antiquity* 68: 398–405.

Langebaek, Carl Henrik 1995. *Regional Archaeology in the Muisca Territory: a Study of the Fúquene and Susa Valleys.* Pittsburgh: University of Pittsburgh (Memoirs in Latin American Archaeology 9).

Larick, Roy, and Russell L. Ciochon 1996. The African emergence and early Asian dispersals of the genus *Homo*. *American Scientist* 84: 538–51.

Larsen, Clark Spencer 1984. Health and disease in prehistoric Georgia: the transition to agriculture. *Palaeopathology at the Origins of Agriculture*, M. N. Cohen and G. J. Armelagos (eds), pp. 367–92. Orlando: Academic Press.

Larsson, Lars 1990. Dogs in fraction – symbols in action. *Contribution to the Mesolithic in Europe*, P. M. Vermeersch and P. van Peer (eds), pp. 153–60. Leuven: Leuven University Press.

—— 1993. The Skateholm Project: late Mesolithic coastal settlement in southern Sweden. *Case Studies in European Prehistory*, P. Bogucki (ed.), pp. 31–62. Boca Raton: CRC Press.

Leakey, Mary D. 1971. *Olduvai Gorge: Excavations in Beds I and II, 1960–1963.* Cambridge: Cambridge University Press.

Leakey, Meave G. 1995. The farthest horizon. *National Geographic* 188: 38–51.

——, Craig S. Feibel, Ian McDougall, and Alan C. Walker 1995. New four-million-year-old hominid species from Kanapoi and Allia Bay, Kenya. *Nature* 376: 565–71.

LeBlanc, Steven A., and Patty Jo Watson 1973. A comparative statistical analysis of painted pottery from seven Halafian sites. *Paléorient* 1: 117–33.

Lee, Richard B. 1979. *The !Kung San*. Cambridge: Cambridge University Press.

——, and Irven DeVore (eds) 1968. *Man the Hunter*. Chicago: Aldine.

——, and —— (eds) 1976. *Kalahari Hunter-Gatherers: Studies of the !Kung San and their Neighbors*. Cambridge: Harvard University Press.

Legge, A. J. 1972. Prehistoric exploitation of the gazelle in Palestine. *Papers in Economic Prehistory*, E. S. Higgs (ed.), pp. 119–24. Cambridge: Cambridge University Press.

——, and Peter A. Rowley-Conwy 1987. Gazelle killing in Stone Age Syria. *Scientific American* 257: 88–95.

Lekson, Stephen H. 1984. *Great Pueblo Architecture of Chaco Canyon*. Albuquerque: National Park Service.

—— 1991. Settlement patterns and the Chaco region. *Chaco & Hohokam. Prehistoric Regional Systems in the American Southwest*, P. L. Crown and W. J. Judge (eds), pp. 31–56. Santa Fe: School of American Research Press.

——, and Catherine M. Cameron 1995. Abandonment of Chaco Canyon, the Mesa Verde migrations, and the reorganization of the Pueblo world. *Journal of Anthropological Archaeology* 14: 184–202.

——, Thomas C. Windes, John R. Stein, and W. James Judge 1988. The Chaco Canyon Community. *Scientific American* 259: 100–9.

Leroi-Gourhan, André 1968. The *Art of Prehistoric Man in Western Europe*. London: Thames and Hudson.

——, and M. Brezillon 1966. L'Habitation Madgalénienne No.1 de Pincevent près Montereau (Seine-et-Marne). *Gallia Préhistoire* 9: 263–385.

——, and —— 1972. Fouilles de Pincevent. Essai d'analyse ethnographique d'un habitat magdalénien. *Gallia Préhistoire (VIIème supplement à Gallia Préhistoire)*. Paris: Éditions du CNRS.

Leroi-Gourhan, Arlette 1975. The flowers found with Shanidar IV, a Neanderthal burial in Iraq. *Science* 190: 562–4.

Levy, Janet E. 1991. Metalworking technology and craft specialization in Bronze Age Denmark. *Archaeomaterials* 5: 55–74.

—— 1995. Heterarchy in Bronze Age Denmark: settlement pattern, gender, and ritual. *Heterarchy and the Analysis of Complex Societies*, R. M. Ehrenreich, C. L. Crumley, and J. E. Levy (eds), pp. 41–53. Washington: American Anthropological Association.

Lewenstein, Suzanne M. 1987. *Stone Tool Use at Cerros. The Ethnoarchaeological and Use-Wear Evidence*. Austin: University of Texas Press.

Lewis, Henry T. 1991. Technological complexity, ecological diversity, and fire regimes in Northern Australia: hunter-gatherer, cowboy, ranger. *Profiles in Cultural Evolution*, A. T. Rambo and K. Gillogly (eds), pp. 261–88. Ann Arbor: Museum of Anthropology (Anthropological Papers 85).

Lewis-Williams, J. David 1983. *The Rock Art of Southern Africa*. Cambridge: Cambridge University Press.

—— 1991. Wrestling with analogy: a methodological dilemma in Upper Palaeolithic art research. *Proceedings of the Prehistoric Society* 57: 149–62.

Lewis-Williams, J. David and T. A. Dowson 1988. Signs of all times: entoptic phenomena in Upper Paleolithic art. *Current Anthropology* 29: 201–45.

Lieberman, Daniel E. 1993. The rise and fall of seasonal mobility among hunter-gatherers. The case of the southern Levant. *Current Anthropology* 34: 599–631.

—— 1995. Cementum increment analyses of teeth from Wadi Hisma: estimations of site seasonality. *Prehistoric Cultural Ecology and Evolution: Insights from Southern Jordan*, D. O. Henry (ed.), pp. 391–8. New York: Plenum Press.

——, and Ofer Bar-Yosef 1994. On sedentism and cereal gathering in the Natufian. *Current Anthropology* 35: 431–4.

Lieberman, Philip, and Edmund S. Crelin 1971. On the speech of Neanderthal man. *Linguistic Inquiry* 2: 203–22.

Liu, Li 1996. Settlement patterns, chiefdom variability, and the development of early states in North China. *Journal of Anthropological Archaeology* 15: 237–88.

Lohof, Eric 1994. Tradition and change. Burial practices in the late Neolithic and Bronze Age in the north-eastern Netherlands. *Archaeological Dialogues* 1: 98–132.

Longacre, William A. 1970. *Archaeology as Anthropology: a Case Study*. Tucson: University of Arizona Press.

Louwe Kooijmans, L. P. 1993a. The Mesolithic/Neolithic transformation in the lower Rhine basin. *Case Studies in European Prehistory*, P. Bogucki (ed.), pp. 95–145. Boca Raton: CRC Press.

—— 1993b. An Early/Middle Bronze Age multiple burial at Wassenaar, the Netherlands. *Analecta Praehistorica Leidensia* 26: 1–20.

Love, Michael W. 1991. Style and social complexity in Formative Mesoamerica. *Formation of Complex Society in Southeastern Mesoamerica*, W. R. Fowler, Jr. (ed.), pp. 47–76. Boca Raton: CRC Press.

Lowe, Gareth 1989. The heartland Olmec: evolution of material culture. *Regional Perspectives on the Olmec*, R. J. Sharer and D. C. Grove (eds), pp. 33–67. Cambridge: Cambridge University Press.

Lumley, Henry de 1969. A Palaeolithic camp at Nice. *Scientific American* 220: 42–50.

Lynch, Thomas F. 1990. Glacial-age man in South America? A critical review. *American Antiquity* 55: 12–36.

MacNeish, Richard S. 1964. Ancient Mesoamerican civilization. *Science* 143: 531–7.

Mainfort, Robert C., Jr., and Lynne P. Sullivan 1998. Explaining earthen enclosures. *Ancient Earthen Enclosures of the Eastern Woodlands*, R. C. Mainfort and L. P. Sullivan (eds), pp. 1–16. Gainesville: University Press of Florida.

Makoto, Sahara 1992. Rice cultivation and the Japanese. *Acta Asiatica* 63: 40–63.

Mandryk, Carole A. Stein 1993. Hunter-gatherer social costs and the nonviability of submarginal environments. *Journal of Anthropological Research* 49: 39–71.

Manzanilla, Linda 1997. Teotihuacan. Urban archetype, cosmic model. *Emergence and Change in Early Urban Societies*, L. Manzanilla (ed.), pp. 109–31. New York: Plenum Press.

Marčenko, Konstantin, and Yuri Vinogradov 1989. The Scythian period in the northern Black Sea region (750–250 BC). *Antiquity* 63: 803–13.

Marcus, Joyce 1976. The origins of Mesoamerican writing. *Annual Review of Anthropology* 5: 35–67.

——— 1983a. The first appearance of Zapotec writing and calendrics. *The Cloud People. Divergent Evolution of the Zapotec and Mixtec Civilizations*, K. V. Flannery and J. Marcus (eds), pp. 91–6. New York: Academic Press.

——— 1983b. The conquest slabs of Building J, Monte Albán. *The Cloud People. Divergent Evolution of the Zapotec and Mixtec Civilizations*, K. V. Flannery and J. Marcus (eds), pp. 106–8. New York: Academic Press.

——— 1989. Zapotec chiefdoms and the nature of Formative religions. *Regional Perspectives on the Olmec*, R. J. Sharer and D. C. Grove (eds), pp. 148–97. Cambridge: Cambridge University Press.

——— 1992. *Mesoamerican Writing Systems: Propaganda, Myth, and History in Four Ancient Civilizations*. Princeton: Princeton University Press.

———, and Kent V. Flannery 1996. *Zapotec Civilization. How Urban Society Evolved in Mexico's Oaxaca Valley*. London: Thames and Hudson.

Marks, Anthony E. 1990. The Middle and Upper Palaeolithic of the Near East and the Nile Valley: the problem of cultural transformations. *The Emergence of Modern Humans: an Archaeological Perspective*, P. Mellars (ed.), pp. 56–80. Ithaca: Cornell University Press.

Martin, Paul S. 1984. Prehistoric overkill: the global model. *Quaternary Extinctions*, P. S. Martin and R. G. Klein (eds), pp. 354–403. Tucson: University of Arizona Press.

Maška, K. 1886. *Der diluviale Mensch in Mähren: ein Beitrag zur Urgeschichte für das Schuljahr 1885/86*. Neutitschen (cited in Svoboda, Ložek, and Vlček 1996).

Masse, W. Bruce 1991. The quest for subsistence sufficiency and civilization in the Sonoran Desert. *Chaco & Hohokam. Prehistoric Regional Systems in the American Southwest*, P. L. Crown and W. J. Judge (eds), pp. 195–223. Santa Fe: School of American Research Press.

Mathers, Clay, and Simon Stoddart (eds) 1994. *Development and Decline in the Mediterranean Bronze Age. Sheffield Archaeological Monographs 8*. Sheffield: J. R. Collis Publications.

Matson, R. G. 1991. *The Origins of Southwestern Agriculture*. Tucson: University of Arizona Press.

——— 1996. Households as economic organization: a comparison between large houses on the Northwest Coast and in the Southwest. *People who Lived in Big Houses. Archaeological Perspectives on Large Domestic Structures*, G. Coupland and E. B. Banning (eds), pp. 107–19. Madison: Prehistory Press.

———, and Gary Coupland 1995. *The Prehistory of the Northwest Coast*. San Diego: Academic Press.

Mazonowicz, Douglas 1975. *Voices from the Stone Age: a Search for Cave and Canyon Art*. London: Allen and Unwin.

McBride, Kevin A., and Robert E. Dewar 1981. Prehistoric settlement in the lower Connecticut River valley. *Man in the Northeast* 22: 37–66.

McCann, James 1984. *Plows, Oxen, and Household Managers: a Reconsideration of the Land Paradigm and the Production Equation in Northeast Ethiopia*. Boston: African Studies Center, Boston University.

McCorriston, Joy, and Frank Hole 1991. The ecology of seasonal stress and the origins of agriculture in the Near East. *American Anthropologist* 93: 46–69.

McIntosh, Susan Keech (ed.) 1995. *Excavations at Jenné-Jeno, Hambarketolo, and Kaniana (Inland Niger Delta, Mali), the 1981 Season*. Berkeley: University of California Press.

——, and Roderick J. McIntosh 1988. From stone to metal: new perspectives on the later prehistory of West Africa. *Journal of World Prehistory* 2: 89–133.

——, and —— 1993. Cities without citadels: understanding urban origins along the middle Niger. *The Archaeology of Africa. Food, Metals, and Towns*, T. Shaw, P. Sinclair, B. Andah, and A. Okpoko (eds), pp. 622–41. London: Routledge.

McKern, W. C. 1939. The Midwestern Taxonomic System as an aid to archaeological study. *American Antiquity* 4: 301–13.

McNett, Charles W., Jr. (ed.) 1985. *Shawnee Minisink: a Stratified Paleoindian-Archaic Site in the Upper Delaware Valley of Pennsylvania*. Orlando: Academic Press.

Mead, Jim I. 1980. Is it really that old? A comment about the Meadowcroft Rockshelter "overview." *American Antiquity* 45: 579–82.

Meadow, Richard H. 1984. Animal domestication in the Middle East: a view from the eastern margin. *Animals and Archaeology 3: Early Herders and their Flocks*, J. Clutton-Brock and C. Grigson (eds), pp. 309–37. Oxford: British Archaeological Reports (BAR International Series 202).

—— 1989. Osteological evidence for the process of animal domestication. *The Walking Larder: Patterns of Domestication, Pastoralism, and Predation*, J. Clutton-Brock (ed.), pp. 80–90. London: Unwin Hyman.

—— 1993. Animal domestication in the Middle East: a revised view from the eastern margin. *Harappan Civilization. A Recent Perspective*, G. L. Possehl (ed.), pp. 295–320. New Delhi: Oxford and IBH Publishing.

Meggers, Betty J. 1954. Environmental limitations on the development of culture. *American Anthropologist* 56: 801–24.

Mehrer, Mark W. 1995. *Cahokia's Countryside. Household Archaeology, Settlement Patterns, and Social Power*. DeKalb: Northern Illinois University Press.

Meignen, Liliane (ed.) 1993. *L'Abri des Canalettes: un Habitat Moustérien sue les Grands Causses (Nant, Aveyron): Fouilles 1980–1986*. Paris: CNRS (cited in Mellars 1996).

Mellaart, James 1975. *The Neolithic of the Near East*. New York: Charles Scribner's Sons.

Mellars, Paul A. 1976. Fire ecology, animal populations and man: a study of some ecological relationships in prehistory. *Proceedings of the Prehistoric Society* 42: 15–45.

—— 1994. The Upper Palaeolithic revolution. *The Oxford Illustrated Prehistory of Europe*. B. Cunliffe (ed.), pp. 42–78. Oxford: Oxford University Press.

—— 1996. *The Neanderthal Legacy: an Archaeological Perspective from Western Europe*. Princeton: Princeton University Press.

Meltzer, David J. 1988. Late Pleistocene human adaptations in eastern North America. *Journal of World Prehistory* 2: 1–52.

—— 1991. On "paradigms" and "paradigm bias" in controversies over human antiquity in America. *The First Americans: Search and Research*, T. D. Dillehay and D. J. Meltzer (eds), pp. 13–49. Boca Raton: CRC Press.

—— 1993a. *Search for the First Americans*. Montreal: St. Remy Press.

—— 1993b. Is there a Clovis adaptation? *From Kostenki to Clovis. Upper Palaeolithic – Palaeo-Indian Adaptations*, O. Soffer and N. D. Praslov (eds), pp. 293–310. New York: Plenum Press.

——, and Bruce D. Smith 1986. Palaeoindian and Early Archaic subsistence strategies in eastern North America. *Foraging, Collecting, and Harvesting: Archaic Period Subsistence and Settlement in the Eastern Woodlands*, S. W. Neusius (ed.), pp. 3–30. Carbondale: Center for Archaeological Investigations.

Midgley, Magdalena S. 1985. *The Origin and Function of the Earthen Long Barrows of Northern Europe*. Oxford: British Archaeological Reports (BAR International Series 259).

Miklaszewska-Balcer, Róża 1991. Datowanie osiedla obronnego kultury łużyckiej w Biskupinie. *Prahistoryczny Gród w Biskupinie. Problematyka Osiedli Obronnych na Początku Epoki Żelaza*, J. Jaskanis (ed.), pp. 107–13. Warsaw: Wydawnictwo Naukowe PWN.

Milisauskas, Sarunas, and Janusz Kruk 1982. Die Wagendarstellung auf einem Trichterbecher aus Bronocice in Polen. *Archäologisches Korrespondenzblatt* 12: 141–4.

——, and —— 1991. Utilization of cattle for traction during the later Neolithic in southeastern Poland. *Antiquity* 65: 562–6.

Miller, George R., and Richard L. Burger 1995. Our father the cayman, our dinner the llama: animal utilization at Chavín de Huántar, Peru. *American Antiquity* 60: 421–58.

Miller, Naomi 1992. The origins of plant cultivation in the Near East. *The Origins of Agriculture: an International Perspective*, C. W. Cowan and P. J. Watson (eds), pp. 39–58. Washington: Smithsonian Institution Press.

Millon, René 1988. The last years of Teotihuacan dominance. *The Collapse of Ancient States and Civilizations*, N. Yoffee and G. L. Cowgill (eds), pp. 102–64. Tucson: University of Arizona Press.

Mills, Barbara J. 1986. Prescribed burning and hunter-gatherer subsistence systems. *Haliksa'i, UNM Contributions to Anthropology* 5: 1–26.

Milner, George R. 1990. The late prehistoric Cahokia cultural system of the Mississippi River valley: foundations, florescence, and fragmentation. *Journal of World Prehistory* 4: 1–43.

—— 1996. Development and dissolution of a Mississippian society in the American Bottom, Illinois. *Political Structure and Change in the Prehistoric Southeastern United States*, J. F. Scarry (ed.), pp. 27–52. Gainesville: University Press of Florida.

Minnis, Paul E. 1985. *Social Adaptation to Food Stress: a Prehistoric Southwestern Example*. Chicago: University of Chicago Press.

—— 1992. Earliest plant cultivation in the desert borderlands of North America. *Origins of Agriculture: an International Perspective*, C. W. Cowan and P. J. Watson (eds), pp. 121–41. Washington: Smithsonian Institution Press.

Mithen, Steven J. 1991. Ecological interpretations of Palaeolithic art. *Proceedings of the Prehistoric Society* 57: 103–14.

—— 1993. Simulating mammoth hunting and extinction: implications for the Late Pleistocene of the Central Russian Plain. *Hunting and Animal Exploitation in the Later Palaeolithic and Mesolithic of Eurasia*, G. L. Peterkin, H. M. Bricker, and P. Mellars (eds), pp. 163–78. Washington: American Anthropological Association.

—— 1994. Technology and society during the Middle Pleistocene: hominid group size, social learning and industrial variability. *Cambridge Archaeological Journal* 4: 3–32.

—— 1996. *The Prehistory of the Mind*. London: Thames and Hudson.

Mochanov, Yuri A., and Svetlana A. Fedoseeva 1996. Berelekh, Allakhovsk region. *American Beginnings. The Prehistory and Palaeoecology of Beringia*, F. H. West (ed.), pp. 218–22. Chicago: University of Chicago Press.

Mohr Chavez, Karen L. 1988. The significance of *chiripa* in Lake Titicaca basin developments. *Expedition* 30: 17–26.

Moore, A. M. T. 1975. The excavation of Tell Abu Hureyra in Syria: a preliminary report. *Proceedings of the Prehistoric Society* 41: 50–77.

—— 1989. The transition from foraging to farming in Southwest Asia: present problems and future directions. *Foraging and Farming. The Evolution of Plant Exploitation*, D. R. Harris and G. C. Hillman (eds), pp. 620–31. London: Unwin Hyman.

—— 1991. Abu Hureyra I and the antecedents of agriculture on the Middle Euphrates. *The Natufian Culture in the Levant*, O. Bar-Yosef and F. R. Valla (eds), pp. 277–94. Ann Arbor: International Monographs in Prehistory.

——1994. On seasonal mobility and agriculture in the Levant. *Current Anthropology* 35: 48–9.

——, G. C. Hillman, and A. J. Legge 1999. *Village on the Euphrates. The Excavation of Abu Hureyra*. New York: Oxford University Press.

Moorey, P. R. S. 1993. Iran: A Sumerian El-Dorado? *Early Mesopotamia and Iran: Contact and Conflict 3500–1600 BC*, John Curtis (ed.), pp. 31–43. London: British Museum Press.

Moseley, Michael E. 1975. *The Maritime Foundations of Andean Civilization*. Menlo Park: Cummings Publishing Company.

Moss, Madonna L., and Jon M. Erlandson 1995. Reflections on North American Pacific Coast prehistory. *Journal of World Prehistory* 9: 1–45.

Movius, Hallam L. 1944. *Early Man and Pleistocene Stratigraphy in Southern and Eastern Asia*. Cambridge: Peabody Museum.

—— 1953. The Mousterian cave of Teshik-Tash, south-eastern Uzbekistan, Central Asia. *American School of Prehistoric Research Bulletin* 17: 11–71.

Mughal, Mohammed Rafique 1990. Further evidence of the Early Harappan culture in the Greater Indus Valley: 1971-1990. *South Asian Studies* 6: 175–200.

Muller, Jon 1986. *Archaeology of the Lower Ohio River Valley*. Orlando: Academic Press.

—— 1987. Salt, chert and shell: Mississippian exchange and economy. *Specialization, Exchange, and Complex Societies*, E. M. Brumfiel and T. K. Earle (eds), pp. 10–21. Cambridge: Cambridge University Press.

—— 1989. The Southern Cult. *The Southeastern Ceremonial Complex: Artifacts Analysis. The Cottonlandia Conference*, P. Galloway (ed.), pp. 11–26. Lincoln: University of Nebraska Press.

—— 1997. *Mississippian Political Economy*. New York: Plenum Press.

Nadel, D., A. Danin, E. Werker, T. Schick, M. E. Kislev, and K. Stewart 1994. 19,000-year-old twisted fibers from Ohalo 11. *Current Anthropology* 35: 451–7.

Nash, D. T., and M. D. Petraglia 1987. *Natural Formation Processes and the Archaeological Record*. Oxford: British Archaeological Reports (BAR International Series 352).

Neitzel, Jill 1991. Hohokam material culture and behavior: the dimensions of organizational change. *Exploring the Hohokam. Prehistoric Desert Peoples of the American Southwest*, G. J. Gumerman (ed.), pp. 177–230. Dragoon, Arizona: Amerind Foundation.

Nelson, Richard S. 1986. Pochtecas and prestige: Mesoamerican artifacts in Hohokam sites. *Ripples in the Chichimec Sea*, F. J. Mathien and R. H. McGuire (eds), pp. 154–82. Carbondale: Southern Illinois University Press.

Nelson, Sarah M. 1991. "Goddess Temple" and the status of women at Niuheliang, China. *Archaeology of Gender*, D. Walde and N. D. Willows (eds), pp. 302–8. Calgary: Archaeological Association, University of Calgary.

—— 1995. Ritualized pigs and the origins of complex society: hypotheses regarding the Hongshan culture. *Early China* 20: 1–16.

—— 1996. Early civilizations of China. *The Oxford Companion to Archaeology*, B. Fagan (ed.), pp. 137–40. New York: Oxford University Press.

Nissen, Hans J. 1988. *The Early History of the Ancient Near East 9000–2000 BC*. Chicago: University of Chicago Press.

—— 1995. Western Asia before the Age of Empires. *Civilizations of the Ancient Near East. Vol. II*, J. M. Sasson et al. (eds), pp. 791–806. New York: Charles Scribner's Sons.

Nobbs, Margaret, and Ronald Dorn 1993. New surface exposure ages for petroglyphs from the Olary Province, South Australia. *Archaeology in Oceania* 28: 18–39.

Nobis, Günter 1975. Zur Fauna des ellerbekzeitlichen Wohnplatzes Rosenhof in Ostholstein. *Archaeozoological Studies*, A. T. Clason (ed.), pp. 160–3. Amsterdam: North Holland Publishing Company.

Noble, William, and Iain Davidson 1996. *Human Evolution, Language and Mind. A Psychological and Archaeological Inquiry*. Cambridge: Cambridge University Press.

Northover, Peter 1982. The metallurgy of the Wilburton hoards. *Oxford Journal of Archaeology* 1: 69–109.

Noy, Tamar 1989. Some aspects of Natufian mortuary behavior at Nahal Oren. *People and Culture in Change: proceedings of the Second Symposium on Upper Palaeolithic, Mesolithic and Neolithic Populations of Europe and the Mediterranean Basin*. I. Hershkovitz, (ed.), pp. 53–7. Oxford: British Archaeological Reports (BAR International Series 508).

O'Brien, Patricia J. 1989. Cahokia: the political capital of the "Ramey" state? *North American Archaeologist* 10: 275–92.

—— 1991. Early state economics: Cahokia, capital of the Ramey state. *Early State Economics*, H. J. M. Claessen and P. van de Velde (eds), pp. 143–75. London: Transaction Publishers.

O'Connor, David 1993. Urbanism in Bronze Age Egypt and northeast Africa. *The Archaeology of Africa. Food, Metals, and Towns*, T. Shaw, P. Sinclair, B. Andah, and A. Okpoko (eds), pp. 570–86. London: Routledge.

O'Connor, Mallory McCane 1995. *Lost Cities of the Ancient Southeast*. Gainesville: University Press of Florida.

O'Shea, John M. 1996. *Villagers of the Maros. A Portrait of an Early Bronze Age Society*. New York: Plenum Press.

Ohnuma, K., and C. A. Bergman 1990. A technological analysis of the Upper Palaeolithic levels (XXV–VI) of Ksar Akil, Lebanon. *The Emergence of Modern Humans: an Archaeological Perspective*, P. Mellars (ed.), pp. 91–138. Ithaca: Cornell University Press.

Olsen, Sandra L. 1995. Pleistocene horse-hunting at Solutré: Why bison jump analogies fail. *Ancient Peoples and Landscapes*, E. Johnson (ed.), pp. 65–75. Lubbock: Museum of Texas Tech University.

Palmatary, Helen C. 1950. *The Pottery of Marajo Island, Brazil. Transactions of the American Philisophical Society*, vol. 39. Philadelphia: American Philosophical Society.

—— 1965. *The River of the Amazons. Its Discovery and Early Exploration 1500–1743*. New York: Carlton Press.

Parker Pearson, Michael 1993. *English Heritage Book of Bronze Age Britain*. London: Batsford/English Heritage.

Parkington, John, and Glen Mills 1991. From space to place: the architecture and social organization of southern African mobile communities. *Ethnoarchaeological Approaches to Mobile Campsites*, C. S. Gamble and W. A. Boismier (eds), pp. 355-70. Ann Arbor: International Monographs in Prehistory.

Pasztory, Esther 1997. *Teotihuacan. An Experiment in Living*. Norman: University of Oklahoma Press.

Patton, Mark 1993. *Statements in Stone. Monuments and Society in Neolithic Brittany*. London: Routledge.

Pauketat, Timothy R. 1987. Mississippian domestic economy and formation processes: a response to Prentice. *MCJA: Midcontinental Journal of Archaeology* 12: 77-88.

—— 1989. Monitoring Mississippian homestead occupation span and economy using ceramic refuse. *American Antiquity* 54: 288–310.

—— 1994. *The Ascent of Chiefs. Cahokia and Mississippian Politics in Native North America*. Tuscaloosa: University of Alabama Press.

—— 1997a. Socialization, political symbols, and the crafty elite of Cahokia. *Southeastern Archaeology* 16: 1–15.

—— 1997b. Cahokian political economy. *Cahokia. Domination and Ideology in the Mississippian World*, T. R. Pauketat and T. E. Emerson (eds), pp. 30–51. Lincoln: University of Nebraska Press.

—— and Thomas E. Emerson 1997a. Conclusion: Cahokia and the Four Winds. *Cahokia. Domination and Ideology in the Mississippian World*, T. R. Pauketat and T. E. Emerson (eds), pp. 269–78. Lincoln: University of Nebraska Press.

——, and —— (eds) 1997b. *Cahokia. Domination and Ideology in the Mississippian World*. Lincoln: University of Nebraska Press.

—— and Neal H. Lopinot 1997. Cahokian population dynamics. *Cahokia. Domination and Ideology in the Mississippian World*, T. R. Pauketat and T. E. Emerson (eds), pp. 103-23. Lincoln: University of Nebraska Press.

Payne, Claudine 1994. Fifty years of archaeological research at the Lake Jackson site. *Florida Anthropologist* 47: 107–19.

Pazdur, Mieczysław F., Róża Miklaszewska-Balcer, Wojciech Piotrowski, and Teresa Węgrzynowicz 1991. Chronologia bezwzględna osady w Biskupinie w świetle datowań radiowęglowych. *Prahistoryczny Gród w Biskupinie. Problematyka Osiedli Obronnych na Początku Epoki Żelaza*, J. Jaskanis (ed.), pp. 115–25. Warsaw: Wydawnictwo Naukowe PWN.

Pearce, R. H., and Mike Barbetti 1981. A 38,000-year-old archaeological site at Upper Swan, Western Australia. *Archaeology in Oceania* 16: 173–8.

Pearson, Richard, and Anne Underhill 1987. Chinese Neolithic: recent trends in research. *American Anthropologist* 89: 807–22.

Peck, Mary 1994. *Chaco Canyon. A Center and its World*. Santa Fe: Museum of New Mexico Press.

Peebles, Christopher S., and Susan Kus 1977. Some archaeological correlates of ranked societies. *American Antiquity* 42: 421–48.

Peregrine, Peter 1992. *Mississippian Evolution: a World-System Perspective*. Madison: Prehistory Press.

Perlès, Catherine 1994. Les débuts du Néolithique en Grèce. *La Recherche* 266: 642–9.

Perrot, Jean, and Daniel Ladiray 1988. *Les Hommes de Mallaha (Eynan) Israel. I. Les Sepultures*. Paris: Association Paléorient.

Peterkin, Gail Larsen, Harvey M. Bricker, and Paul Mellars (eds) 1993. *Hunting and Animal Exploitation in the Late Palaeolithic and Mesolithic of Eurasia*. Washington: American Anthropological Association.

Petersen, Glenn 1982. *One Man Cannot Rule a Thousand: Fission in a Ponapean Chiefdom.* Ann Arbor: University of Michigan Press.

—— 1993. Kanengamah and Pohnpei's politics of concealment. *American Anthropologist* 95: 334–52.

Peterson, Jean Treloggen 1978a. Hunter-gatherer/farmer exchange. *American Anthropologist* 80: 335–51.

—— 1978b. *The Ecology of Social Boundaries: Agta Foragers of the Philippines.* Urbana: University of Illinois Press.

Petrie, W. M. Flinders 1920. *Prehistoric Egypt* (Egyptian Research Account). London: British School of Archaeology.

Phillipson, David W. 1993. *African Archaeology.* 2nd edn. Cambridge: Cambridge University Press.

Piggott, Stuart 1938. The early Bronze Age in Wessex. *Proceedings of the Prehistoric Society* 4: 52–106.

Pigott, Vincent C., and S. Natapintu 1988. Archaeological investigations into prehistoric copper production: the Thailand Archaeometallurgy Project 1984–1986. *The Beginning of the Use of Metals and Alloys,* R. Maddin (ed.), pp. 156–62. Cambridge: MIT Press.

Pike-Tay, Anne 1991. *Red Deer Hunting in the Upper Palaeolithic of South-West France: A Study in Seasonality.* Oxford: Tempvs Reparatvm (BAR International Series 569).

Pineda, Rosa Fung 1988. The Late Preceramic and Initial Period. *Peruvian Prehistory,* R. W. Keatinge (ed.), pp. 67–96. Cambridge: Cambridge University Press.

Piperno, Dolores 1989. Non-affluent foragers: resource availability, seasonal shortages, and the emergence of agriculture in Panamanian tropical forests. *Foraging and Farming. The Evolution of Plant Exploitation,* D. R. Harris and G. C. Hillman (eds), pp. 538–54. London: Unwin Hyman.

——, and Deborah M. Pearsall 1998. *The Origins of Agriculture in the Lowland Neotropics.* San Diego: Academic Press.

Politis, Gustavo G., José L. Prado, and Roelf P. Beukens 1995. The human impact in Pleistocene-Holocene extinctions in South America – the Pampean Case. *Ancient People and Landscapes,* E. Johnson (ed.), pp. 187–205. Lubbock: Museum of Texas Tech University.

Pollock, Susan 1992. Bureaucrats and managers, peasants and pastoralists, imperialists and traders: research on the Uruk and Jemdet Nasr periods in Mesopotamia. *Journal of World Prehistory* 6: 297–336.

Polosmak, Natalya 1994. A mummy unearthed from the Pastures of Heaven. *National Geographic* 186(4): 80–103.

Possehl, Gregory L. 1986. *Kulli. An Exploration of Ancient Civilization in Asia.* Durham: Carolina Academic Press.

—— 1990. Revolution in the urban revolution: the emergence of Indus urbanism. *Annual Review of Anthropology* 19: 261–82.

—— (ed.) 1993. *Harappan Civilization. A Recent Perspective.* New Delhi: Oxford and IHB Publishing.

—— 1996. *Indus Age. The Writing System.* Philadelphia: University of Pennsylvania Press.

——, and M. H. Raval 1989. *Harappan Civilization and Rojdi*. Leiden: E. J. Brill.

Postgate, J. N. 1992. *Early Mesopotamia. Society and Economy at the Dawn of History*. London: Routledge.

Potts, D. T. 1990. *The Arabian Gulf in Antiquity*. Oxford: Clarendon Press.

—— 1993. The late prehistoric, protohistoric, and early historic period in Eastern Arabia (ca. 5000–1200 BC). *Journal of World Prehistory* 7: 163–212.

—— 1997. *Mesopotamian Civilization. The Material Foundations*. London: The Athlone Press.

Potts, Richard 1988. *Early Hominid Activities at Olduvai*. New York: A. de Gruyter.

—— 1996. *Humanity's Descent. The Consequences of Ecological Instability*. New York: William Morrow and Company.

Potts, Timothy 1994. *Mesopotamia and the East. An Archaeological and Historical Study of Foreign Relations, ca. 3400–2000, BC*. Oxford: Oxford University Committee for Archaeology.

Powers, William R., and John F. Hoffecker 1989. Late Pleistocene settlement in the Nenana Valley, central Alaska. *American Antiquity* 54: 263–87.

Pozorski, Shelia 1987. Theocracy vs. militarism: the significance of the Casma Valley in understanding early state formation. *The Origins and Development of the Andean State*, J. Haas, S. Pozorski, and T. Pozorski (eds), pp. 15–30. Cambridge: Cambridge University Press.

——, and Thomas Pozorski 1979. Alto Salaverry: a Peruvian coastal preceramic site. *Annals of the Carnegie Museum of Natural History* 49: 337–75.

——, and —— 1987. *Early Settlement and Subsistence in the Casma Valley, Peru*. Iowa City: University of Iowa Press.

——, and —— 1992. Early civilization in the Casma Valley, Peru. *Antiquity* 66: 845–70.

Prentice, Guy 1983. Cottage industries: concepts and implications. *MCJA: Midcontinental Journal of Archaeology* 8: 17–48.

—— 1985. Economic differentiation among Mississippian farmsteads. *MCJA: Midcontinental Journal of Archaeology* 10: 77–122.

Price, Barbara J. 1984. Competition, productive intensification, and ranked society: speculations from evolutionary theory. *Warfare, Culture, and Environment*, R. B. Ferguson (ed.), pp. 209–40. Orlando: Academic Press.

Price, T. Douglas 1991. Mesolithic of Northern Europe. *Annual Review of Anthropology* 20: 211–33.

—— (ed.) 1999. *Europe's First Farmers*. Cambridge: Cambridge University Press.

——, and Gary M. Feinman 1995. Foundations of prehistoric social inequality. *Foundations of Social Inequality*, T. D. Price and G. M. Feinman (eds), pp. 3–14. New York: Plenum Press.

——, and Anne Birgitte Gebauer 1992. The final frontier: first farmers in northern Europe. *Transitions to Agriculture in Prehistory*, A. B. Gebauer and T. D. Price (eds), pp. 97–117. Madison: Prehistory Press.

——, ——, and Lawrence H. Keeley 1995. The spread of farming into Europe north of the Alps. *Last Hunters – First Farmers. New Perspectives on the Prehistoric Transition to Agriculture*, T. D. Price and A. B. Gebauer (eds), pp. 95–126. Santa Fe: School of American Research Press.

Pryor, Francis 1991. *The English Heritage Book of Flag Fen: Prehistoric Fenland Centre*. London: Batsford.

Pumpelly, Raphael 1908. *Explorations in Turkestan. Expedition of 1904. Prehistoric Civilizations of Anau: Origins, Growth, and Influence of Environment*. Washington: Carnegie Institution.

Pyranarn, Kosum 1989. New evidence on plant exploitation and environment during the Hoabinhian (Late Stone Age) from Ban Kao caves, Thailand. *Foraging and Farming. The Evolution of Plant Exploitation*, D. R. Harris and G. C. Hillman (eds), pp. 282–91. London: Unwin Hyman.

Quilter, Jeffrey 1989. Households and societies in Preceramic Peru: Paloma and El Paraíso. *Households and Communities*, S. MacEacherm, D. J. W. Archer, and R. D. Garvin (eds), pp. 469–77. Calgary: Archaeological Association, University of Calgary (Proceedings, Chacmool Annual Conference, no. 21).

—— 1991. Late Preceramic Peru. *Journal of World Prehistory* 5: 439–80.

——, Bernardino Ojeda E., Deborah M. Pearsall, Daniel H. Sandweiss, John G. Jones, and Elizabeth S. Wing 1991. Subsistence economy of El Paraíso, an early Peruvian site. *Science* 251: 277–83.

Rasmussen, Kaare Lund 1993. Radiocarbon dates from late Neolithic and Early Bronze Age Settlements at Hemmed, Højgard, and Trappendal, Jutland, Denmark. *Journal of Danish Archaeology* 10: 156–62.

Rasmussen, Marianne 1995. Settlement structure and economic variation in the Early Bronze Age. *Journal of Danish Archaeology* 11: 87–107.

Raymond, J. Scott 1981. The maritime foundations of Andean civilization: a reconsideration of the evidence. *American Antiquity* 46: 806–21.

Raynal, Jean-Paul, Lionel Magoga, and Peter Bindon 1995. Tephrofacts and the first human occupation of the French Massif Central. *Analecta Praehistorica Leidensia* 27: 129–46.

Reader, John 1981. *Missing Links*. Boston: Little, Brown.

Redmond, Elsa M. 1994. *Tribal and Chiefly Warfare in South America*. Ann Arbor: Museum of Anthropology (Memoirs of the Museum of Anthropology 28).

——, and Charles S. Spencer 1983. The Cuicatlán Canada and the Period II frontier of the Zapotec state. *The Cloud People. Divergent Evolution of the Zapotec and Mixtec Civilizations*, K. V. Flannery and J. Marcus (eds), pp. 117–20. New York: Academic Press.

——, and —— 1994. Pre-Columbian chiefdoms. *National Geographic Research & Exploration* 10: 422–39.

Reeves, B. O. K. 1973. The nature and age of the contact between the Laurentide and Cordilleran ice sheets in the western interior of North America. *Arctic and Alpine Research* 5: 1–16.

Renfrew, Colin 1972. *The Emergence of Civilisation*. London: Methuen.

—— 1973. *Before Civilization. The Radiocarbon Revolution and Prehistoric Europe*. New York: Knopf.

—— 1974. Beyond a subsistence economy: the evolution of social organization in prehistoric Europe. *Reconstructing Complex Societies*, C. B. Moore (ed.), pp. 69–95. Cambridge: American Schools of Oriental Research.

—— 1975. Trade as action at a distance: questions of integration and communication. *Ancient Civilization and Trade*, J. A. Sabloff and C. C. Lamberg-Karlovsky (eds), pp. 3–59. Albuquerque: University of New Mexico Press.

—— 1976. Megaliths, territories, and populations. *Acculturation and Continuity in Atlantic Europe*, S. J. de Laet (ed.), pp. 298–320. Brugge: De Tempel.

—— 1993. *The Roots of Ethnicity, Archaeology, Genetics and the Origins of Europe*. Rome: Unione Internazionale degli Istituti di Archeologia, Storia e Storia dell'Arte.

——, and Paul G. Bahn 1996. *Archaeology: Theories, Methods and Practice*. 2nd edn. London: Thames and Hudson.

——, and John Cherry (eds) 1986. *Peer-Polity Interaction and Socio-Political Change*. Cambridge: Cambridge University Press.

Rensink, Eelco 1995. On Magdalenian mobility and land use in north-west Europe. Some methodological considerations. *Archaeological Dialogues* 2: 85–119.

Révillion, Stéphane, and Alain Tuffreau 1994. *Les Industries Laminaires au Paléolithique Moyen*. Paris: Éditions du CNRS.

Richardson, James B., III 1994. *People of the Andes*. Montreal: St. Remy Press.

Rigaud, Jean-Philippe, and Jean-Michel Geneste 1988. L'utilisation de l'espace dans la Grotte Vaufrey. *La Grotte Vaufrey: Paleoenvironnement, Chronologie, Activites Humaines*, J.-Ph. Rigaud (ed.), pp. 593–612. Paris: Éditions du CNRS (Memoires de la Society Préhistoriques Française 19).

——, and Jan F. Simek 1991. Interpreting spatial patterns at the Grotte XV. A multiple-method approach. *The Interpretation of Archaeological Spatial Patterning*, E. M. Kroll and T. D. Price (eds), pp. 199–220. New York: Plenum Press.

Rindos, David 1984. *The Origins of Agriculture: an Evolutionary Perspective*. Orlando: Academic Press.

Rissman, Paul C., and Y. M. Chitalwala 1990. *Harappan Civilization and Oriyo Timbo*. New Delhi: Oxford & IBH Publishing Co.

Ritchie, William A. 1932. *The Lamoka Lake Site: the Type Station of the Archaic Algonkin Period in New York*. Researches and Transactions of the New York State Archaeological Association 8(1). Rochester: NY State Archaeological Association.

Rønne, Preben 1986. Stilvariationer i ældre bronzealder: undersøgelser over lokalforskelle i brug af ornamenter og oldsager i ældre bronzealders anden periode. *Aarbøger for Nordisk Oldkyndighed og Historie* 1986: 71–124.

Roberts, Mark B., Clive S. Gamble, and David R. Bridgland 1995. The earliest occupation of Europe: the British Isles. *Analecta Praehistorica Leidensia* 27: 165–91.

Roberts, Richard G., Rhys Jones, and M. A. Smith 1994. Beyond the radiocarbon barrier in Australian prehistory. *Antiquity* 68: 611–16.

——, Michael Bird, Jon Olley, Rex Galbraih, Ewan Lawson, Geoff Laslett, Hiroyuki Yoshida, Rhys Jones, Richard Fullagar, Geraldine Jacobsen, and Quan Hua 1998. Optical and radiocarbon dating at Jinmium rock shelter in northern Australia. *Nature* 393: 358–62.

Robertson, Robin A., and David A. Freidel (eds) 1986. *Archaeology at Cerros, Belize, Central America. Volume I: an Interim Report*. Dallas: Southern Methodist University Press.

Robinson, Andrew 1995. *The Story of Writing*. London: Thames and Hudson.

Robinson, Brian S. 1992. Early and Middle Archaic Period occupation in the Guly of Maine region: mortuary and technological patterning. *Early Holocene Occupation in Northern New England*, B. S. Robinson, J. B. Petersen, and A. K. Robinson (eds), pp. 63–116. Augusta: Maine Historic Preservation Commission (Occasional Publications in Maine Archaeology 9).

Roebroeks, Wil, and Thijs van Kolfschoten 1995. The earliest occupation of Europe: a reappraisal of the artefactual and chronological evidence. *Analecta Praehistorica Leidensia* 27: 297–315.

Rogers, J. Daniel 1996. Markers of social integration: the development of centralized authority in the Spiro region. *Political Structure and Change in the Prehistoric Southeastern United States*, J. F. Scarry (ed.), pp. 53–68. Gainesville: University Press of Florida.

——, and Bruce D. Smith (eds) 1995. *Mississippian Communities and Households*. Tuscaloosa: University of Alabama Press.

Rolland, Nicolas, and Harold L. Dibble 1990. A new synthesis of Middle Palaecolithic variability. *American Antiquity* 55: 480–99.

Rolle, Renate 1989. *The World of the Scythians*. London: Batsford.

Roney, John R. 1992. Prehistoric roads and regional integration in the Chacoan system. *Anasazi Regional Organization and the Chaco System*, D. E. Doyel, (ed.), pp. 123–32. Albuquerque: Maxwell Museum of Anthropology.

Roosevelt, Anna Curtenius 1987. Chiefdoms in the Amazon and Orinoco. *Chiefdoms in the Americas*, R. D. Drennan and C. A. Uribe (eds), pp. 153–84. Lanham: University Press of America.

—— 1991. *Moundbuilders of the Amazon: Geophysical Archaeology, on Marajo Island, Brazil*. San Diego: Academic Press.

—— 1993. The rise and fall of the Amazon chiefdoms. *L'Homme* 33: 255–83.

——, M. Lima da Costa, C. Lopes Machado, M. Michab, N. Mercier, H. Valladas, J. Feathers, W. Barnett, I. Imazio da Silveira, A. Henderson, J. Silva, B. Chernoff, D. S. Reese, J. A. Holman, N. Toth, and K. Schick 1996. Palaeoindian cave dwellers in the Amazon: the peopling of the Americas. *Science* 272: 373–84.

Rose, Lisa, and Fiona Marshall 1996. Meat eating, hominid sociality, and home bases revisited. *Current Anthropology* 37: 307–38.

Rosenberg, Michael, R. Mark Nesbitt, Richard, W. Redding, and Thomas F. Strasser 1995. Hallan Çemi Tepesi: some preliminary observations concerning Early Neolithic subsistence behaviors in eastern Anatolia. *Anatolica* 21: 1–12.

Rothman, Mitchell S. 1994. Introduction Part I. Evolutionary typologies and cultural complexity. *Chiefdoms and Early States in the Near East. The Organizational Dynamics of Complexity*, G. Stein and M. S. Rothman (eds), pp. 1–10. Madison: Prehistory Press.

Rothschild, Nan A. 1979. Mortuary behavior and social organization at Indian Knoll and Dickson Mounds. *American Antiquity* 44: 658–75.

Rowlands, Michael J. 1976. *The Production and Distribution of Metalwork in the Middle Bronze Age in Southern Britain*. Oxford: British Archaeological Reports (BAR British Series 32).

Rowley-Conwy, Peter 1983. Sedentary hunters: the Ertebølle example. *Hunter-Gatherer Economy in Prehistory: A European Perspective*, G. Bailey (ed.), pp. 111–26. Cambridge: Cambridge University Press.

—— 1984. Postglacial foraging and early farming economies in Japan and Korea: a west European perspective. *World Archaeology* 16: 28–42.

—— 1995. Wild or domestic? On the evidence for the earliest domestic cattle and pigs in south Scandinavia and Iberia. *International Journal of Osteoarchaeology* 5: 115–26.

Rudenko, Sergei I. 1970. *Frozen Tombs of Siberia. The Pazyryk Burials of Iron Age Horsemen*. Berkeley: University of California Press.

Runnels, Curtis, and Tjeerd H. van Andel 1988. Trade and the origins of agriculture in the Eastern Mediterranean. *Journal of Mediterranean Archaeology* 1: 83–109.

Russo, Michael 1994. Why we don't believe in Archaic ceremonial mounds and why we should: the case from Florida. *Southeastern Archaeology* 13: 93–109.

—— 1996. Southeastern Archaic mounds. *Archaeology of the Mid-Holocene Southeast*, K. E. Sassaman and D. G. Anderson (eds), pp. 259–87. Gainesville: University Press of Florida.

Rust, William F., and Robert J. Sharer 1988. Olmec settlement data from La Venta, Tabasco, Mexico. *Science* 242: 102–4.

Ruvolo, Maryellen 1996. A new approach to studying modern human origins: hypothesis testing with coalescence time distributions. *Molecular Phylogenetics and Evolution* 5: 202–19.

Sabloff, Jeremy 1994. *The New Archaeology and the Ancient Maya*. 2nd edn. New York: W. H. Freeman.

Safar, Fuad, Mohammed Ali Mustafa, and Seton Lloyd 1981. *Eridu*. Baghdad: State Organization of Antiquities and Heritage.

Sahlins, Marshal D. 1958. *Social Stratification in Polynesia*. Seattle: American Ethnological Society.

—— 1972. *Stone Age Economics*. Chicago: Aldine-Atherton.

Sand, Christophe 1993. A preliminary study of the impact of the Tongan maritime chiefdom on the late prehistoric society of 'Uvea, western Polynesia. *The Evolution and Organization of Prehistoric Society in Polynesia*, M. W. Graves and R. C. Green (eds), pp. 43–51. Auckland: New Zealand Archaeological Association (Monograph 19).

Sanders, William T., and Barbara J. Price 1968. *Mesoamerica: the Evolution of a Civilization*. New York: Random House.

Sandweiss, Daniel H., Heather McInnis, Richard L. Burger, Asunción Cano, Bernardino Ojeda, Rolando Paredes, María del Carmen Sandweiss, Michael D. Glascock 1998. Quebrada Jaguay: early South American maritime adaptations. *Science* 281: 1830–5.

Sanger, David 1975. Culture change as an adaptive process in the Maine-Maritimes region. *Arctic Anthropology* 12: 60–75.

Santley, Robert S. 1980. Disembedded capitals reconsidered. *American Antiquity* 45: 132–45.

—— 1993. Late Formative Period society at Loma Torremote: a consideration of the Redistribution vs. the Great Provider models as a basis for the emergence of complexity in the Basin of Mexico. *Prehispanic Domestic Units in Western Mesoamerica. Studies of the Household, Compound, and Residence*, R. S. Santley and K. G. Hirth (eds), pp. 67–86. Boca Raton: CRC Press.

Sasaki, Ken'ichi 1992. Chōhōji-Minamibara investigations in the framework of Kofun Period archaeology. *Chōhōji-Minamibara Tumulus: a Fourth Century Burial Mound in Southwestern Kyoto, Japan*. Osaka University Studies in Archaeology 2. Osaka: Faculty of Letters, Osaka University.

Sassaman, Kenneth E. 1993. *Early Pottery in the Southeast. Tradition and Innovation in Cooking Technology*. Tuscaloosa: University of Alabama Press.

Sasson, Jack M. (ed.) 1995. *Civilizations of the Ancient Near East*. New York: Charles Scribner's Sons.

Saunders, Joe W., Thurman Allen, and Roger T. Saucier 1994. Four Archaic? Mound complexes in northeast Louisiana. *Southeastern Archaeology* 13: 134–53.

Savage, Stephen Howard 1989. *Late Archaic Landscapes. A Geographic Informations Systems Approach to the Late Archaic Landscape of the Savannah River Valley, Georgia and South Carolina*. Columbia: Institute of Archaeology and Anthropology.

Scarborough, Vernon L. 1994. Maya water management. *National Geographic Research & Exploration* 10: 184–99.

Scarre, Christopher (ed.) 1983. *Ancient France*. Edinburgh: Edinburgh University Press.

Scarry, C. Margaret 1993a. Variability in Mississippian crop production strategies. *Foraging and Farming in the Eastern Woodlands*, C. M. Scarry (ed.), pp. 78–90. Gainesville: University Press of Florida.

—— 1993b. Agricultural risk and the development of the Moundville chiefdom. *Foraging and Farming in the Eastern Woodlands*, C. M. Scarry (ed.), pp. 157–81. Gainesville: University Press of Florida.

——, and Vincas P. Steponaitis 1997. Between farmstead and center: the natural and social landscape of Moundville. *People, Plants, and Landscapes: Studies in Paleoethnobotany*, K. J. Gremillion (ed.), pp. 107–22. Tuscaloosa: University of Alabama Press.

Scarry, John F. 1995. Apalachee homesteads: the basal social and economic units of a Mississippian chiefdom. *Mississippian Communities and Households*, J. D. Rogers and B. D. Smith (eds), pp. 201–23. Tuscaloosa: University of Alabama Press.

—— 1996. Stability and change in the Apalachee chiefdom. *Political Structure and Change in the Prehistoric Southeastern United States*, J. F. Scarry (ed.), pp. 192–227. Gainesville: University Press of Florida.

——, and Claudine Payne 1986. Mississippian polities in the Fort Walton area: a model generated from the Renfrew-Level XTENT algorithm. *Southeastern Archaeology* 5: 79–90.

Scheparts, L. A. 1993. Language and modern human origins. *Yearbook of Physical Anthropology* 36: 91–126.

Schick, Kathy 1987. Modeling the formation of early stone age artifact concentrations. *Journal of Human Evolution* 16: 789–808.

——, and Nicholas Toth 1993. *Making Silent Stones Speak: How the Dawn of Technology Changed the Course of Human Evolution Two and a Half Million Years Ago*. New York: Simon & Schuster.

——, and Dong Zhuan 1993. Early Paleolithic of China and Eastern Asia. *Evolutionary Anthropology* 2: 22–35.

Schild, Romuald 1996. The North European Plain and eastern Sub-Balticum between 12,700 and 8000 BP. *Humans at the End of the Ice Age. The Archaeology of the Pleistocene-Holocene Transition*, L. G. Straus, B. V. Eriksen, J. M. Erlandson and D. R. Yesner (eds), pp. 129–57. New York: Plenum Press.

Schmandt-Besserat, Denise 1978. The earliest precursor of writing. *Scientific American* 238 June: 50–9.

—— 1992. *Before Writing. From Counting to Cuneiform*. Austin: University of Texas Press.

Scott, Katherine 1986. The bone assemblages of layers 3 and 6. *La Cotte de St. Brelade 1961-1978. Excavations by C. B. M. McBurney*, P. Callow and J. M. Comford (eds), pp. 159–83. Norwich: Geo Books.

Sebastian, Lynne 1991. Sociopolitical complexity and the Chaco system. *Chaco & Hohokam. Prehistoric Regional Systems in the American Southwest*, P. L. Crown and W. J. Judge (eds), pp. 109–34. Santa Fe: School of American Research Press.

—— 1992. *The Chaco Anasazi. Sociopolitical Evolution in the Prehistoric Southwest*. Cambridge: Cambridge University Press.

Seeman, Mark F. 1979a. Feasting with the dead: Ohio Hopewell charnel house ritual as a context for redistribution. *Hopewell Archaeology*, D. S. Brose and N. Greber (eds), pp. 39–46. Kent, Ohio: Kent State University Press.

—— 1979b. *The Hopewell Interaction Sphere: Evidence for Interregional trade and Structural Complexity*. Indianapolis: Indiana Historical Society (Prehistory Research Series 5/2).

—— 1992. Woodland traditions in the Midcontinent: a comparison of three regional sequences. *Long-Term Subsistence Change in Prehistoric North America*, D. Croes, R. Hawkins, and B. Isaac (eds), pp. 3–46. Greenwich: JAI Press (Research in Economic Anthropology, supplement 6).

Semaw, S., P. Renne, J. W. K. Harris, C. S. Feibel, R. L. Bernor, N. Fesseha, and K. Mowbray 1997. 2.5-million-year-old stone tools from Gona, Ethiopia. *Nature* 385: 333–6.

Service, Elman 1962. *Primitive Social Organization*. New York: Random House.

Sharer, Robert 1994. *The Ancient Maya*. 5th edn. Stanford: Stanford University Press.

—— 1996. *Daily Life in Maya Civilization*. Westport: Greenwood Press.

——, and David C. Grove (eds) 1989. *Regional Perspectives on the Olmec*. Cambridge: Cambridge University Press.

Shaw, Thurstan 1970. *Igbo-Ukwu*. London: Faber.

Shea, John J. 1993. Lithic use-wear evidence for hunting by Neanderthals and early modern humans from the Levantine Mousterian. *Hunting and Animal Eploitation in the Late Palaeolithic and Mesolithic of Eurasia*, G. L. Peterkin, H. M. Bricker, and P. Mellars (eds), pp. 189–97. Washington: American Anthropological Association.

—— 1997. Middle Palaeolithic spear point technology. *Projectile Technology*, H. Knecht (ed.), pp. 79–106. New York: Plenum Press.

Shennan, Stephen J. 1986. Central Europe in the Third Millenium BC: an evolutionary trajectory for the beginning of the European Bronze Age. *Journal of Anthropological Archaeology* 5: 115–46.

—— 1993a. Settlement and social change in central Europe, 3500–1500 BC. *Journal of World Prehistory* 7: 121–61.

—— 1993b. Commodities, transactions, and growth in the central-European early Bronze Age. *Journal of European Archaeology* 1: 59–72.

—— 1994. Grounding arguments about burials. *Archaeological Dialogues* 1: 124–5.

Shennan, Susan 1975. The social organization at Branč. *Antiquity* 49: 279–88.

Sherratt, Andrew G. 1981. Plough and pastoralism: aspects of the secondary products revolution. *Pattern of the Past: Studies in Honour of David Clarke*, I. Hodder, G. Isaac, and N. Hammond (eds), pp. 261–305. Cambridge: Cambridge University Press.

—— 1983. The secondary exploitation of animals in the Old World. *World Archaeology* 15: 90–104.

—— 1990. The genesis of megaliths: monumentality, ethnicity and social complexity in Neolithic north-west Europe. *World Archaeology* 22: 147–67.

—— 1993. What would a Bronze-Age world system look like? Relations between temperate Europe and the Mediterranean in later prehistory. *Journal of European Archaeology* 1: 1–58.

Shimada, Izumi 1994. *Pampa Grande and the Mochica Culture*. Austin: University of Texas Press.

Shipek, Florence C. 1989. An example of intensive plant husbandry: the Kumeyaay of southern California. *Foraging and Farming. The Evolution of Plant Exploitation*, D. R. Harris and G. C. Hillman (eds), pp. 159–70. London: Unwin Hyman.

Shipman, Pat 1986. Studies of hominid-faunal interactions at Olduvai Gorge. *Journal of Human Evolution* 15: 691–706.

Shott, Michael J. 1992. On recent trends in the anthropology of foragers: Kalahari revisionism and its archaeological implications. *Man* 27: 843–71.

Silverman, Helaine 1993. *Cahuachi in the Ancient Nasca World*. Iowa City: University of Iowa Press.

—— 1996. The Formative Period on the south coast of Peru: a critical review. *Journal of World Prehistory* 10: 95–146.

Simmons, Alan H. 1986. New evidence for the early use of cultigens in the American Southwest. *American Antiquity* 51: 73–89.

Sinclair, Paul J., Innocent Pikirayi, Gilbert Pwiti, and Robert Soper 1993. Urban trajectories on the Zimbabwean plateau. *The Archaeology of Africa. Food, Metals and Towns*, T. Shaw, P. Sinclair, B. Andah, and A. Okpoko (eds), pp. 705–31. London: Routledge.

Singh, Ram D. 1988. *Economics of the Family and Farming Systems in Sub-Saharan Africa: Development Perspectives*. Boulder: Westview Press.

Skinner, G. William 1964. Marketing and social structure in rural China. Part I–III. *Journal of Asian Studies* 24: 3–43, 195–228, 363–99.

Smirnov, Yuri 1989. Intentional human burial: Middle Paleolithic (last glaciation) beginnings. *Journal of World Prehistory* 3: 199–233.

Smith, Bruce D. 1978. *Prehistoric Patterns of Human Behavior: a Case Study in the Mississippi Valley*. New York: Academic Press.

—— 1989. Origins of agriculture in eastern north America. *Science* 246: 1566–71.

—— 1990. Introduction. Research on the origins of Mississippian chiefdoms in eastern North America. *The Mississippian Emergence*, B. D. Smith (ed.), pp. 1–8. Washington: Smithsonian Institution Press.

—— 1992. *Rivers of Change. Essays on Early Agriculture in Eastern North America*. Washington: Smithsonian Institution Press.

—— 1993. Reconciling the Gender-Credit Critique and the Floodplain Weed Theory of plant domestication. *Archaeology of Eastern North America. Papers in Honor of Stephen Williams*, J. B. Stoltman (ed.), pp. 111–25. Jackson, Mississippi: Mississippi Department of Archives and History.

—— 1995a. *The Emergence of Agriculture*. New York: W. H. Freeman (Scientific American Library).

—— 1995b. Seed plant domestication in eastern North America. *Last Hunters, First Farmers. New Perspectives on the Prehistoric Transition to Agriculture*, T. D. Price and A. B. Gebauer (eds), pp. 193–213. Santa Fe: School of American Research Press.

—— 1995c. The analysis of Mississippian single-household settlements. *Mississippian Communities and Households*, J. D. Rogers and B. D. Smith, (eds), pp. 224–49. Tuscaloosa: University of Alabama Press.

Smith, Fred H. 1992. The role of continuity in modern human origins. *Continuity or Replacement? Controversies in* Homo sapiens *Evolution*, G. Bräuer and F. H. Smith (eds), pp. 145–56. Rotterdam: A. A. Balkema.

Smith, Fred H., and Erik Trinkaus 1992. Modern human origins in central Europe: a case of continuity. *Aux Origines de la Diversité Humaine*, J.-J. Hublin and A.-M. Tillier (eds), pp. 251–90. Paris: Presses Universitaires de France.

Smith, K., J. Coppen, G. J. Wainwright, and S. Beckett 1981. The Shaugh Moor Project: third report, settlement and environmental investigations. *Proceedings of the Prehistoric Society* 47: 205–73.

Smith, Patricia 1991. The dental evidence for nutritional status in the Natufians. *The Natufian Culture in the Levant*, O. Bar-Yosef and F. R. Valla (eds), pp. 425–32. Ann Arbor: International Monographs in Prehistory.

Smith, Philip E. L., and T. Cuyler Young 1972. The evolution of early agriculture and culture in Greater Mesopotamia. *Population Growth: Anthropological Implications*, B. Spooner (ed.), pp. 1–59. Cambridge: MIT Press.

Smith, Shelley L., and Francis B. Harrold 1997. A paradigm's worth of difference? Understanding the impasse over modern human origins. *Yearbook of Physical Anthropology* 40: 113–39.

Smyth, Michael P., and Christopher D. Dore 1994. Maya urbanism. *National Geographic Research & Exploration* 10: 38–55.

Soffer, Olga 1985. *The Upper Palaeolithic of the Central Russian Plain*. Orlando: Academic Press.

—— 1987. Upper Palaeolithic connubia, refugia, and the archaeological record. *The Pleistocene Old World*, O. Soffer (ed.), pp. 333–48. New York: Plenum Press.

—— 1990. The Russian Plain at the Last Glacial Maximum. *The World at 18 000 BP. Volume One: High Latitudes*, O. Soffer and C. Gamble (eds), pp. 228–52. London: Unwin Hyman.

—— 1993. Upper Palaeolithic adaptations in central and eastern Europe and man–mammoth interactions. *From Kostenki to Clovis. Upper Palaeolithic – Palaeo-Indian Adaptations*, O. Soffer and N. D. Praslov (eds), pp. 31–49. New York: Plenum Press.

——, and Clive Gamble (eds) 1990. *The World at 18 000 BP. Volume I: High Latitudes*. London: Unwin Hyman.

——, James M. Adovasio, and D. C. Hyland 1999. Perishable industries from Upper Palaeolithic Moravia: new insights into the origin and nature of the Gravettian. *Archeologické Rozhledy* (in press).

——, Pamela Vandiver, Bohuslav Klíma, and Jiři Svoboda 1993. The pyrotechnology of performance art: Moravian Venuses and wolverines. *Before Lascaux. The Complex Record of the Early Upper Palaeolithic*, H. Knecht, A. Pike-Tay, and R. White (eds), pp. 259–75. Boca Raton: CRC Press.

Solecki, Ralph S. 1971. *Shanidar, the First Flower People*. New York: Knopf.

—— 1995. The cultural significance of the fire hearths in the Middle Palaeolithic at Shanidar Cave, Iraq. *Ancient Peoples and Landscapes*, E. Johnson (ed.), pp. 51–63. Lubbock: Museum of Texas Tech University.

Solheim, Wilhelm G. 1968. Early bronze in northeastern Thailand. *Current Anthropology* 9: 59–62.

—— 1972. An earlier agricultural revolution. *Scientific American* 226: 34–41.

Sollas, W. J. 1911. *Ancient Hunters and their Modern Representatives*. London: Macmillan.

Spencer, Charles S. 1987. Rethinking the chiefdom. *Chiefdoms in the Americas*, R. D. Drennan and C. A. Uribe (eds), pp. 369–89. Lanham: University Press of America.

—— 1993. Human agency, biased transmission, and the cultural evolution of chiefly authority. *Journal of Anthropological Archaeology* 12: 41–74.

—— 1994. Factional ascendance, dimensions of leadership and the development of centralized authority. *Factional Competition and Political Development in the New World*, E. M. Brumfiel and J. W. Fox (eds), pp. 31–43. Cambridge: Cambridge University Press.

——, and Elsa M. Redmond 1983. A Middle Formative elite residence and associated structures at la Coyotera, Oaxaca. *The Cloud People. Divergent Evolution of the Zapotec and Mixtec Civilizations*, K. V. Flannery and J. Marcus (eds), pp. 71–2. New York: Academic Press.

——, and —— 1992. Prehispanic chiefdoms of the western Venezuelan llanos. *World Archaeology* 24: 134–57.

Spiess, Arthur E. 1979. *Reindeer and Caribou Hunters: an Archaeological Study*. San Francisco: Academic Press.

—— 1992. Archaic period subsistence in New England and the Atlantic Provinces. *The Early Holocene Occupation in Northern New England*, B. Robinson, J. Petersen, and A. Robinson (eds), pp. 163–85. Augusta: Maine Historic Preservation Commission (Occasional Publications in Maine Archaeology 9).

—— 1993. Caribou, walrus, and seals: Maritime Archaic subsistence in Labrador and Newfoundland. *Archaeology of Eastern North America. Papers in Honor of Stephen Williams*, J. B. Stoltman (ed.), pp. 73–100. Jackson, Mississippi: Mississippi Department of Archives and History.

Spooner, Nigel A. 1998. Human occupation at Jinmium, northern Australia: 116,000 years ago or much less? *Antiquity* 72: 173–9.

Spores, Ronald 1983. Middle and Late Formative settlement patterns in the Mixteca Alta. *The Cloud People. Divergent Evolution of the Zapotec and Mixtec Civilizations*, K. V. Flannery and J. Marcus (eds), pp. 72–4. New York: Academic Press.

Srejović, Dragoslav 1969. *Lepenski Vir*. London: Thames and Hudson.

Stark, Barbara 1986. Origins of food production in the New World. *American Archaeology Past and Future*, D. Meltzer, D. Fowler, and J. Sabloff (eds), pp. 277–321. Washington: Smithsonian Institution Press.

Starr, Marthan A. 1987. Risk, environmental variability and drought-induced impoverishment: the pastoral economy of central Niger. *Africa* 57: 29–50.

Stech, Tamara, and Vincent C. Pigott 1986. Metals trade in Southwest Asia in the third millennium BC. *Iraq* 48: 39–64.

Stein, Gil 1994. Economy, ritual, and power in 'Ubaid Mesopotamia. *Chiefdoms and Early States in the Near East: the Organizational Dynamics of Complexity*, G. Stein and M. S. Rothman (eds), pp. 35–46. Madison: Prehistory Press.

Steponaitis, Vincas P. 1983. *Ceramics, Chronology, and Community Patterns. An Archaeological Study at Moundville*. San Diego: Academic Press.

—— 1991. Constrasting patterns of Mississippian development. *Chiefdoms: Power, Economy, and Ideology*, T. K. Earle (ed.), pp. 193–228. Cambridge: Cambridge University Press.

Stiner, Mary C. 1991. Faunal remains from Grotta Guattari: a taphonomic perspective. *Current Anthropology* 32: 103–17.

—— 1993. Small animal exploitation and its relation to hunting, scavenging, and gathering in the Italian Mousterian. *Hunting and Animal Exploitation in the Later Palaeolithic and Mesolithic of Eurasia*, G. L. Peterkin, H. M. Bricker, and P. Mellars (eds), pp. 101–19. Washington: American Anthropological Association.

—— 1994. *Honor Among Thieves. A Zooarchaeological Study of Neanderthal Ecology*. Princeton: Princeton University Press.

Straus, Lawrence Guy 1986. Late Würm adaptive systems in Cantabrian Spain: the case of eastern Asturias. *Journal of Anthropological Archaeology* 5: 330–68.

—— 1991. Epipalaeolithic and Mesolithic adaptations in Cantabrian Spain and Pyrenean France. *Journal of World Prehistory* 5: 83–104.

—— 1993. Upper Palaeolithic hunting tactics and weapons in western Europe. *Hunting and Animal Exploitation in the Later Palaeolithic and Mesolithic of Eurasia*, G. L. Peterkin, H. M. Bricker, and P. Mellars (eds), pp. 83–93. Washington: American Anthropological Association.

Streuver, Stuart 1964. The Hopewell Interaction Sphere in riverine-western Great Lakes culture history. *Hopewellian Studies*, J. R. Caldwell and R. Hall (eds), pp. 85–106. Springfield (Illinois): Springfield Science Museum.

——, and Gail L. Houart 1972. An analysis of the Hopewell Interaction Sphere. *Social Exchange and Interaction*, E. Wilmsen (ed.), pp. 47–80. Ann Arbor: Museum of Anthropology (Anthropological Papers 46).

Stringer, Christopher B. 1994. Out of Africa – a personal history. *Origins of Anatomically Modern Humans*, M. H. Nitecki and D. V. Nitecki (eds), pp. 149–72. New York: Plenum Press.

—— 1995. The evolution and distribution of later Pleistocene human populations. *Palaeoclimate and Evolution with Emphasis on Human Origins*, E. S. Vrba, G. H. Denton, T. C. Partridge, and L. H. Burckle (eds), pp. 524–31. New Haven: Yale University Press.

——, and Clive Gamble 1993. *In Search of the Neanderthals: Solving the Puzzle of Human Origins*. London: Thames and Hudson.

——, and Robin McKie 1996. *African Exodus*. London: Jonathan Cape.

Stuart, David, and Stephen D. Houston 1989. Maya writing. *Scientific American* 261(2): 82–9.

Stuart, David E., and Rory P. Gauthier 1988. *Prehistoric New Mexico. Background for Survey*. Albuquerque: University of New Mexico Press.

Stuart George 1993. New light on the Olmec. *National Geographic* 184: 88–115.

Stuchlík, Stanislav, and Jana Stuchlíkova 1996. Aunjetizer Gräberfeld in Velké Pavlovice, Südmähren. *Praehistorische Zeitschrift* 71: 123–69.

Styles, Bonnie Whatley 1986. Aquatic exploitation in the Lower Illinois River Valley: the role of palaeoecological change. *Foraging, Collecting, and Harvesting: Archaic Period Subsistence and Settlement in the Eastern Woodlands*, S. W. Neusius (ed.), pp. 145–74. Carbondale: Center for Archaeological Investigations.

——, Steven R. Ahler, and Melvin L. Fowler. 1983. Modoc Rock Shelter revisited. *Archaic Hunters and Gatherers in the American Midwest*, J. L. Phillips and J. A. Brown (eds), pp. 261–97. New York: Academic Press.

Svoboda, Jiři, Vojen Ložek, and Emanuel Vlček 1996. *Hunters Between East and West. The Palaeolithic of Moravia.* New York: Plenum Press.

Swisher, C. C., III, G. H. Curtis, T. Jacob, A. G. Getty, A. Suprijo Widiasmoro 1994. Age of the earliest known hominids in Java, Indonesia. *Science* 263: 1118–21.

Taçon, Paul, and Christopher Chippindale 1994. Australia's ancient warriors: changing depictions of fighting in the rock art of Arnhem Land, N.T. *Cambridge Archaeological Journal* 4: 211–48.

Tainter, Joseph A. 1988. *The Collapse of Complex Societies.* Cambridge: Cambridge University Press.

——, and Bonnie Bagley Tainter (eds) 1996. *Evolving Complexity and Environmental Risk in the Prehistoric Southwest: Proceedings of the Workshop "Resource Stress, Economic Uncertainty, and Human Response in the Prehistoric Southwest."* Reading, MA: Addison-Wesley Publishing Company.

Tanaka, Migaku, Ken'ichi Sasaki, and Masatoshi Sagawa 1998. Archaeology. *An Introductory Bibliography for Japanese Studies, Volume 10, Part 2: Humanities 1993–94*, pp. 1–30. Tokyo: The Japan Foundation.

Tankersley, Kenneth B. 1994. Was Clovis a colonizing population in eastern North America? *The First Discovery of America*, W. S. Dancey (ed.), pp. 95–109. Columbus: The Ohio Archaeological Council.

Tattersall, Ian 1995. *The Last Neanderthal: the Rise, Success, and Mysterious Extinction of Our Closest Human Relatives.* New York: Macmillan.

Taylor, Walter W. 1948. *A Study of Archaeology.* Washington: American Anthropological Association.

Tchernov, Eitan 1991. Biological evidence for human sedentism in south-west Asia during the Natufian. *The Natufian Culture in the Levant*, O. Bar-Yosef and F. R. Valla (eds), pp. 315–40. Ann Arbor: International Monographs in Prehistory.

Templeton, Alan R. 1993. "Eve" hypotheses: a genetic critique and reanalysis. *American Anthropologist* 95: 51–72.

Testart, Alain 1982. The significance of food storage among hunter-gatherers: residence patterns, population densities, and social inequalities. *Current Anthropology* 23: 523–30.

—— 1988. Food storage among hunter-gatherers: more or less security in the way of life? *Coping with Uncertainty in the Food Supply*, I. de Garine and G. A. Harrison (eds), pp. 170–4. Oxford: Clarendon Press.

Thom, Alexander 1971. *Megalithic Lunar Observatories.* Oxford: Clarendon Press.

Thomas, Julian 1991. *Rethinking the Neolithic.* Cambridge: Cambridge University Press.

Thorpe, I. J. 1996. *The Origins of Agriculture in Europe.* London: Routledge.

Tilley, Christopher 1996. *An Ethnography of the Neolithic: Early Prehistoric Societies in Southern Scandinavia.* Cambridge: Cambridge University Press.

Tishkoff, S. A., E. Dietzsch, W. Speed, A. J. Pakstis, J. R. Kidd, K. Cheung, B. Monné-Tamir, A. S. Santachiara-Benercetti, P. Moral, M. Krings, S. Pääbo, E. Waltson, N. Risch, T. Jenkins, and K. K. Kidd 1996. Global patterns of linkage disequilibrium at the CD4 locus and modern human origins. *Science* 271: 1380–7.

Toll, H. Wolcott 1991. Material distributions and exchange in the Chaco system. *Chaco & Hohokam. Prehistoric Regional Systems in the American Southwest*, P. L. Crown and W. J. Judge (eds), pp. 77–108. Santa Fe: School of American Research Press.

Topic, Theresa L. 1982. The Early Intermediate period and its legacy. *Chan Chan: Andean Desert City*, M. E. Moseley and K. C. Day (eds), pp. 255–84. Albuquerque: University of New Mexico Press.

Toth, Nicholas 1985. Oldowan reassessed: a close look at early stone artifacts. *Journal of Archaeological Science* 12: 101–20.

Trigger, Bruce G. 1989. *A History of Archaeological Thought*. Cambridge: Cambridge University Press.

Tringham, Ruth E. 1974. The concept of "civilization" in European archaeology. *The Rise and Fall of Civilizations*, J. A. Sabloff and C. C. Lamberg-Karlovsky (eds), pp. 470–86. Menlo Park: Cummings Publishing.

——, and Dušan Krstić 1990. Conclusion: Selevac in the wider context of European prehistory. *Selevac, a Neolithic Village in Yugoslavia*, R. Tringham and D. Krstić (eds), pp. 567–616. Los Angeles: Institute of Archaeology.

Trinkaus, Erik 1983. *The Shanidar Neanderthals*. New York: Academic Press.

—— 1989. Comment on "Grave shortcomings. The evidence for Neandertal Burial" by Robert H. Gargett. *Current Anthropology* 30: 183–4.

——, and Pat Shipman 1993. *The Neandertals: Changing the Image of Mankind*. New York: Knopf.

Tuck, James A. 1976. *Ancient People of Port au Choix: the Excavation of an Archaic Indian Cemetery in Newfoundland*. St John's (Nfld.): Institute of Social and Economic Research.

—— 1978. Regional cultural development, 3,000 to 300 BC. *Handbook of North American Indians* 15: 28–43. Washington: Smithsonian Institution.

Tylecote, R. F. 1987. *The Early History of Metallurgy in Europe*. London: Longman.

Uerpmann, Hans-Peter 1979. Probleme der Neolithisierung des Mittelmeerraums. *Beihefte zum Tübinger Atlas des Vorderen Orients, Reihe B, nr. 28*. Wiesbaden: Ludwig Reichert Verlag.

—— 1987. The Ancient Distribution of Ungulate Mammals in the Middle East. *Beihefte zum Tübinger Atlas des vorderen Orients, Reihe A, no. 27*. Wiesbaden: Ludwig Reichert Verlag.

—— 1989. Animal exploitation and the phasing of the transition from the Palaeolithic to the Neolithic. *The Walking Larder*, J. Clutton-Brock (ed.), pp. 91-6. London: Unwin Hyman.

Ukraintseva, Valentina V., Larry D. Agenbroad, and Jim I. Mead 1996. A palaeoenvironmental reconstruction of the "Mammoth Epoch" of Siberia. *American Beginnings. The Prehistory and Palaeoecology of Beringia*, F. H. West (ed.), pp. 129–36. Chicago: University of Chicago Press.

Underhill, Anne P. 1991. Pottery production in chiefdoms: the Longshan Period in northern China. *World Archaeology* 23: 12–27.

—— 1994. Variation in settlements during the Longshan period of northern China. *Asian Perspectives* 33: 197–228.

—— 1996. Craft production and social evolution during the Longshan period of northern China. *Craft Specialization and Social Evolution: in Memory of V. Gordon Childe*, B. Wailes (ed.), pp. 133–50. Philadelphia: University Museum of Archaeology and Anthropology.

—— 1997. Current issues in Chinese Neolithic archaeology. *Journal of World Prehistory* 11 (2): 103–60.

Valla, F. R. 1991. Les Natoufiens de Mallaha et l'espace. *The Natufian Culture in the Levant*, O. Bar-Yosef and F. R. Valla (eds), pp. 111–12. Ann Arbor: International Monographs in Prehistory.

van Andel, Tjeerd H. 1994. *New Views on an Old Planet. A History of Global Change*. 2nd edn. Cambridge: Cambridge University Press.

——, and Curtis Runnels 1995. The earliest farmers in Europe. *Antiquity* 69: 481–500.

Van De Mieroop, Marc 1997. *The Ancient Mesopotamian City*. Oxford: Oxford University Press.

Vandermeersch, Bernard 1989. The evolution of modern humans: recent evidence from southwest Asia. *The Human Revolution*, P. Mellars and C. Stringer (eds), pp. 155–64. Edinburgh: Edinburgh University Press.

Vandiver, Pamela B., Olga Soffer, Bohuslav Klima, and Jiří Svoboda 1989. The origins of ceramic technology at Dolní Věstonice, Czechoslovakia. *Science* 246: 1001–8.

Vang Petersen, Peter and Lykke Johansen 1991. Sølbjerg I-an Ahrensburgian Site on a reindeer migration route through eastern Denmark. *Journal of Danish Archaeology* 10: 20–37.

Vavilov, Nikolai I. 1992 [1926]. *The Origin and Geography of Cultivated Plants*. Cambridge: Cambridge University Press.

Velichko, A. A., and E. I. Kurenkova 1990. Environmental conditions and human occupations of northern Eurasia during the Late Valdai. *The World at 18 000 BP. Volume One. High Latitudes*, O. Soffer and C. Gamble (eds), pp. 255–65. London: Unwin Hyman.

Villa, Paola 1983. *Terra Amata and the Middle Pleistocene Archaeological Record of Southern France*. Berkeley: University of California Press.

Vivian, R. Gwinn 1991. Chacoan subsistence. *Chaco & Hohokam. Prehistoric Regional Systems in the American Southwest*, P. L. Crown and W. J. Judge (eds), pp. 57–75. Santa Fe: School of American Research Press.

—— 1997a. Chacoan roads: morphology. *The Kiva* 63: 7–34.

—— 1997b. Chacoan roads: function. *The Kiva* 63: 35–67.

von Däniken, Erich 1970. *Chariots of the Gods?* New York: Bantam.

Voorhies, Barbara 1976. The Chantuto people: an Archaic period society of the Chiapas littoral, Mexico. *Papers of the New World Archaeological Foundation* 41: 1–147.

Vrba, Elisabeth S. 1996. Climate, heterochrony, and human evolution. *Journal of Anthropological Research* 52: 1–28.

Wadley, Lyn 1993. The Pleistocene Later Stone Age south of the Limpopo River. *Journal of World Prehistory* 7: 243–96.

Wailes, Bernard (ed.) 1995. *Craft Specialization and Social Evolution: In Memory of V. Gordon Childe*. Philadelphia: University Museum of Archaeology and Anthropology.

Walker, Alan, and Richard Leakey 1993. *The Nariokotome* Homo erectus *skeleton*. Cambridge: Harvard University Press.

——, and Pat Shipman 1996. *The Wisdom of the Bones: In Search of Human Origins*. New York: Knopf.

Waring, Antonio J., and Preston Holder 1945. A prehistoric ceremonial complex in the southeastern United States. *American Anthropologist* 47: 1–34.

Watchman, Alan 1993. Evidence of a 25,000-year-old pictograph in Northern Australia. *Geoarchaeology* 8: 465–73.

Waters, Michael R., Stevel L. Forman, and James M. Pierson 1997. Diring Yuriakh, a Lower Palaeolithic site in central Siberia. *Science* 275: 1281–3.

Watkins, Trevor 1992. Pushing back the frontiers of Mesopotamian prehistory. *Biblical Archaeologist* December: 176–81.

Watson, Patty Jo 1983. The Halafian Culture: a review and synthesis. *The Hilly Flanks and Beyond. Essays on the Prehistory of Southwestern Asia*, pp. 231–49. Chicago: The Oriental Institute (Studies in Ancient Oriental Civilization 36).

—— 1985. The impact of early horticulture in the upland drainages of the Midwest and Midsouth. *Prehistoric Food Production in North America*, R. I. Ford (ed.), pp. 99–148. Ann Arbor: Museum of Anthropology (Anthropological Papers 75).

—— 1995. Explaining the transition to agriculture. *Last Hunters, First Farmers. New Perspectives on the Prehistoric Transition to Agriculture*, T. D. Price and A. B. Gebauer (eds), pp. 3–37. Santa Fe: School of American Research Press.

——, and Mary C. Kennedy 1991. Development of horticulture in the eastern woodlands of North America: women's role. *Engendering Archaeology: Women and Prehistory*, J. M. Gero and M. W. Conkey (eds), pp. 255–75. Oxford: Blackwell.

——, and Steven A. LeBlanc 1990. *Girikihaciyan: a Halafian Site in Southeastern Turkey*. Los Angeles: Institute of Archaeology.

Webb, Clarence H. 1982. *The Poverty, Point Culture*. Baton Rouge: Louisiana State University (*Geoscience and Man*, vol. 17, 2nd edn revised).

Webb, William S. 1974 [1946]. *Indian Knoll*. Knoxville: University of Tennessee Press.

Weber, Steven A. 1992. South Asian archaeobotanical variability. *South Asian Archaeology 1989: Papers from the Tenth International Conference of South Asian Archaeologists in Western Europe, Musée National des Arts Asiatiques – Guimet, Paris, France, 3–7 July 1989*, C. Jarrige (ed.), pp. 283–90. Madison: Prehistory Press.

Weiner, Steve, Qinqi Xu, Paul Goldberg, Jinyi Liu, and Ofer Bar-Yosef 1998. Evidence for the use of fire at Zhoukoudian, China. *Science* 281: 251–3.

Welch, John R. 1991. From horticulture to agriculture in the late prehistory of the Grasshopper region, Arizona. *Proceedings of the Fifth Biannual*

Mogollon Conference, P. H. Beckett (ed.), pp. 75–92. Las Cruces: COAS Publishing and Research.

Welch, Paul D. 1991. *Moundville's Economy*. Tuscaloosa: University of Alabama Press.

—— 1996. Control over goods and the political stability of the Moundville chiefdom. *Political Structure and Change in the Prehistoric Southeastern United States*, J. F. Scarry (ed.), pp. 69–91. Gainesville: University Press of Florida.

Wells, Peter S. 1983. Rural Economy in the Early Iron Age: Excavations at Hascherkeller, 1978–1981. *American School of Prehistoric Research Bulletin* 36. Cambridge: Peabody Museum.

—— 1984. *Farms, Villages, and Cities*: Commerce and Urban Origins in Late Prehistoric Europe. Ithaca: Cornell University Press.

—— 1993. Investigating the origins of temperate Europe's first towns: excavations at Hascherkeller, 1978 to 1981. *Case Studies in European Prehistory*, P. Bogucki (ed.), pp. 181–205. Boca Raton: CRC Press.

Wenke, Robert J. 1991. The evolution of early Egyptian civilization: issues and evidence. *Journal of World Prehistory* 5: 279–329.

Wesler, Kit W. 1996. An elite burial mound at Wickliffe? *Mounds, Embankments, and Ceremonialism in the Midsouth*, R. C. Mainfort and R. Walling (eds), pp. 50–3. Fayetteville: Arkansas Archaeological Survey.

West, Frederick Hadleigh 1996a. The study of Beringia. *American Beginnings: the Prehistory and Palaeoecology of Beringia*, F. H. West (ed.), pp. 1–10. Chicago: University of Chicago Press.

—— 1996b. The archaeological evidence. *American Beginnings. The Prehistory and Palaeoecology of Beringia*, F. H. West (ed.), pp. 537–59. Chicago: University of Chicago Press.

Wetterstrom, Wilma 1993. Foraging and farming in Egypt: the transition from hunting and gathering to horticulture in the Nile Valley. *The Archaeology of Africa. Food, Metals, and Towns*, T. Shaw, P. Sinclair, B. Andah, and A. Okpoko (eds), pp. 165–226. London: Routledge.

Whallon, Robert 1989. Elements of cultural change in the later Palaeolithic. *The Human Revolution*, P. Mellars and C. Stringer (eds), pp. 433–54. Edinburgh: Edinburgh University Press.

White, Joyce C. 1995. Incorporating heterarchy into theory on socio-political development: the case from Southeast Asia. *Heterarchy and the Analysis of Complex Societies*, R. M. Ehrenreich, C. L. Crumley, and J. E. Levy (eds), pp. 101–23. Washington: American Anthropological Association.

——, and Vincent C. Pigott 1996. From community craft to regional specialization: intensification of copper production in pre-state Thailand. *Craft Specialization and Social Evolution: In Memory of V. Gordon Childe*, B. Wailes (ed.), pp. 151–75. Philadelphia: University Museum of Archaeology and Anthropology.

White, Randall 1989. Visual thinking in the Ice Age. *Scientific American* 260: 92–9.

—— 1992. Beyond art: toward an understanding of the origins of material representation in Europe. *Annual Review of Anthropology* 21: 537–64.

White, Randall 1993. Technological and social dimensions of "Aurignacian-age" body ornaments across Europe. *Before Lascaux. The Complex Record of the Early Upper Palaeolithic*, H. Knecht, A. Pike-Tay, and R. White (eds), pp. 277–99. Boca Raton: CRC Press.

White, Tim D., Gen Suwa, and Berhane Asfaw 1994. *Australopithecus ramidus*, a new species of early hominid from Aramis, Ethiopia. *Nature* 371: 306–12.

——, ——, and —— 1995. Corrigendum. *Nature* 375: 88.

Whitelaw, Todd 1991. Some dimensions of variability in the social organisation of community space among foragers. *Ethnoarchaeological Approaches to Mobile Campsites*, C. S. Gamble and W. A. Boismier (eds), pp. 139–88. Ann Arbor: International Monographs in Prehistory.

Whittle, Alasdair 1996. *Europe in the Neolithic*. Cambridge: Cambridge University Press.

Wieshieu, Walburga 1997. China's first cities. The walled site of Wangchenggang in the central plain region of North China. *Emergence and Change in Early Urban Societies*, L. Manzanilla (ed.), pp. 87–105. New York: Plenum Press.

Wilcox, David R. 1991. Hohokam social complexity. *Chaco & Hohokam. Prehistoric Regional Systems in the American Southwest*, P. L. Crown and W. J. Judge (eds), pp. 253–75. Santa Fe: School of American Research Press.

——, Thomas R. McGuire, and Charles Sternberg 1981. *Snaketown Revisited*. Tucson: Arizona State Museum, University of Arizona.

Wilhelmi, Klaus 1985. *Ausgrabungen in Niedersachsen*. Stuttgart: Konrad Theiss.

Wilk, Richard R., and Robert M. Netting 1984. Households: changing forms and functions. *Households: Comparative and Historical Studies of the Domestic Group*, R. M. Netting, R. R. Wilk and E. J. Arnould (eds), pp. 1–28. Berkeley: University of California Press.

——, and William L. Rathje 1982. Household archaeology. *Archaeology of the Household*, R. R. Wilk and W. L. Rathje (eds), pp. 617–39 (American Behavioral Scientist vol. 25).

——, and Harold L. Wilhite, Jr. 1991. The community of Cuello: patterns of household and settlement change. *Cuello. An Early Maya Community in Belize*, N. Hammond (ed.), pp. 118–33. Cambridge: Cambridge University Press.

Wilkerson, S. Jeffrey K. 1994. The garden city of El Pital. *National Geographic Research & Exploration* 10: 56–71.

Willey, Gordon R. 1962. The early great styles and the rise of the pre-Columbian civilizations. *American Anthropologist* 64: 1–14.

Williams, Stephen, and Jeffrey P. Brain 1983. *Excavations at the Lake George Site, Yazoo County, Mississippi, 1958–1960*. Cambridge MA: Peabody Museum of Archaeology and Ethnology (Papers of the Peabody Museum of Archaeology and Ethnology 74).

Wills, W. H. 1988. *Early Prehistoric Agriculture in the American Southwest*. Santa Fe: School of American Research Press.

—— 1992. Foraging systems and plant cultivation during the emergence of agricultural economies in the prehistoric American Southwest. *Transitions to Agriculture in Prehistory*, A. B. Gebauer and T. D. Price (eds), pp. 153–76. Madison: Prehistory Press.

—— 1995. Archaic foraging and the beginnings of food production in the American Southwest. *Last Hunters, First Farmers. New Perspectives on the Prehistoric Transition to Agriculture*, T. D. Price and A. B. Gebauer (eds), pp. 215–42. Santa Fe: School of American Research Press.

Wilmsen, Edwin N. 1989. *Land Filled with Flies: a Political Economy of the Kalahari*. Chicago: University of Chicago Press.

Wilson, David J. 1981. Of maize and men: a critique of the maritime hypothesis of state origins on the coast of Peru. *American Anthropologist* 83: 93–120.

Wilson, J. A. 1960. Egypt to the New Kingdom: civilization without cities. *City Invincible*, C. Kraeling and R. M. Adams (eds), pp. 124–64. Chicago: University of Chicago Press.

Winter, Marcus C. 1976. The archeological household cluster in the Valley of Oaxaca. *The Early Mesoamerican Village*, K. V. Flannery (ed.), pp. 25–31. New York: Academic Press.

Winters, Howard D. 1974. Introduction to the new edition. *Indian Knoll* by William S. Webb, pp. v–xxvii. Knoxville: University of Tennessee Press.

Wintle, A. G., and M. J. Aiken 1977. Thermoluminescence dating of burnt flint: application to a Lower Paleolithic site, Terra Amata. *Archaeometry* 19: 111–30.

Witthoft, John 1952. A Paleo-Indian site in eastern Pennsylvania: an early hunting culture. *American Philosophical Society Library Bulletin*: 464–95.

Wobst, H. Martin 1978. The archaeo-ethnology of hunter-gatherers or the tyranny of the ethnographic record in archaeology. *American Antiquity* 43: 303–9.

Wolpoff, Milford H., Alan G. Thorne, Fred H. Smith, David W. Frayer, and Geoffrey G. Pope 1994. Multiregional evolution: a world-wide source for modern human populations. *Origins of Anatomically Modern Humans*, M. H. Nitecki and D. V. Nitecki (eds), pp. 175–99. New York: Plenum Press.

Wood, Bernard 1992. Origin and evolution of the genus *Homo*. *Nature* 355: 783–90.

Woodburn, James 1982. Egalitarian societies. *Man* 17: 431–51.

Wright, Rita P. 1989. New tracks on ancient frontiers: ceramic technology on the Indo-Iranian borderlands. *Archaeological Thought in America*, C. C. Lamberg-Karlovsky (ed.), pp. 268–79. Cambridge: Cambridge University Press.

Wymer, John 1968. *Lower Palaeolithic Archaeology in Britain as Represented by the Thames Valley*. London: John Baker.

Yellen, John E. 1996. Behavioral and taphonomic patterning at Katanda 9: a Middle Stone Age site, Kivu Province, Zaire. *Journal of Archaeological Science* 23: 915–32.

Yen, Douglas E. 1977. Hoabinhian horticulture: the evidence and the questions from northwest Thailand. *Sunda and Sahul: Prehistoric Studies in*

Southeast Asia, J. Allen, J. Golson, and R. Jones (eds), pp. 567–99. London: Academic Press.

Yerkes, Richard W. 1989. Mississippian craft specialization on the American Bottom. *Southeastern Archaeology* 8: 93–106.

—— 1991. Specialization in shell artifact production at Cahokia. *New Perspectives on Cahokia: Views from the Periphery*, J. Stoltman (ed.), pp. 49–64. Madison: Prehistory Press.

Yesner, Devid R. 1996. Human adaptation at the Pleistocene–Holocene boundary (circa 13,000 to 8000 BP) in eastern Beringia. *Humans at the End of the Ice Age. The Archaeology of the Pleistocene–Holocene Transition*, L. G. Straus, B. V. Eriksen, J. M. Erlandson, and D. R. Yesner (eds), pp. 255–76. New York: Plenum Press.

Yoffee, Norman 1985. Perspectives on "Trends toward Social Complexity in Prehistoric Australia and Papua New Guinea." *Archaeology in Oceania* 20: 41–9.

—— 1993. Too many chiefs? (or, safe texts for the '90s). *Archaeological Theory: Who Sets the Agenda?* N. Yoffee and A. Sherratt (eds), pp. 60–78. Cambridge: Cambridge University Press.

——, and George L. Cowgill (eds) 1988. *The Collapse of Ancient States and Civilizations*. Tucson: University of Arizona Press.

Zeitlin, Robert N., and Judith Francis Zeitlin in press. The Palaeoindian and Archaic cultures of Mesoamerica. *The Cambridge History of the Native Peoples of the Americas. Mesoamerica*, R. E. W. Adams and M. MacLeod (eds). Cambridge: Cambridge University Press.

Zhimin, An 1989. Prehistoric agriculture in China. *Foraging and Farming. The Evolution of Plant Exploitation*, D. R. Harris and G. C. Hillman (eds), pp. 643–49. London: Unwin Hyman.

Zilhão, João 1993. The spread of agro-pastoral economies across Mediterranean Europe: a view from the far west. *Journal of Mediterranean Archaeology* 6: 5–63.

—— (ed.) 1998. *Arte Rupestre e Pré-História do Vale do Côa*. 2nd edn. Lisbon: Ministério da Cultura.

Zohary, Daniel 1992. Domestication of the Neolithic Near Eastern crop assemblage. *Préhistoire de l'Agriculture: Nouvelles Approches Expérimentales et Ethnographiques*, P. C. Anderson, (ed.), pp. 81–6. Paris: Éditions du CNRS.

——, and Maria Hopf 1993. *Domestication of Plants in the Old World: the Origin and Spread of Cultivated Plants in West Asia, Europe, and the Nile Valley*. 2nd edn. Oxford: Clarendon Press.

Zvelebil, Marek 1994. Plant use in the mesolithic and its role in the transition to farming. *Proceedings of the Prehistoric Society* 60: 35–74.

INDEX